D1133379

Paradise
Kiss

Paradise
Kiss

Paradise Kiss

2

Ai Yazawa

Santa Fe Springs City Library
11700 Telegraph Road
Santa Fe Springs, CA 90670

• Contents •

Santa Fe Springs City Library
11700 Telegraph Road
Santa Fe Springs, CA 90670

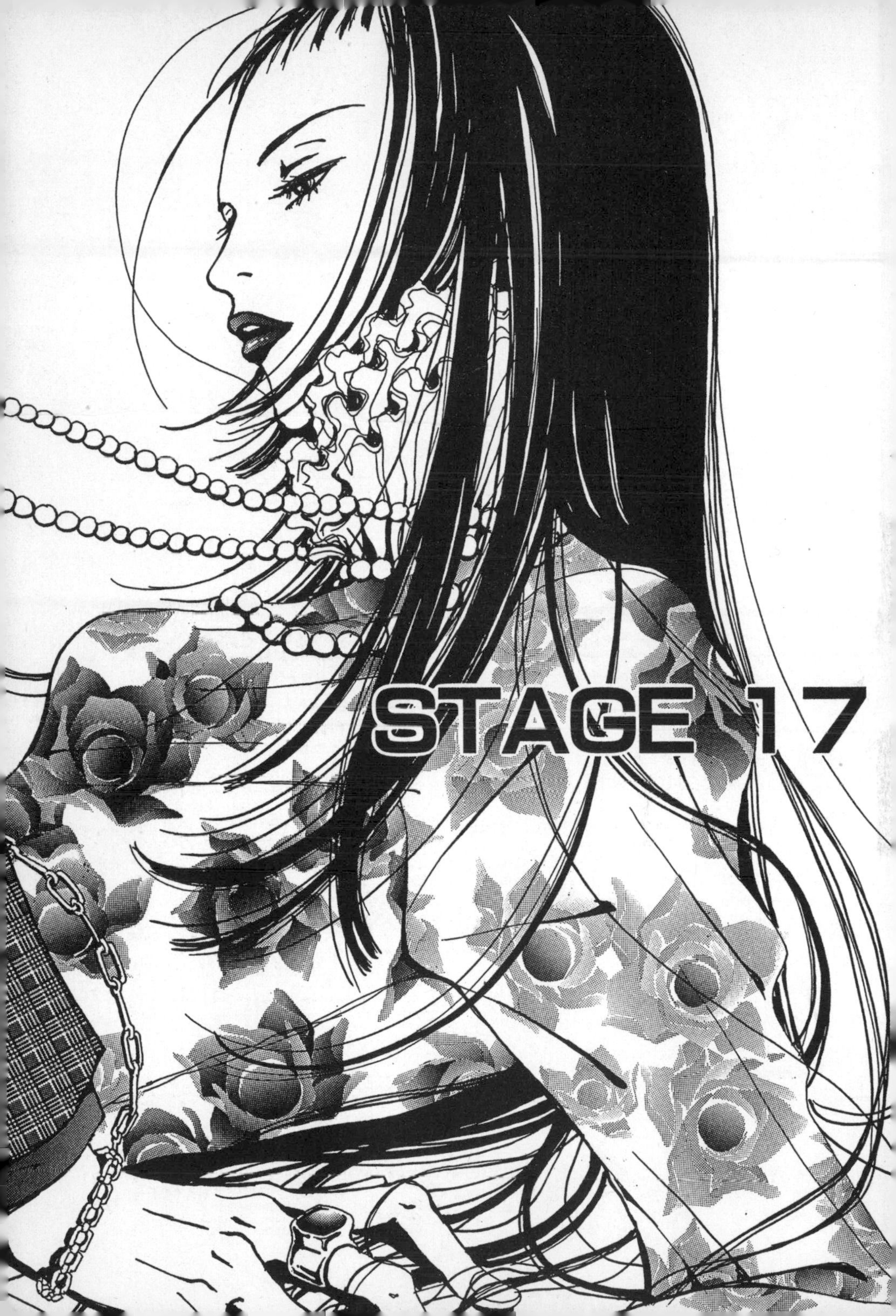
STAGE 17

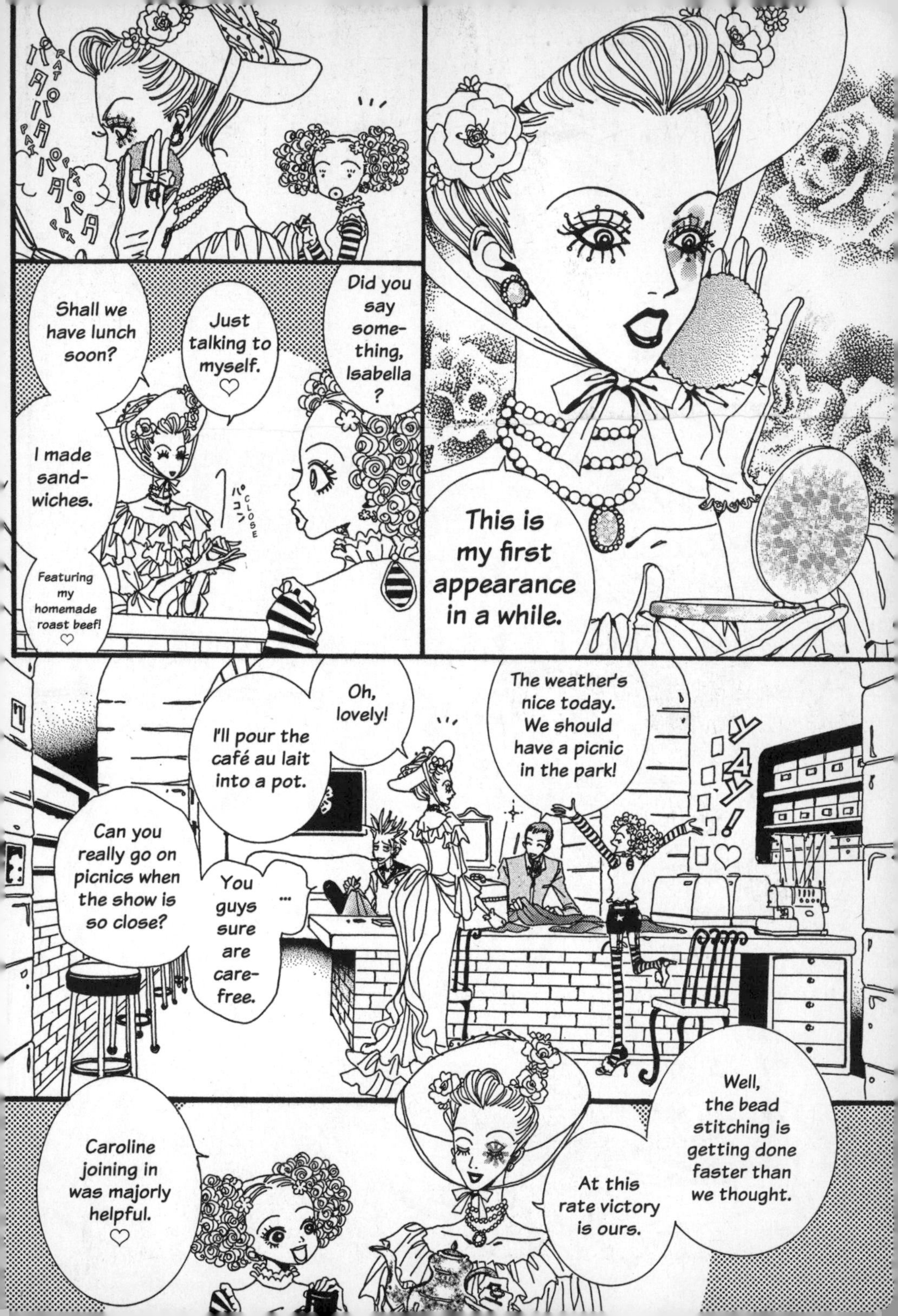
This is my first appearance in a while.
PAT
PAT
PAT
PAT
Did you say something, Isabella?
Just talking to myself. ♡
Shall we have lunch soon?
CLOSE
I made sandwiches.
Featuring my homemade roast beef! ♡
The weather's nice today. We should have a picnic in the park!
YAY!
Oh, lovely!
I'll pour the café au lait into a pot.
...
You guys sure are carefree.
Can you really go on picnics when the show is so close?
Well, the bead stitching is getting done faster than we thought.
At this rate victory is ours.
Caroline joining in was majorly helpful. ♡

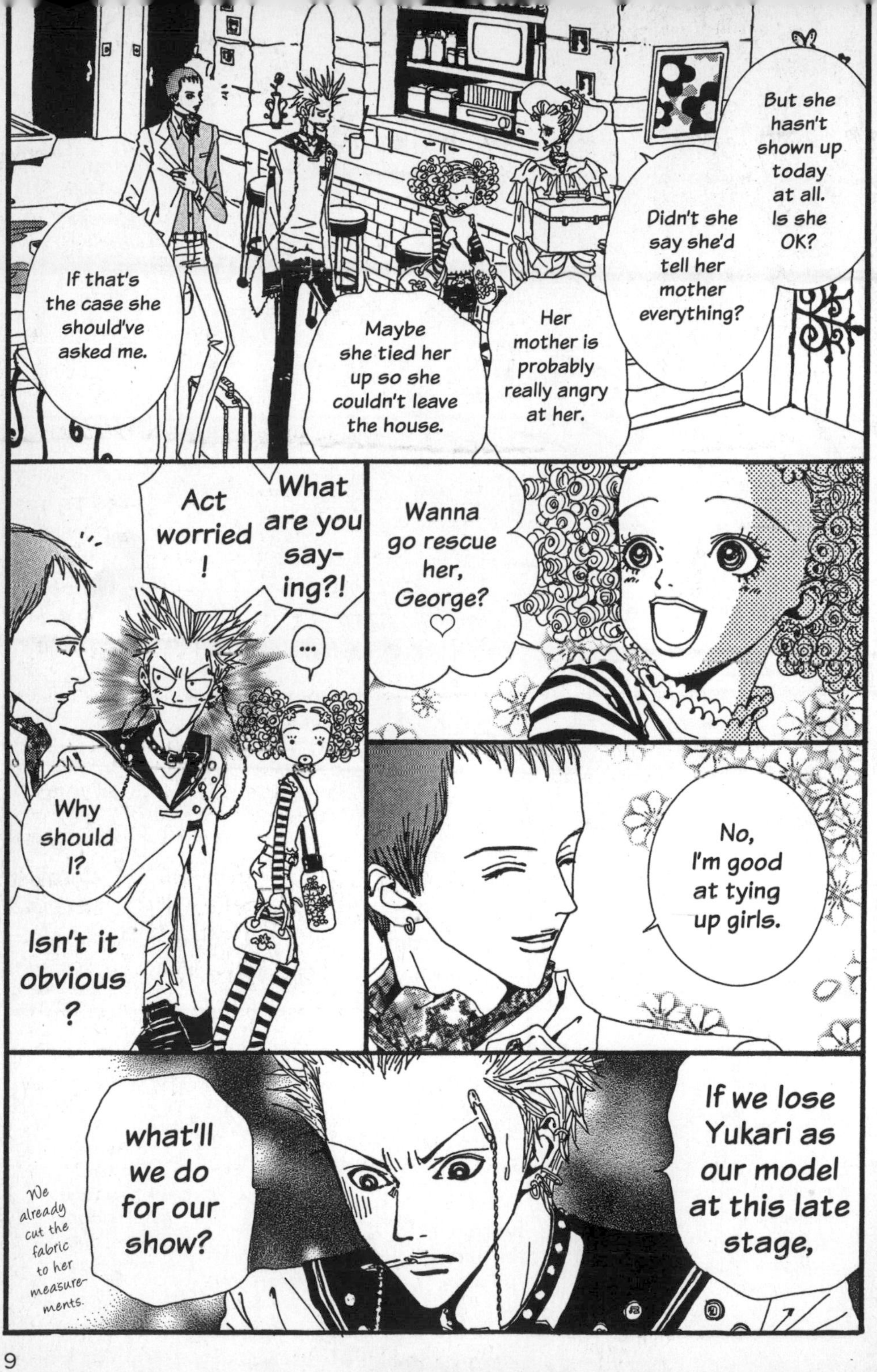
But she hasn't shown up today at all. Is she OK?
Didn't she say she'd tell her mother everything?
Her mother is probably really angry at her.
Maybe she tied her up so she couldn't leave the house.
If that's the case she should've asked me.
Wanna go rescue her, George? ♡
No, I'm good at tying up girls.
What are you saying?!
Act worried!
...
Why should I?
Isn't it obvious?
If we lose Yukari as our model at this late stage,
what'll we do for our show?
We already cut the fabric to her measurements.

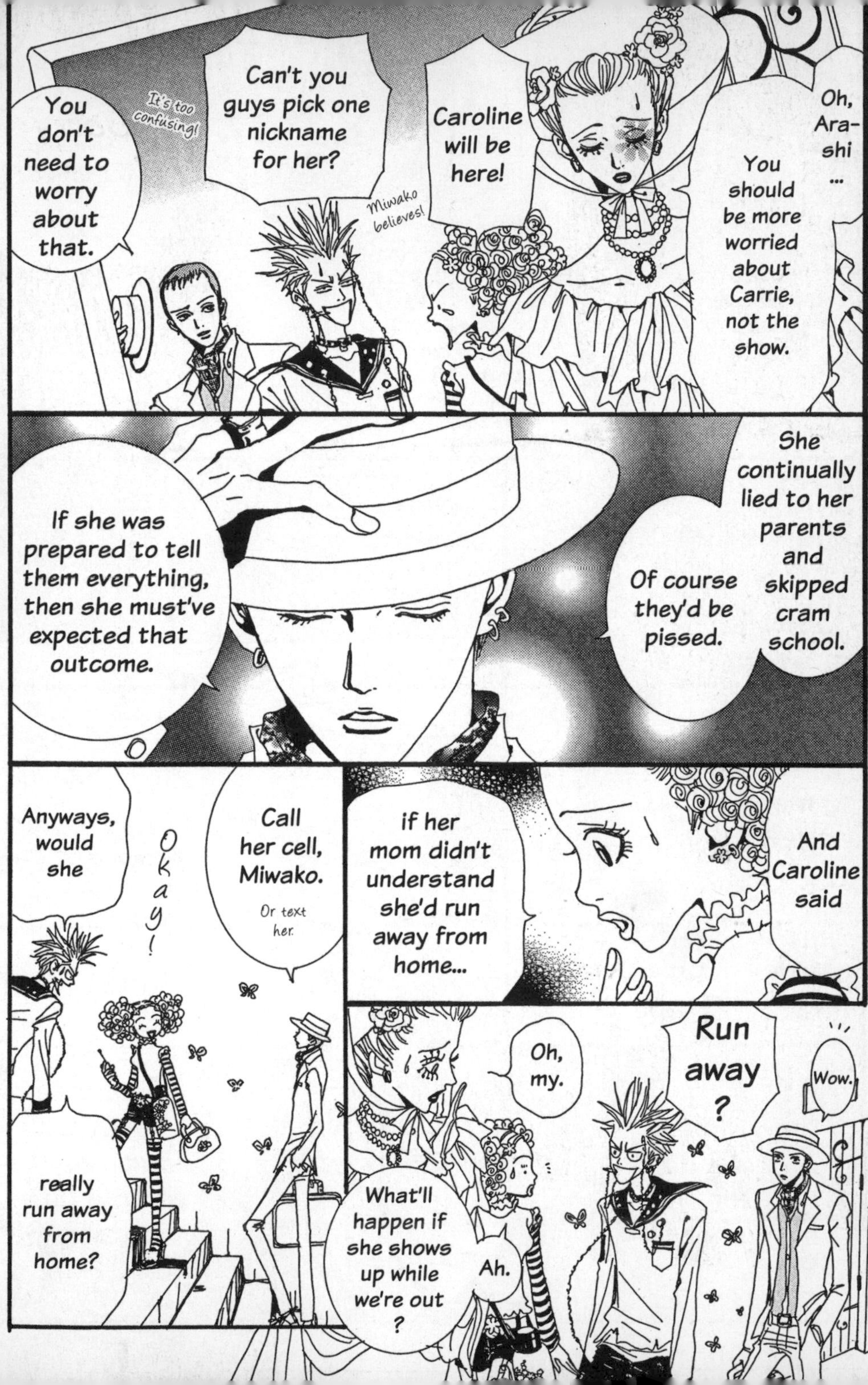
Oh, Arashi ...
You should be more worried about Carrie, not the show.
Caroline will be here!
Miwako believes!
Can't you guys pick one nickname for her?
It's too confusing!
You don't need to worry about that.
She continually lied to her parents and skipped cram school.
Of course they'd be pissed.
If she was prepared to tell them everything, then she must've expected that outcome.
And Caroline said
if her mom didn't understand she'd run away from home...
Wow.
Run away?
Oh, my.
Ah.
What'll happen if she shows up while we're out?
Call her cell, Miwako.
Or text her.
Okay!
Anyways, would she
really run away from home?

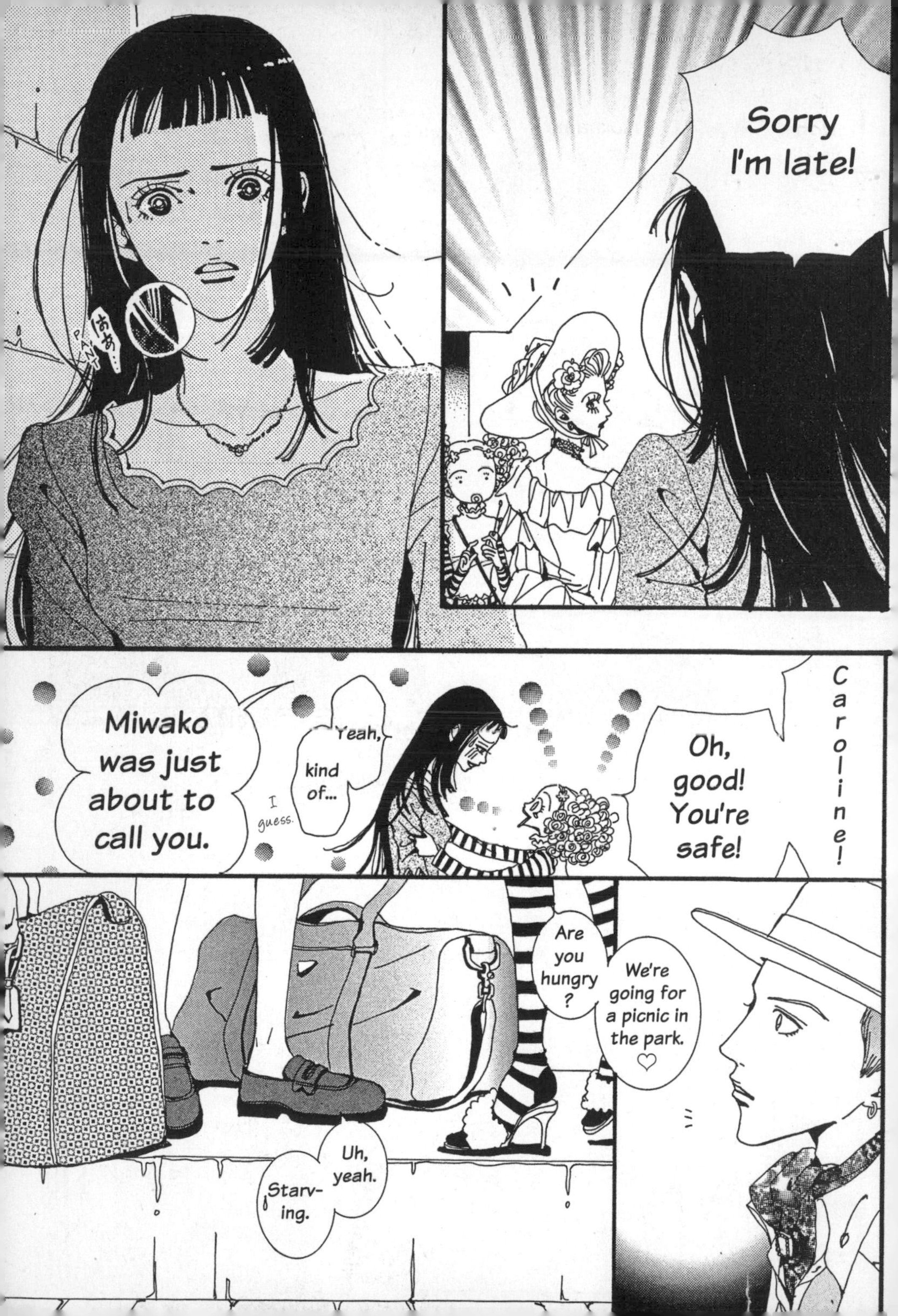
Sorry I'm late!
おあ…
PANT
Caroline!
Oh, good! You're safe!
Yeah, kind of...
I guess.
Miwako was just about to call you.
We're going for a picnic in the park. ♡
Are you hungry?
Uh, yeah.
Starv-ing.

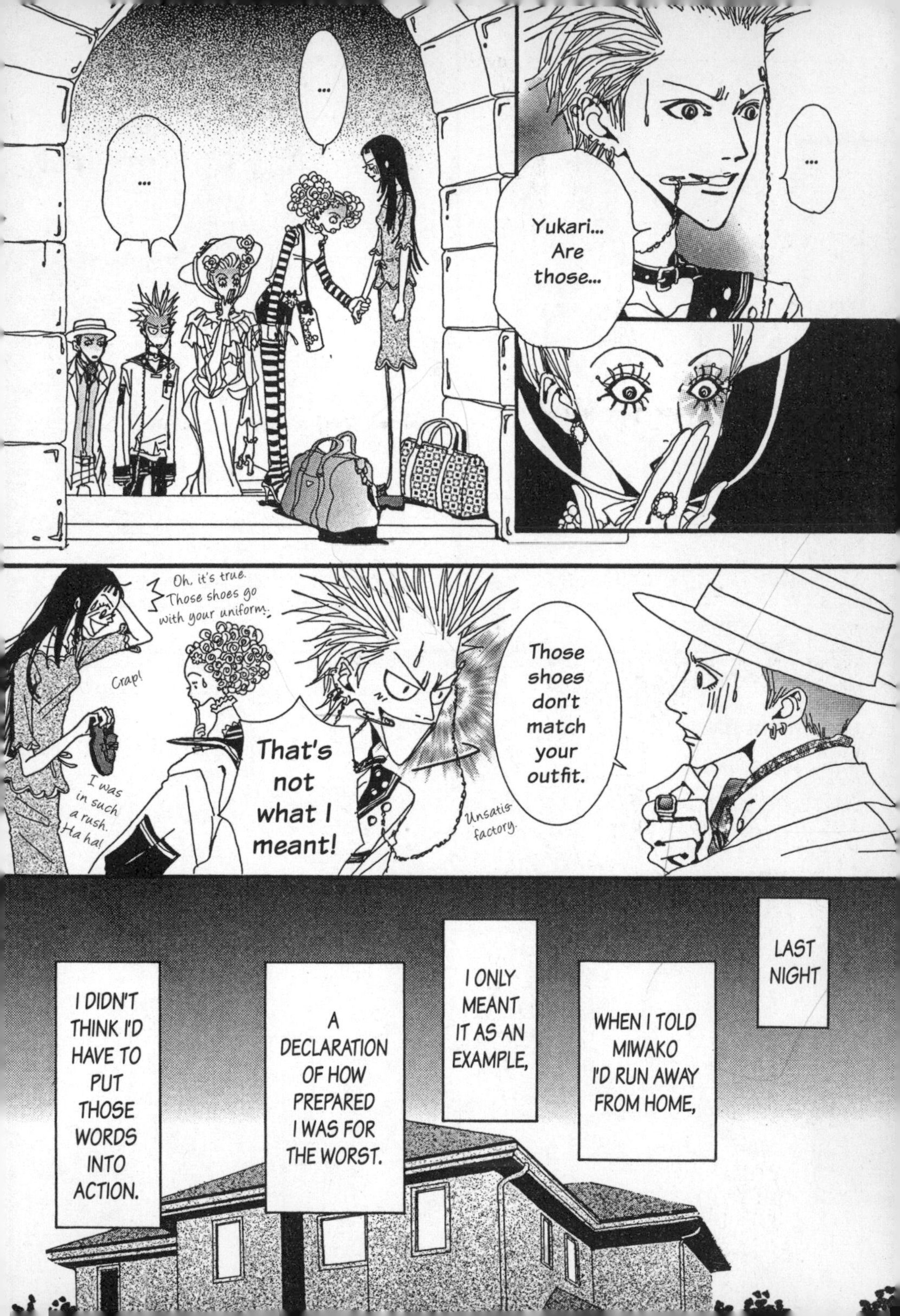
...
Yukari... Are those...
...
...
Those shoes don't match your outfit.
Unsatisfactory.
That's not what I meant!
Oh, it's true. Those shoes go with your uniform.
Crap!
I was in such a rush. Ha ha!
LAST NIGHT
WHEN I TOLD MIWAKO I'D RUN AWAY FROM HOME,
I ONLY MEANT IT AS AN EXAMPLE,
A DECLARATION OF HOW PREPARED I WAS FOR THE WORST.
I DIDN'T THINK I'D HAVE TO PUT THOSE WORDS INTO ACTION.

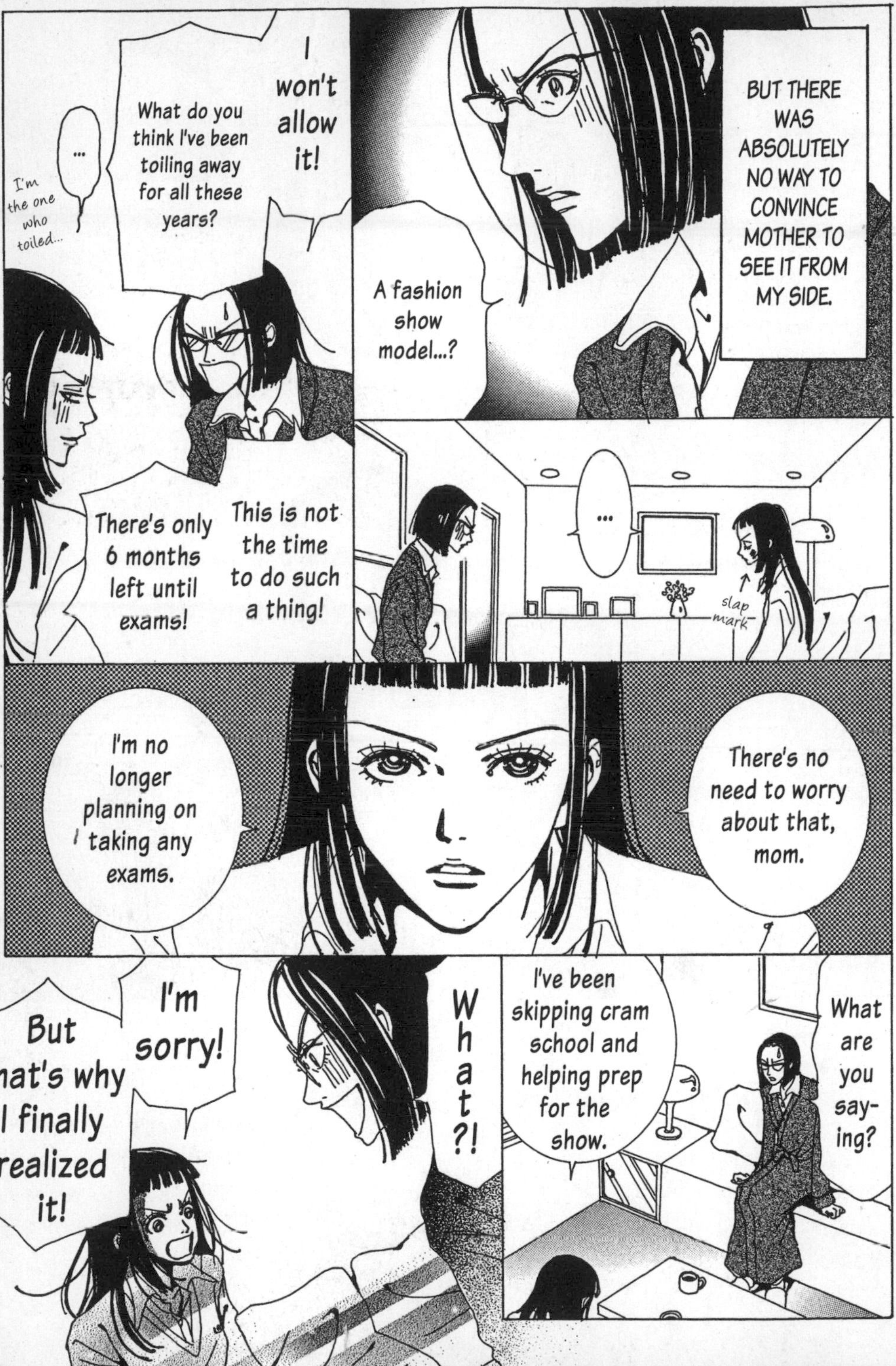
BUT THERE WAS ABSOLUTELY NO WAY TO CONVINCE MOTHER TO SEE IT FROM MY SIDE.
A fashion show model...?
...
slap mark
I won't allow it!
What do you think I've been toiling away for all these years?
...
I'm the one who toiled...
This is not the time to do such a thing!
There's only 6 months left until exams!
There's no need to worry about that, mom.
I'm no longer planning on taking any exams.
What are you say-ing?
I've been skipping cram school and helping prep for the show.
What?!
I'm sorry!
But that's why I finally realized it!

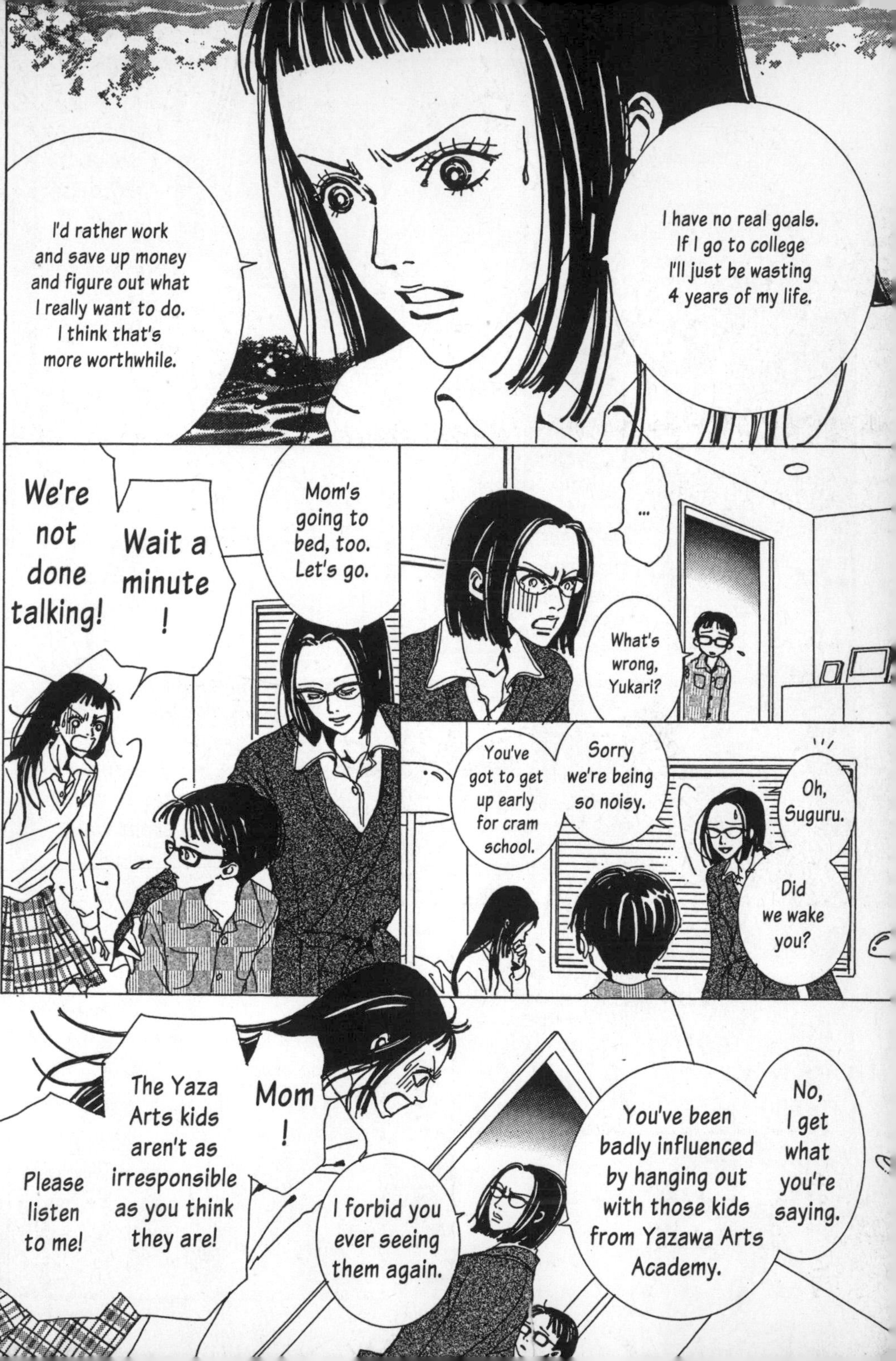
I have no real goals. If I go to college I'll just be wasting 4 years of my life.
I'd rather work and save up money and figure out what I really want to do. I think that's more worthwhile.
...
What's wrong, Yukari?
Oh, Suguru.
Did we wake you?
Sorry we're being so noisy.
You've got to get up early for cram school.
Mom's going to bed, too. Let's go.
Wait a minute!
We're not done talking!
No, I get what you're saying.
You've been badly influenced by hanging out with those kids from Yazawa Arts Academy.
I forbid you ever seeing them again.
Mom!
The Yaza Arts kids aren't as irresponsible as you think they are!
Please listen to me!

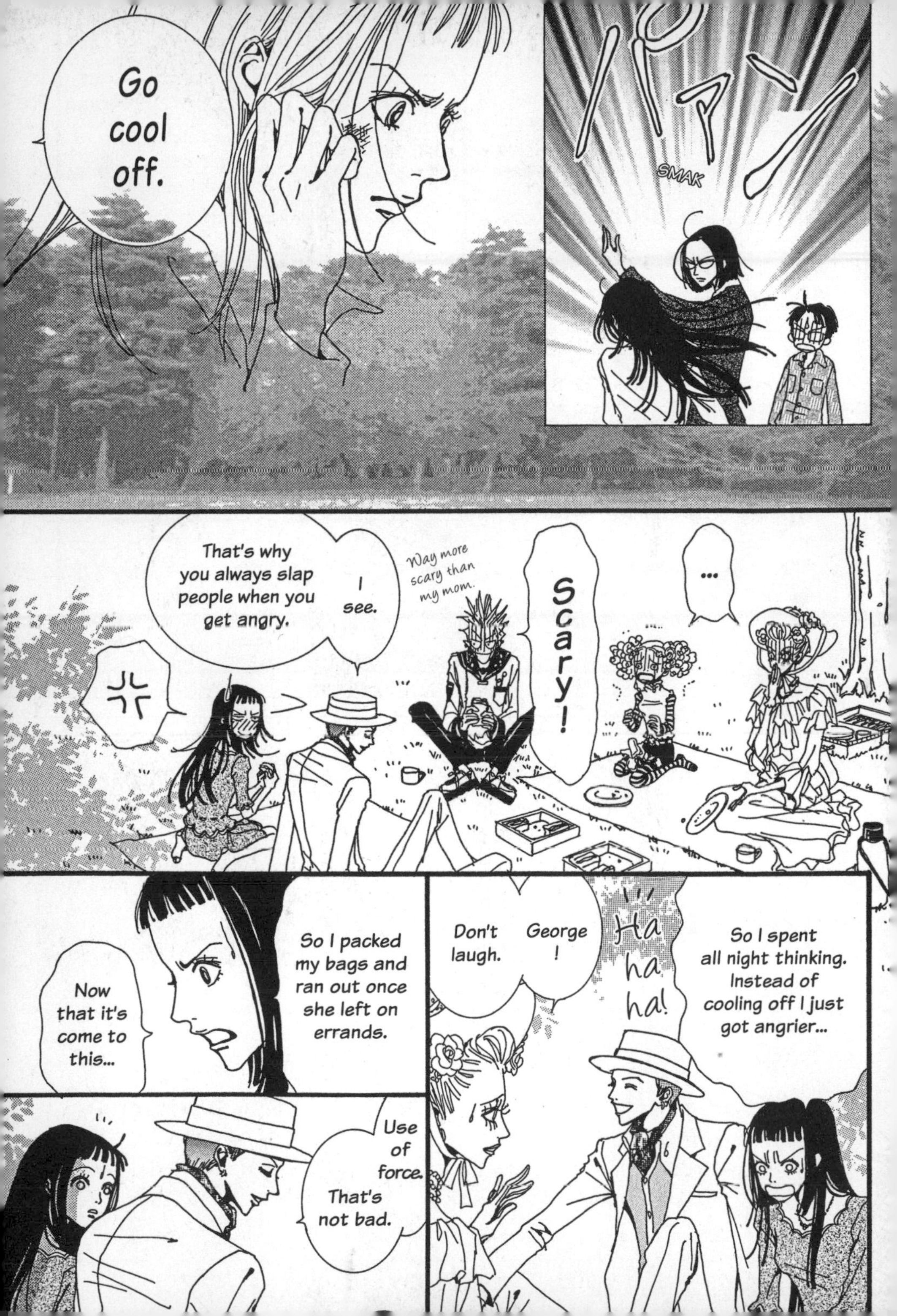

パァーン
SMAK
Go cool off.
...
Scary!
Way more scary than my mom.
I see.
That's why you always slap people when you get angry.
So I spent all night thinking. Instead of cooling off I just got angrier...
Ha ha ha!
George!
Don't laugh.
So I packed my bags and ran out once she left on errands.
Now that it's come to this...
Use of force. That's not bad.

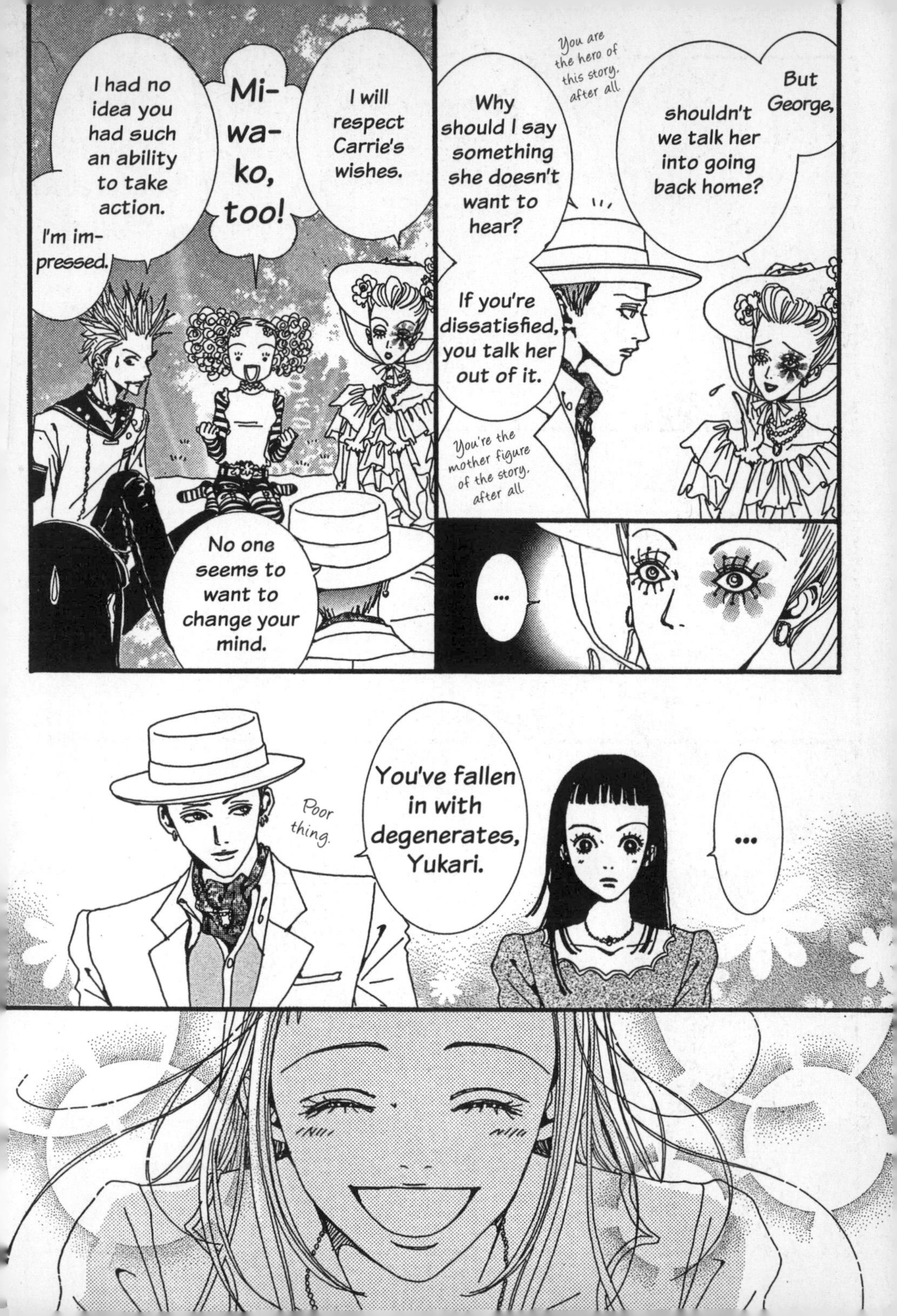

But George, shouldn't we talk her into going back home?
You are the hero of this story, after all
Why should I say something she doesn't want to hear?
If you're dissatisfied, you talk her out of it.
You're the mother figure of the story, after all.
...
I will respect Carrie's wishes.
Mi-wa-ko, too!
I had no idea you had such an ability to take action.
I'm im-pressed.
No one seems to want to change your mind.
...
You've fallen in with degenerates, Yukari.
Poor thing.

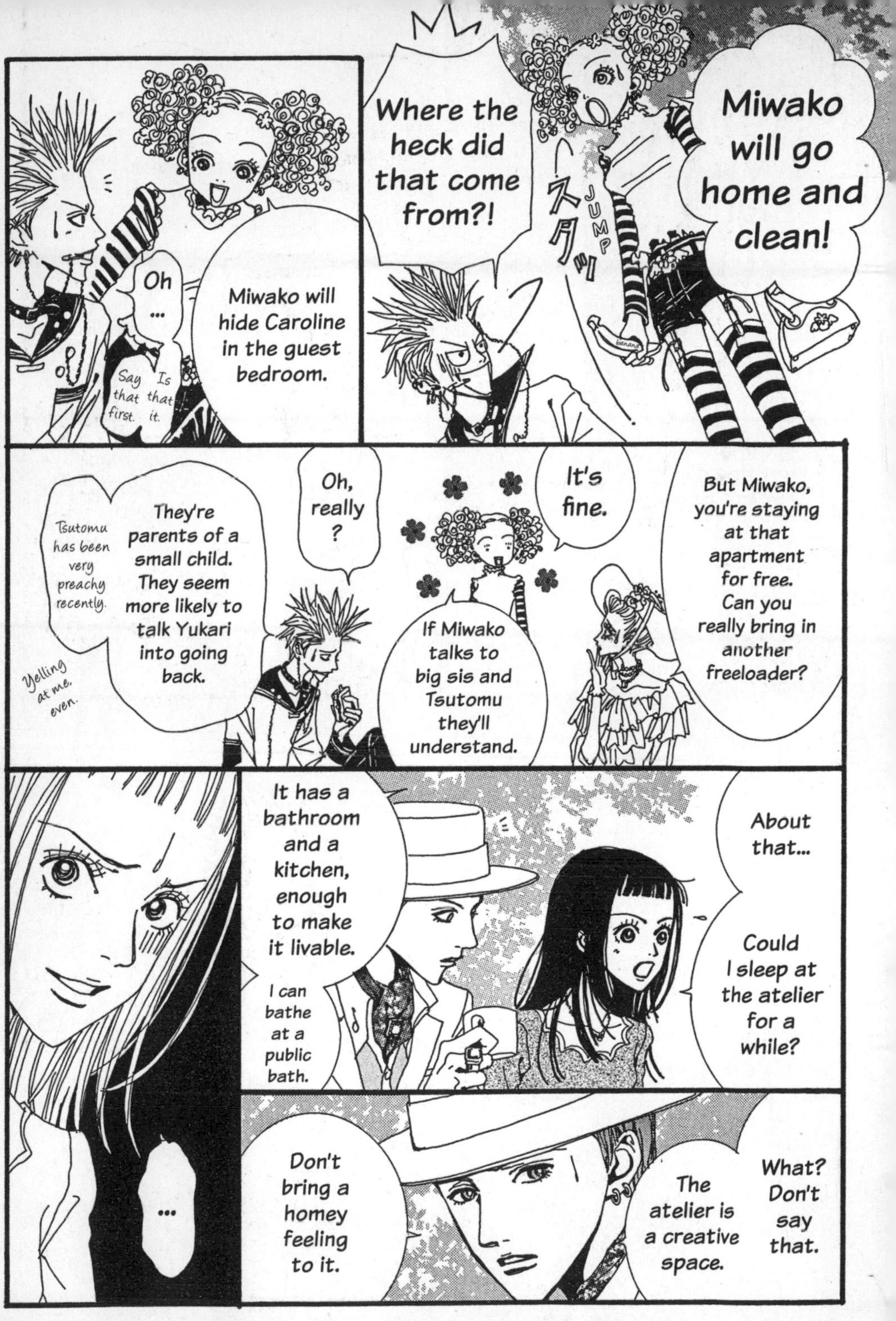

Miwako will go home and clean!
JUMP
Where the heck did that come from?!
Miwako will hide Caroline in the guest bedroom.
Oh ...
Is that it.
Say that first.
But Miwako, you're staying at that apartment for free. Can you really bring in another freeloader?
It's fine.
If Miwako talks to big sis and Tsutomu they'll understand.
Oh, really?
They're parents of a small child. They seem more likely to talk Yukari into going back.
Tsutomu has been very preachy recently.
Yelling at me, even.
About that...
Could I sleep at the atelier for a while?
It has a bathroom and a kitchen, enough to make it livable.
I can bathe at a public bath.
What? Don't say that.
The atelier is a creative space.
Don't bring a homey feeling to it.
...

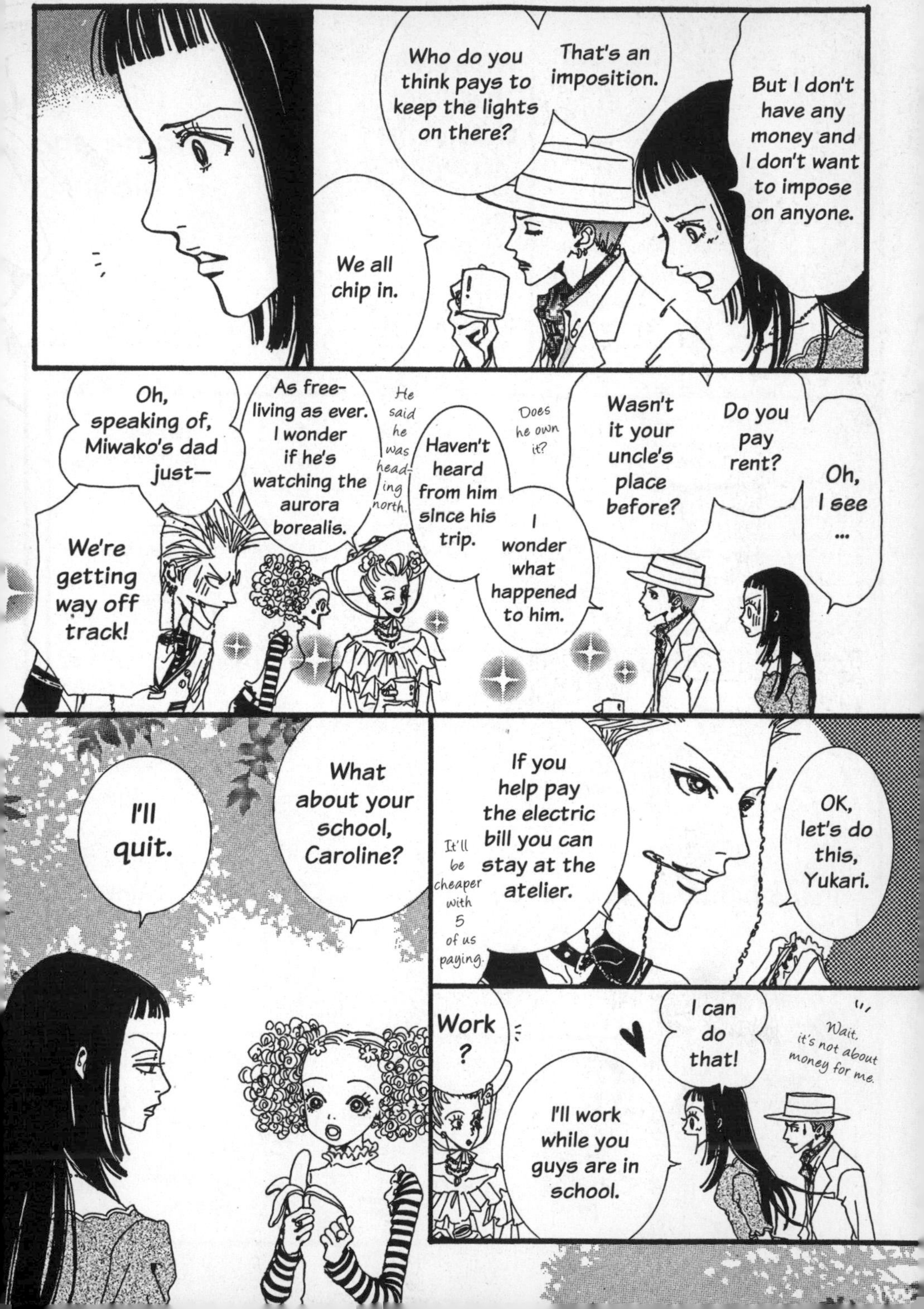

But I don't have any money and I don't want to impose on anyone.
That's an imposition.
Who do you think pays to keep the lights on there?
We all chip in.
Oh, I see ...
Do you pay rent?
Wasn't it your uncle's place before?
Does he own it?
I wonder what happened to him.
Haven't heard from him since his trip.
He said he was head-ing north.
As free-living as ever. I wonder if he's watching the aurora borealis.
Oh, speaking of, Miwako's dad just—
We're getting way off track!
OK, let's do this, Yukari.
If you help pay the electric bill you can stay at the atelier.
It'll be cheaper with 5 of us paying.
Wait, it's not about money for me.
I can do that!
I'll work while you guys are in school.
Work?
What about your school, Caroline?
I'll quit.

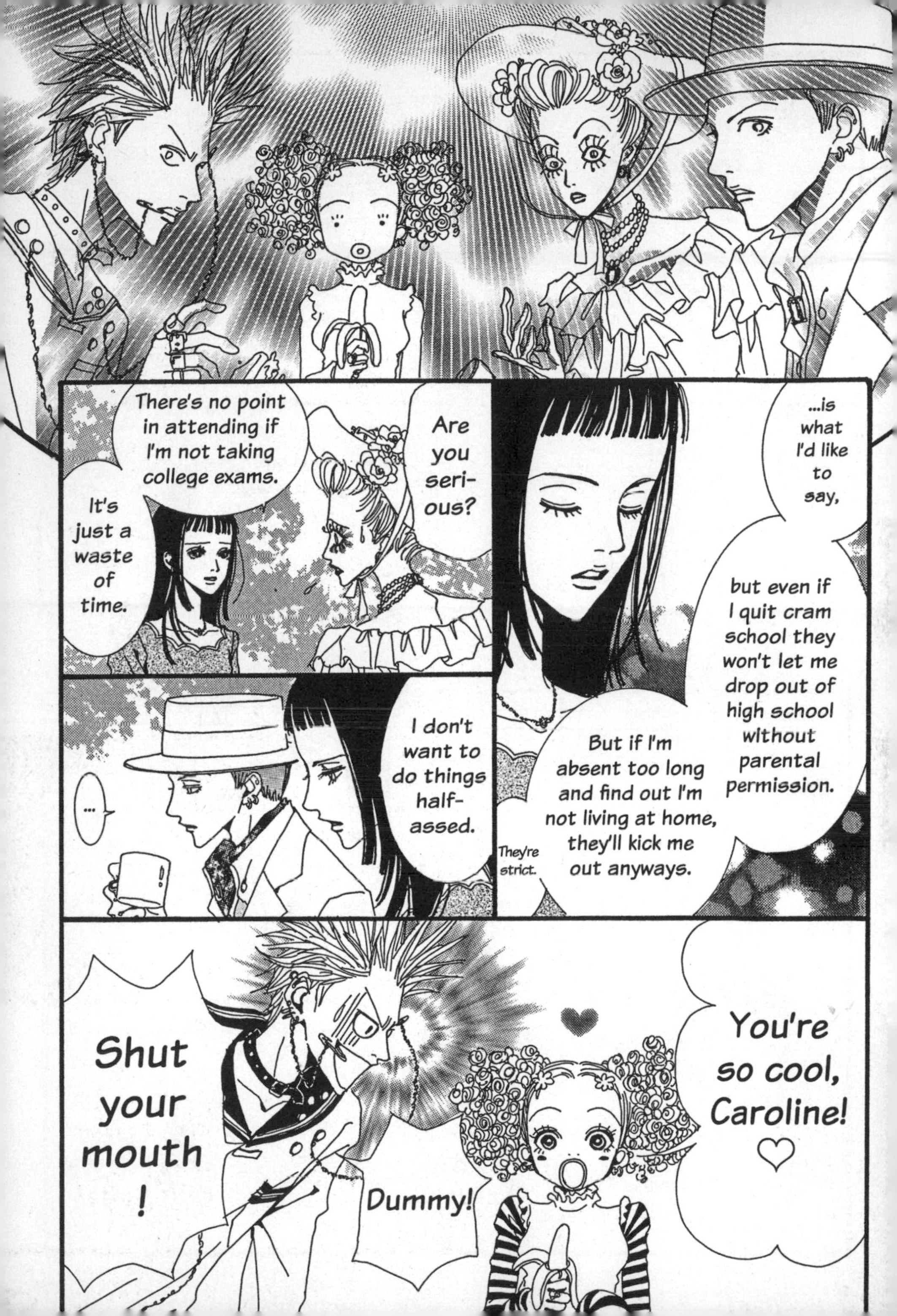
...is what I'd like to say,
but even if I quit cram school they won't let me drop out of high school without parental permission.
But if I'm absent too long and find out I'm not living at home, they'll kick me out anyways.
They're strict.
Are you seri-ous?
There's no point in attending if I'm not taking college exams.
It's just a waste of time.
I don't want to do things half-assed.
...
You're so cool, Caroline! ♡
Dummy!
Shut your mouth!

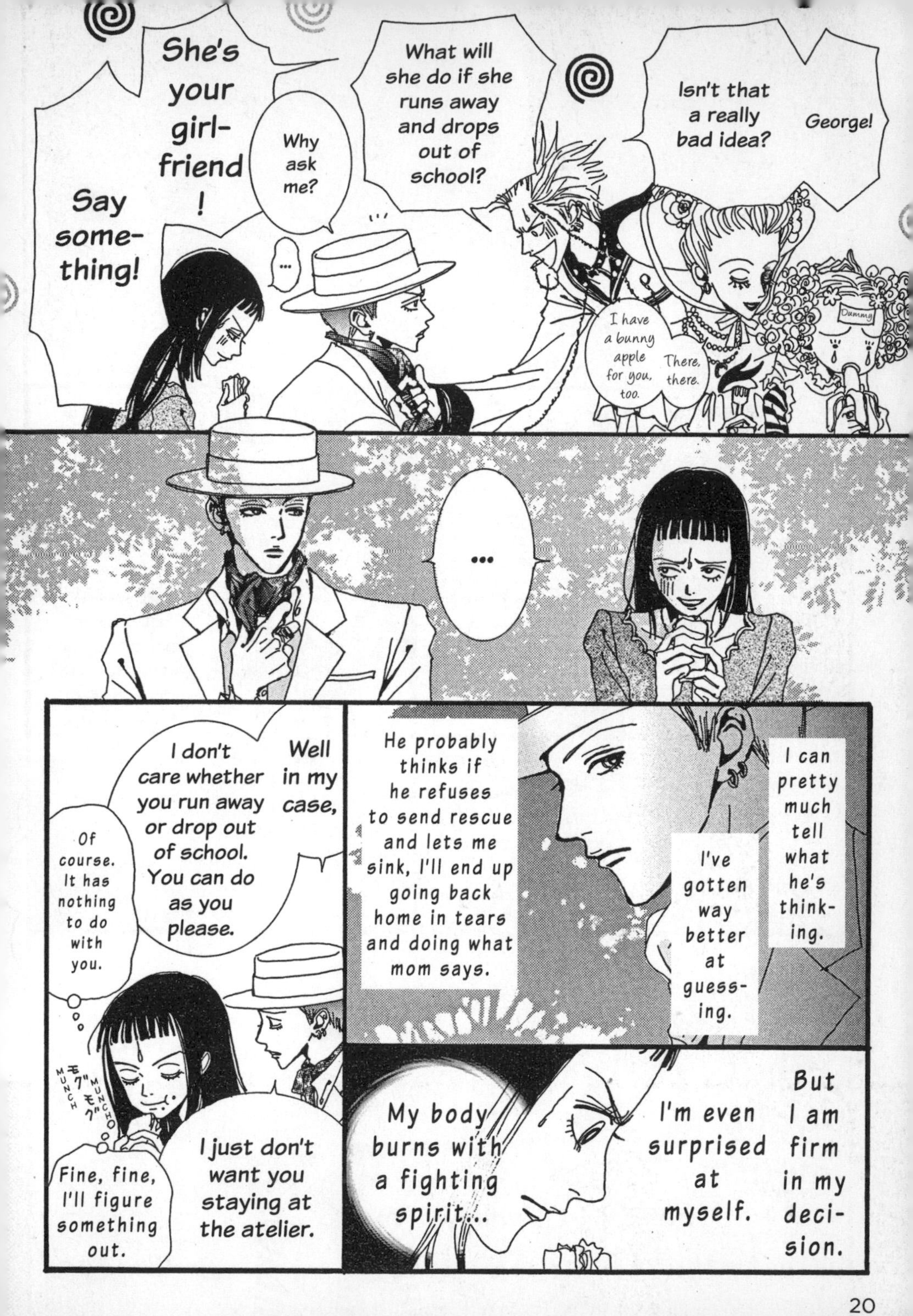
Isn't that a really bad idea? George!
What will she do if she runs away and drops out of school?
She's your girl-friend! Say some-thing!
Why ask me?
...
There, there.
I have a bunny apple for you, too.
Dummy
...
I can pretty much tell what he's think-ing.
I've gotten way better at guess-ing.
He probably thinks if he refuses to send rescue and lets me sink, I'll end up going back home in tears and doing what mom says.
But I am firm in my deci-sion.
I'm even surprised at myself.
My body burns with a fighting spirit...
Well in my case,
I don't care whether you run away or drop out of school. You can do as you please.
Of course. It has nothing to do with you.
I just don't want you staying at the atelier.
Fine, fine, I'll figure something out.
MUNCH MUNCH

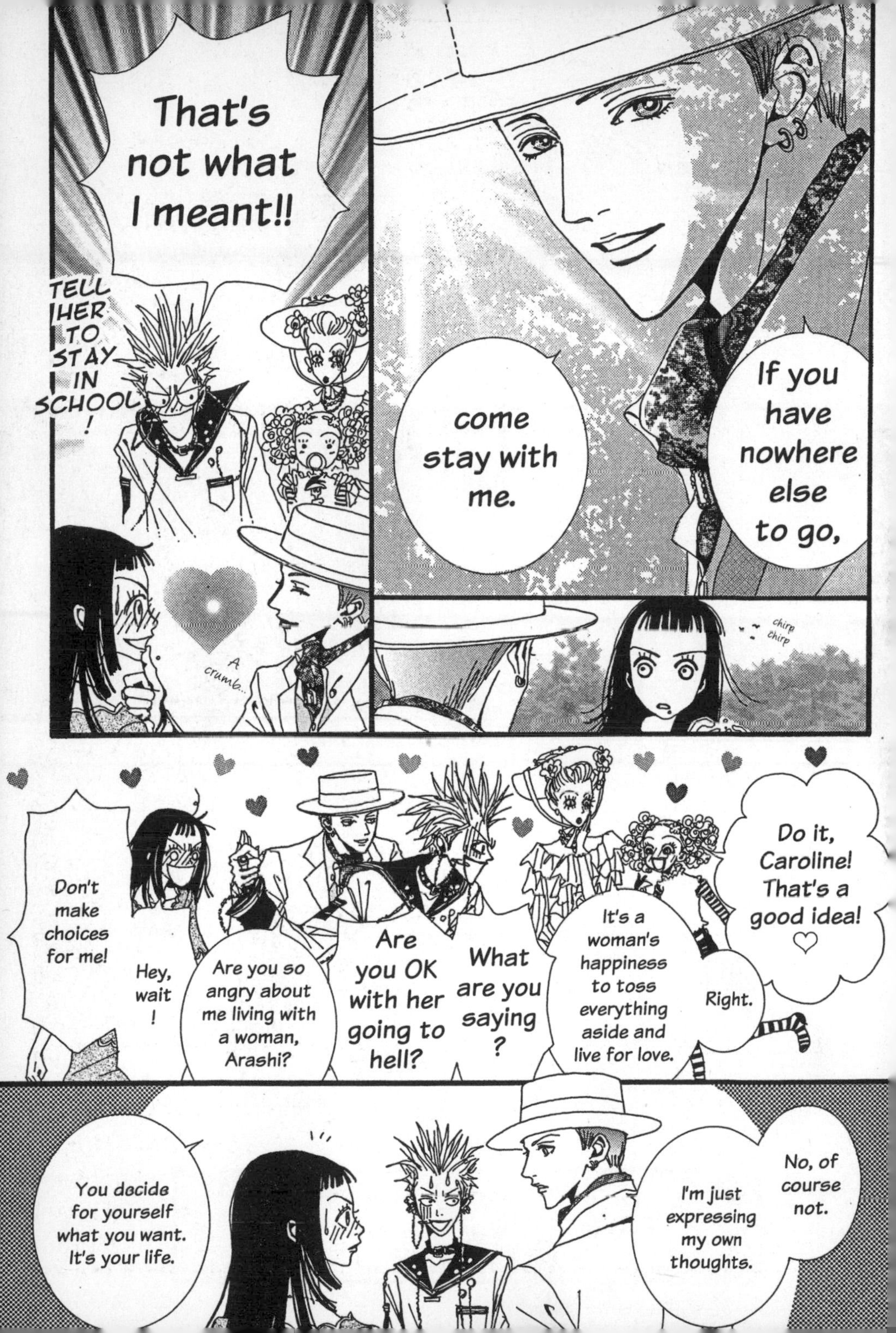
If you have nowhere else to go,
come stay with me.
chirp chirp
That's not what I meant!!
TELL HER TO STAY IN SCHOOL!
A crumb...
Do it, Caroline! That's a good idea! ♡
Right.
It's a woman's happiness to toss everything aside and live for love.
What are you saying?
Are you OK with her going to hell?
Are you so angry about me living with a woman, Arashi?
Hey, wait!
Don't make choices for me!
No, of course not.
I'm just expressing my own thoughts.
You decide for yourself what you want. It's your life.

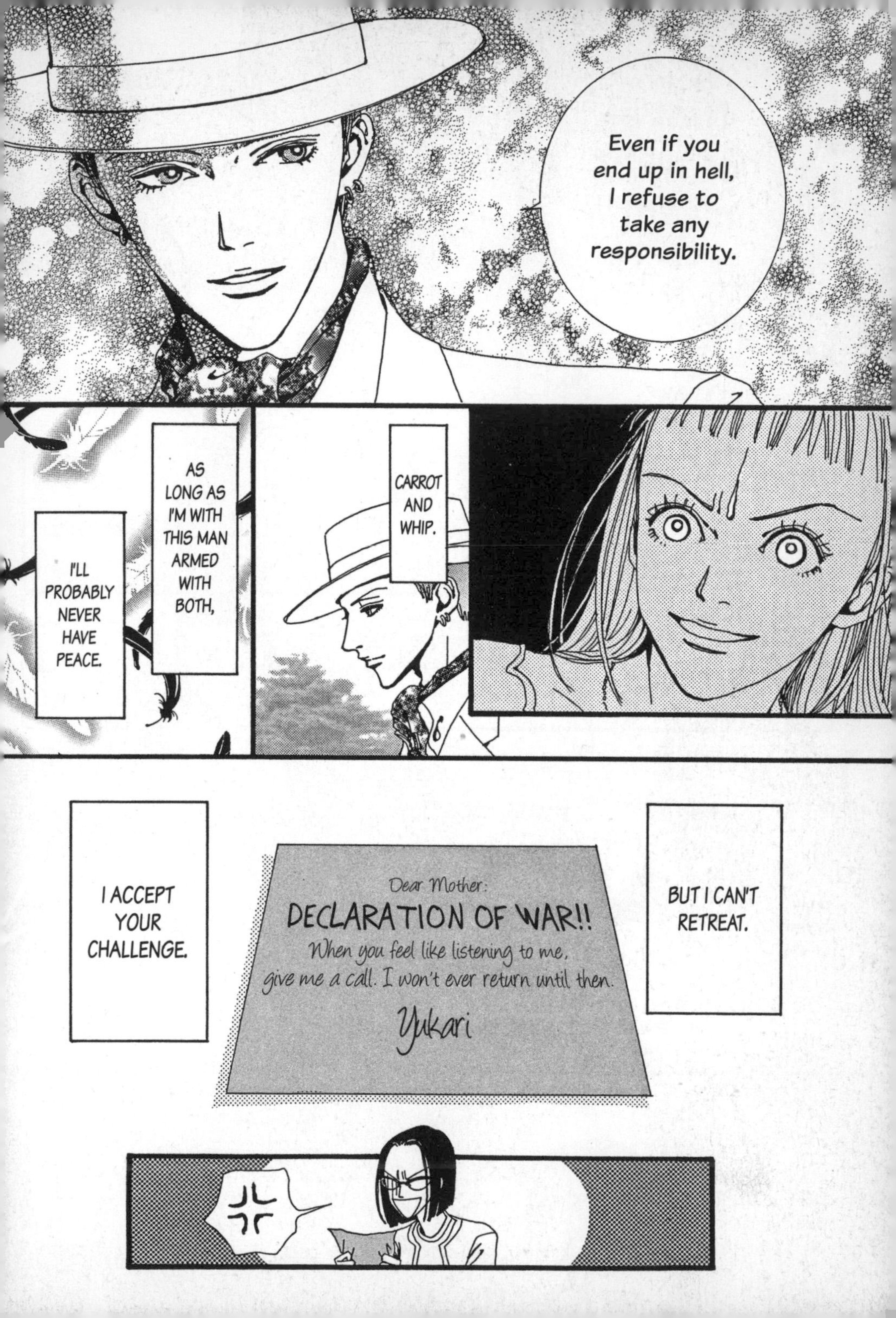
Even if you end up in hell, I refuse to take any responsibility.
CARROT AND WHIP.
AS LONG AS I'M WITH THIS MAN ARMED WITH BOTH,
I'LL PROBABLY NEVER HAVE PEACE.
BUT I CAN'T RETREAT.
Dear Mother:
DECLARATION OF WAR!!
When you feel like listening to me, give me a call. I won't ever return until then.
Yukari
I ACCEPT YOUR CHALLENGE.

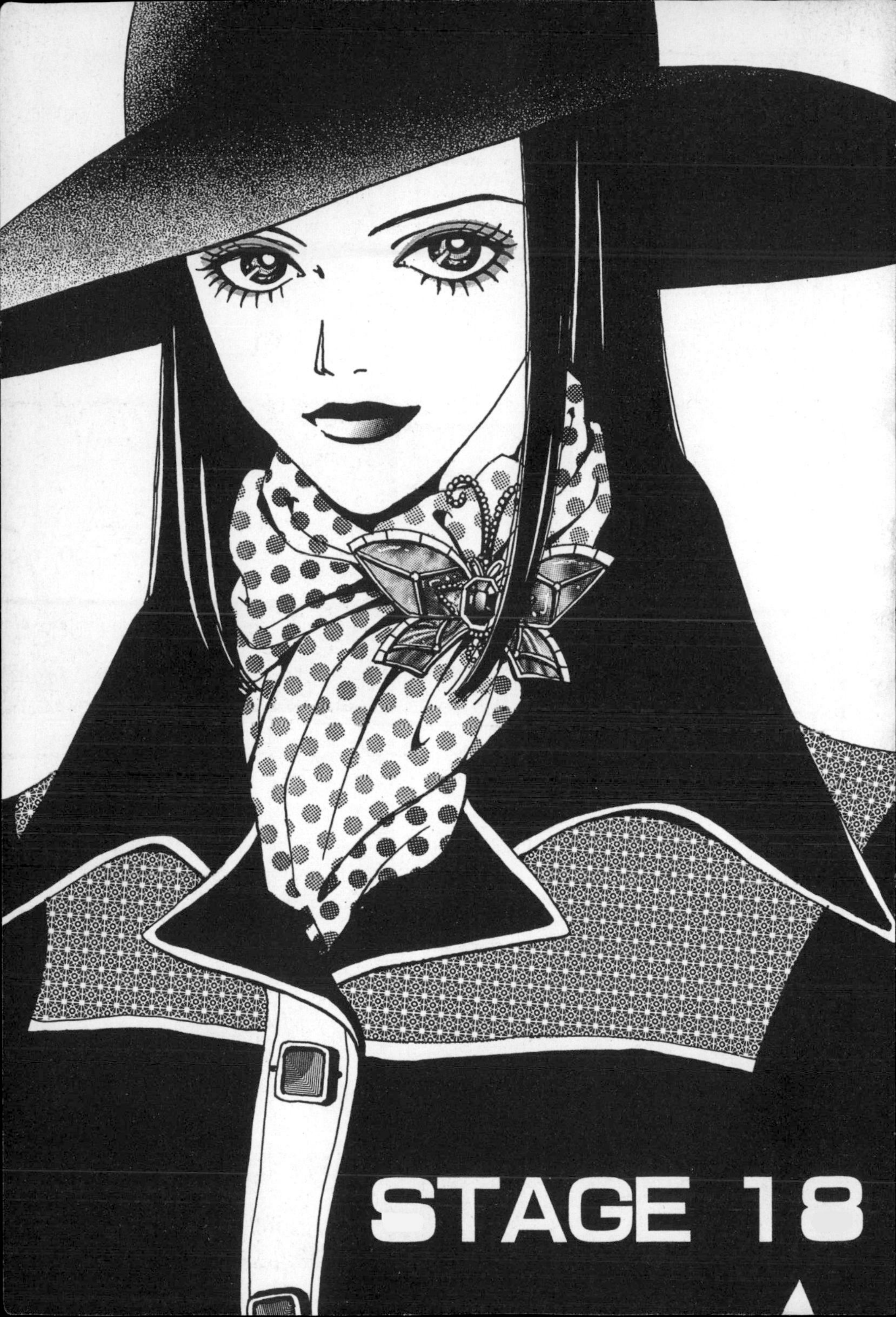
STAGE 18

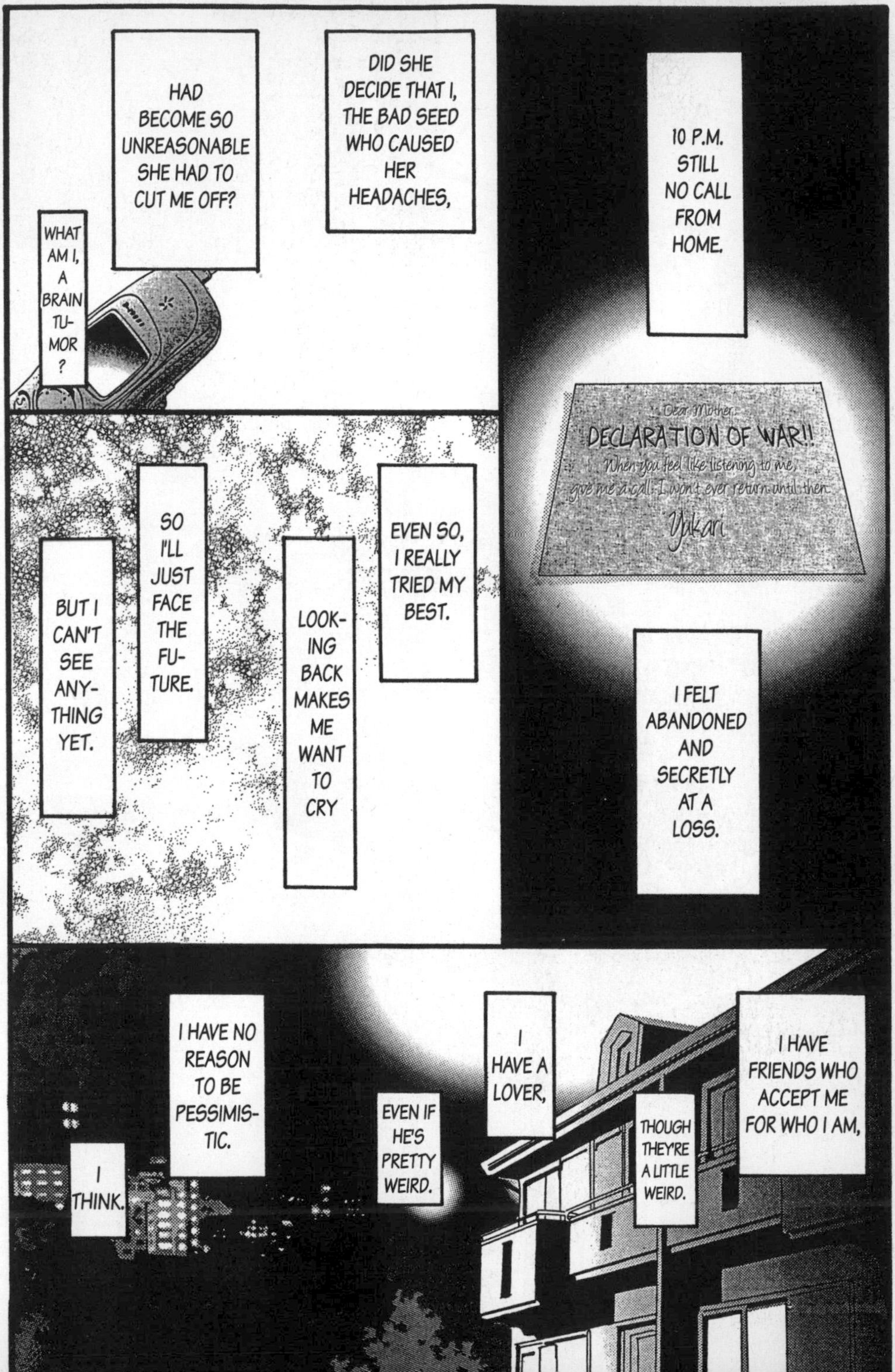
10 P.M. STILL NO CALL FROM HOME.
Dear Mother,
DECLARATION OF WAR!!
When you feel like listening to me, give me a call. I won't ever return until then
Yukari
I FELT ABANDONED AND SECRETLY AT A LOSS.
DID SHE DECIDE THAT I, THE BAD SEED WHO CAUSED HER HEADACHES,
HAD BECOME SO UNREASONABLE SHE HAD TO CUT ME OFF?
WHAT AM I, A BRAIN TU-MOR?
EVEN SO, I REALLY TRIED MY BEST.
LOOK-ING BACK MAKES ME WANT TO CRY
SO I'LL JUST FACE THE FU-TURE.
BUT I CAN'T SEE ANY-THING YET.
I HAVE FRIENDS WHO ACCEPT ME FOR WHO I AM,
THOUGH THEY'RE A LITTLE WEIRD.
I HAVE A LOVER,
EVEN IF HE'S PRETTY WEIRD.
I HAVE NO REASON TO BE PESSIMIS-TIC.
I THINK.

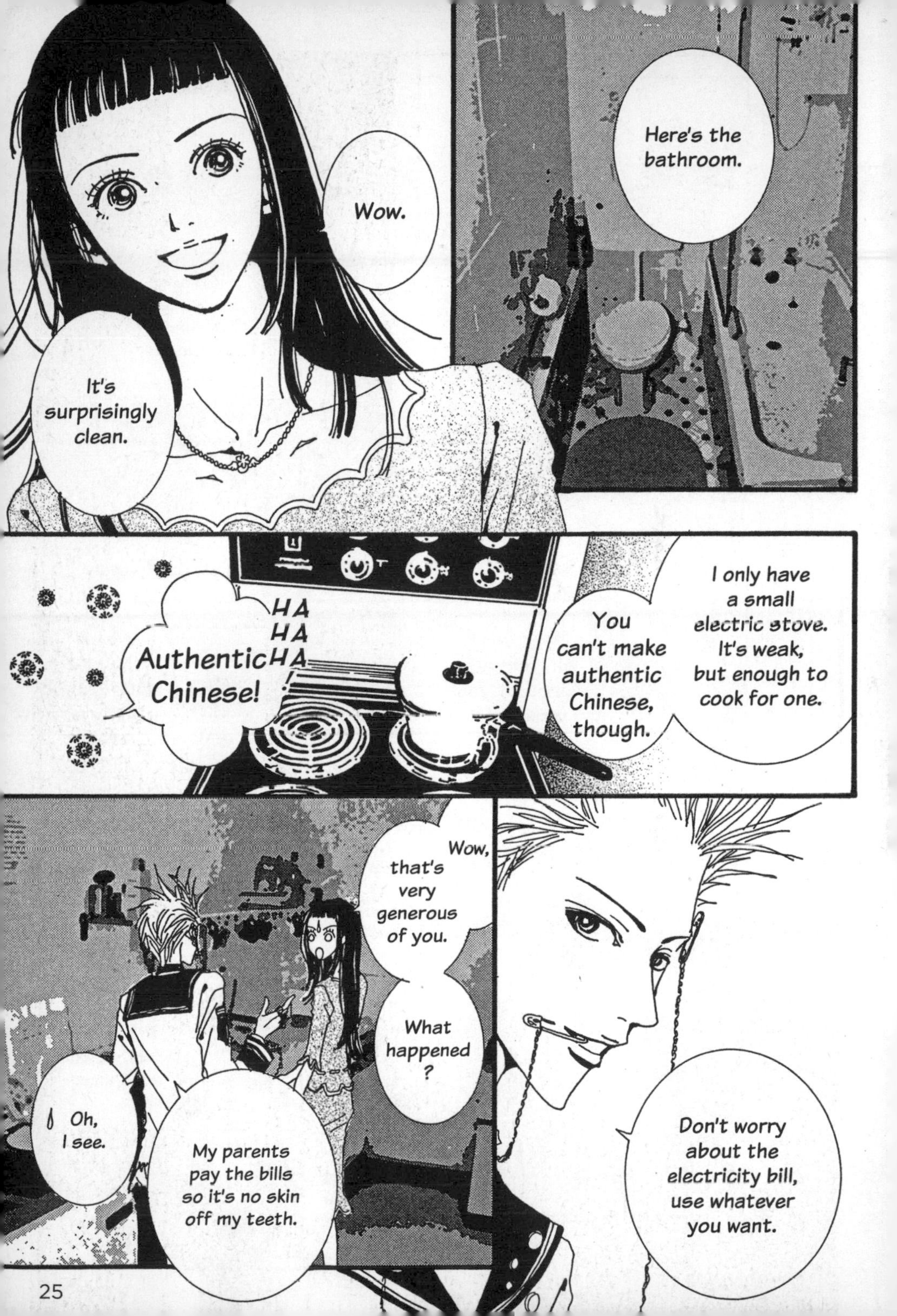
Here's the bathroom.
Wow.
It's surprisingly clean.
I only have a small electric stove. It's weak, but enough to cook for one.
You can't make authentic Chinese, though.
HA HA HA
Authentic Chinese!
Don't worry about the electricity bill, use whatever you want.
Wow, that's very generous of you.
What happened?
My parents pay the bills so it's no skin off my teeth.
Oh, I see.

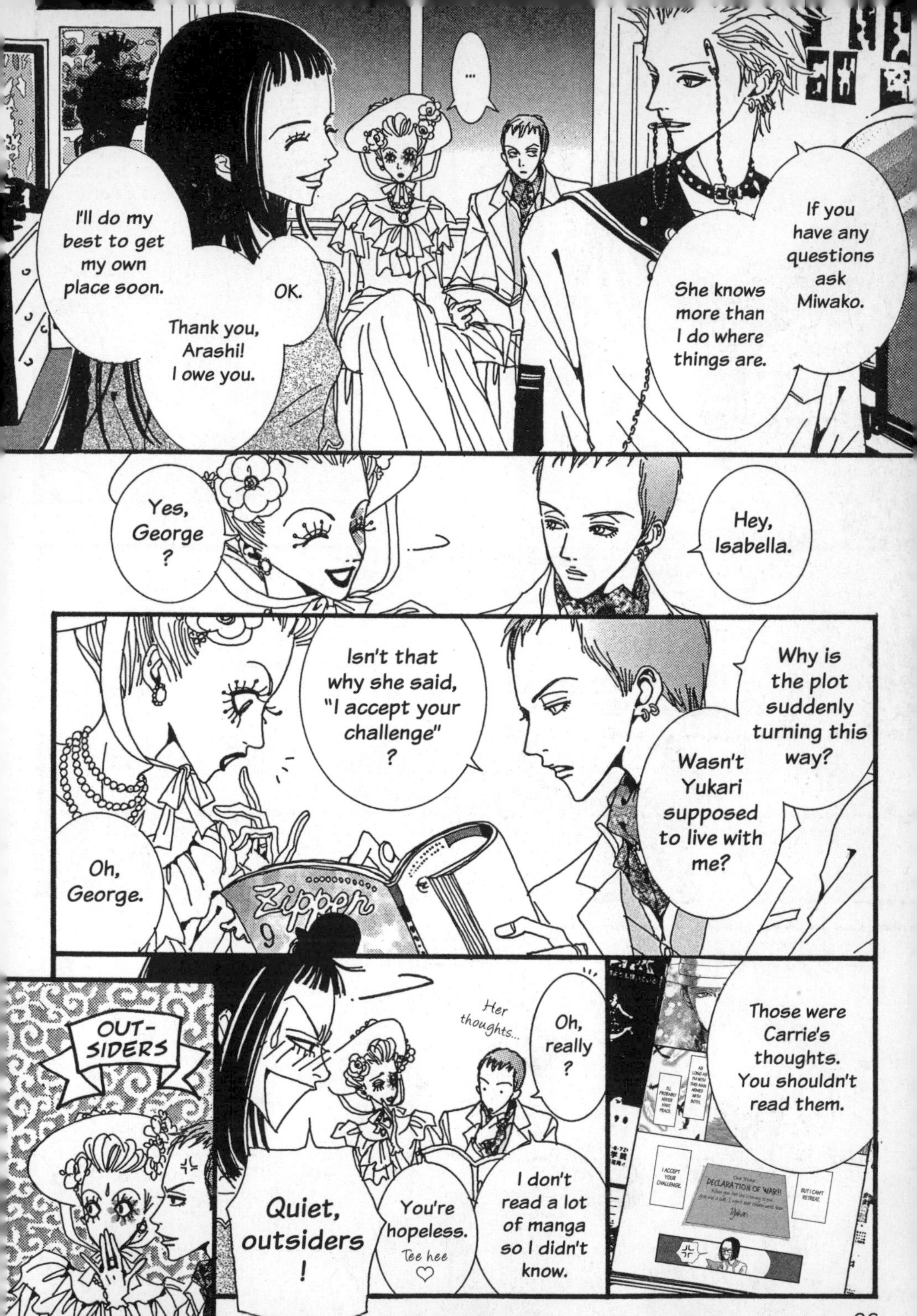

If you have any questions ask Miwako.
She knows more than I do where things are.
...
Thank you, Arashi! I owe you.
OK.
I'll do my best to get my own place soon.
Hey, Isabella.
Yes, George?
Why is the plot suddenly turning this way?
Wasn't Yukari supposed to live with me?
Isn't that why she said, "I accept your challenge"?
Oh, George.
Zipper
Those were Carrie's thoughts. You shouldn't read them.
AS LONG AS I'M WITH THIS MAN ARMED WITH BOTH,
I'LL PROBABLY NEVER HAVE PEACE.
I ACCEPT YOUR CHALLENGE.
DECLARATION OF WAR!!
Yukari
BUT I CAN'T RETREAT.
Oh, really?
Her thoughts...
I don't read a lot of manga so I didn't know.
You're hopeless.
Tee hee
Quiet, outsiders!
OUT-SIDERS

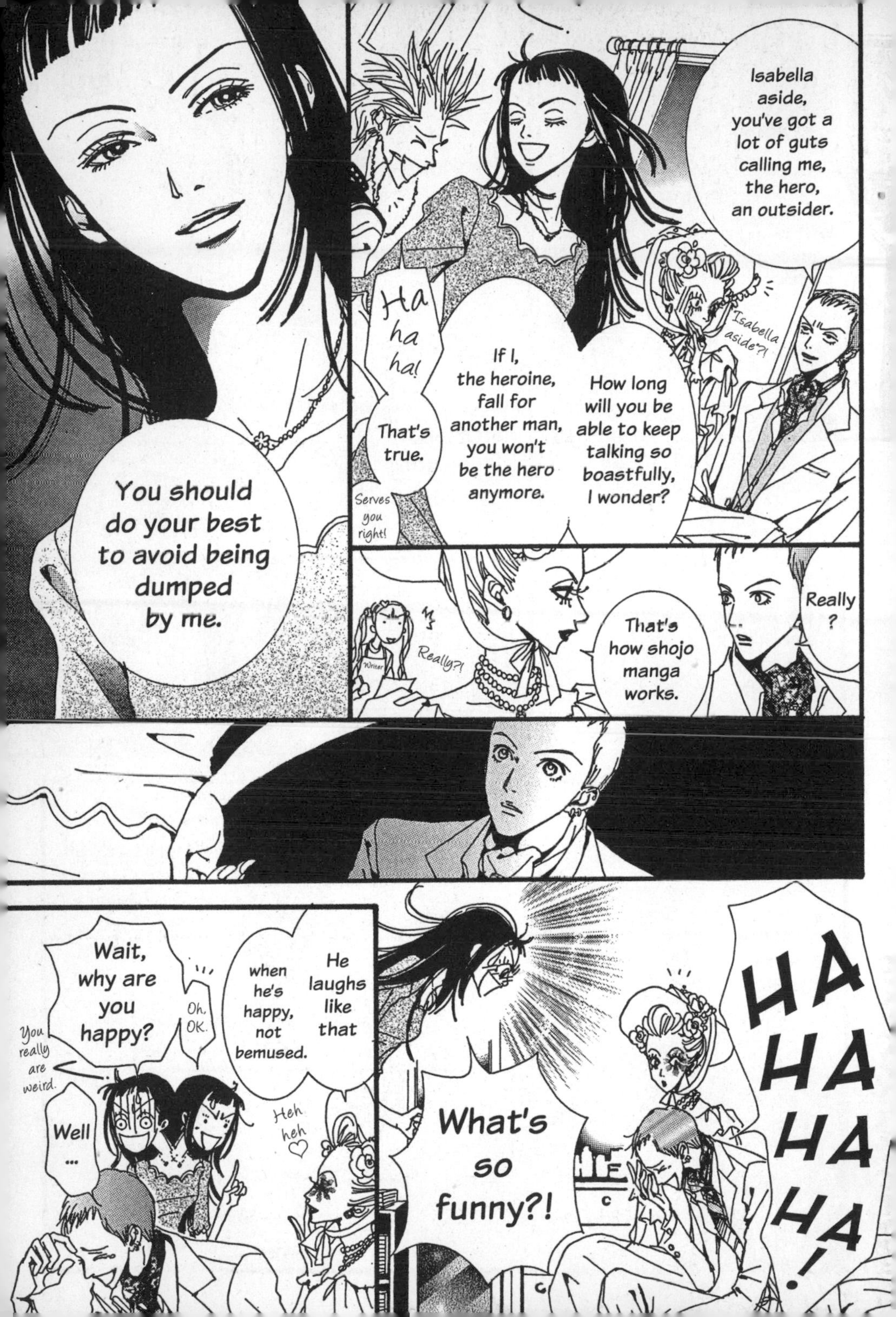
Isabella aside, you've got a lot of guts calling me, the hero, an outsider.
"Isabella aside"?!
How long will you be able to keep talking so boastfully, I wonder?
If I, the heroine, fall for another man, you won't be the hero anymore.
Ha ha ha!
That's true.
Serves you right!
Really?
That's how shojo manga works.
Really?!
Writer
You should do your best to avoid being dumped by me.
HA HA HA HA HA!
What's so funny?!
He laughs like that when he's happy, not bemused.
Oh, OK.
Wait, why are you happy?
You really are weird.
Heh heh ♡
Well ...

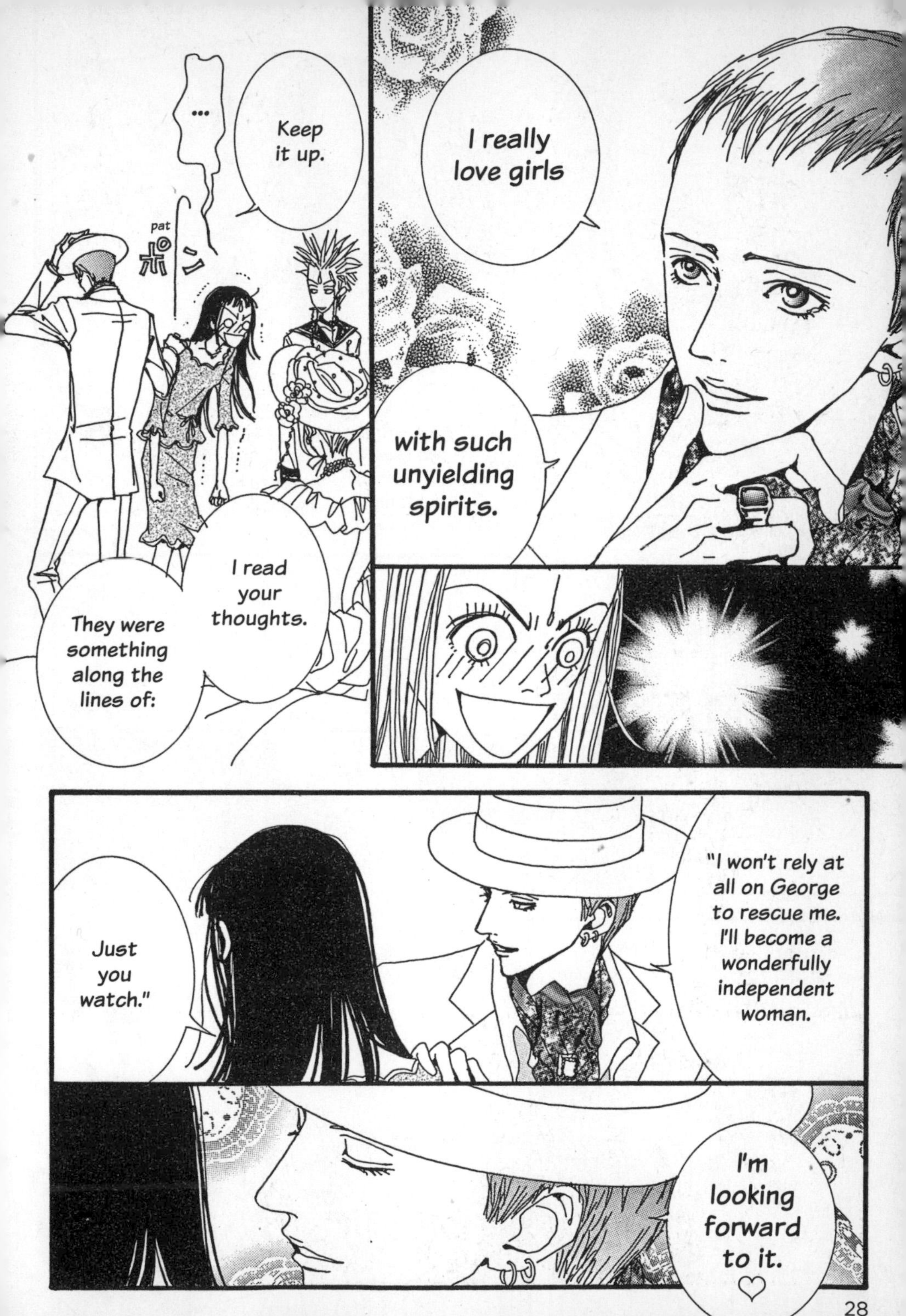

I really love girls
with such unyielding spirits.
...
Keep it up.
pat
ポン
I read your thoughts.
They were something along the lines of:
"I won't rely at all on George to rescue me. I'll become a wonderfully independent woman.
Just you watch."
I'm looking forward to it. ♡

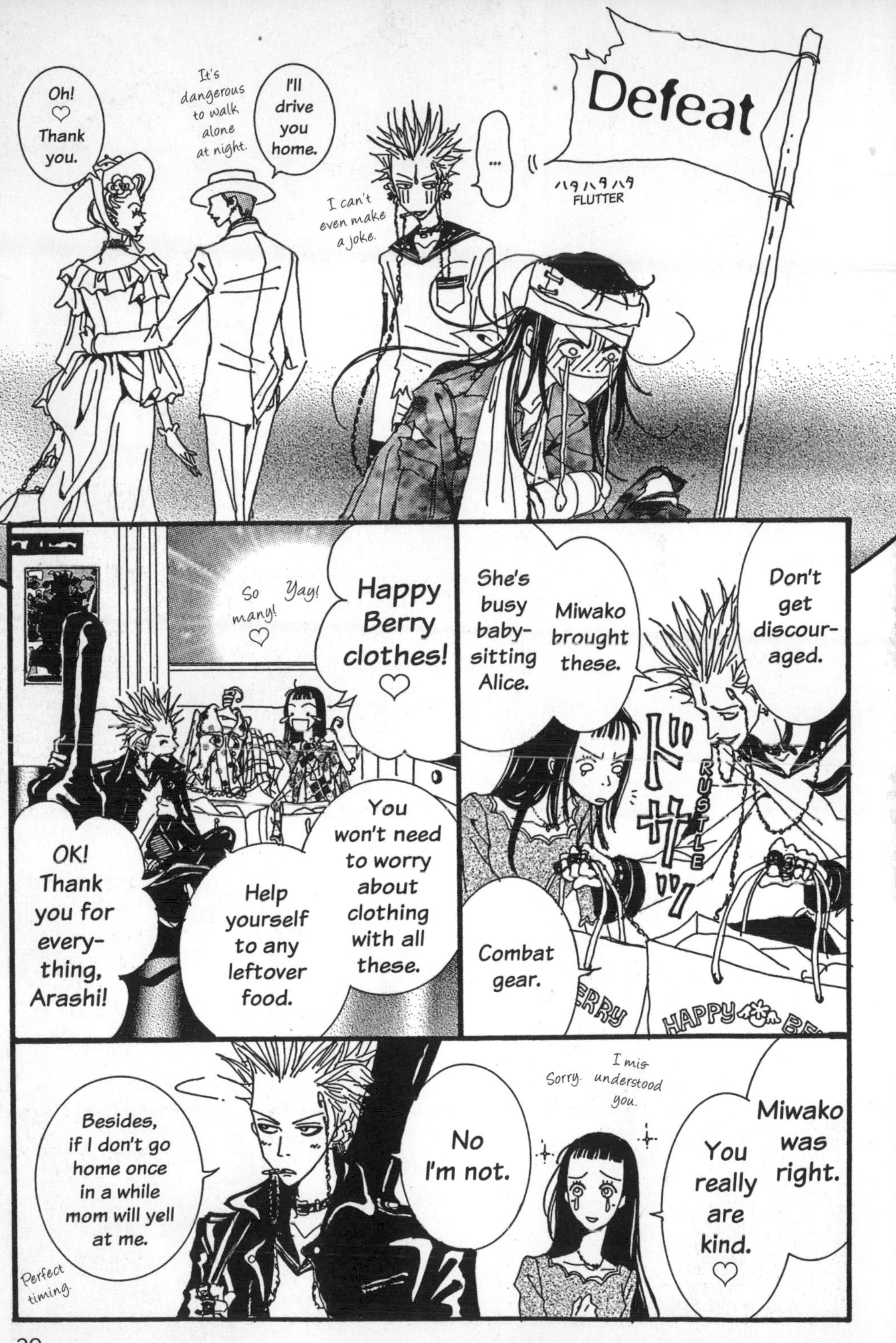
Defeat
ハタハタハタ
FLUTTER
...
I can't even make a joke.
I'll drive you home.
It's dangerous to walk alone at night.
Oh! ♡ Thank you.
Don't get discour-aged.
Miwako brought these.
She's busy baby-sitting Alice.
RUSTLE
Combat gear.
HAPPY
Happy Berry clothes! ♡
Yay!
So many! ♡
You won't need to worry about clothing with all these.
Help yourself to any leftover food.
OK! Thank you for every-thing, Arashi!
Miwako was right.
You really are kind. ♡
I mis understood you.
Sorry.
No I'm not.
Besides, if I don't go home once in a while mom will yell at me.
Perfect timing.

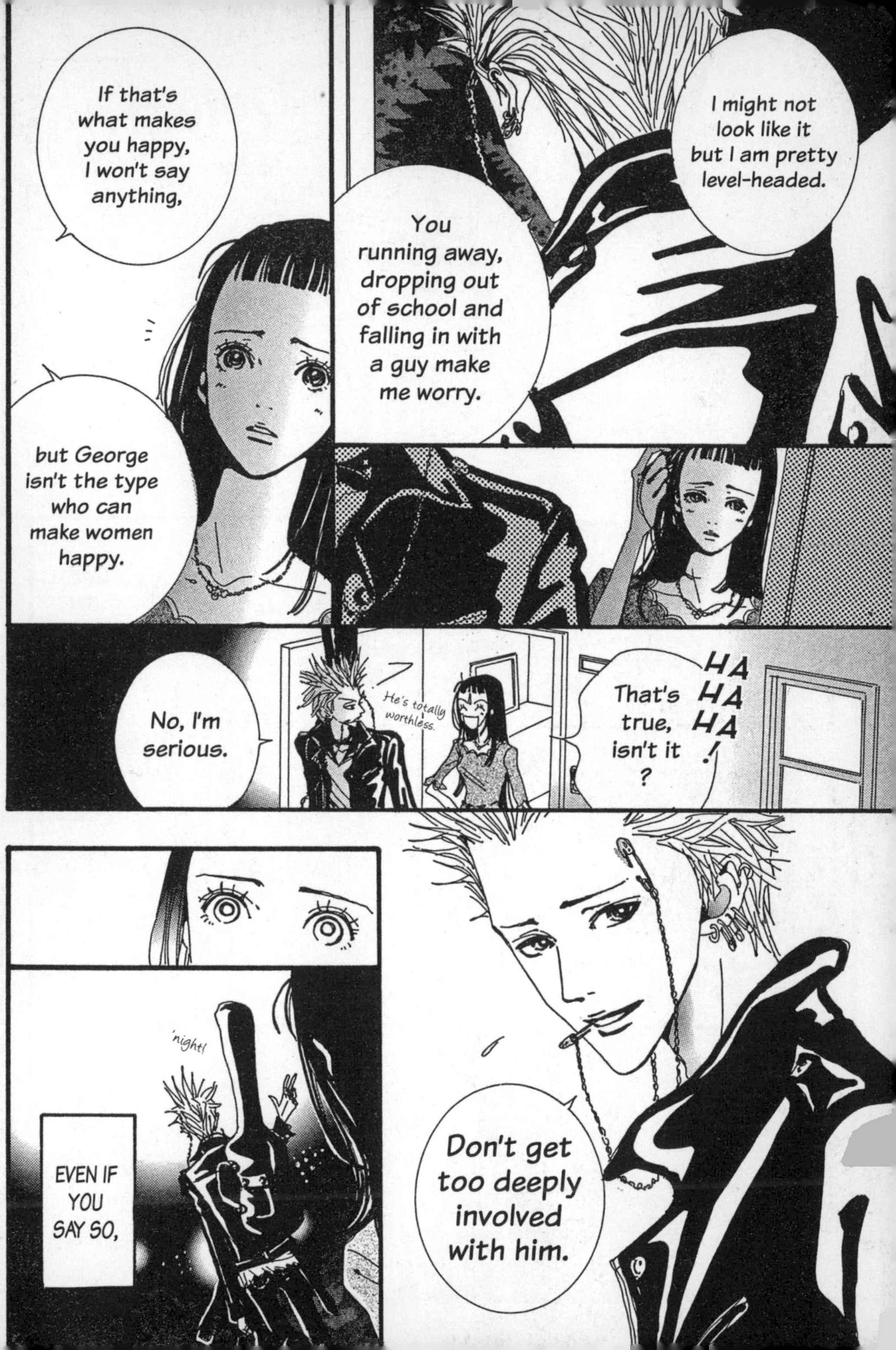
I might not look like it but I am pretty level-headed.
You running away, dropping out of school and falling in with a guy make me worry.
If that's what makes you happy, I won't say anything,
but George isn't the type who can make women happy.
That's true, isn't it?
HA HA HA!
He's totally worthless.
No, I'm serious.
Don't get too deeply involved with him.
'night!
EVEN IF YOU SAY SO,

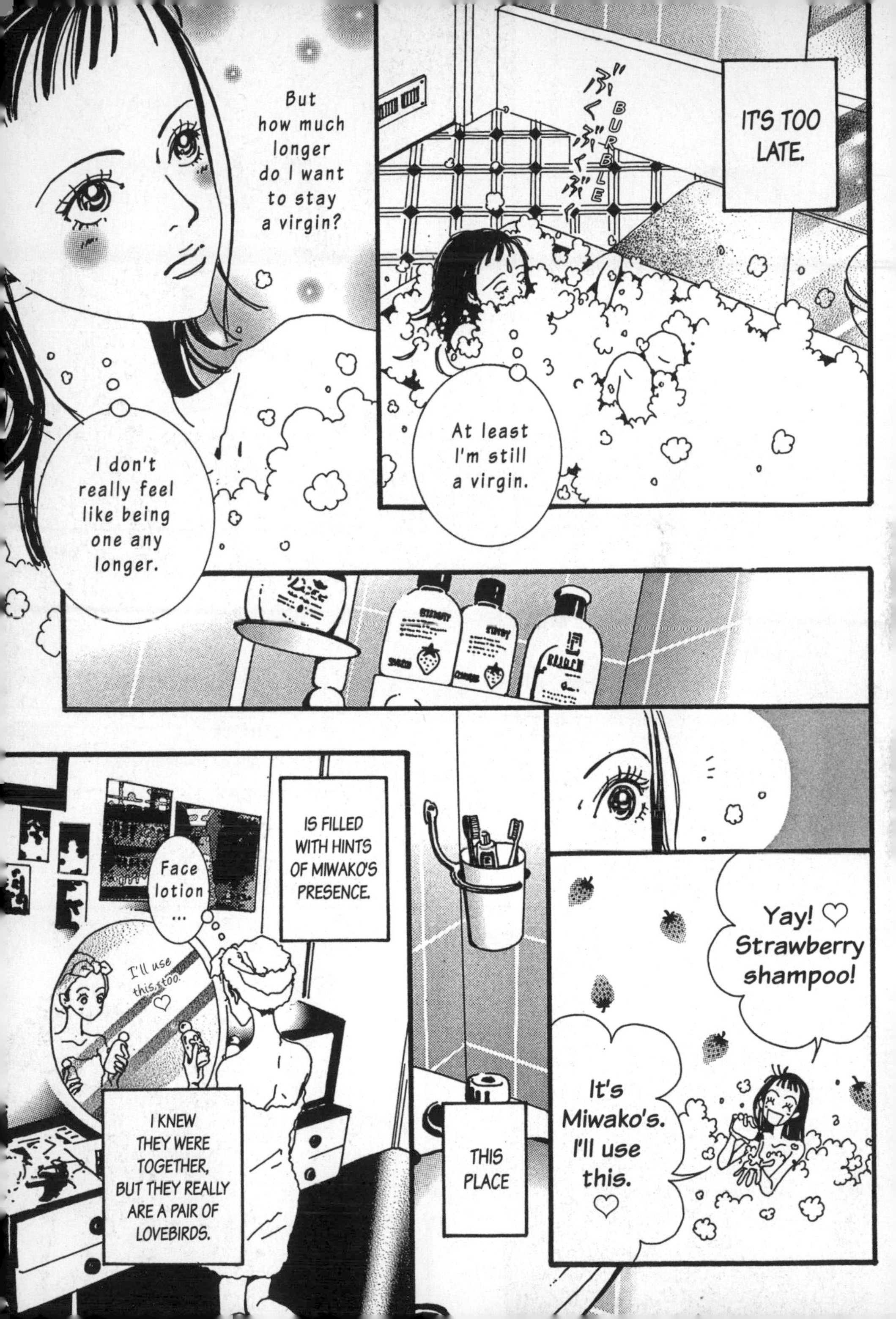
IT'S TOO LATE.
BURBLE
At least I'm still a virgin.
But how much longer do I want to stay a virgin?
I don't really feel like being one any longer.
Yay! ♡ Strawberry shampoo!
It's Miwako's. I'll use this. ♡
THIS PLACE
IS FILLED WITH HINTS OF MIWAKO'S PRESENCE.
Face lotion ...
I'll use this, too. ♡
I KNEW THEY WERE TOGETHER, BUT THEY REALLY ARE A PAIR OF LOVEBIRDS.

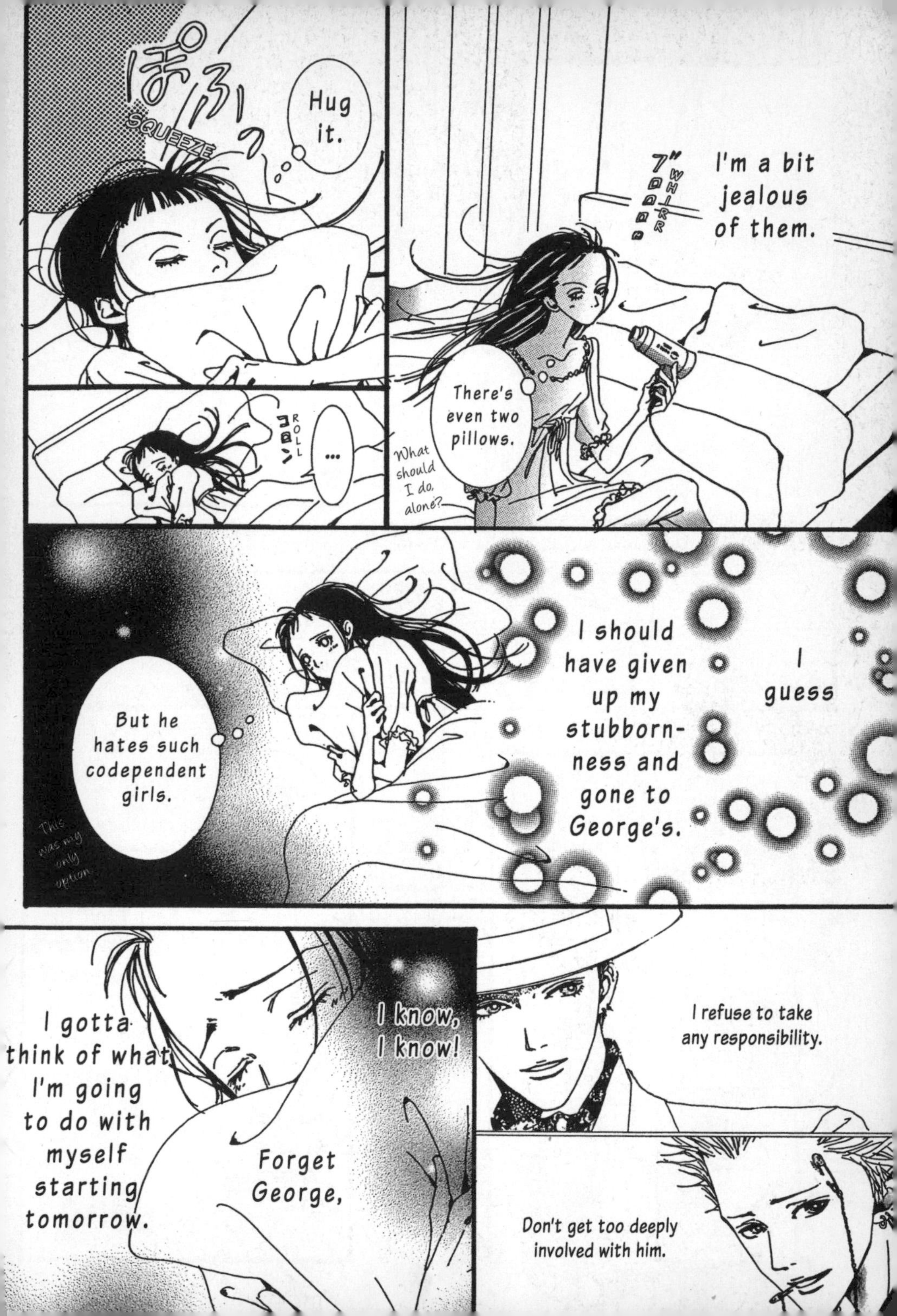
I'm a bit jealous of them.
WHIRR
There's even two pillows.
What should I do, alone?
SQUEEZE
Hug it.
ROLL
...
I guess
I should have given up my stubborn-ness and gone to George's.
But he hates such codependent girls.
This was my only option
I refuse to take any responsibility.
Don't get too deeply involved with him.
I know, I know!
Forget George,
I gotta think of what I'm going to do with myself starting tomorrow.

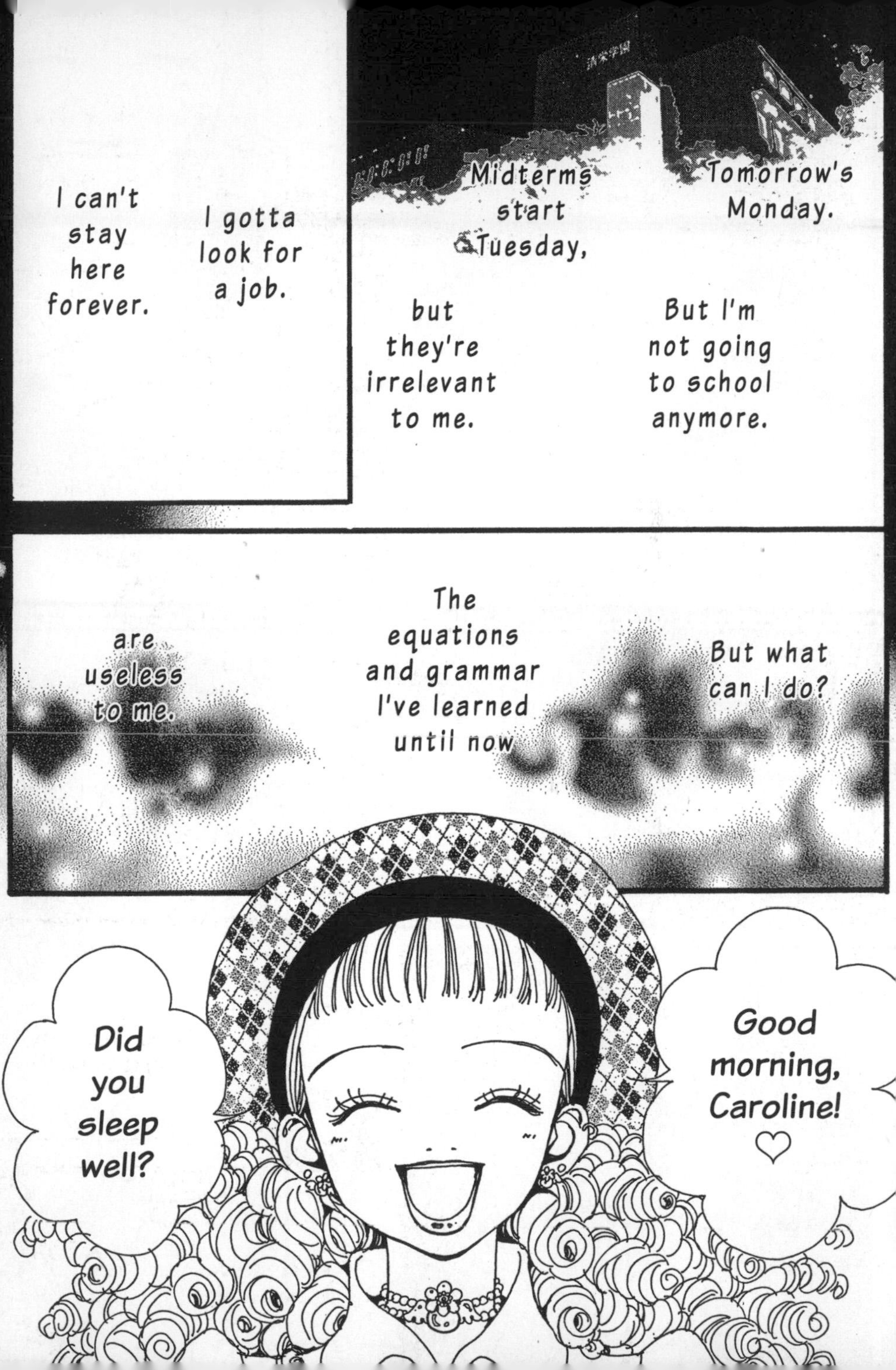
Tomorrow's Monday.
But I'm not going to school anymore.
Midterms start Tuesday,
but they're irrelevant to me.
I gotta look for a job.
I can't stay here forever.
But what can I do?
The equations and grammar I've learned until now
are useless to me.
Good morning, Caroline! ♡
Did you sleep well?

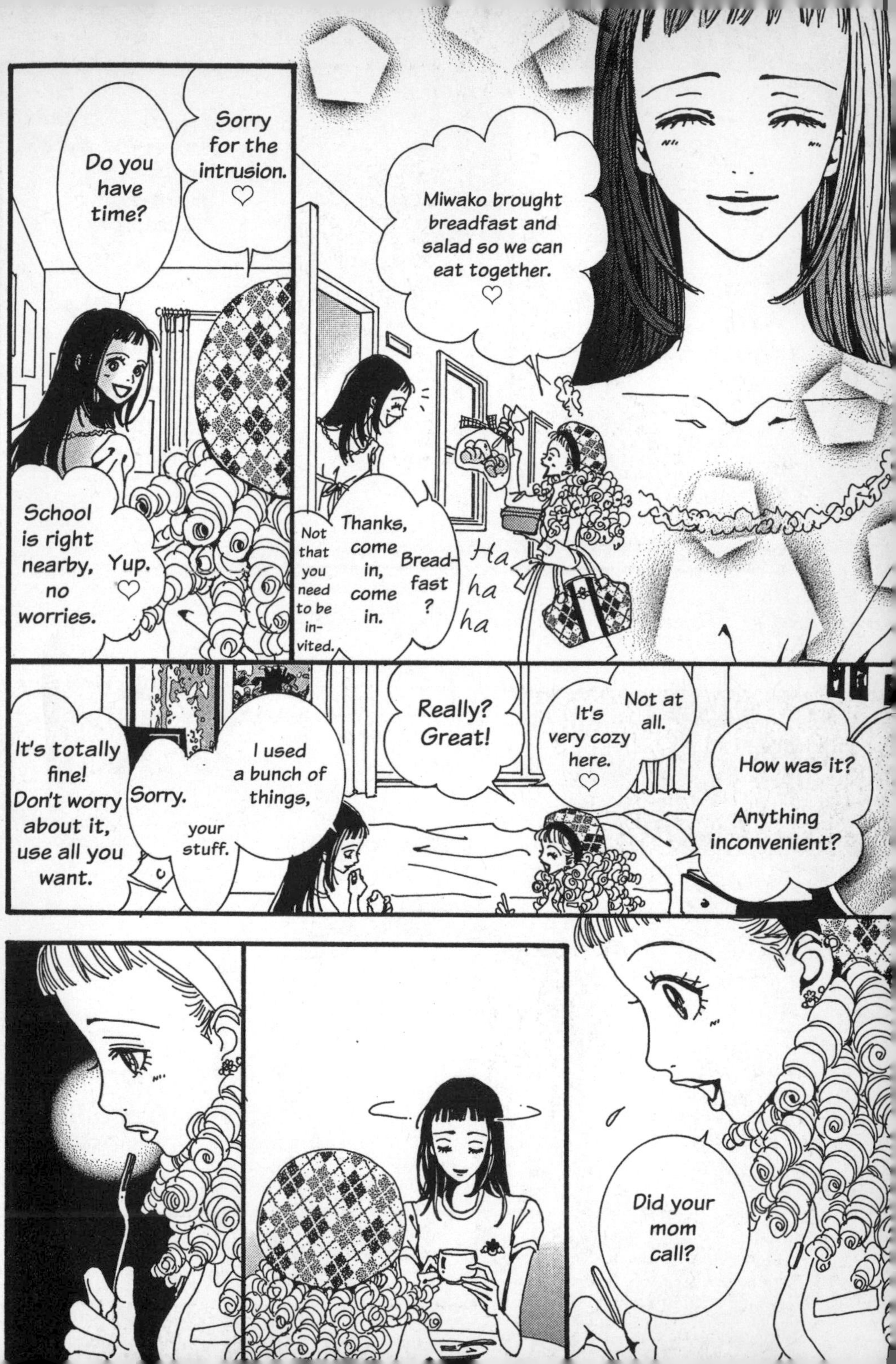
Miwako brought breadfast and salad so we can eat together. ♡
Ha ha ha
Breadfast?
Thanks, come in, come in.
Not that you need to be invited.
Sorry for the intrusion. ♡
Do you have time?
Yup. ♡
School is right nearby, no worries.
How was it? Anything inconvenient?
Not at all. It's very cozy here. ♡
Really? Great!
I used a bunch of things, your stuff.
Sorry.
It's totally fine! Don't worry about it, use all you want.
Did your mom call?

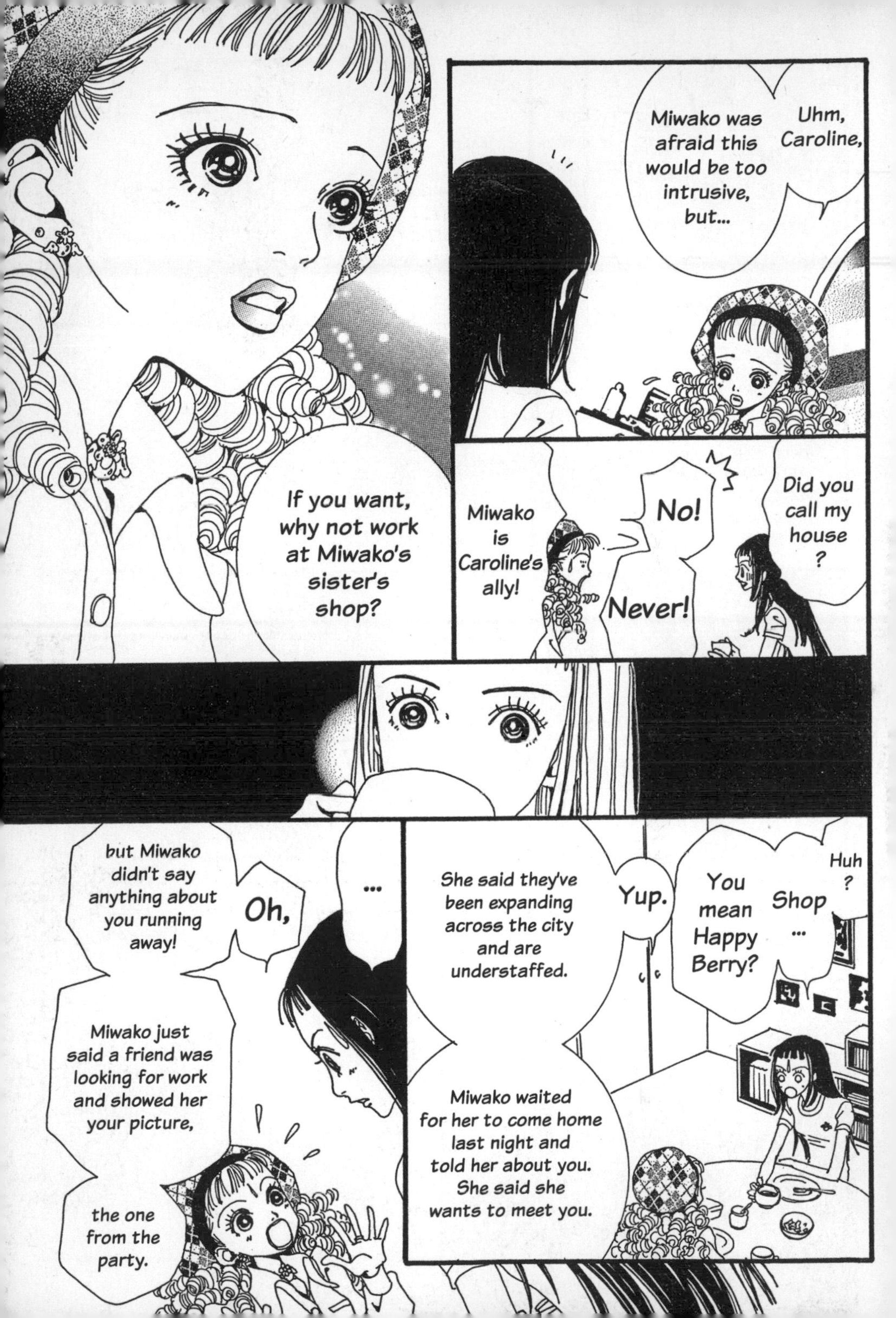
Uhm, Caroline,
Miwako was afraid this would be too intrusive, but...
Did you call my house?
No!
Never!
Miwako is Caroline's ally!
If you want, why not work at Miwako's sister's shop?
Huh?
Shop...
You mean Happy Berry?
Yup.
She said they've been expanding across the city and are understaffed.
Miwako waited for her to come home last night and told her about you. She said she wants to meet you.
...
Oh,
but Miwako didn't say anything about you running away!
Miwako just said a friend was looking for work and showed her your picture,
the one from the party.

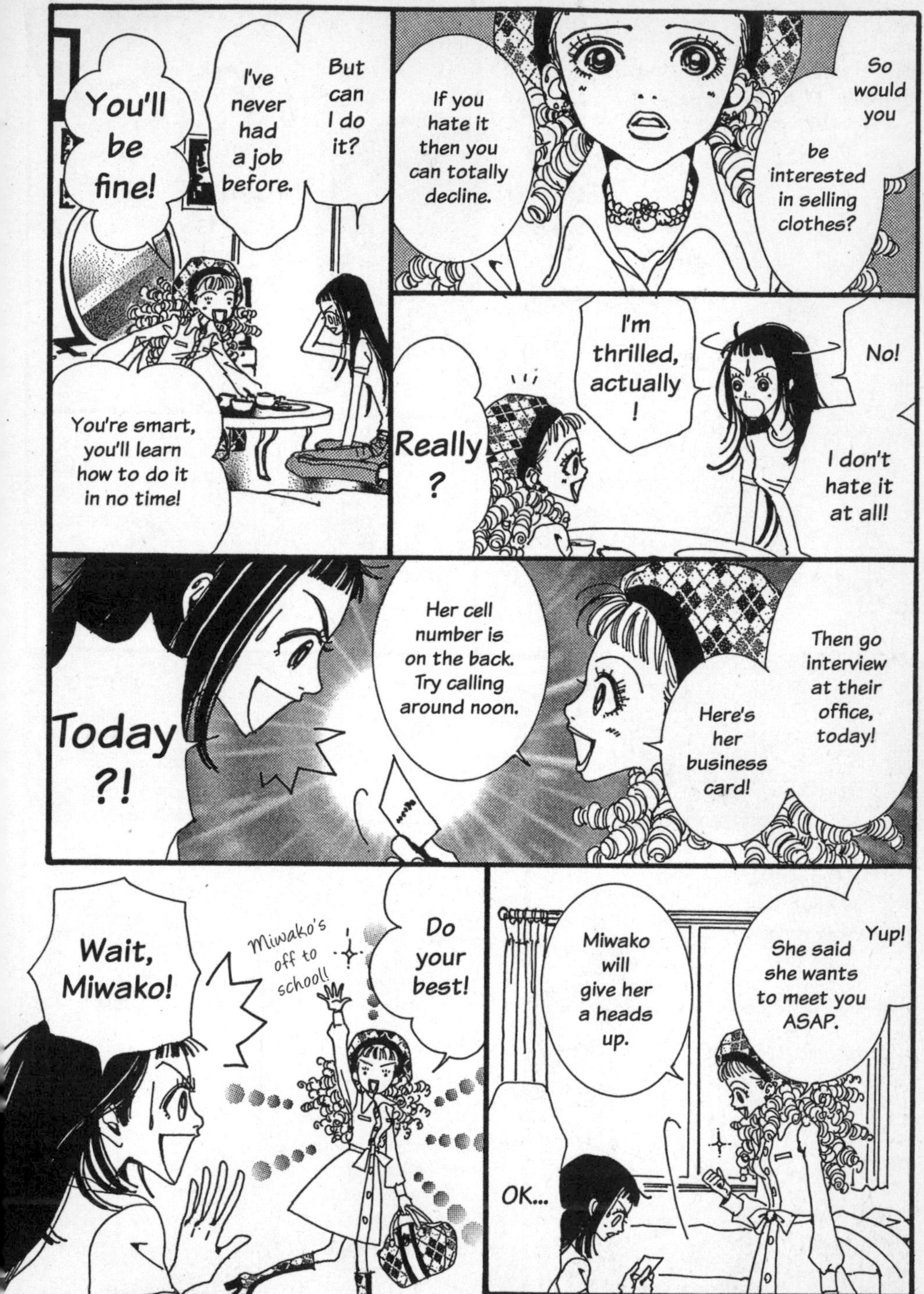
So would you
be interested in selling clothes?
If you hate it then you can totally decline.
No!
I don't hate it at all!
I'm thrilled, actually!
Really?
But can I do it?
I've never had a job before.
You'll be fine!
You're smart, you'll learn how to do it in no time!
Then go interview at their office, today!
Here's her business card!
Her cell number is on the back. Try calling around noon.
Today?!
Yup!
She said she wants to meet you ASAP.
Miwako will give her a heads up.
OK...
Do your best!
Miwako's off to school!
Wait, Miwako!

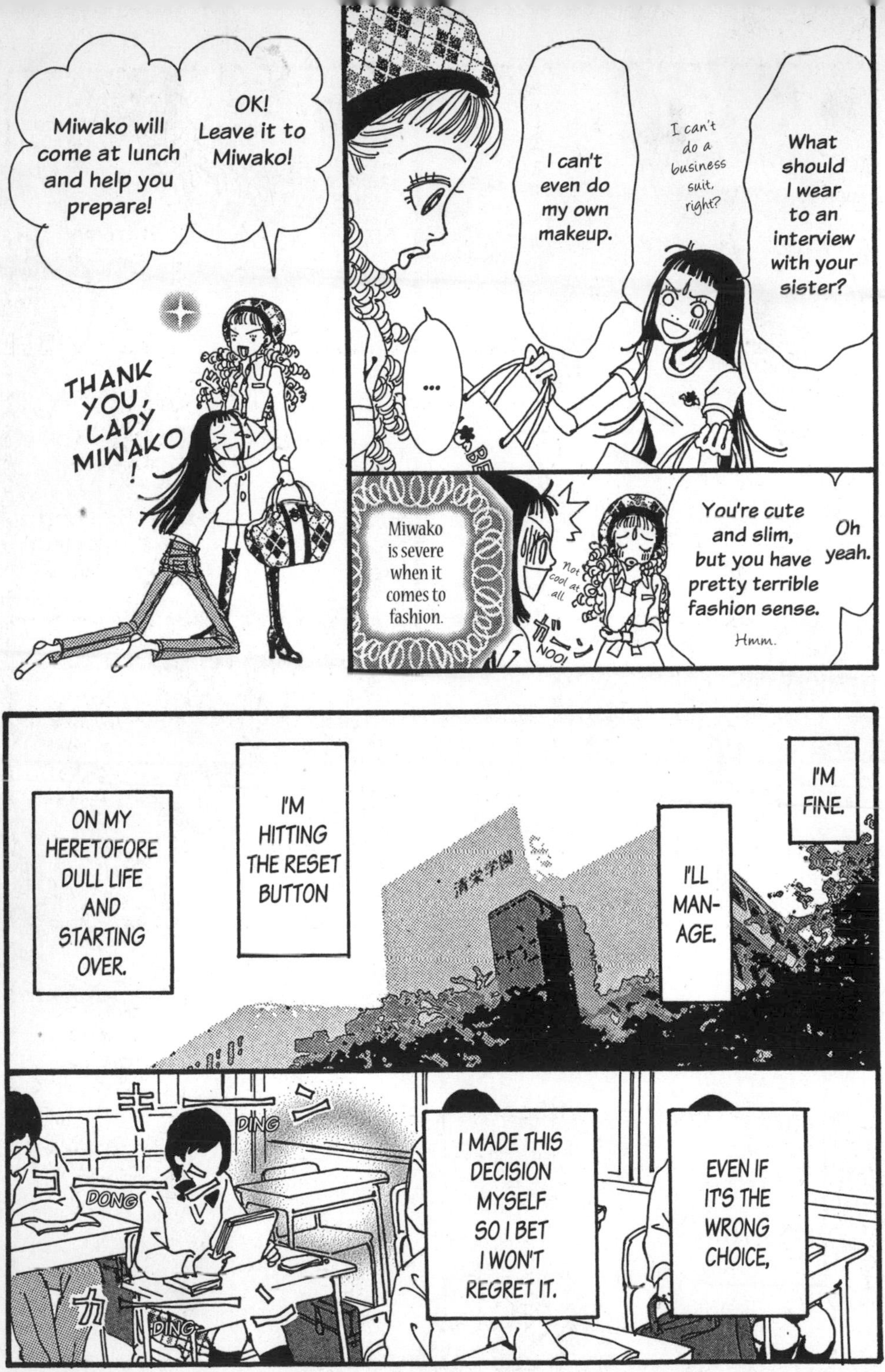
What should I wear to an interview with your sister?
I can't do a business suit, right?
I can't even do my own makeup.
...
Oh yeah.
You're cute and slim, but you have pretty terrible fashion sense.
Hmm.
Not cool at all
NOO!
Miwako is severe when it comes to fashion.
OK! Leave it to Miwako!
Miwako will come at lunch and help you prepare!
THANK YOU, LADY MIWAKO!
I'M FINE.
I'LL MAN-AGE.
I'M HITTING THE RESET BUTTON
ON MY HERETOFORE DULL LIFE AND STARTING OVER.
EVEN IF IT'S THE WRONG CHOICE,
I MADE THIS DECISION MYSELF SO I BET I WON'T REGRET IT.
DING
DONG
DING

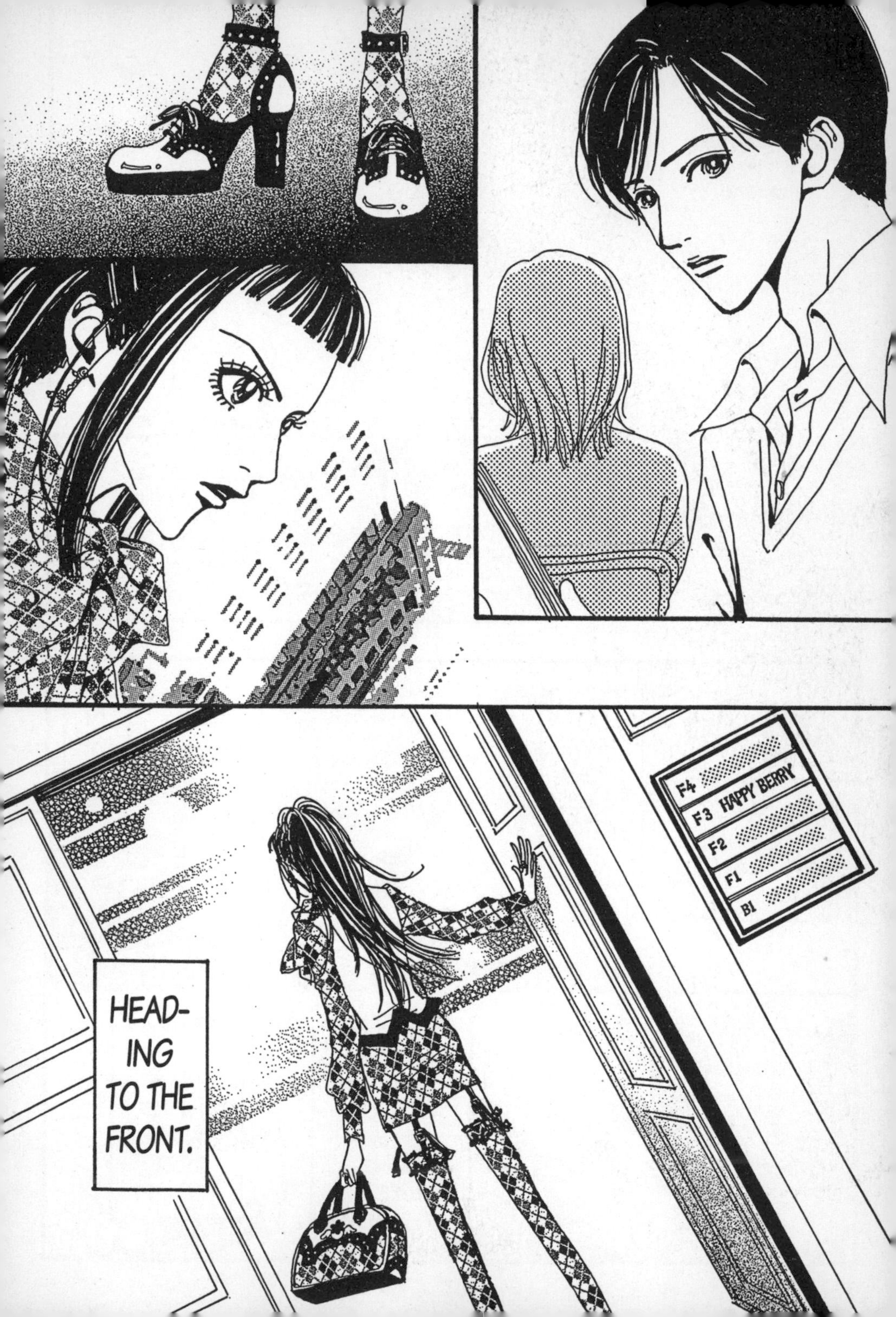
F4
F3 HAPPY BERRY
F2
F1
B1
HEAD-
ING
TO THE
FRONT.

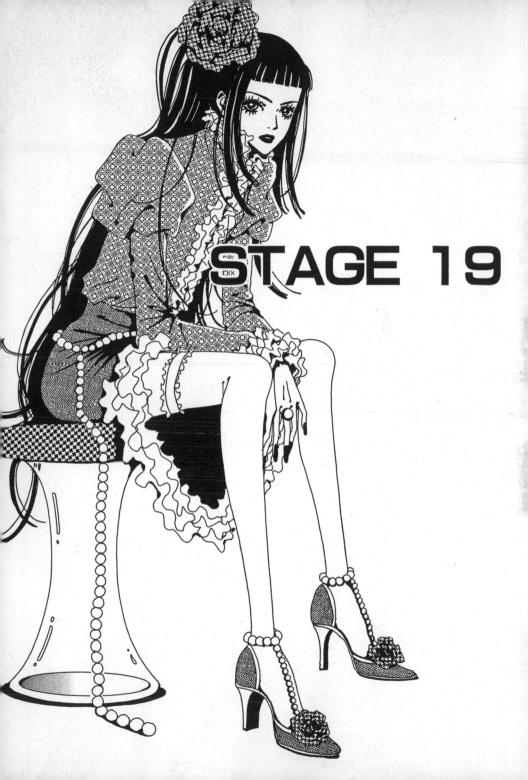

STAGE 19

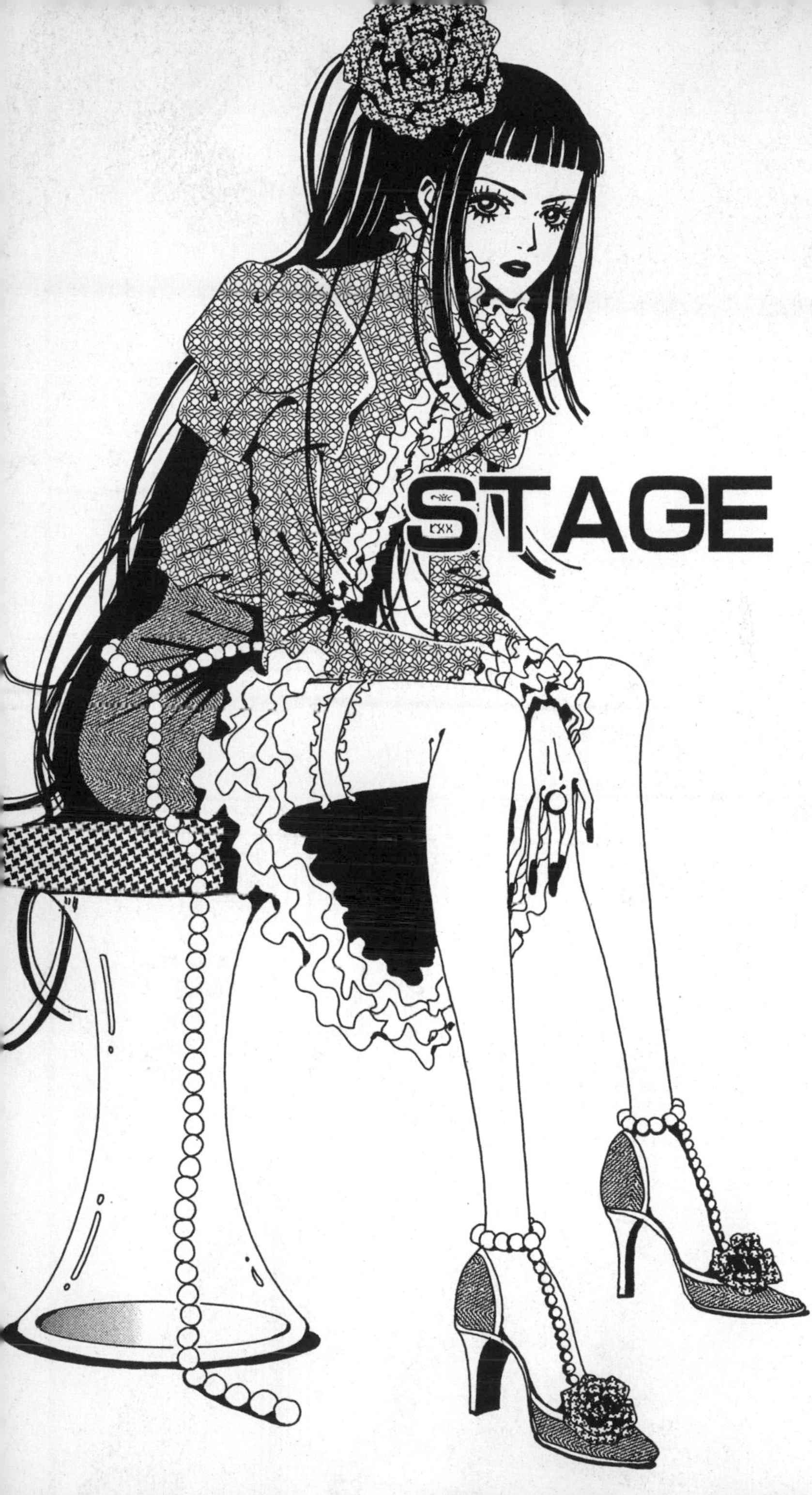

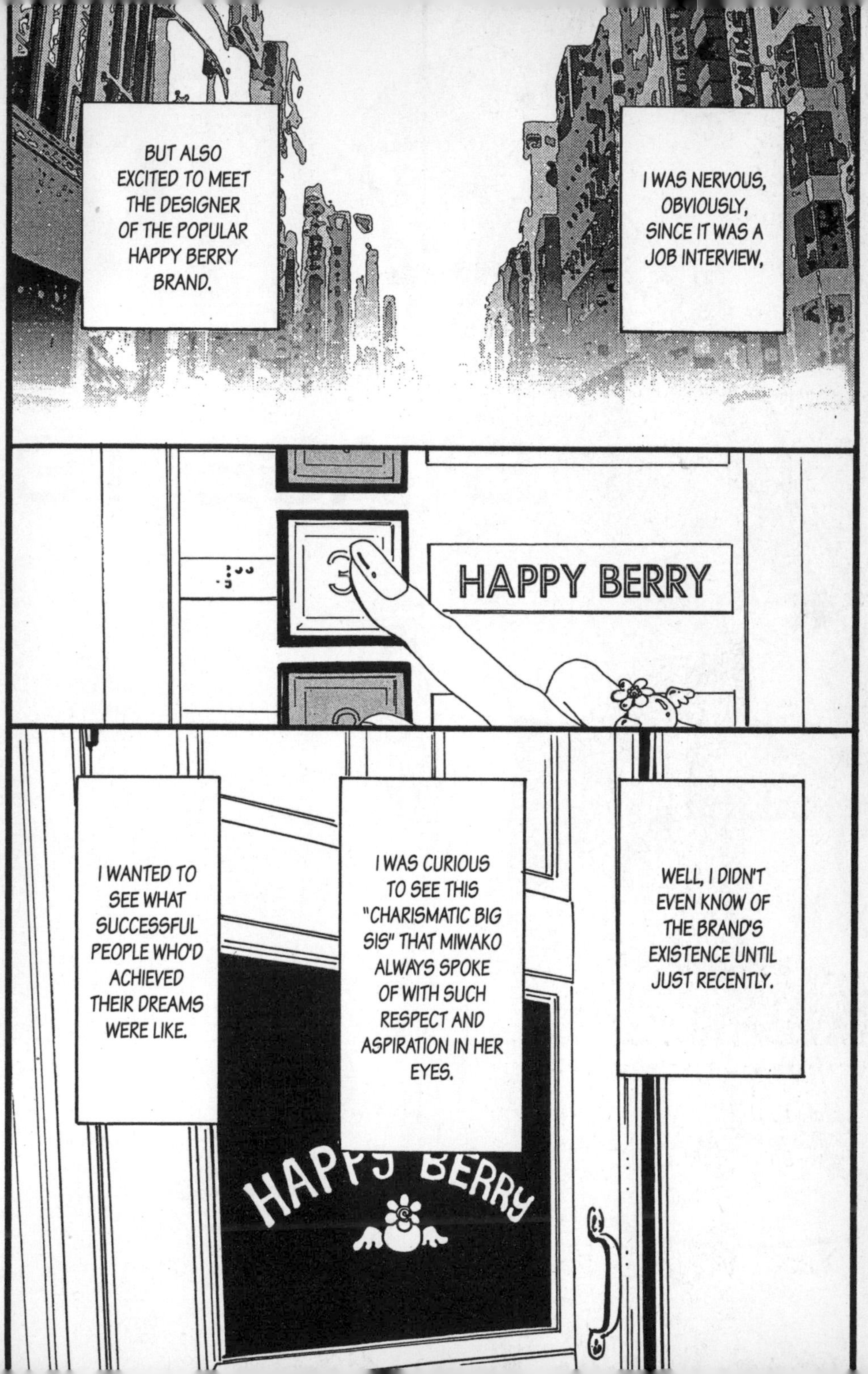
I WAS NERVOUS, OBVIOUSLY, SINCE IT WAS A JOB INTERVIEW,
BUT ALSO EXCITED TO MEET THE DESIGNER OF THE POPULAR HAPPY BERRY BRAND.
HAPPY BERRY
WELL, I DIDN'T EVEN KNOW OF THE BRAND'S EXISTENCE UNTIL JUST RECENTLY.
I WAS CURIOUS TO SEE THIS "CHARISMATIC BIG SIS" THAT MIWAKO ALWAYS SPOKE OF WITH SUCH RESPECT AND ASPIRATION IN HER EYES.
I WANTED TO SEE WHAT SUCCESSFUL PEOPLE WHO'D ACHIEVED THEIR DREAMS WERE LIKE.

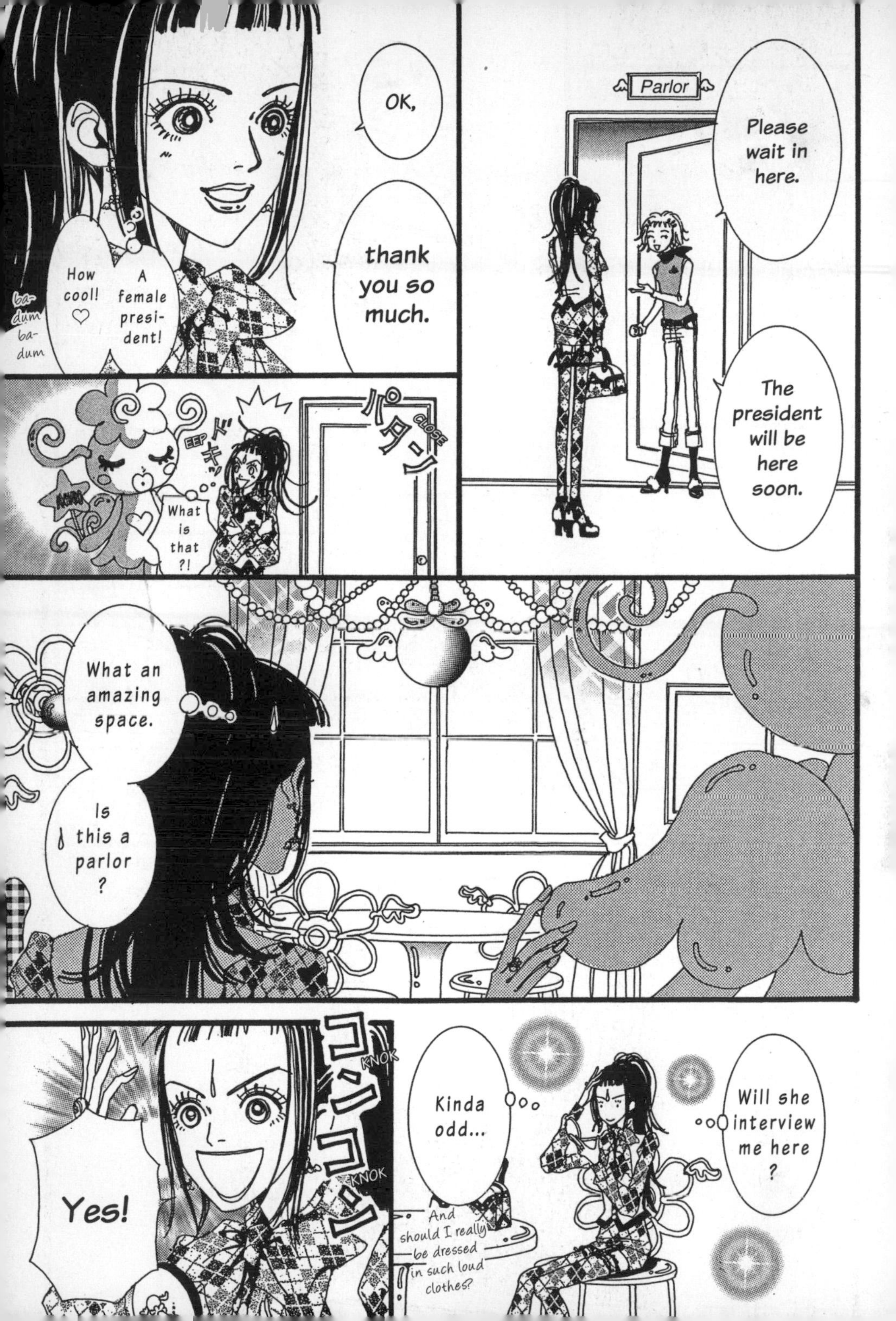
Parlor
Please wait in here.
The president will be here soon.
OK,
thank you so much.
How cool! ♡ A female president!
ba-dum ba-dum
CLOSE
EEP
What is that ?!
What an amazing space.
Is this a parlor ?
Will she interview me here ?
Kinda odd...
And should I really be dressed in such loud clothes?
KNOK
KNOK
Yes!

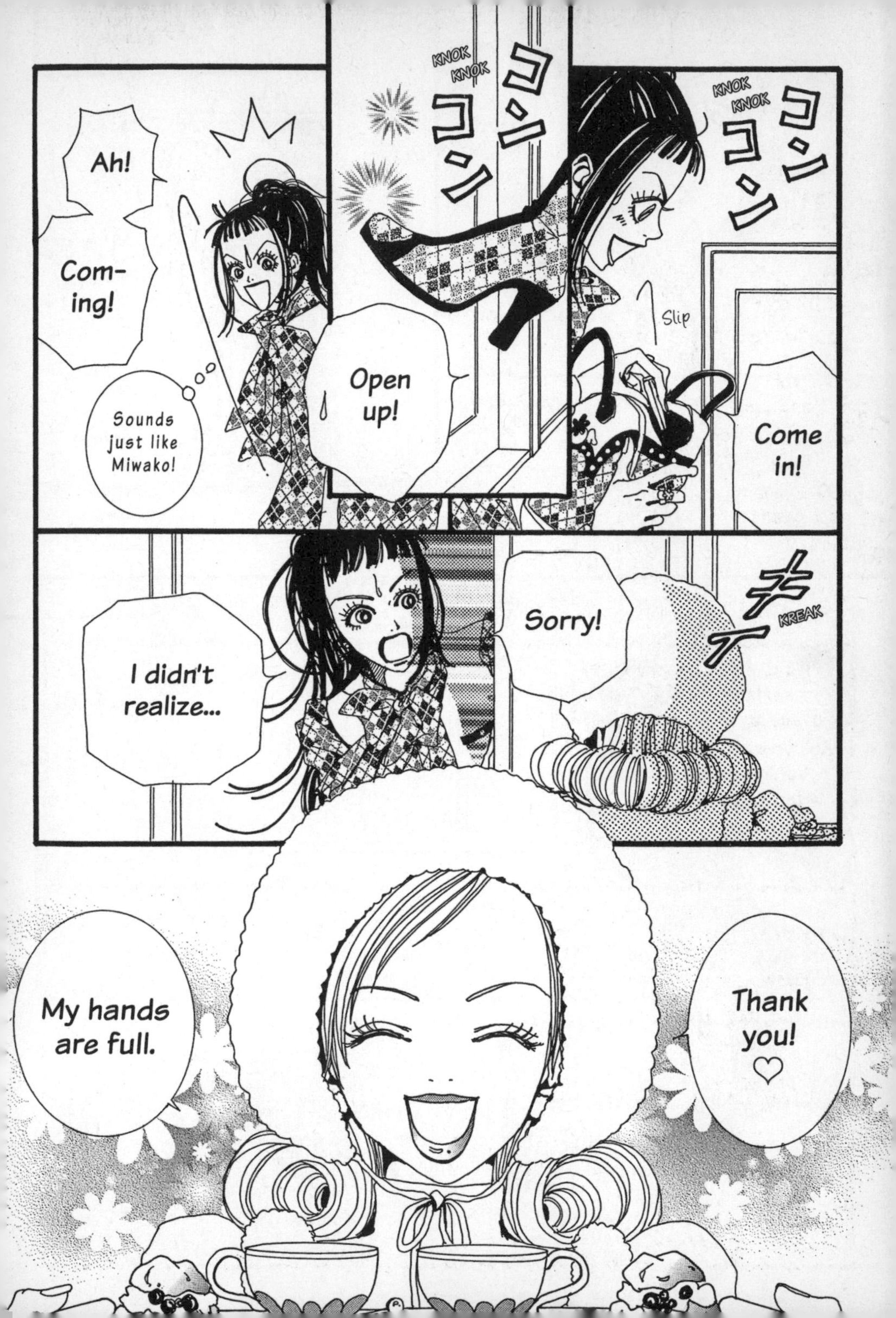
KNOK KNOK
コン
コン
Slip
Come in!
KNOK KNOK
コン
コン
Open up!
Ah!
Coming!
Sounds just like Miwako!
キィ
KREAK
Sorry!
I didn't realize...
Thank you! ♡
My hands are full.

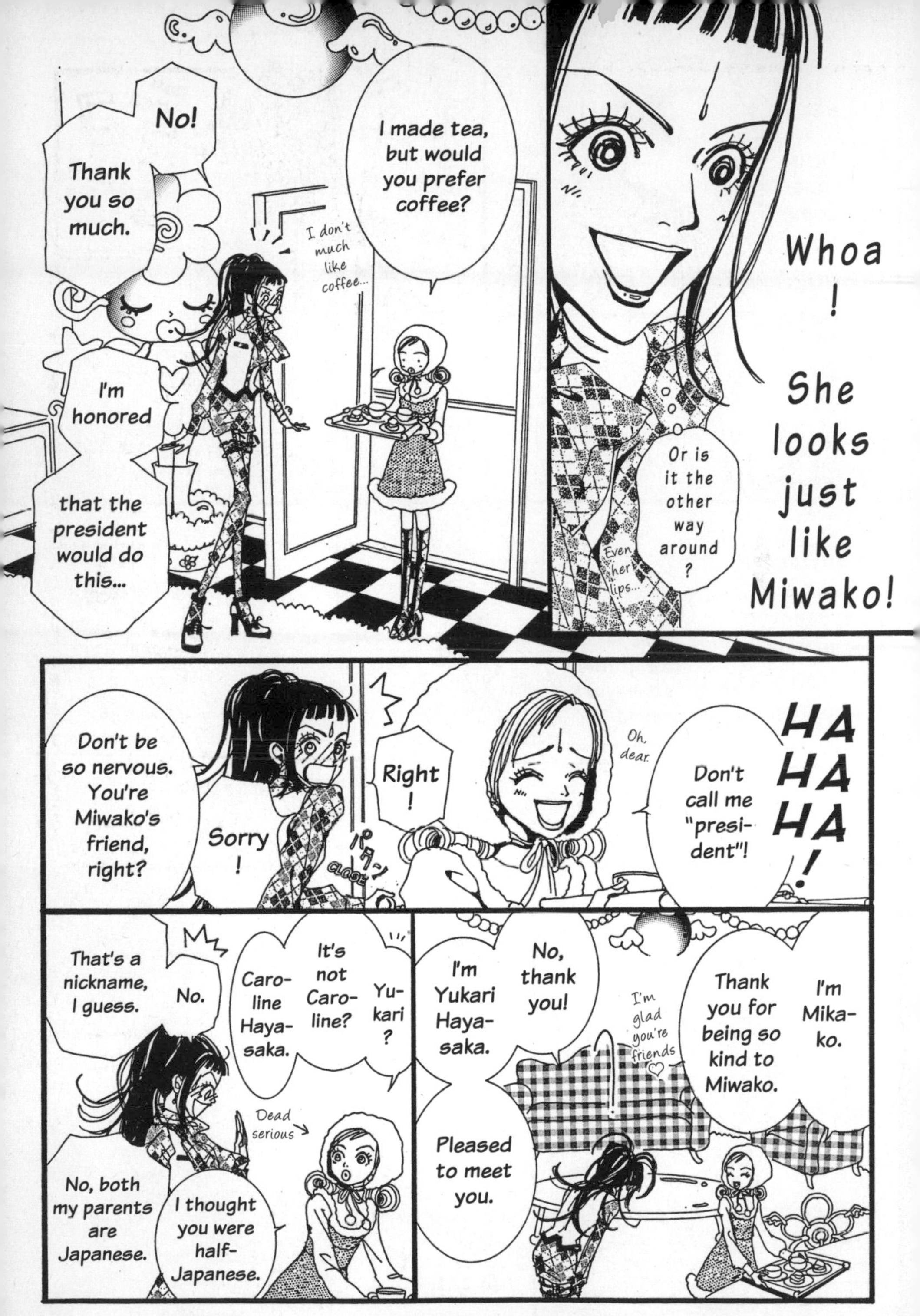
Whoa!
She looks just like Miwako!
Or is it the other way around?
Even her lips...
I made tea, but would you prefer coffee?
I don't much like coffee...
No!
Thank you so much.
I'm honored
that the president would do this...
HA HA HA!
Don't call me "president"!
Oh, dear.
Right!
Sorry!
CLOSE
Don't be so nervous. You're Miwako's friend, right?
I'm Mikako.
Thank you for being so kind to Miwako.
I'm glad you're friends
No, thank you!
I'm Yukari Hayasaka.
Pleased to meet you.
Yu-kari?
It's not Caro-line?
Caro-line Hayasaka.
No.
That's a nickname, I guess.
Dead serious
I thought you were half-Japanese.
No, both my parents are Japanese.

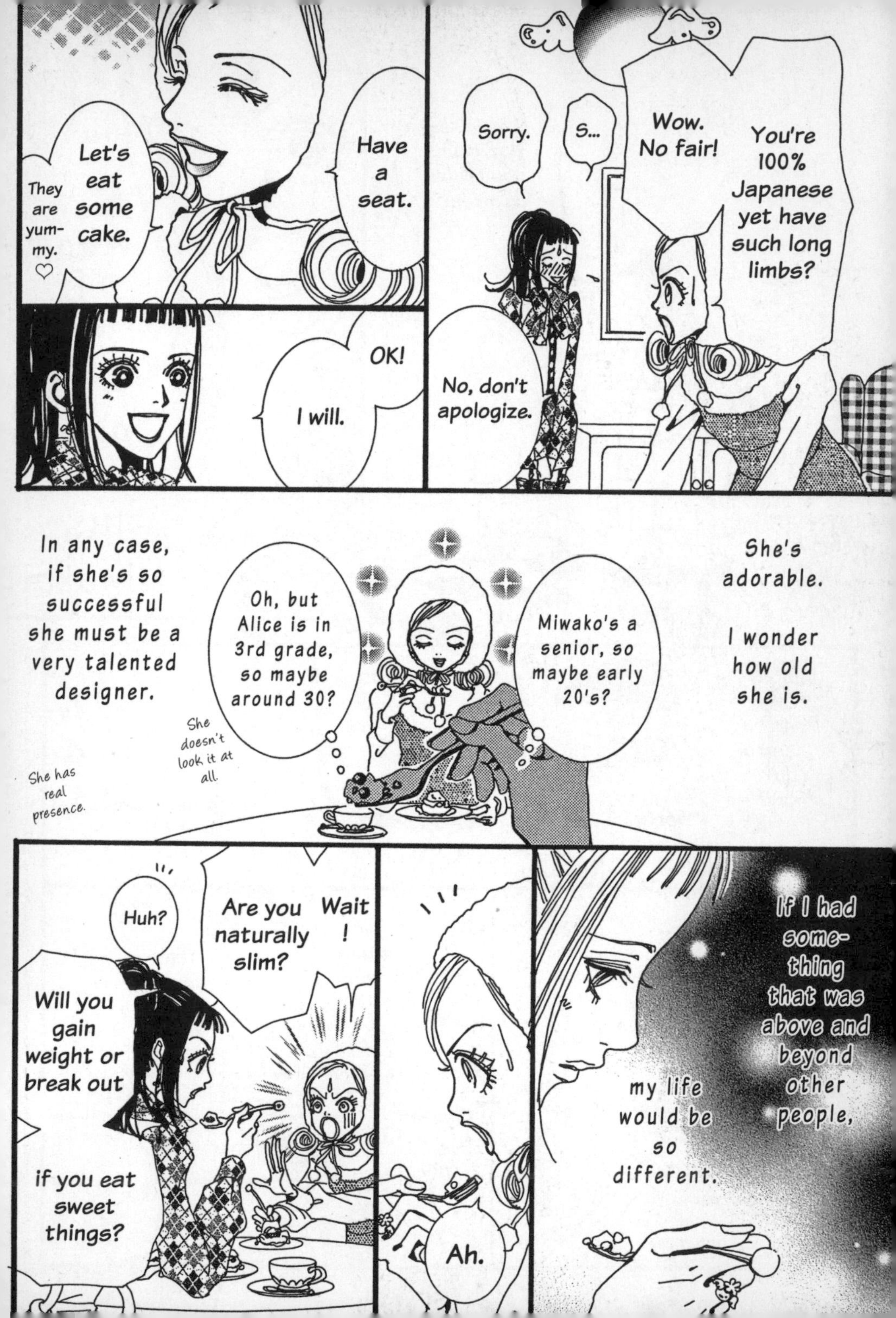

You're 100% Japanese yet have such long limbs?
Wow. No fair!
S...
Sorry.
No, don't apologize.
Have a seat.
Let's eat some cake.
They are yum-my. ♡
OK! I will.
She's adorable. I wonder how old she is.
Miwako's a senior, so maybe early 20's?
Oh, but Alice is in 3rd grade, so maybe around 30?
She doesn't look it at all.
In any case, if she's so successful she must be a very talented designer.
She has real presence.
If I had something that was above and beyond other people,
my life would be so different.
Ah.
Wait!
Are you naturally slim?
Huh?
Will you gain weight or break out
if you eat sweet things?

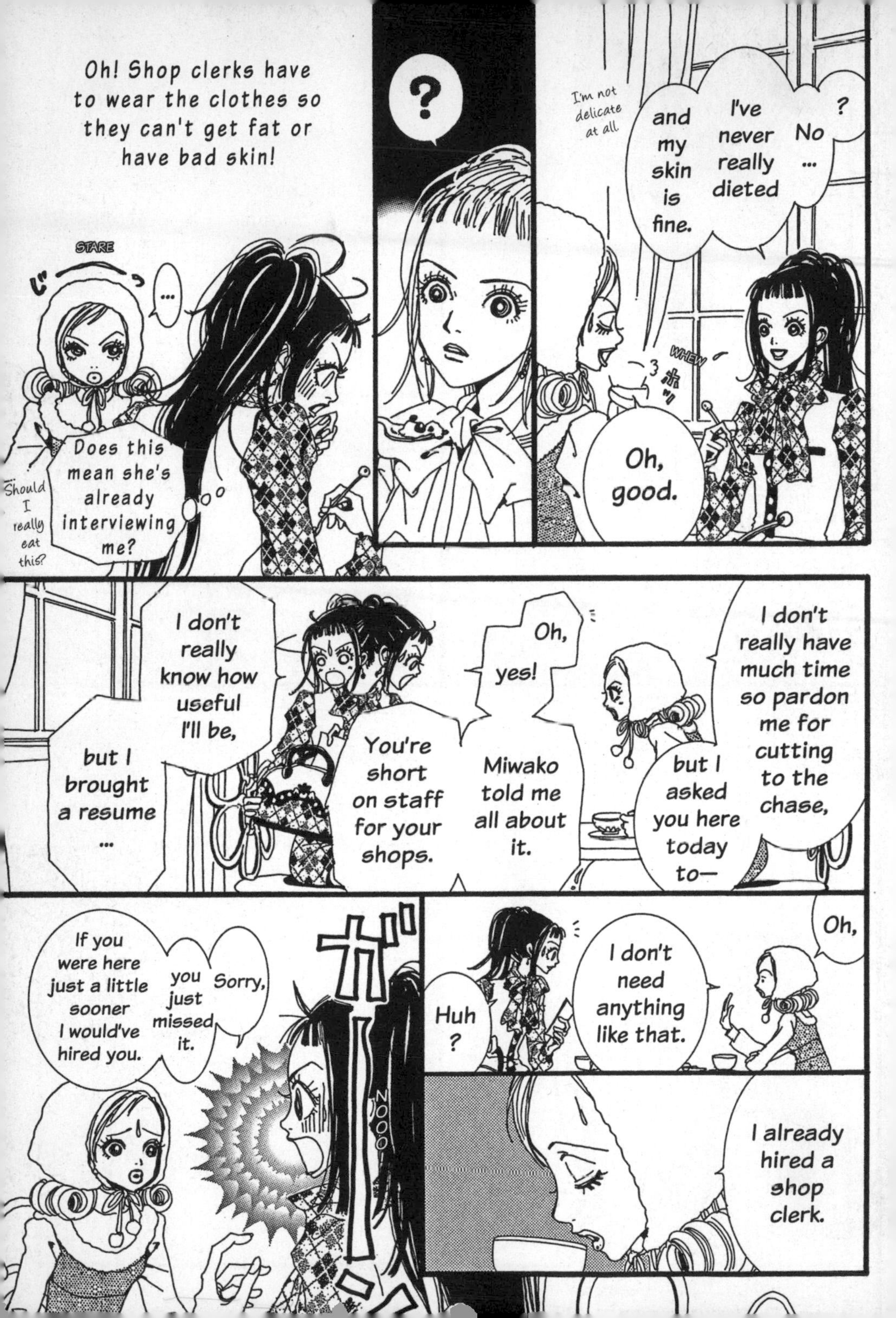

No ...?
I've never really dieted
and my skin is fine.
I'm not delicate at all.
WHEW
Oh, good.
?
Oh! Shop clerks have to wear the clothes so they can't get fat or have bad skin!
STARE
...
Does this mean she's already interviewing me?
Should I really eat this?
I don't really have much time so pardon me for cutting to the chase,
but I asked you here today to—
Oh,
yes!
Miwako told me all about it.
You're short on staff for your shops.
I don't really know how useful I'll be,
but I brought a resume ...
Oh,
I don't need anything like that.
Huh?
I already hired a shop clerk.
Sorry,
you just missed it.
If you were here just a little sooner I would've hired you.
NOOO

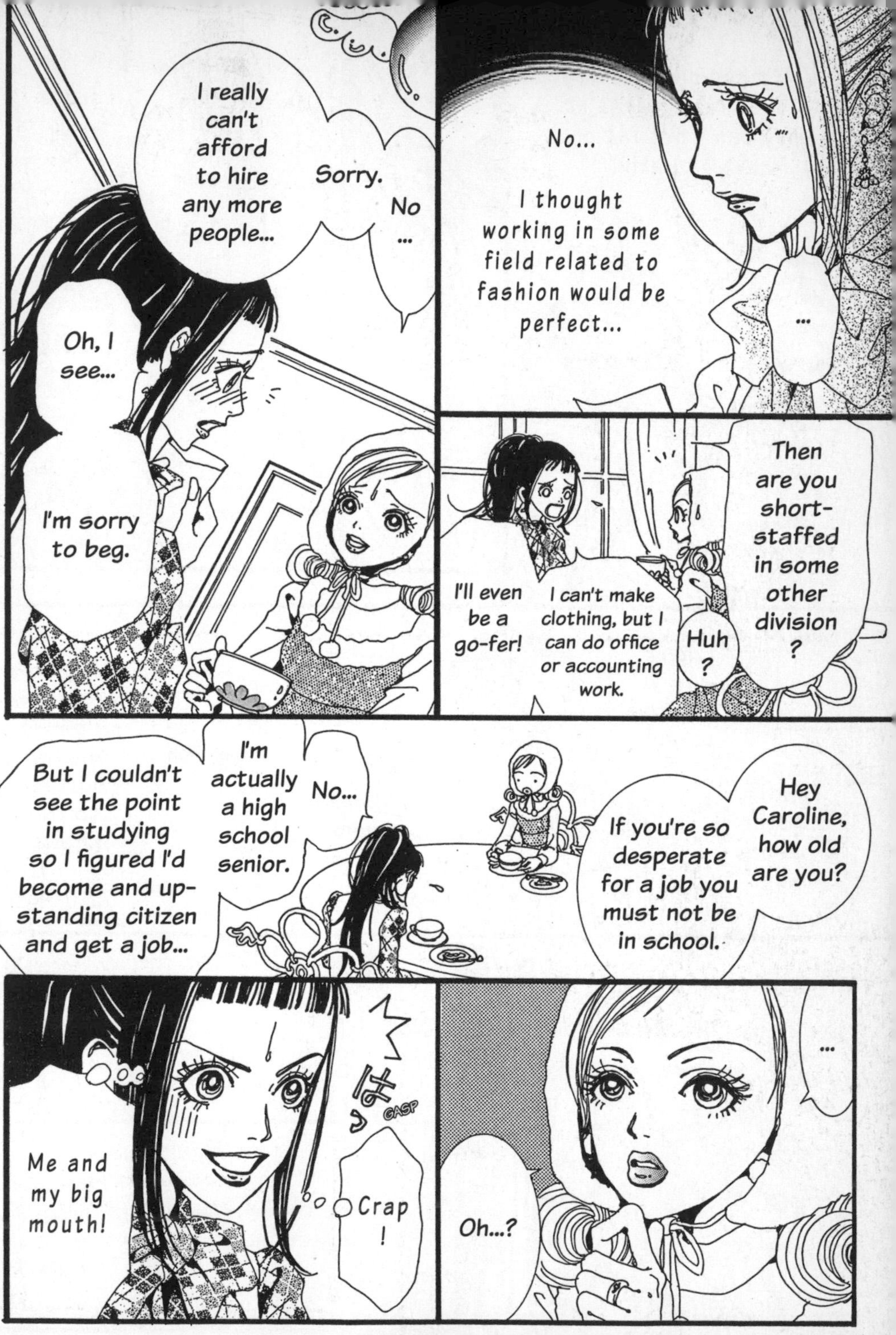

No...
I thought working in some field related to fashion would be perfect...
...
Then are you short-staffed in some other division?
Huh?
I can't make clothing, but I can do office or accounting work.
I'll even be a go-fer!
I really can't afford to hire any more people...
Sorry.
No ...
Oh, I see...
I'm sorry to beg.
Hey Caroline, how old are you?
If you're so desperate for a job you must not be in school.
No...
I'm actually a high school senior.
But I couldn't see the point in studying so I figured I'd become and up-standing citizen and get a job...
...
Oh...?
はっ
GASP
Crap!
Me and my big mouth!

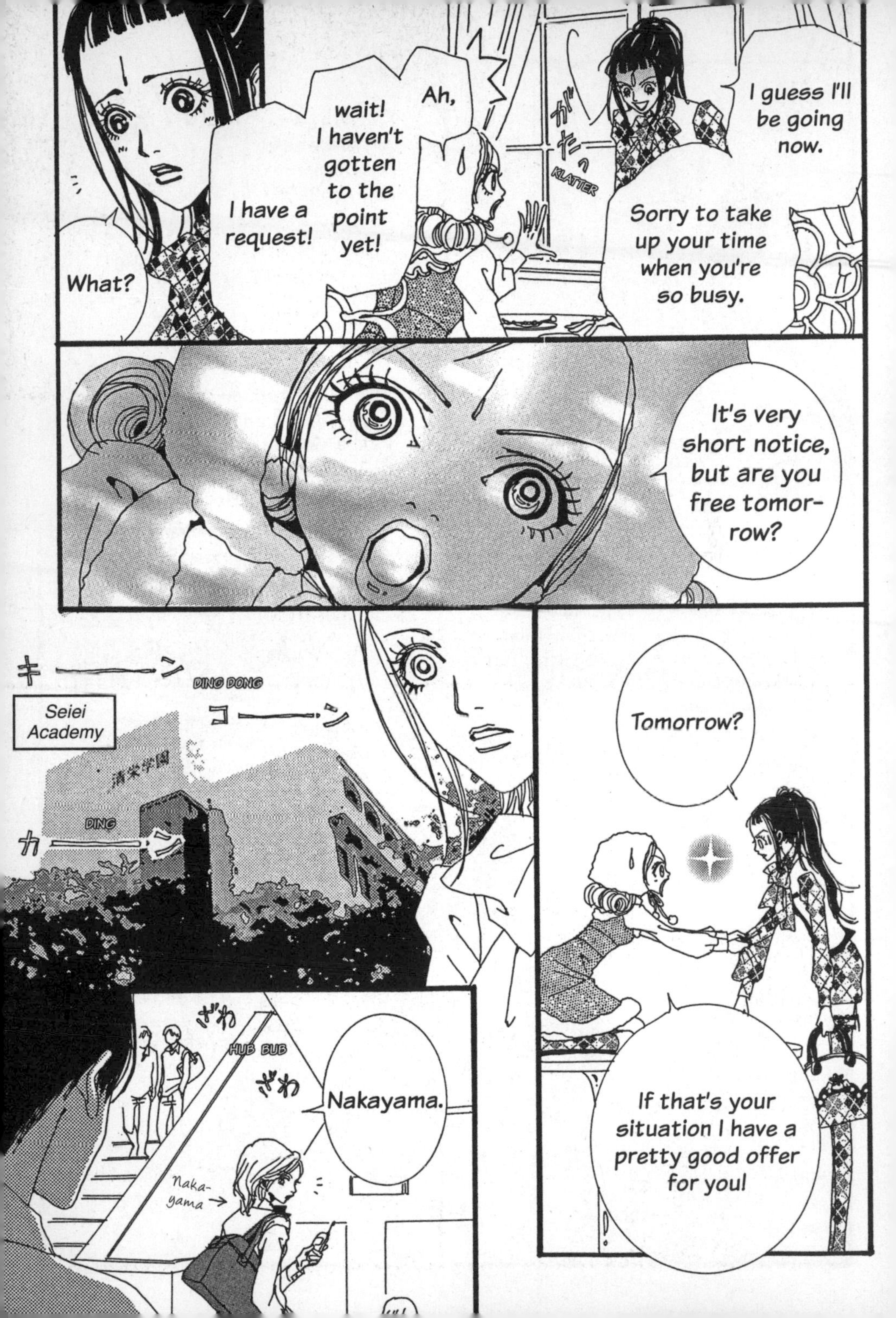
I guess I'll be going now.
Sorry to take up your time when you're so busy.
ガタッ
KLATTER
Ah, wait! I haven't gotten to the point yet!
I have a request!
What?
It's very short notice, but are you free tomorrow?
Tomorrow?
If that's your situation I have a pretty good offer for you!
キーン
DING DONG
コーン
Seiei Academy
清栄学園
カーン
DING
ざわ
HUB BUB
ざわ
Nakayama.
Naka-yama

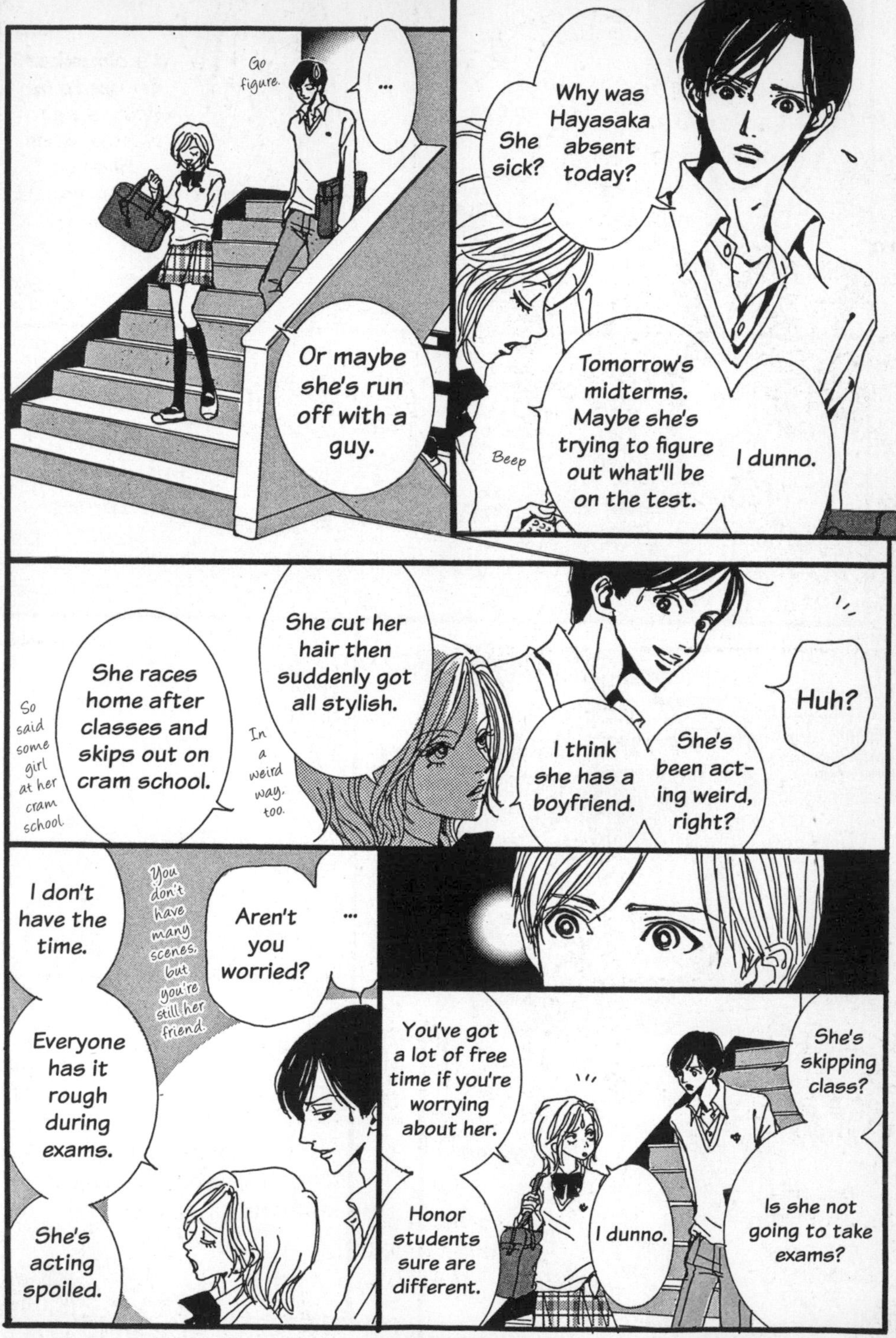
Why was Hayasaka absent today?
She sick?
I dunno.
Tomorrow's midterms. Maybe she's trying to figure out what'll be on the test.
Beep
...
Go figure.
Or maybe she's run off with a guy.
Huh?
She's been act-ing weird, right?
I think she has a boyfriend.
She cut her hair then suddenly got all stylish.
In a weird way, too.
She races home after classes and skips out on cram school.
So said some girl at her cram school.
She's skipping class?
Is she not going to take exams?
I dunno.
You've got a lot of free time if you're worrying about her.
Honor students sure are different.
...
Aren't you worried?
You don't have many scenes, but you're still her friend.
I don't have the time.
Everyone has it rough during exams.
She's acting spoiled.

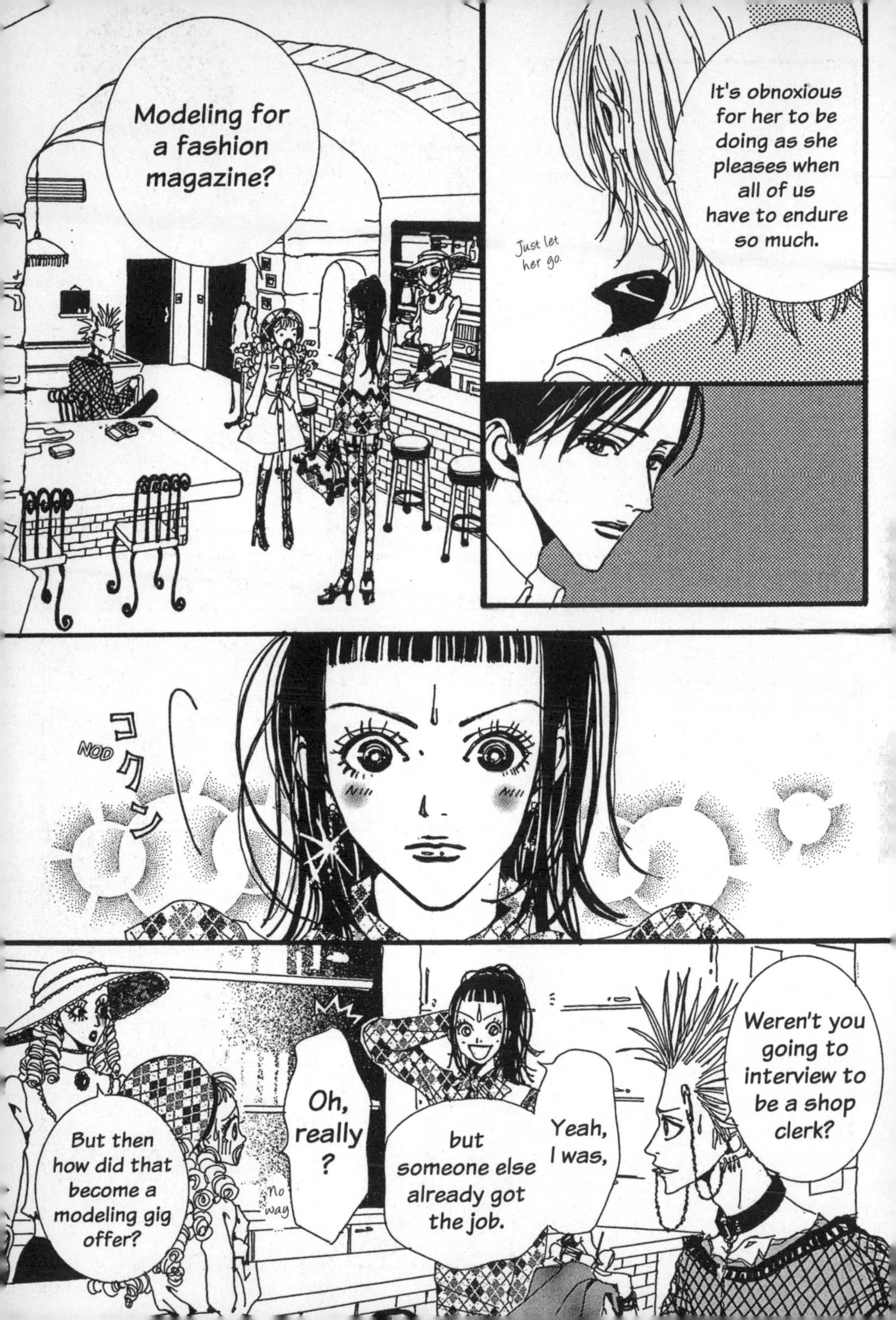
It's obnoxious for her to be doing as she pleases when all of us have to endure so much.
Just let her go.
Modeling for a fashion magazine?
コクン
NOD
Weren't you going to interview to be a shop clerk?
Yeah, I was,
but someone else already got the job.
Oh, really?
No way
But then how did that become a modeling gig offer?

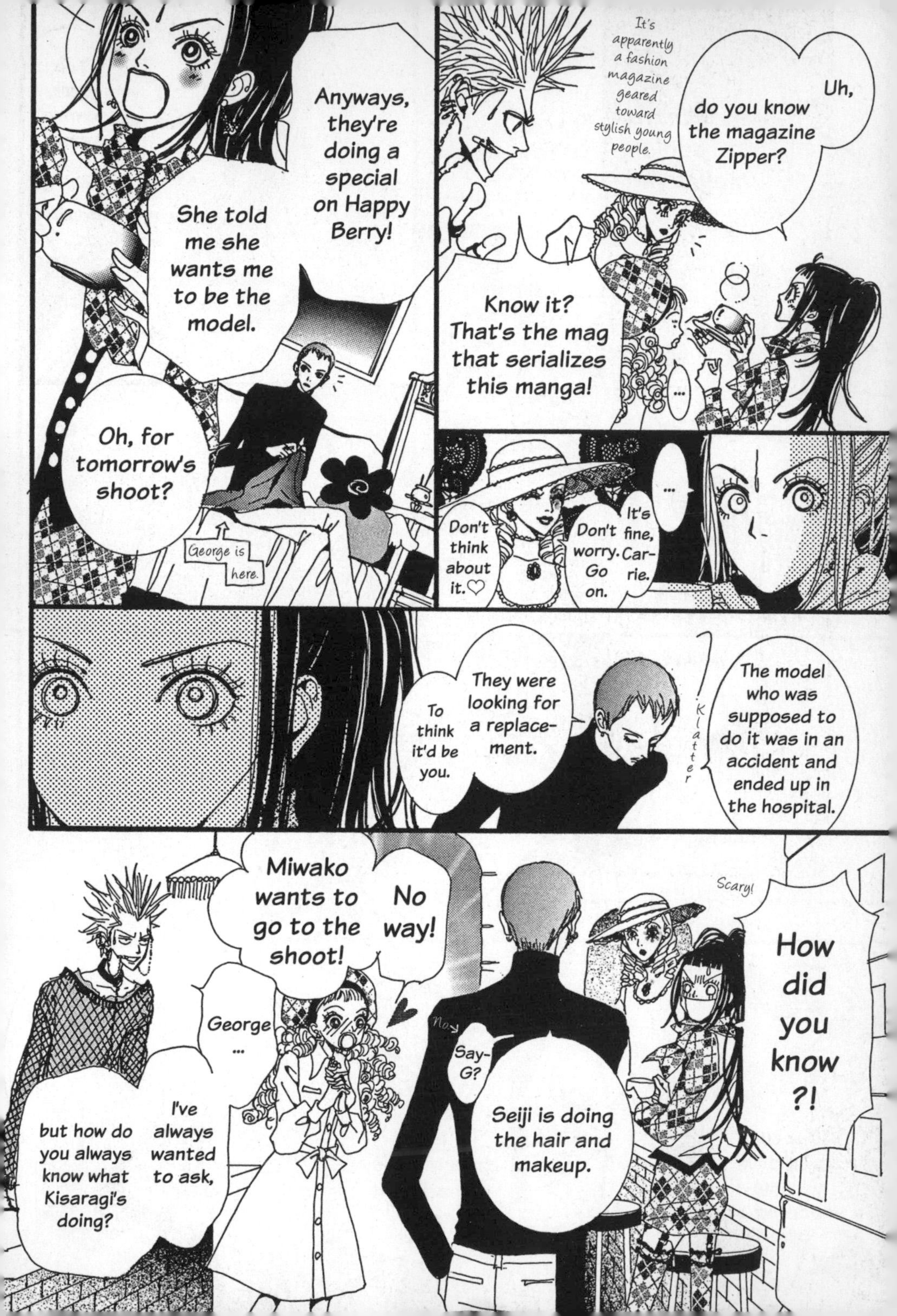
Uh, do you know the magazine Zipper?
It's apparently a fashion magazine geared toward stylish young people.
Know it? That's the mag that serializes this manga!
...
...
It's fine, Carrie.
Don't worry. Go on.
Don't think about it.♡
Anyways, they're doing a special on Happy Berry!
She told me she wants me to be the model.
Oh, for tomorrow's shoot?
George is here.
The model who was supposed to do it was in an accident and ended up in the hospital.
Klatter
They were looking for a replacement.
To think it'd be you.
How did you know?!
Scary!
Seiji is doing the hair and makeup.
Say-G?
No
Miwako wants to go to the shoot!
No way!
George...
I've always wanted to ask,
but how do you always know what Kisaragi's doing?

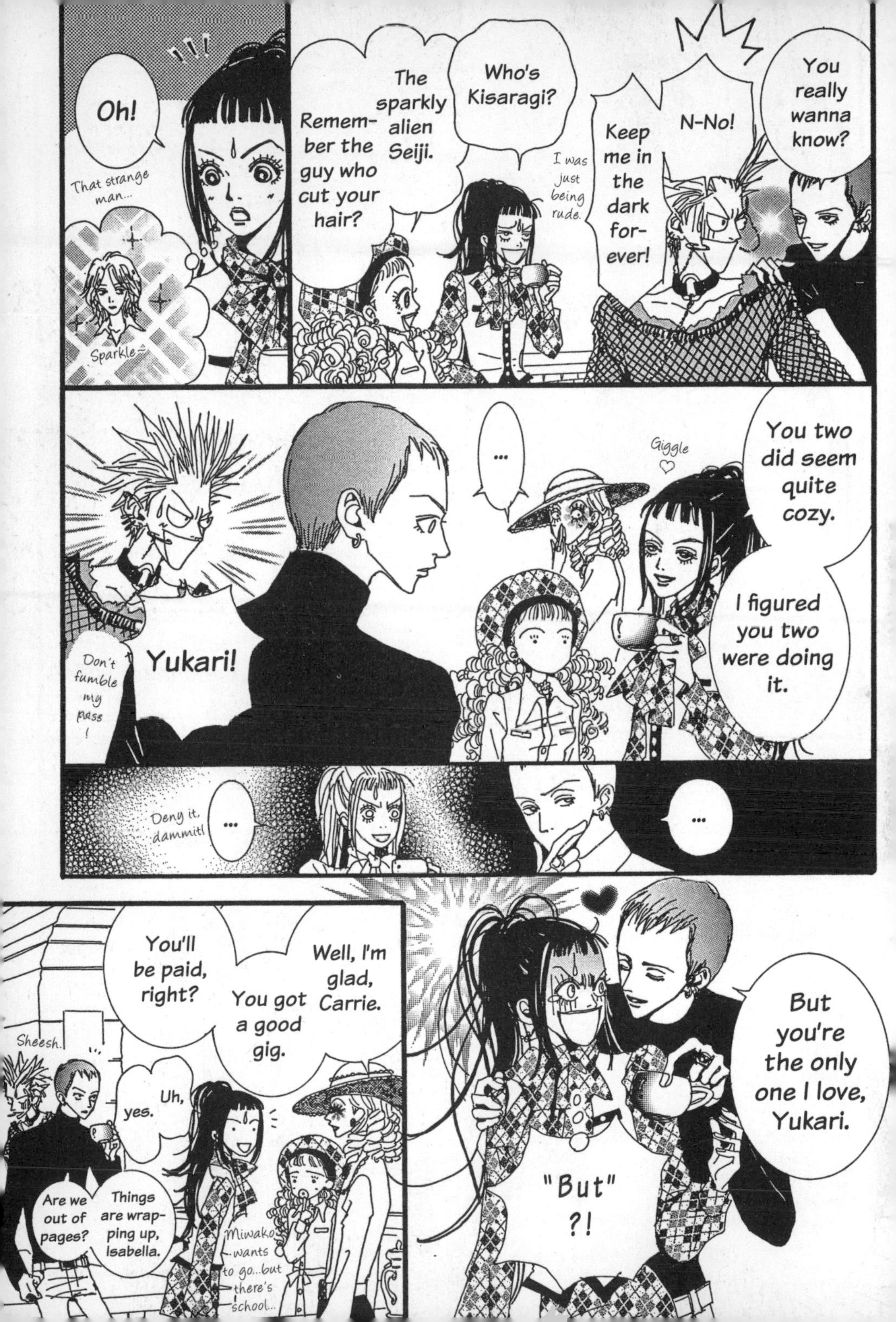
You really wanna know?
N-No!
Keep me in the dark forever!
Who's Kisaragi?
I was just being rude.
The sparkly alien Seiji.
Remember the guy who cut your hair?
Oh!
That strange man...
Sparkle
You two did seem quite cozy.
Giggle
I figured you two were doing it.
...
Yukari!
Don't fumble my pass!
...
...
Deny it, dammit!
But you're the only one I love, Yukari.
"But" ?!
Well, I'm glad, Carrie.
You'll be paid, right?
You got a good gig.
Uh, yes.
Sheesh.
Things are wrap-ping up, Isabella.
Are we out of pages?
Miwako wants to go...but there's school...

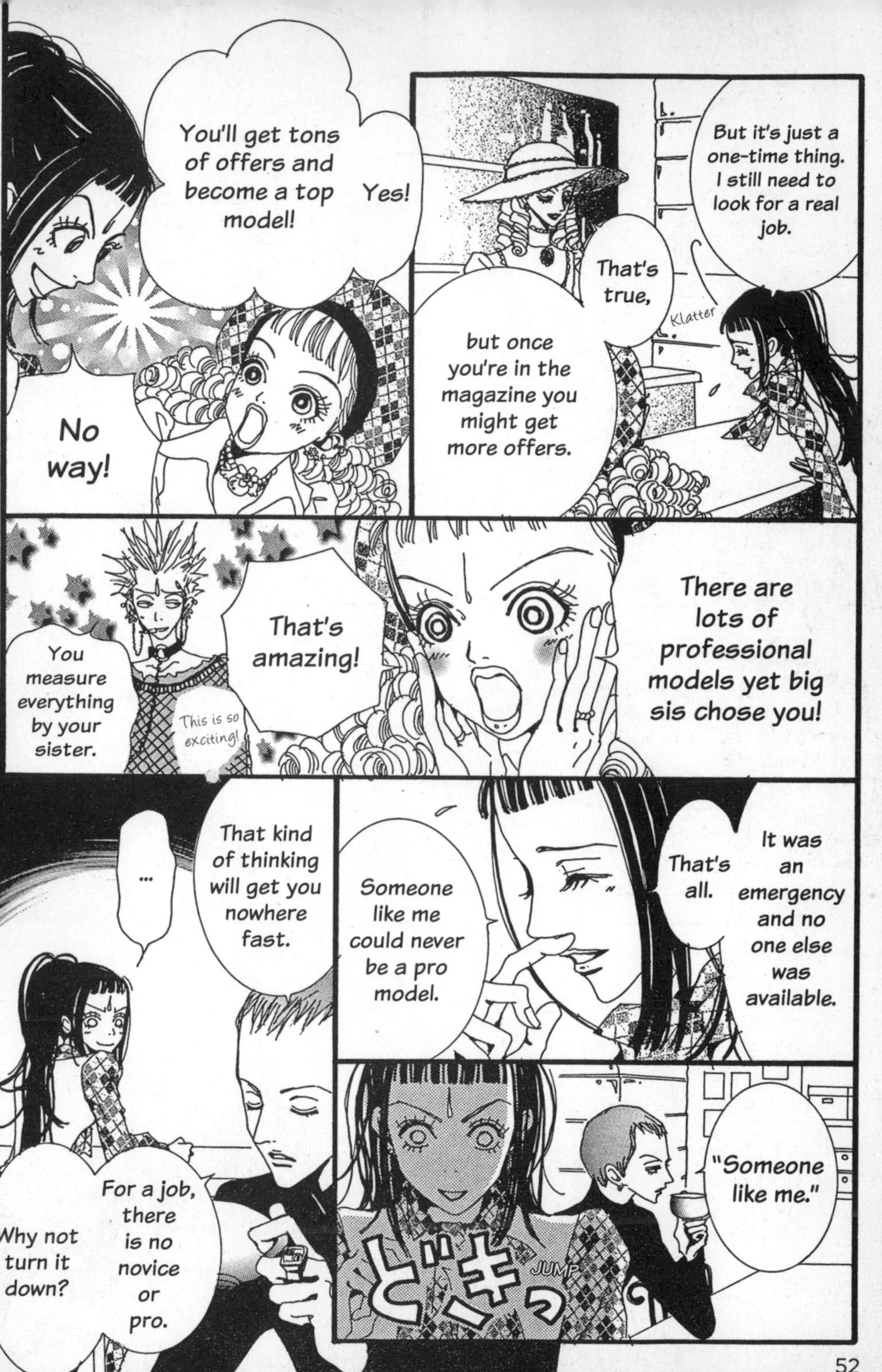
But it's just a one-time thing. I still need to look for a real job.
That's true,
but once you're in the magazine you might get more offers.
Klatter
You'll get tons of offers and become a top model!
Yes!
No way!
There are lots of professional models yet big sis chose you!
That's amazing!
This is so exciting!
You measure everything by your sister.
It was an emergency and no one else was available.
That's all.
Someone like me could never be a pro model.
"Someone like me."
JUMP
That kind of thinking will get you nowhere fast.
...
For a job, there is no novice or pro.
Why not turn it down?

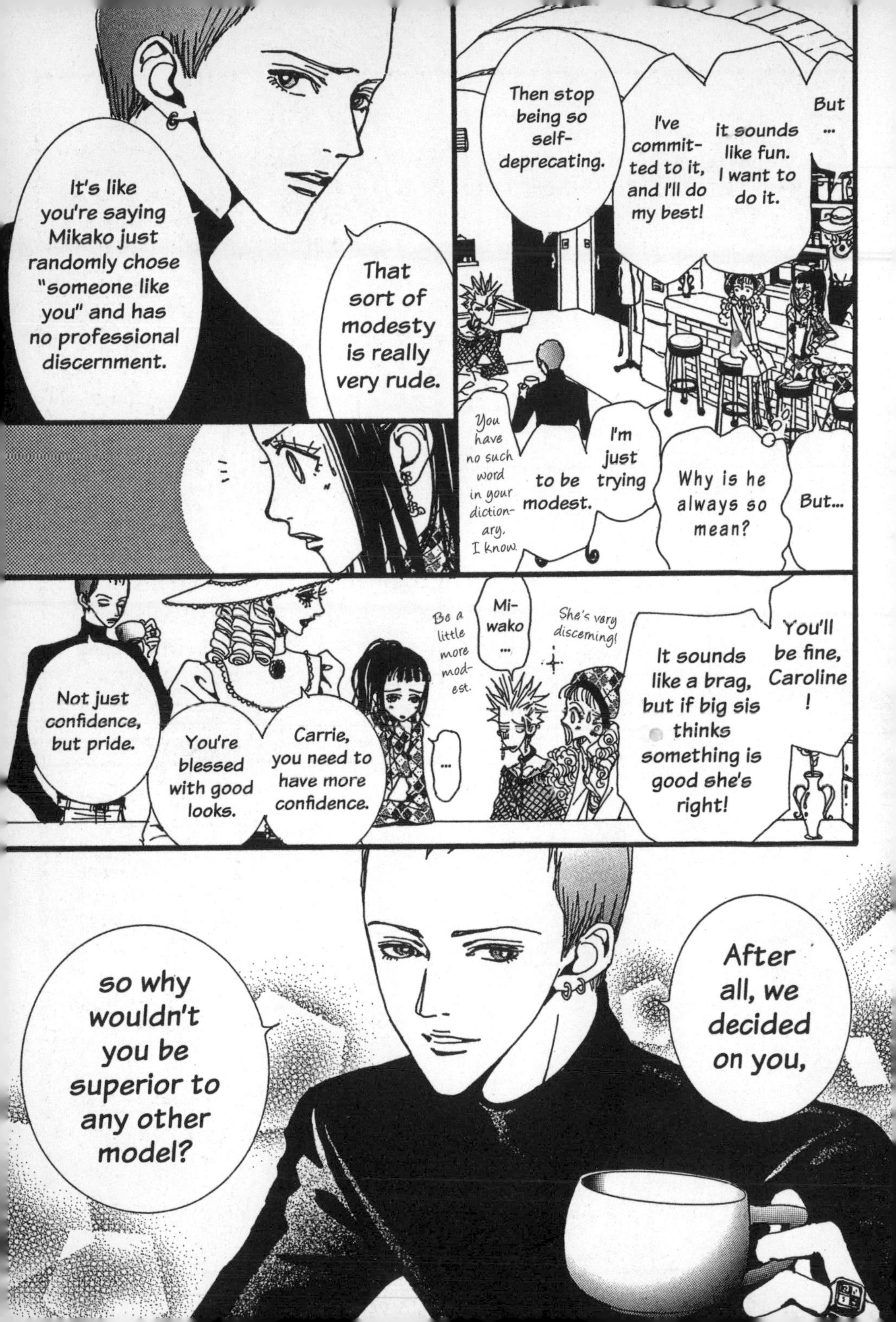
But ...
it sounds like fun. I want to do it.
I've commit-ted to it, and I'll do my best!
Then stop being so self-deprecating.
But...
Why is he always so mean?
I'm just trying to be modest.
You have no such word in your diction-ary, I know.
That sort of modesty is really very rude.
It's like you're saying Mikako just randomly chose "someone like you" and has no professional discernment.
You'll be fine, Caroline!
It sounds like a brag, but if big sis thinks something is good she's right!
She's very discerning!
Mi-wako ...
Be a little more mod-est.
...
Carrie, you need to have more confidence.
You're blessed with good looks.
Not just confidence, but pride.
After all, we decided on you,
so why wouldn't you be superior to any other model?

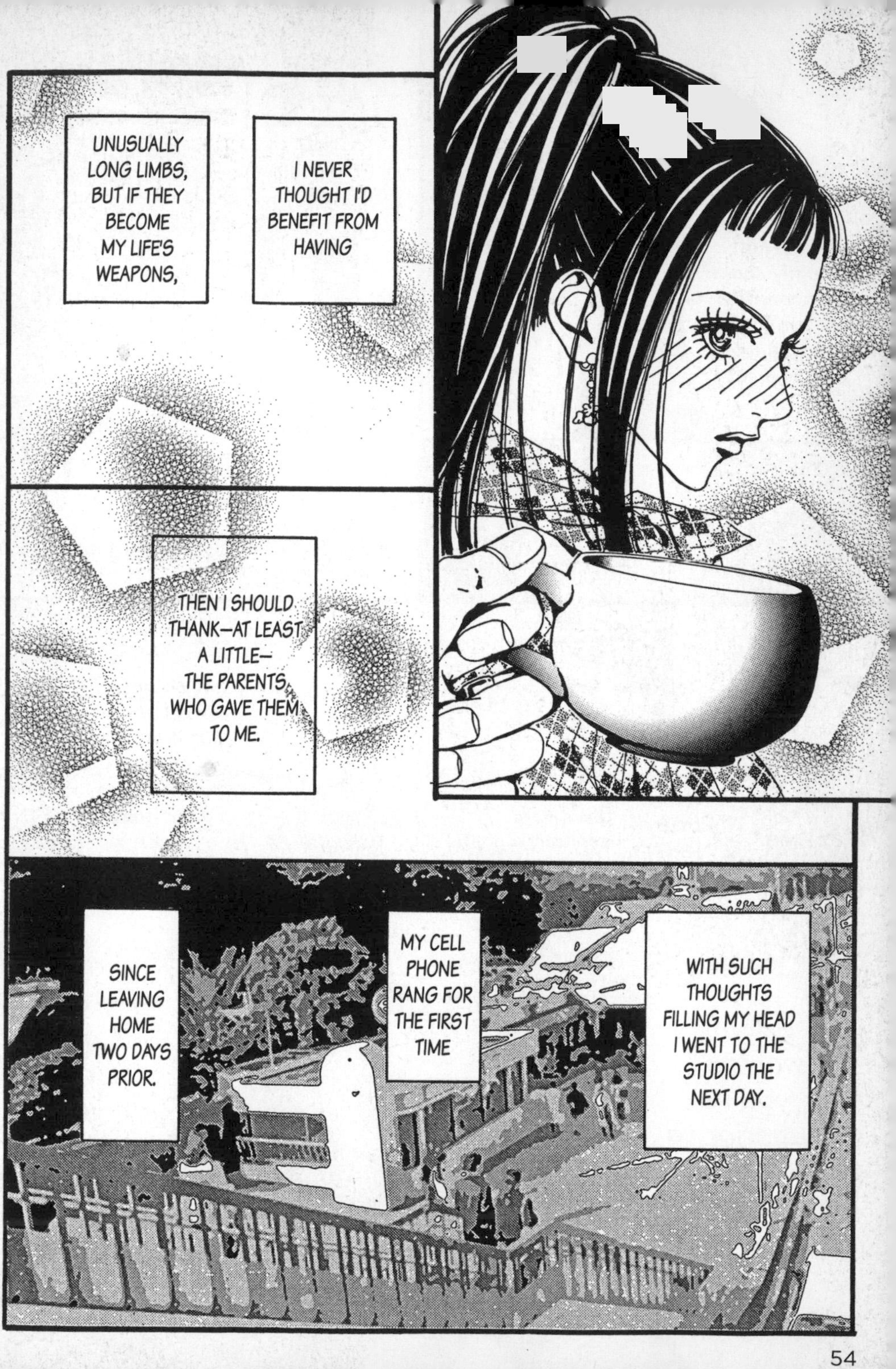
I NEVER THOUGHT I'D BENEFIT FROM HAVING
UNUSUALLY LONG LIMBS, BUT IF THEY BECOME MY LIFE'S WEAPONS,
THEN I SHOULD THANK—AT LEAST A LITTLE— THE PARENTS WHO GAVE THEM TO ME.
WITH SUCH THOUGHTS FILLING MY HEAD I WENT TO THE STUDIO THE NEXT DAY.
MY CELL PHONE RANG FOR THE FIRST TIME
SINCE LEAVING HOME TWO DAYS PRIOR.

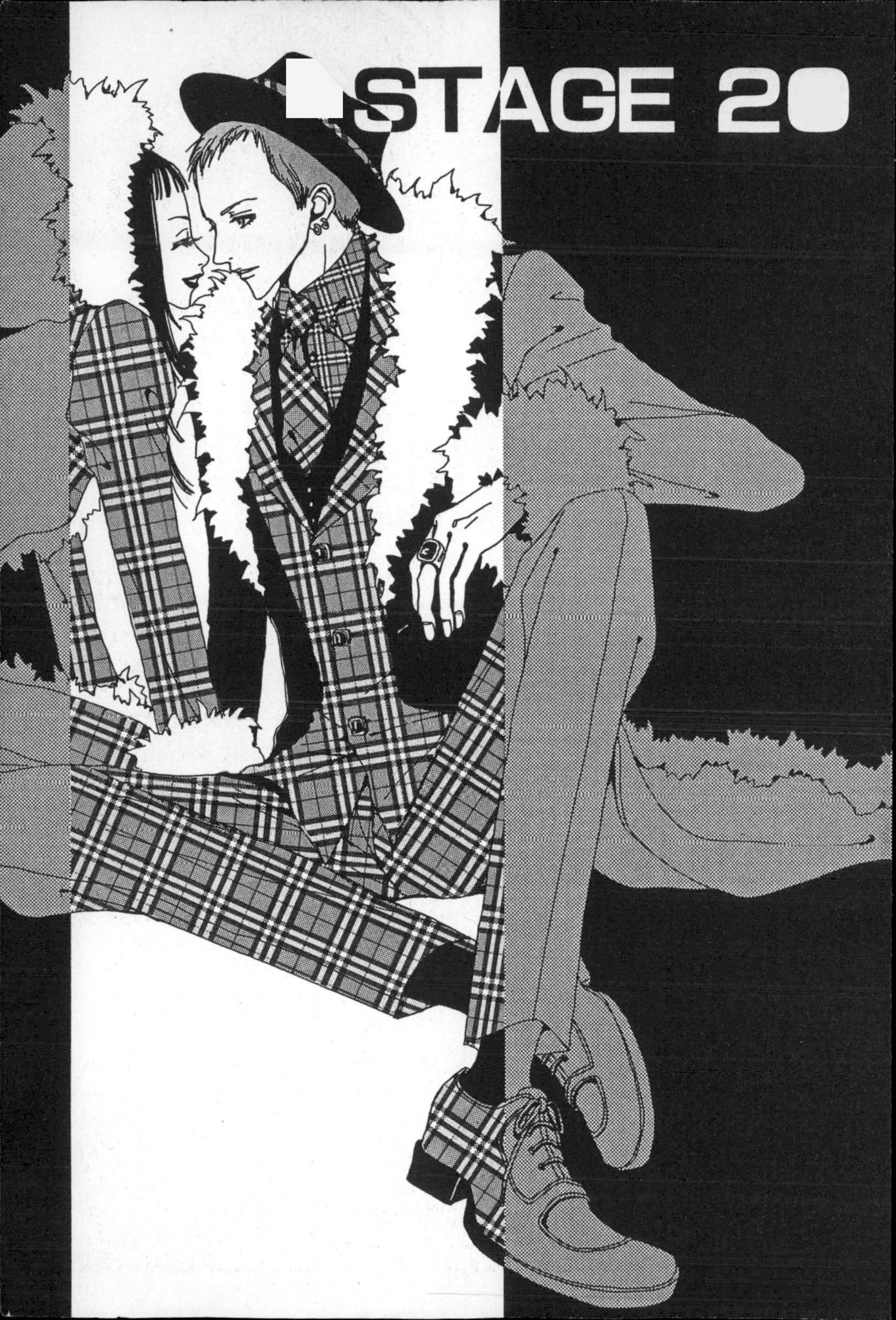
STAGE 20

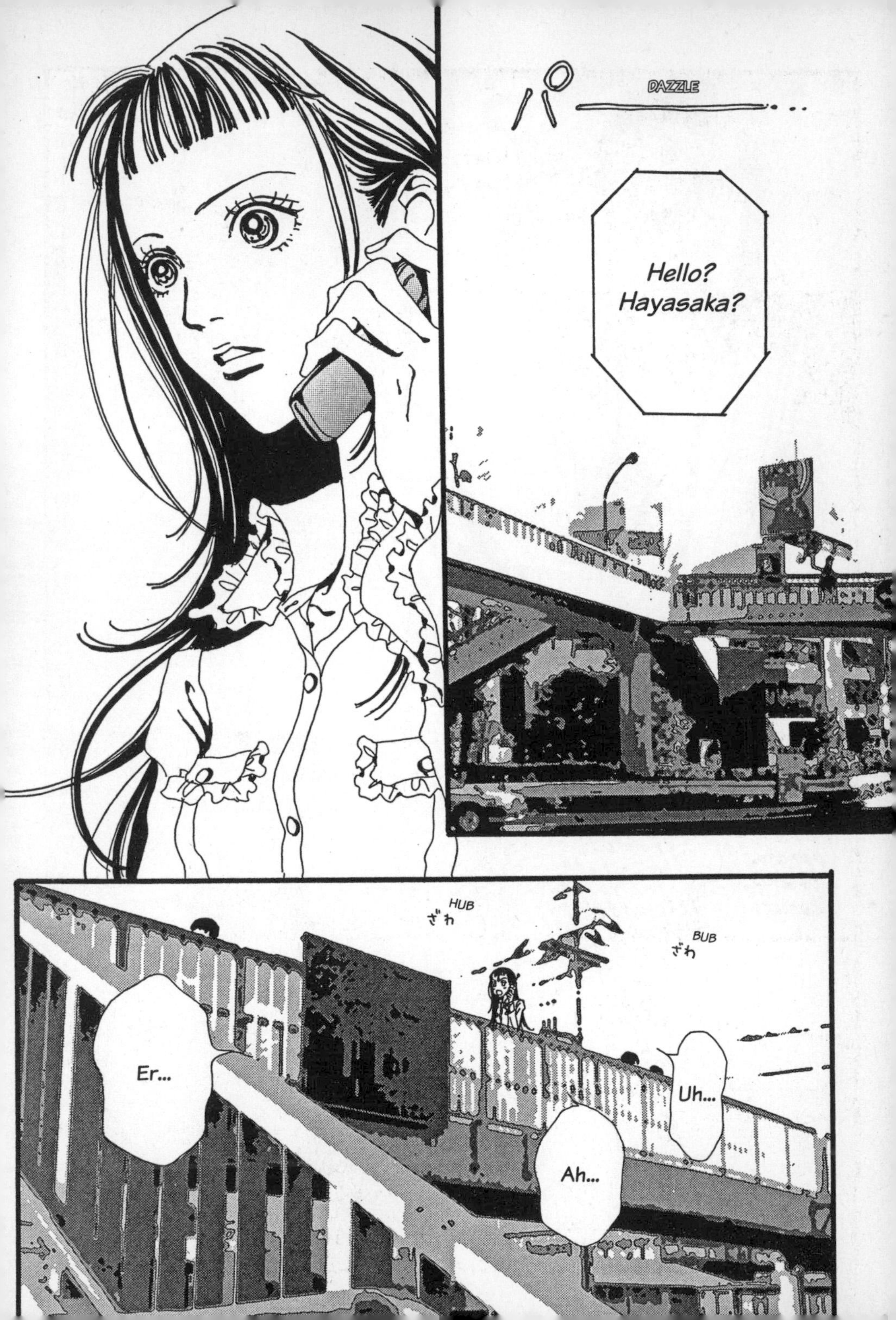
パ
DAZZLE
Hello? Hayasaka?
ざわ BUB
ざわ HUB
Uh...
Ah...
Er...

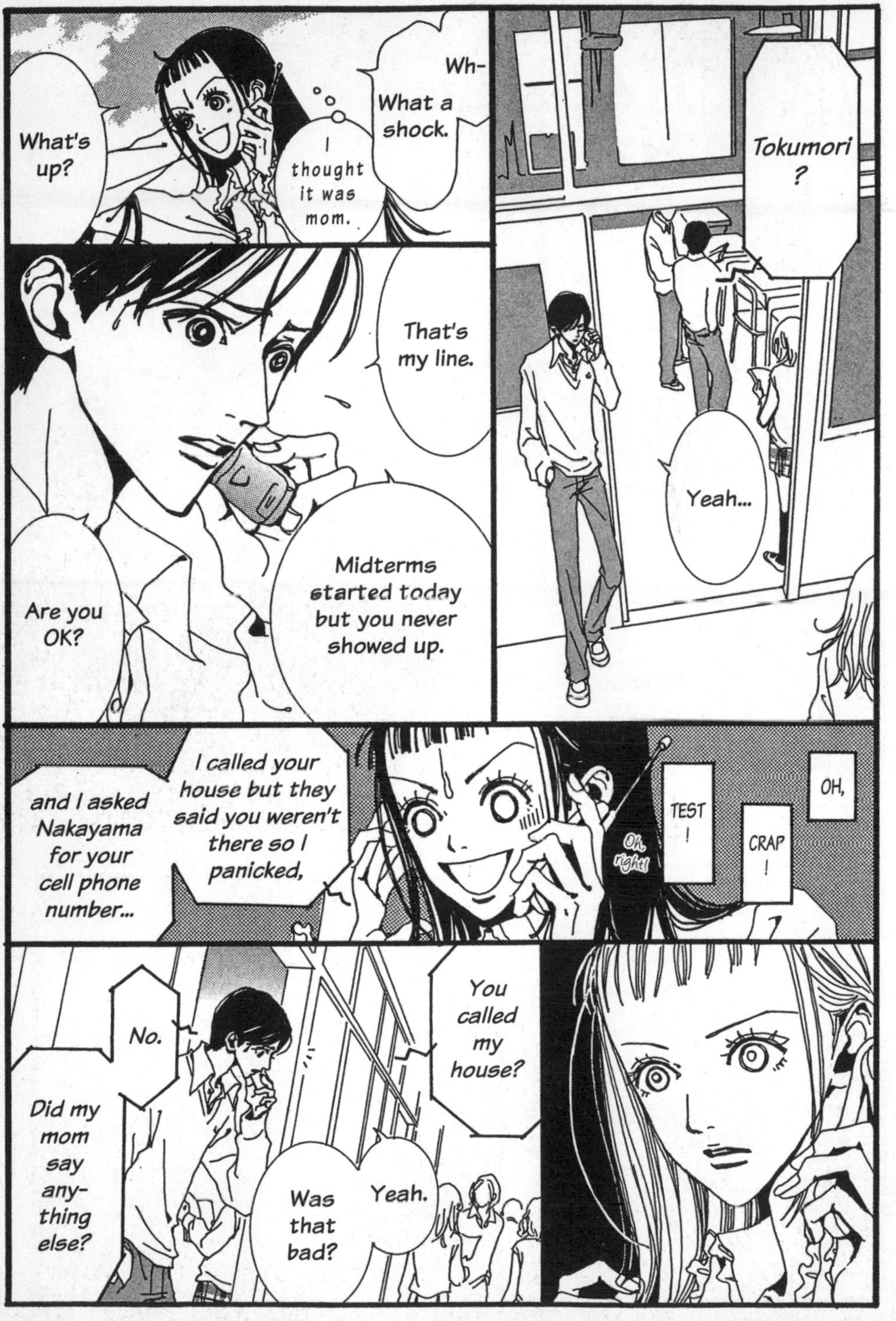
Tokumori?
Yeah...
Wh- What a shock.
I thought it was mom.
What's up?
That's my line.
Midterms started today but you never showed up.
Are you OK?
OH,
CRAP!
TEST!
Oh, right!
I called your house but they said you weren't there so I panicked,
and I asked Nakayama for your cell phone number...
You called my house?
Yeah.
Was that bad?
No.
Did my mom say anything else?

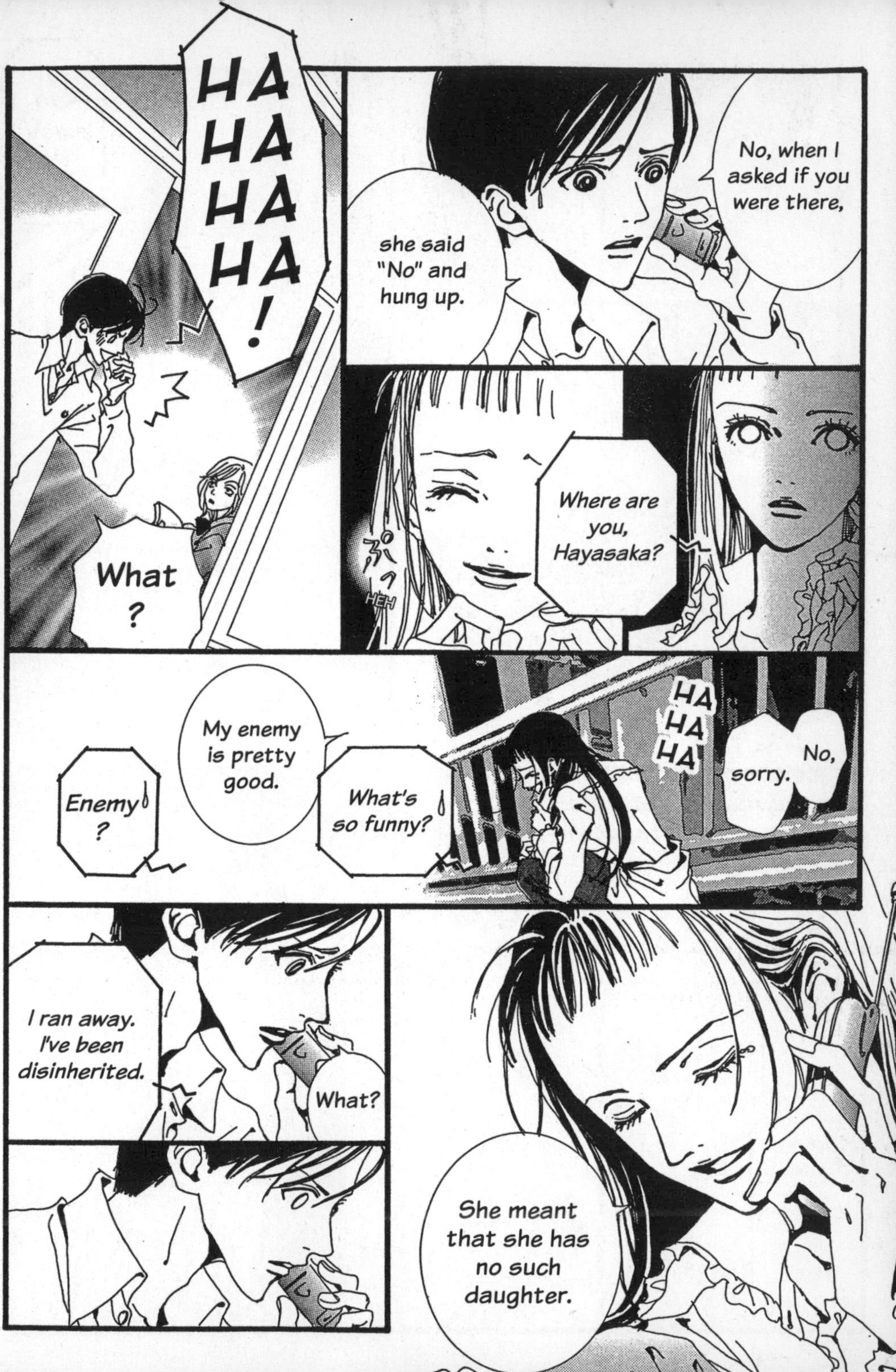
No, when I asked if you were there,
she said "No" and hung up.
Where are you, Hayasaka?
HEH
HA HA HA HA!
What ?
HA HA HA
No, sorry.
What's so funny?
My enemy is pretty good.
Enemy ?
She meant that she has no such daughter.
I ran away. I've been disinherited.
What?

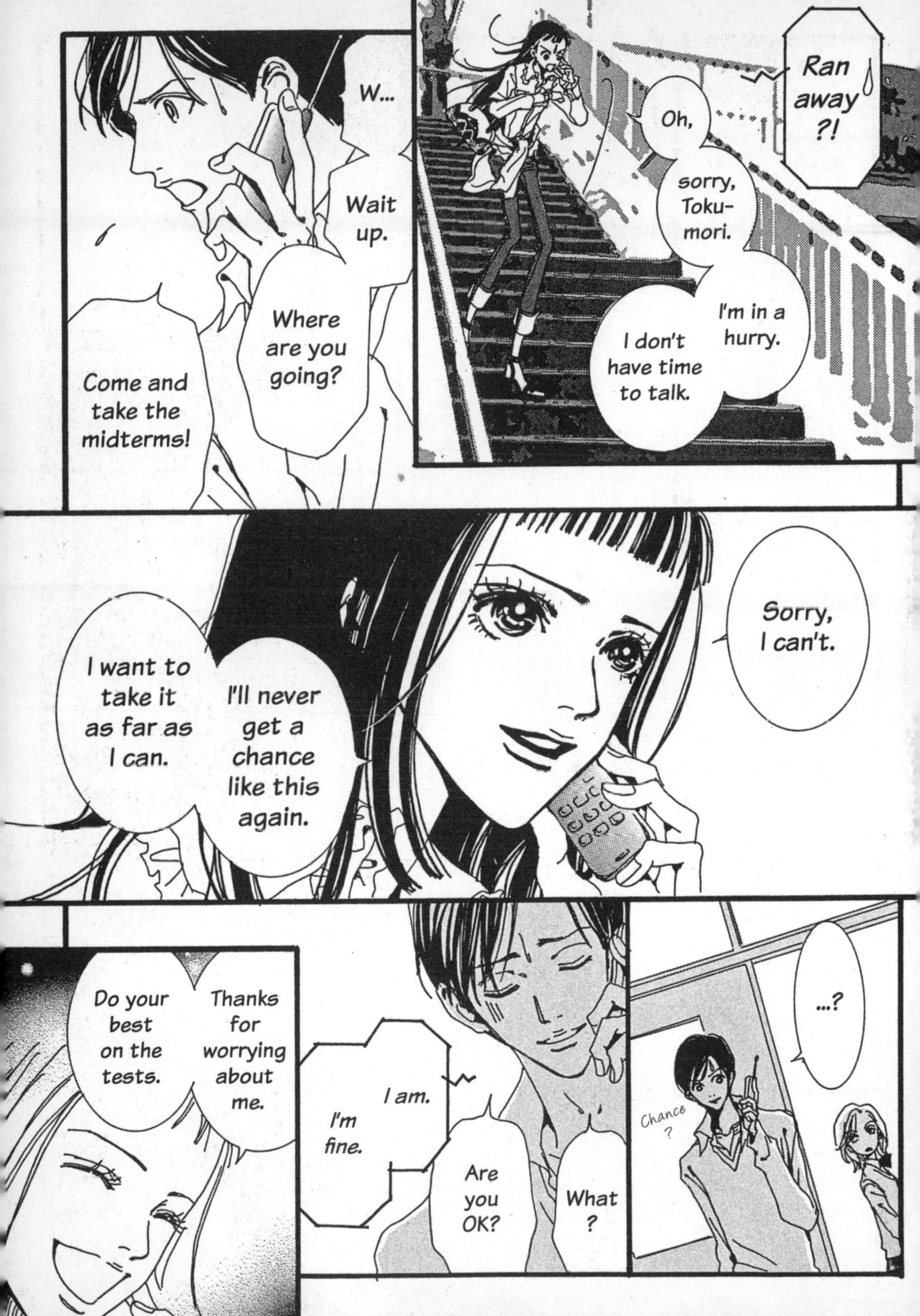
Ran away ?!
Oh, sorry, Toku-mori.
I'm in a hurry.
I don't have time to talk.
W...
Wait up.
Where are you going?
Come and take the midterms!
Sorry, I can't.
I'll never get a chance like this again.
I want to take it as far as I can.
...?
Chance ?
What ?
Are you OK?
I am.
I'm fine.
Thanks for worrying about me.
Do your best on the tests.

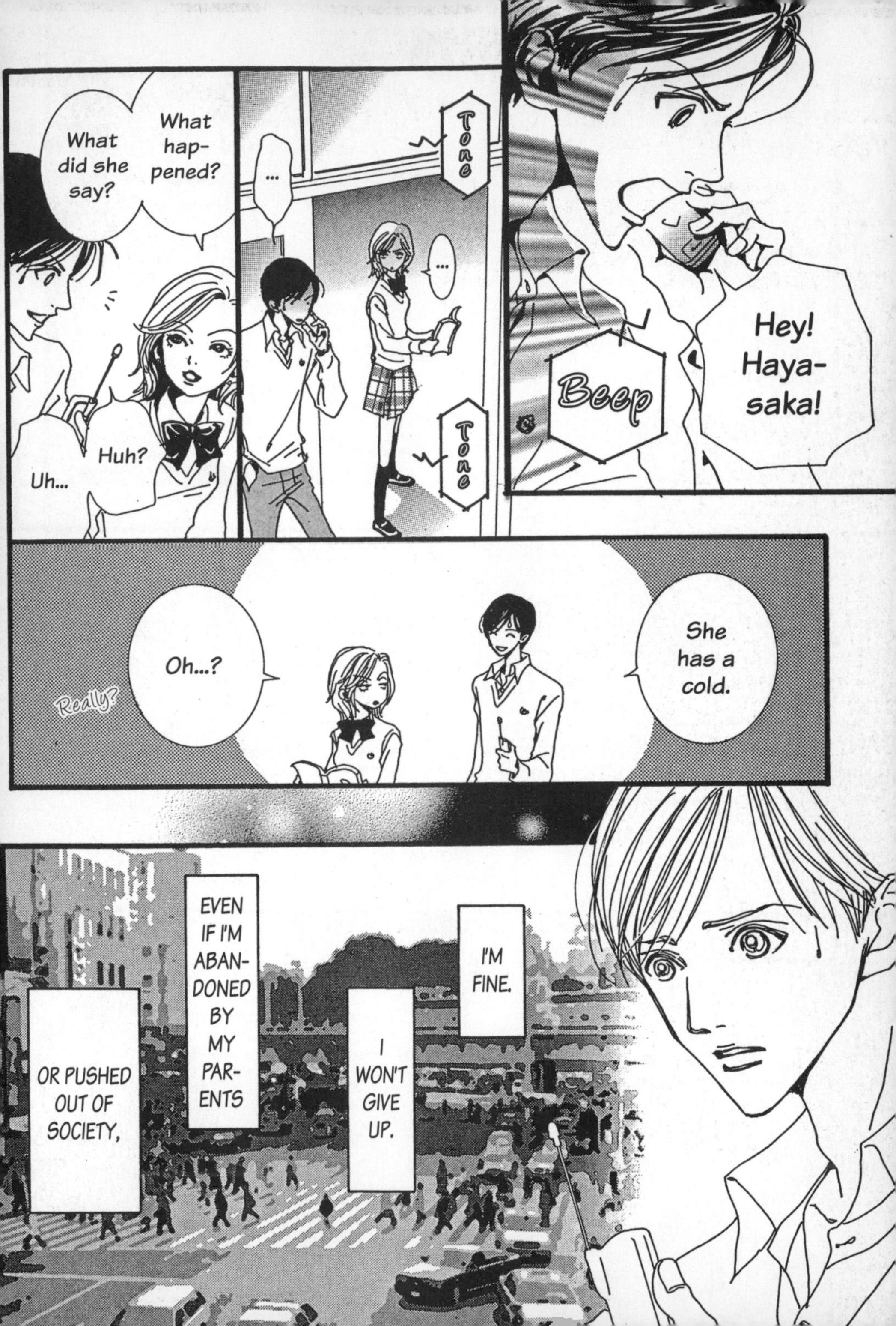
Hey! Haya-saka!
Beep
Tone
...
...
Tone
What hap-pened?
What did she say?
Huh?
Uh...
She has a cold.
Oh...?
Really?
I'M FINE.
I WON'T GIVE UP.
EVEN IF I'M ABAN-DONED BY MY PAR-ENTS
OR PUSHED OUT OF SOCIETY,

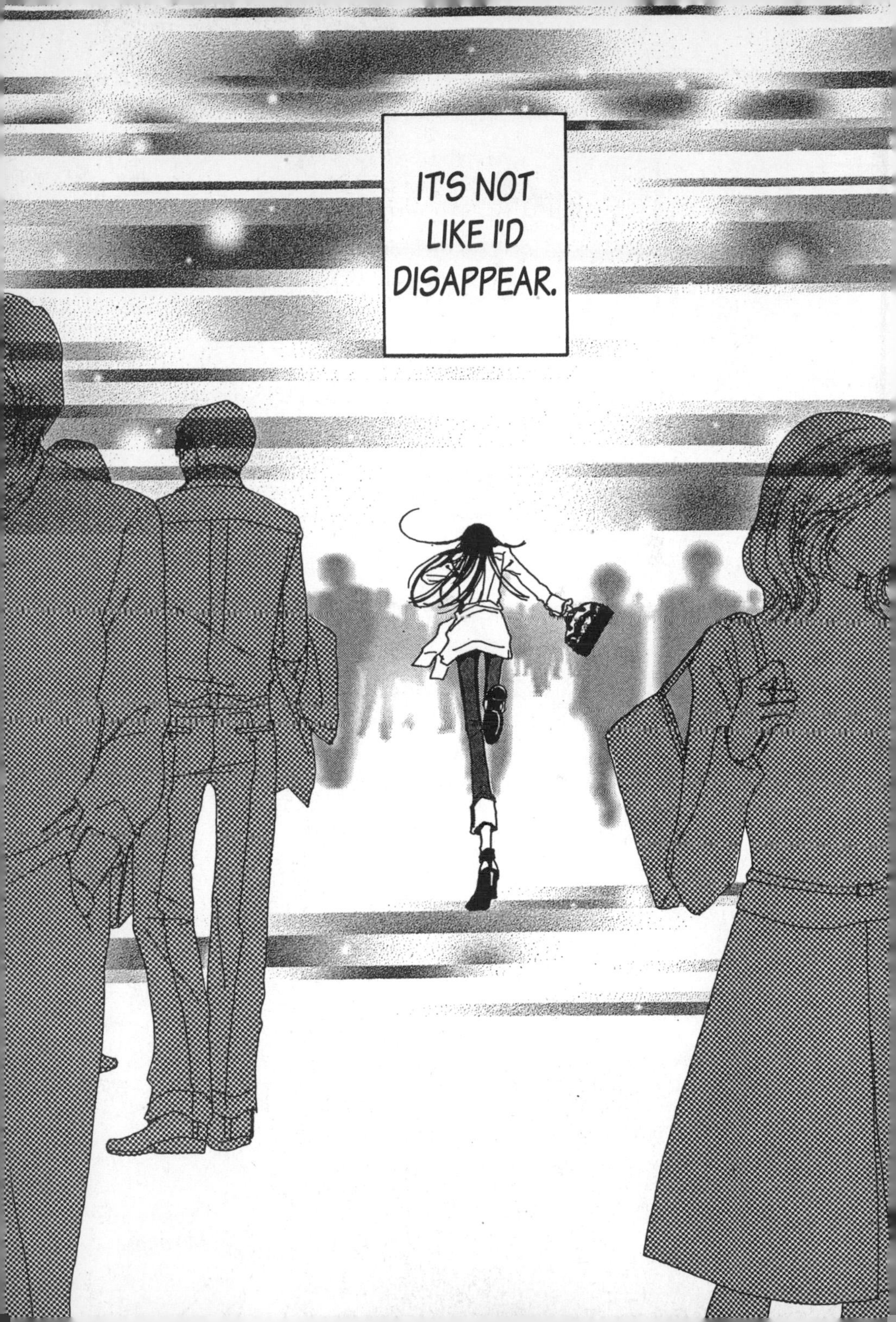
IT'S NOT LIKE I'D DISAPPEAR.

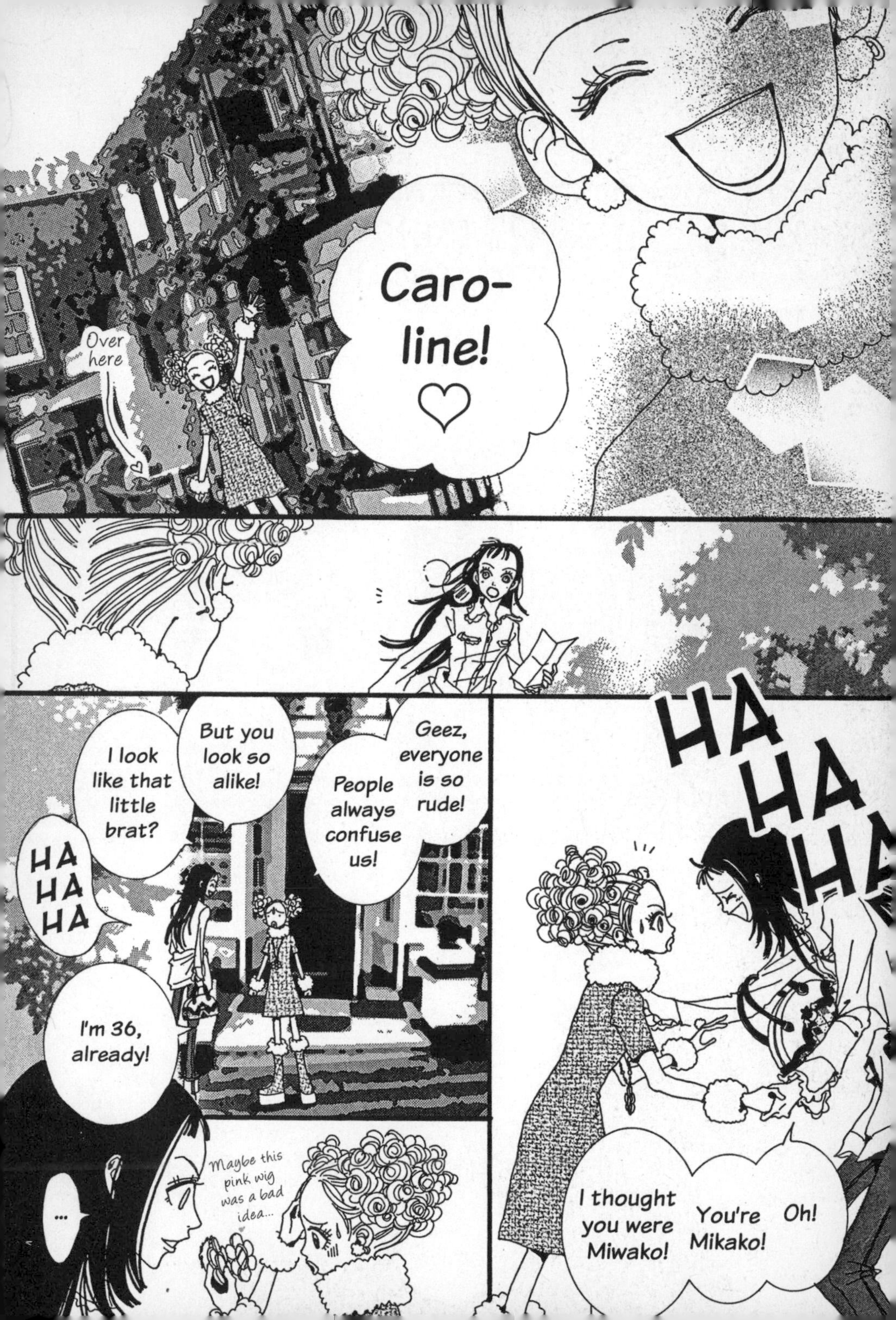
Caro-line! ♡
Over here
HA HA HA
Oh! You're Mikako! I thought you were Miwako!
Geez, everyone is so rude!
People always confuse us!
But you look so alike!
I look like that little brat?
HA HA HA
I'm 36, already!
Maybe this pink wig was a bad idea...
...

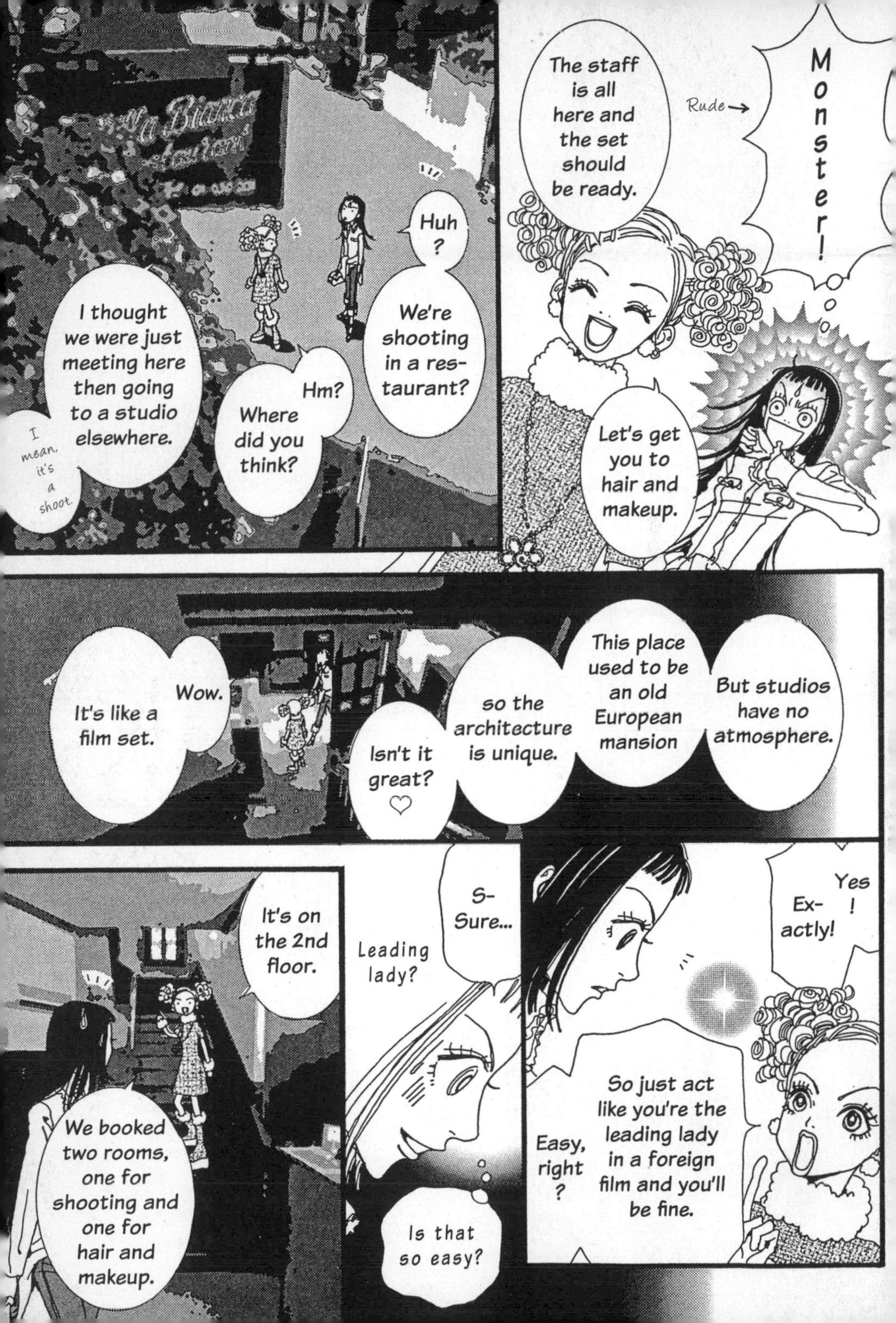
Monster!
Rude →
The staff is all here and the set should be ready.
Let's get you to hair and makeup.
Huh?
We're shooting in a restaurant?
Hm? Where did you think?
I thought we were just meeting here then going to a studio elsewhere.
I mean, it's a shoot.
But studios have no atmosphere.
This place used to be an old European mansion
so the architecture is unique.
Isn't it great? ♡
Wow.
It's like a film set.
Yes! Exactly!
So just act like you're the leading lady in a foreign film and you'll be fine.
Easy, right?
S-Sure...
Leading lady?
Is that so easy?
It's on the 2nd floor.
We booked two rooms, one for shooting and one for hair and makeup.

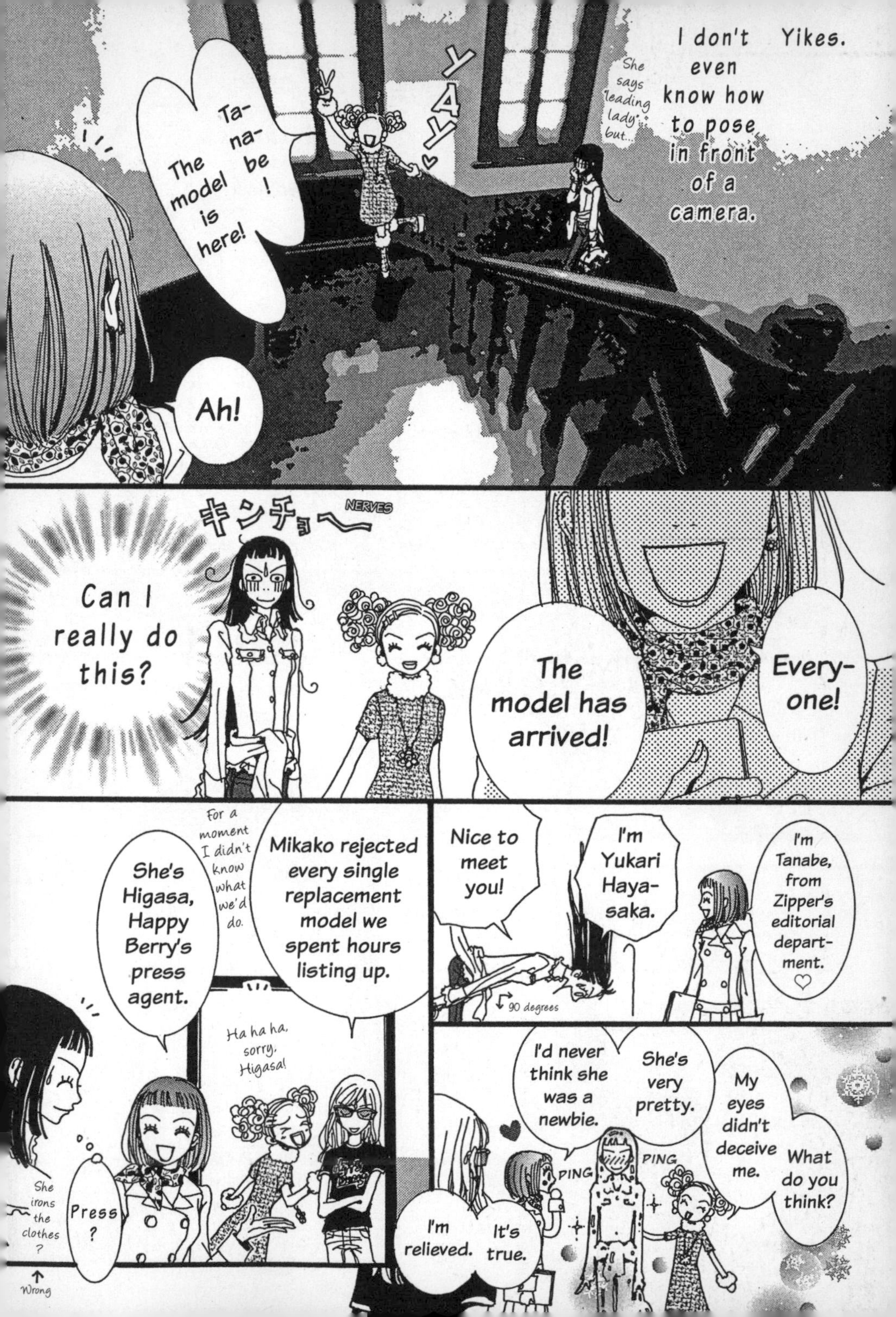

Yikes.
I don't even know how to pose in front of a camera.
She says "leading lady" but...
YAY
Ta-na-be!
The model is here!
Ah!
Every-one!
The model has arrived!
キンチョ〜
NERVES
Can I really do this?
I'm Tanabe, from Zipper's editorial depart-ment. ♡
I'm Yukari Haya-saka.
Nice to meet you!
90 degrees
What do you think?
My eyes didn't deceive me.
She's very pretty.
I'd never think she was a newbie.
PING
PING
It's true.
I'm relieved.
Mikako rejected every single replacement model we spent hours listing up.
For a moment I didn't know what we'd do.
She's Higasa, Happy Berry's press agent.
Ha ha ha, sorry, Higasa!
Press?
She irons the clothes?
Wrong

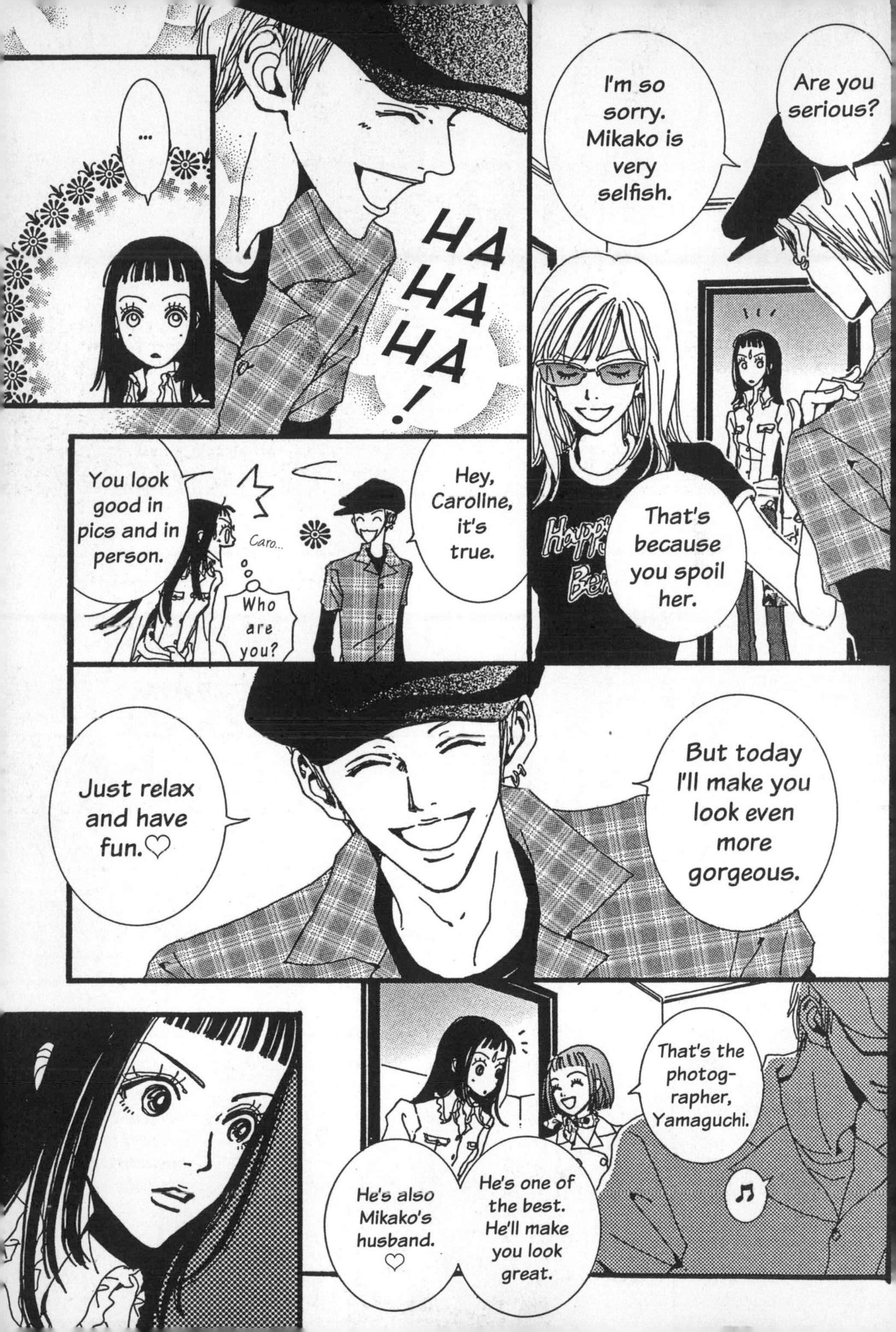
Are you serious?
I'm so sorry. Mikako is very selfish.
That's because you spoil her.
HA HA HA!
...
Hey, Caroline, it's true.
Caro...
Who are you?
You look good in pics and in person.
But today I'll make you look even more gorgeous.
Just relax and have fun.♡
That's the photographer, Yamaguchi.
♫
He's one of the best. He'll make you look great.
He's also Mikako's husband. ♡

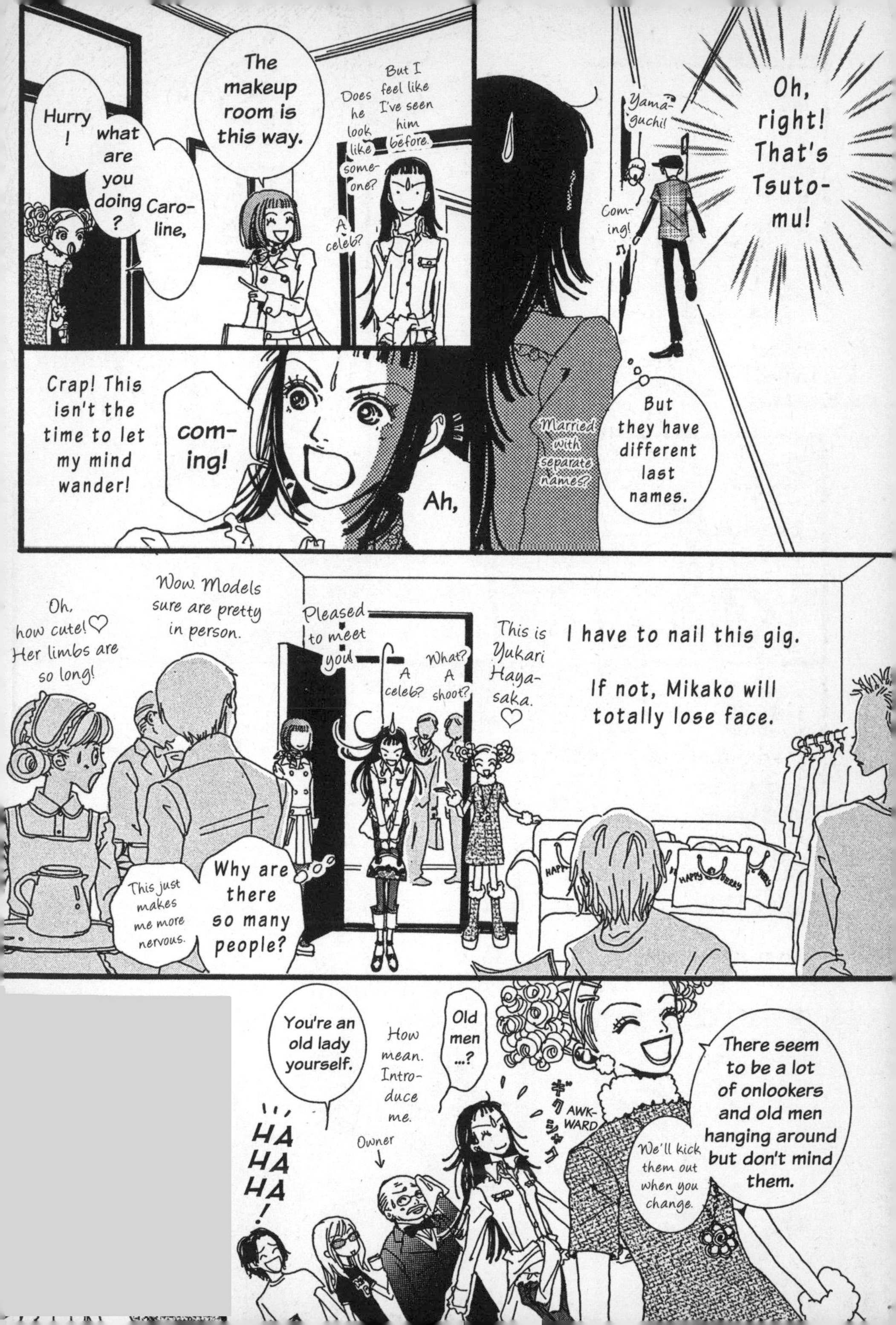
Oh, right! That's Tsutomu!
Yamaguchi!
Coming!
But they have different last names.
Married with separate names?
But I feel like I've seen him before.
Does he look like someone?
A celeb?
The makeup room is this way.
Caroline, what are you doing? Hurry!
Ah,
coming!
Crap! This isn't the time to let my mind wander!
I have to nail this gig.
If not, Mikako will totally lose face.
This is Yukari Hayasaka. ♡
What? A shoot?
A celeb?
Pleased to meet you
Wow. Models sure are pretty in person.
Oh, how cute! ♡ Her limbs are so long!
Why are there so many people?
This just makes me more nervous.
There seem to be a lot of onlookers and old men hanging around but don't mind them.
We'll kick them out when you change.
AWKWARD
Old men ...?
How mean. Introduce me.
You're an old lady yourself.
Owner
HA HA HA!

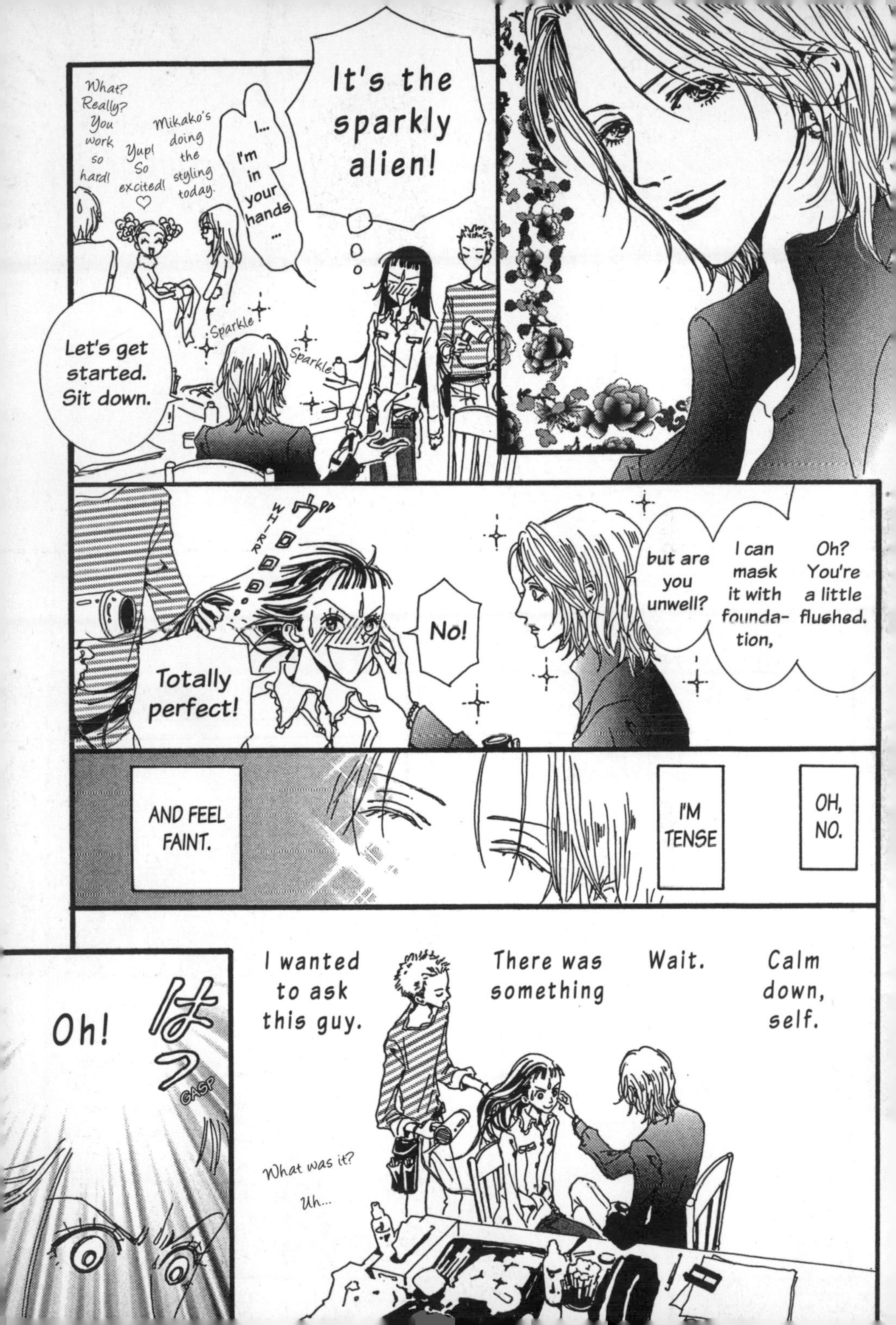
It's the sparkly alien!
I... I'm in your hands...
Mikako's doing the styling today.
What? Really? You work so hard!
Yup! So excited! ♡
Sparkle
Sparkle
Let's get started. Sit down.
Oh? You're a little flushed.
I can mask it with foundation,
but are you unwell?
No!
WHIRR
Totally perfect!
OH, NO.
I'M TENSE
AND FEEL FAINT.
Calm down, self.
Wait.
There was something
I wanted to ask this guy.
What was it?
Uh...
はっ
GASP
Oh!

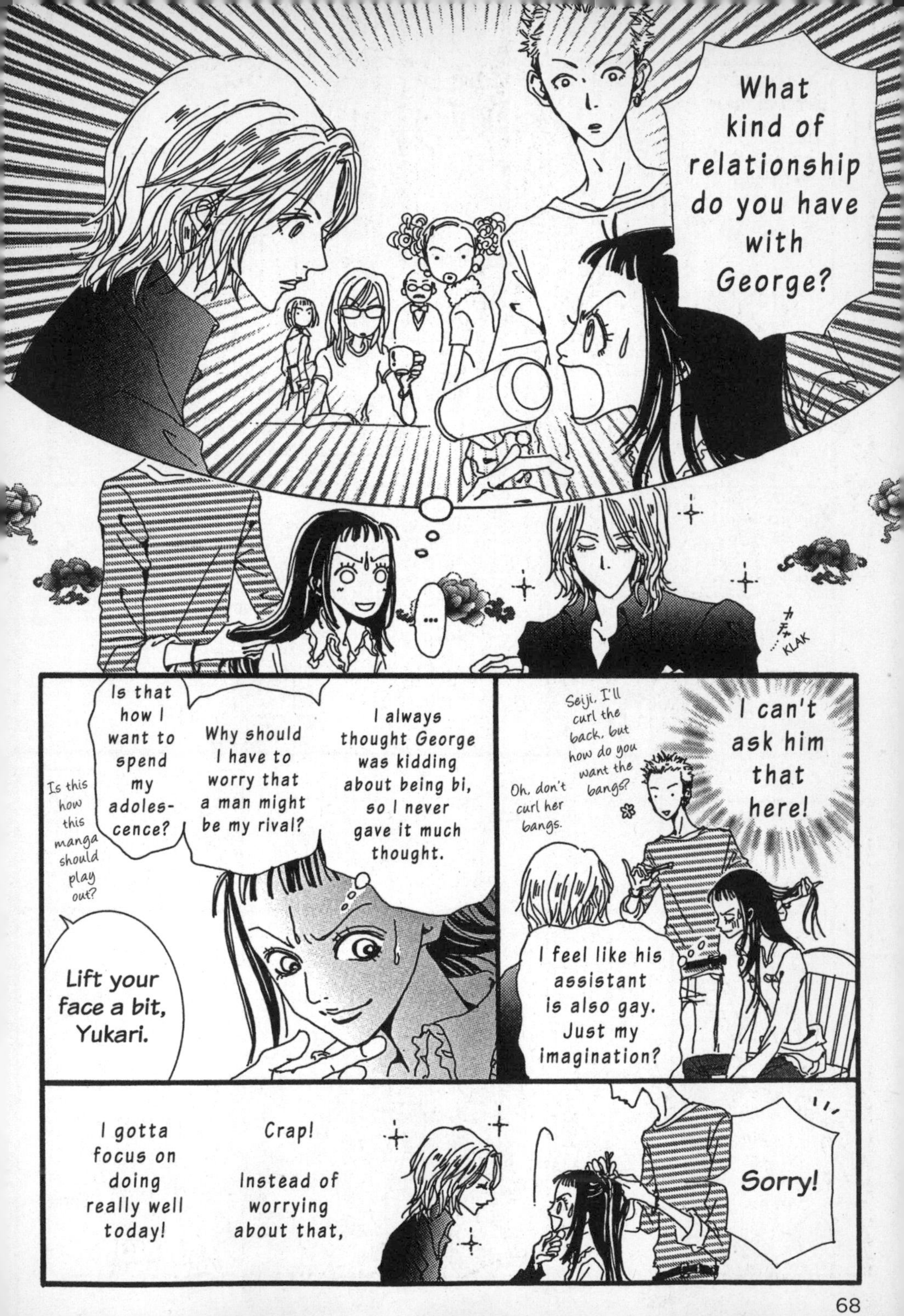
What kind of relationship do you have with George?
...
カチャ KLAK
I can't ask him that here!
Seiji, I'll curl the back, but how do you want the bangs?
Oh, don't curl her bangs.
I feel like his assistant is also gay. Just my imagination?
I always thought George was kidding about being bi, so I never gave it much thought.
Why should I have to worry that a man might be my rival?
Is that how I want to spend my adolescence?
Is this how this manga should play out?
Lift your face a bit, Yukari.
Sorry!
Crap!
Instead of worrying about that,
I gotta focus on doing really well today!

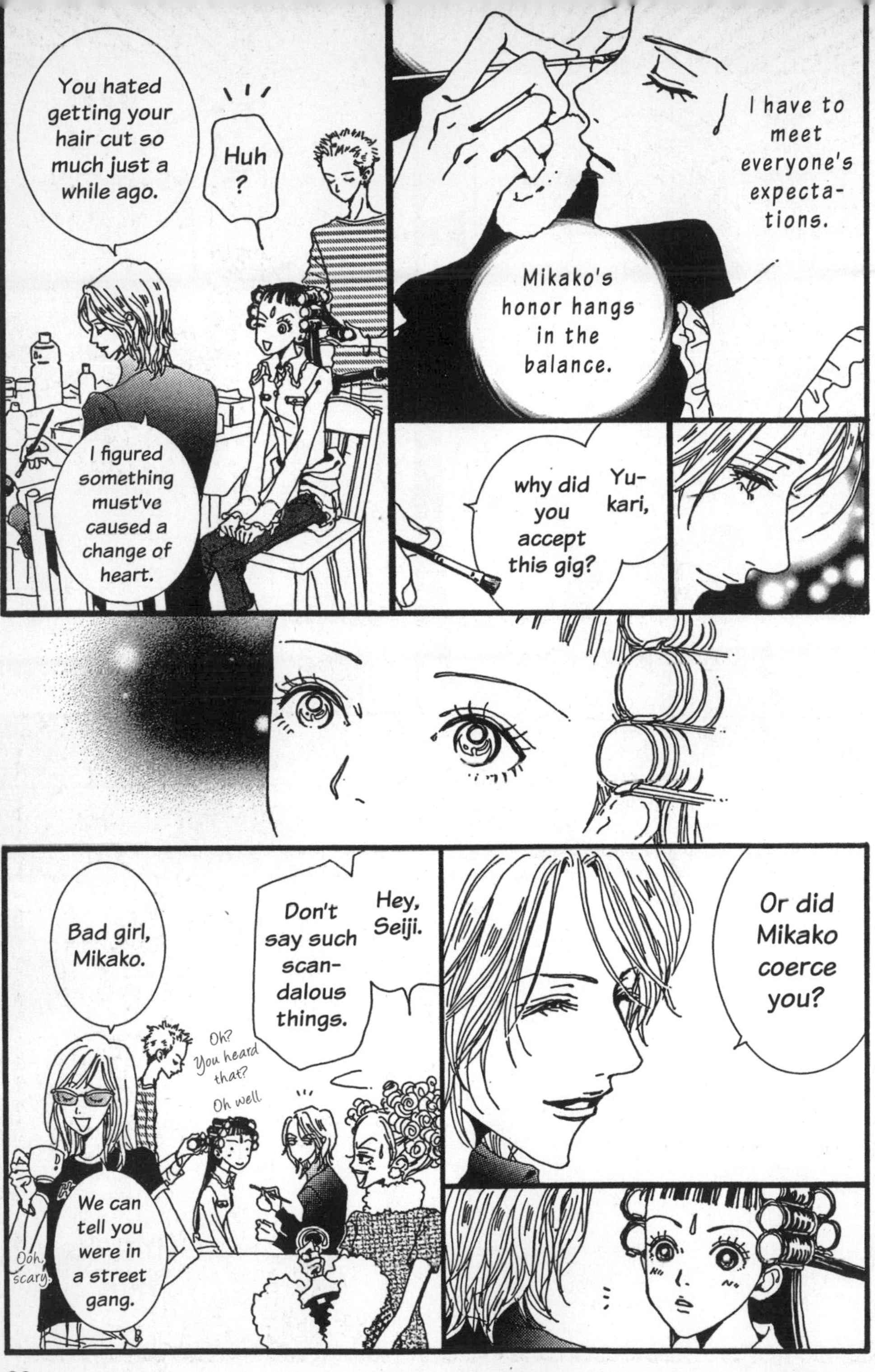
I have to meet everyone's expectations.
Mikako's honor hangs in the balance.
Yukari, why did you accept this gig?
You hated getting your hair cut so much just a while ago.
Huh?
I figured something must've caused a change of heart.
Or did Mikako coerce you?
Hey, Seiji. Don't say such scandalous things.
Bad girl, Mikako.
Oh? You heard that? Oh well
We can tell you were in a street gang.
Ooh, scary.

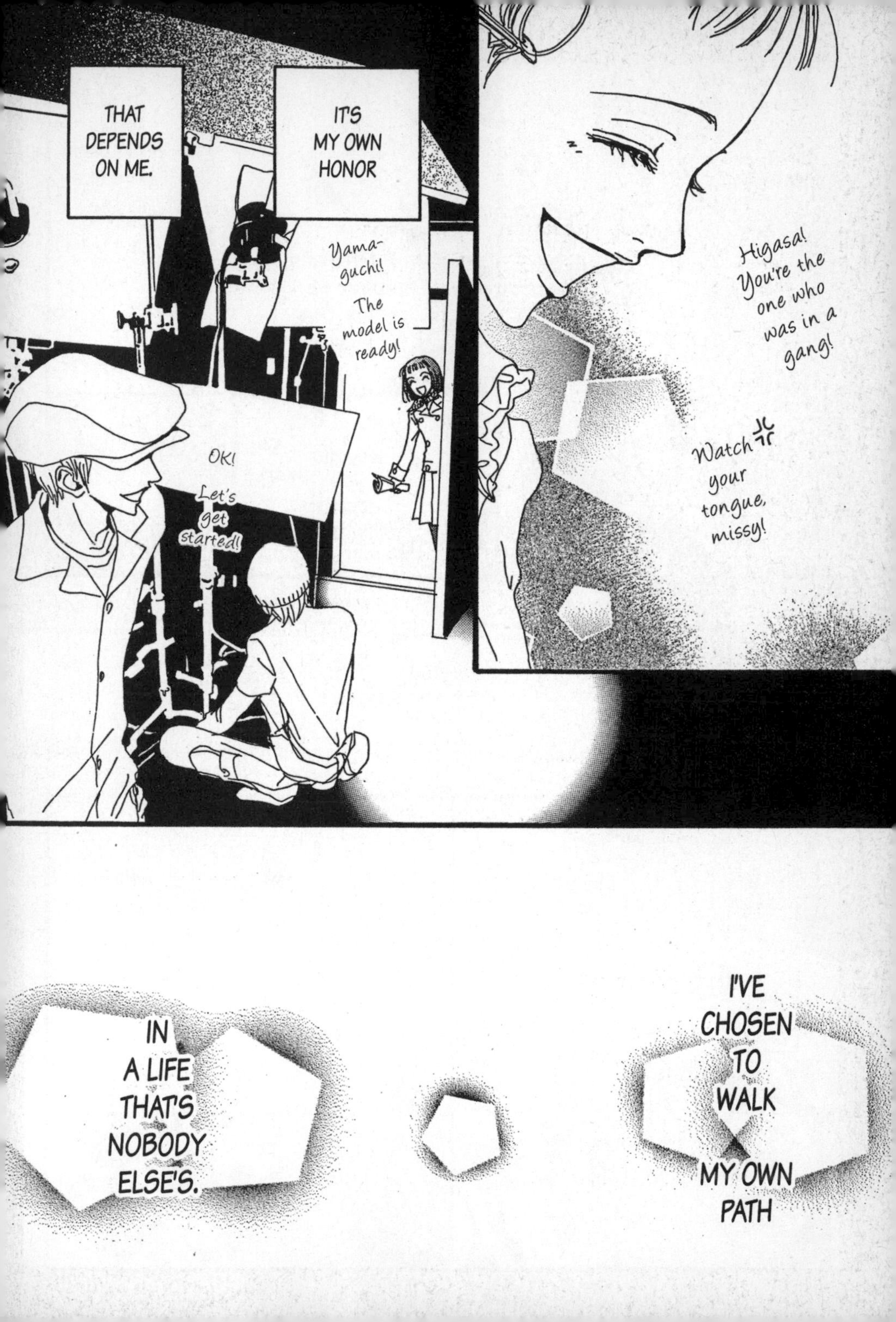
Higasa! You're the one who was in a gang!
Watch your tongue, missy!
IT'S MY OWN HONOR
THAT DEPENDS ON ME.
Yama-guchi! The model is ready!
OK! Let's get started!
I'VE CHOSEN TO WALK MY OWN PATH
IN A LIFE THAT'S NOBODY ELSE'S.

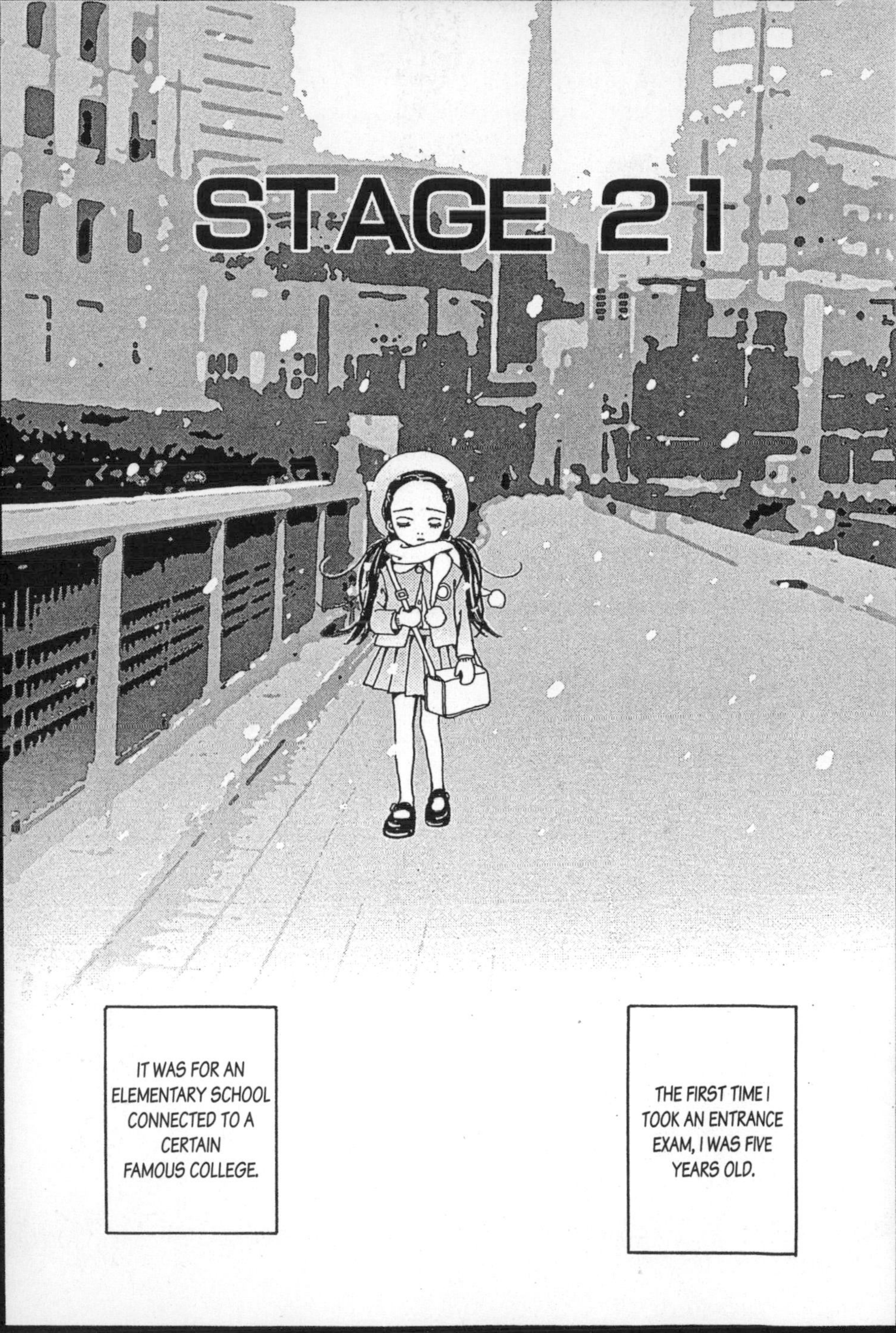
STAGE 21
THE FIRST TIME I TOOK AN ENTRANCE EXAM, I WAS FIVE YEARS OLD.
IT WAS FOR AN ELEMENTARY SCHOOL CONNECTED TO A CERTAIN FAMOUS COLLEGE.

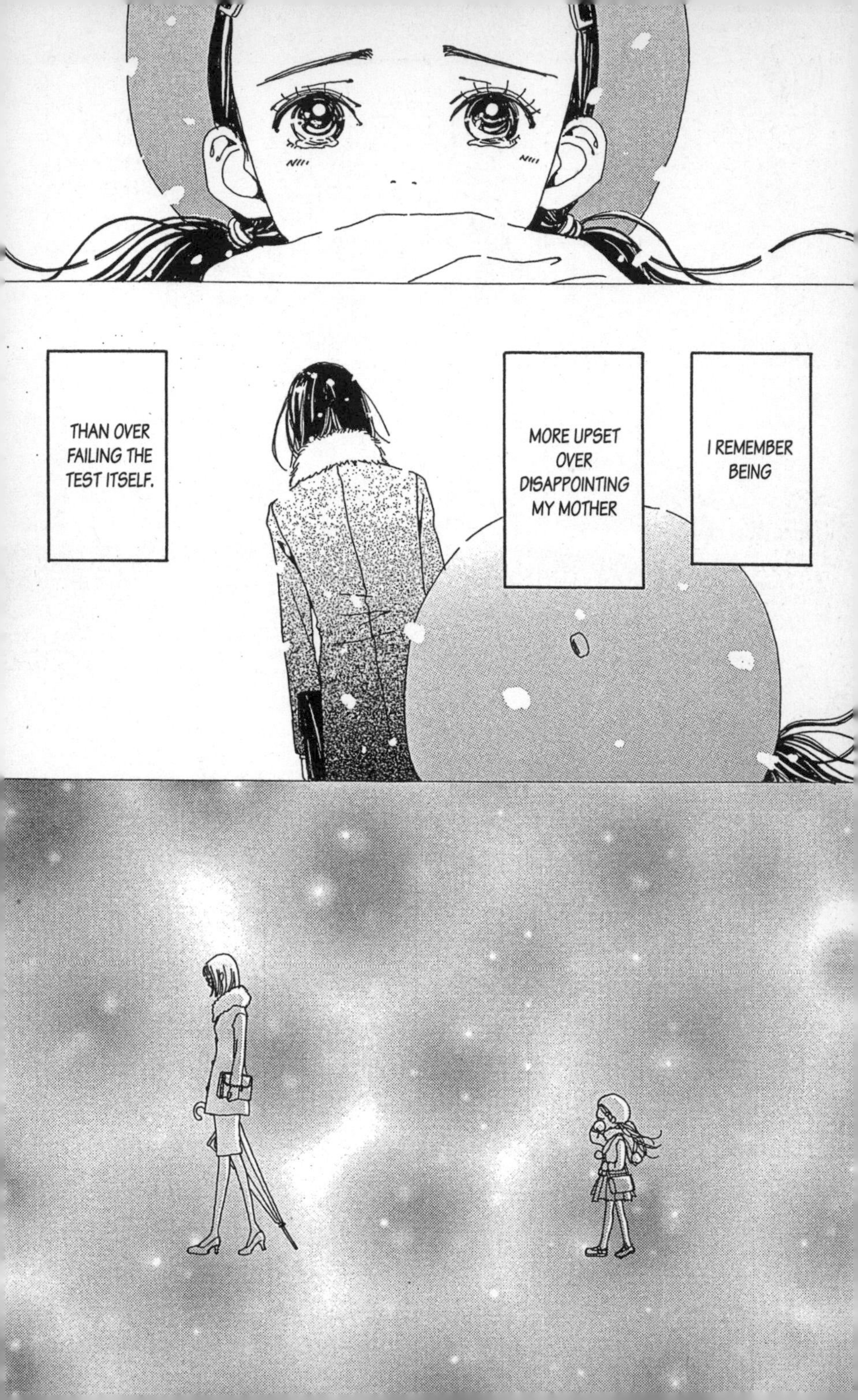
I REMEMBER BEING
MORE UPSET OVER DISAPPOINTING MY MOTHER
THAN OVER FAILING THE TEST ITSELF.

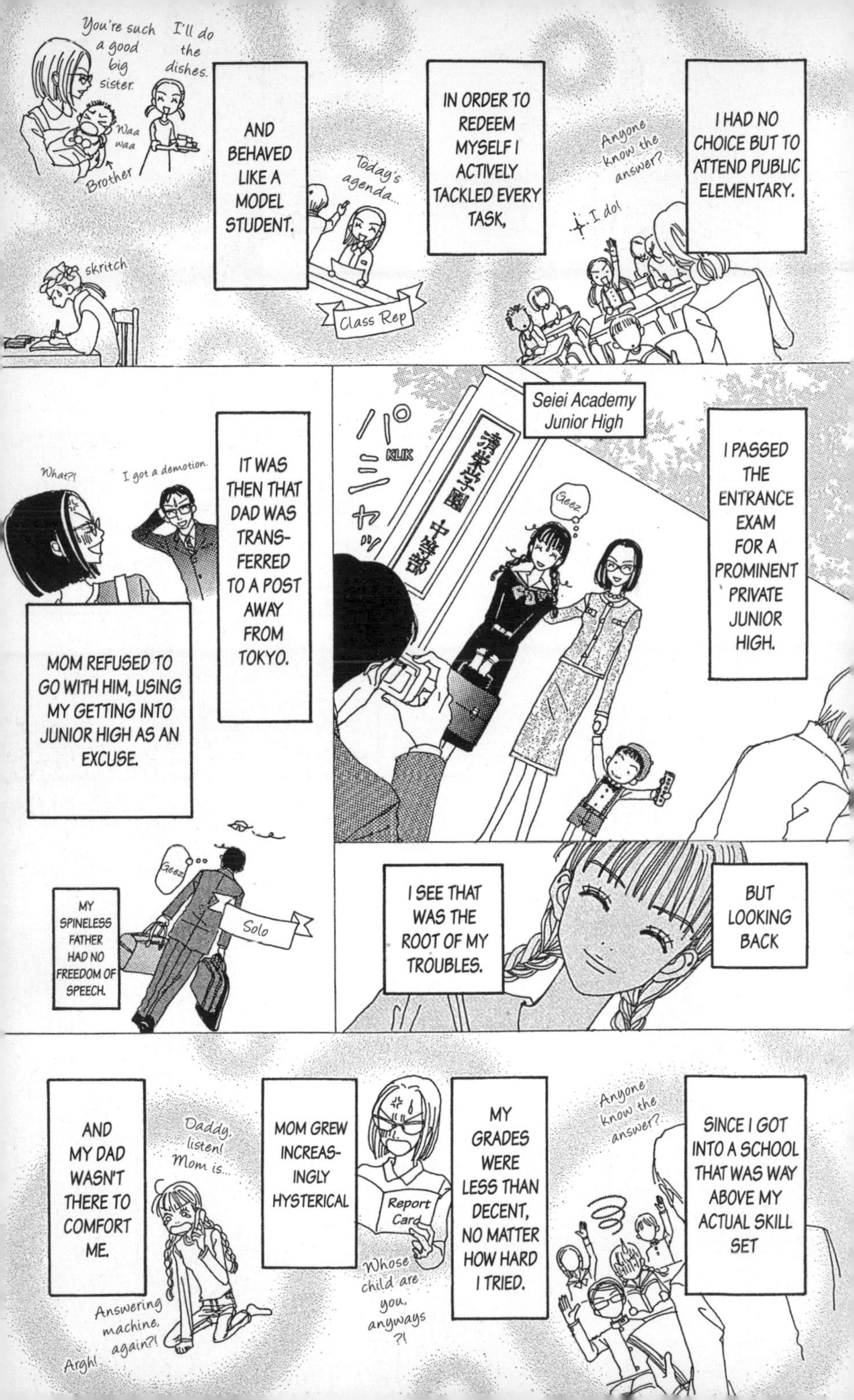
I HAD NO CHOICE BUT TO ATTEND PUBLIC ELEMENTARY.
Anyone know the answer?
I do!
IN ORDER TO REDEEM MYSELF I ACTIVELY TACKLED EVERY TASK,
Today's agenda...
Class Rep
AND BEHAVED LIKE A MODEL STUDENT.
I'll do the dishes.
You're such a good big sister.
Waa waa
Brother
skritch
Seiei Academy Junior High
I PASSED THE ENTRANCE EXAM FOR A PROMINENT PRIVATE JUNIOR HIGH.
清栄学園 中等部
Geez
パシャ
KLIK
IT WAS THEN THAT DAD WAS TRANSFERRED TO A POST AWAY FROM TOKYO.
I got a demotion.
What?!
MOM REFUSED TO GO WITH HIM, USING MY GETTING INTO JUNIOR HIGH AS AN EXCUSE.
BUT LOOKING BACK
I SEE THAT WAS THE ROOT OF MY TROUBLES.
MY SPINELESS FATHER HAD NO FREEDOM OF SPEECH.
Geez
Solo
SINCE I GOT INTO A SCHOOL THAT WAS WAY ABOVE MY ACTUAL SKILL SET
Anyone know the answer?
MY GRADES WERE LESS THAN DECENT, NO MATTER HOW HARD I TRIED.
Report Card
Whose child are you, anyways?!
MOM GREW INCREASINGLY HYSTERICAL
Daddy, listen! Mom is...
AND MY DAD WASN'T THERE TO COMFORT ME.
Answering machine, again?!
Argh!

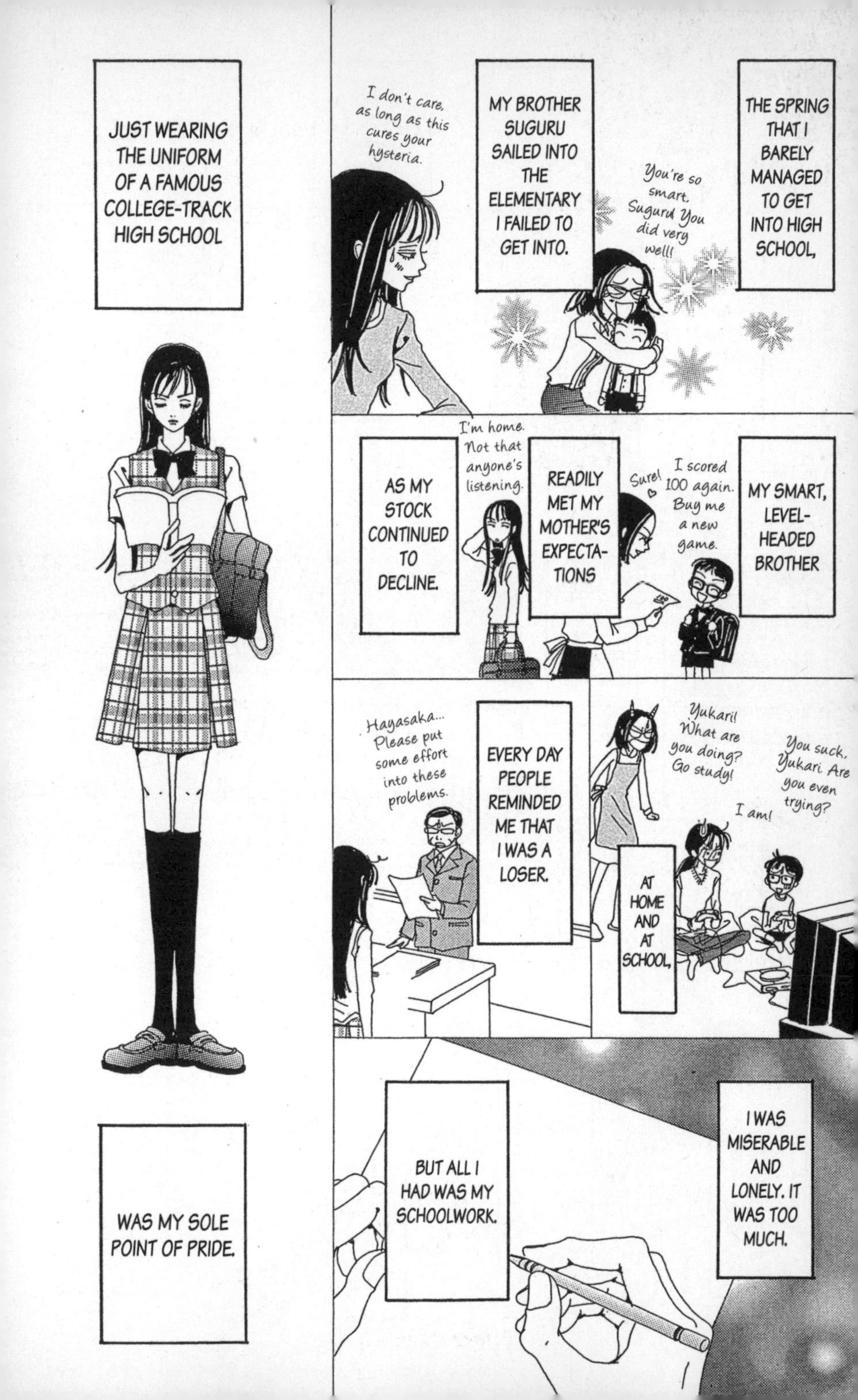
THE SPRING THAT I BARELY MANAGED TO GET INTO HIGH SCHOOL,
MY BROTHER SUGURU SAILED INTO THE ELEMENTARY I FAILED TO GET INTO.
You're so smart, Suguru! You did very well!
I don't care, as long as this cures your hysteria.
MY SMART, LEVEL-HEADED BROTHER
I scored 100 again. Buy me a new game.
Sure! ♡
READILY MET MY MOTHER'S EXPECTATIONS
I'm home. Not that anyone's listening.
AS MY STOCK CONTINUED TO DECLINE.
Yukari! What are you doing? Go study!
You suck, Yukari. Are you even trying?
I am!
AT HOME AND AT SCHOOL,
EVERY DAY PEOPLE REMINDED ME THAT I WAS A LOSER.
Hayasaka... Please put some effort into these problems.
I WAS MISERABLE AND LONELY. IT WAS TOO MUCH.
BUT ALL I HAD WAS MY SCHOOLWORK.
JUST WEARING THE UNIFORM OF A FAMOUS COLLEGE-TRACK HIGH SCHOOL
WAS MY SOLE POINT OF PRIDE.

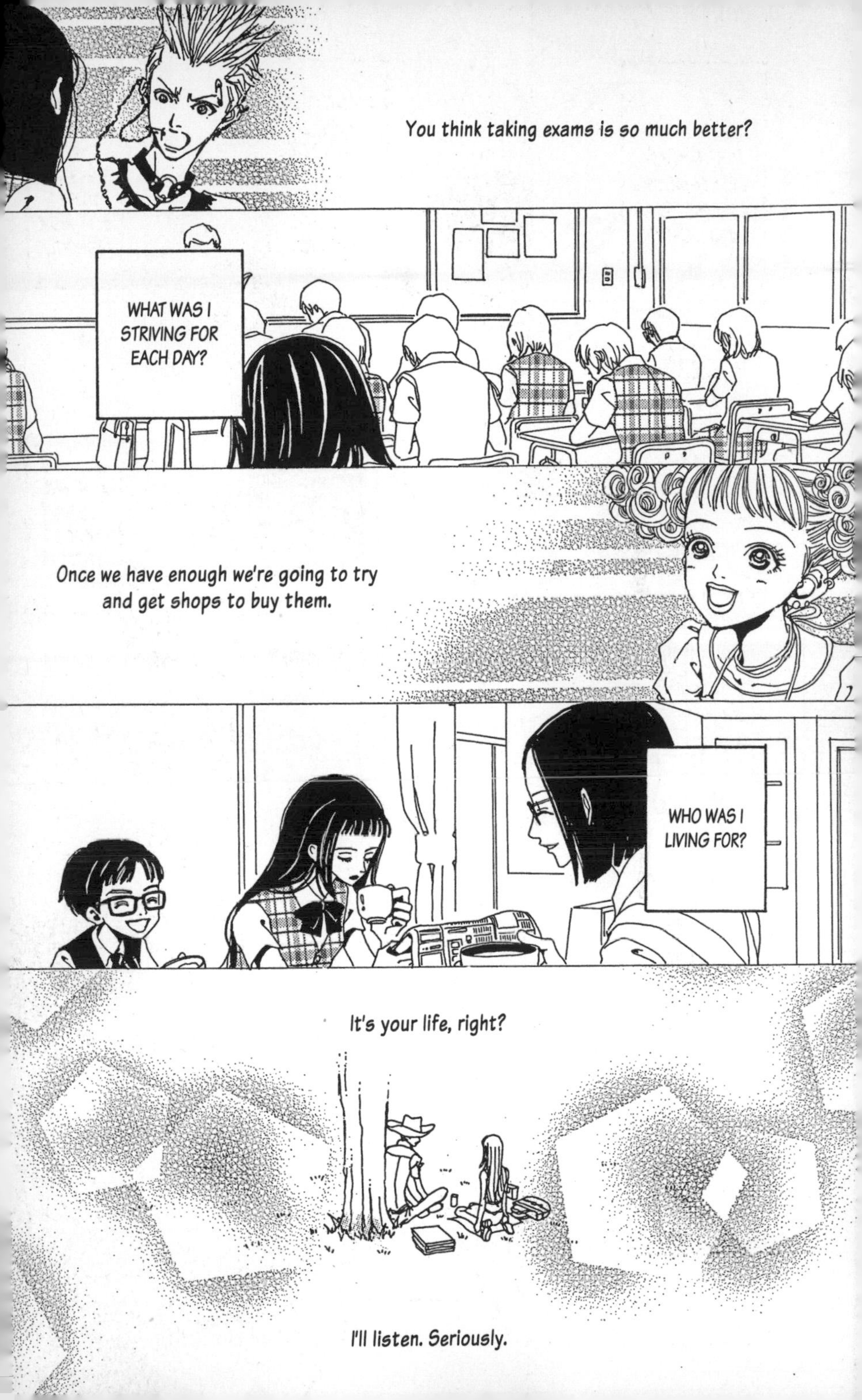
You think taking exams is so much better?
WHAT WAS I STRIVING FOR EACH DAY?
Once we have enough we're going to try and get shops to buy them.
WHO WAS I LIVING FOR?
It's your life, right?
I'll listen. Seriously.

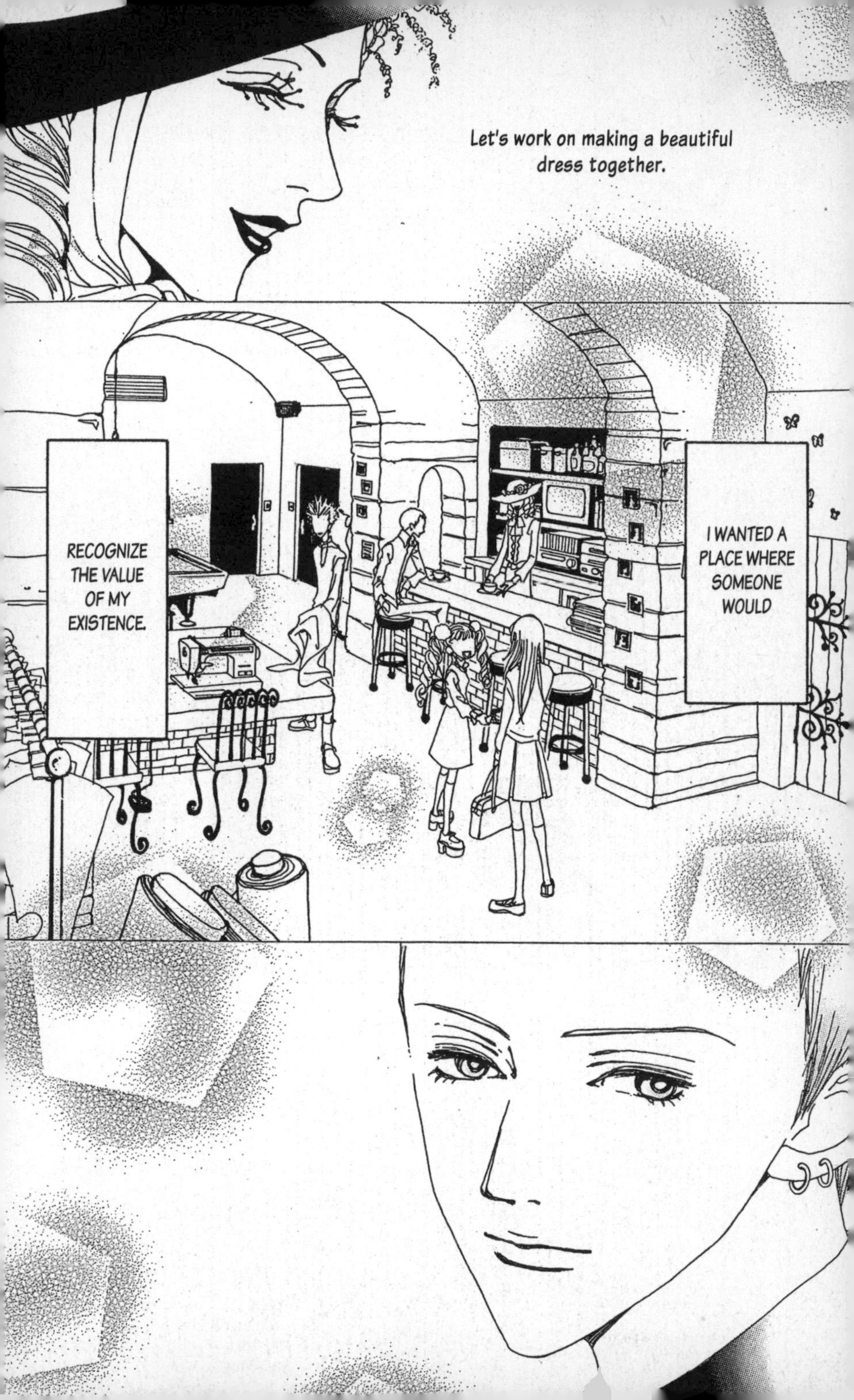
Let's work on making a beautiful dress together.
I WANTED A PLACE WHERE SOMEONE WOULD
RECOGNIZE THE VALUE OF MY EXISTENCE.

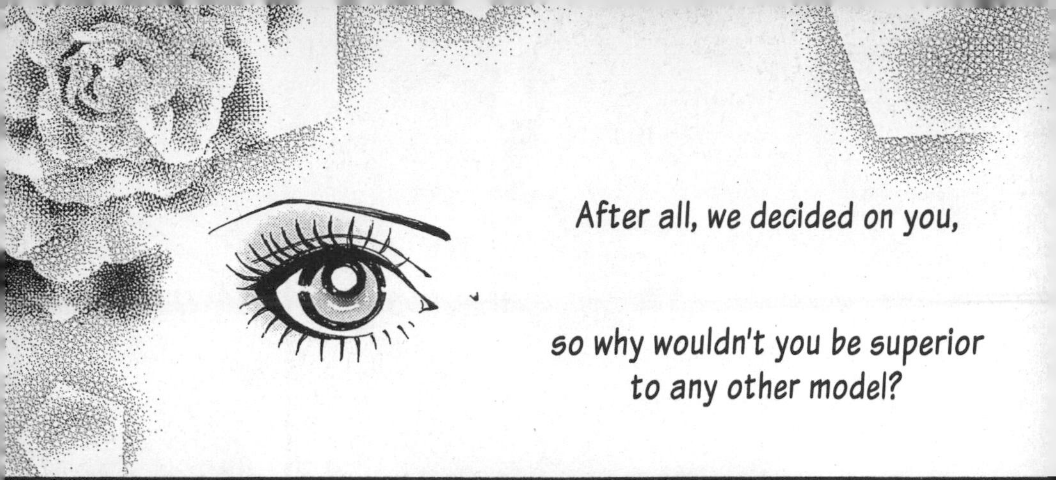
After all, we decided on you,
so why wouldn't you be superior
to any other model?

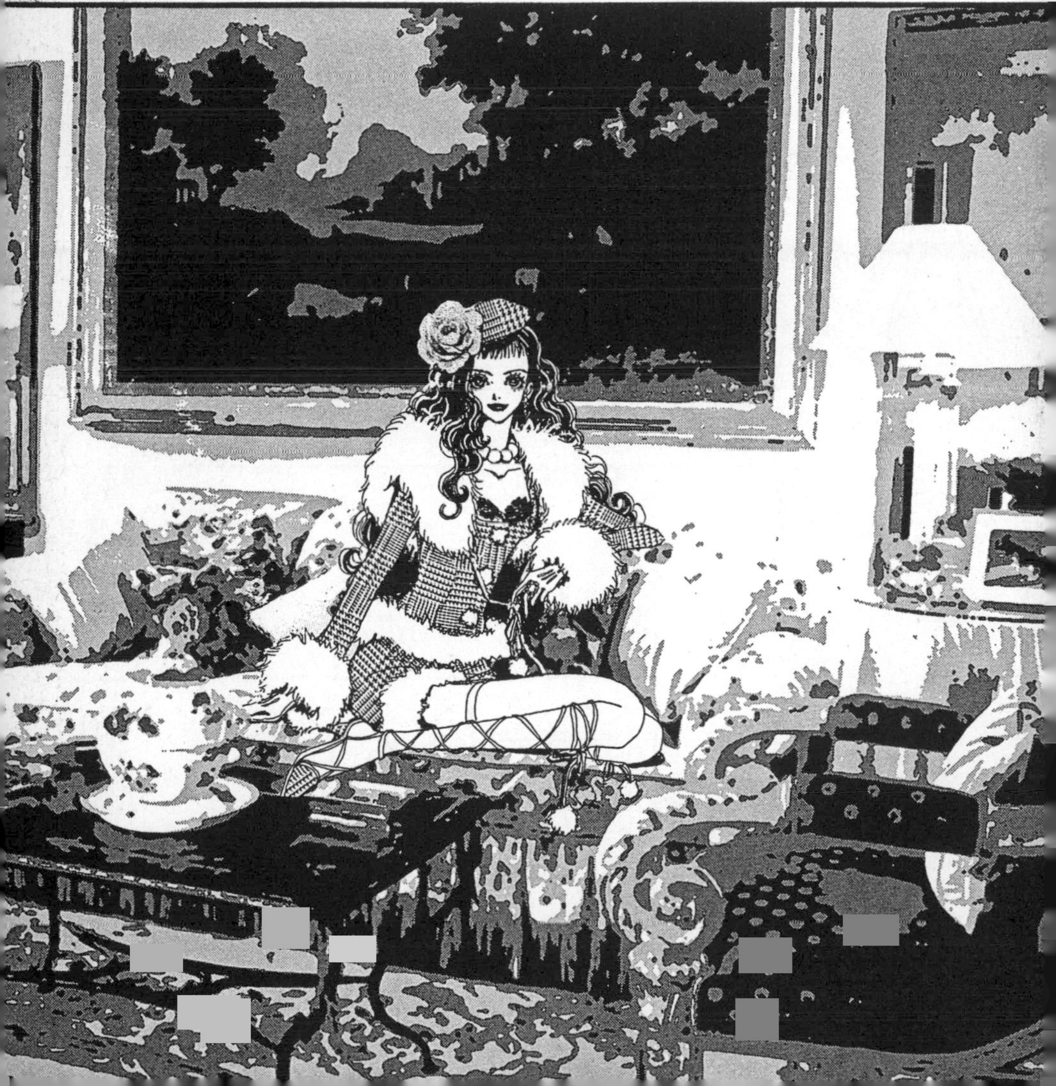

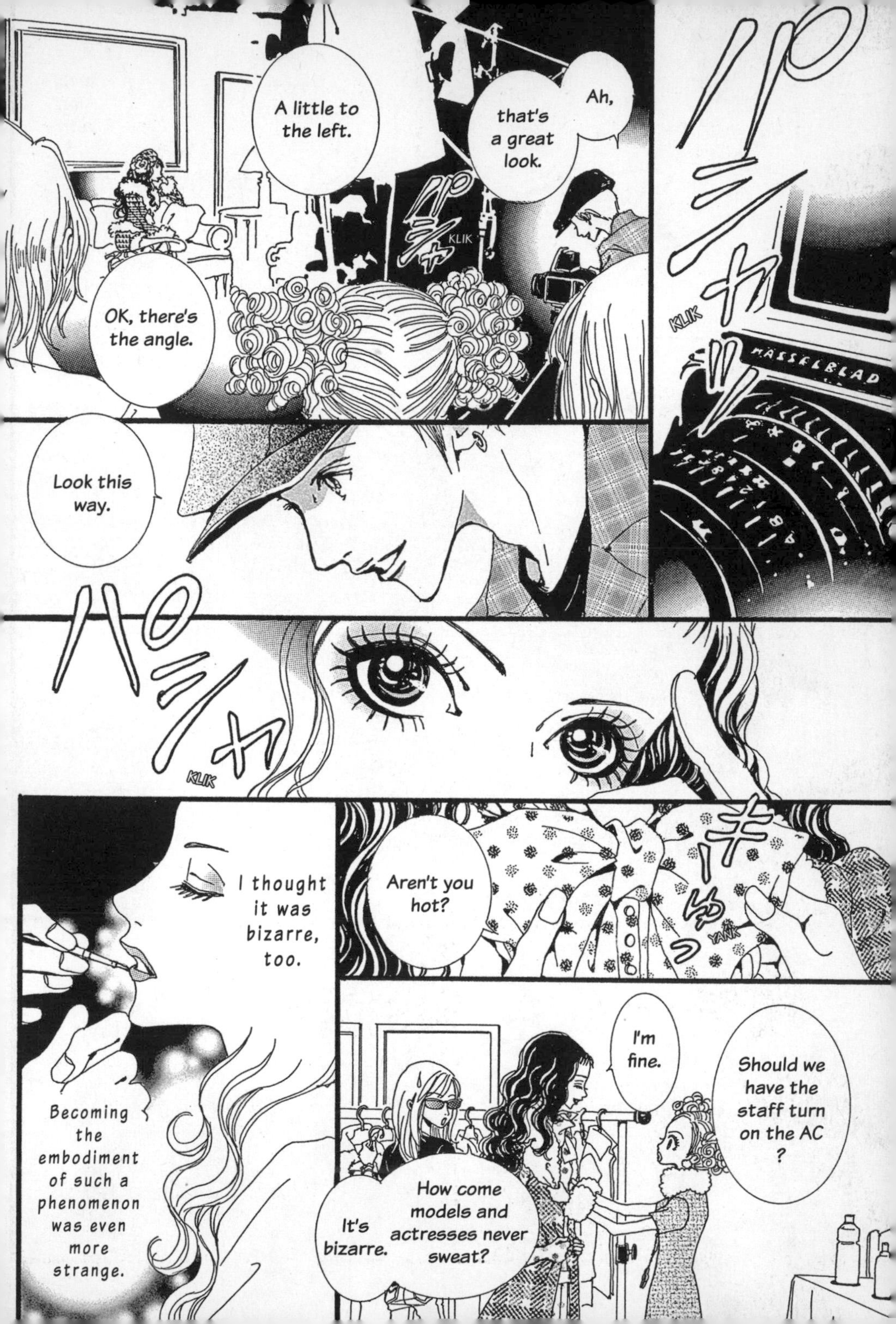
KLIK
Ah, that's a great look.
A little to the left.
KLIK
OK, there's the angle.
Look this way.
KLIK
Aren't you hot?
YANK
Should we have the staff turn on the AC?
I'm fine.
How come models and actresses never sweat?
It's bizarre.
I thought it was bizarre, too.
Becoming the embodiment of such a phenomenon was even more strange.

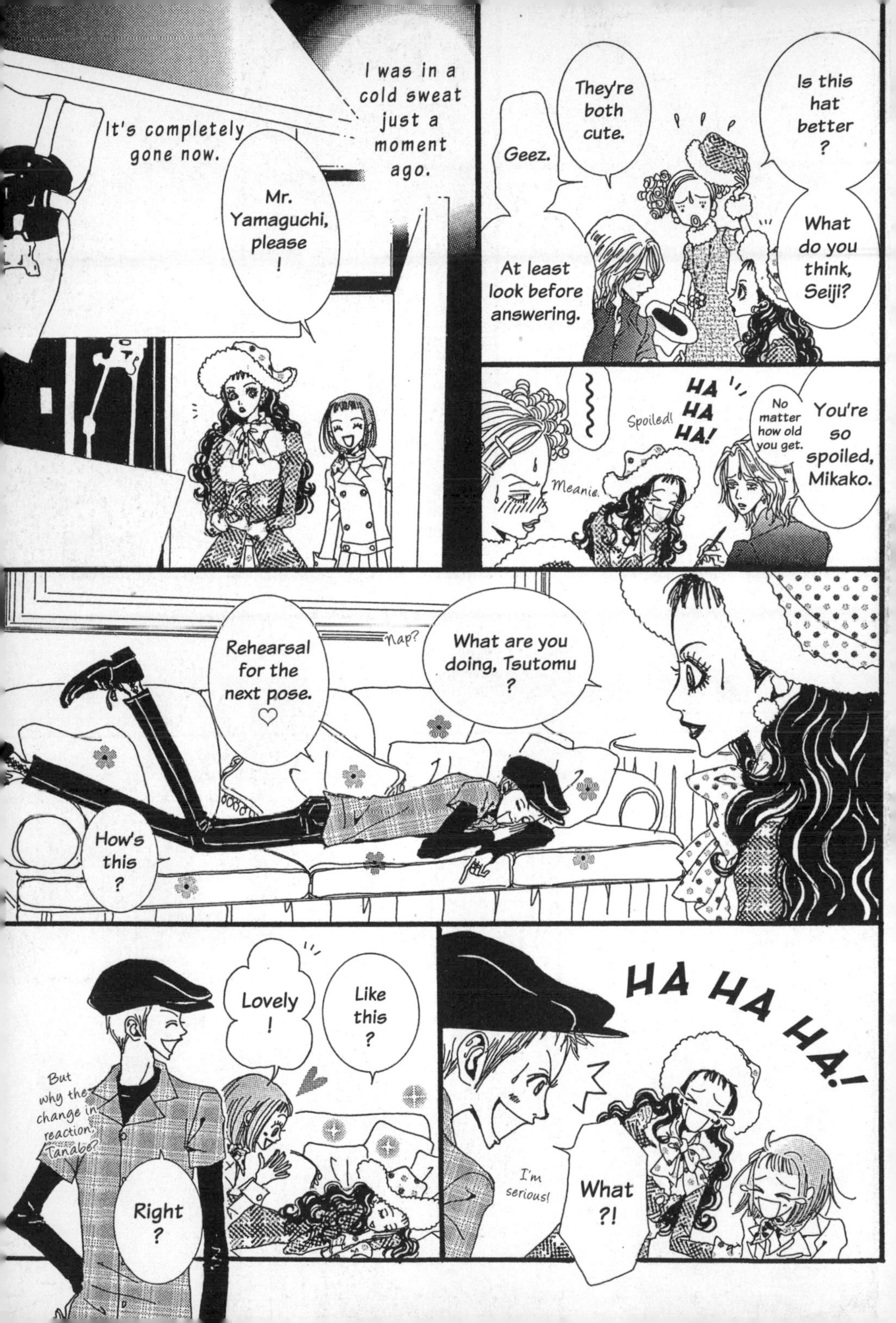
Is this hat better?
What do you think, Seiji?
They're both cute.
Geez.
At least look before answering.
You're so spoiled, Mikako.
No matter how old you get.
HA HA HA!
Spoiled!
Meanie.
I was in a cold sweat just a moment ago.
It's completely gone now.
Mr. Yamaguchi, please!
What are you doing, Tsutomu?
Nap?
Rehearsal for the next pose. ♡
How's this?
HA HA HA!
What?!
I'm serious!
Like this?
Lovely!
Right?
But why the change in reaction, Tanabe?

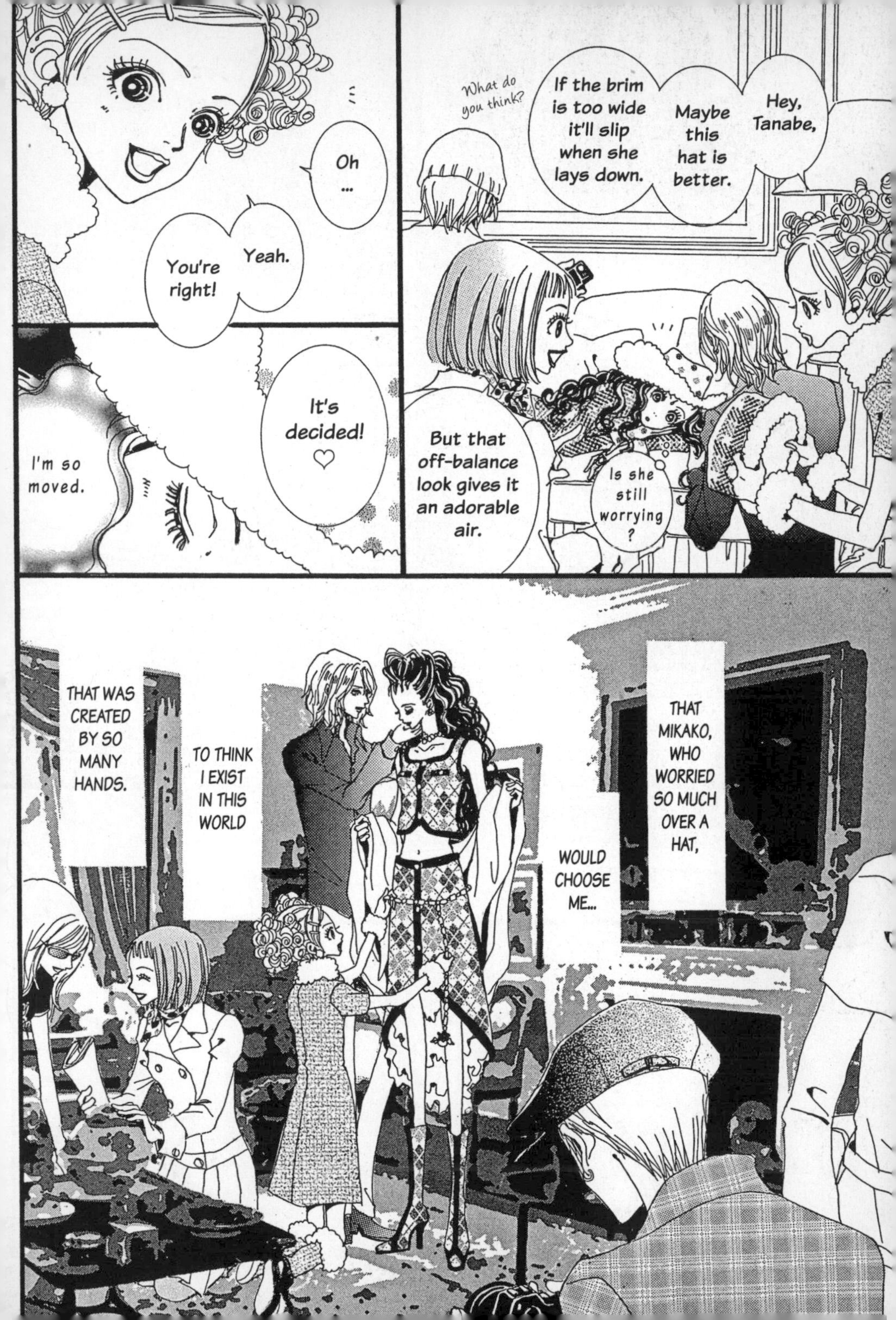
Hey, Tanabe,
Maybe this hat is better.
If the brim is too wide it'll slip when she lays down.
What do you think?
But that off-balance look gives it an adorable air.
Is she still worrying ?
Oh ...
Yeah.
You're right!
It's decided! ♡
I'm so moved.
THAT MIKAKO, WHO WORRIED SO MUCH OVER A HAT,
WOULD CHOOSE ME...
TO THINK I EXIST IN THIS WORLD
THAT WAS CREATED BY SO MANY HANDS.

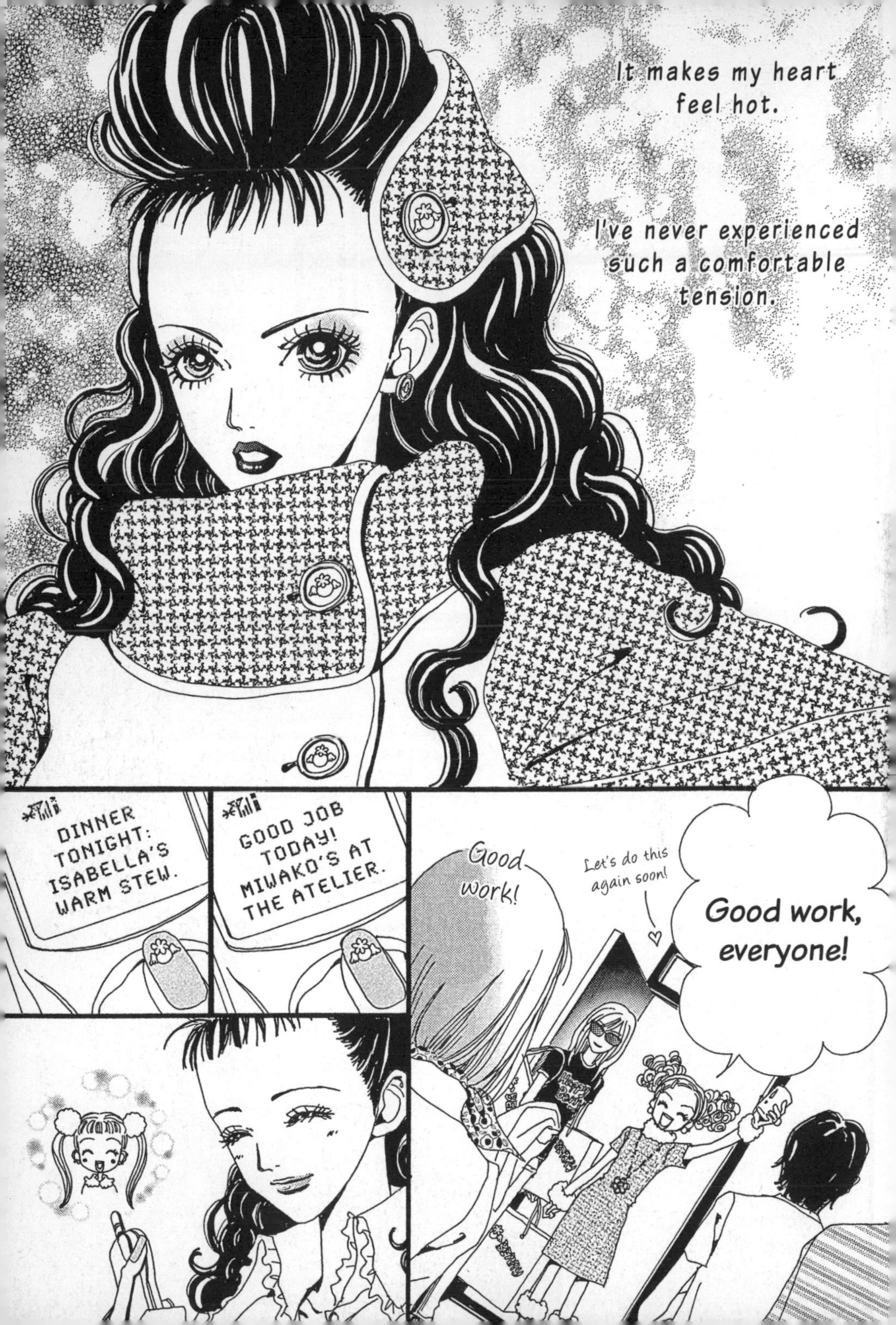
It makes my heart feel hot.
I've never experienced such a comfortable tension.
Good work, everyone!
Let's do this again soon! ♥
Good work!
GOOD JOB TODAY! MIWAKO'S AT THE ATELIER.
DINNER TONIGHT: ISABELLA'S WARM STEW.

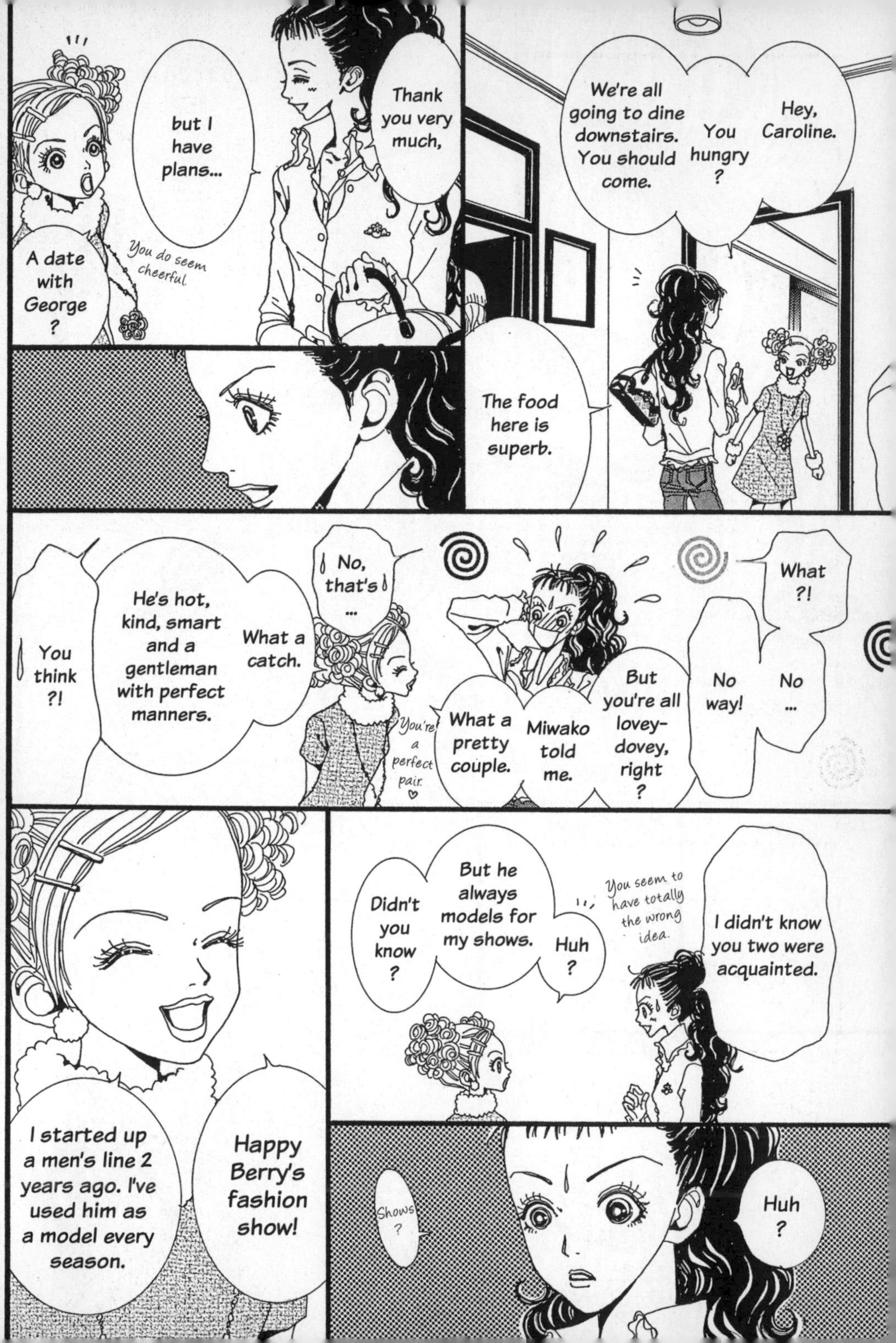
Hey, Caroline.
You hungry?
We're all going to dine downstairs. You should come.
The food here is superb.
Thank you very much,
but I have plans...
A date with George?
You do seem cheerful.
What?!
No...
No way!
But you're all lovey-dovey, right?
Miwako told me.
What a pretty couple.
You're a perfect pair.
No, that's...
What a catch.
He's hot, kind, smart and a gentleman with perfect manners.
You think?!
I didn't know you two were acquainted.
You seem to have totally the wrong idea.
Huh?
But he always models for my shows.
Didn't you know?
Huh?
Shows?
Happy Berry's fashion show!
I started up a men's line 2 years ago. I've used him as a model every season.

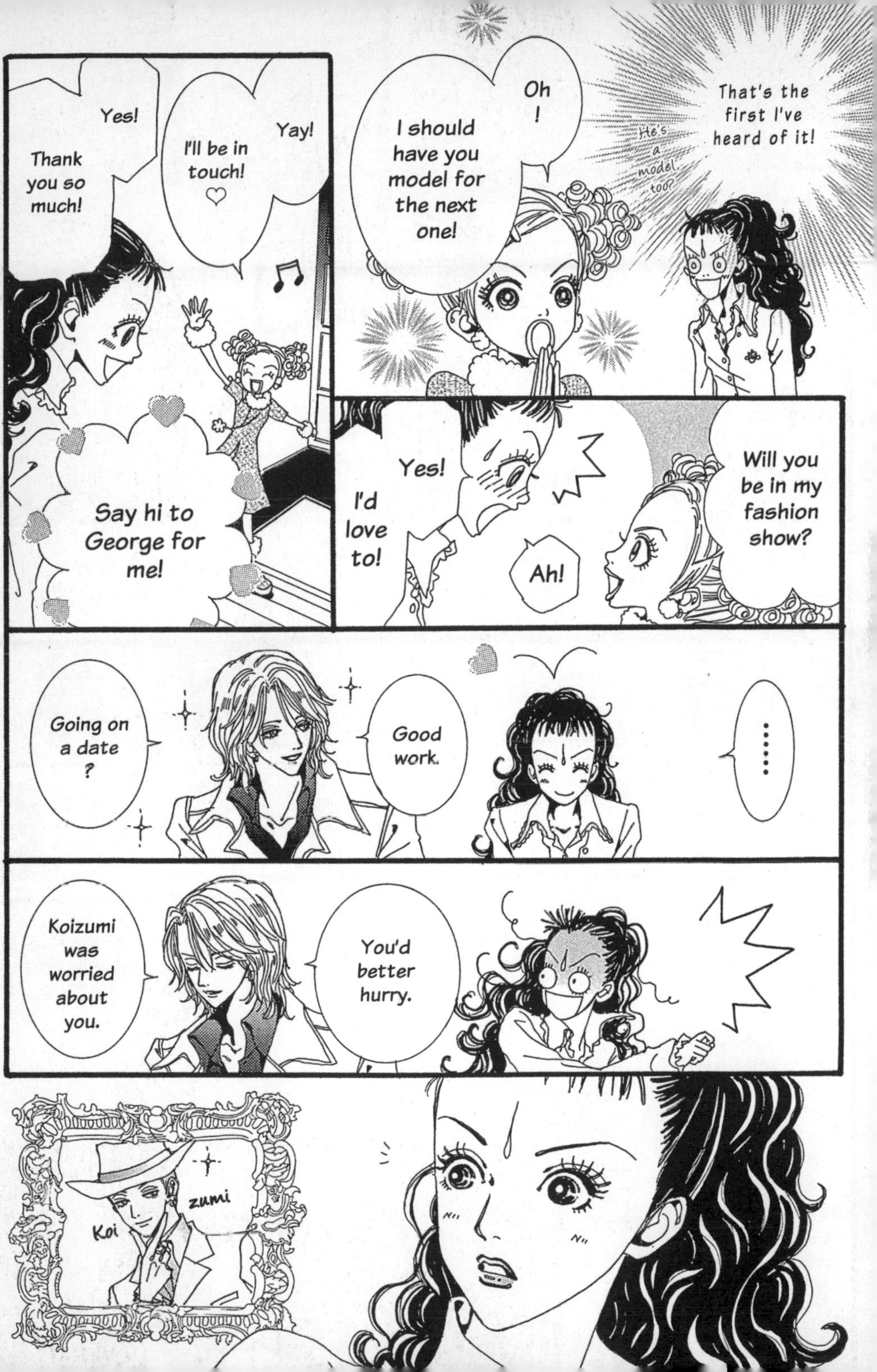
That's the first I've heard of it!
He's a model too?
Oh!
I should have you model for the next one!
Will you be in my fashion show?
Ah!
Yes!
I'd love to!
Yay!
I'll be in touch! ♡
Yes!
Thank you so much!
Say hi to George for me!
......
Good work.
Going on a date?
You'd better hurry.
Koizumi was worried about you.
Koi
zumi

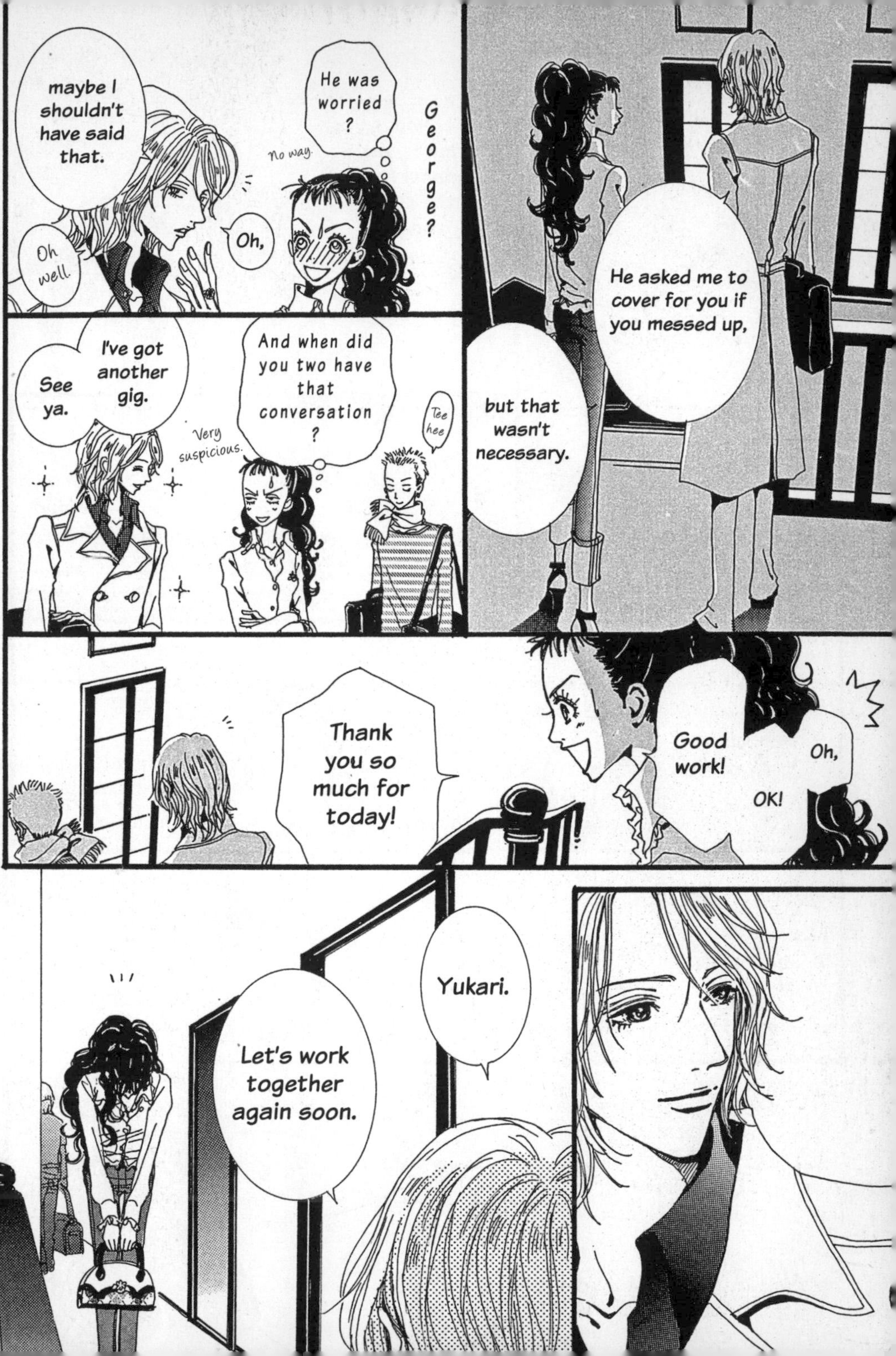
He asked me to cover for you if you messed up,
but that wasn't necessary.
George?
He was worried?
No way.
Oh,
maybe I shouldn't have said that.
Oh well.
Tee hee
And when did you two have that conversation?
Very suspicious.
I've got another gig.
See ya.
Oh, OK!
Good work!
Thank you so much for today!
Yukari.
Let's work together again soon.

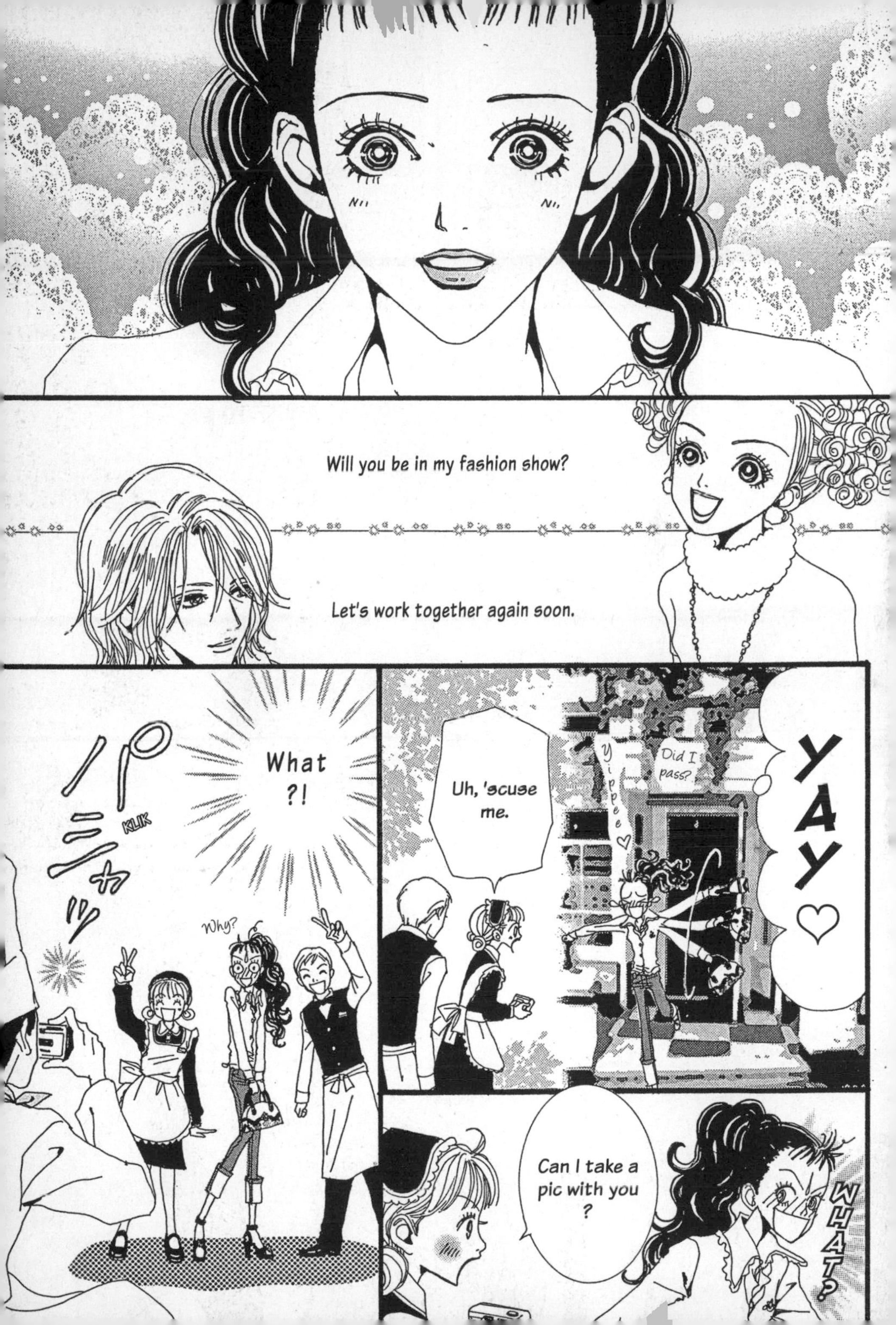
Will you be in my fashion show?
Let's work together again soon.
YAY ♡
Did I pass?
Yippee ♡
Uh, 'scuse me.
What ?!
パシャッ
KLIK
Why?
Can I take a pic with you ?
WHAT?

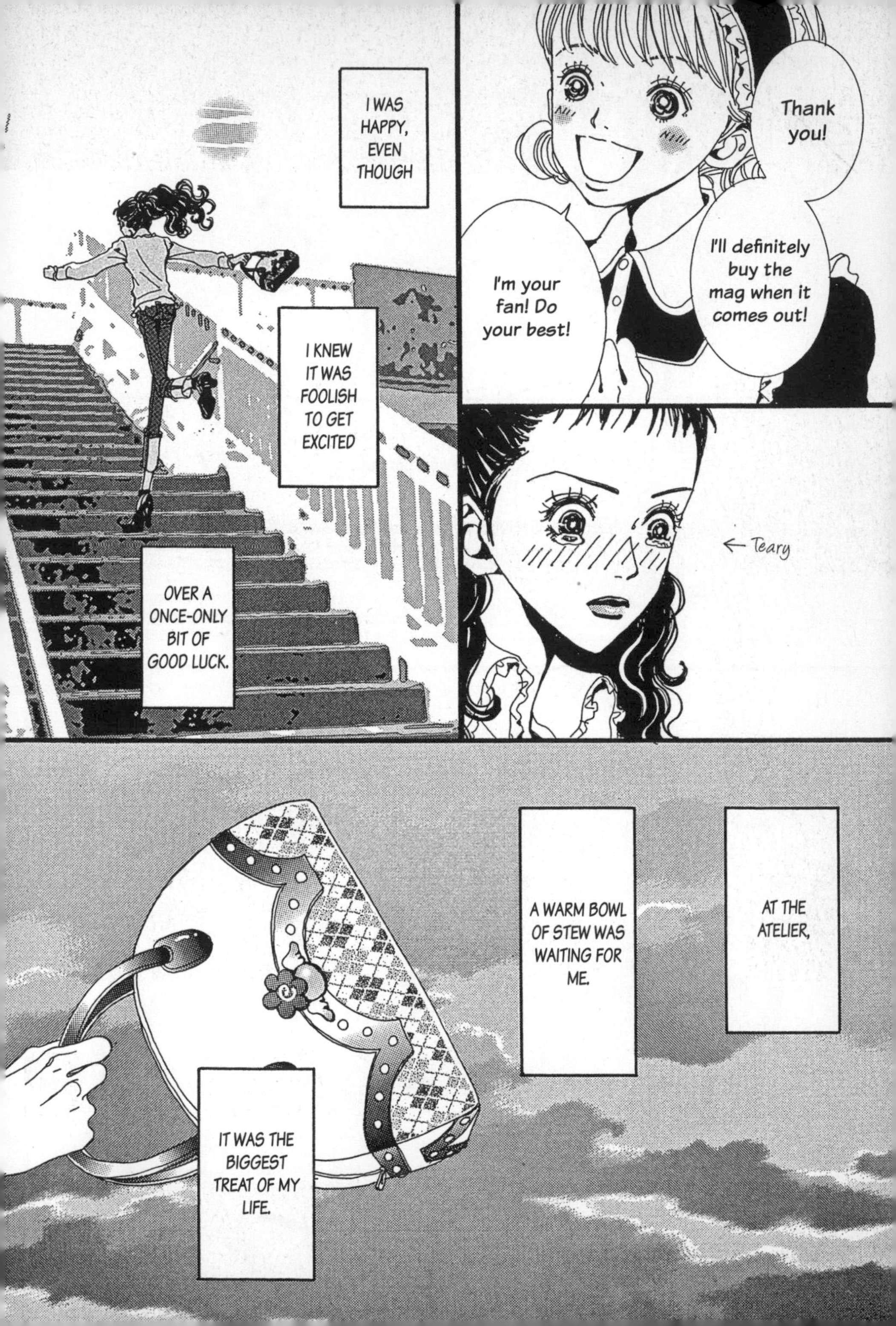
Thank you!
I'll definitely buy the mag when it comes out!
I'm your fan! Do your best!
← Teary
I WAS HAPPY, EVEN THOUGH
I KNEW IT WAS FOOLISH TO GET EXCITED
OVER A ONCE-ONLY BIT OF GOOD LUCK.
AT THE ATELIER,
A WARM BOWL OF STEW WAS WAITING FOR ME.
IT WAS THE BIGGEST TREAT OF MY LIFE.

STAGE 22

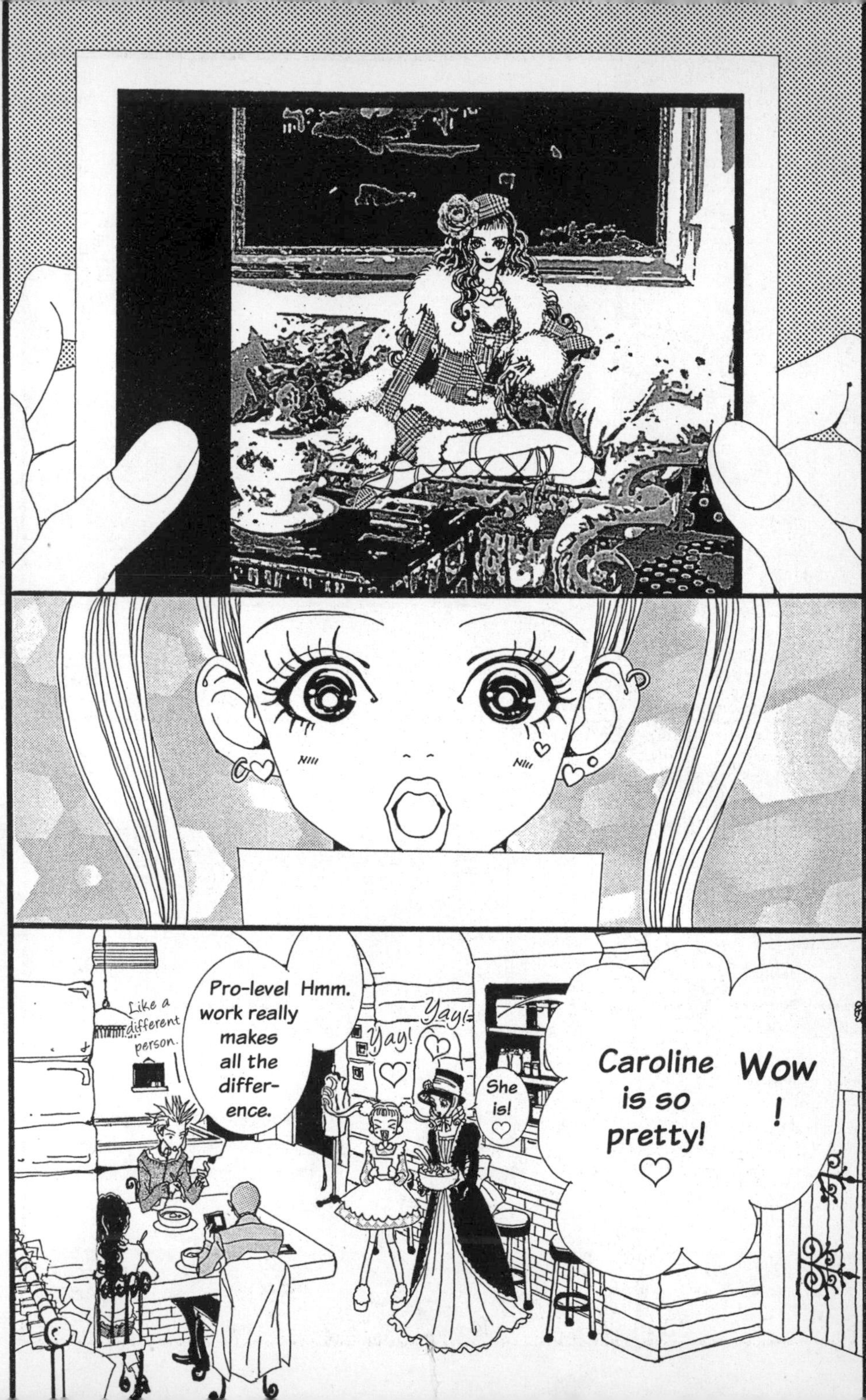
Wow!
Caroline is so pretty! ♡
Yay!
She is! ♡
Yay!
Hmm.
Pro-level work really makes all the differ-ence.
Like a different person.

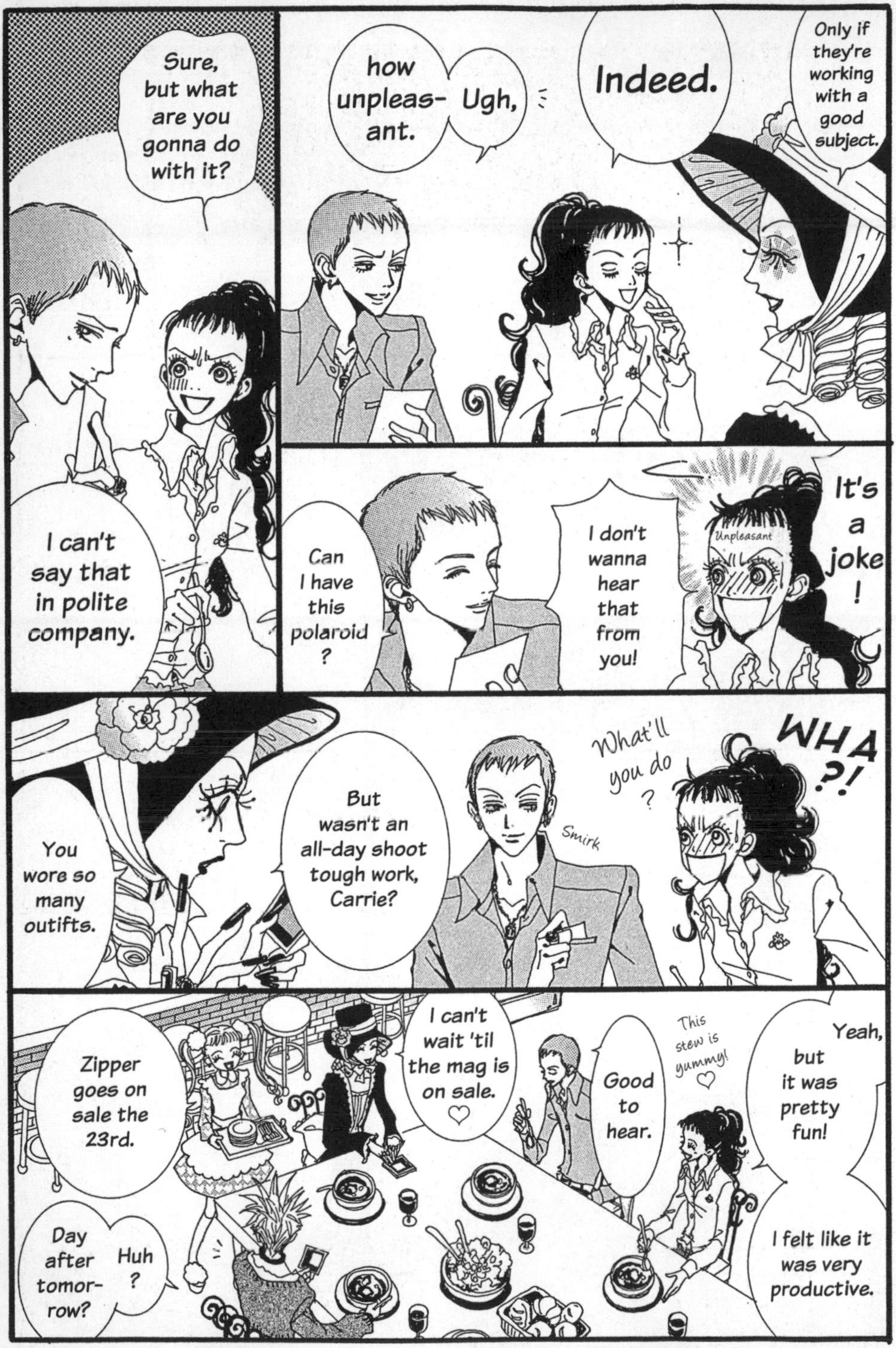
Only if they're working with a good subject.
Indeed.
Ugh,
how unpleasant.
It's a joke!
Unpleasant
I don't wanna hear that from you!
Can I have this polaroid?
Sure, but what are you gonna do with it?
I can't say that in polite company.
WHA?!
What'll you do?
Smirk
But wasn't an all-day shoot tough work, Carrie?
You wore so many outfits.
Yeah, but it was pretty fun!
I felt like it was very productive.
This stew is yummy! ♡
Good to hear.
I can't wait 'til the mag is on sale. ♡
Zipper goes on sale the 23rd.
Huh?
Day after tomorrow?

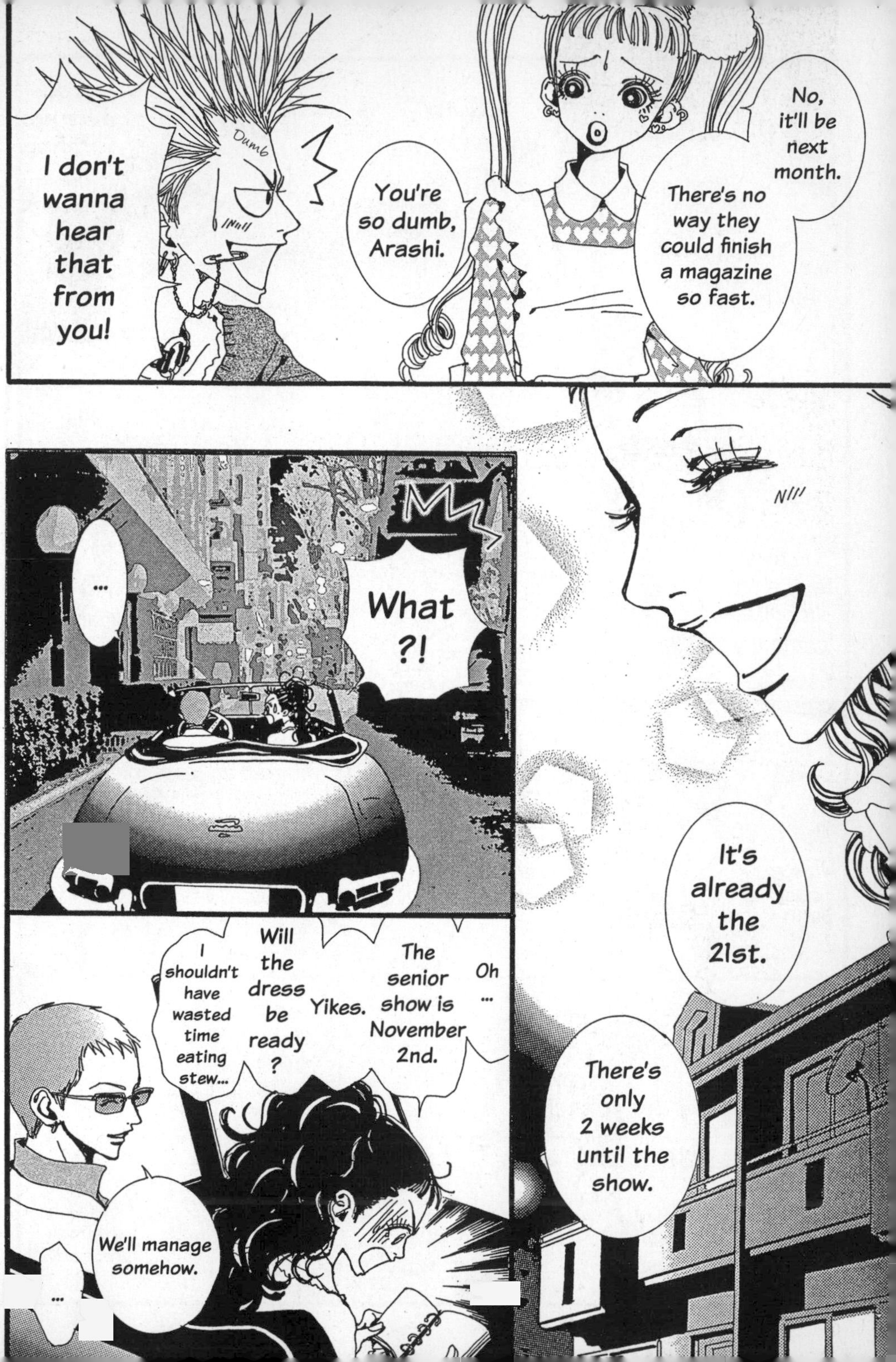
No, it'll be next month.
There's no way they could finish a magazine so fast.
You're so dumb, Arashi.
Dumb
I don't wanna hear that from you!
It's already the 21st.
There's only 2 weeks until the show.
What ?!
...
Oh ...
The senior show is November 2nd.
Yikes.
Will the dress be ready ?
I shouldn't have wasted time eating stew...
We'll manage somehow.
...

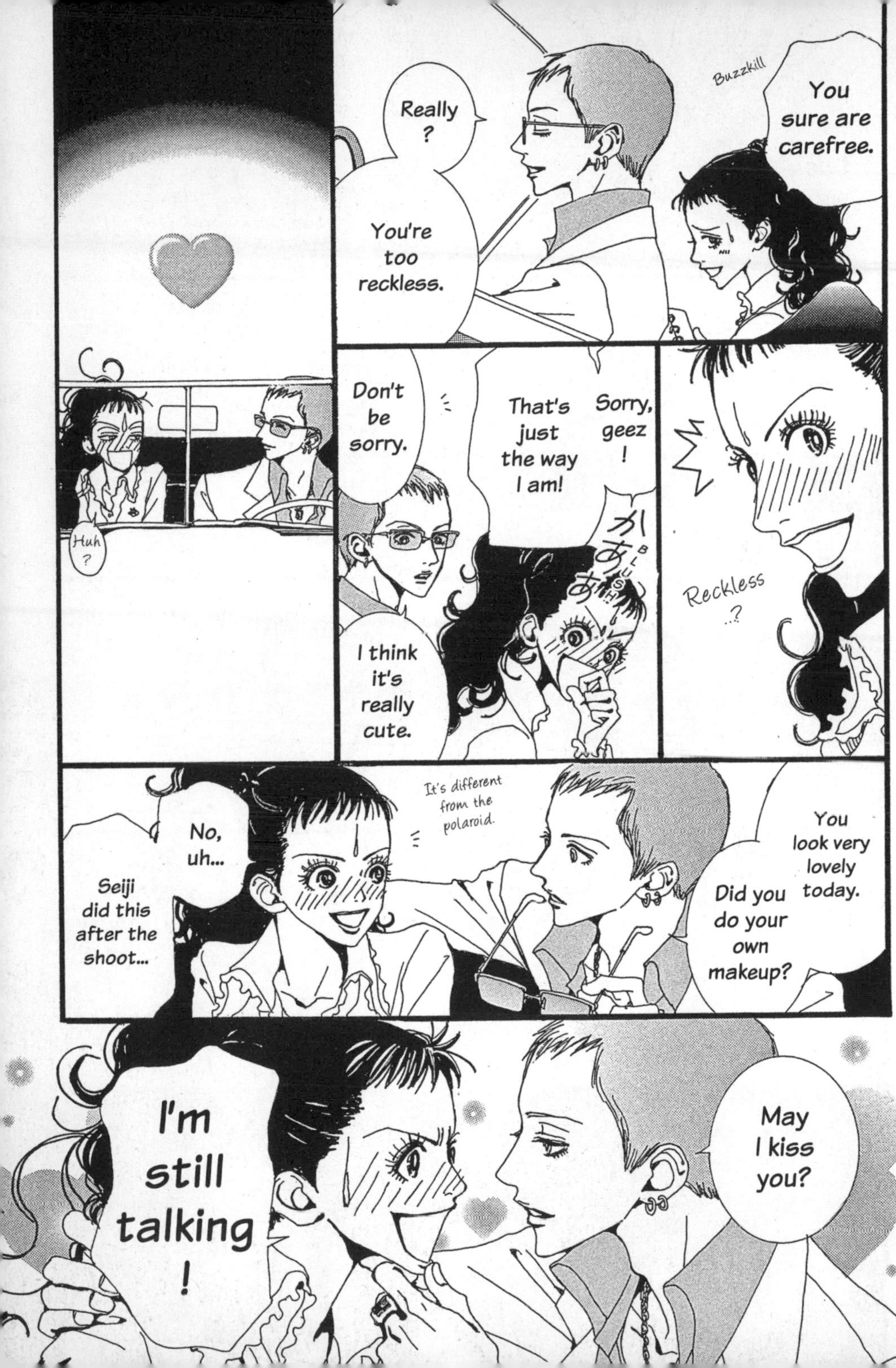
Buzzkill
You sure are carefree.
Really?
You're too reckless.
Reckless..?
Sorry, geez!
That's just the way I am!
BLUSH
Don't be sorry.
I think it's really cute.
Huh?
You look very lovely today.
Did you do your own makeup?
It's different from the polaroid.
No, uh...
Seiji did this after the shoot...
May I kiss you?
I'm still talking!

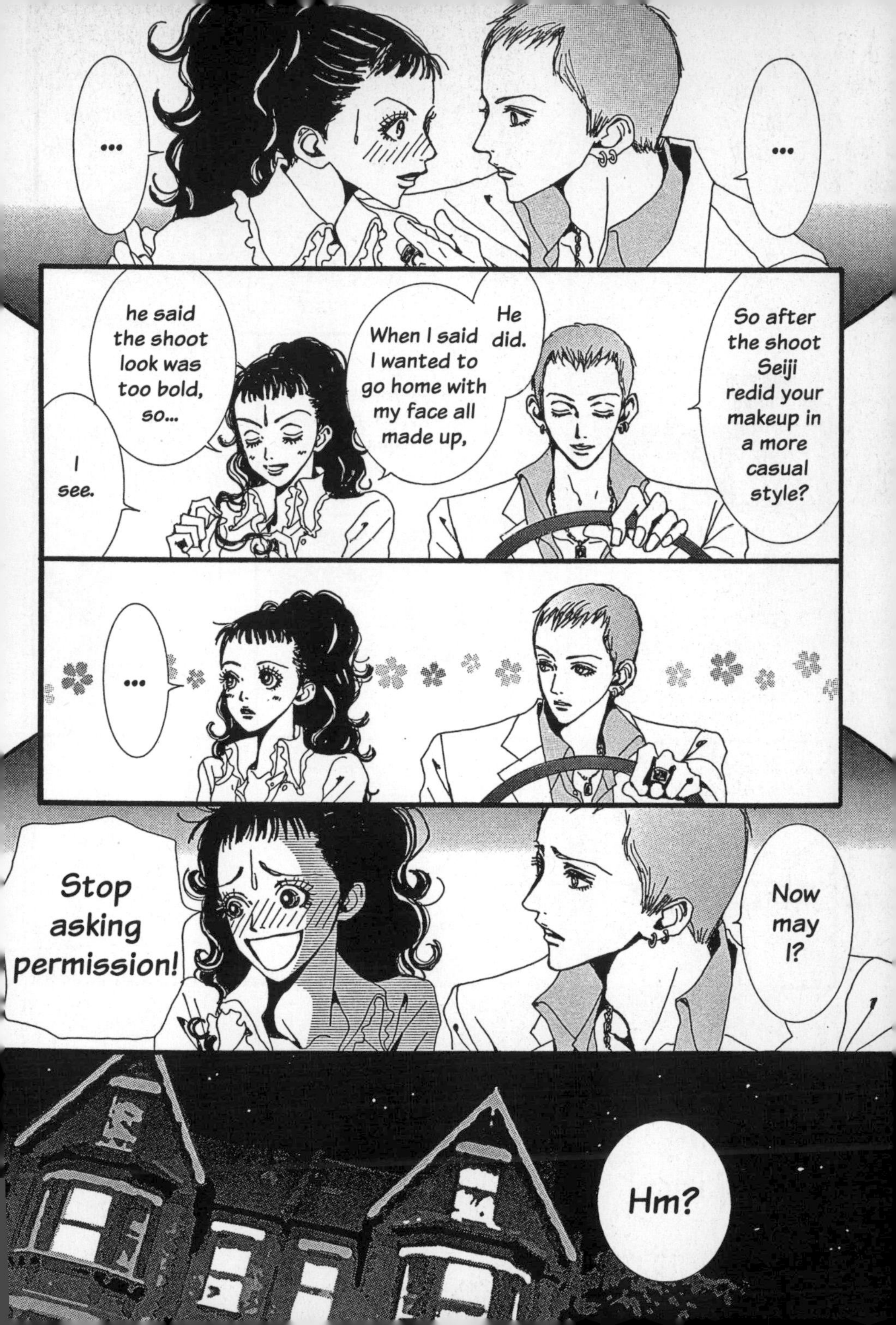
...
...
So after the shoot Seiji redid your makeup in a more casual style?
He did.
When I said I wanted to go home with my face all made up,
he said the shoot look was too bold, so...
I see.
...
Now may I?
Stop asking permission!
Hm?

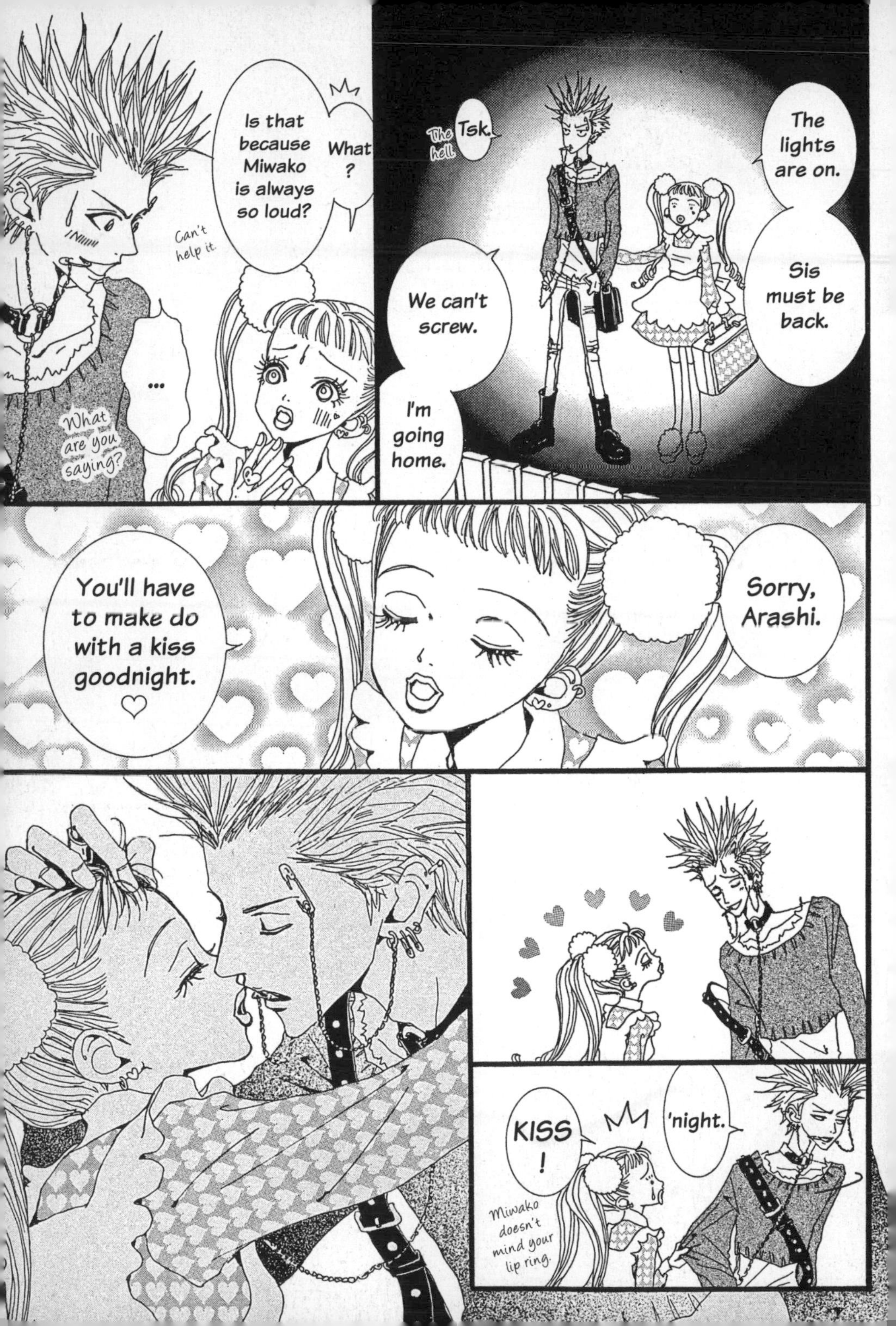
The lights are on.
Sis must be back.
Tsk.
The hell
We can't screw.
I'm going home.
What ?
Is that because Miwako is always so loud?
Can't help it.
...
What are you saying?
Sorry, Arashi.
You'll have to make do with a kiss goodnight. ♡
'night.
KISS !
Miwako doesn't mind your lip ring.

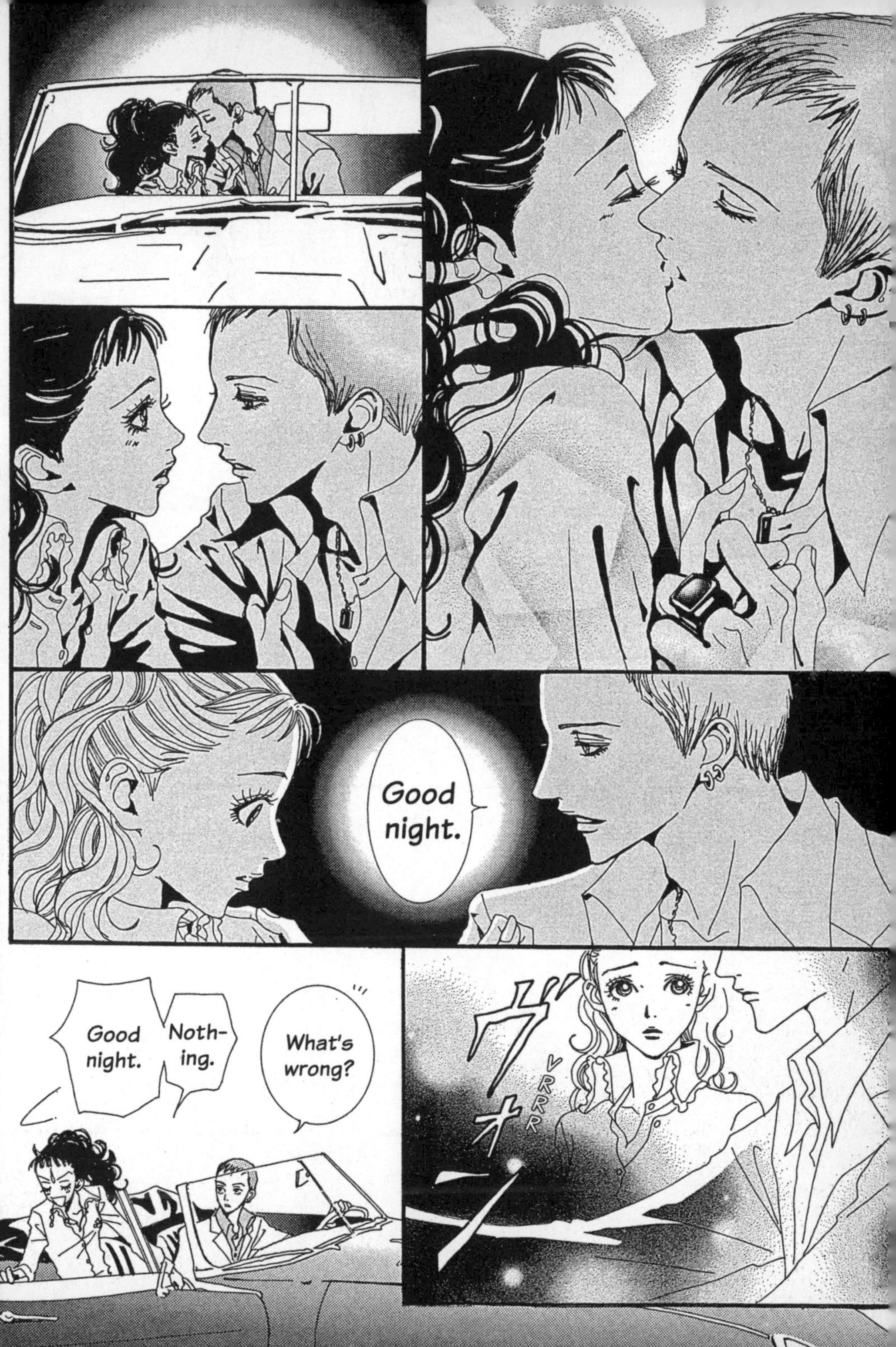
Good night.
ヴォ
VRRR
What's wrong?
Noth-ing.
Good night.

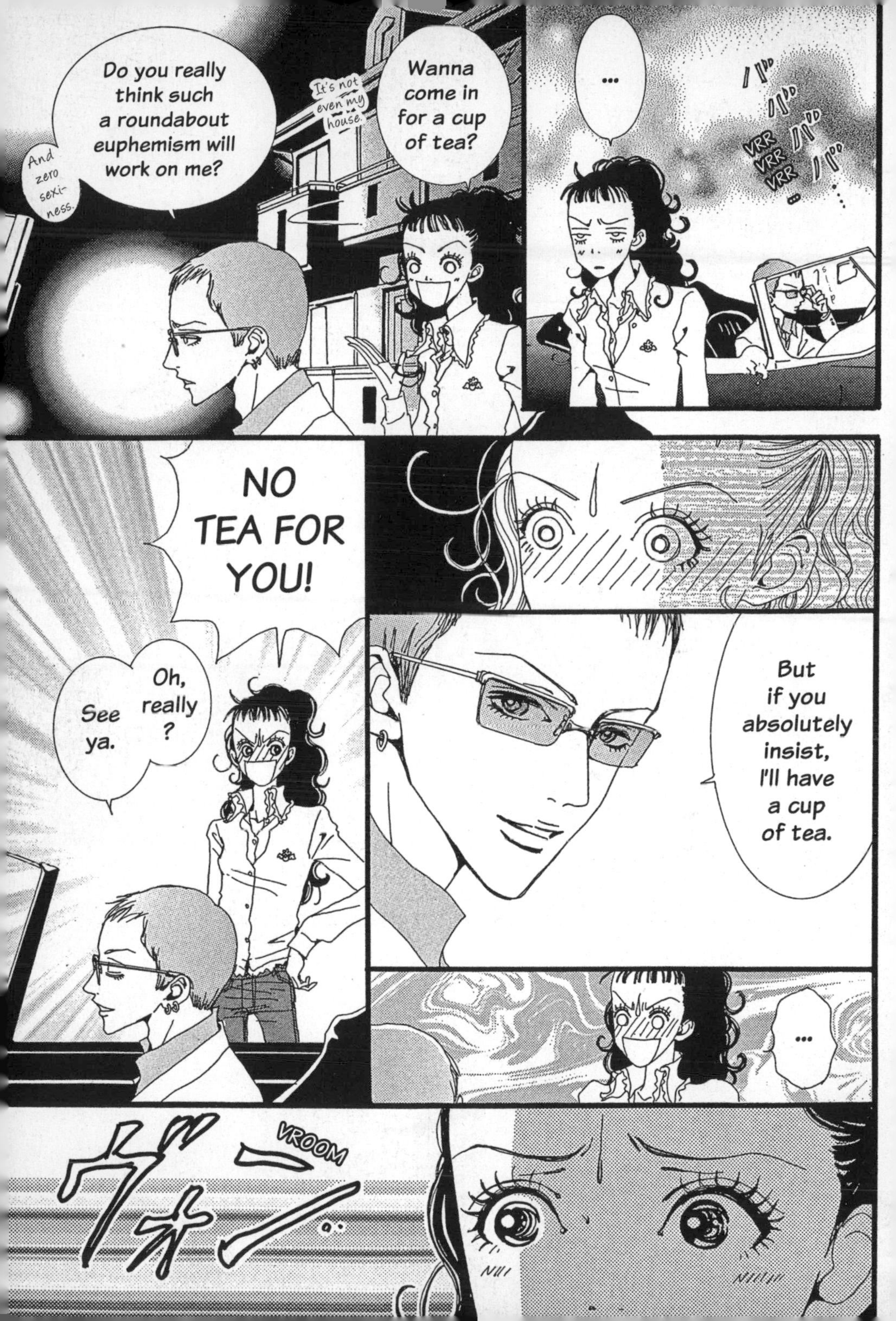
...
VRR VRR VRR
slip
Wanna come in for a cup of tea?
It's not even my house.
Do you really think such a roundabout euphemism will work on me?
And zero sexi-ness.
But if you absolutely insist, I'll have a cup of tea.
...
NO TEA FOR YOU!
Oh, really?
See ya.
VROOM
ヴォン

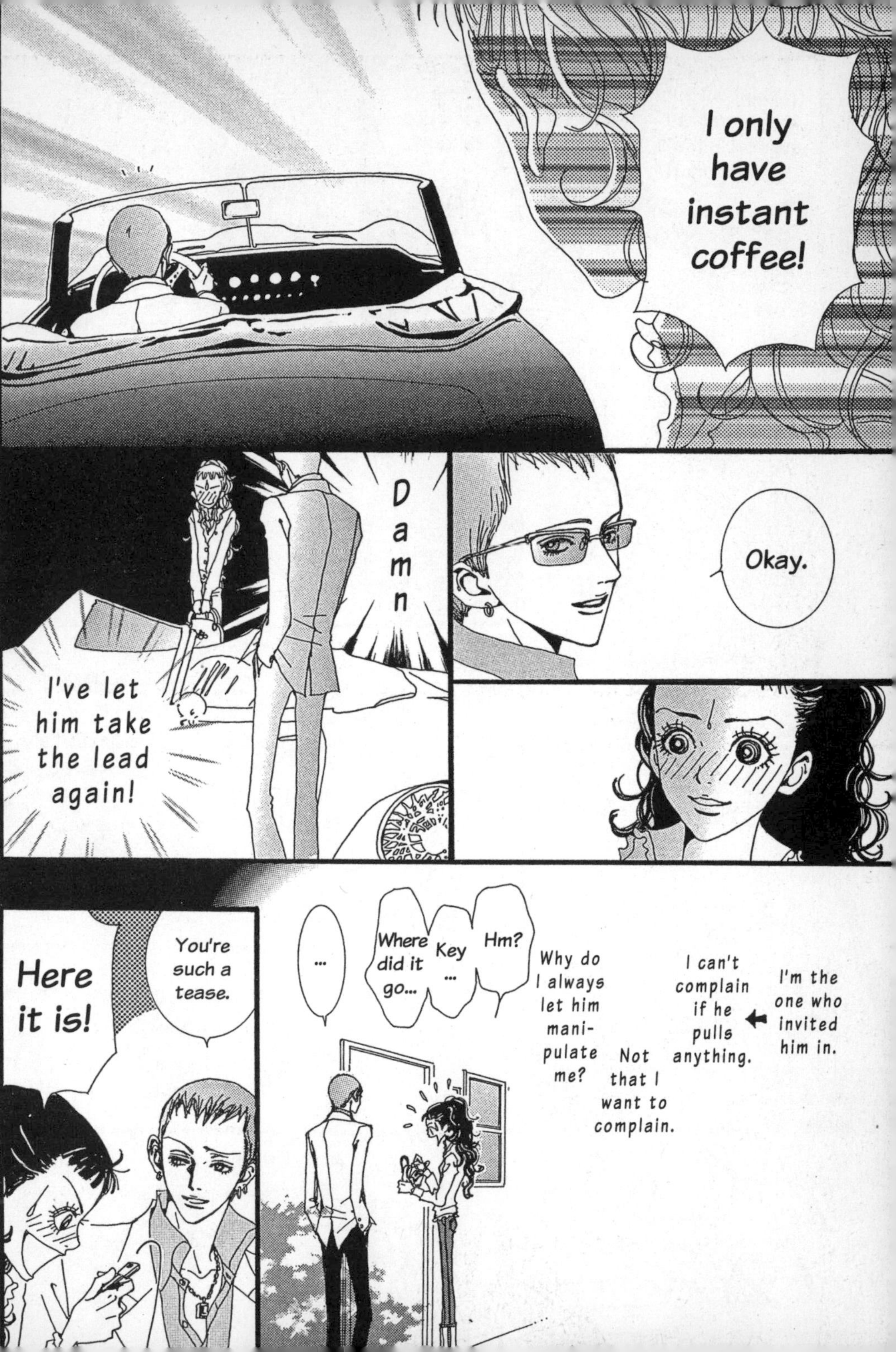
I only have instant coffee!
Okay.
Damn
I've let him take the lead again!
I'm the one who invited him in.
I can't complain if he pulls anything.
Not that I want to complain.
Why do I always let him manipulate me?
Hm?
Key...
Where did it go...
...
Here it is!
You're such a tease.

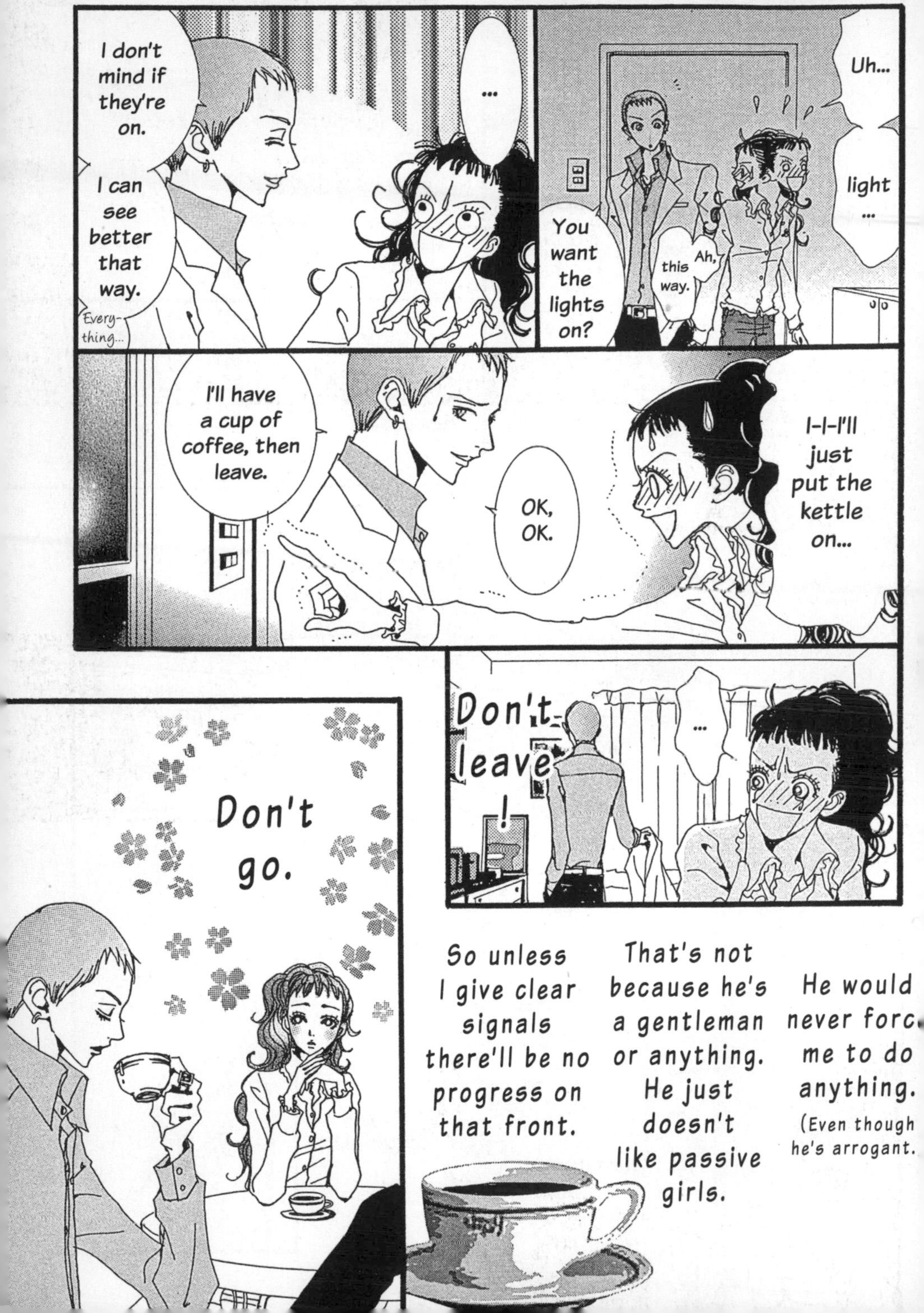
Uh...
light...
Ah, this way.
You want the lights on?
...
I don't mind if they're on.
I can see better that way.
Every-thing...
I-I-I'll just put the kettle on...
OK, OK.
I'll have a cup of coffee, then leave.
...
Don't leave!
Don't go.
He would never forc me to do anything.
(Even though he's arrogant.
That's not because he's a gentleman or anything. He just doesn't like passive girls.
So unless I give clear signals there'll be no progress on that front.

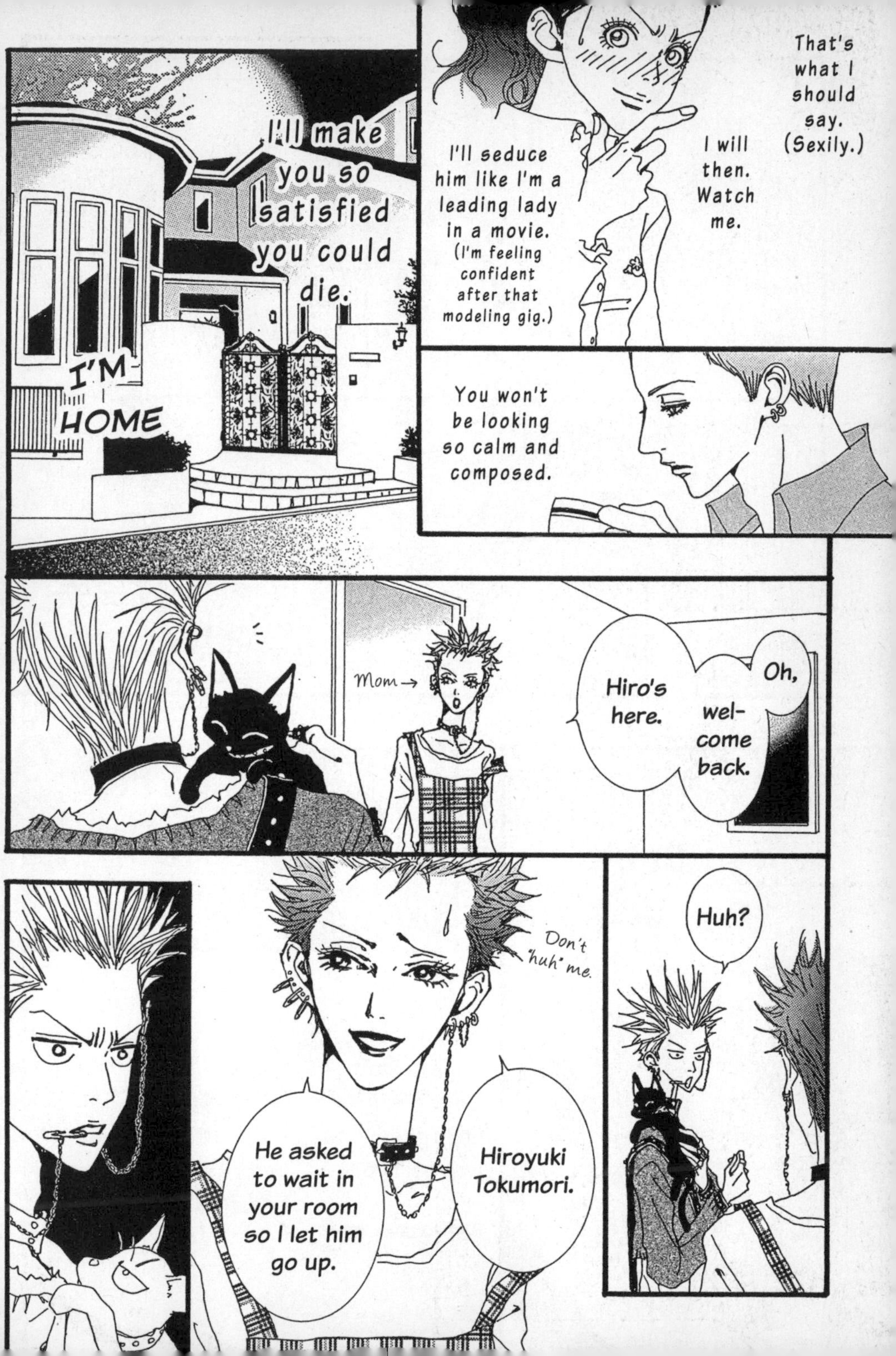

That's what I should say. (Sexily.)
I will then. Watch me.
I'll seduce him like I'm a leading lady in a movie.
(I'm feeling confident after that modeling gig.)
You won't be looking so calm and composed.
I'll make you so satisfied you could die.
I'M HOME
Oh, welcome back.
Hiro's here.
Mom →
Huh?
Don't "huh" me.
Hiroyuki Tokumori.
He asked to wait in your room so I let him go up.

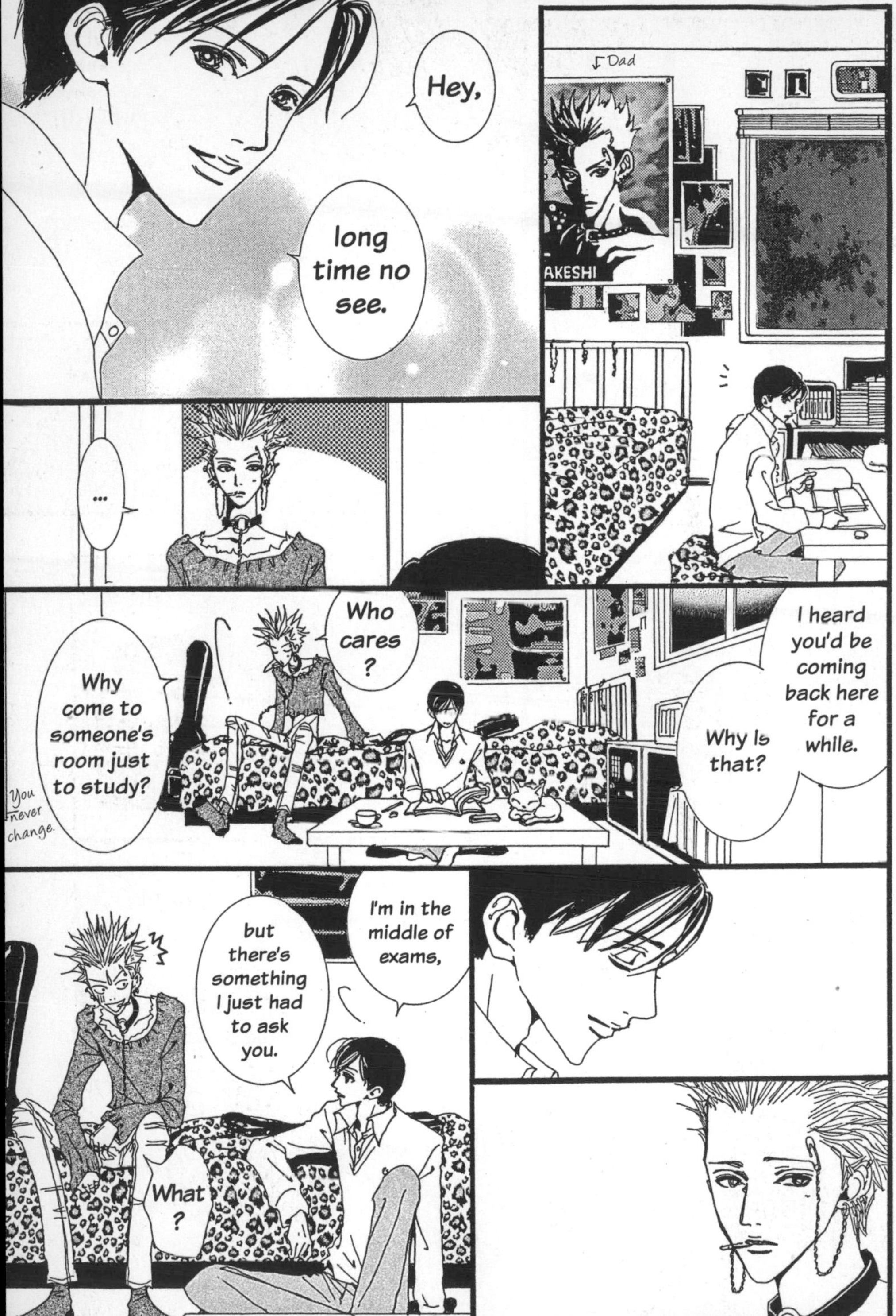
Dad
AKESHI
Hey,
long time no see.
...
I heard you'd be coming back here for a while.
Why is that?
Who cares?
Why come to someone's room just to study?
You never change.
I'm in the middle of exams,
but there's something I just had to ask you.
What?

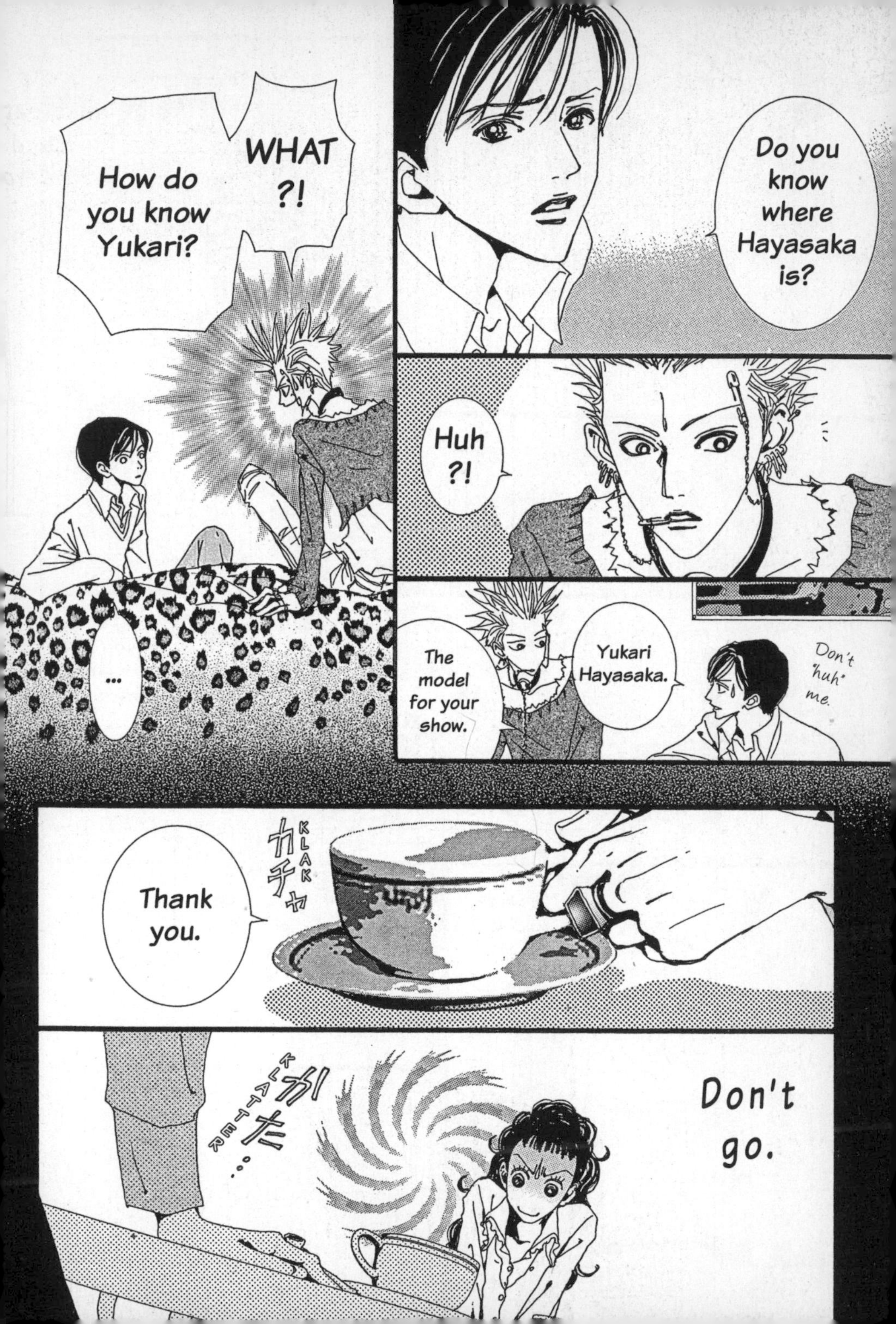
Do you know where Hayasaka is?
Huh ?!
Don't "huh" me.
Yukari Hayasaka.
The model for your show.
WHAT ?!
How do you know Yukari?
...
KLAK
カチャ
Thank you.
Don't go.
がた
KLATTER...

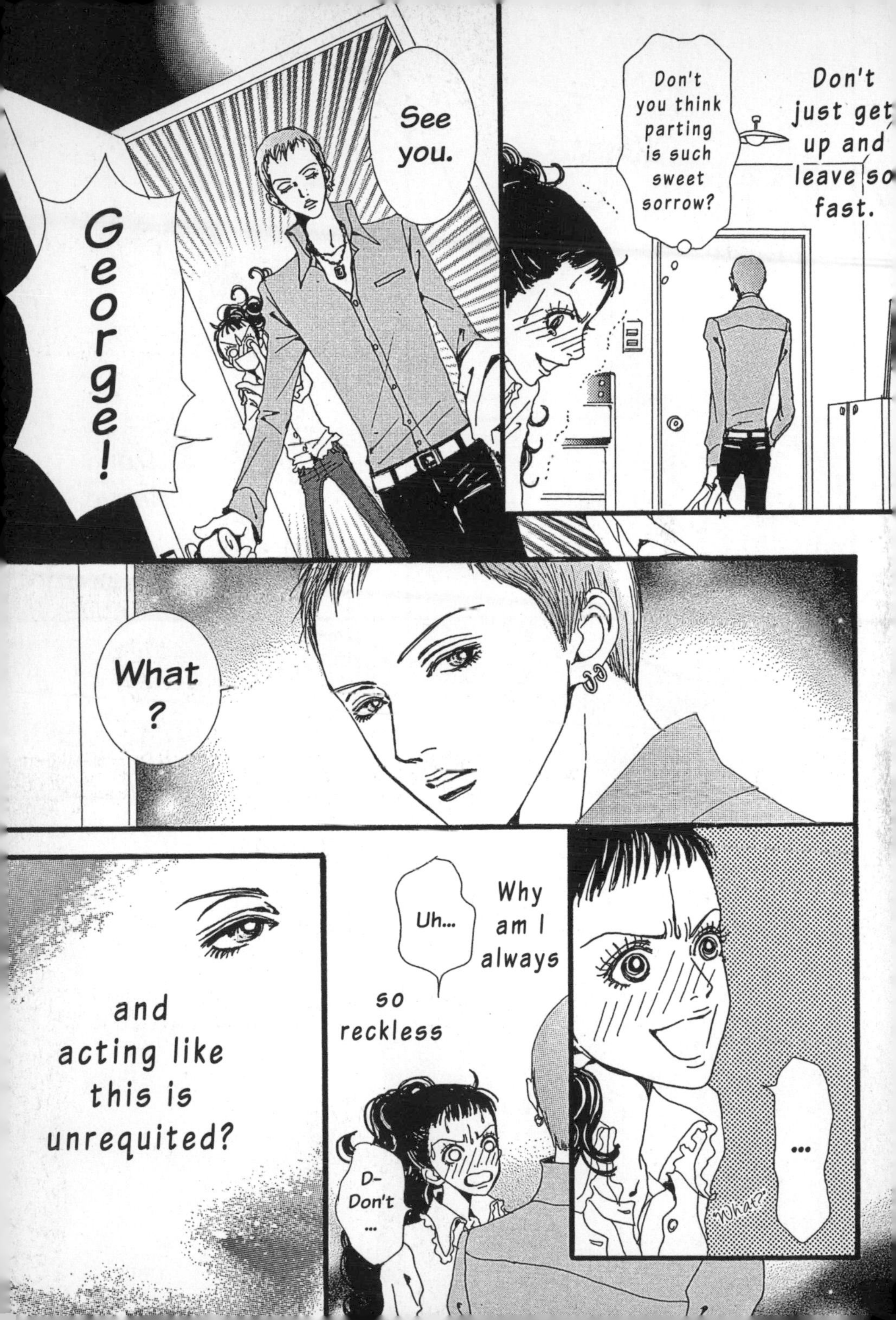
Don't just get up and leave so fast.
Don't you think parting is such sweet sorrow?
See you.
George!
What?
...
What?
Why am I always
Uh...
so reckless
D- Don't ...
and acting like this is unrequited?

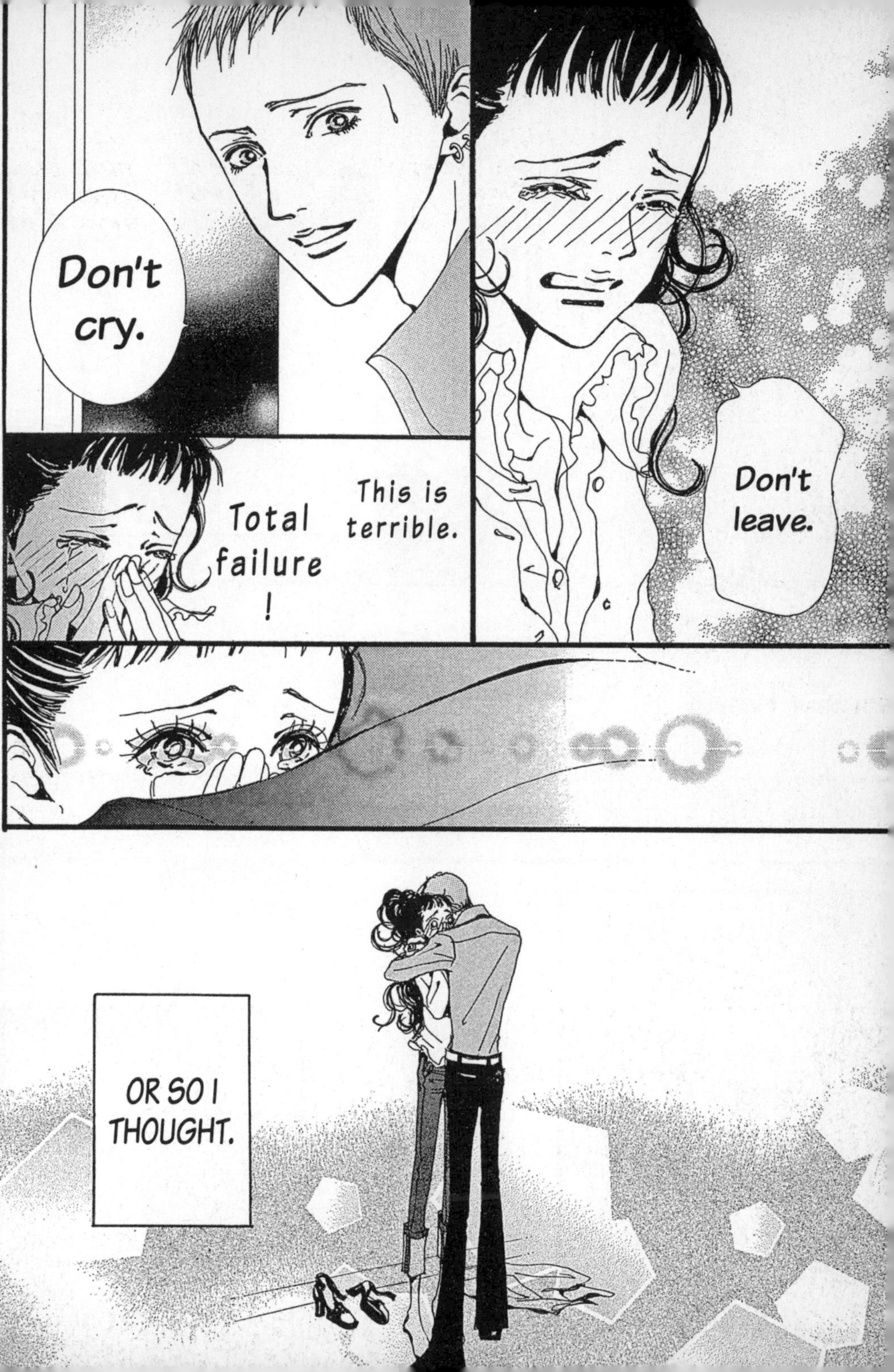
Don't leave.
Don't cry.
This is terrible.
Total failure!
OR SO I THOUGHT.

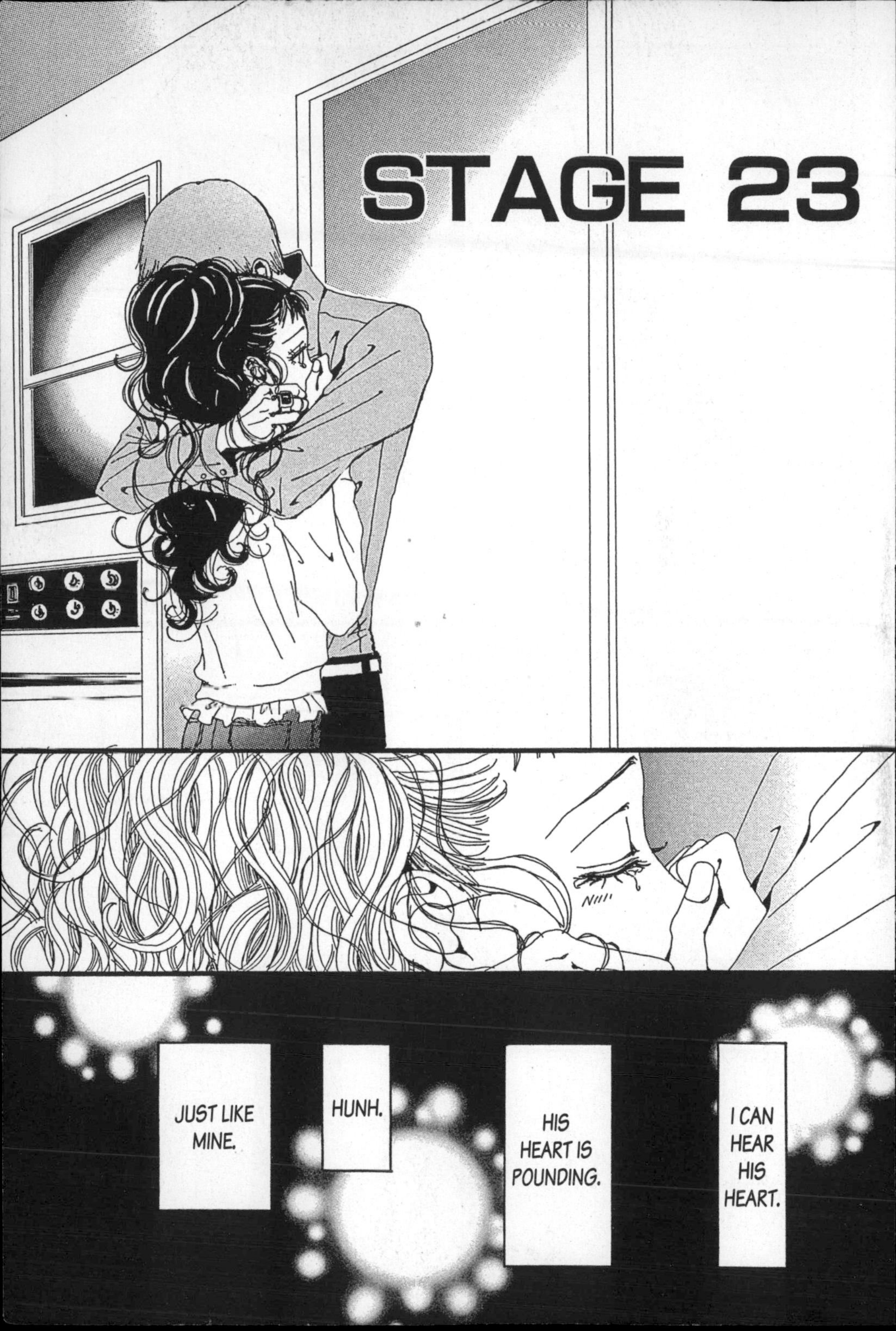
STAGE 23
I CAN HEAR HIS HEART.
HIS HEART IS POUNDING.
HUNH.
JUST LIKE MINE.

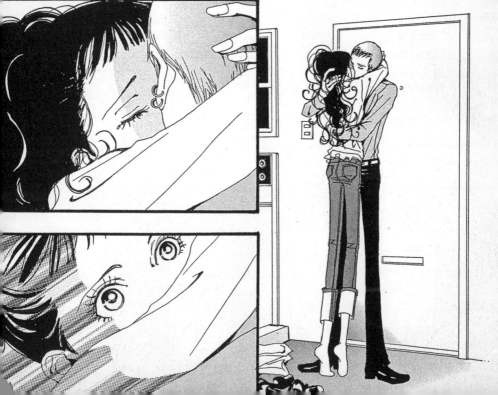

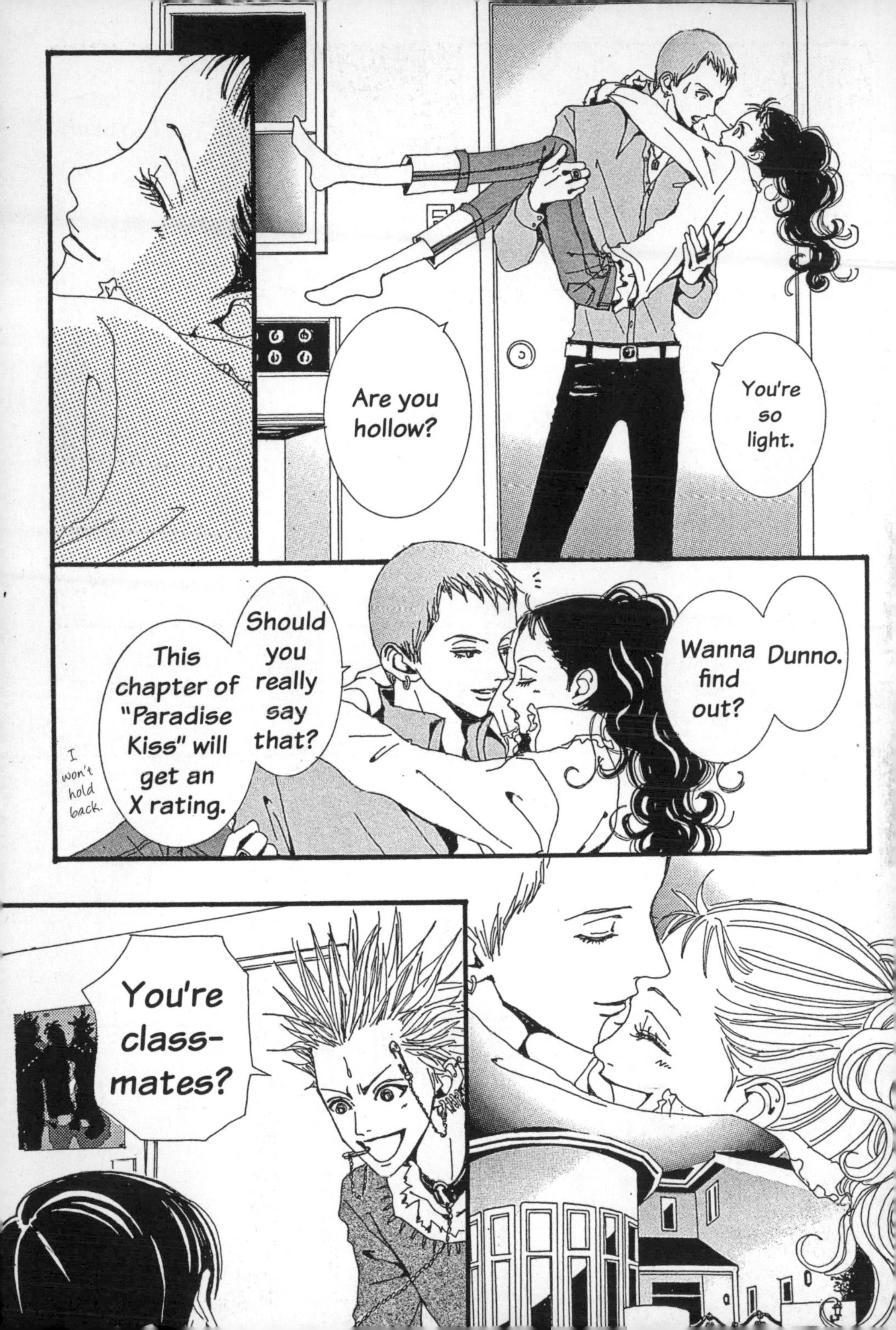
You're so light.
Are you hollow?
Dunno.
Wanna find out?
Should you really say that?
This chapter of "Paradise Kiss" will get an X rating.
I won't hold back.
You're class-mates?

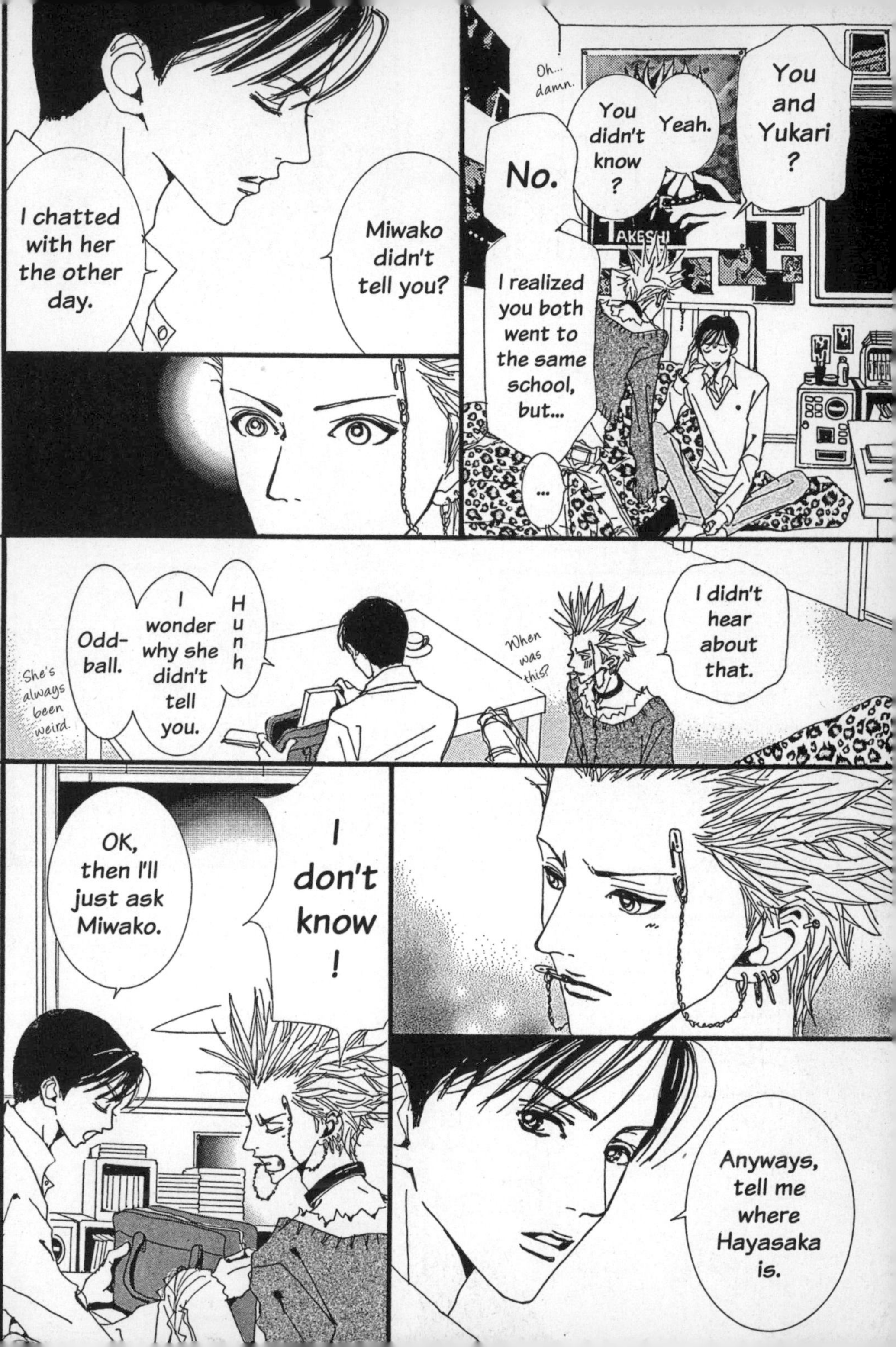
You and Yukari ?
Yeah.
You didn't know ?
Oh... damn.
No.
I realized you both went to the same school, but...
...
Miwako didn't tell you?
I chatted with her the other day.
I didn't hear about that.
When was this?
Hunh
I wonder why she didn't tell you.
Odd-ball.
She's always been weird.
Anyways, tell me where Hayasaka is.
I don't know !
OK, then I'll just ask Miwako.

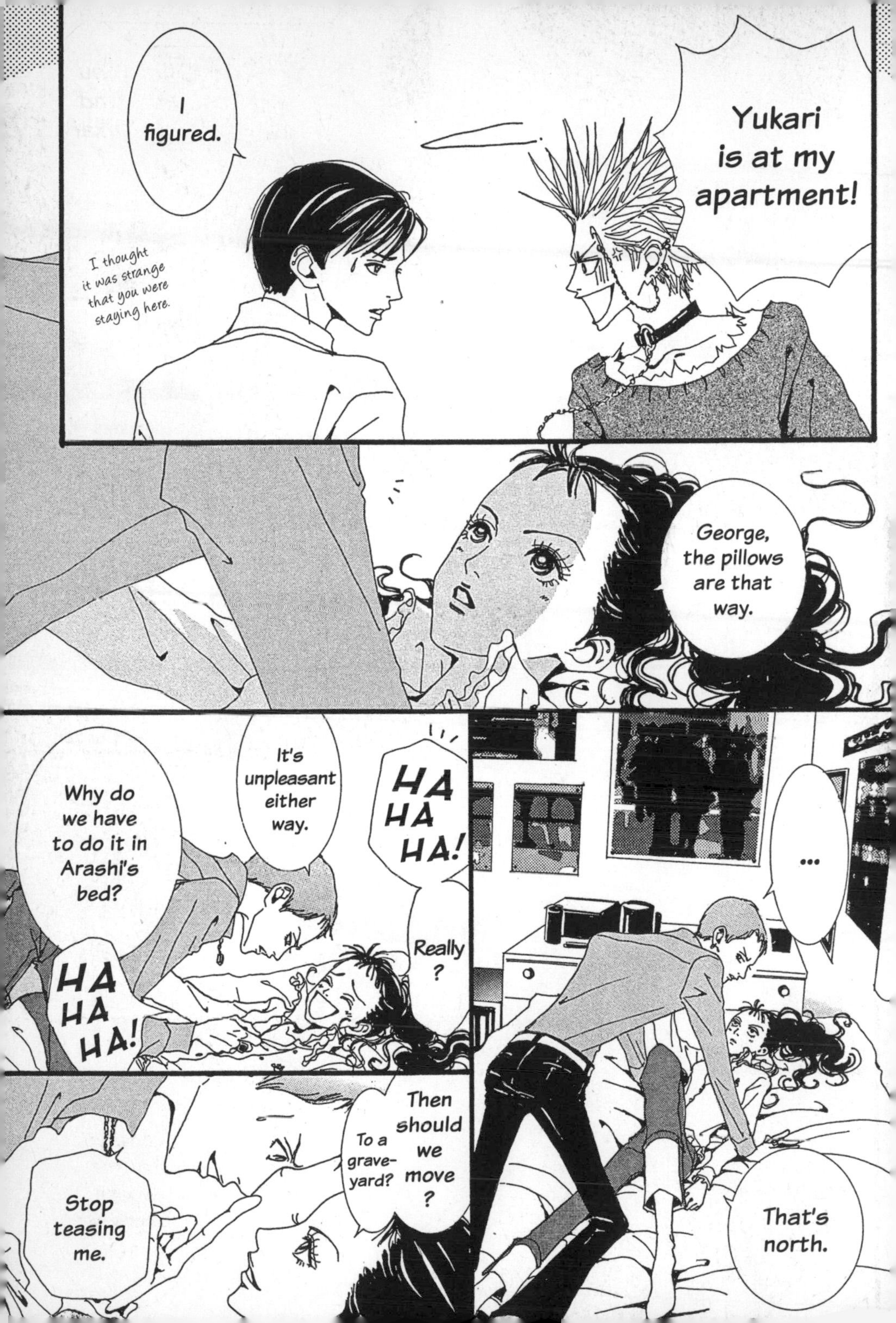
Yukari is at my apartment!
I figured.
I thought it was strange that you were staying here.
George, the pillows are that way.
...
That's north.
Why do we have to do it in Arashi's bed?
It's unpleasant either way.
HA HA HA!
Really?
HA HA HA!
Then should we move?
To a graveyard?
Stop teasing me.

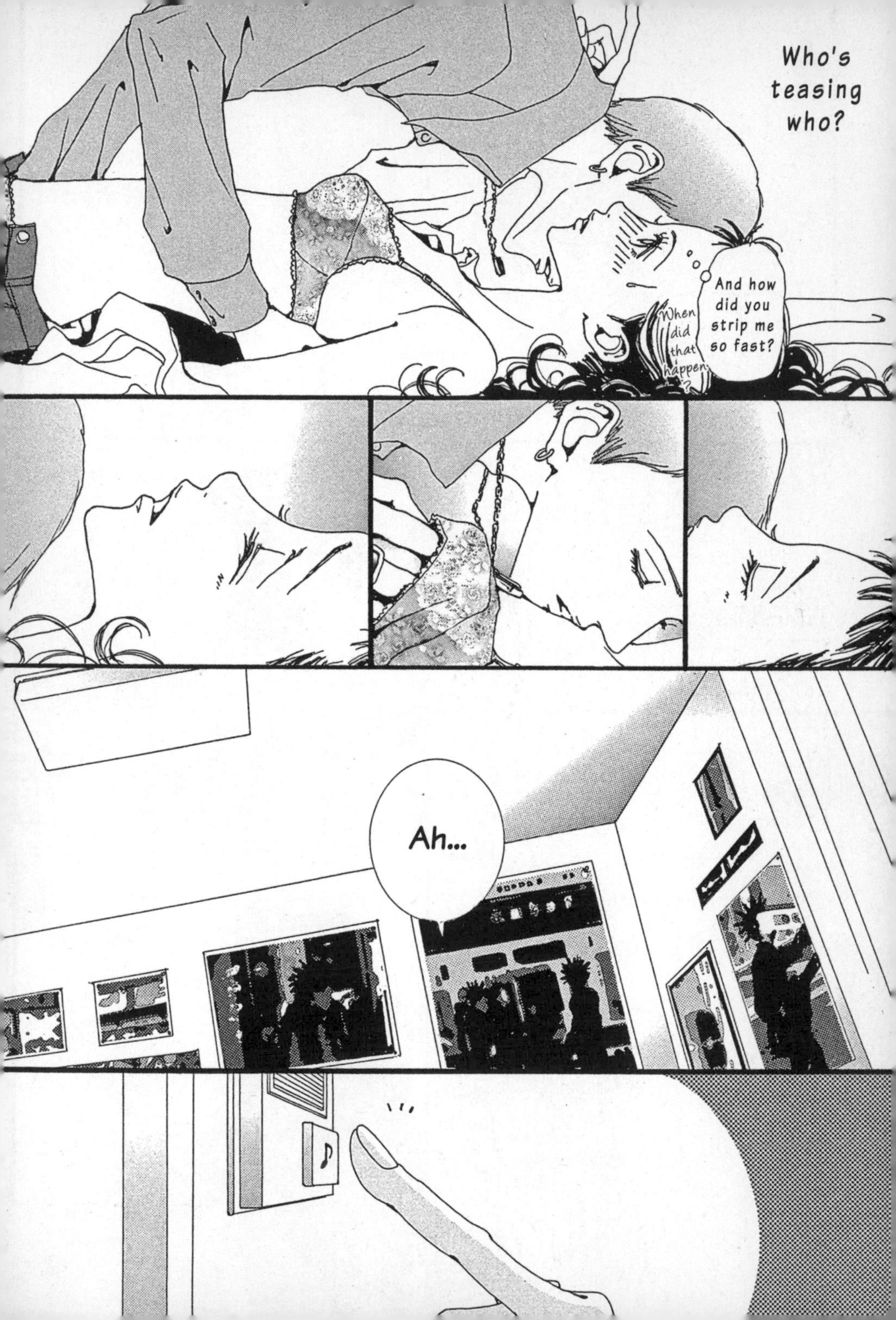
Who's teasing who?
And how did you strip me so fast?
When did that happen?
Ah...

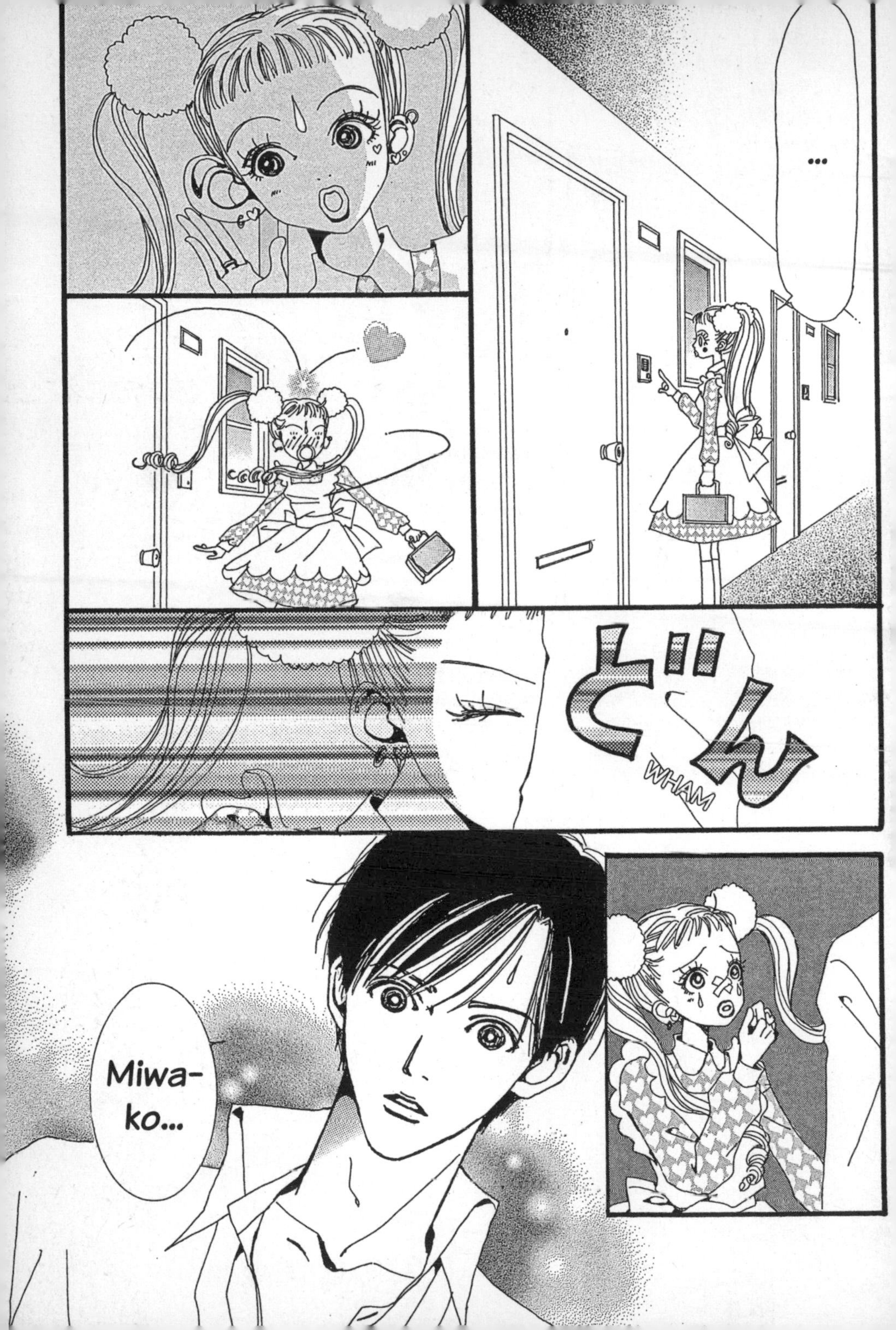
...
どん
WHAM
Miwa-
ko...

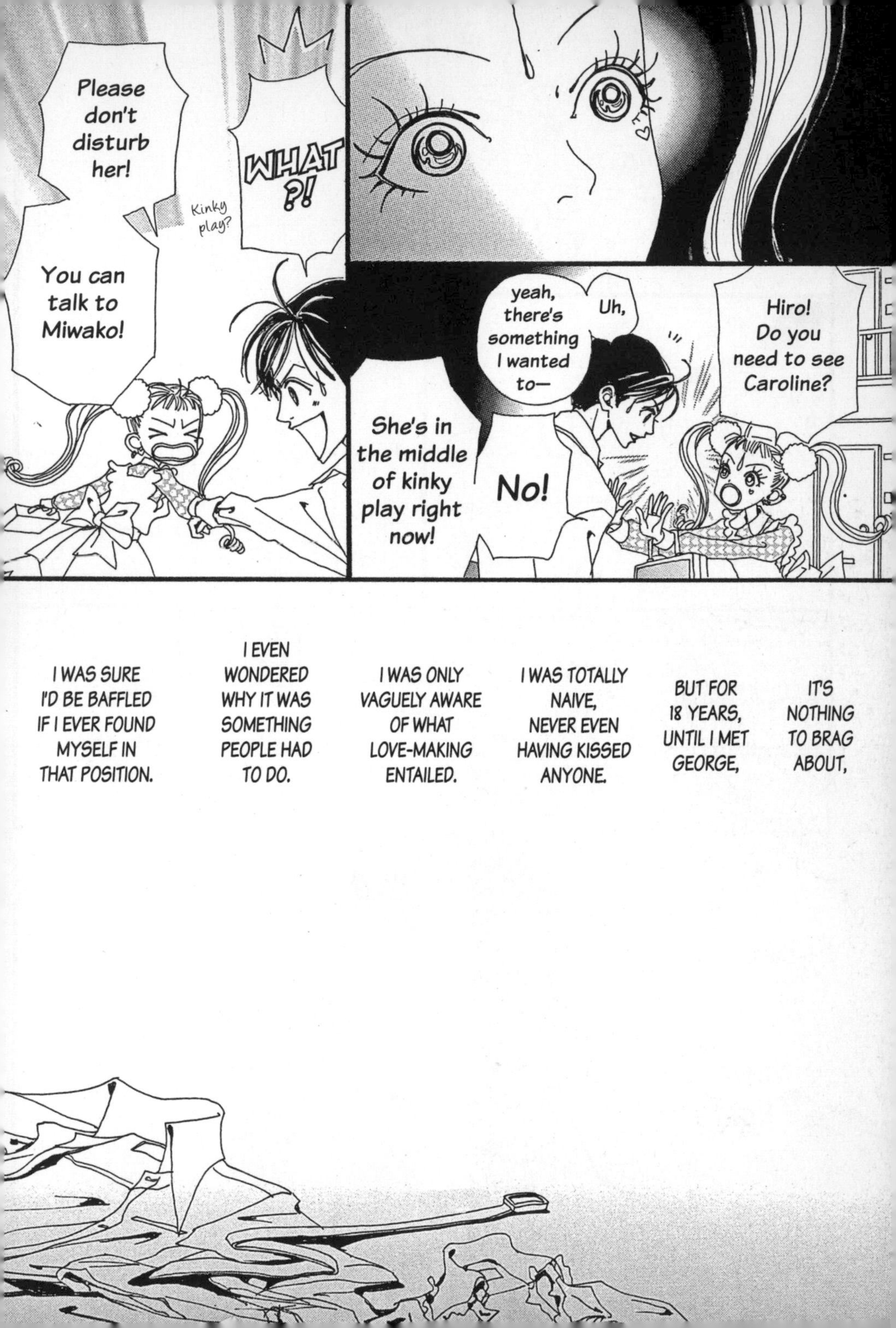
Hiro! Do you need to see Caroline?
Uh, yeah, there's something I wanted to—
No!
She's in the middle of kinky play right now!
WHAT?!
Kinky play?
Please don't disturb her!
You can talk to Miwako!
IT'S NOTHING TO BRAG ABOUT,
BUT FOR 18 YEARS, UNTIL I MET GEORGE,
I WAS TOTALLY NAIVE, NEVER EVEN HAVING KISSED ANYONE.
I WAS ONLY VAGUELY AWARE OF WHAT LOVE-MAKING ENTAILED.
I EVEN WONDERED WHY IT WAS SOMETHING PEOPLE HAD TO DO.
I WAS SURE I'D BE BAFFLED IF I EVER FOUND MYSELF IN THAT POSITION.

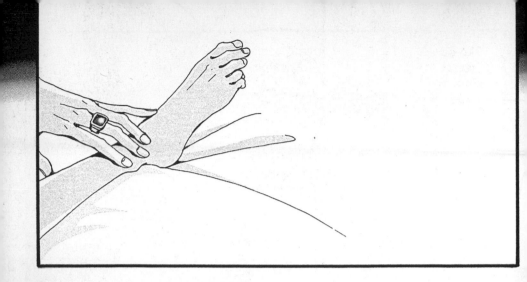

Yukari
...

ON
ITS
OWN

BUT
MY
BODY

RESPONDED
TO HIS
FINGERS,
HIS LIPS.

I REALIZED
THAT PEOPLE
ARE BORN
WITH THOSE
INSTINCTS.

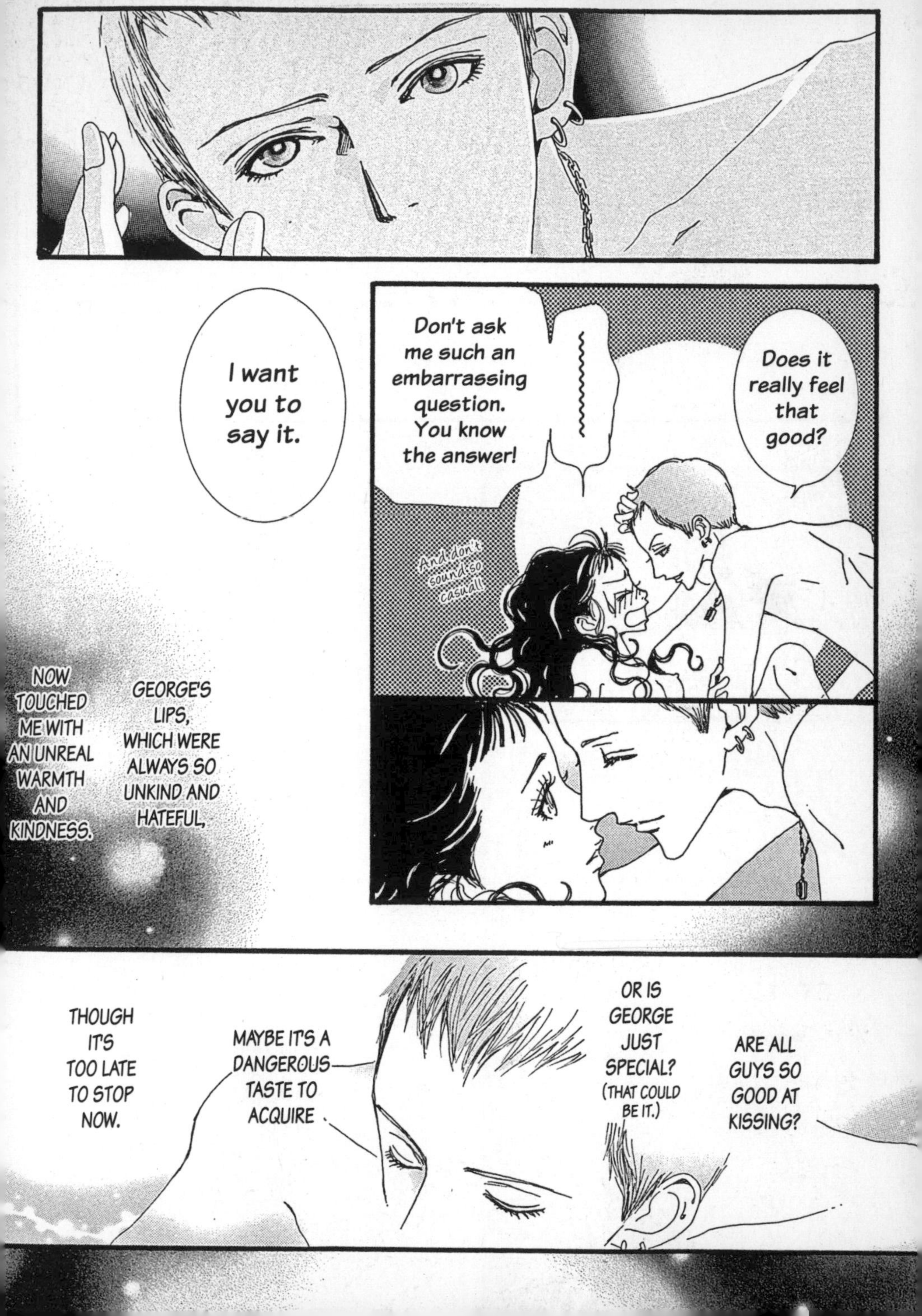
Does it really feel that good?
Don't ask me such an embarrassing question. You know the answer!
And don't sound so casual!
I want you to say it.
GEORGE'S LIPS, WHICH WERE ALWAYS SO UNKIND AND HATEFUL,
NOW TOUCHED ME WITH AN UNREAL WARMTH AND KINDNESS.
ARE ALL GUYS SO GOOD AT KISSING?
OR IS GEORGE JUST SPECIAL? (THAT COULD BE IT.)
MAYBE IT'S A DANGEROUS TASTE TO ACQUIRE
THOUGH IT'S TOO LATE TO STOP NOW.

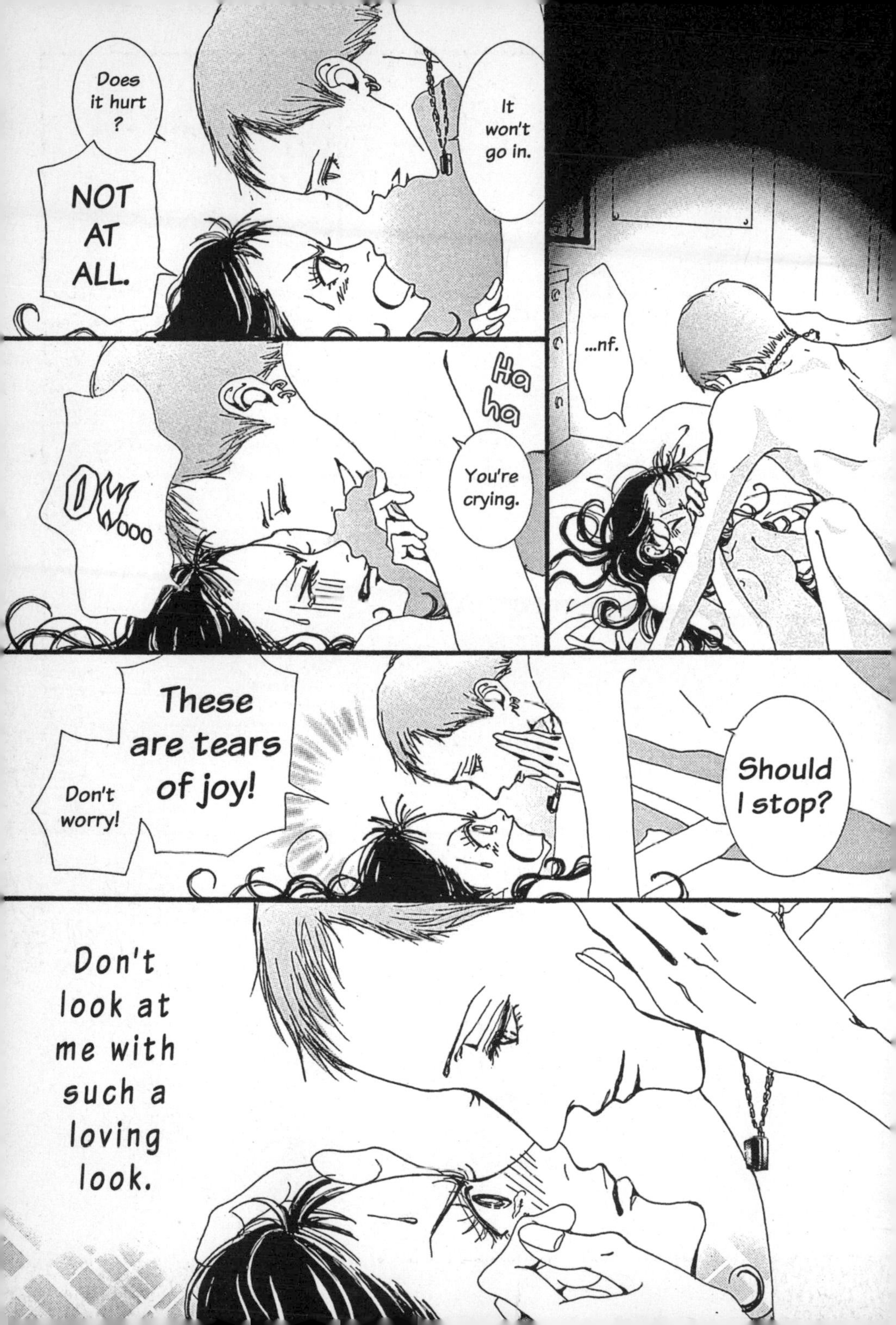
...nf.
It won't go in.
Does it hurt?
NOT AT ALL.
Ha ha
You're crying.
OWWOOO
Should I stop?
These are tears of joy!
Don't worry!
Don't look at me with such a loving look.

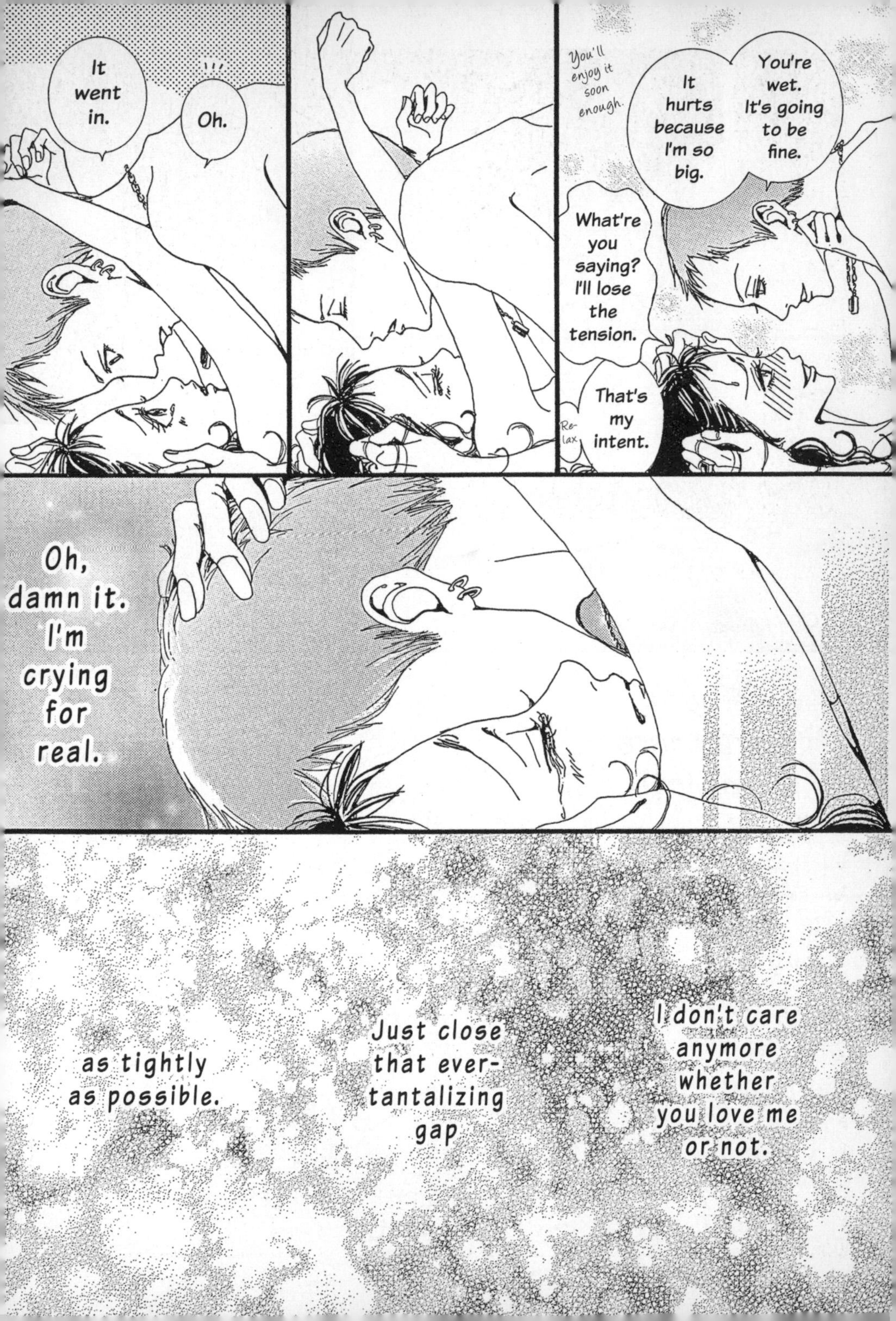
You're wet. It's going to be fine.
It hurts because I'm so big.
You'll enjoy it soon enough.
What're you saying? I'll lose the tension.
That's my intent.
Re-lax
Oh.
It went in.
Oh, damn it. I'm crying for real.
I don't care anymore whether you love me or not.
Just close that ever-tantalizing gap
as tightly as possible.

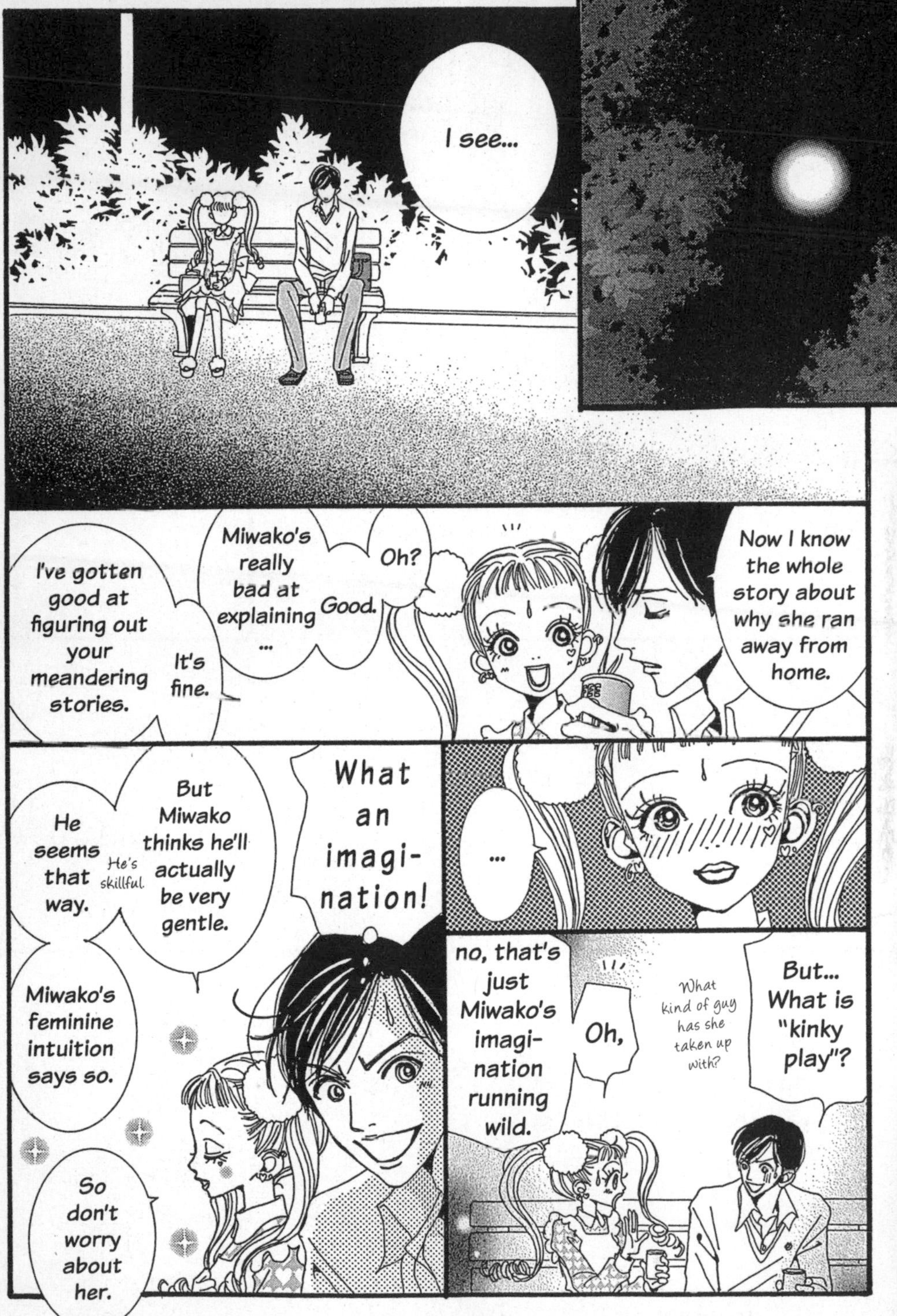
I see...
Now I know the whole story about why she ran away from home.
Oh?
Good.
Miwako's really bad at explaining ...
It's fine.
I've gotten good at figuring out your meandering stories.
...
But... What is "kinky play"?
What kind of guy has she taken up with?
Oh,
no, that's just Miwako's imagination running wild.
What an imagi-nation!
But Miwako thinks he'll actually be very gentle.
He's skillful.
He seems that way.
Miwako's feminine intuition says so.
So don't worry about her.

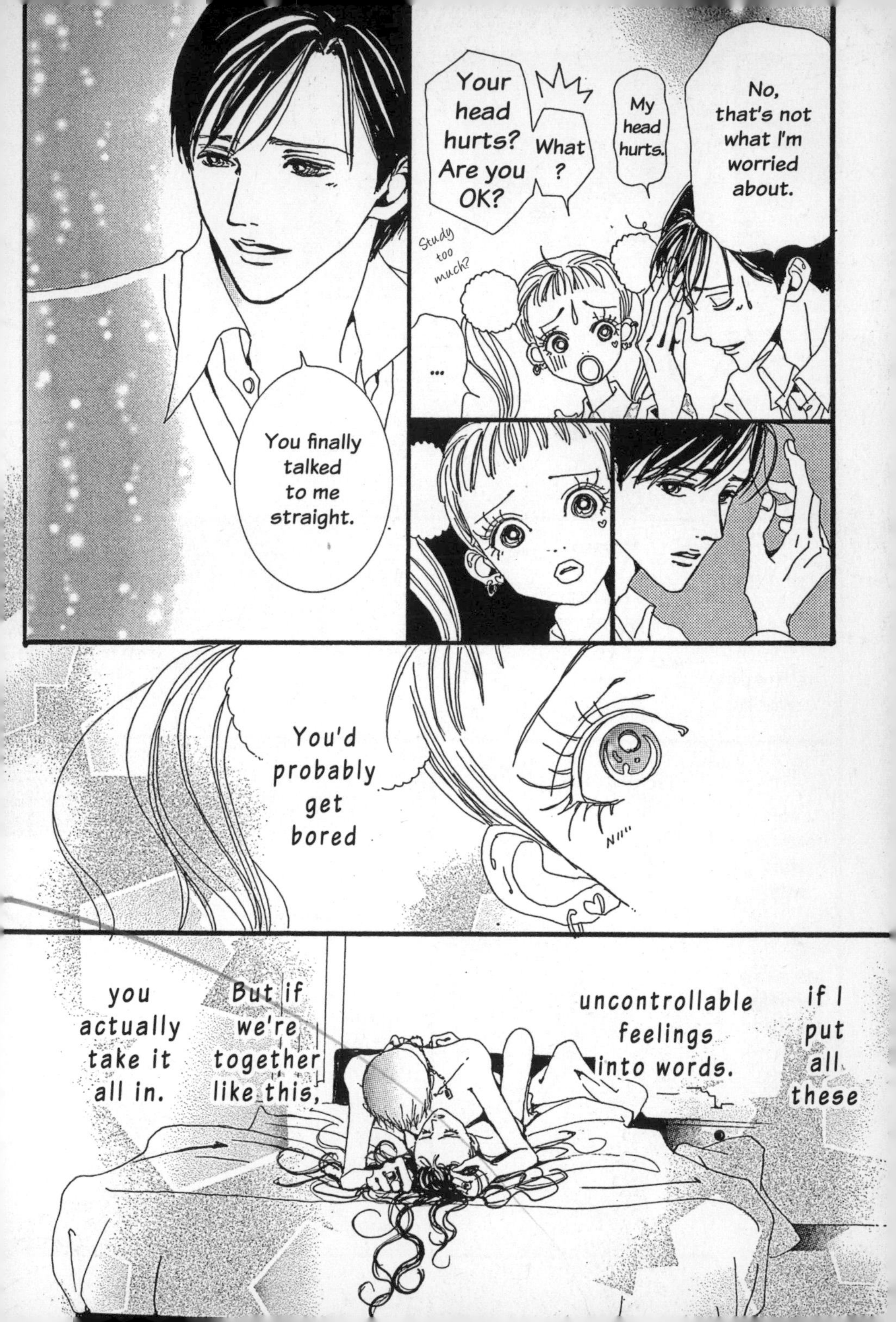
No, that's not what I'm worried about.
My head hurts.
What?
Your head hurts? Are you OK?
Study too much?
...
You finally talked to me straight.
You'd probably get bored
if I put all these
uncontrollable feelings into words.
But if we're together like this,
you actually take it all in.

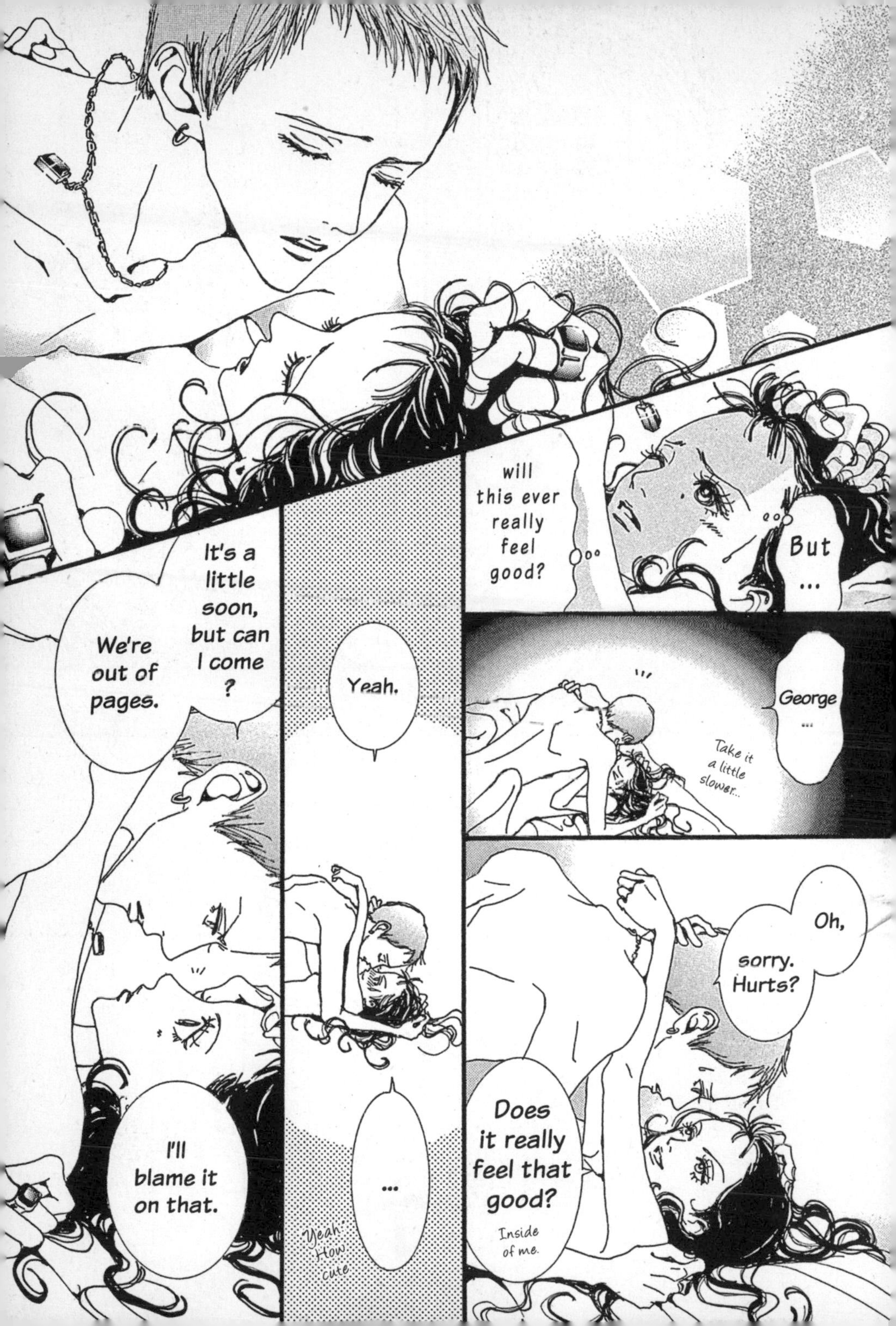

But ...
will this ever really feel good?
George ...
Take it a little slower...
Oh, sorry. Hurts?
Does it really feel that good?
Inside of me.
Yeah.
...
Yeah How cute
It's a little soon, but can I come?
We're out of pages.
I'll blame it on that.

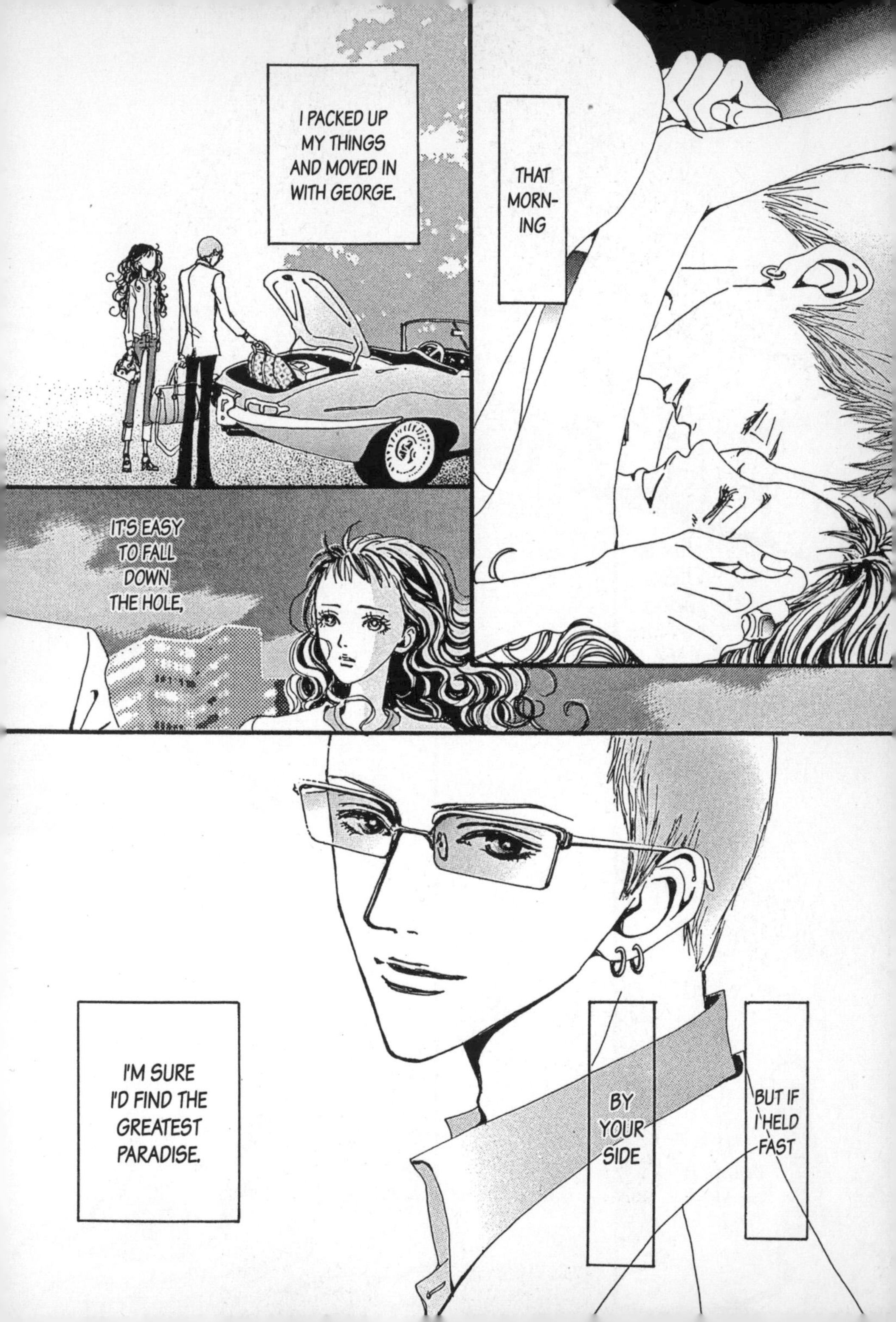
THAT MORNING
I PACKED UP MY THINGS AND MOVED IN WITH GEORGE.
IT'S EASY TO FALL DOWN THE HOLE,
BUT IF I HELD FAST
BY YOUR SIDE
I'M SURE I'D FIND THE GREATEST PARADISE.

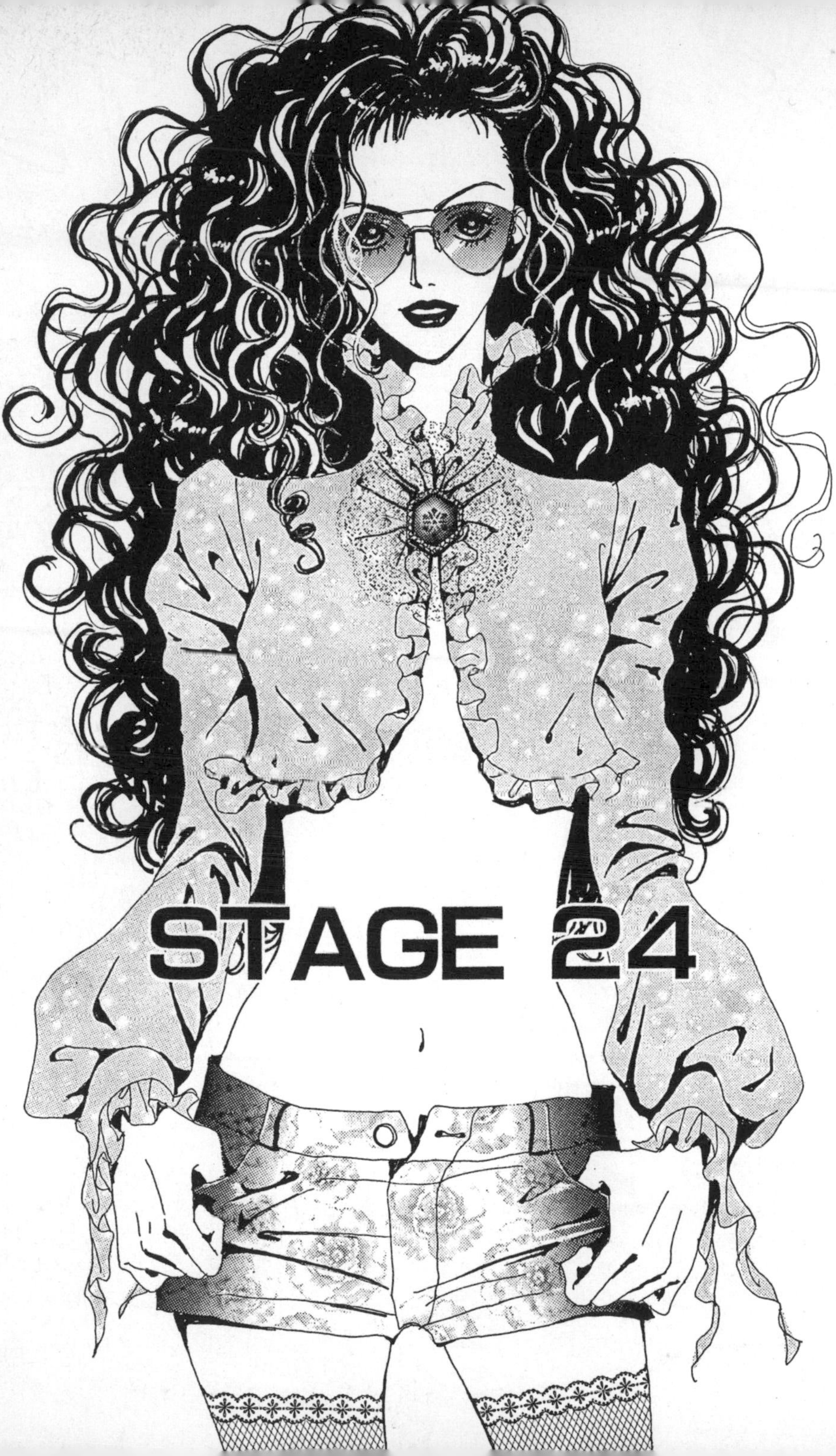
STAGE 24

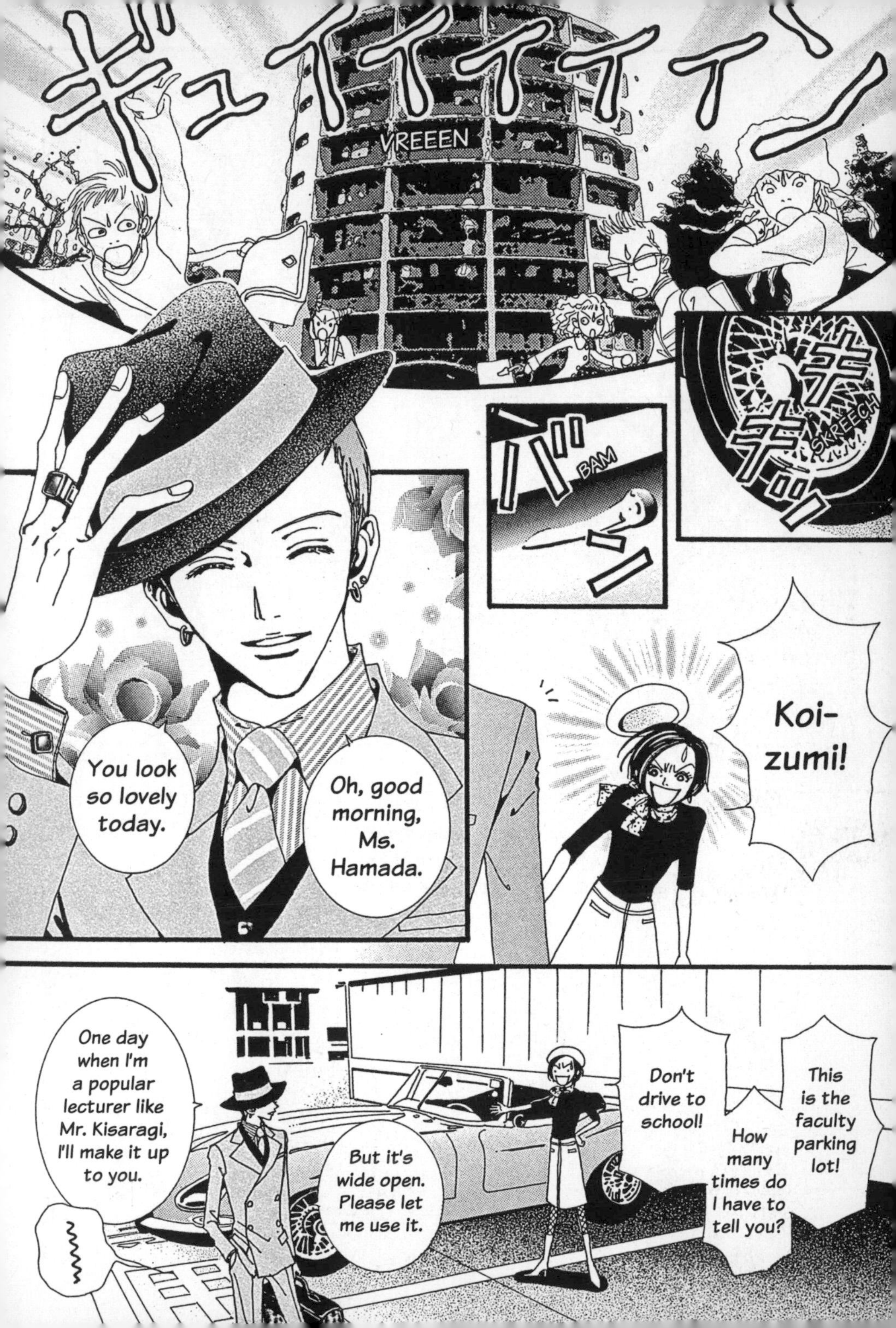

ギュイイイイン
VREEEN
SKREECH
BAM
Koi-zumi!
Oh, good morning, Ms. Hamada.
You look so lovely today.
This is the faculty parking lot!
Don't drive to school!
How many times do I have to tell you?
But it's wide open. Please let me use it.
One day when I'm a popular lecturer like Mr. Kisaragi, I'll make it up to you.

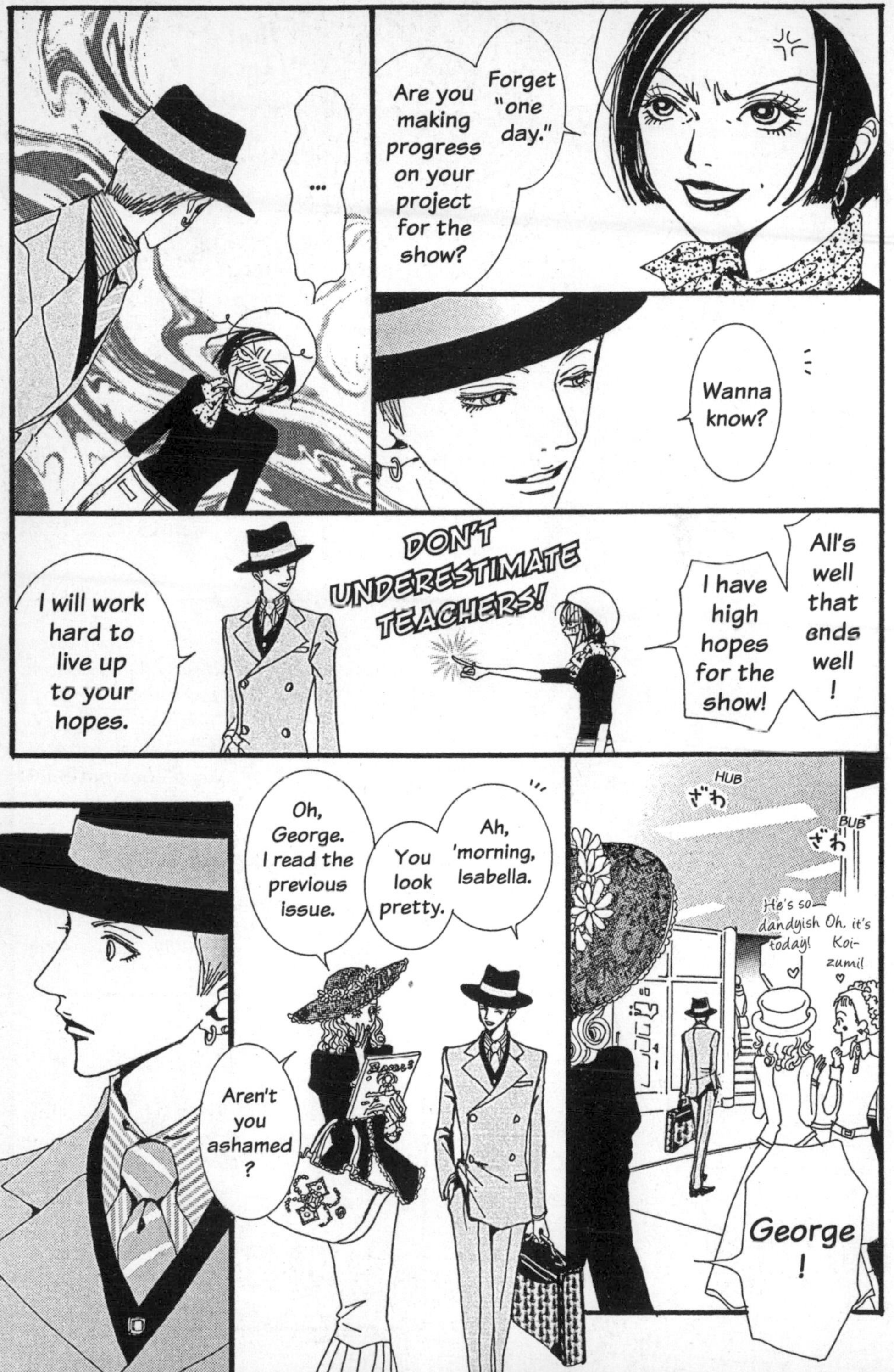
Forget "one day."
Are you making progress on your project for the show?
Wanna know?
...
All's well that ends well!
I have high hopes for the show!
DON'T UNDERESTIMATE TEACHERS!
I will work hard to live up to your hopes.
HUB ざわ
BUB ざわ
Oh, it's Koi-zumi!
He's so dandyish today!
George!
Ah, 'morning, Isabella.
You look pretty.
Oh, George. I read the previous issue.
Aren't you ashamed?

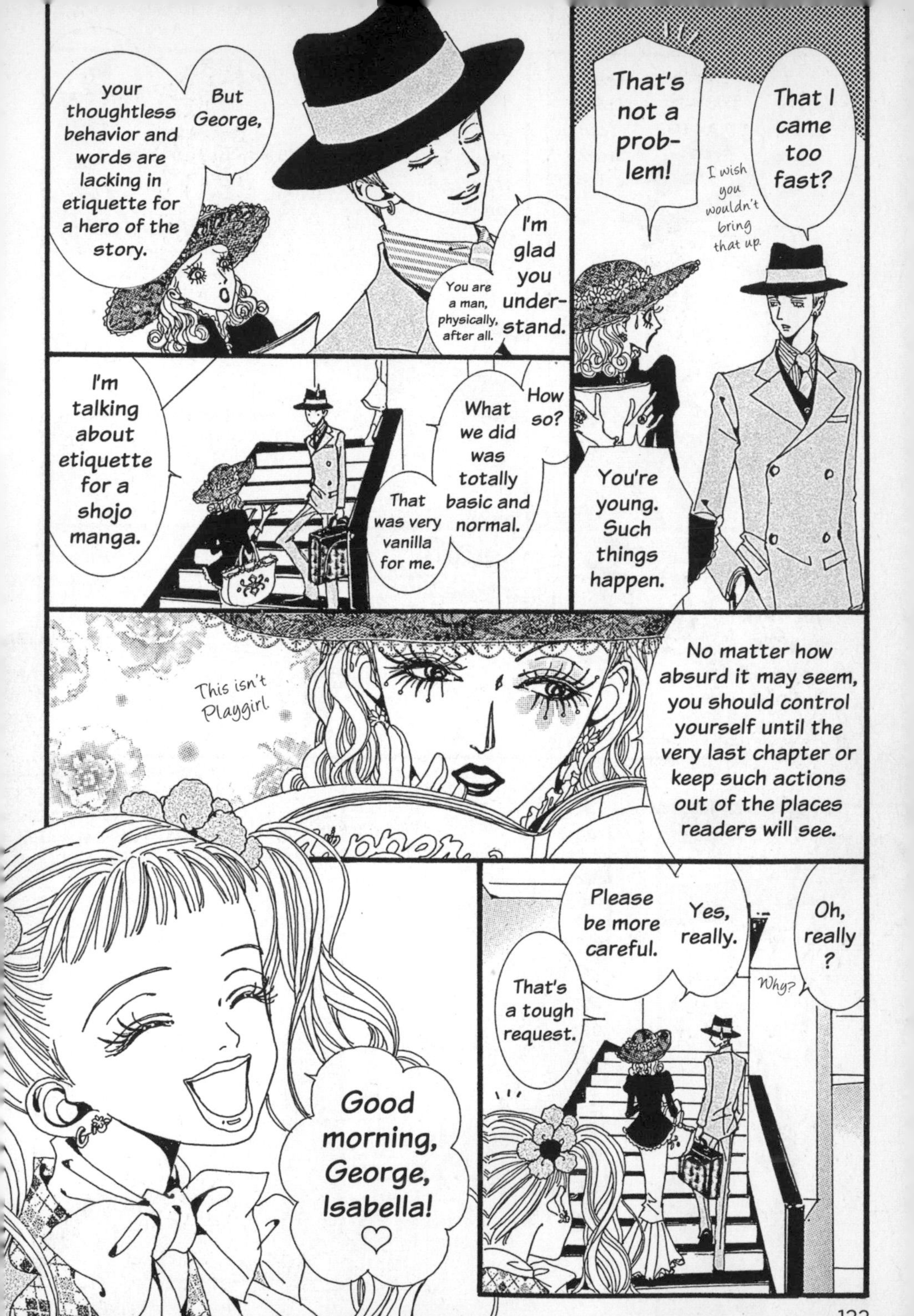
That I came too fast?
That's not a prob-lem!
I wish you wouldn't bring that up.
You're young. Such things happen.
I'm glad you under-stand.
You are a man, physically, after all.
But George,
your thoughtless behavior and words are lacking in etiquette for a hero of the story.
How so?
What we did was totally basic and normal.
That was very vanilla for me.
I'm talking about etiquette for a shojo manga.
No matter how absurd it may seem, you should control yourself until the very last chapter or keep such actions out of the places readers will see.
This isn't Playgirl.
Oh, really?
Why?
Yes, really.
Please be more careful.
That's a tough request.
Good morning, George, Isabella! ♡

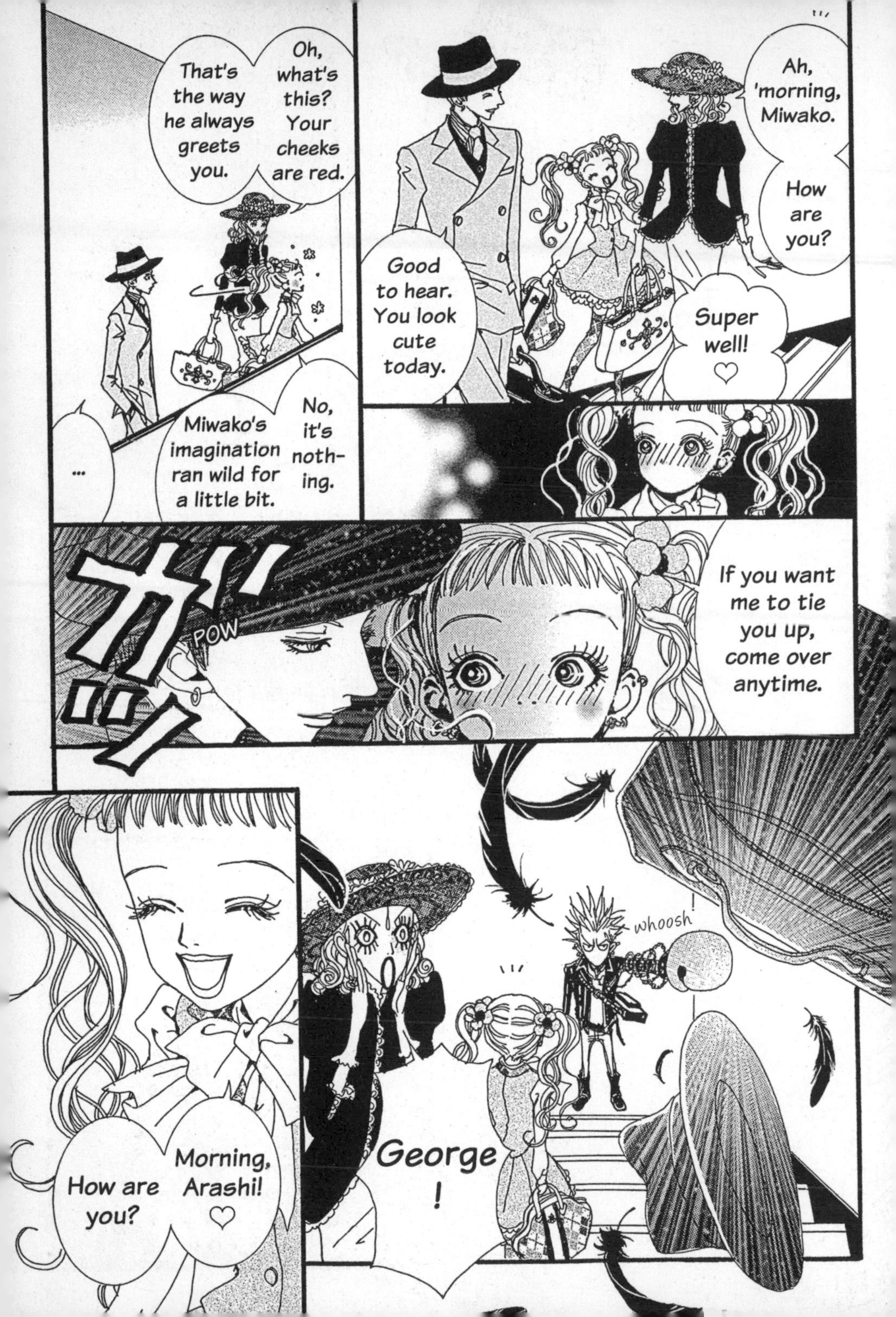
Ah, 'morning, Miwako.
How are you?
Super well! ♡
Good to hear. You look cute today.
Oh, what's this? Your cheeks are red.
That's the way he always greets you.
No, it's nothing.
Miwako's imagination ran wild for a little bit.
...
If you want me to tie you up, come over anytime.
POW
whoosh
George!
Morning, Arashi! ♡
How are you?

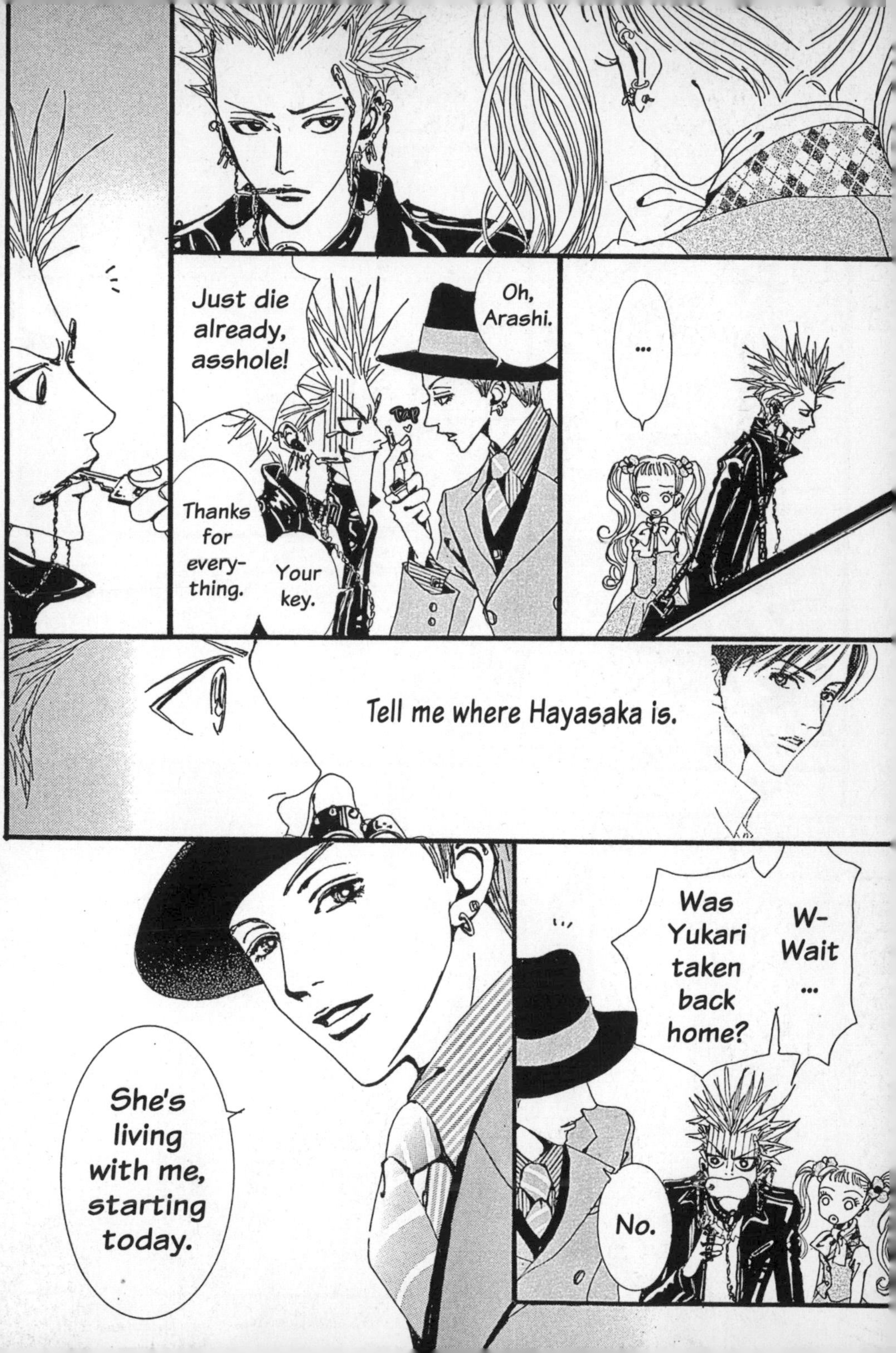
...
Oh, Arashi.
Just die already, asshole!
Your key.
Thanks for every-thing.
Tell me where Hayasaka is.
W-Wait...
Was Yukari taken back home?
No.
She's living with me, starting today.

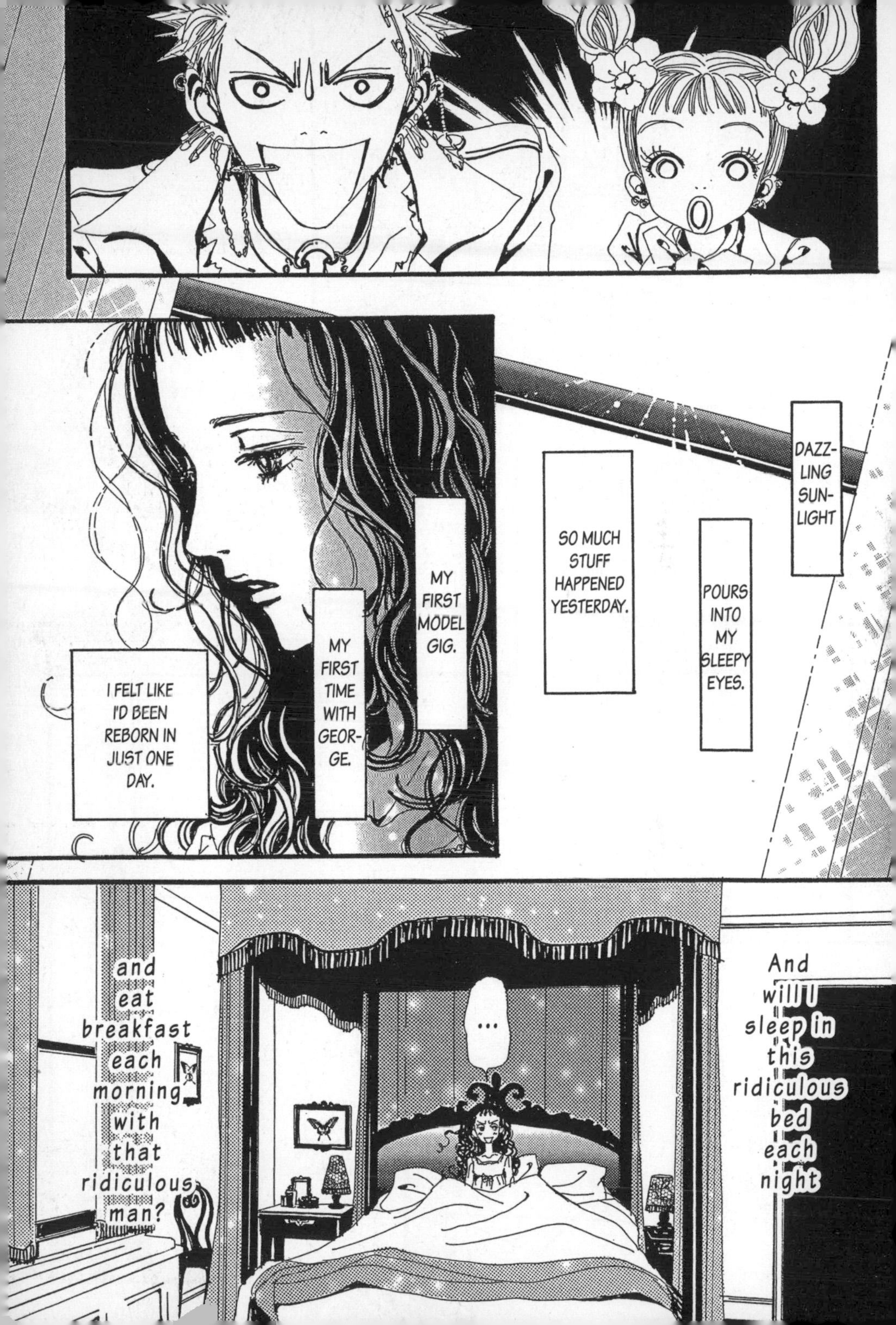
DAZZ-LING SUN-LIGHT
POURS INTO MY SLEEPY EYES.
SO MUCH STUFF HAPPENED YESTERDAY.
MY FIRST MODEL GIG.
MY FIRST TIME WITH GEOR-GE.
I FELT LIKE I'D BEEN REBORN IN JUST ONE DAY.
And will I sleep in this ridiculous bed each night
...
and eat breakfast each morning with that ridiculous man?

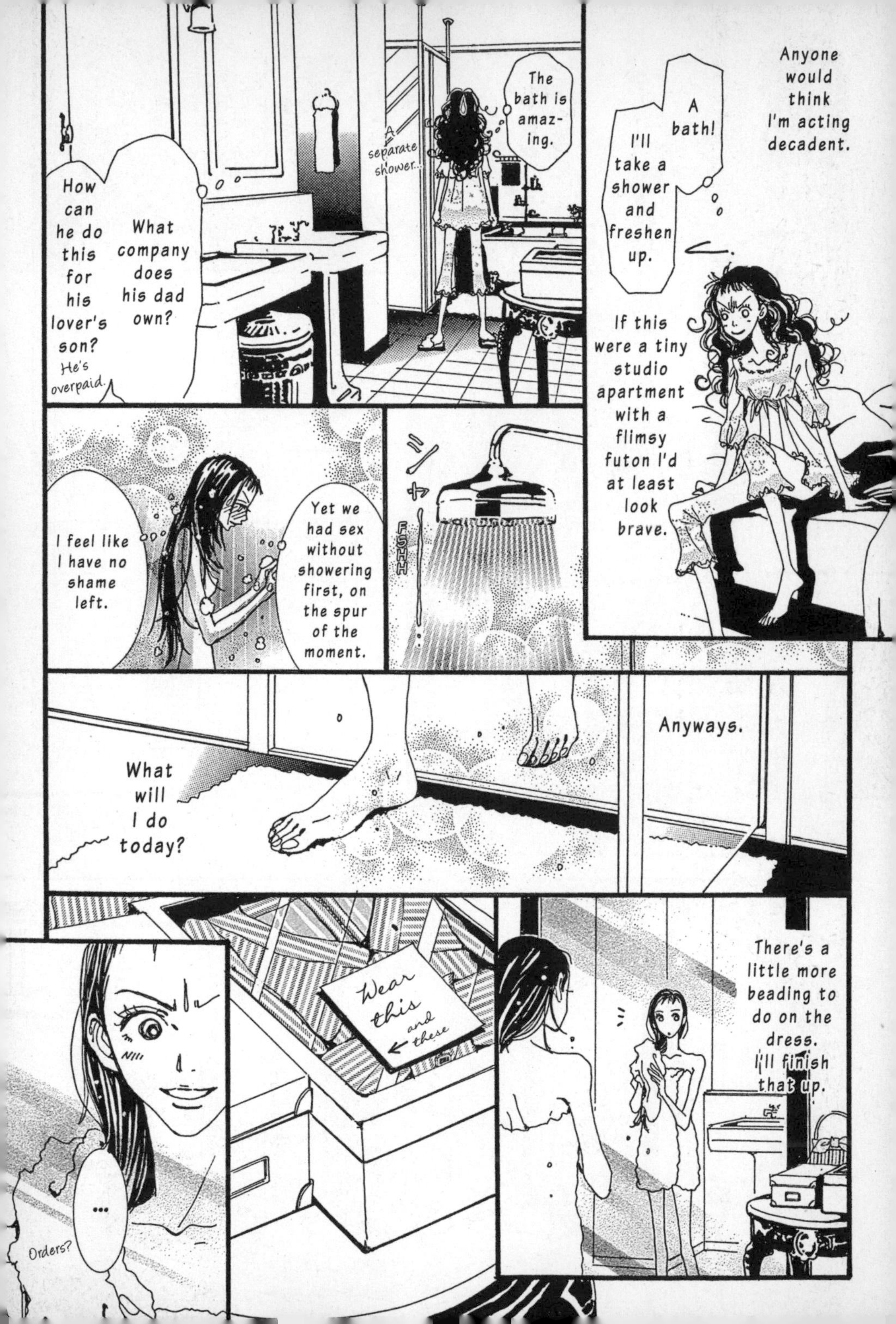
Anyone would think I'm acting decadent.
A bath!
I'll take a shower and freshen up.
If this were a tiny studio apartment with a flimsy futon I'd at least look brave.
The bath is amazing.
A separate shower...
What company does his dad own?
How can he do this for his lover's son?
He's overpaid.
FSHH
Yet we had sex without showering first, on the spur of the moment.
I feel like I have no shame left.
Anyways.
What will I do today?
There's a little more beading to do on the dress. I'll finish that up.
Wear this
and these
...
Orders?

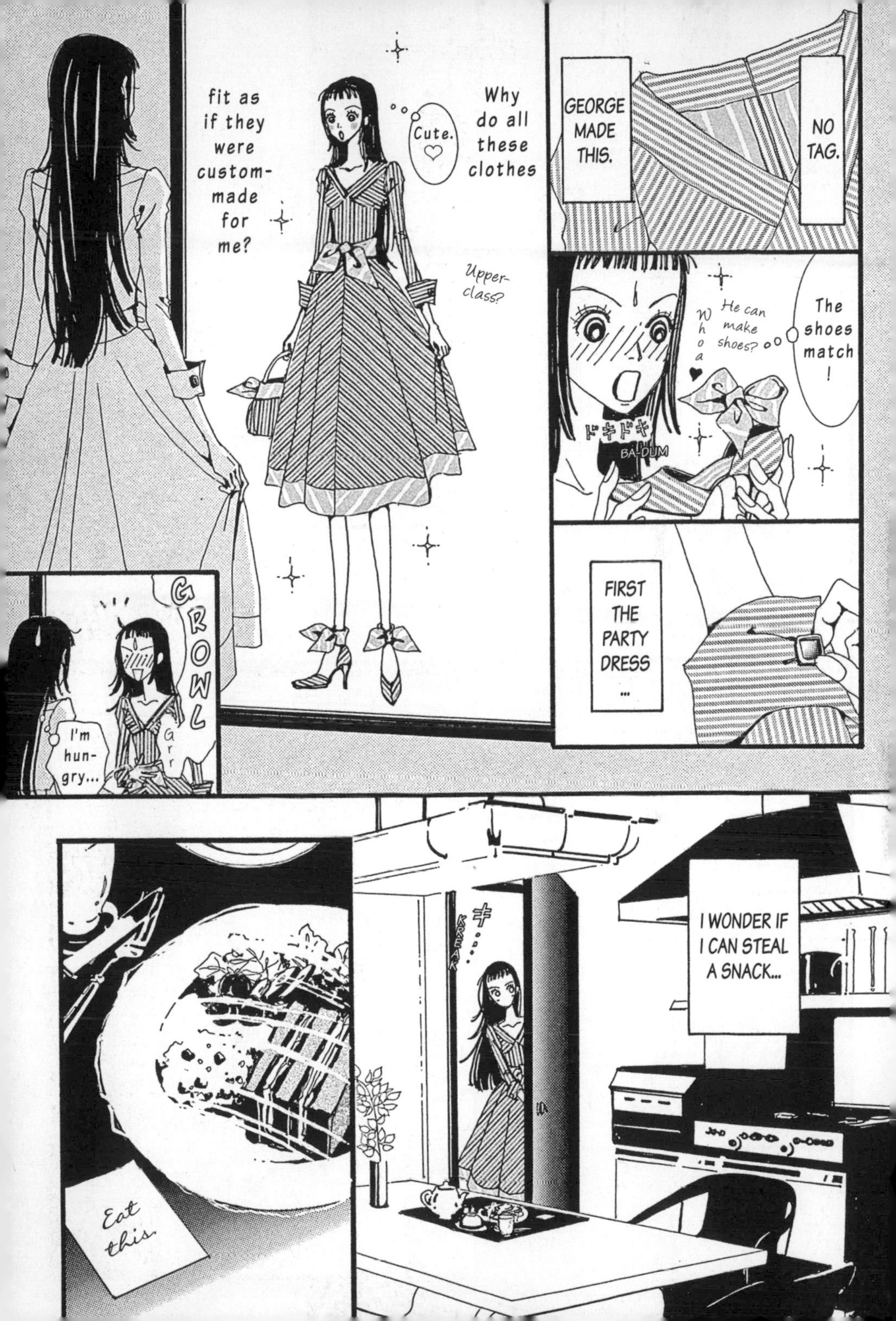
NO TAG.
GEORGE MADE THIS.
The shoes match!
He can make shoes?
Whoa
ドキドキ
BA-DUM
FIRST THE PARTY DRESS...
Why do all these clothes
fit as if they were custom-made for me?
Cute.
Upper-class?
GROWL
Grr
I'm hungry...
I WONDER IF I CAN STEAL A SNACK...
キ
KREAK
Eat this.

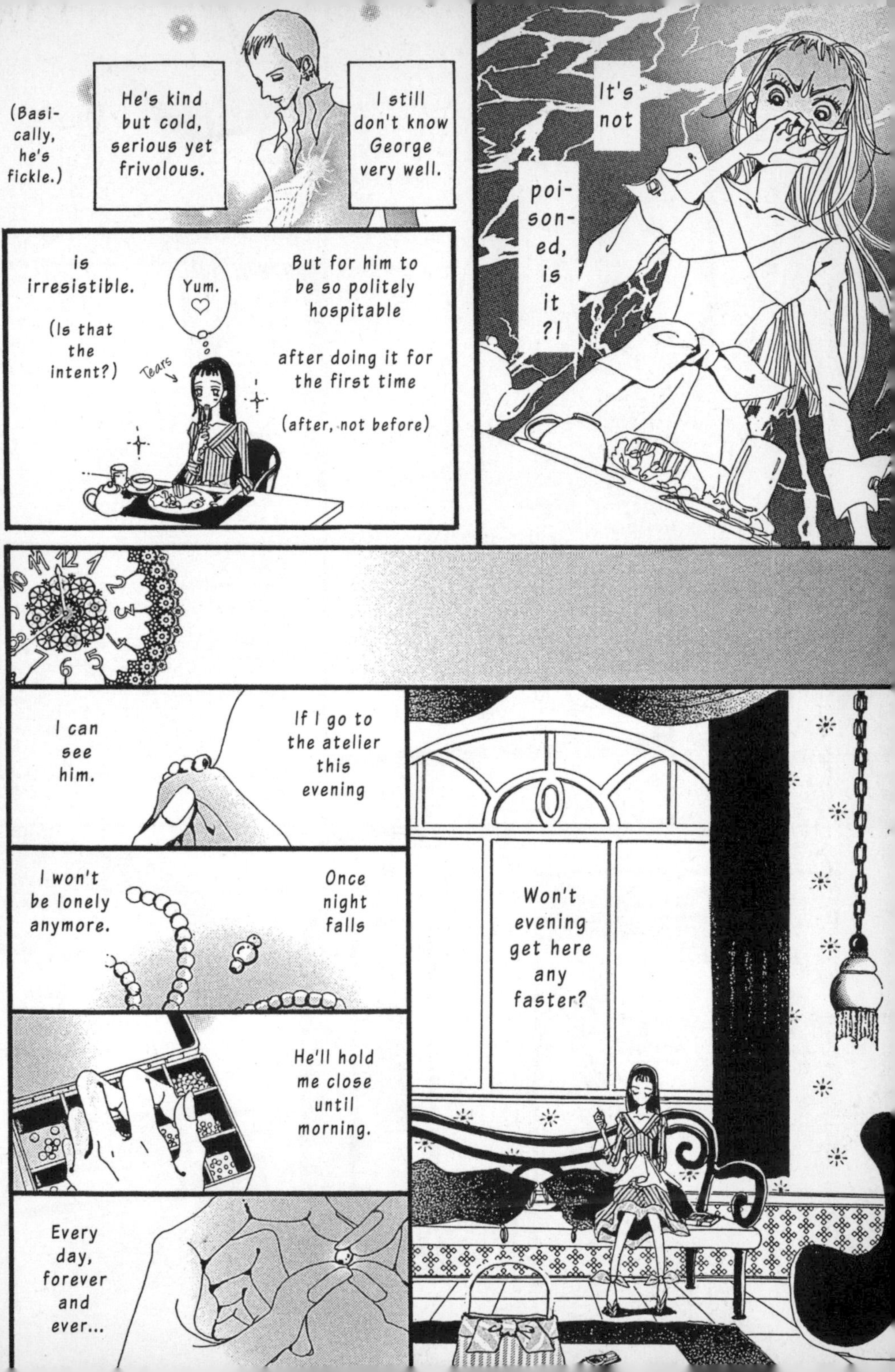
It's not
poi-son-ed, is it?!
I still don't know George very well.
He's kind but cold, serious yet frivolous.
(Basi-cally, he's fickle.)
But for him to be so politely hospitable
after doing it for the first time
(after, not before)
Yum. ♡
is irresistible.
(Is that the intent?)
Tears
Won't evening get here any faster?
If I go to the atelier this evening
I can see him.
Once night falls
I won't be lonely anymore.
He'll hold me close until morning.
Every day, forever and ever...

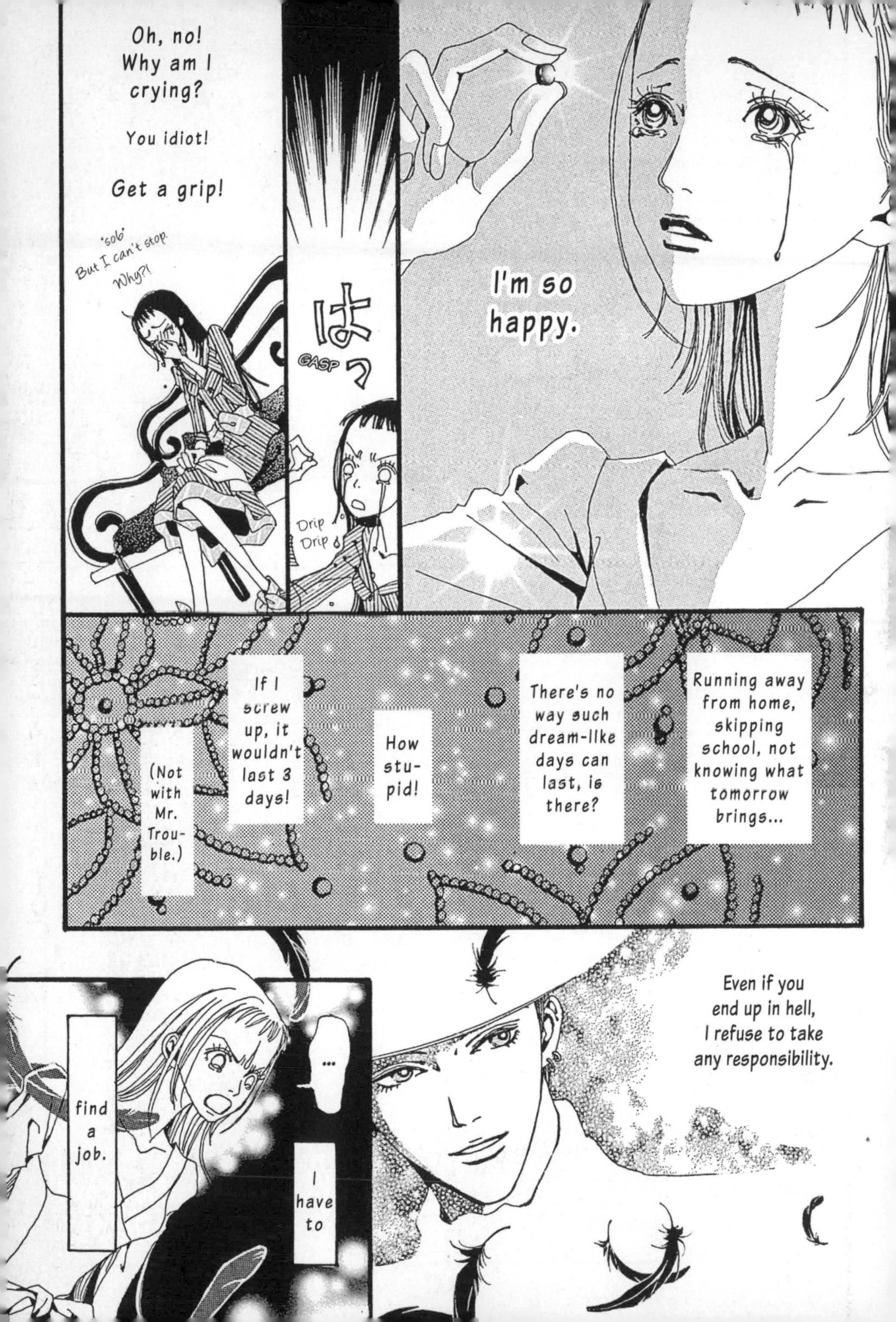
I'm so happy.
はっ
GASP
Drip Drip
Oh, no! Why am I crying?
You idiot!
Get a grip!
sob But I can't stop. Why?!
Running away from home, skipping school, not knowing what tomorrow brings...
There's no way such dream-like days can last, is there?
How stu-pid!
If I screw up, it wouldn't last 3 days!
(Not with Mr. Trou-ble.)
Even if you end up in hell, I refuse to take any responsibility.
...
I have to
find a job.

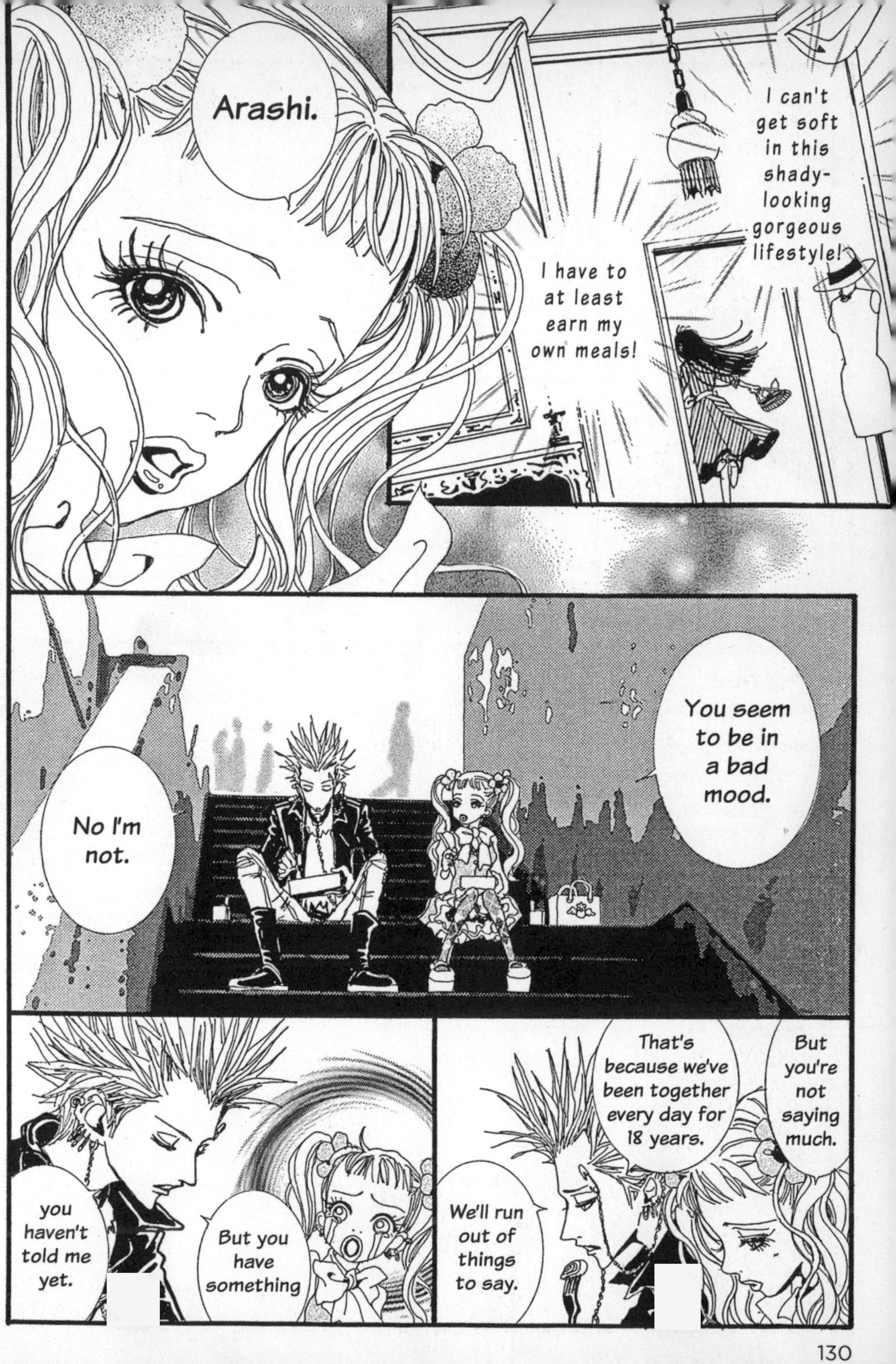

I can't get soft in this shady-looking gorgeous lifestyle!
I have to at least earn my own meals!
Arashi.
You seem to be in a bad mood.
No I'm not.
But you're not saying much.
That's because we've been together every day for 18 years.
We'll run out of things to say.
But you have something
you haven't told me yet.

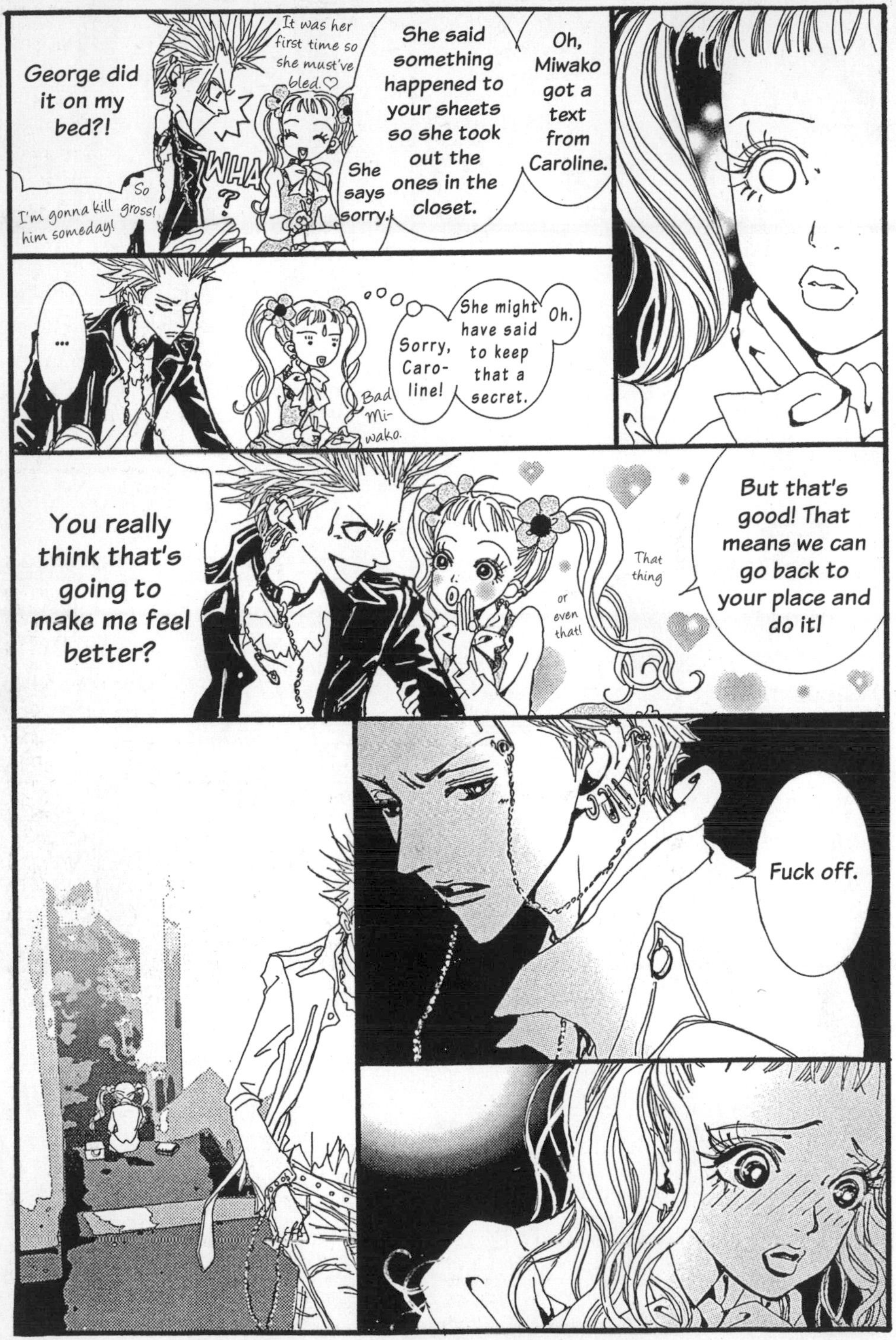
Oh, Miwako got a text from Caroline.
She said something happened to your sheets so she took out the ones in the closet.
She says sorry.
It was her first time so she must've bled.♡
George did it on my bed?!
WHA ?
So gross!
I'm gonna kill him someday!
Oh.
She might have said to keep that a secret.
Sorry, Caroline!
Bad Miwako.
...
But that's good! That means we can go back to your place and do it!
That thing
or even that!
You really think that's going to make me feel better?
Fuck off.

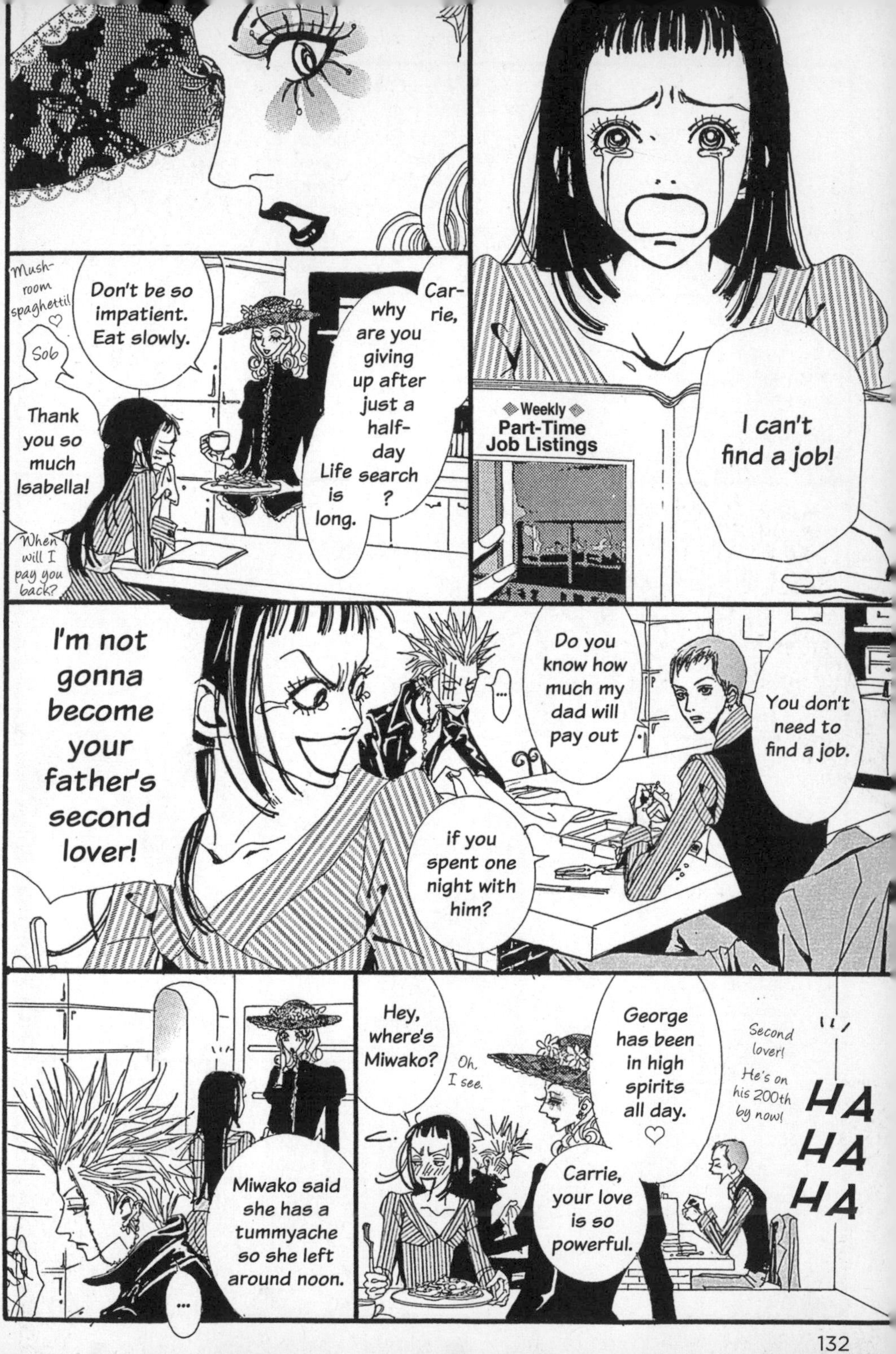
◆Weekly◆
Part-Time Job Listings
I can't find a job!
Carrie, why are you giving up after just a half-day search?
Life is long.
Don't be so impatient. Eat slowly.
Mushroom spaghetti! ♡
Sob
Thank you so much Isabella!
When will I pay you back?
You don't need to find a job.
Do you know how much my dad will pay out
if you spent one night with him?
...
I'm not gonna become your father's second lover!
HA HA HA
Second lover!
He's on his 200th by now!
George has been in high spirits all day. ♡
Carrie, your love is so powerful.
Hey, where's Miwako?
Oh, I see.
Miwako said she has a tummyache so she left around noon.
...

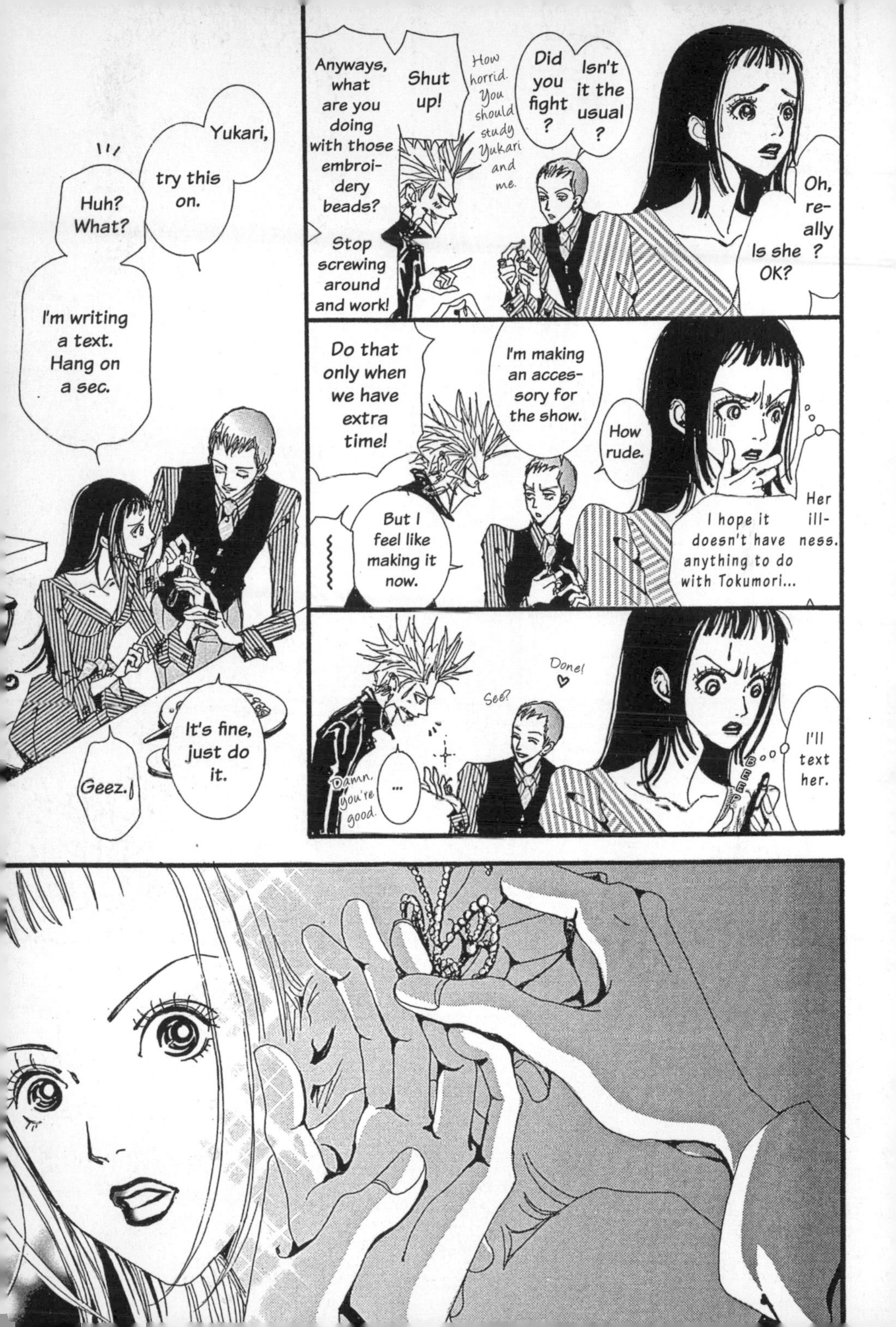
Oh, really?
Is she OK?
Isn't it the usual?
Did you fight?
How horrid. You should study Yukari and me.
Shut up!
Anyways, what are you doing with those embroidery beads?
Stop screwing around and work!
Her illness.
I hope it doesn't have anything to do with Tokumori...
How rude.
I'm making an accessory for the show.
Do that only when we have extra time!
But I feel like making it now.
I'll text her.
BEEP
Done! ♥
See?
...
Damn, you're good.
Yukari,
try this on.
Huh? What?
I'm writing a text. Hang on a sec.
It's fine, just do it.
Geez.

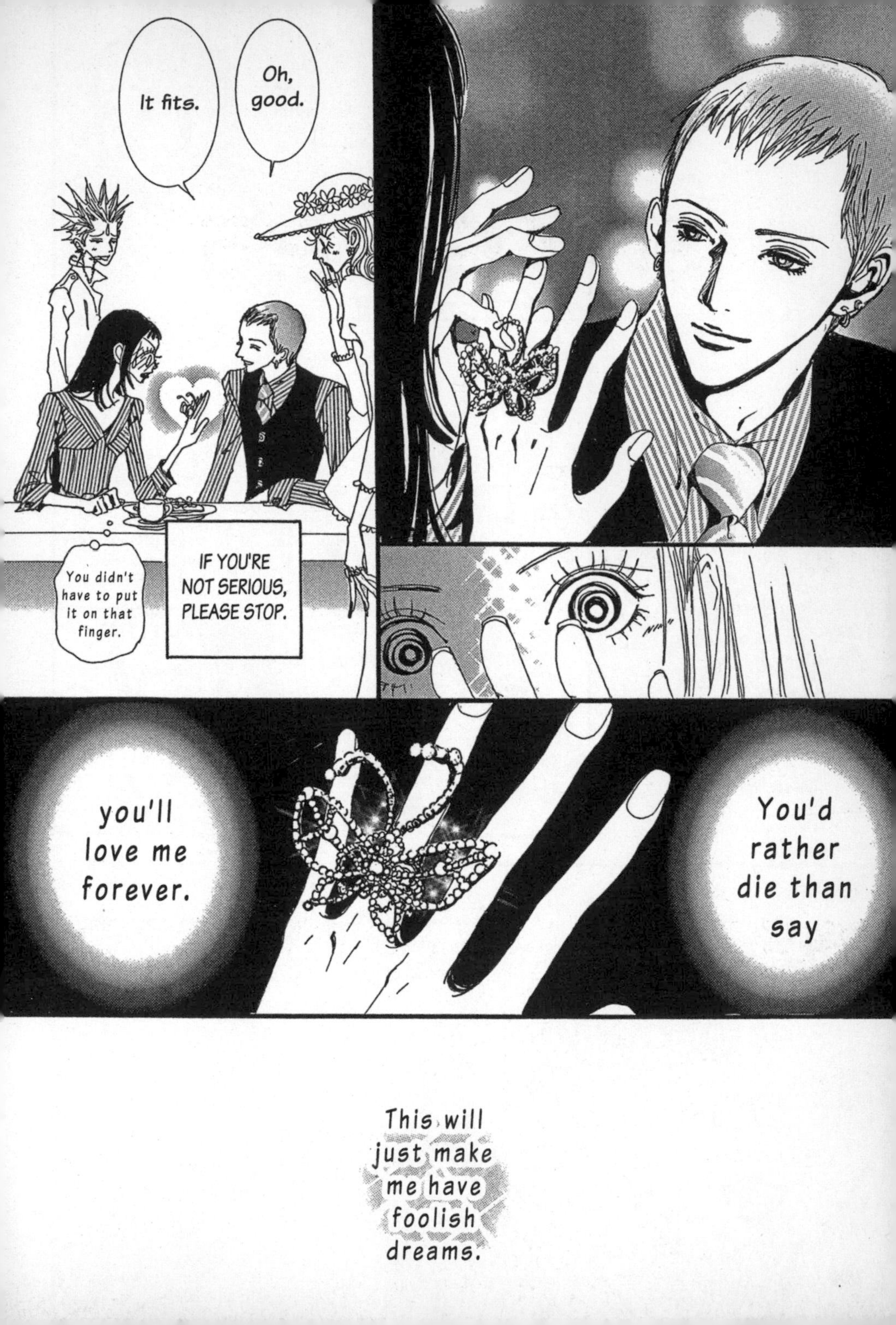
Oh, good.
It fits.
IF YOU'RE NOT SERIOUS, PLEASE STOP.
You didn't have to put it on that finger.
You'd rather die than say
you'll love me forever.
This will just make me have foolish dreams.

STAGE 25

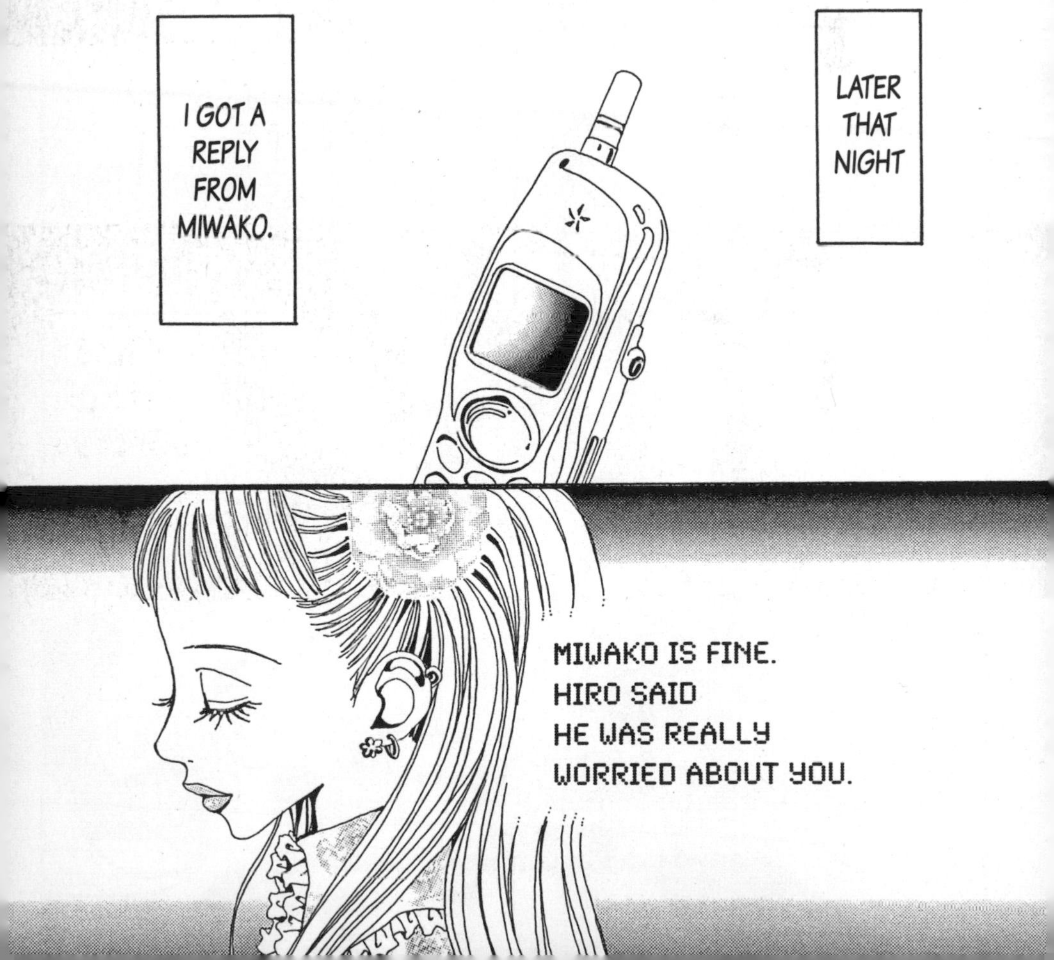
LATER THAT NIGHT
I GOT A REPLY FROM MIWAKO.
MIWAKO IS FINE. HIRO SAID HE WAS REALLY WORRIED ABOUT YOU.

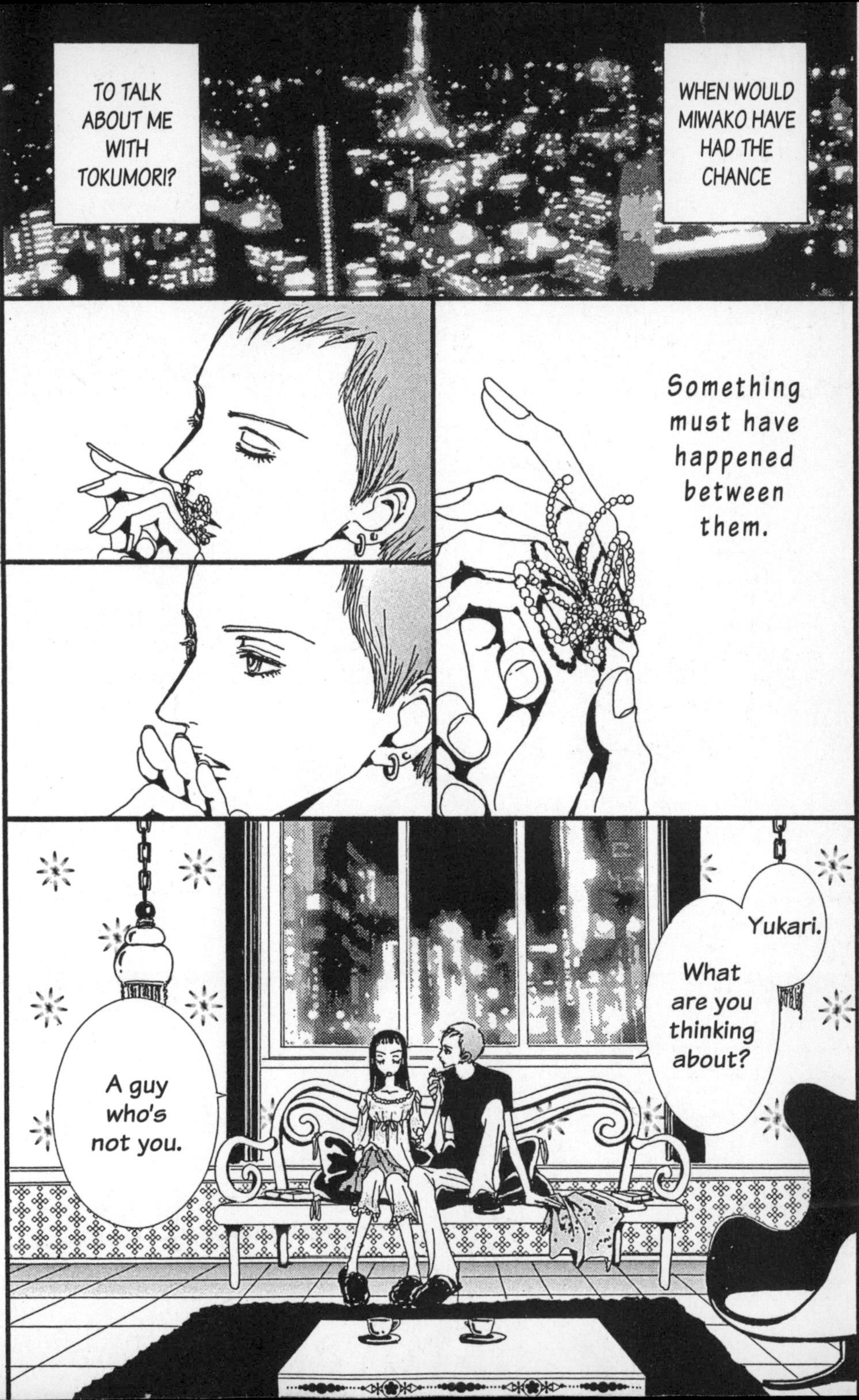
WHEN WOULD MIWAKO HAVE HAD THE CHANCE
TO TALK ABOUT ME WITH TOKUMORI?
Something must have happened between them.
Yukari.
What are you thinking about?
A guy who's not you.

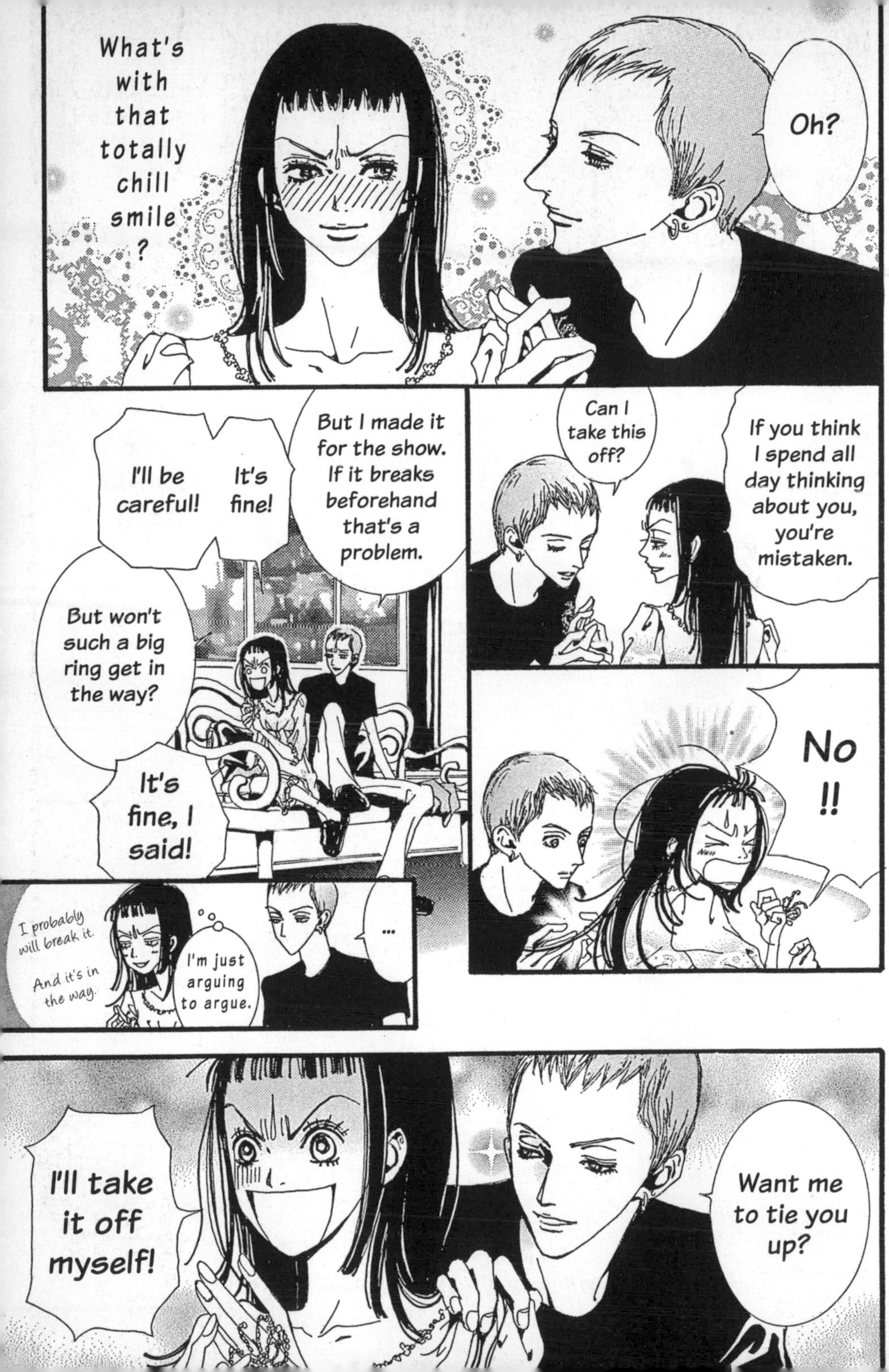
Oh?
What's with that totally chill smile?
If you think I spend all day thinking about you, you're mistaken.
Can I take this off?
No !!
But I made it for the show. If it breaks beforehand that's a problem.
It's fine!
I'll be careful!
But won't such a big ring get in the way?
It's fine, I said!
...
I'm just arguing to argue.
I probably will break it.
And it's in the way.
Want me to tie you up?
I'll take it off myself!

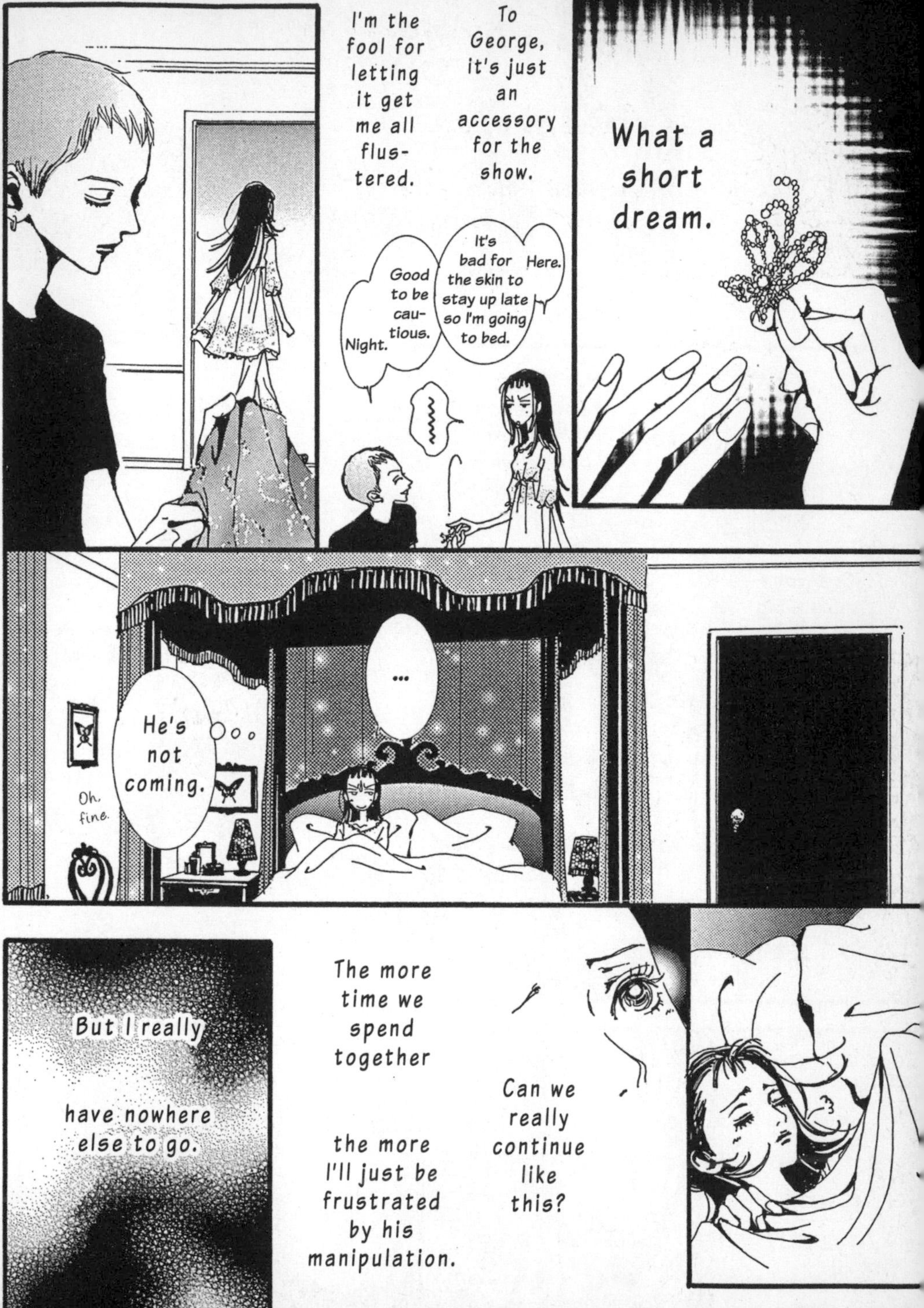
What a short dream.
To George, it's just an accessory for the show.
I'm the fool for letting it get me all flus-tered.
Here.
It's bad for the skin to stay up late so I'm going to bed.
Good to be cau-tious. Night.
...
He's not coming.
Oh, fine.
Can we really continue like this?
The more time we spend together
the more I'll just be frustrated by his manipulation.
But I really
have nowhere else to go.

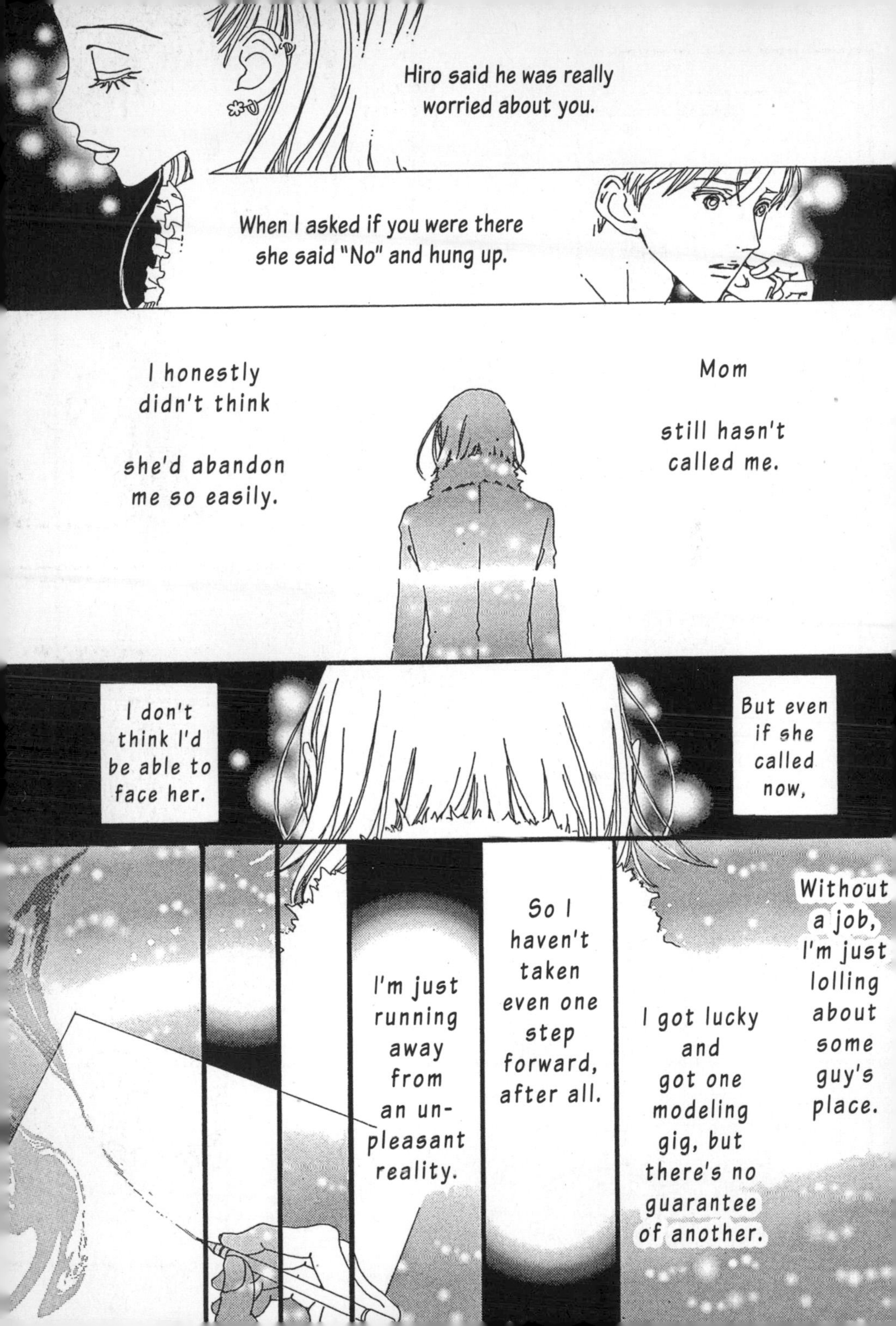
Hiro said he was really worried about you.
When I asked if you were there she said "No" and hung up.
Mom still hasn't called me.
I honestly didn't think she'd abandon me so easily.
But even if she called now,
I don't think I'd be able to face her.
Without a job, I'm just lolling about some guy's place.
I got lucky and got one modeling gig, but there's no guarantee of another.
So I haven't taken even one step forward, after all.
I'm just running away from an unpleasant reality.

合格者発表

It's
not
there.
I
failed.

Why?

I
tried.

I
tried
so
hard.

I'm sorry.

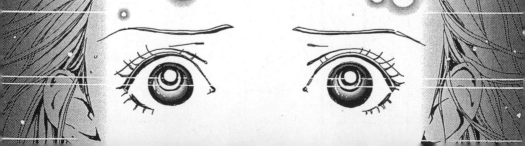

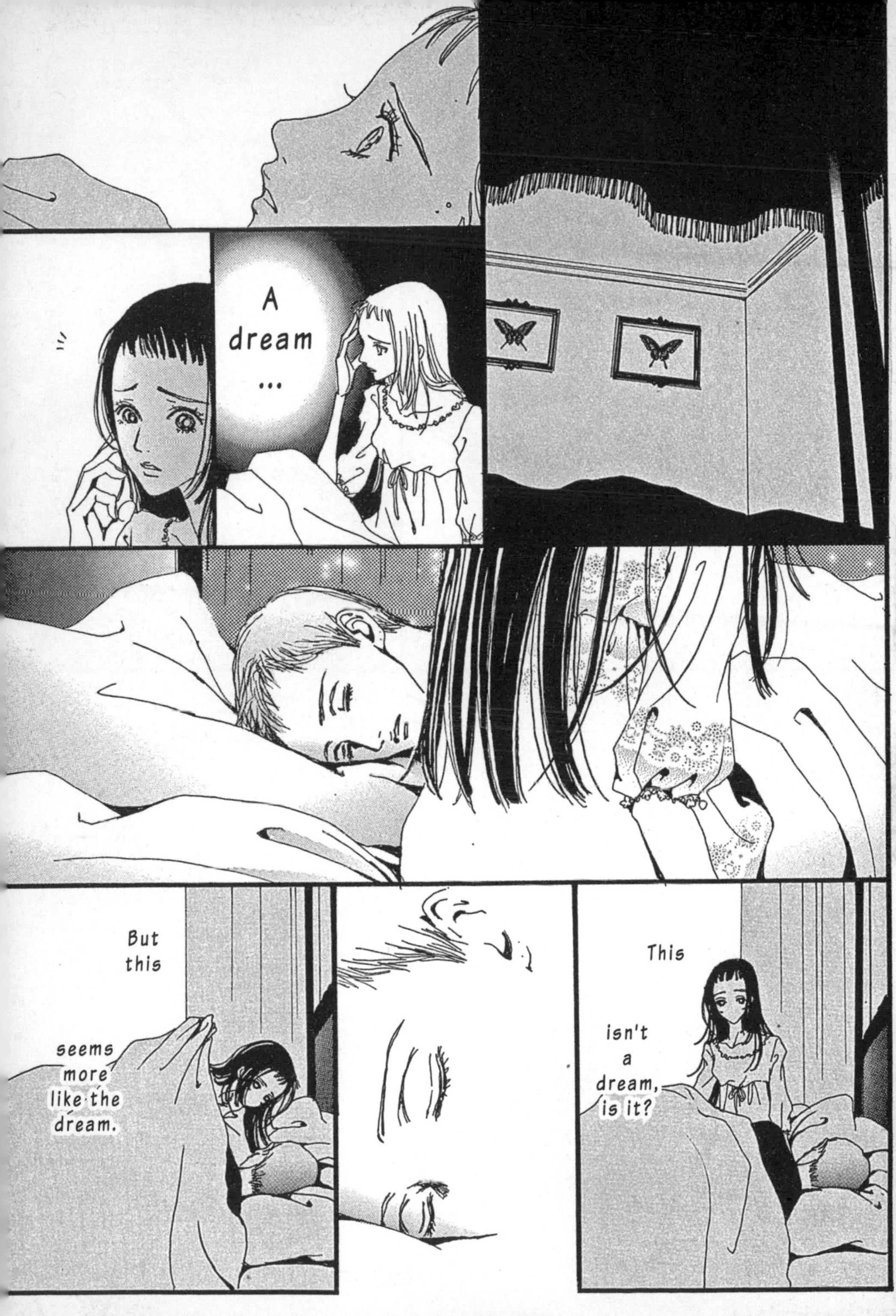
A dream ...
This
isn't a dream, is it?
But this
seems more like the dream.

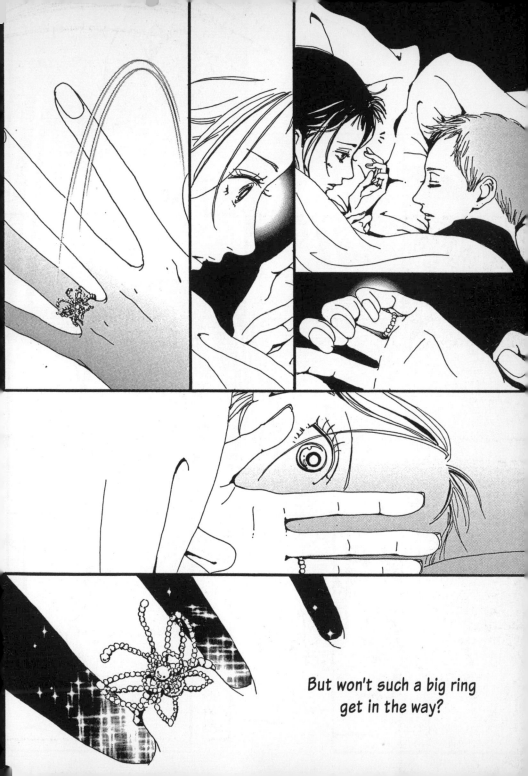

But won't such a big ring
get in the way?

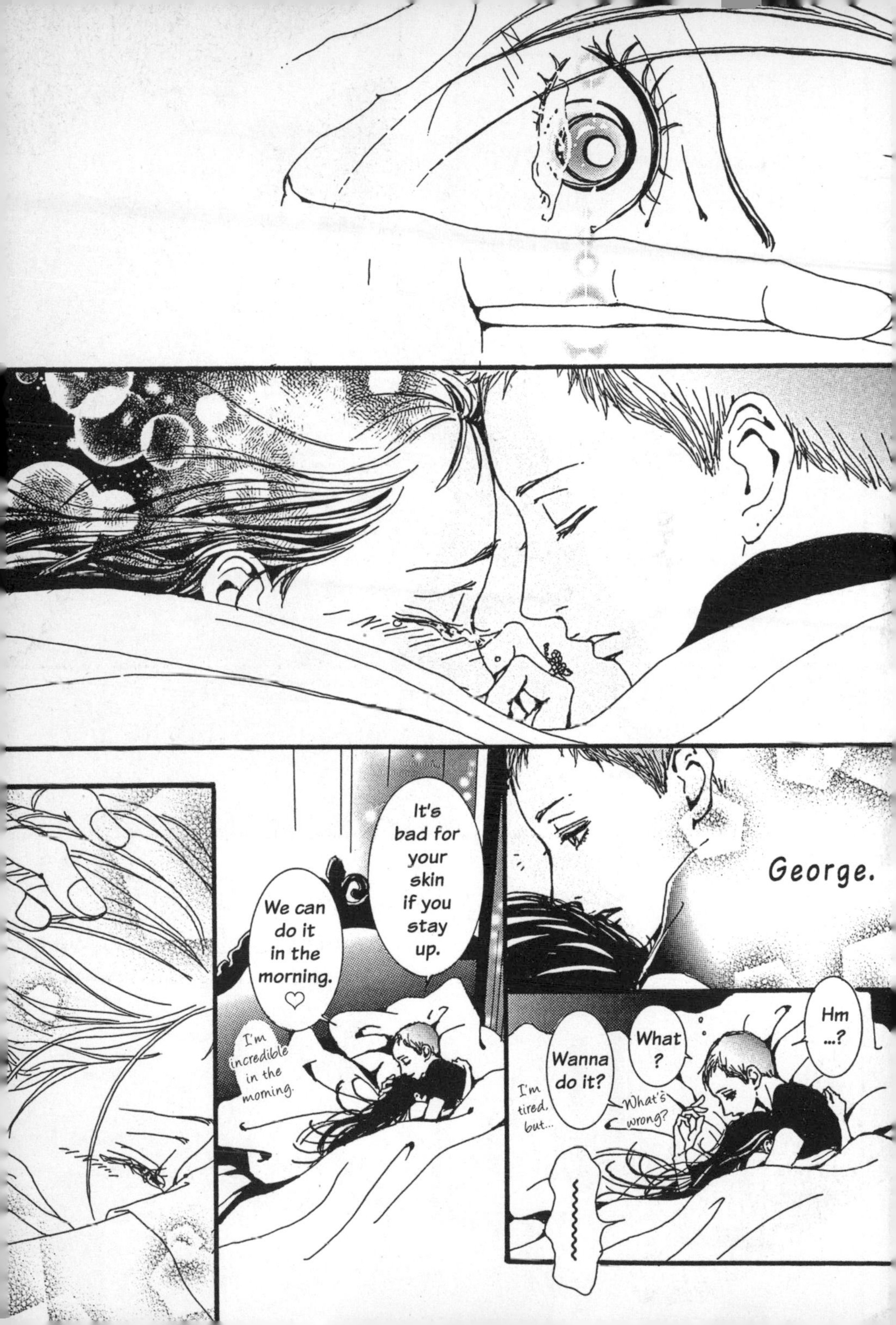
George.
Hm ...?
What?
What's wrong?
Wanna do it?
I'm tired, but...
~~~~~
It's bad for your skin if you stay up.
We can do it in the morning. ♡
I'm incredible in the morning.
~~~~~

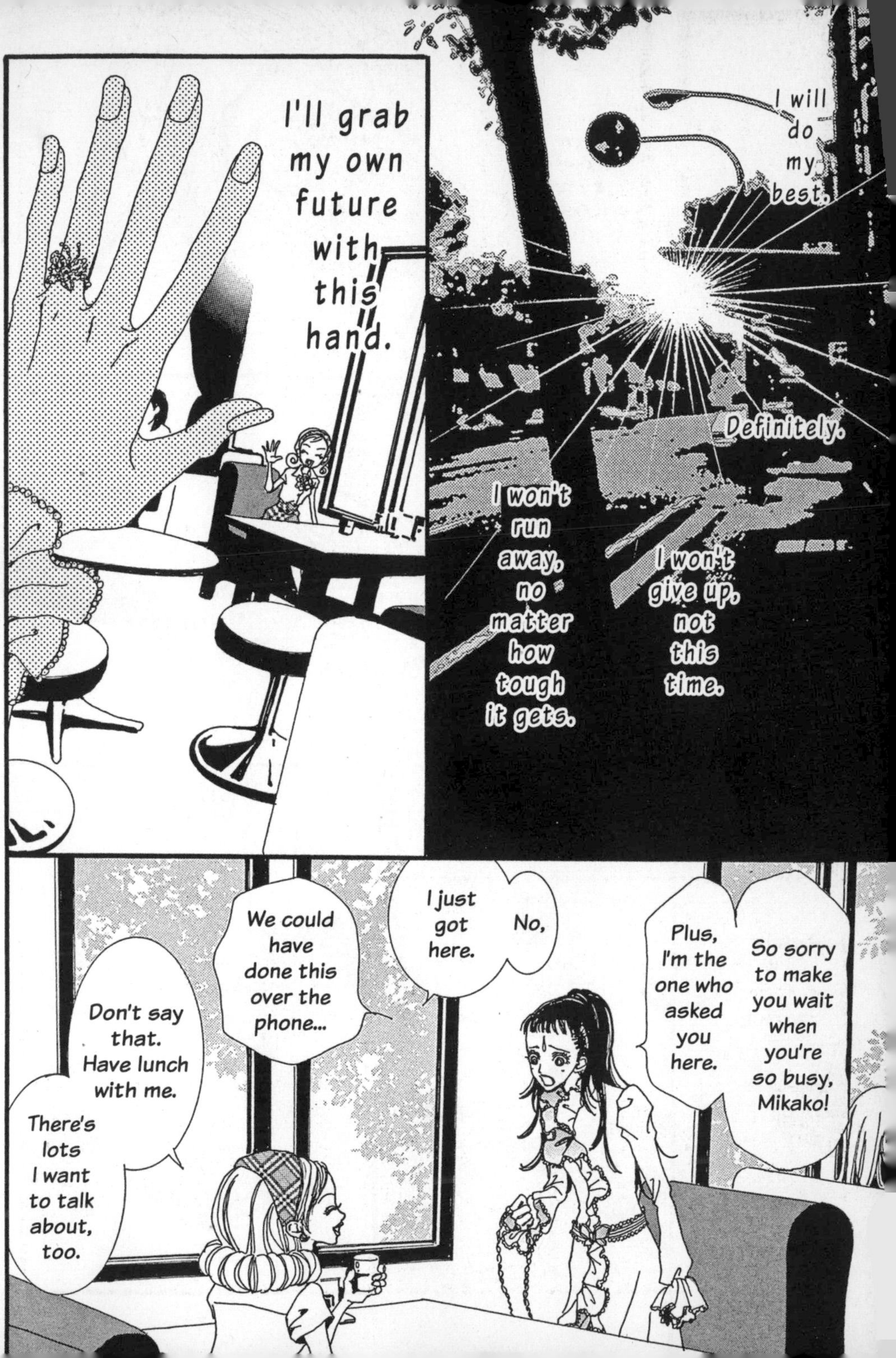
I will do my best.
Definitely.
I won't give up, not this time.
I won't run away, no matter how tough it gets.
I'll grab my own future with this hand.
So sorry to make you wait when you're so busy, Mikako!
Plus, I'm the one who asked you here.
No, I just got here.
We could have done this over the phone...
Don't say that. Have lunch with me.
There's lots I want to talk about, too.

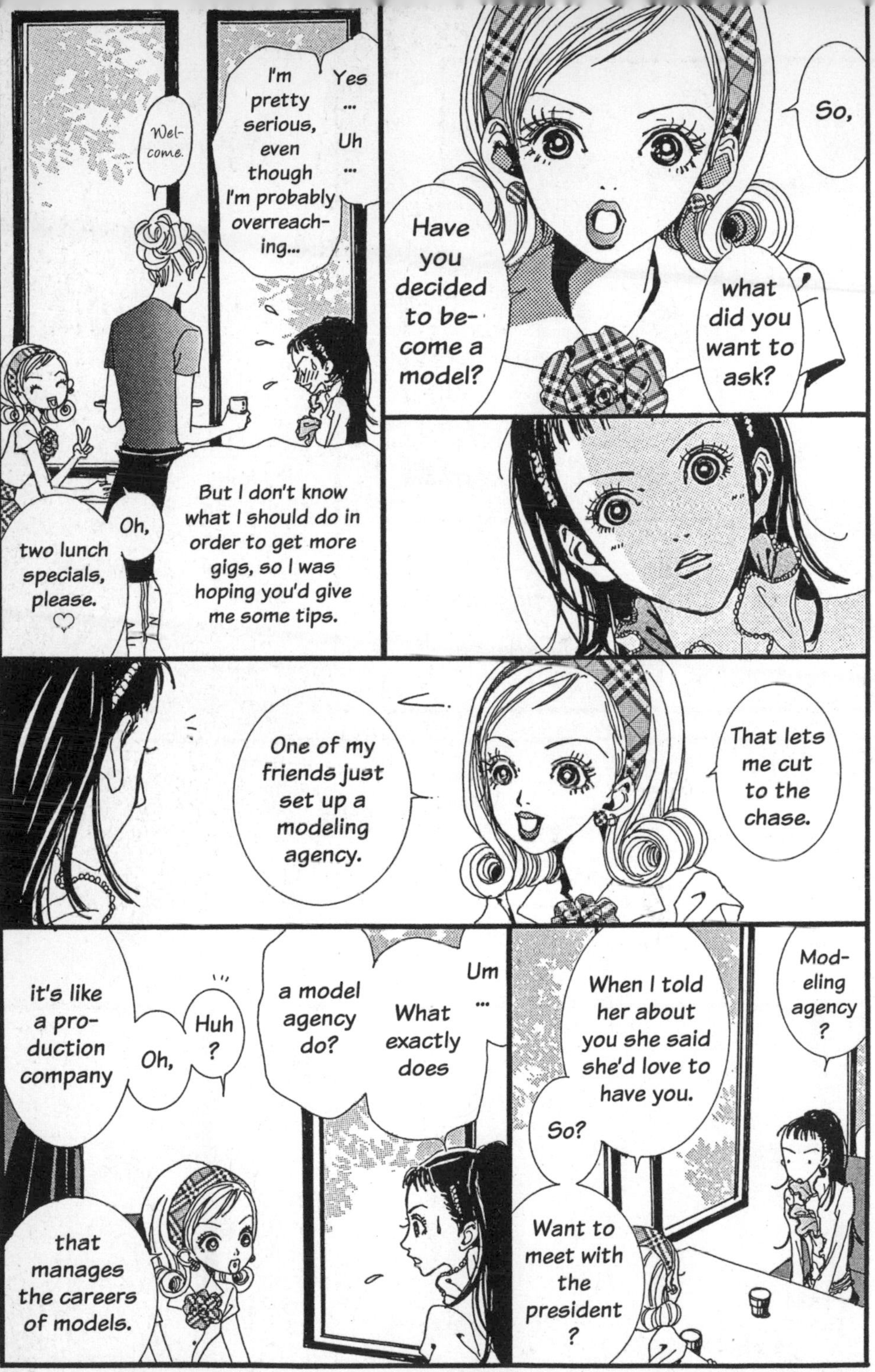
So,
what did you want to ask?
Have you decided to become a model?
Yes ... Uh ...
I'm pretty serious, even though I'm probably overreaching...
Welcome.
But I don't know what I should do in order to get more gigs, so I was hoping you'd give me some tips.
Oh, two lunch specials, please. ♡
That lets me cut to the chase.
One of my friends just set up a modeling agency.
Modeling agency?
When I told her about you she said she'd love to have you.
So?
Want to meet with the president?
Um ...
What exactly does a model agency do?
Huh?
Oh, it's like a production company that manages the careers of models.

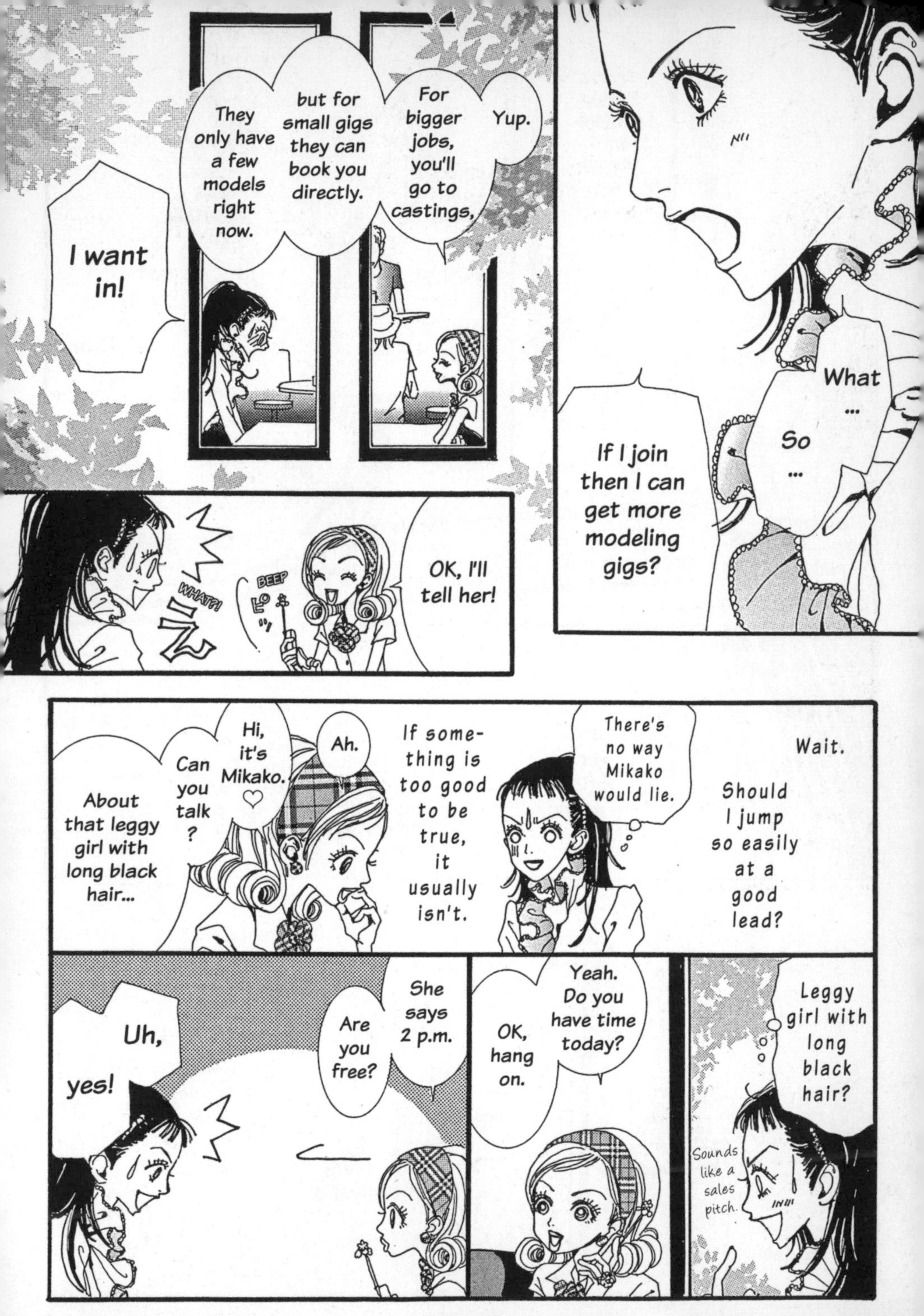
What ...
So ...
If I join then I can get more modeling gigs?
Yup.
For bigger jobs, you'll go to castings,
but for small gigs they can book you directly.
They only have a few models right now.
I want in!
OK, I'll tell her!
BEEP
WHAT?!
Wait.
Should I jump so easily at a good lead?
There's no way Mikako would lie.
If some-thing is too good to be true, it usually isn't.
Ah.
Hi, it's Mikako. ♡
Can you talk?
About that leggy girl with long black hair...
Leggy girl with long black hair?
Sounds like a sales pitch.
Yeah. Do you have time today?
OK, hang on.
She says 2 p.m.
Are you free?
Uh,
yes!

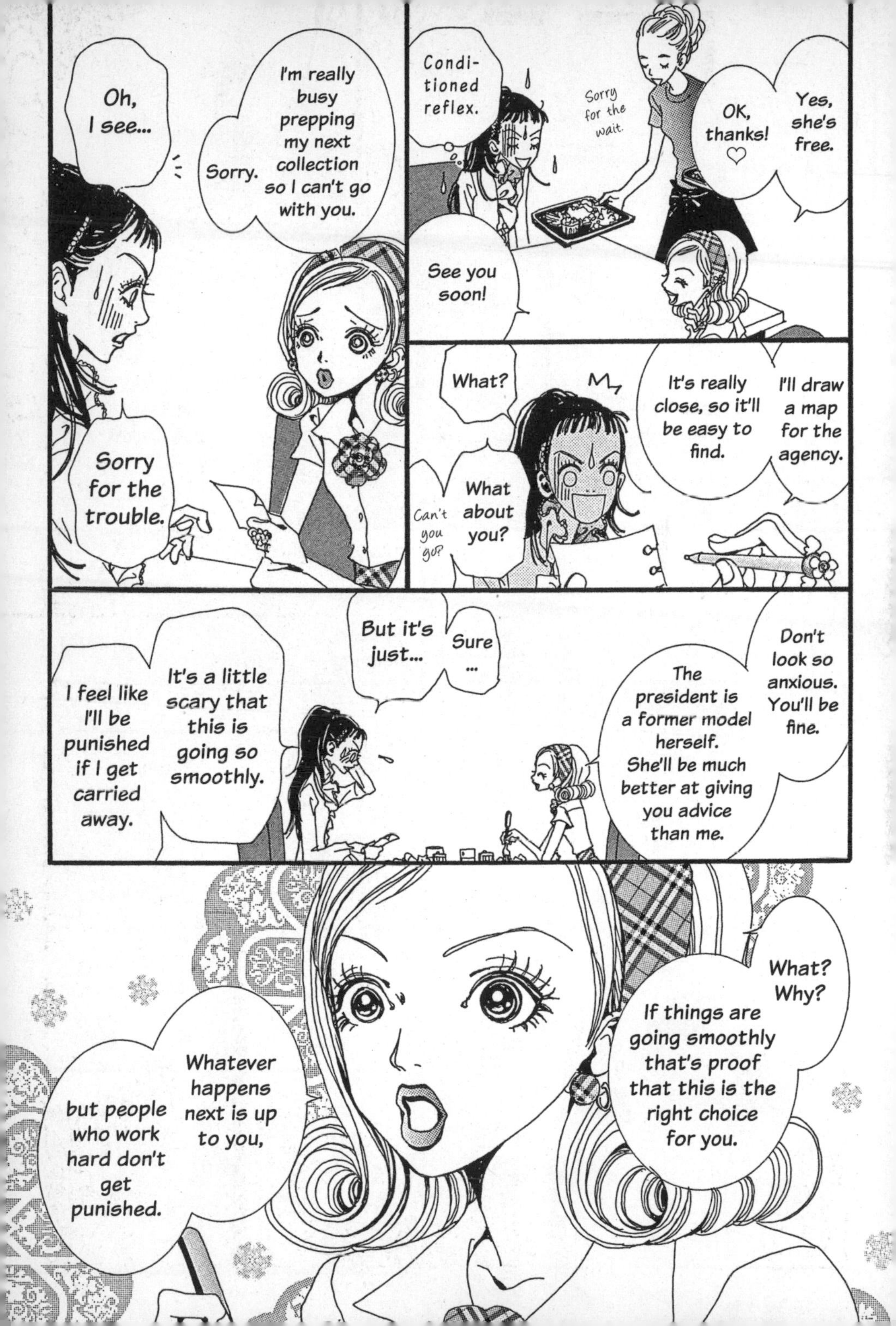
Yes, she's free.
OK, thanks! ♡
Sorry for the wait.
Conditioned reflex.
See you soon!
I'll draw a map for the agency.
It's really close, so it'll be easy to find.
What?
What about you?
Can't you go?
I'm really busy prepping my next collection so I can't go with you.
Sorry.
Oh, I see...
Sorry for the trouble.
Don't look so anxious. You'll be fine.
The president is a former model herself. She'll be much better at giving you advice than me.
Sure...
But it's just...
It's a little scary that this is going so smoothly.
I feel like I'll be punished if I get carried away.
What? Why?
If things are going smoothly that's proof that this is the right choice for you.
Whatever happens next is up to you,
but people who work hard don't get punished.

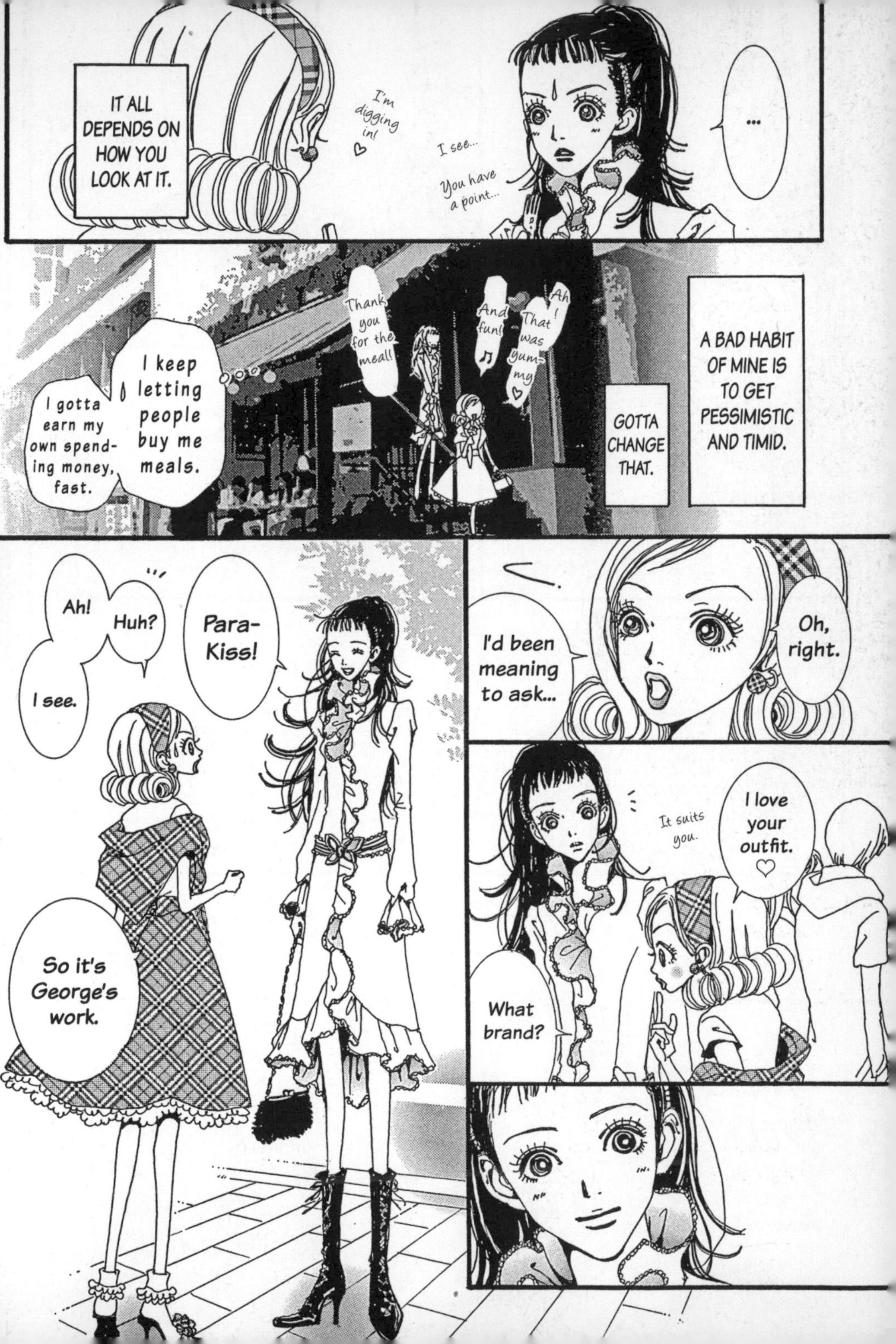
...
I see...
You have a point...
I'm digging in!
IT ALL DEPENDS ON HOW YOU LOOK AT IT.
A BAD HABIT OF MINE IS TO GET PESSIMISTIC AND TIMID.
GOTTA CHANGE THAT.
Ah! That was yum-my
And fun!
Thank you for the meal!
I keep letting people buy me meals.
I gotta earn my own spend-ing money, fast.
Oh, right.
I'd been meaning to ask...
I love your outfit.
It suits you.
What brand?
Para-Kiss!
Huh?
Ah!
I see.
So it's George's work.

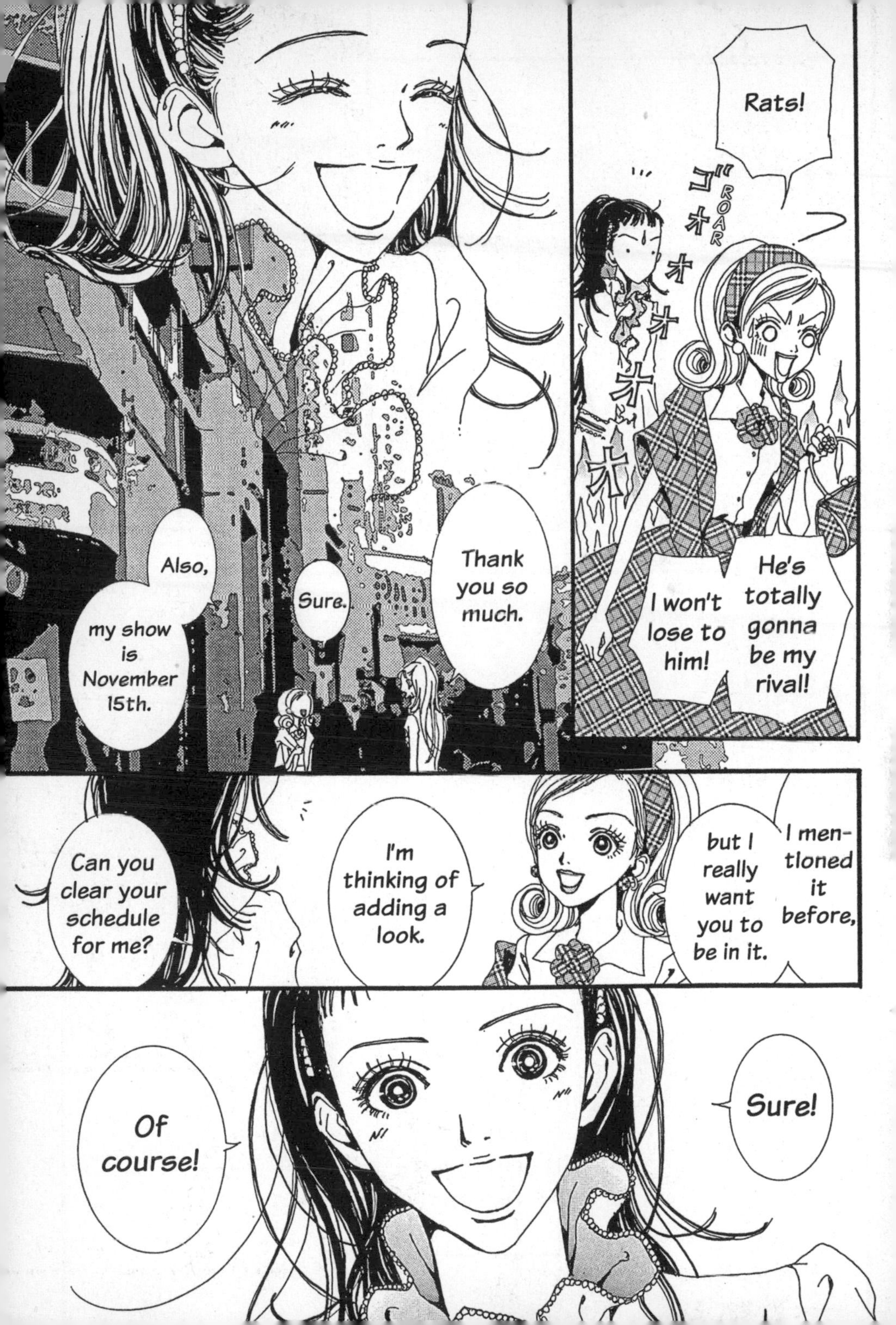
Rats!
ゴオオオオオオ
ROAR
He's totally gonna be my rival!
I won't lose to him!
Thank you so much.
Sure.
Also,
my show is November 15th.
I men-tioned it before,
but I really want you to be in it.
I'm thinking of adding a look.
Can you clear your schedule for me?
Sure!
Of course!

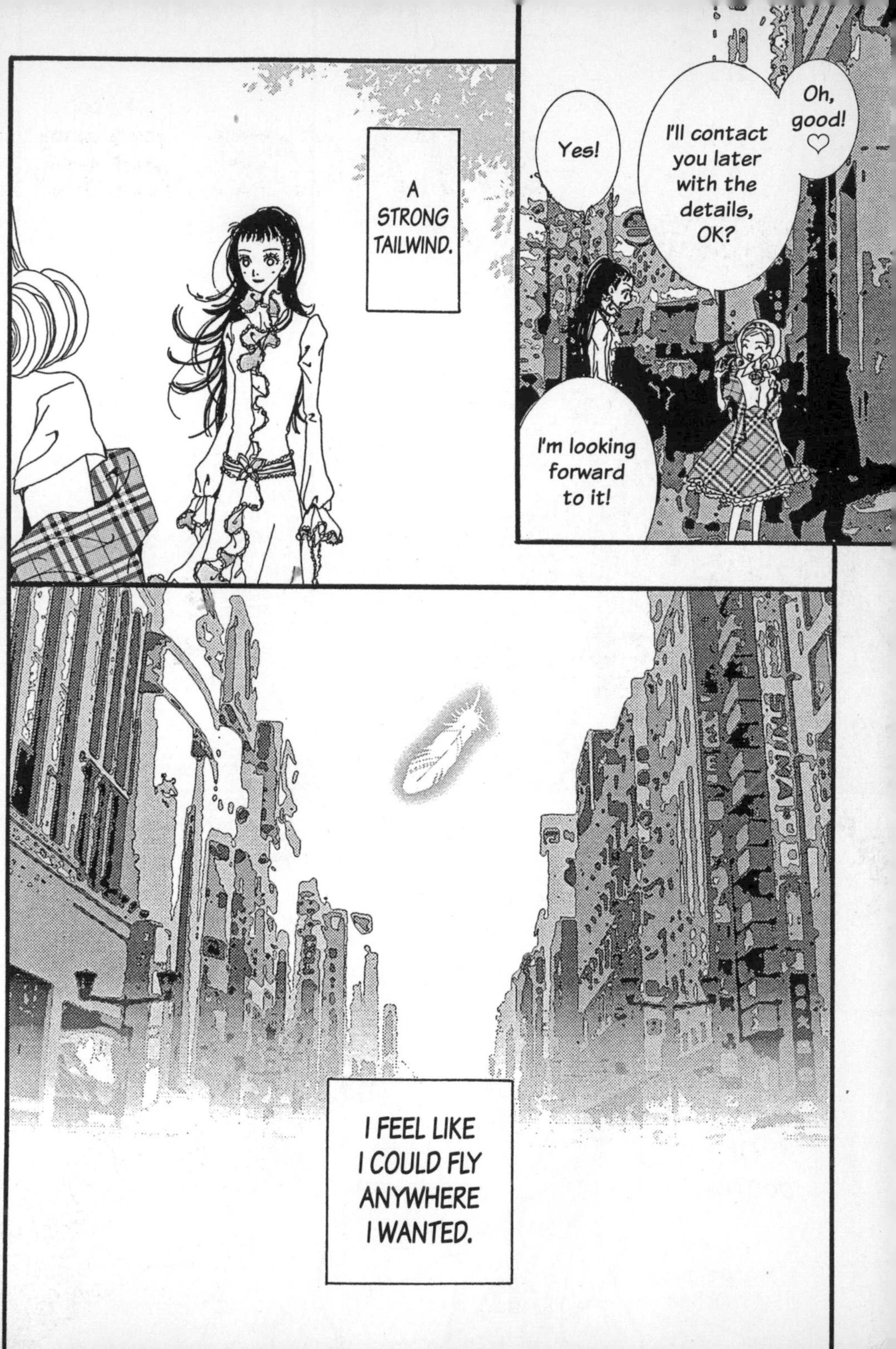
Oh, good! ♡
I'll contact you later with the details, OK?
Yes!
I'm looking forward to it!
A STRONG TAILWIND.
I FEEL LIKE I COULD FLY ANYWHERE I WANTED.

STAGE 26

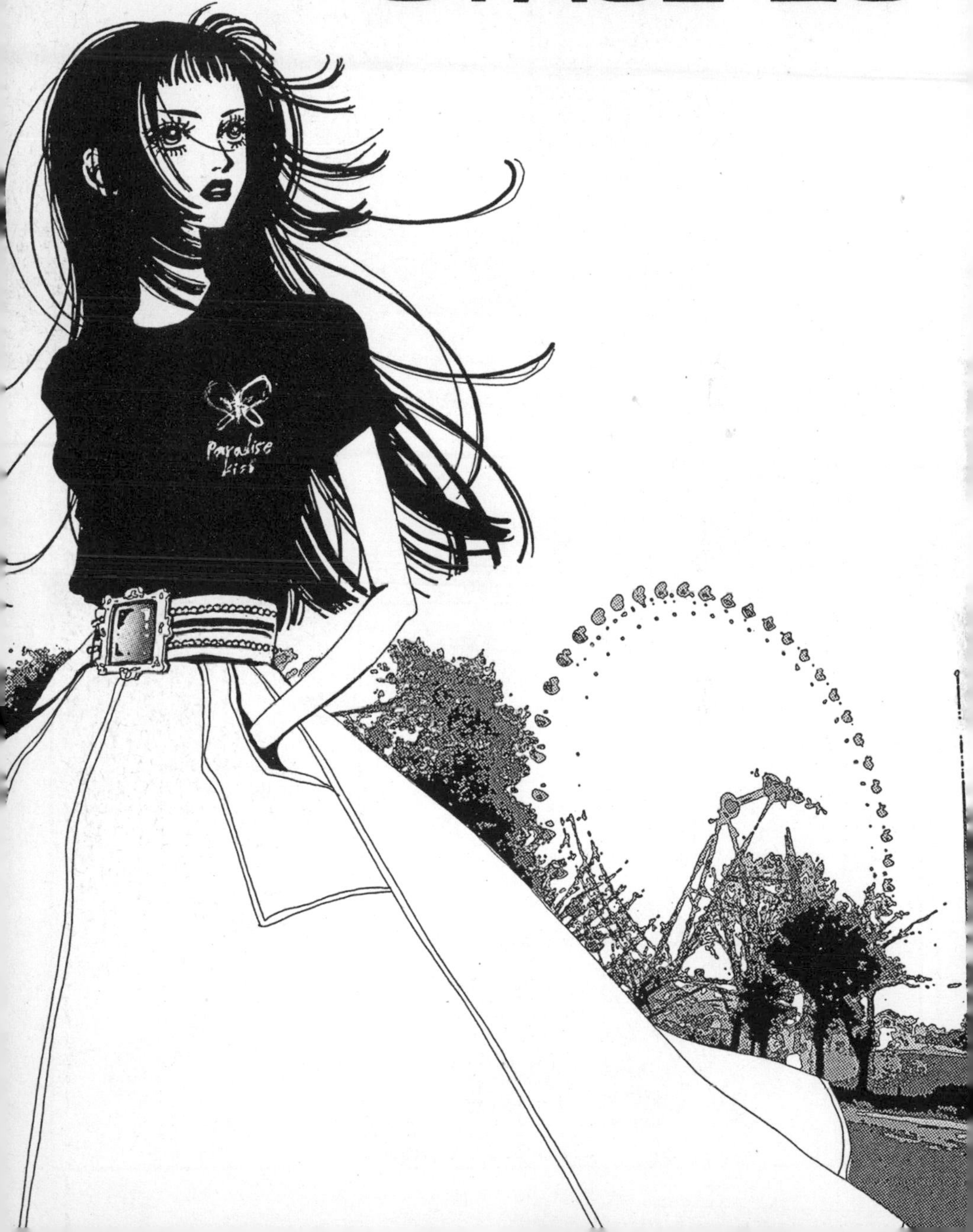
Paradise Kiss

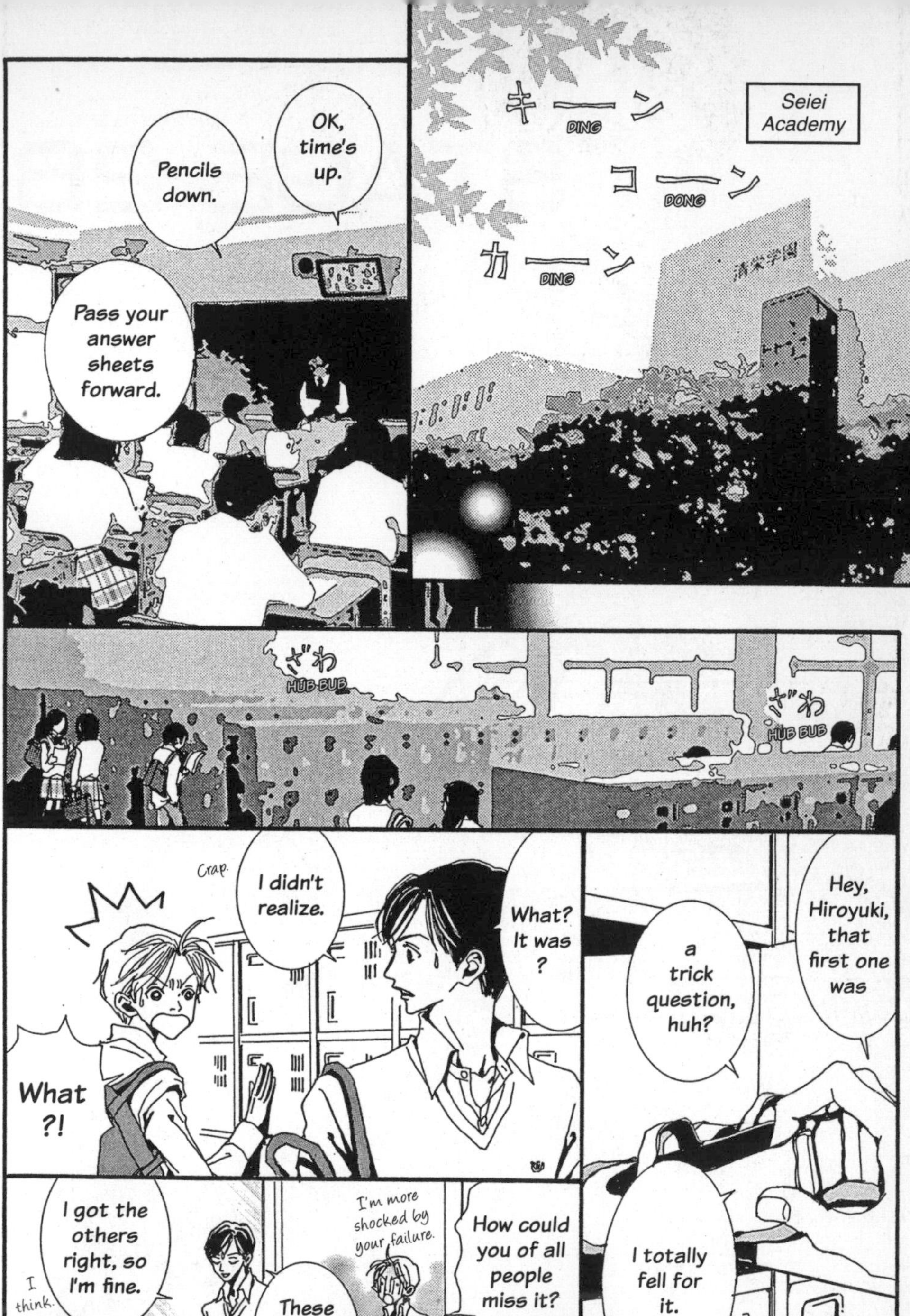
Seiei Academy
キーーン
DING
コーーン
DONG
カーーン
DING
OK, time's up.
Pencils down.
Pass your answer sheets forward.
ざわ
HUB BUB
ざわ
HUB BUB
Hey, Hiroyuki, that first one was
a trick question, huh?
What? It was ?
I didn't realize.
Crap.
What ?!
I totally fell for it.
How could you of all people miss it?
I'm more shocked by your failure.
These things happen.
I got the others right, so I'm fine.
I think.
...

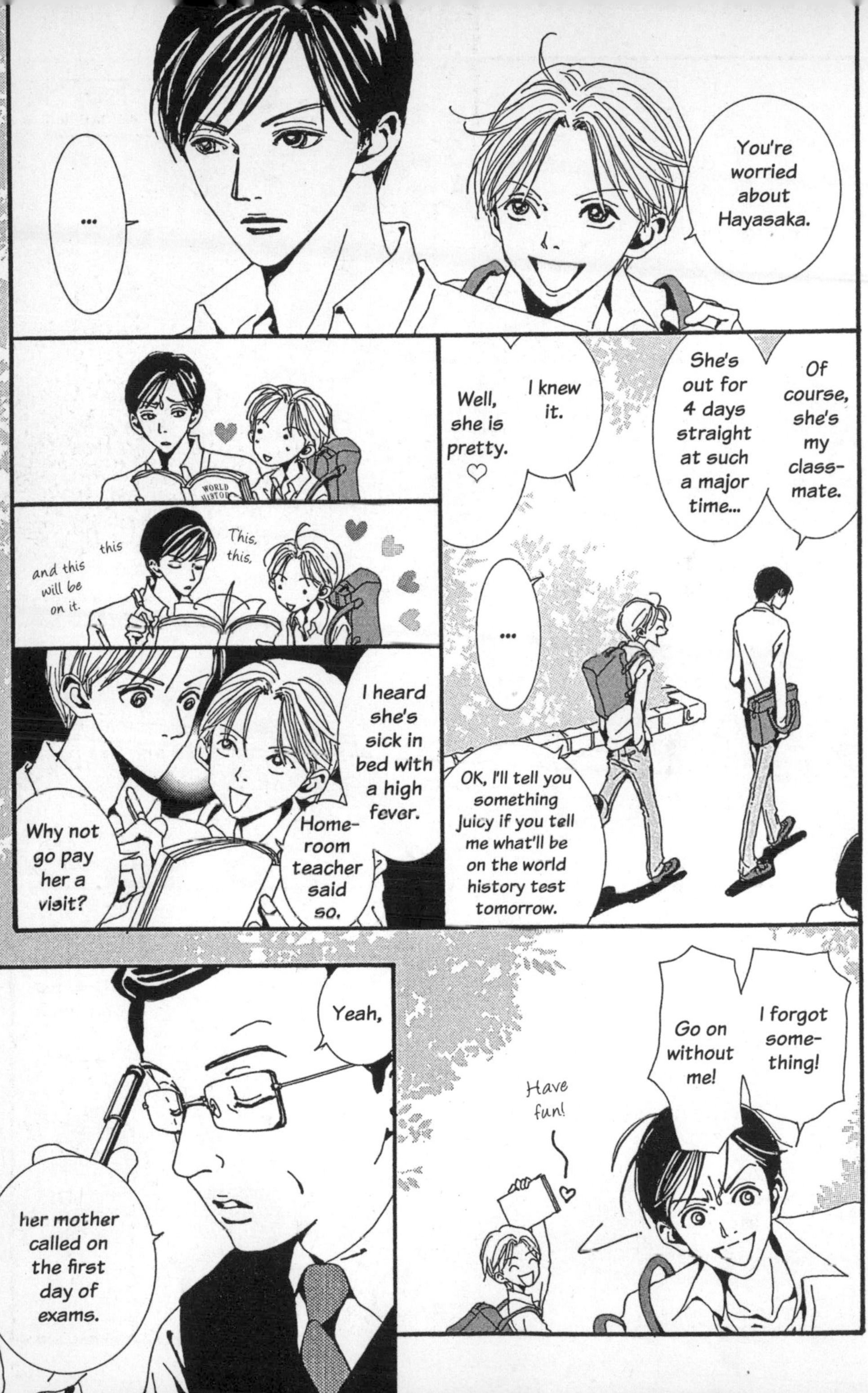
You're worried about Hayasaka.
...
Of course, she's my class-mate.
She's out for 4 days straight at such a major time...
I knew it.
Well, she is pretty. ♡
...
OK, I'll tell you something juicy if you tell me what'll be on the world history test tomorrow.
WORLD HISTO
This, this,
this
and this will be on it.
I heard she's sick in bed with a high fever.
Home-room teacher said so.
Why not go pay her a visit?
I forgot some-thing!
Go on without me!
Have fun! ♡
Yeah,
her mother called on the first day of exams.

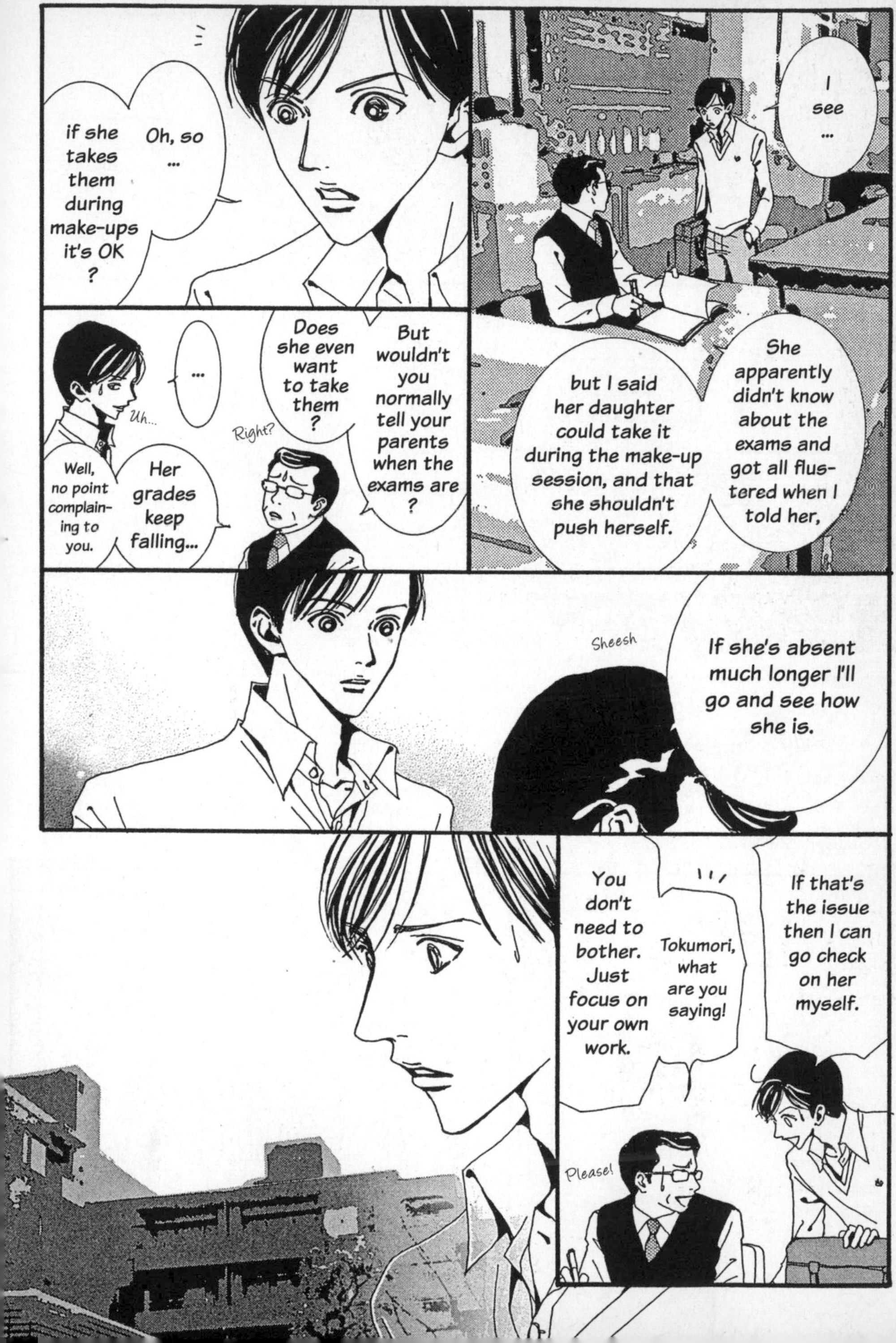

I see ...
Oh, so ...
if she takes them during make-ups it's OK ?
She apparently didn't know about the exams and got all flustered when I told her,
but I said her daughter could take it during the make-up session, and that she shouldn't push herself.
But wouldn't you normally tell your parents when the exams are ?
Does she even want to take them ?
Right?
...
Uh...
Her grades keep falling...
Well, no point complaining to you.
If she's absent much longer I'll go and see how she is.
Sheesh
If that's the issue then I can go check on her myself.
Tokumori, what are you saying!
You don't need to bother. Just focus on your own work.
Please!

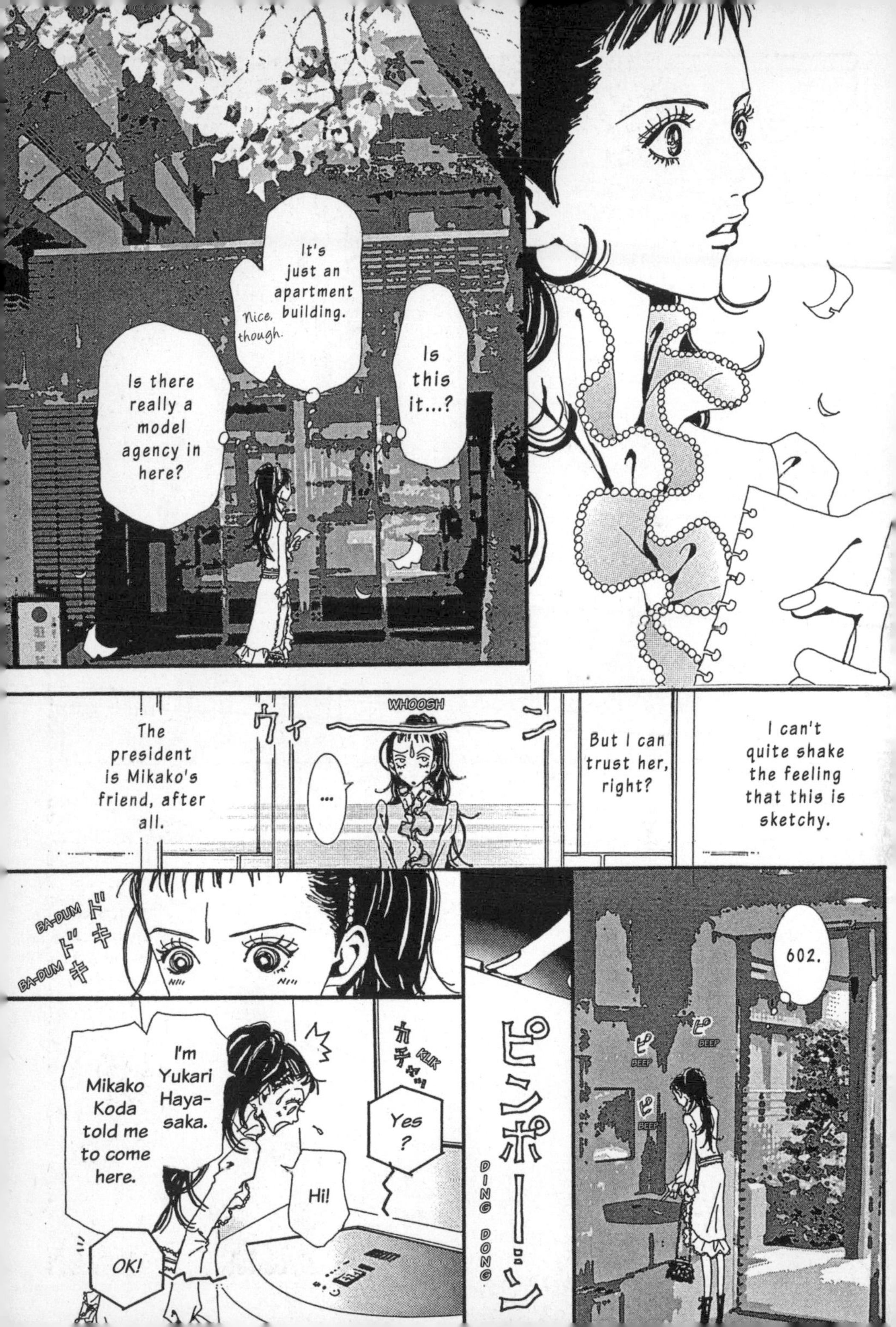
Is this it...?
It's just an apartment building.
Nice, though.
Is there really a model agency in here?
I can't quite shake the feeling that this is sketchy.
But I can trust her, right?
WHOOSH
ウィーン
...
The president is Mikako's friend, after all.
602.
ピ
BEEP
ピ
BEEP
ピ
BEEP
BA-DUM
ドキ
BA-DUM
ドキ
ピンポーン
DING DONG
カチャ
KLIK
Yes?
Hi!
I'm Yukari Haya-saka.
Mikako Koda told me to come here.
OK!

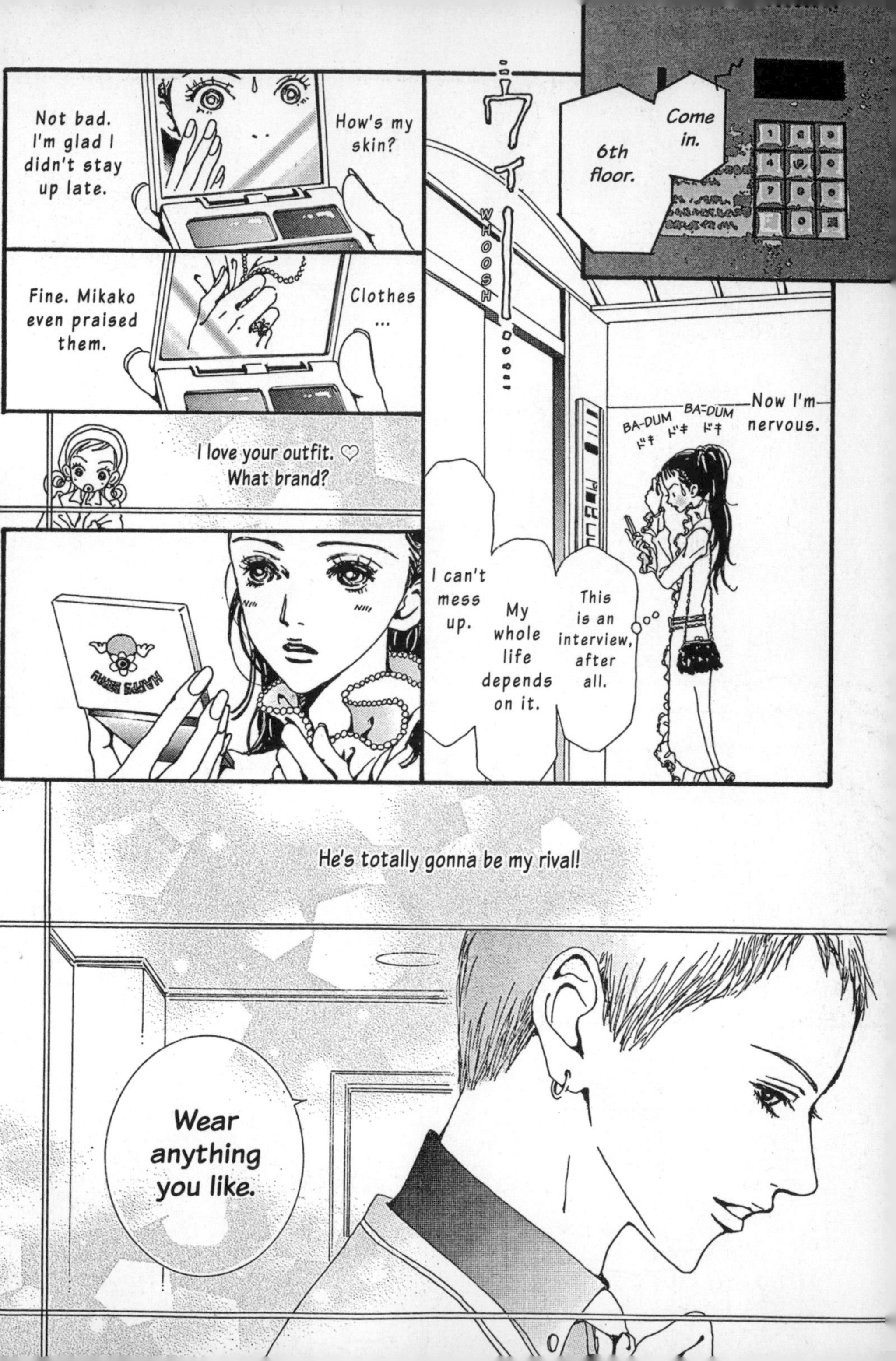
Come in.
6th floor.
WHOOSH
Now I'm nervous.
BA-DUM BA-DUM
ドキ ドキ ドキ
This is an interview, after all.
My whole life depends on it.
I can't mess up.
How's my skin?
Not bad. I'm glad I didn't stay up late.
Clothes...
Fine. Mikako even praised them.
I love your outfit. ♡ What brand?
He's totally gonna be my rival!
Wear anything you like.

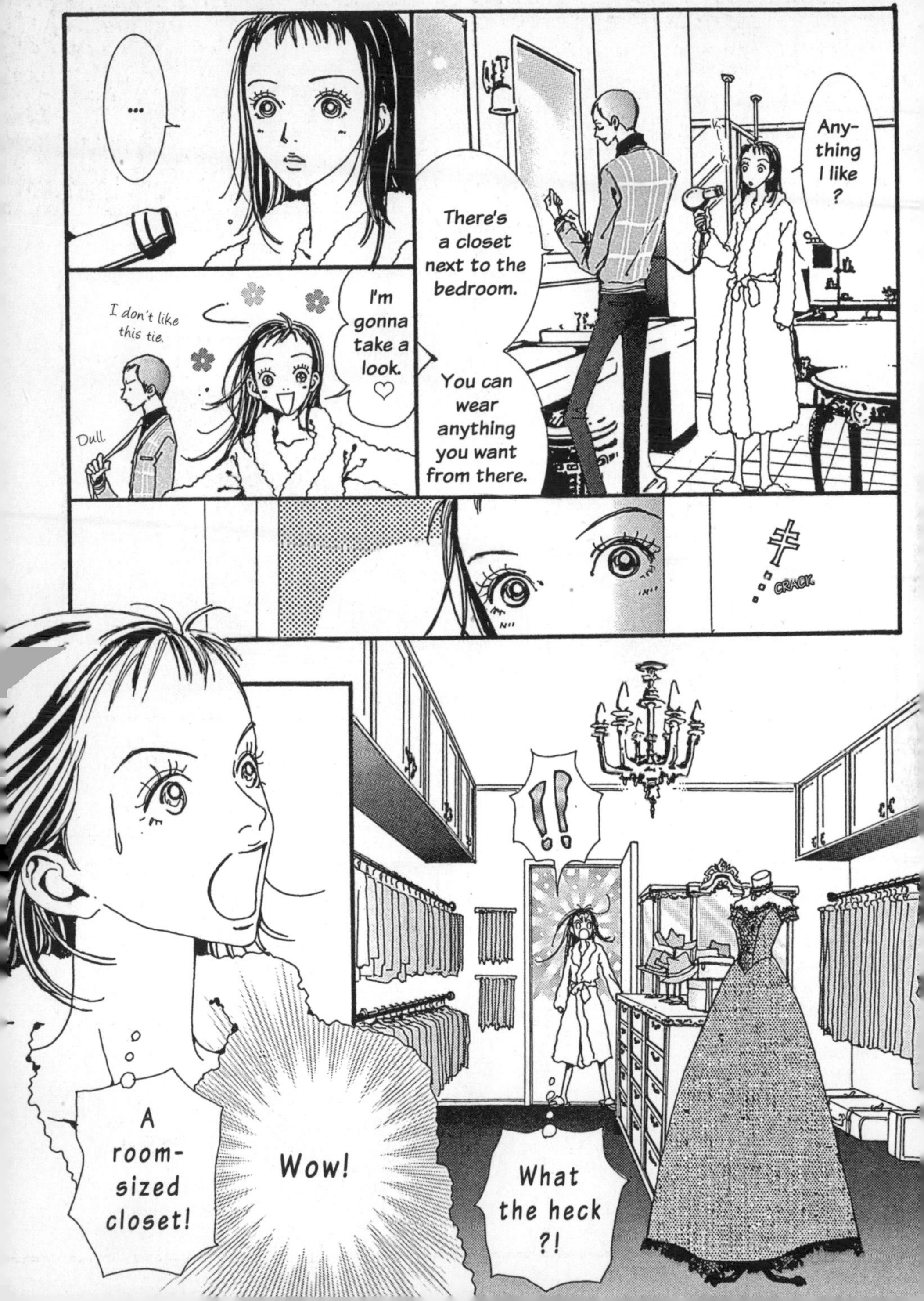
Any-thing I like?
There's a closet next to the bedroom.
You can wear anything you want from there.
...
I'm gonna take a look. ♡
I don't like this tie.
Dull.
CRACK
!!
What the heck?!
Wow!
A room-sized closet!

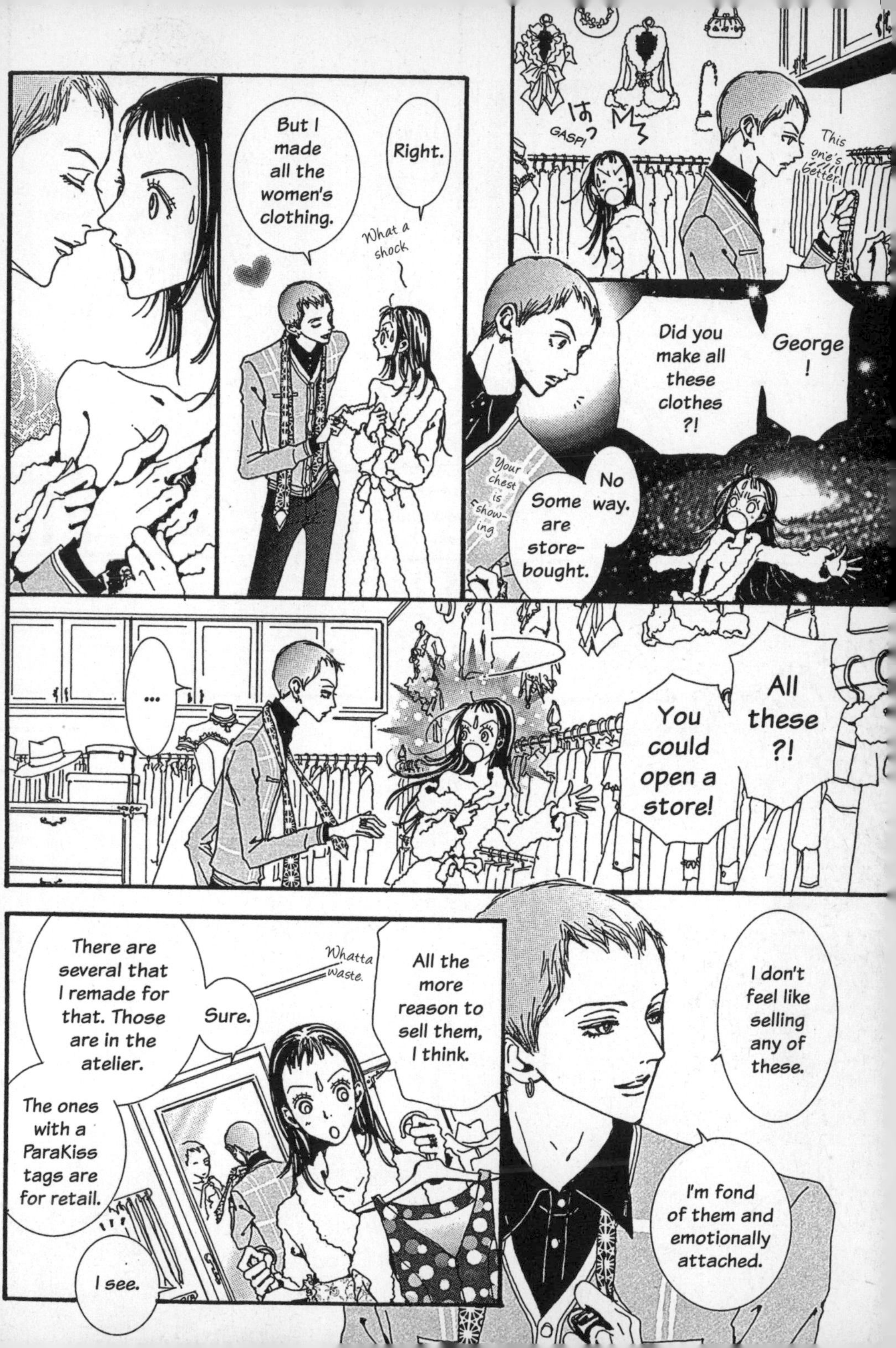

はっ
GASP!
This one's better.
George!
Did you make all these clothes?!
No way.
Some are store-bought.
Your chest is showing
Right.
But I made all the women's clothing.
What a shock
All these?!
You could open a store!
...
I don't feel like selling any of these.
I'm fond of them and emotionally attached.
All the more reason to sell them, I think.
Whatta waste.
Sure.
There are several that I remade for that. Those are in the atelier.
The ones with a ParaKiss tags are for retail.
I see.

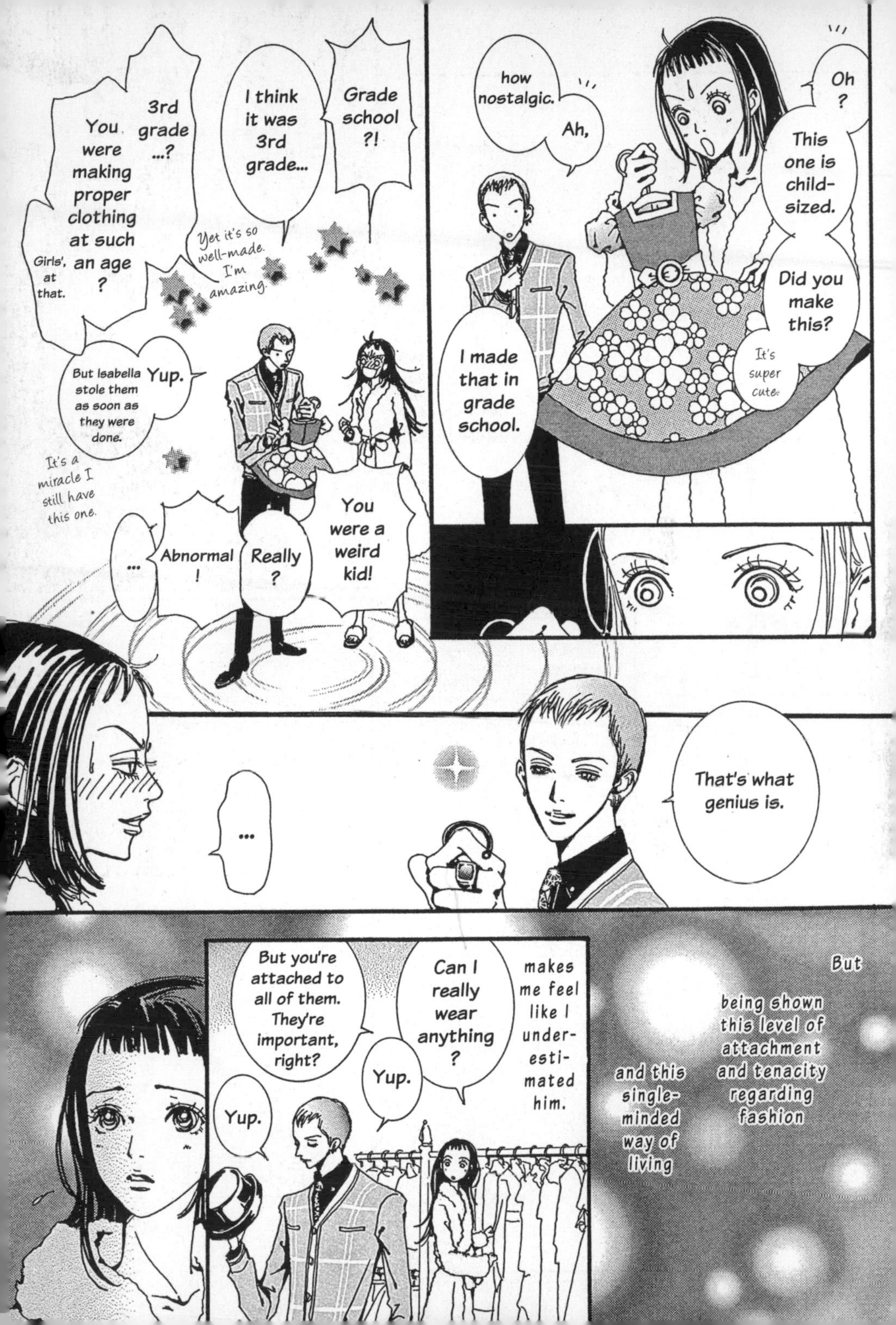
Oh?
This one is child-sized.
Did you make this?
It's super cute.
Ah,
how nostalgic.
I made that in grade school.
Grade school?!
I think it was 3rd grade...
3rd grade...?
You were making proper clothing at such an age?
Girls', at that.
Yet it's so well-made. I'm amazing.
Yup.
But Isabella stole them as soon as they were done.
It's a miracle I still have this one.
You were a weird kid!
Really?
Abnormal!
...
That's what genius is.
...
But
being shown this level of attachment and tenacity regarding fashion
and this single-minded way of living
makes me feel like I under-esti-mated him.
Can I really wear anything?
But you're attached to all of them. They're important, right?
Yup.
Yup.

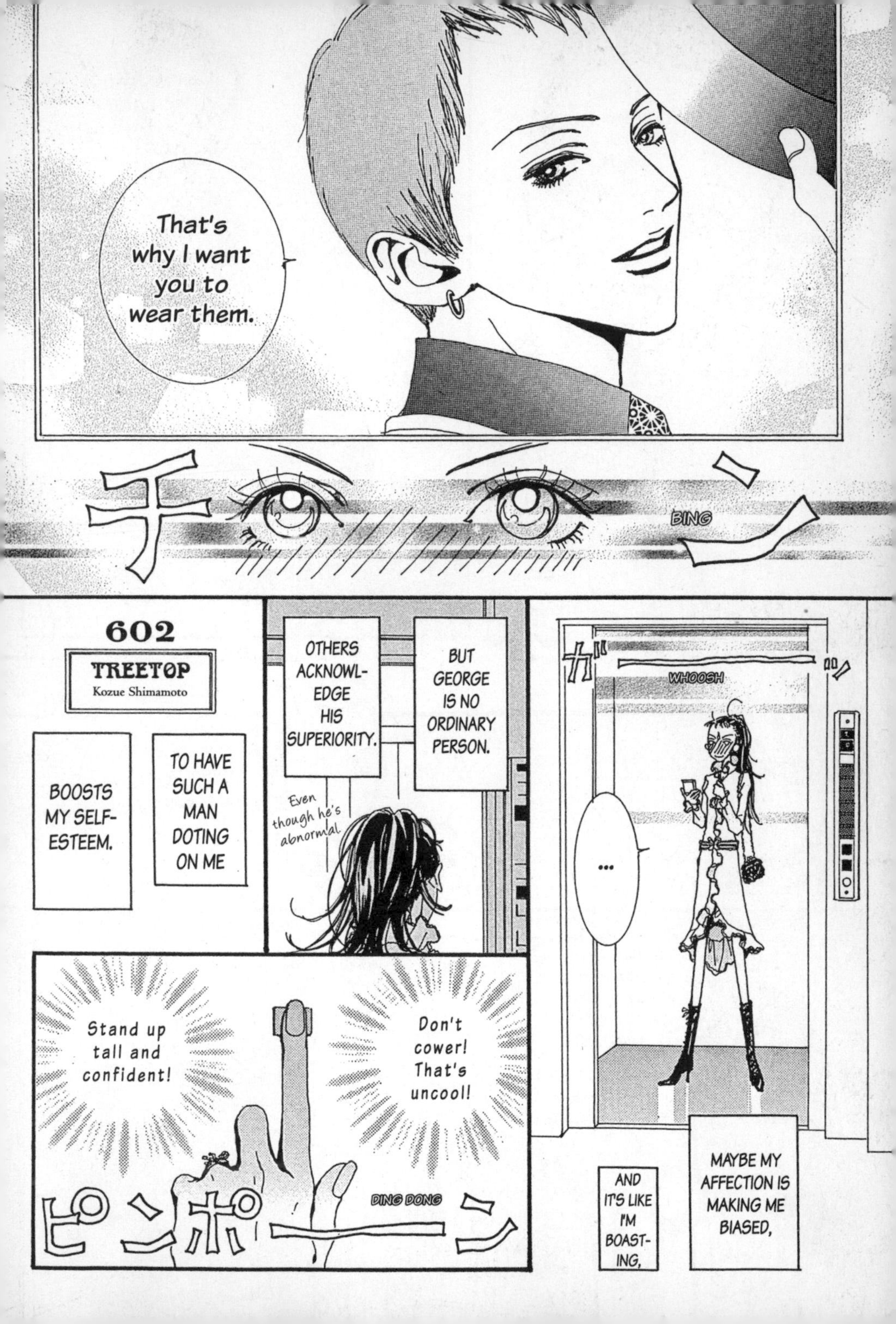
That's why I want you to wear them.
チーン
BING
WHOOSH
...
MAYBE MY AFFECTION IS MAKING ME BIASED,
AND IT'S LIKE I'M BOAST-ING,
BUT GEORGE IS NO ORDINARY PERSON.
OTHERS ACKNOWL-EDGE HIS SUPERIORITY.
Even though he's abnormal.
602
TREETOP
Kozue Shimamoto
TO HAVE SUCH A MAN DOTING ON ME
BOOSTS MY SELF-ESTEEM.
Don't cower! That's uncool!
Stand up tall and confident!
ピンポーン
DING DONG

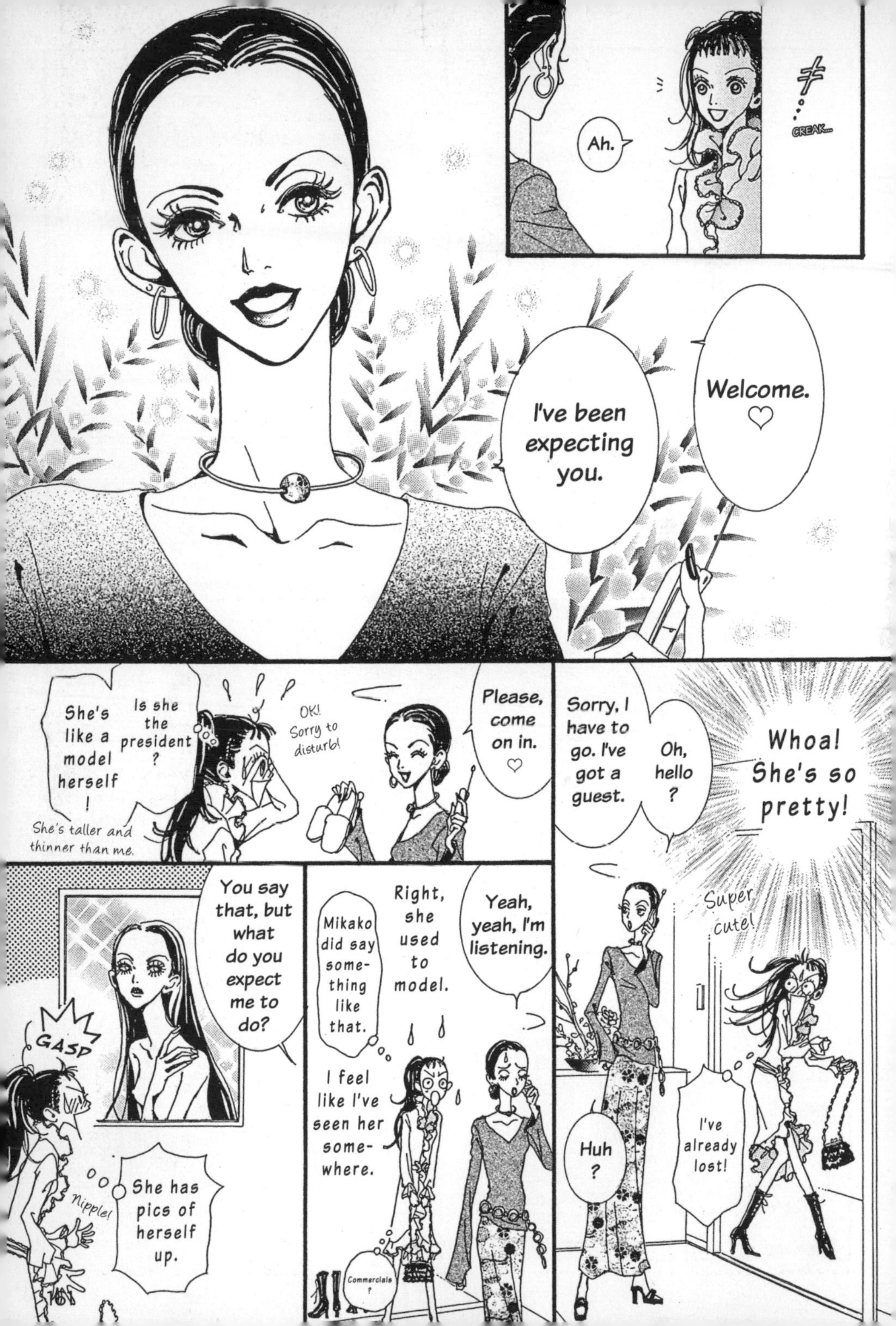
CREAK...
Ah.
Welcome. ♡
I've been expecting you.
Whoa! She's so pretty!
Oh, hello?
Sorry, I have to go. I've got a guest.
Super cute!
I've already lost!
Huh?
Please, come on in. ♡
OK! Sorry to disturb!
Is she the president?
She's like a model herself!
She's taller and thinner than me.
Yeah, yeah, I'm listening.
Right, she used to model.
Mikako did say something like that.
I feel like I've seen her somewhere.
Commercials?
You say that, but what do you expect me to do?
GASP
She has pics of herself up.
Nipple!

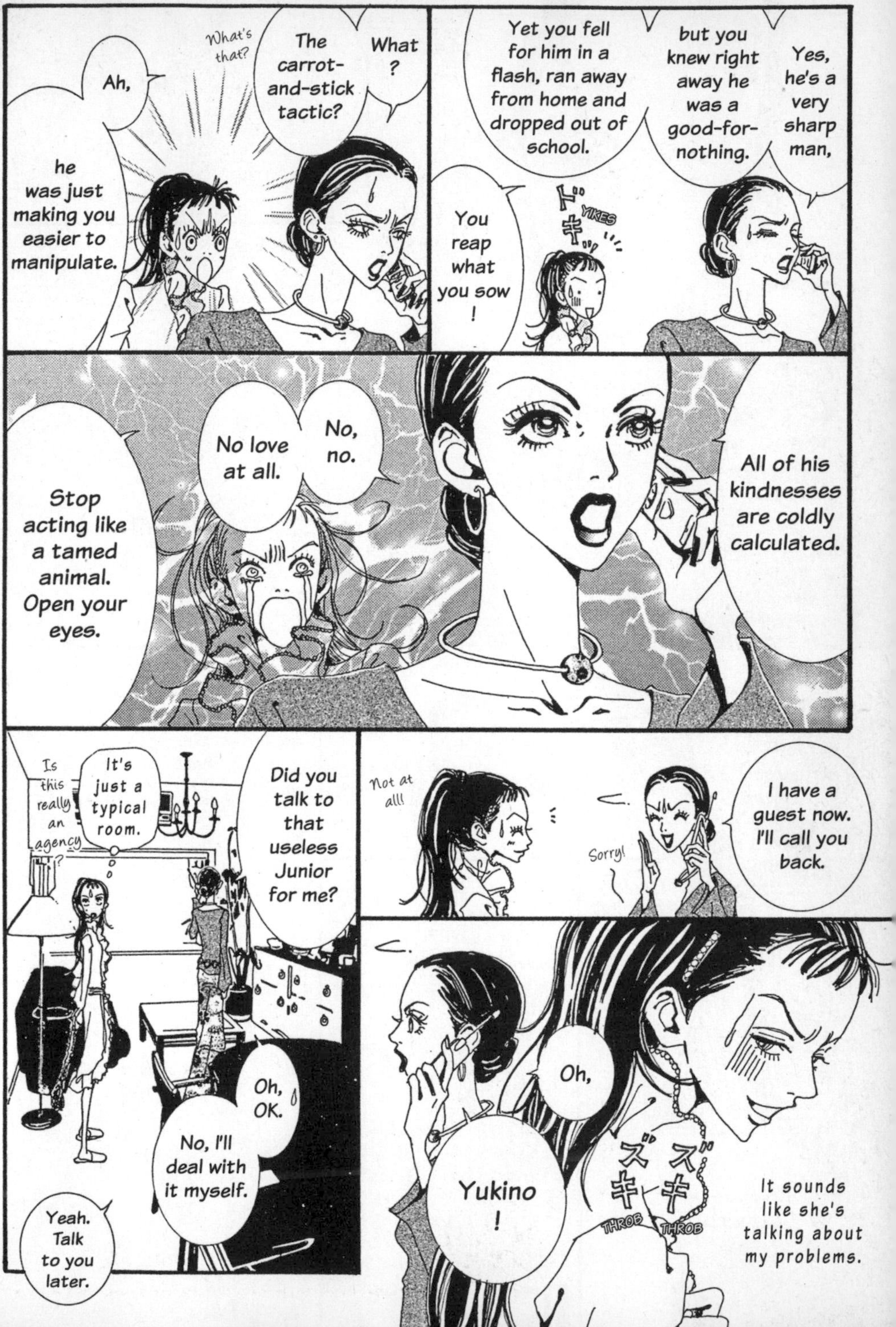
Yes, he's a very sharp man,
but you knew right away he was a good-for-nothing.
Yet you fell for him in a flash, ran away from home and dropped out of school.
YIKES
You reap what you sow!
What?
The carrot-and-stick tactic?
What's that?
Ah,
he was just making you easier to manipulate.
All of his kindnesses are coldly calculated.
No, no.
No love at all.
Stop acting like a tamed animal. Open your eyes.
I have a guest now. I'll call you back.
Sorry!
Not at all!
It sounds like she's talking about my problems.
THROB THROB
Oh,
Yukino!
Did you talk to that useless Junior for me?
It's just a typical room.
Is this really an agency?
Oh, OK.
No, I'll deal with it myself.
Yeah. Talk to you later.

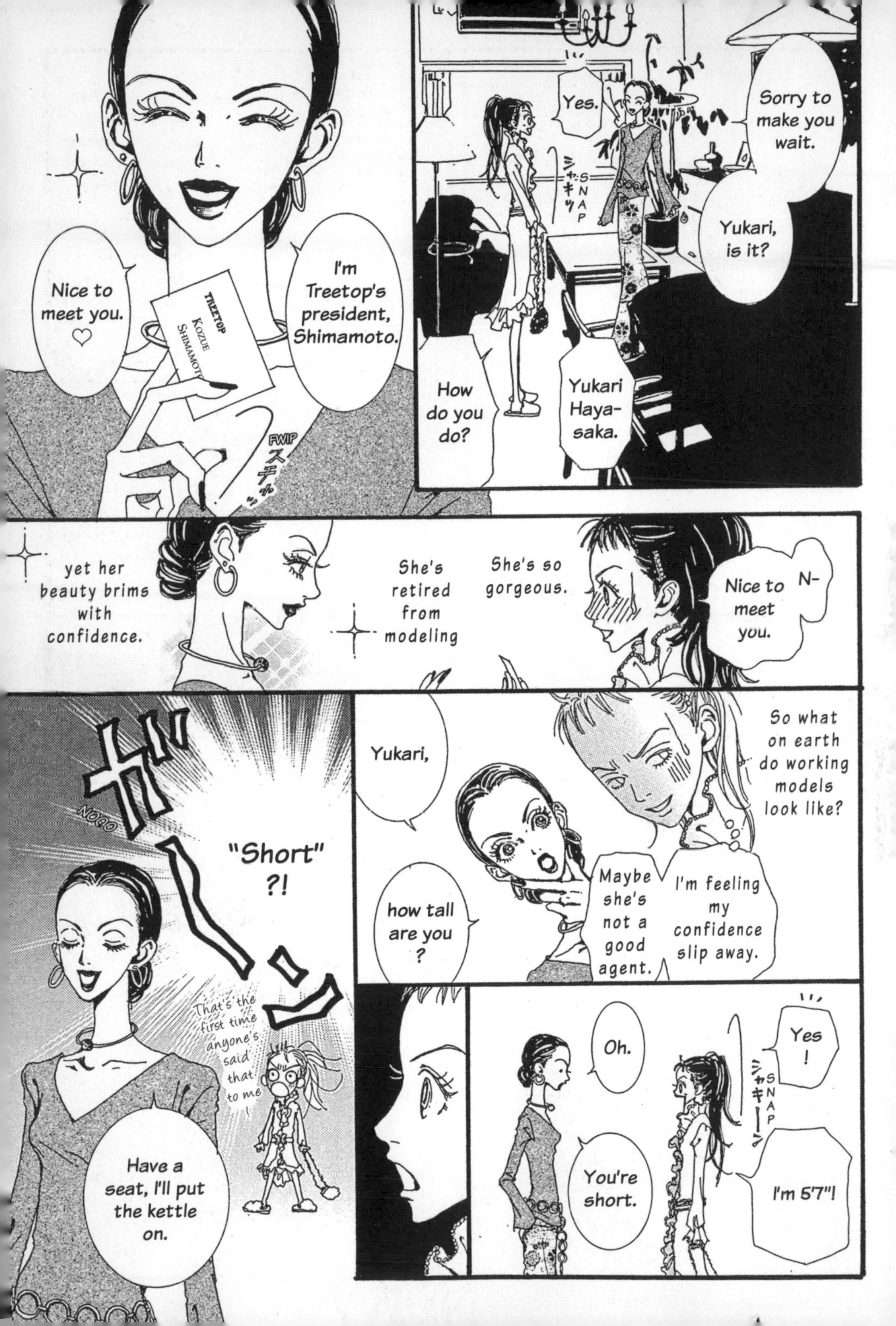
Sorry to make you wait.
Yukari, is it?
Yes.
SNAP
Yukari Haya-saka.
How do you do?
I'm Treetop's president, Shimamoto.
TREETOP KOZUE SHIMAMOTO
Nice to meet you. ♡
FWIP
N- Nice to meet you.
She's so gorgeous.
She's retired from modeling
yet her beauty brims with confidence.
So what on earth do working models look like?
Yukari,
how tall are you?
I'm feeling my confidence slip away.
Maybe she's not a good agent.
Yes!
SNAP
I'm 5'7"!
Oh.
You're short.
"Short" ?!
That's the first time anyone's said that to me!
Have a seat, I'll put the kettle on.

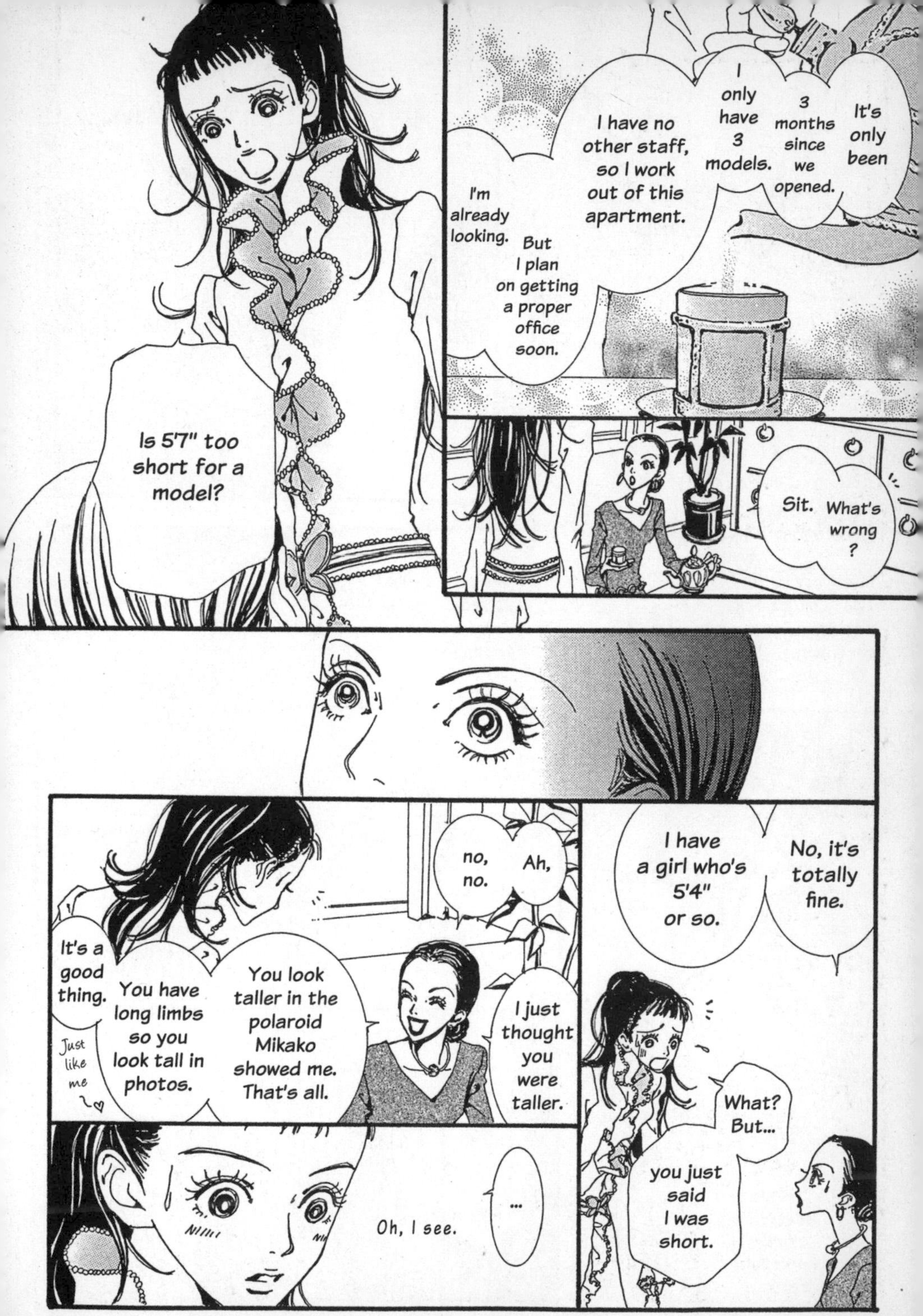
It's only been 3 months since we opened.
I only have 3 models.
I have no other staff, so I work out of this apartment.
But I plan on getting a proper office soon.
I'm already looking.
What's wrong?
Sit.
Is 5'7" too short for a model?
No, it's totally fine.
I have a girl who's 5'4" or so.
What? But...
you just said I was short.
Ah,
no, no.
I just thought you were taller.
You look taller in the polaroid Mikako showed me. That's all.
You have long limbs so you look tall in photos.
It's a good thing.
Just like me ~♡
...
Oh, I see.

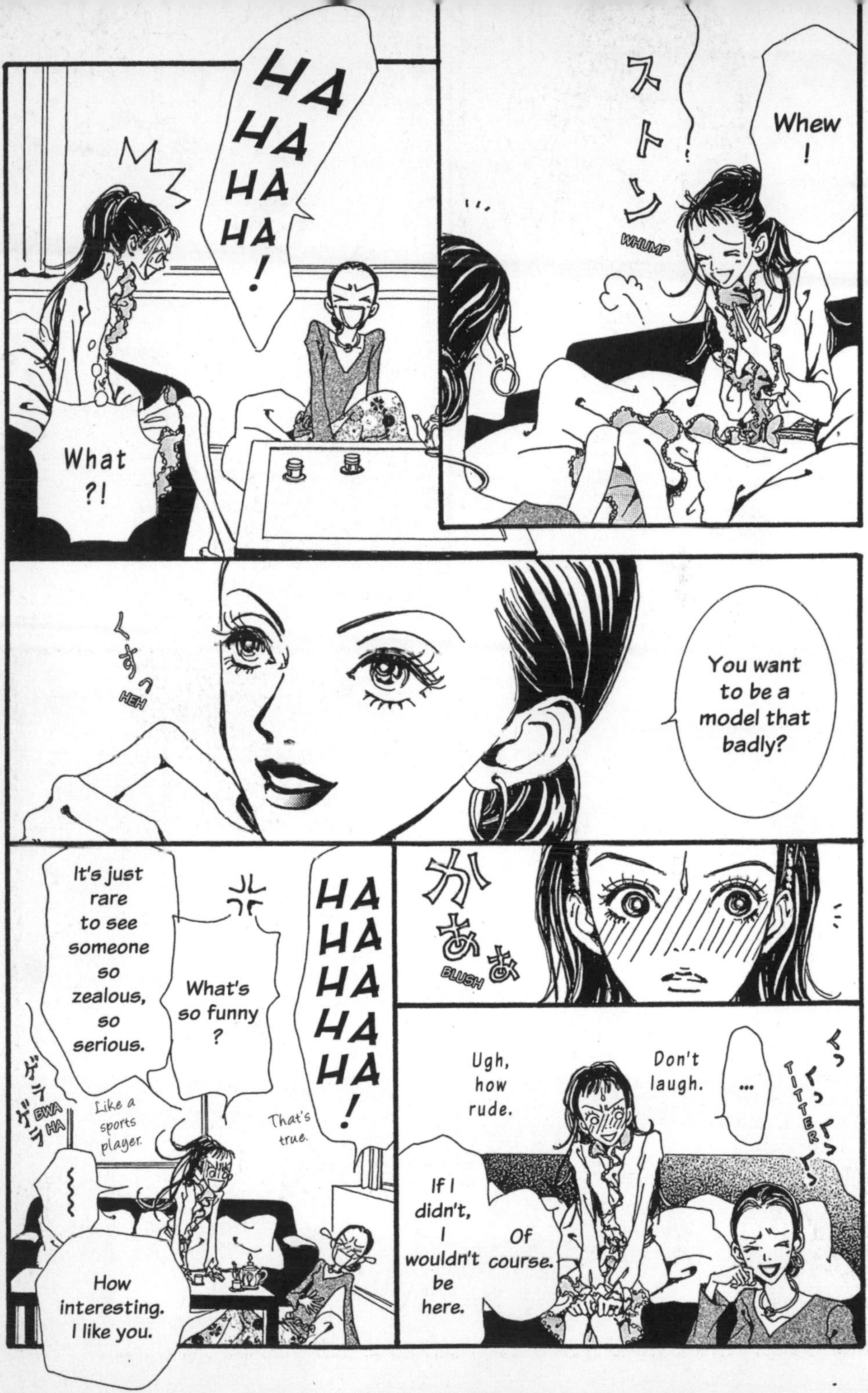
Whew!
ストン
WHUMP
...
HA HA HA HA!
What?!
くすっ
HEH
You want to be a model that badly?
かぁぁ
BLUSH
Don't laugh.
...
くっくっくっくっ
TITTER
Ugh, how rude.
Of course.
If I didn't, I wouldn't be here.
HA HA HA HA HA!
What's so funny?
It's just rare to see someone so zealous, so serious.
That's true.
Like a sports player.
ゲラゲラ
BWA HA
How interesting. I like you.

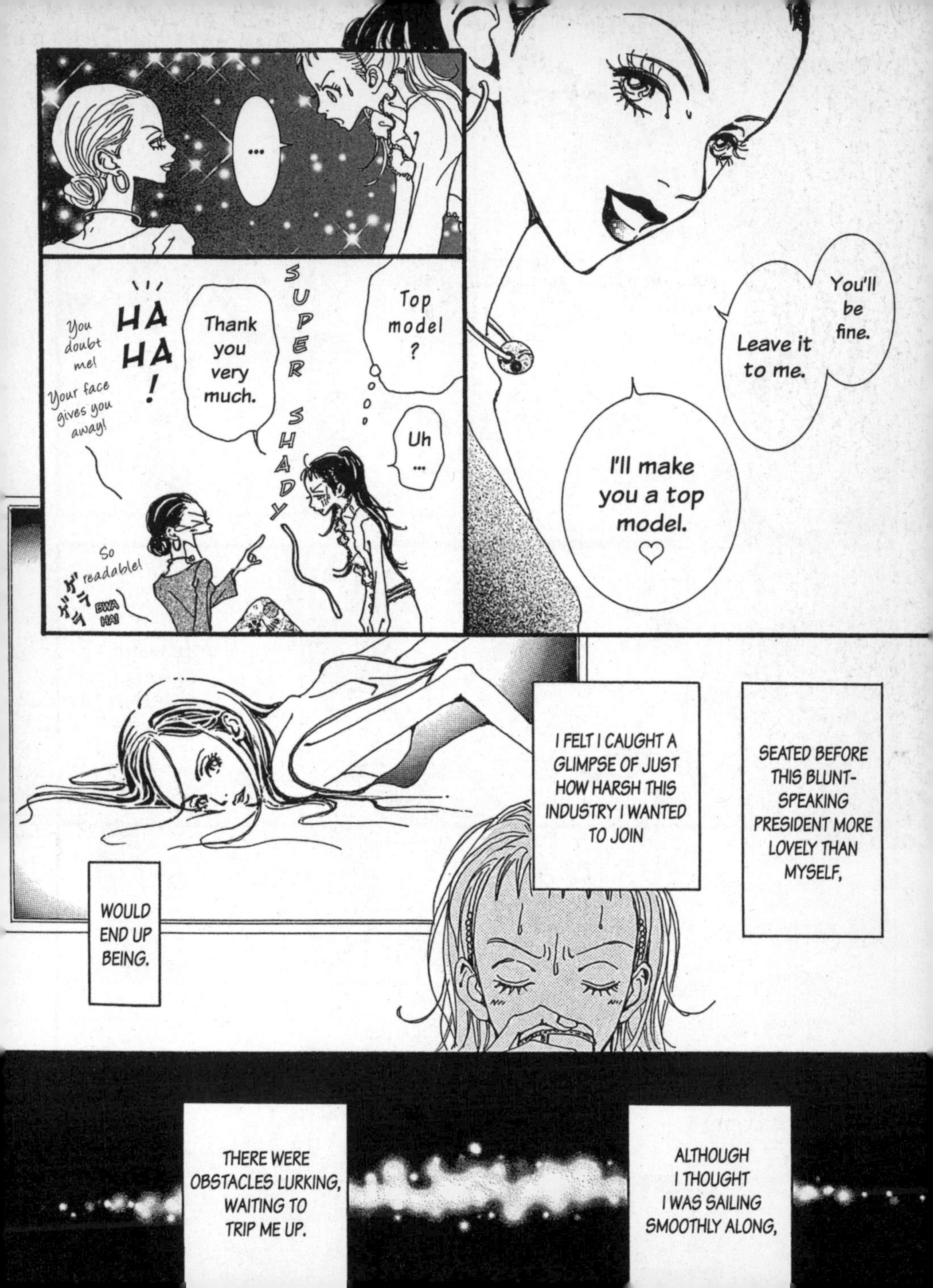
You'll be fine.
Leave it to me.
I'll make you a top model. ♡
...
Top model?
Uh ...
SUPER SHADY
Thank you very much.
HA HA!
You doubt me! Your face gives you away!
So readable!
BWA HA!
SEATED BEFORE THIS BLUNT-SPEAKING PRESIDENT MORE LOVELY THAN MYSELF,
I FELT I CAUGHT A GLIMPSE OF JUST HOW HARSH THIS INDUSTRY I WANTED TO JOIN
WOULD END UP BEING.
ALTHOUGH I THOUGHT I WAS SAILING SMOOTHLY ALONG,
THERE WERE OBSTACLES LURKING, WAITING TO TRIP ME UP.

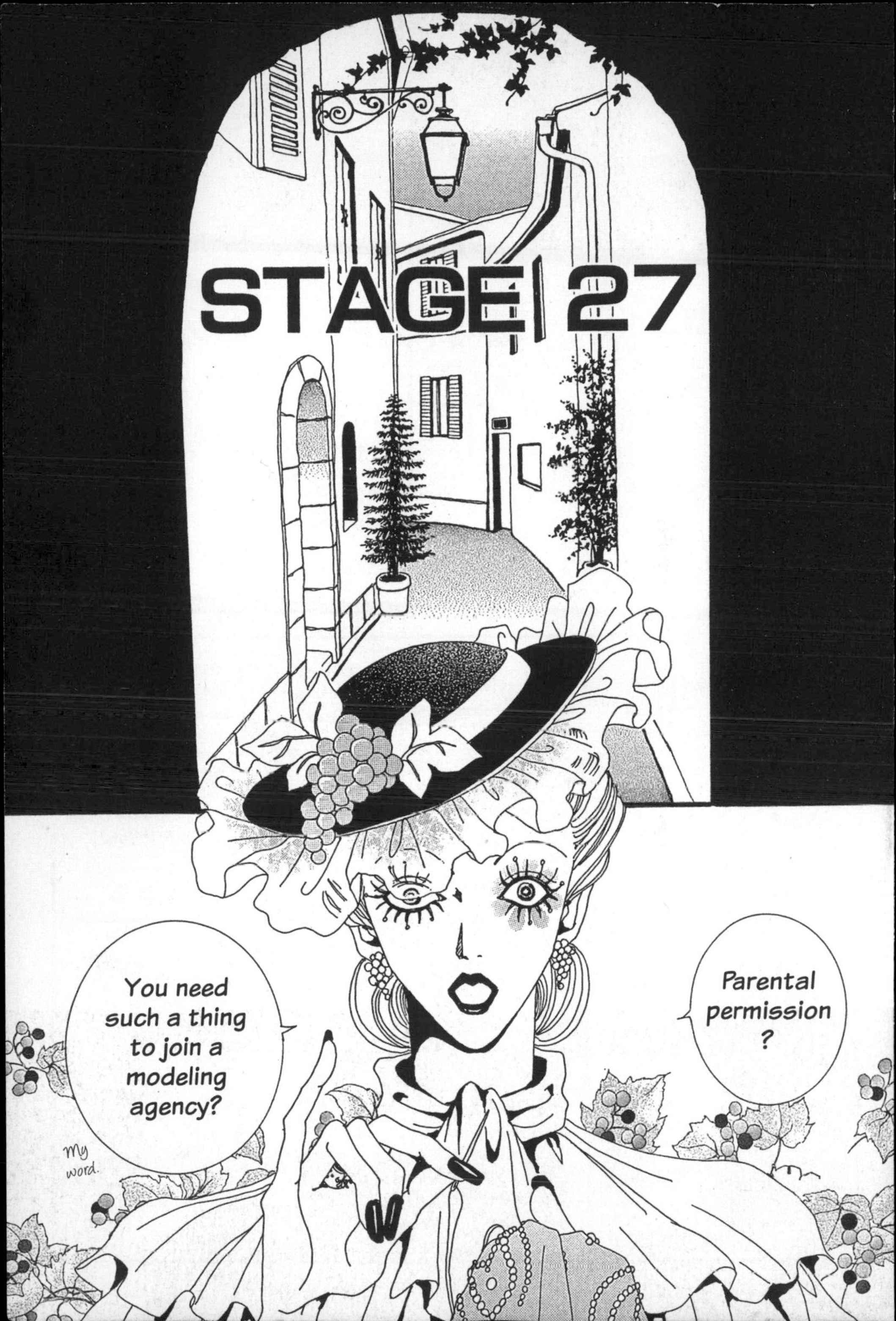
STAGE 27
Parental permission ?
You need such a thing to join a modeling agency?
My word.

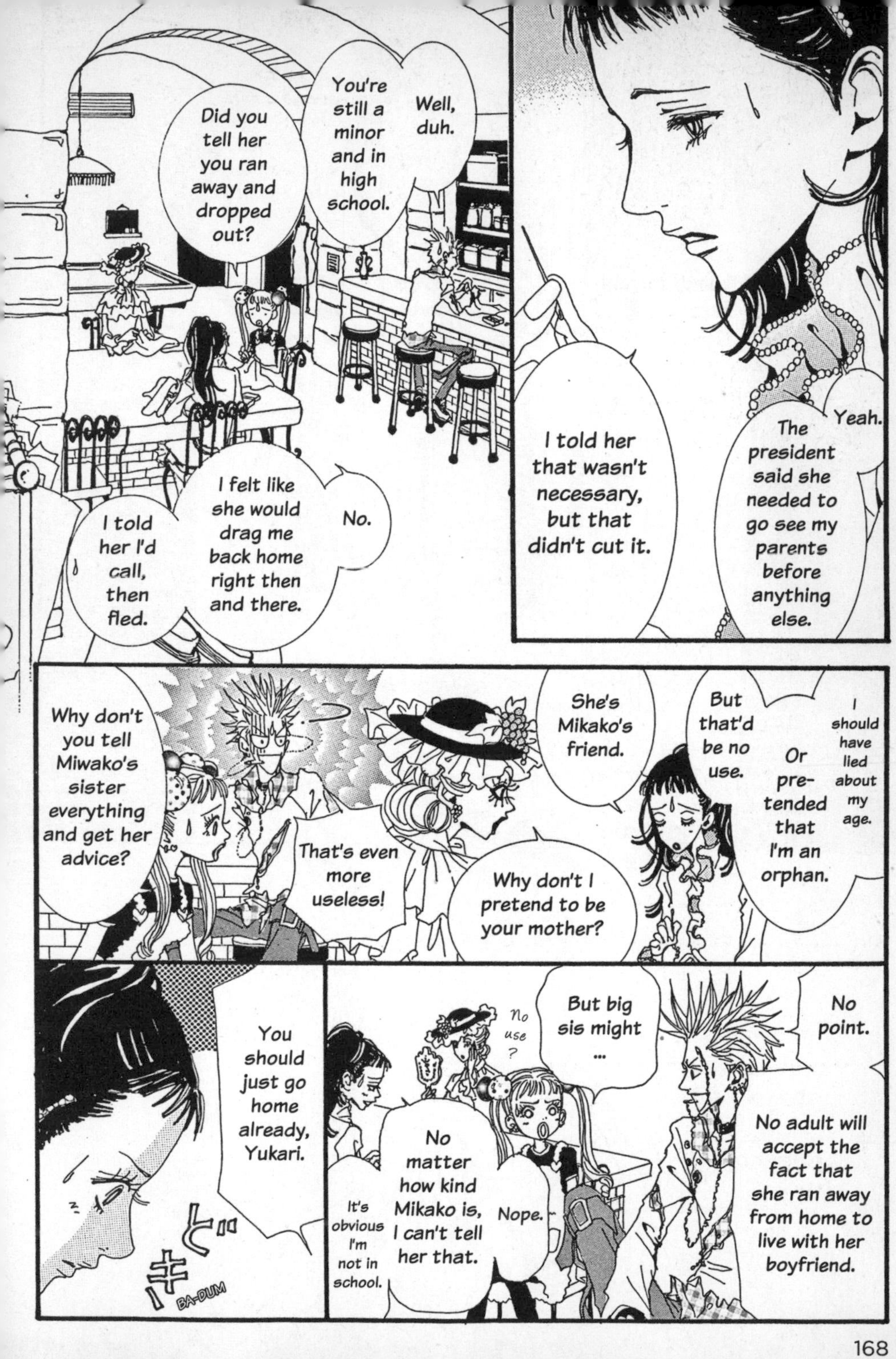

Yeah.
The president said she needed to go see my parents before anything else.
I told her that wasn't necessary, but that didn't cut it.
Well, duh.
You're still a minor and in high school.
Did you tell her you ran away and dropped out?
No.
I felt like she would drag me back home right then and there.
I told her I'd call, then fled.
I should have lied about my age.
Or pretended that I'm an orphan.
But that'd be no use.
She's Mikako's friend.
Why don't I pretend to be your mother?
That's even more useless!
Why don't you tell Miwako's sister everything and get her advice?
No point.
No adult will accept the fact that she ran away from home to live with her boyfriend.
But big sis might ...
No use ?
Nope.
No matter how kind Mikako is, I can't tell her that.
It's obvious I'm not in school.
You should just go home already, Yukari.
BA-DUM

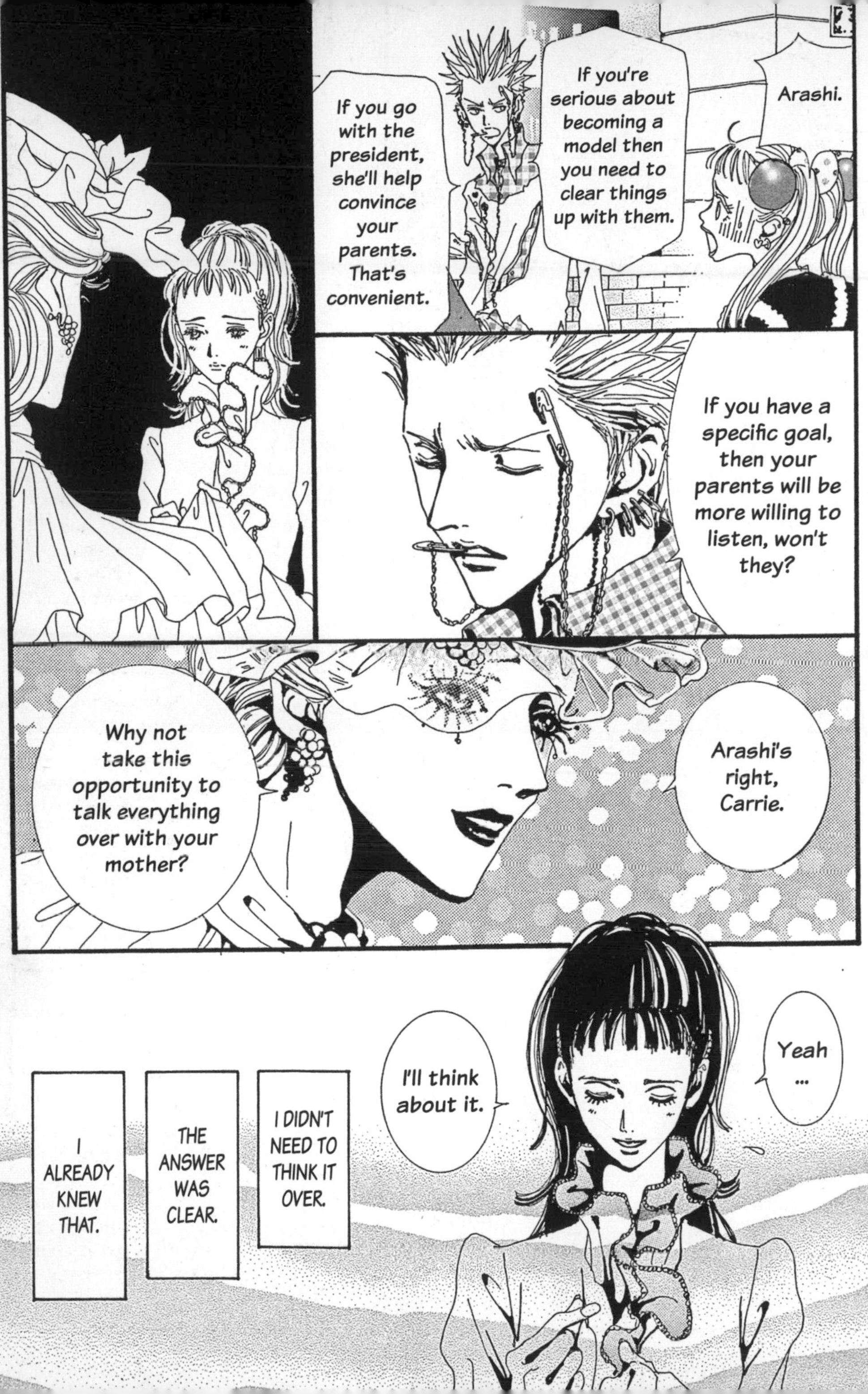
Arashi.
If you're serious about becoming a model then you need to clear things up with them.
If you go with the president, she'll help convince your parents. That's convenient.
If you have a specific goal, then your parents will be more willing to listen, won't they?
Arashi's right, Carrie.
Why not take this opportunity to talk everything over with your mother?
Yeah ...
I'll think about it.
I DIDN'T NEED TO THINK IT OVER.
THE ANSWER WAS CLEAR.
I ALREADY KNEW THAT.

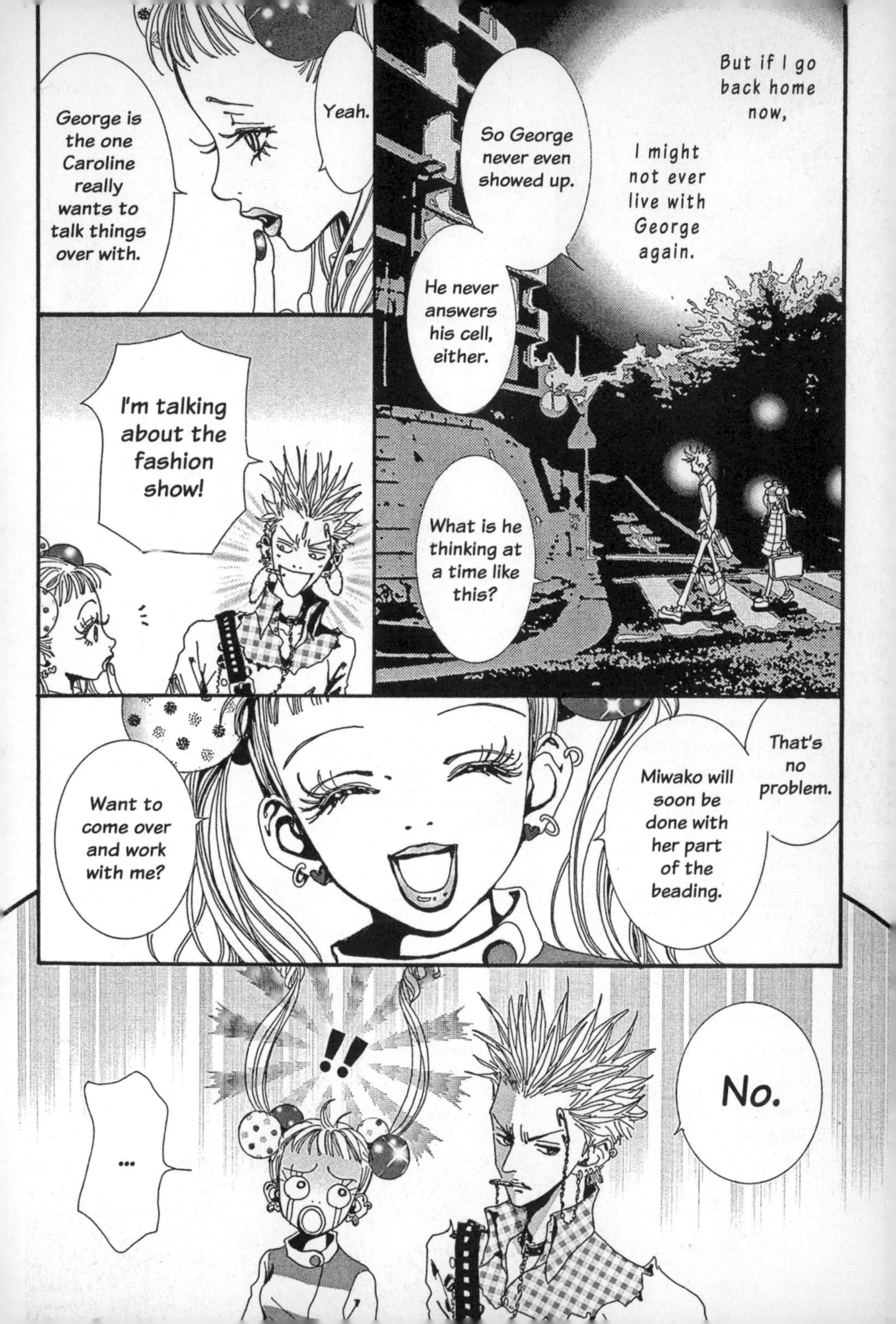

But if I go back home now,
I might not ever live with George again.
So George never even showed up.
He never answers his cell, either.
What is he thinking at a time like this?
Yeah.
George is the one Caroline really wants to talk things over with.
I'm talking about the fashion show!
That's no problem.
Miwako will soon be done with her part of the beading.
Want to come over and work with me?
No.
!!
...

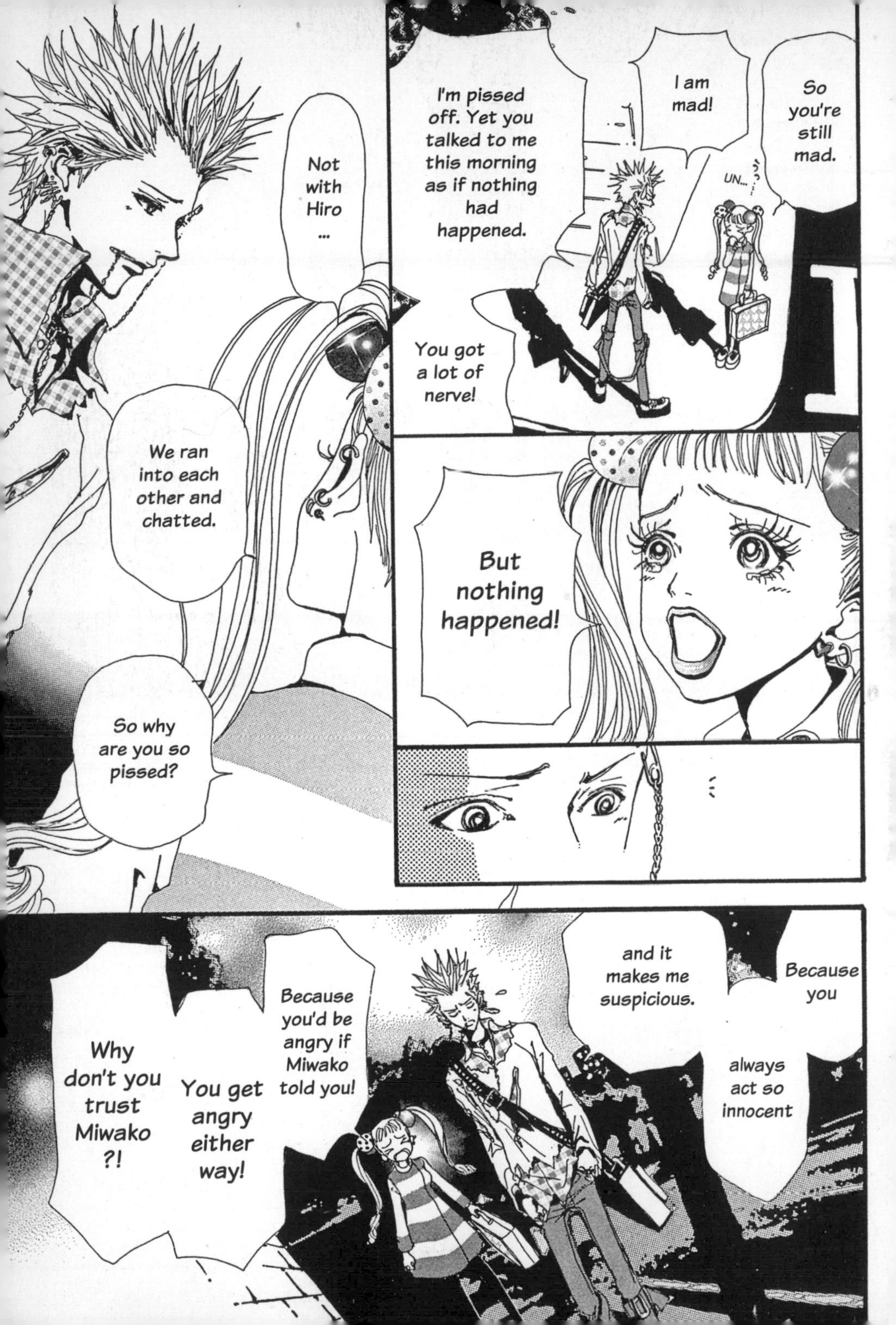
So you're still mad.
UN...
I am mad!
I'm pissed off. Yet you talked to me this morning as if nothing had happened.
You got a lot of nerve!
But nothing happened!
Not with Hiro ...
We ran into each other and chatted.
So why are you so pissed?
Because you
always act so innocent
and it makes me suspicious.
Because you'd be angry if Miwako told you!
You get angry either way!
Why don't you trust Miwako ?!

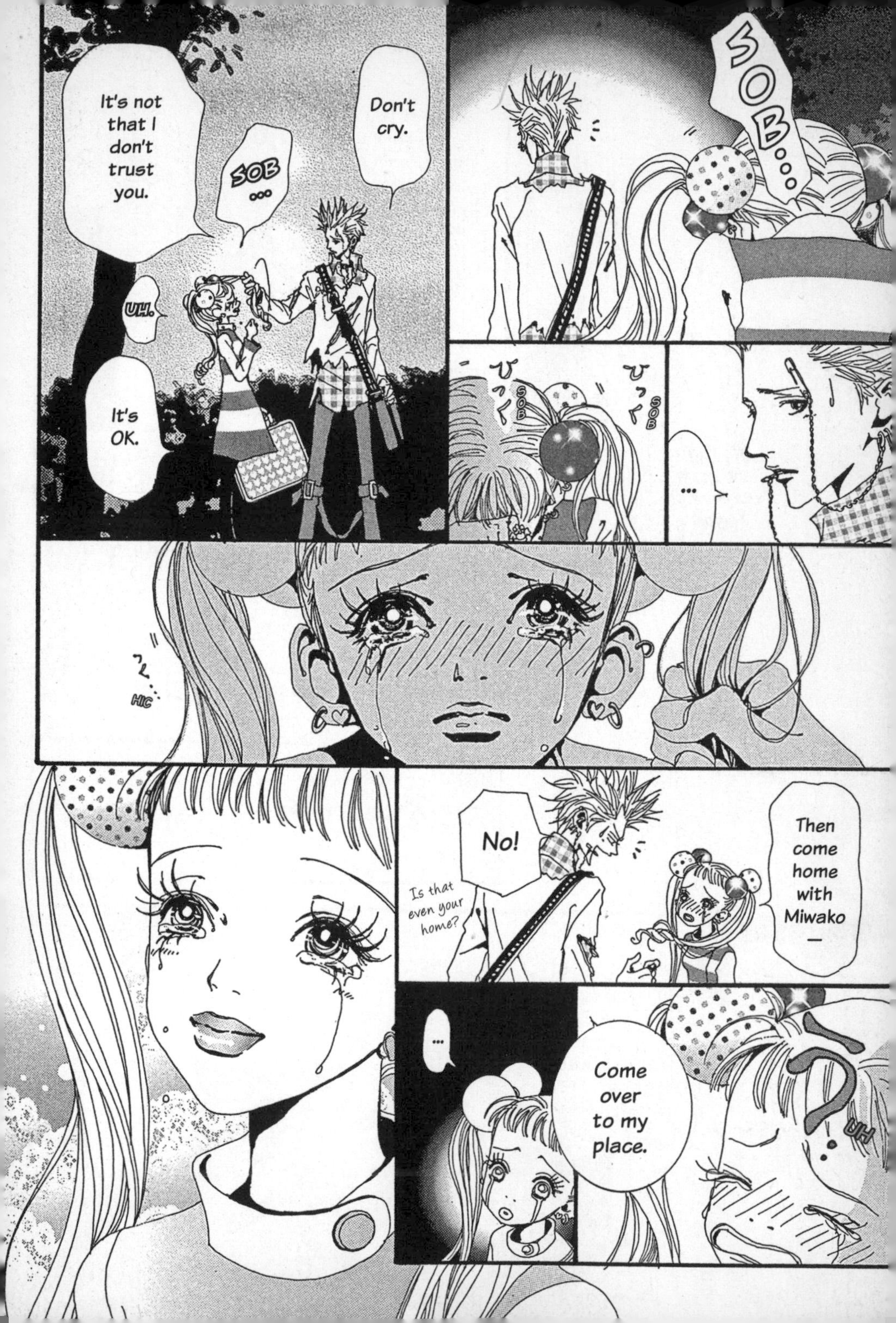
SOB...
...
SOB
SOB
Don't cry.
SOB...
It's not that I don't trust you.
UH.
It's OK.
HIC...
Then come home with Miwako —
No!
Is that even your home?
UH
Come over to my place.
...

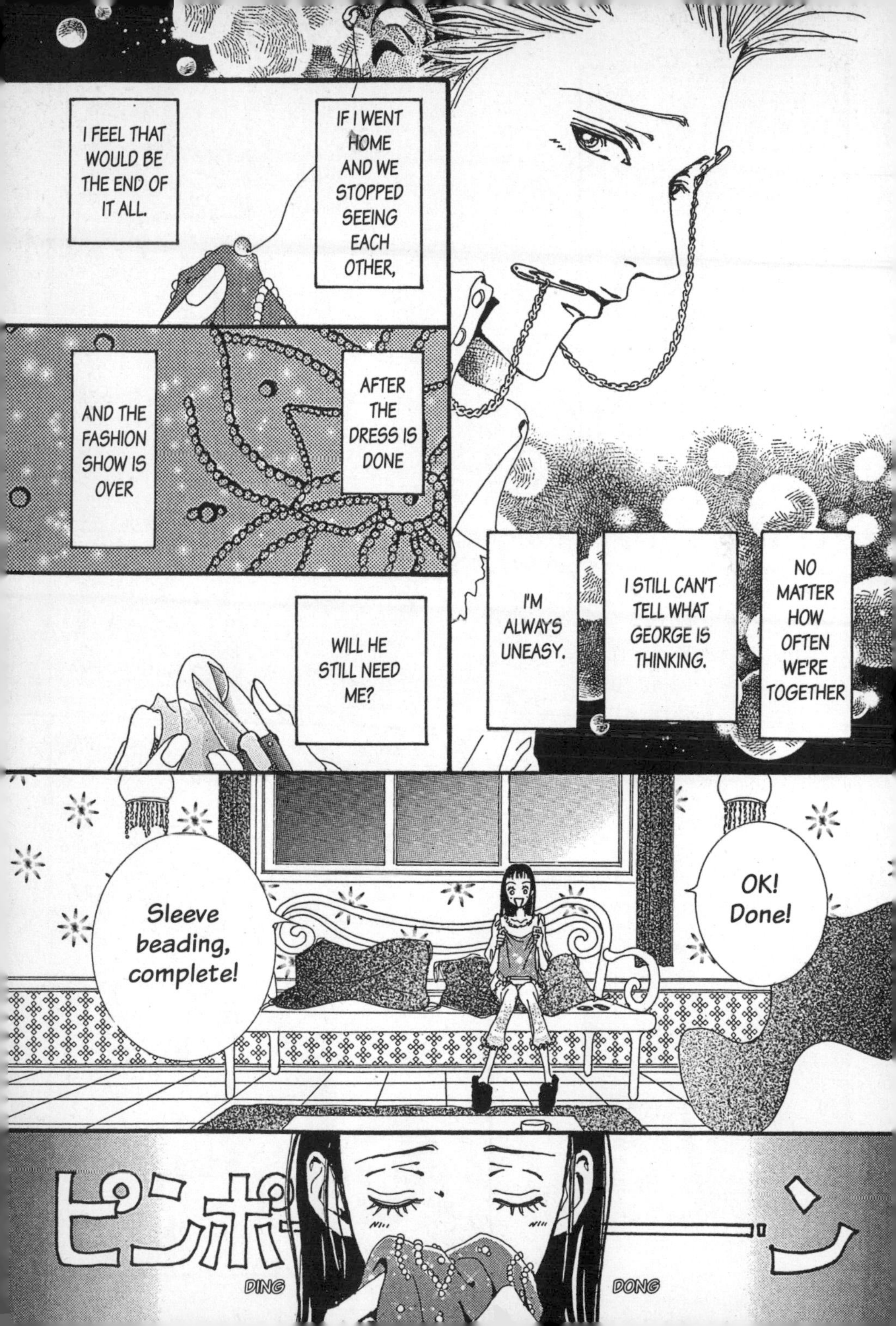
NO MATTER HOW OFTEN WE'RE TOGETHER
I STILL CAN'T TELL WHAT GEORGE IS THINKING.
I'M ALWAYS UNEASY.
IF I WENT HOME AND WE STOPPED SEEING EACH OTHER,
I FEEL THAT WOULD BE THE END OF IT ALL.
AFTER THE DRESS IS DONE
AND THE FASHION SHOW IS OVER
WILL HE STILL NEED ME?
OK! Done!
Sleeve beading, complete!
ピンポーン
DING
DONG

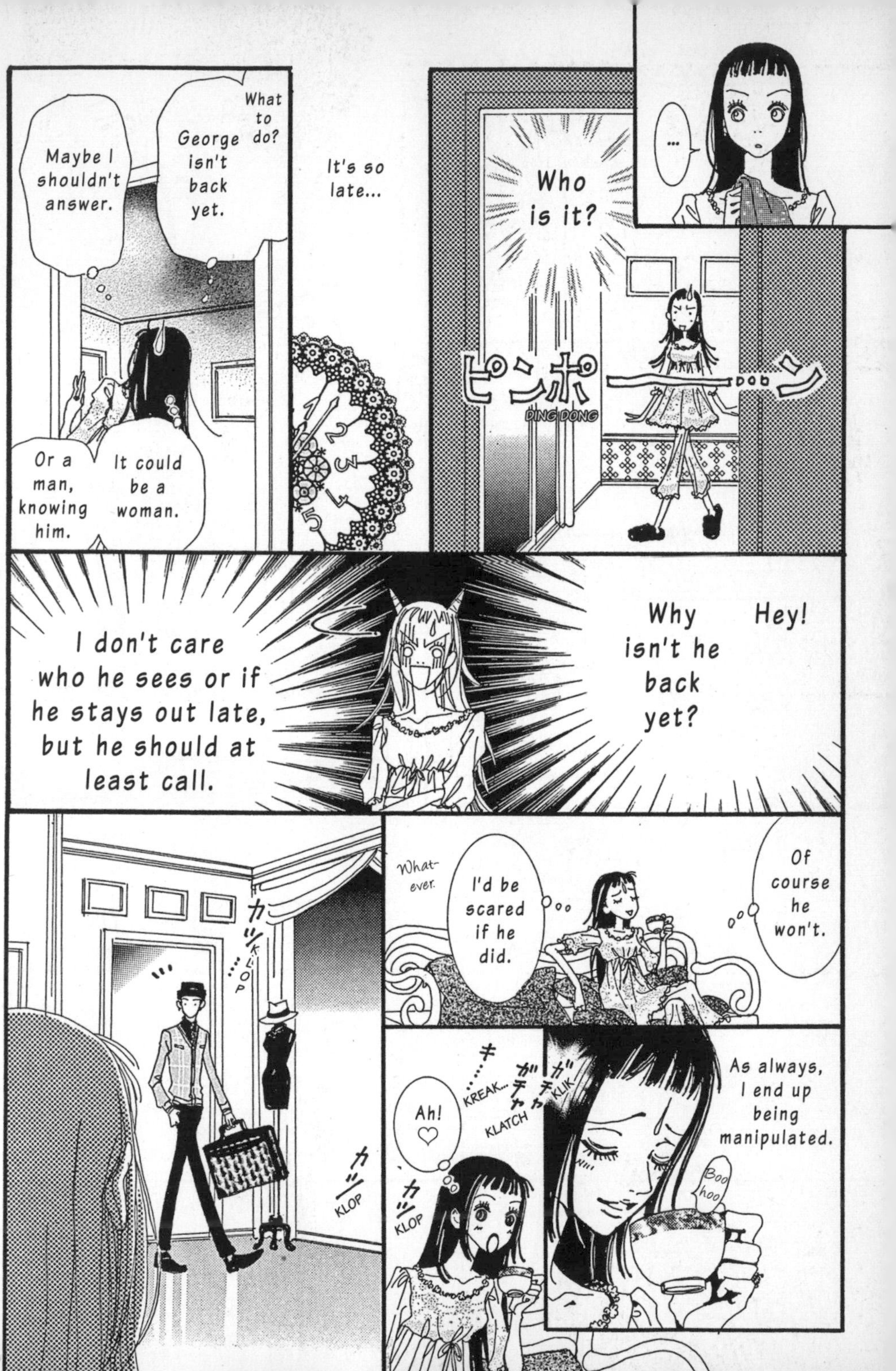
...
Who is it?
ピンポーン
DING DONG
It's so late...
What to do?
George isn't back yet.
Maybe I shouldn't answer.
It could be a woman.
Or a man, knowing him.
Hey!
Why isn't he back yet?
I don't care who he sees or if he stays out late, but he should at least call.
Of course he won't.
I'd be scared if he did.
Whatever.
As always, I end up being manipulated.
Boo hoo
ガチャ KLIK
ガチャ KLATCH
キ... KREAK...
Ah! ♡
カッ KLOP
カッ KLOP
カッ... KLOP

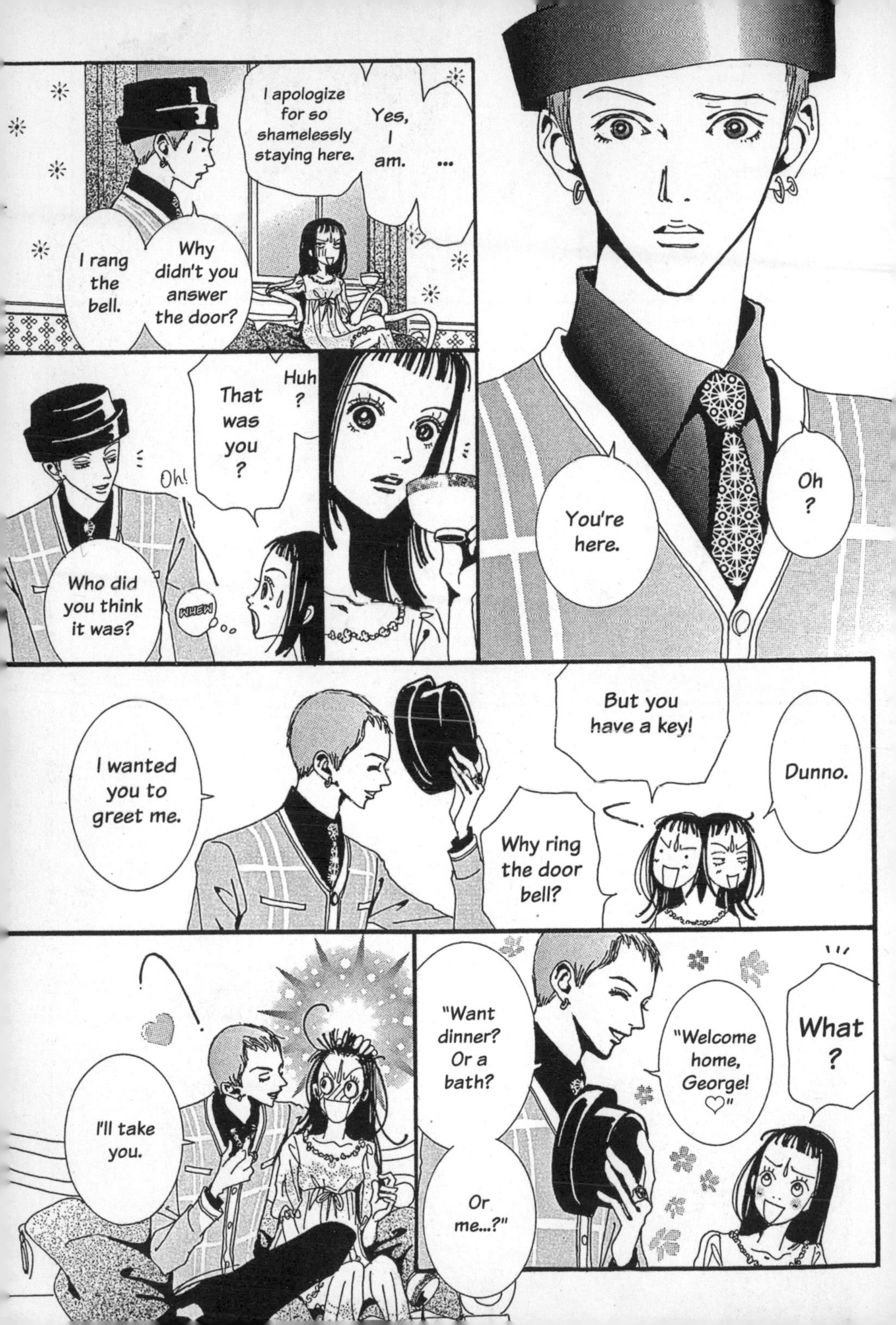
Oh?
You're here.
...
Yes, I am.
I apologize for so shamelessly staying here.
Why didn't you answer the door?
I rang the bell.
Huh?
That was you?
Oh!
WHEW
Who did you think it was?
Dunno.
But you have a key!
Why ring the door bell?
I wanted you to greet me.
What?
"Welcome home, George! ♡"
"Want dinner? Or a bath?
Or me...?"
I'll take you.

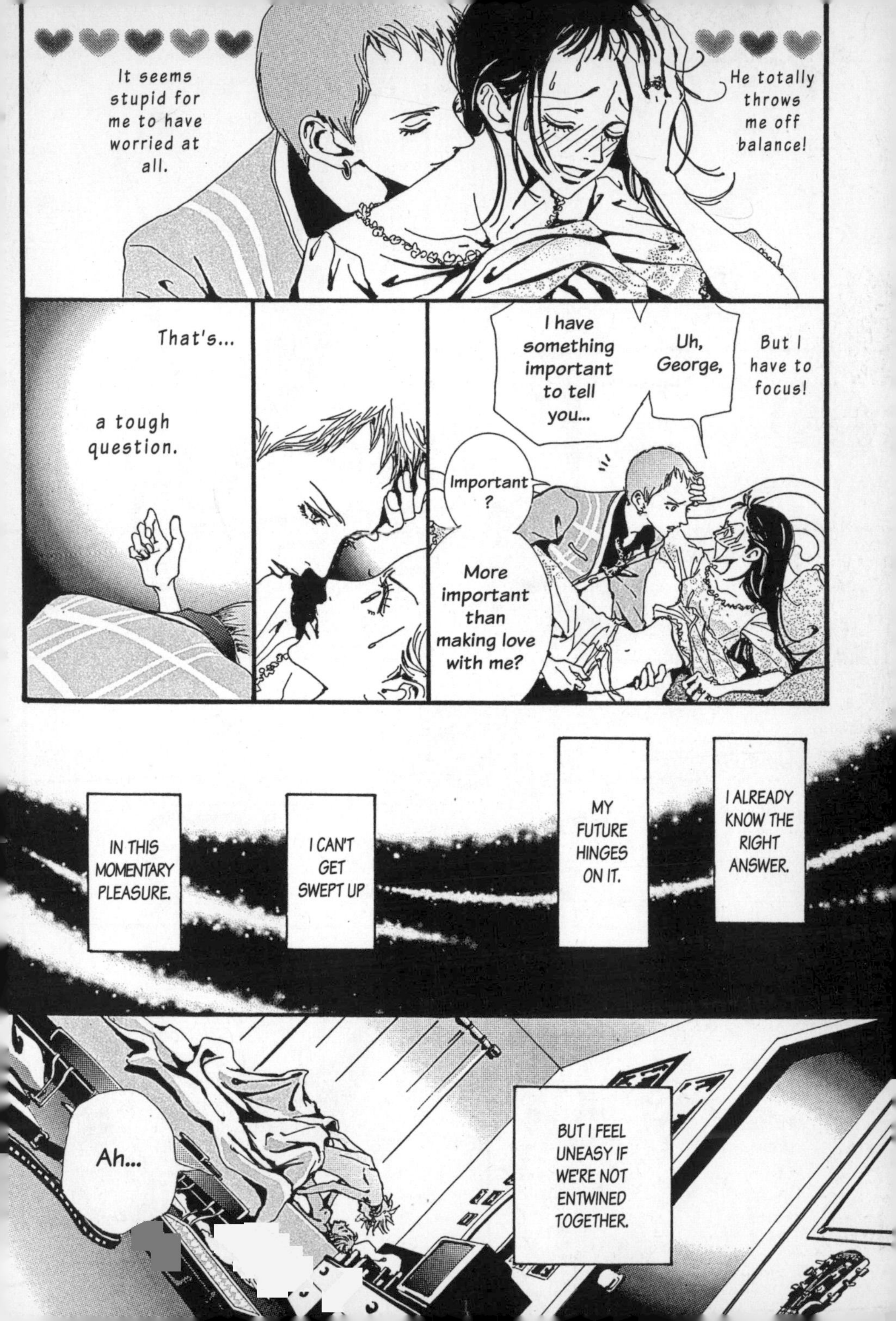
He totally throws me off balance!
It seems stupid for me to have worried at all.
But I have to focus!
Uh, George,
I have something important to tell you...
Important ?
More important than making love with me?
That's...
a tough question.
I ALREADY KNOW THE RIGHT ANSWER.
MY FUTURE HINGES ON IT.
I CAN'T GET SWEPT UP
IN THIS MOMENTARY PLEASURE.
BUT I FEEL UNEASY IF WE'RE NOT ENTWINED TOGETHER.
Ah...

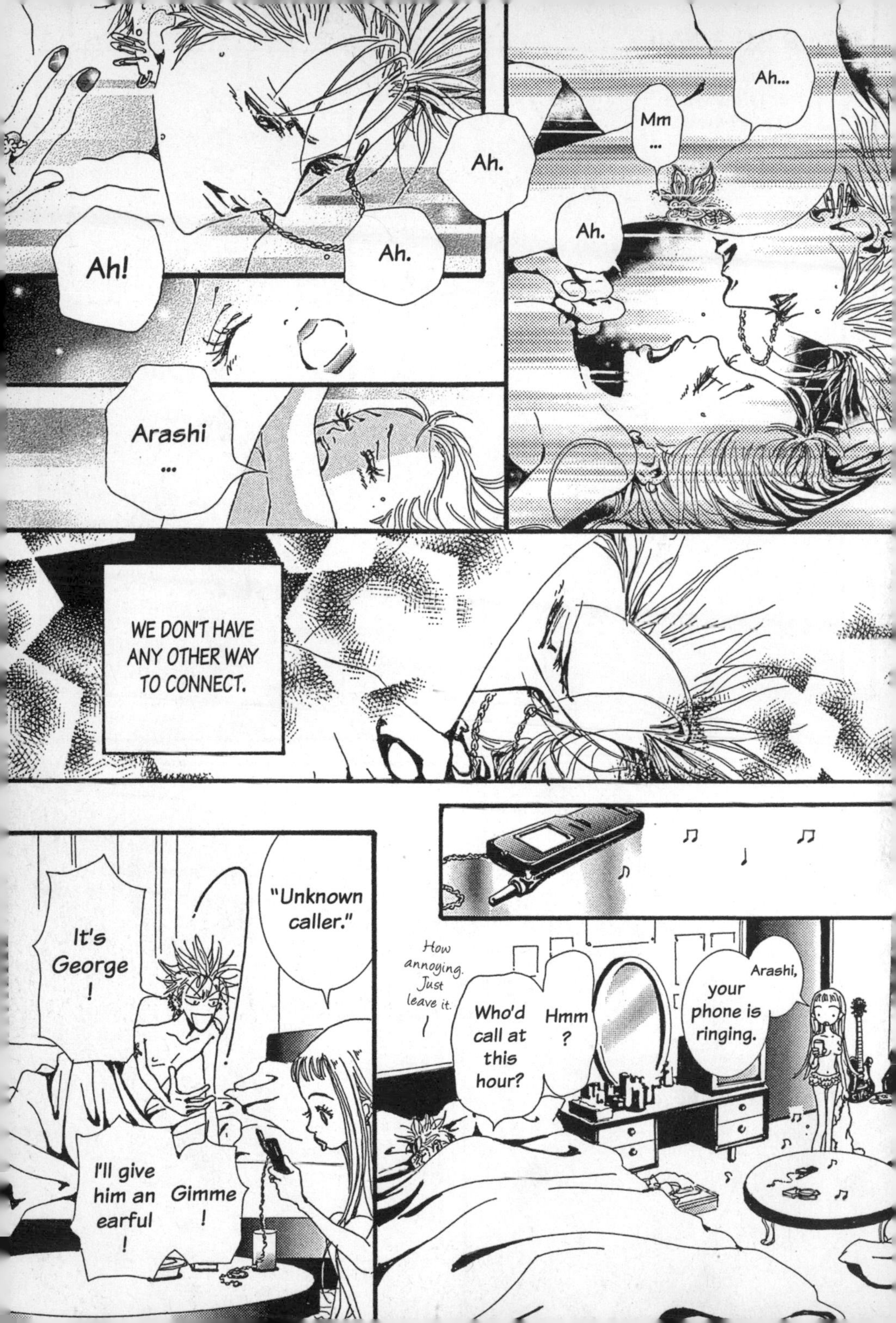
Ah...
Mm ...
Ah.
Ah.
Ah.
Ah!
Arashi ...
WE DON'T HAVE ANY OTHER WAY TO CONNECT.
Arashi, your phone is ringing.
Hmm ?
Who'd call at this hour?
How annoying. Just leave it.
"Unknown caller."
It's George !
Gimme !
I'll give him an earful !

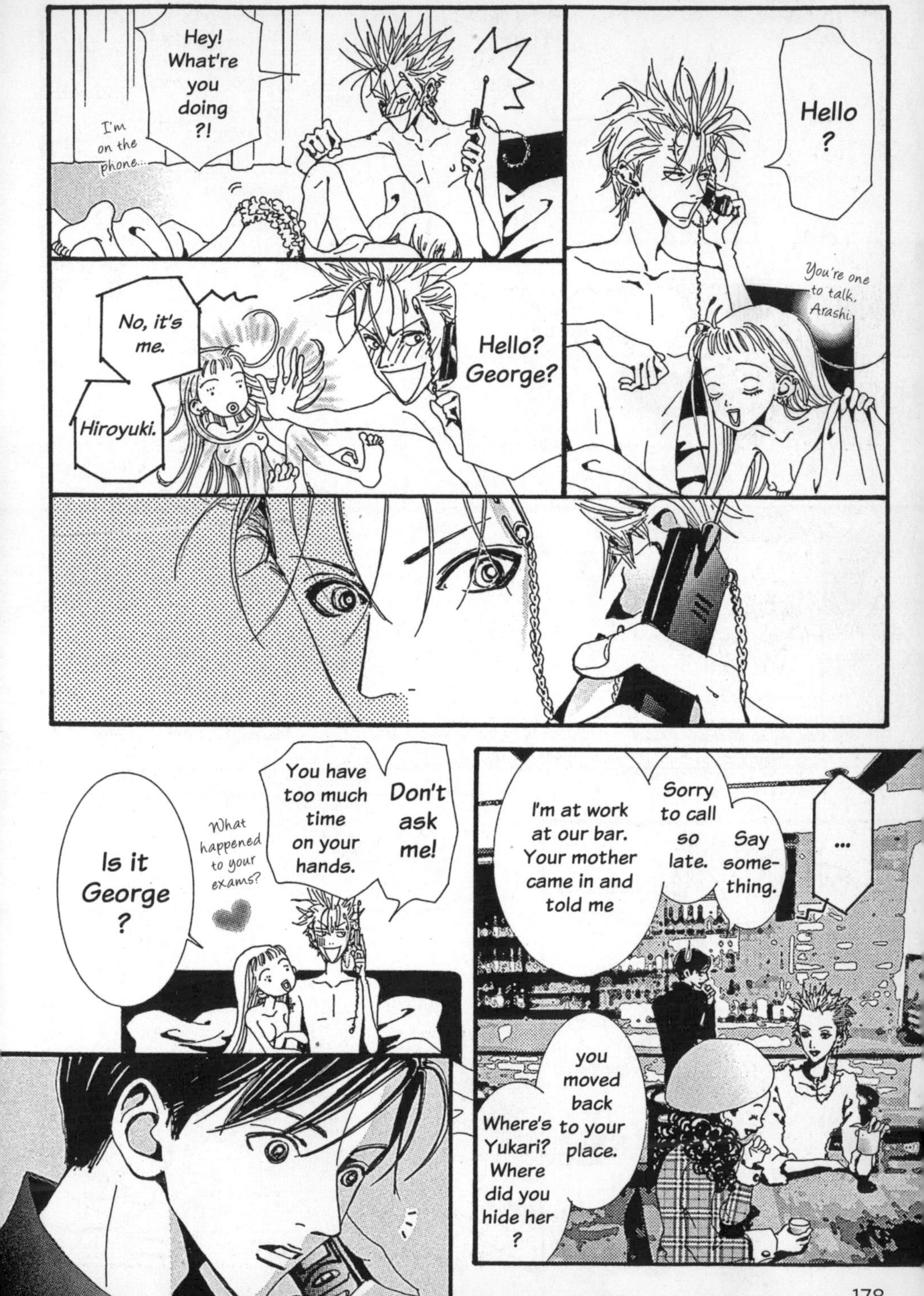
Hello?
You're one to talk, Arashi.
Hey! What're you doing ?!
I'm on the phone...
Hello? George?
No, it's me.
Hiroyuki.
...
Say some-thing.
Sorry to call so late.
I'm at work at our bar. Your mother came in and told me
you moved back to your place.
Where's Yukari? Where did you hide her ?
Don't ask me!
You have too much time on your hands.
What happened to your exams?
Is it George ?

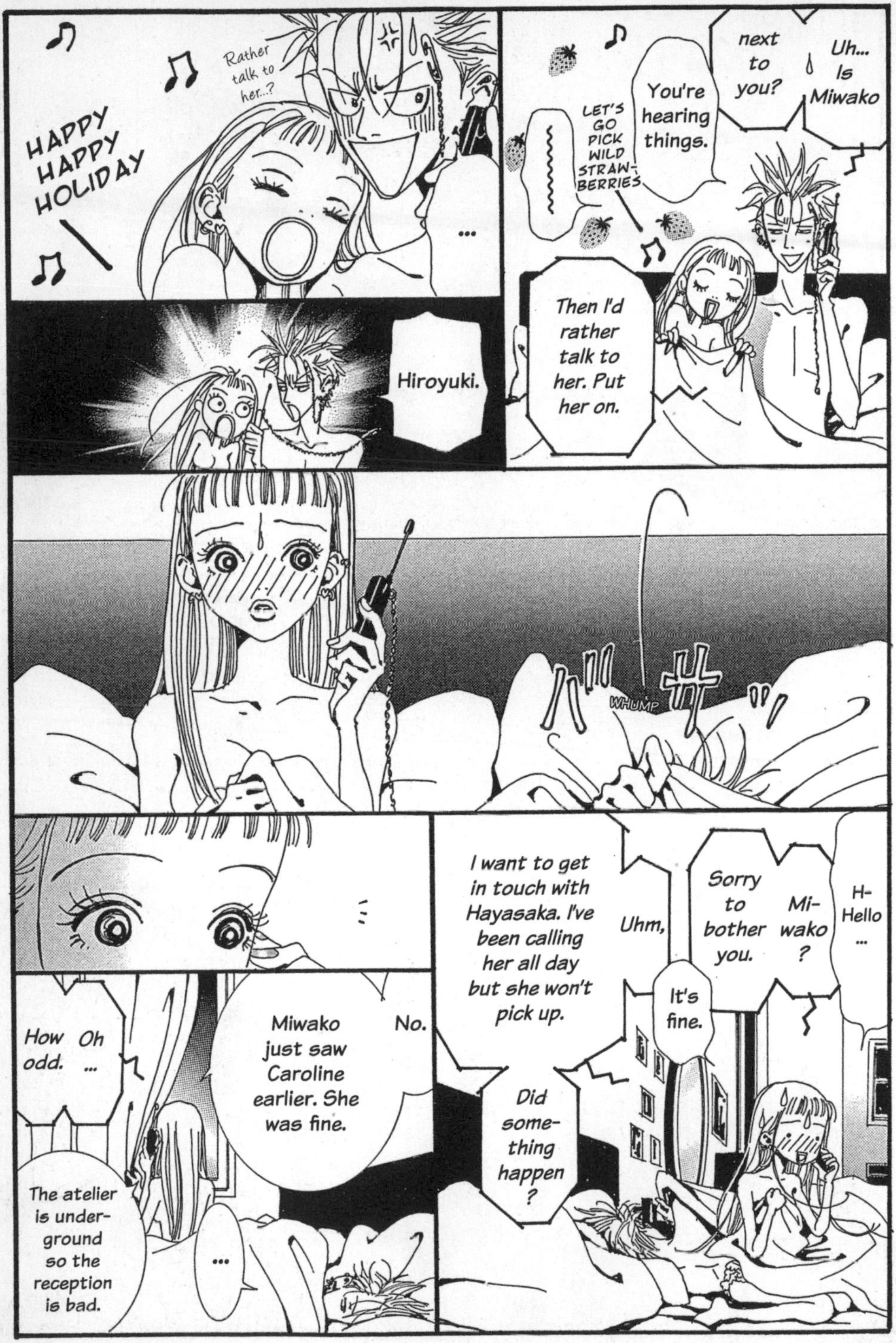
Uh... Is Miwako
next to you?
You're hearing things.
LET'S GO PICK WILD STRAWBERRIES
HAPPY HAPPY HOLIDAY
Rather talk to her..?
...
Then I'd rather talk to her. Put her on.
Hiroyuki.
WHUMP
H-Hello ...
Miwako?
Sorry to bother you.
It's fine.
Uhm,
I want to get in touch with Hayasaka. I've been calling her all day but she won't pick up.
Did something happen?
No.
Miwako just saw Caroline earlier. She was fine.
Oh ...
How odd.
The atelier is underground so the reception is bad.
...

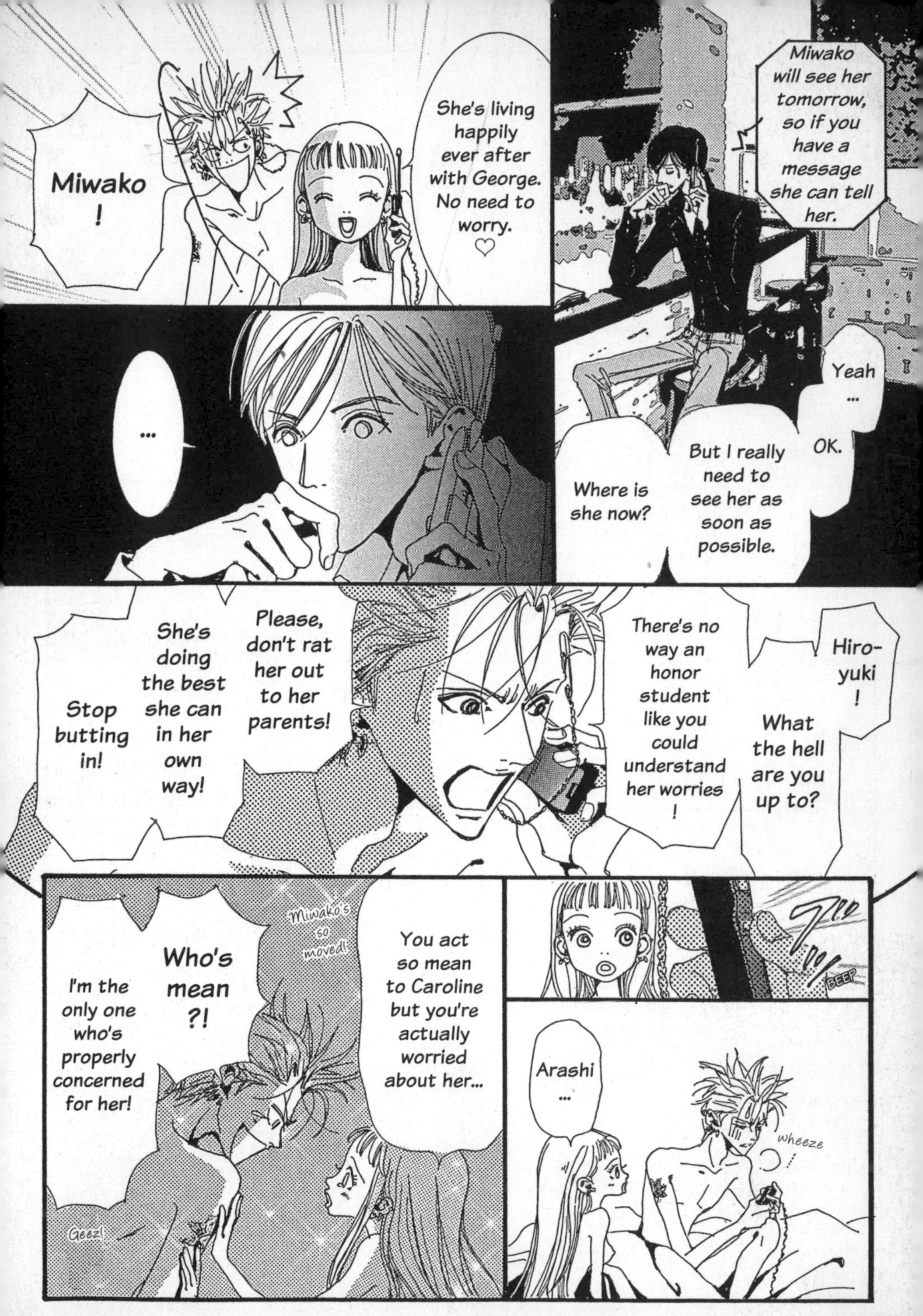
Miwako will see her tomorrow, so if you have a message she can tell her.
Yeah... OK.
But I really need to see her as soon as possible.
Where is she now?
She's living happily ever after with George. No need to worry. ♡
Miwako!
...
Hiro-yuki!
What the hell are you up to?
There's no way an honor student like you could understand her worries!
Please, don't rat her out to her parents!
She's doing the best she can in her own way!
Stop butting in!
BEEP
Arashi...
wheeze...
You act so mean to Caroline but you're actually worried about her...
Miwako's so moved!
Who's mean?!
I'm the only one who's properly concerned for her!
Geez!

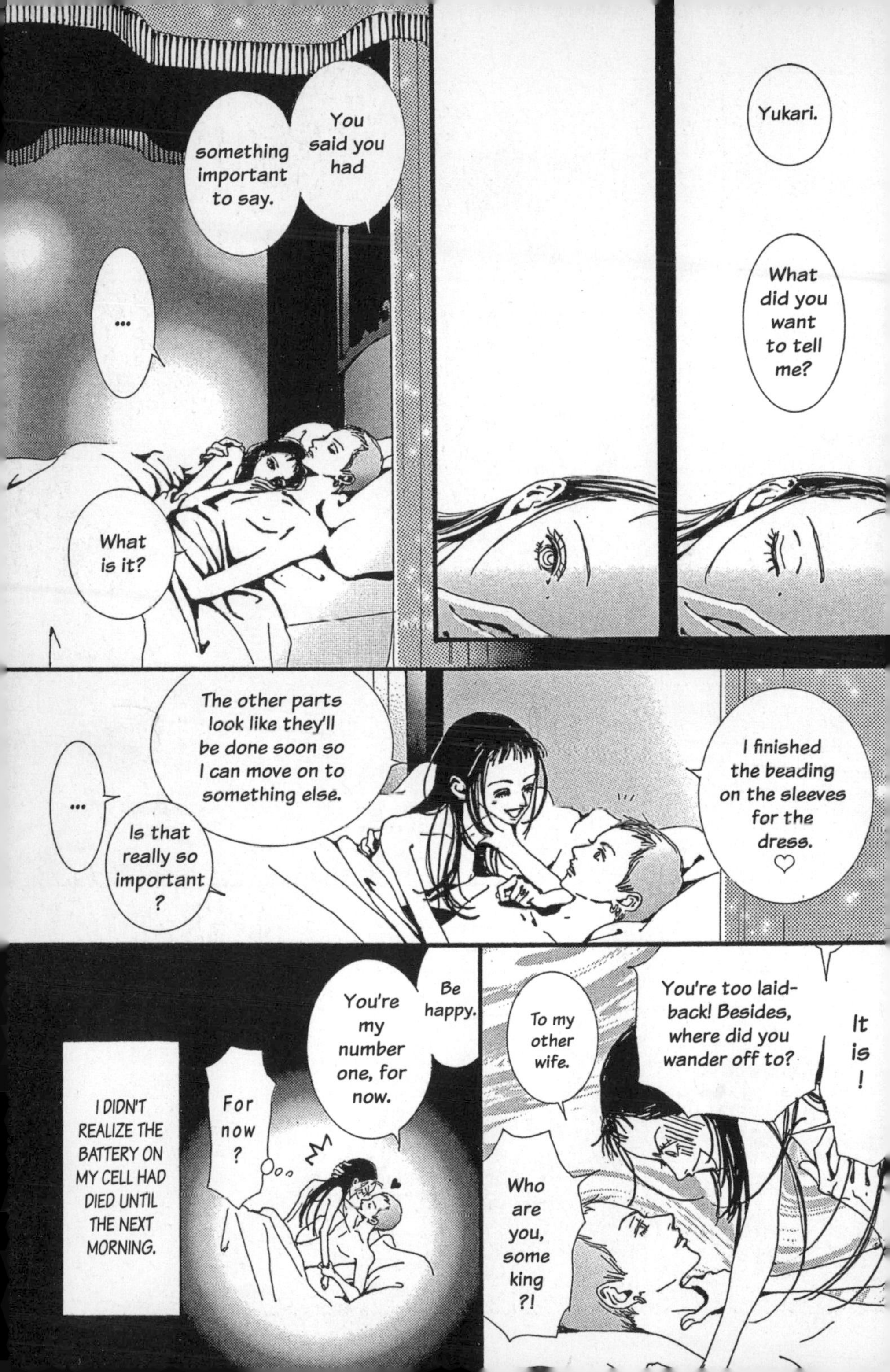
Yukari.
What did you want to tell me?
You said you had
something important to say.
...
What is it?
I finished the beading on the sleeves for the dress. ♡
The other parts look like they'll be done soon so I can move on to something else.
...
Is that really so important?
It is!
You're too laid-back! Besides, where did you wander off to?
To my other wife.
Who are you, some king?!
Be happy.
You're my number one, for now.
For now?
I DIDN'T REALIZE THE BATTERY ON MY CELL HAD DIED UNTIL THE NEXT MORNING.

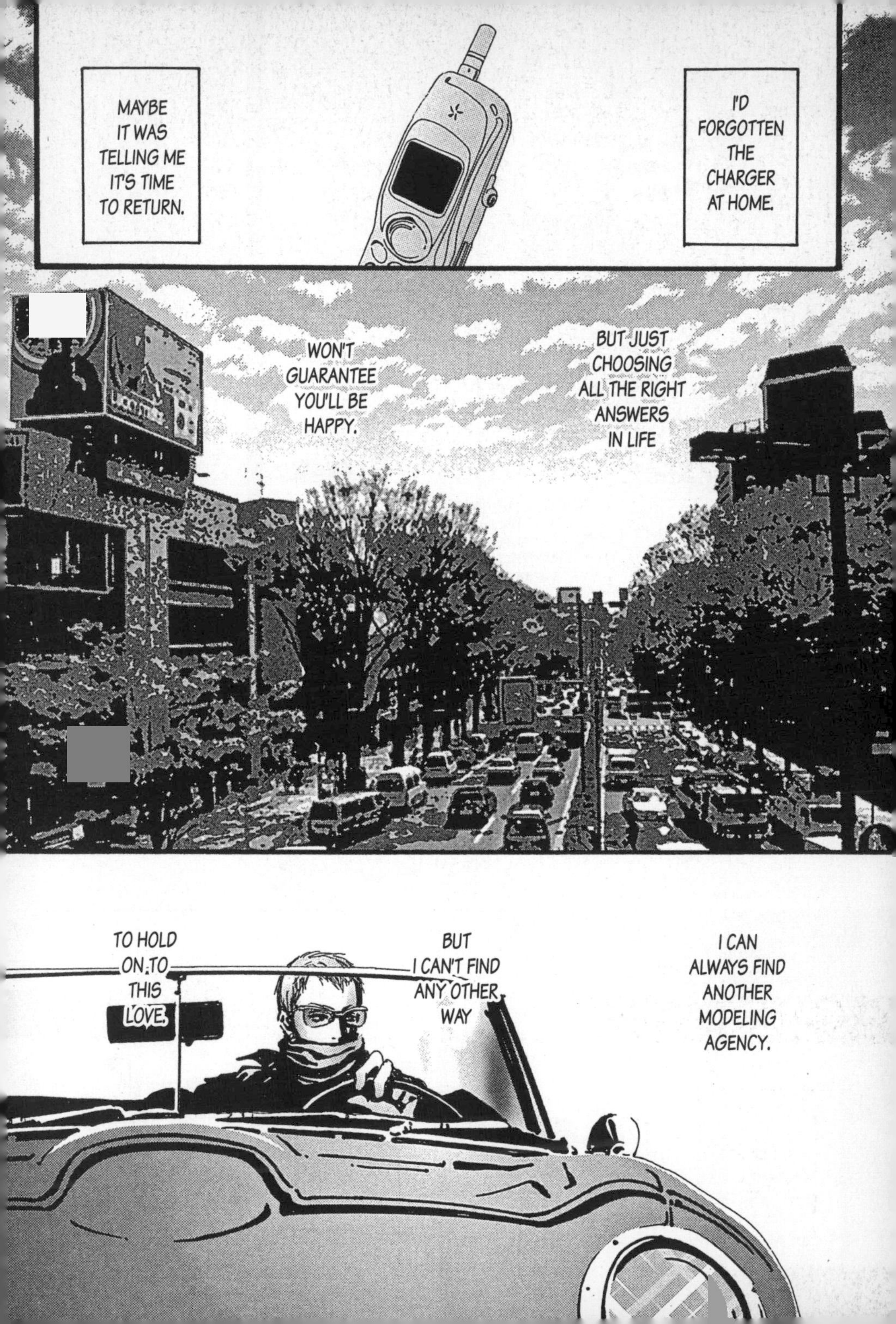
I'D FORGOTTEN THE CHARGER AT HOME.
MAYBE IT WAS TELLING ME IT'S TIME TO RETURN.
BUT JUST CHOOSING ALL THE RIGHT ANSWERS IN LIFE
WON'T GUARANTEE YOU'LL BE HAPPY.
I CAN ALWAYS FIND ANOTHER MODELING AGENCY.
BUT I CAN'T FIND ANY OTHER WAY
TO HOLD ON TO THIS LOVE.

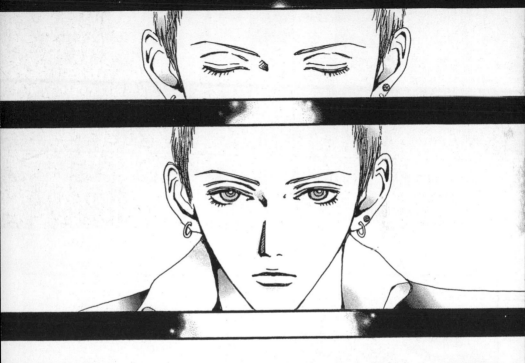

THOSE EYES. YES.

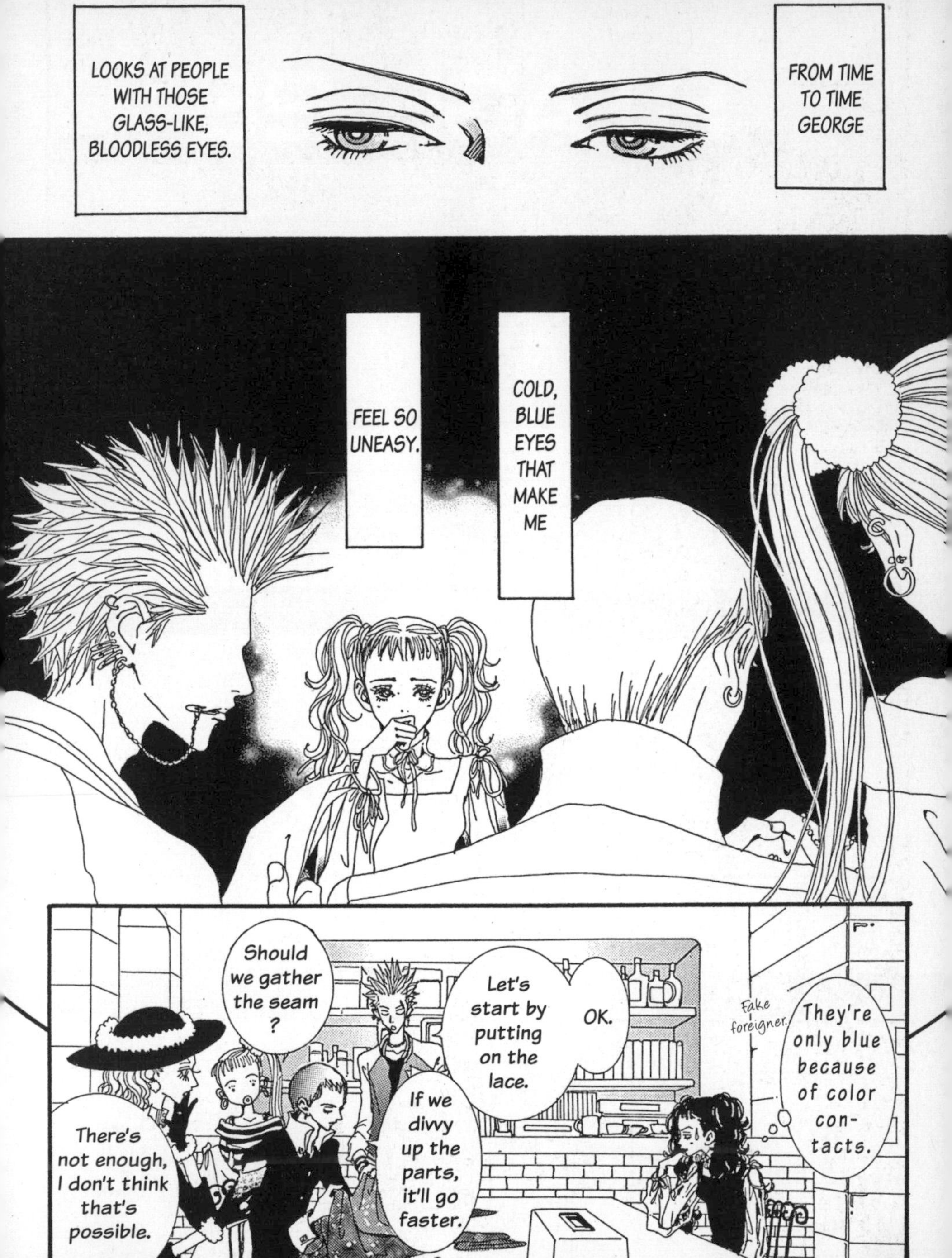
FROM TIME TO TIME GEORGE
LOOKS AT PEOPLE WITH THOSE GLASS-LIKE, BLOODLESS EYES.
COLD, BLUE EYES THAT MAKE ME
FEEL SO UNEASY.
Fake foreigner.
They're only blue because of color con-tacts.
OK.
Let's start by putting on the lace.
Should we gather the seam ?
If we divvy up the parts, it'll go faster.
There's not enough, I don't think that's possible.

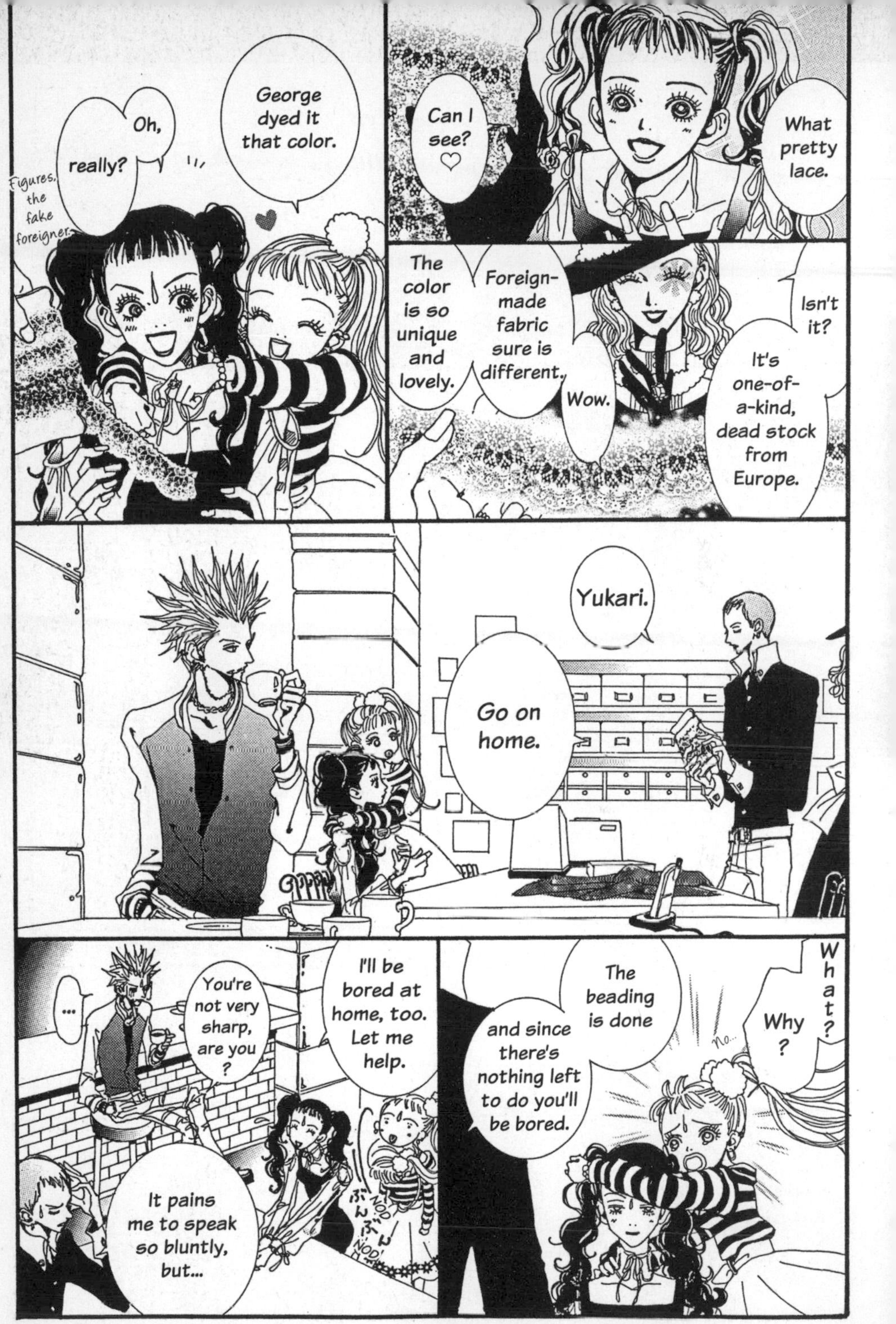
What pretty lace.
Can I see? ♡
Isn't it?
It's one-of-a-kind, dead stock from Europe.
Wow.
Foreign-made fabric sure is different.
The color is so unique and lovely.
George dyed it that color.
Oh, really?
Figures, the fake foreigner.
Yukari.
Go on home.
What?
Why?
No...
The beading is done
and since there's nothing left to do you'll be bored.
I'll be bored at home, too. Let me help.
You're not very sharp, are you?
...
It pains me to speak so bluntly, but...
NOD NOD
ぶんぶん

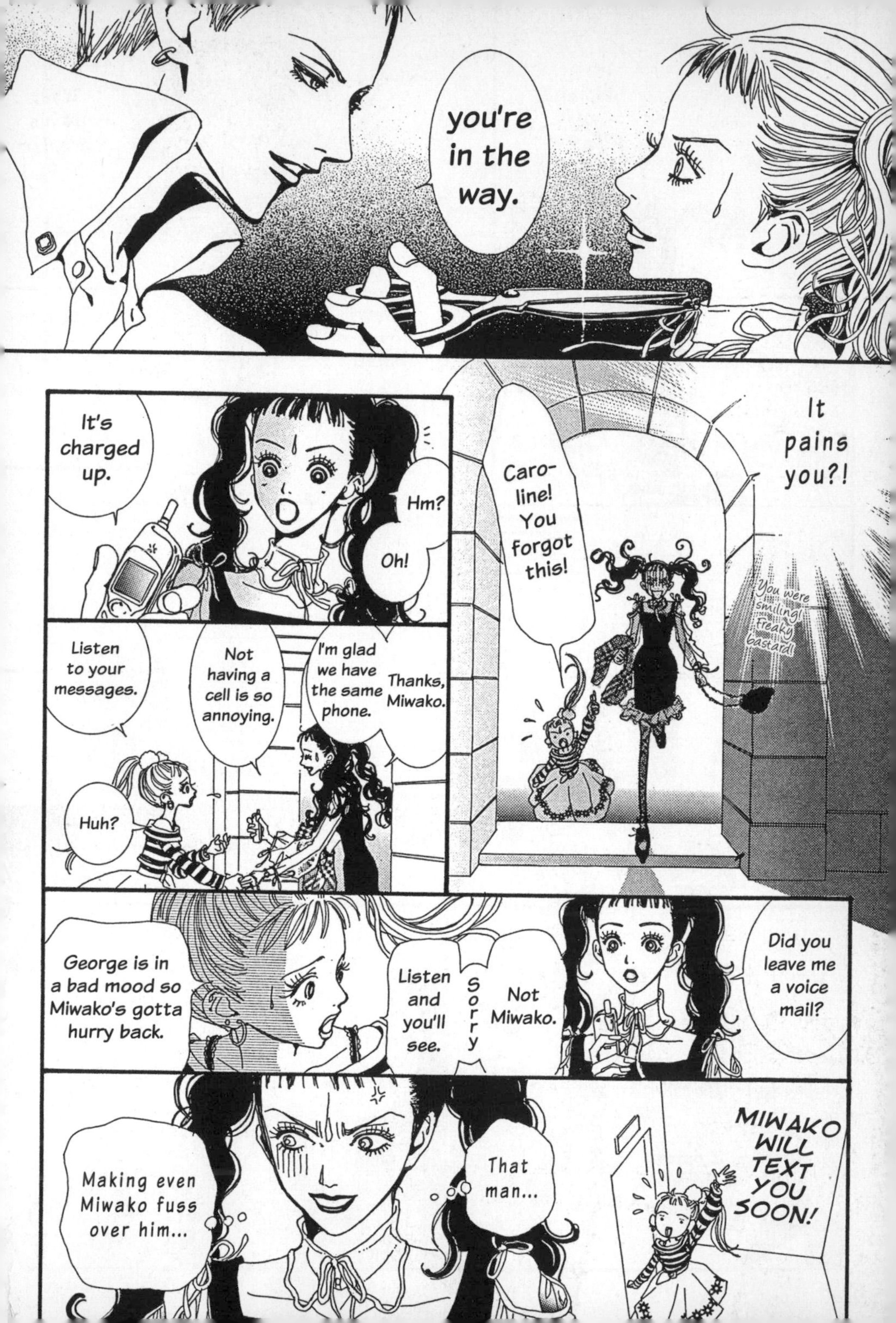
you're in the way.
It pains you?!
You were smiling! Freaky bastard!
Caroline! You forgot this!
Hm?
Oh!
It's charged up.
Thanks, Miwako.
I'm glad we have the same phone.
Not having a cell is so annoying.
Listen to your messages.
Huh?
Did you leave me a voice mail?
Not Miwako.
Sorry
Listen and you'll see.
George is in a bad mood so Miwako's gotta hurry back.
MIWAKO WILL TEXT YOU SOON!
That man...
Making even Miwako fuss over him...

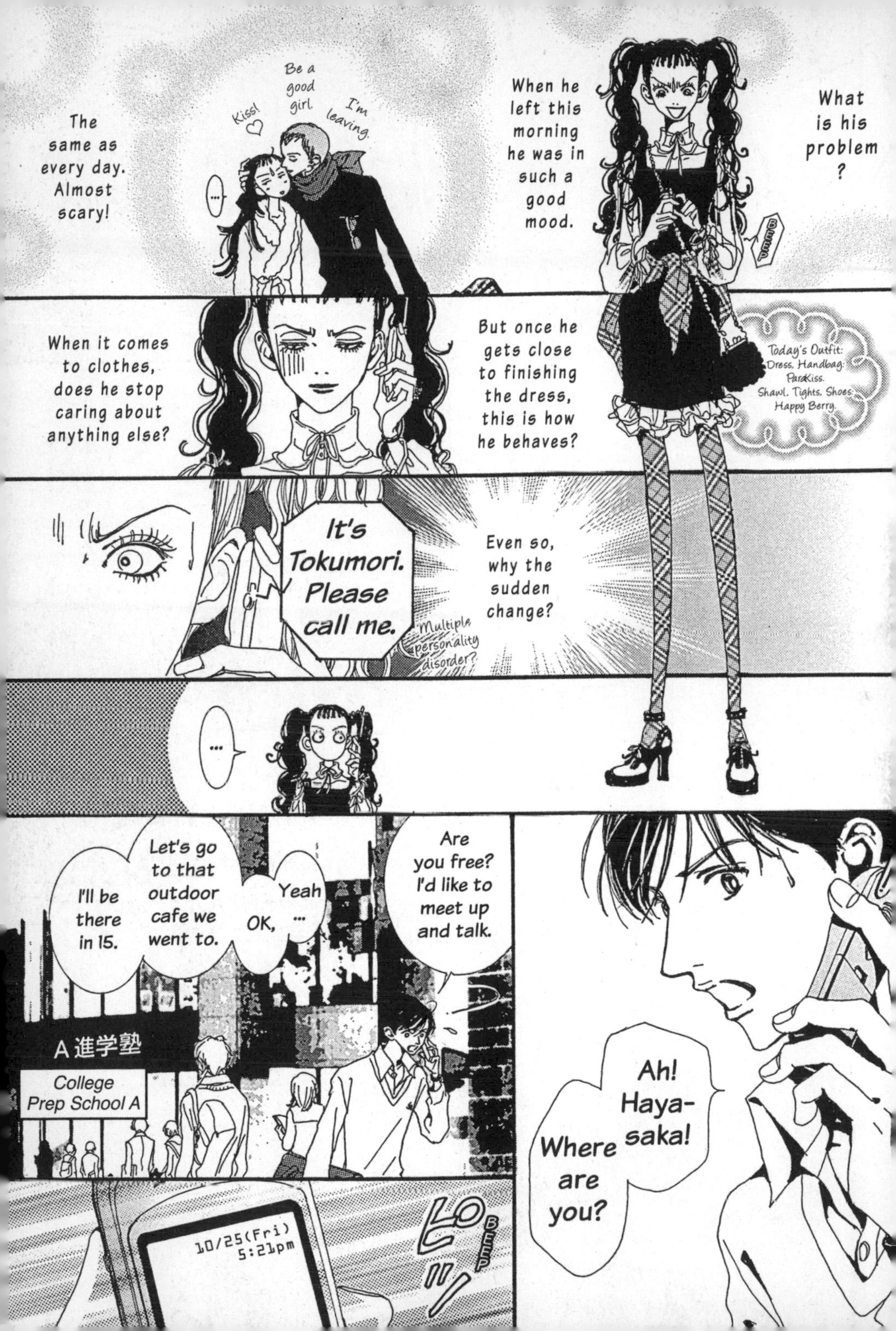
What is his problem?
BEEP
When he left this morning he was in such a good mood.
Today's Outfit: Dress, Handbag: ParaKiss. Shawl, Tights, Shoes: Happy Berry.
I'm leaving.
Be a good girl.
Kiss! ♡
...
The same as every day. Almost scary!
But once he gets close to finishing the dress, this is how he behaves?
When it comes to clothes, does he stop caring about anything else?
Even so, why the sudden change?
Multiple personality disorder?
It's Tokumori. Please call me.
...
Ah! Haya-saka!
Where are you?
Are you free? I'd like to meet up and talk.
Yeah ...
OK,
Let's go to that outdoor cafe we went to.
I'll be there in 15.
A 進学塾
College Prep School A
BEEP
10/25(Fri) 5:21pm

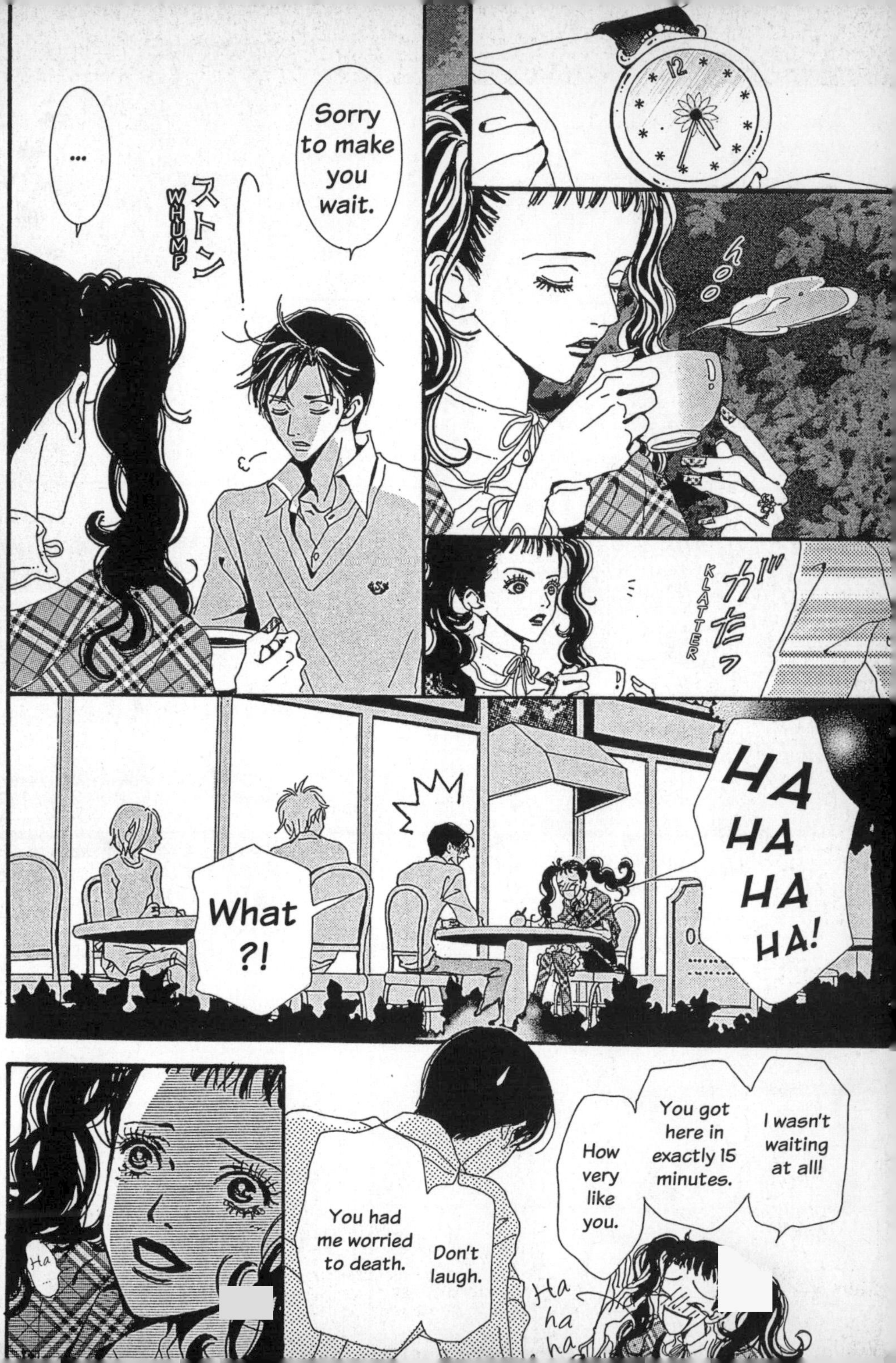
hoo
がたっ
KLATTER
Sorry to make you wait.
ストン
WHUMP
...
HA HA HA HA!
What?!
I wasn't waiting at all!
You got here in exactly 15 minutes.
How very like you.
Ha ha ha
Don't laugh.
You had me worried to death.
Ha ...

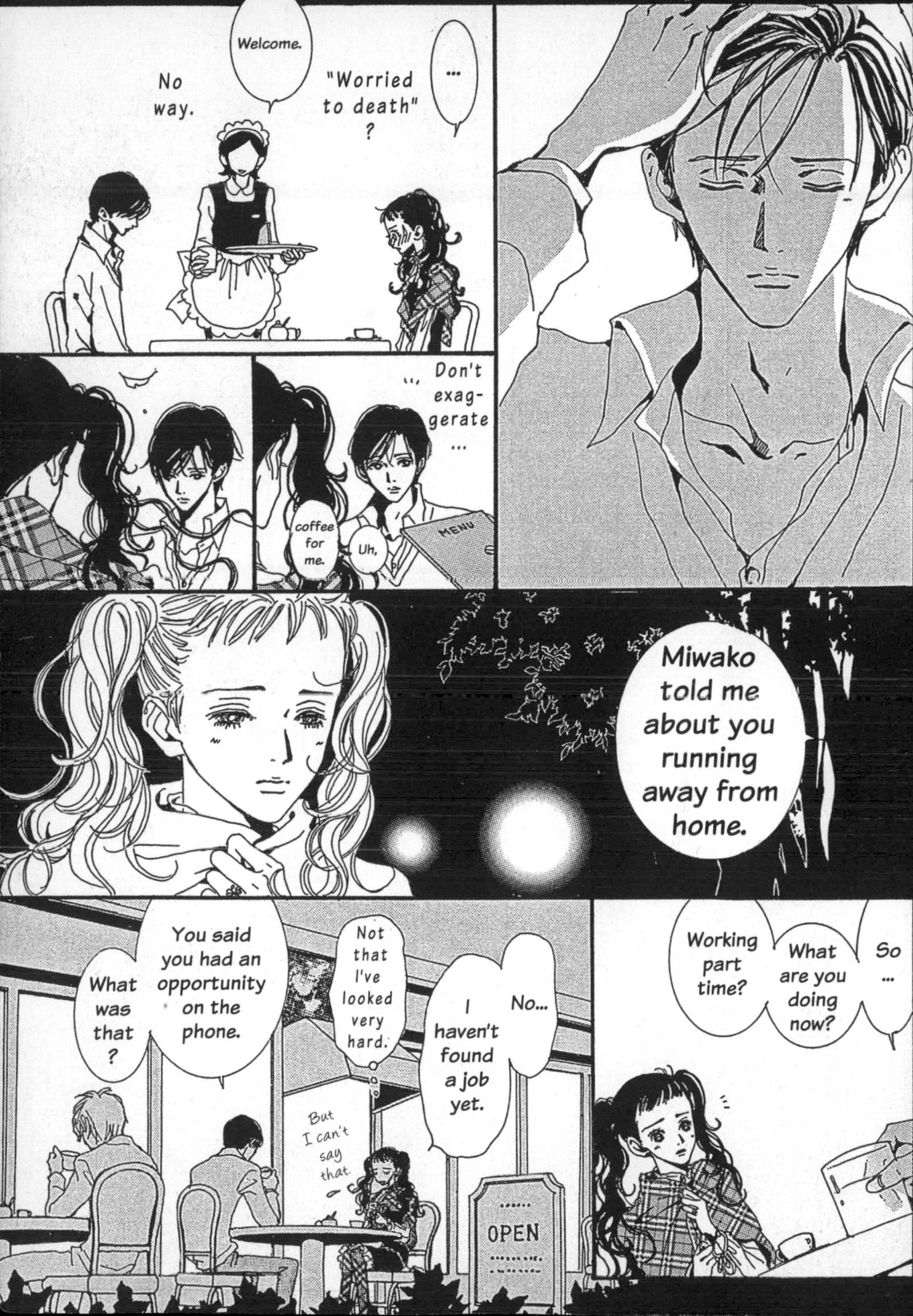
...
"Worried to death"?
Welcome.
No way.
Don't exag-gerate...
Uh,
coffee for me.
Miwako told me about you running away from home.
So...
What are you doing now?
Working part time?
No...
I haven't found a job yet.
Not that I've looked very hard.
But I can't say that.
You said you had an opportunity on the phone.
What was that?
OPEN

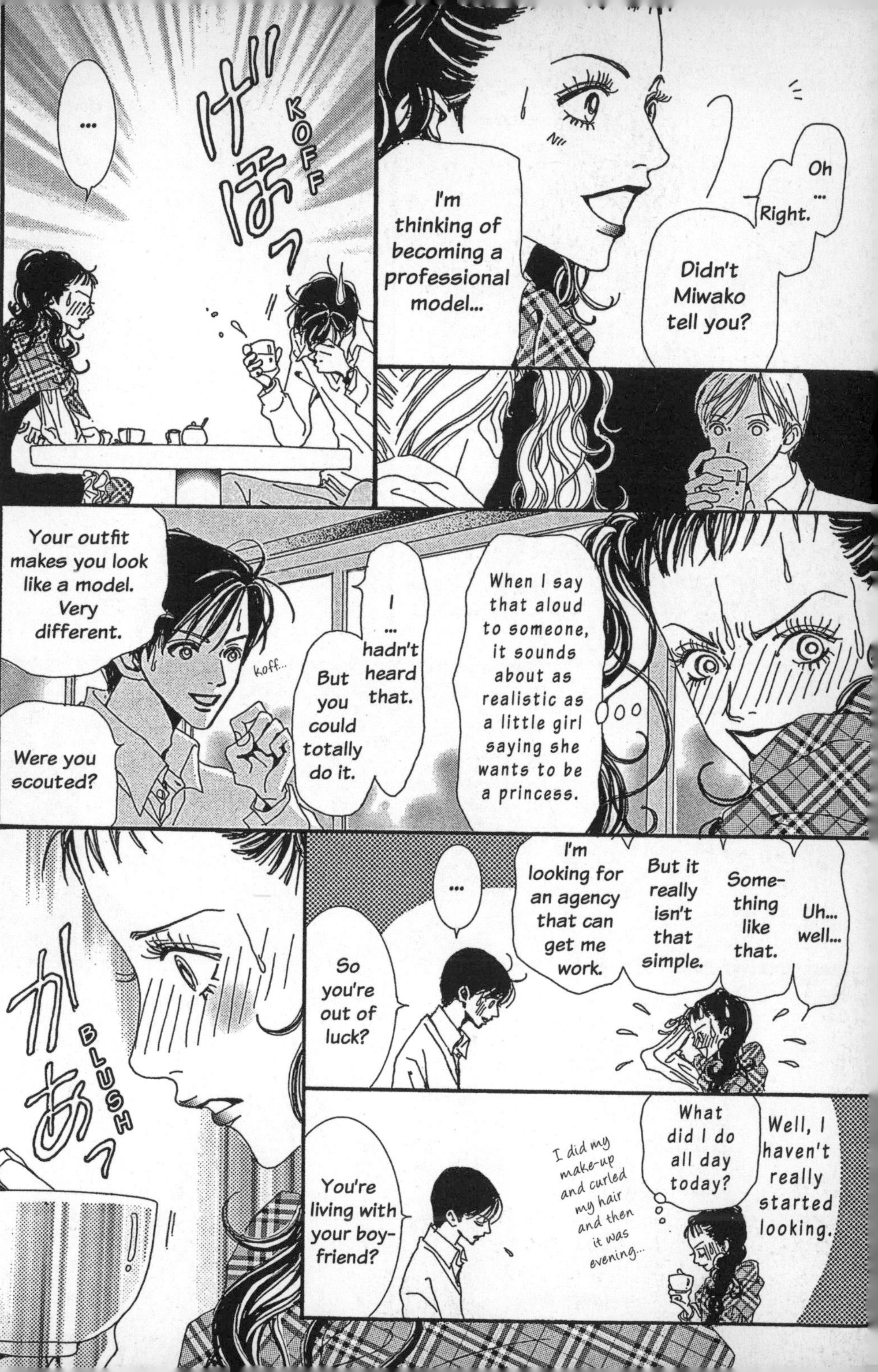
Oh ... Right.
Didn't Miwako tell you?
I'm thinking of becoming a professional model...
...
KOFF
When I say that aloud to someone, it sounds about as realistic as a little girl saying she wants to be a princess.
I ... hadn't heard that.
But you could totally do it.
koff...
Your outfit makes you look like a model. Very different.
Were you scouted?
Uh... well...
Something like that.
But it really isn't that simple.
I'm looking for an agency that can get me work.
...
So you're out of luck?
Well, I haven't really started looking.
What did I do all day today?
I did my make-up and curled my hair and then it was evening...
You're living with your boy-friend?
BLUSH
!

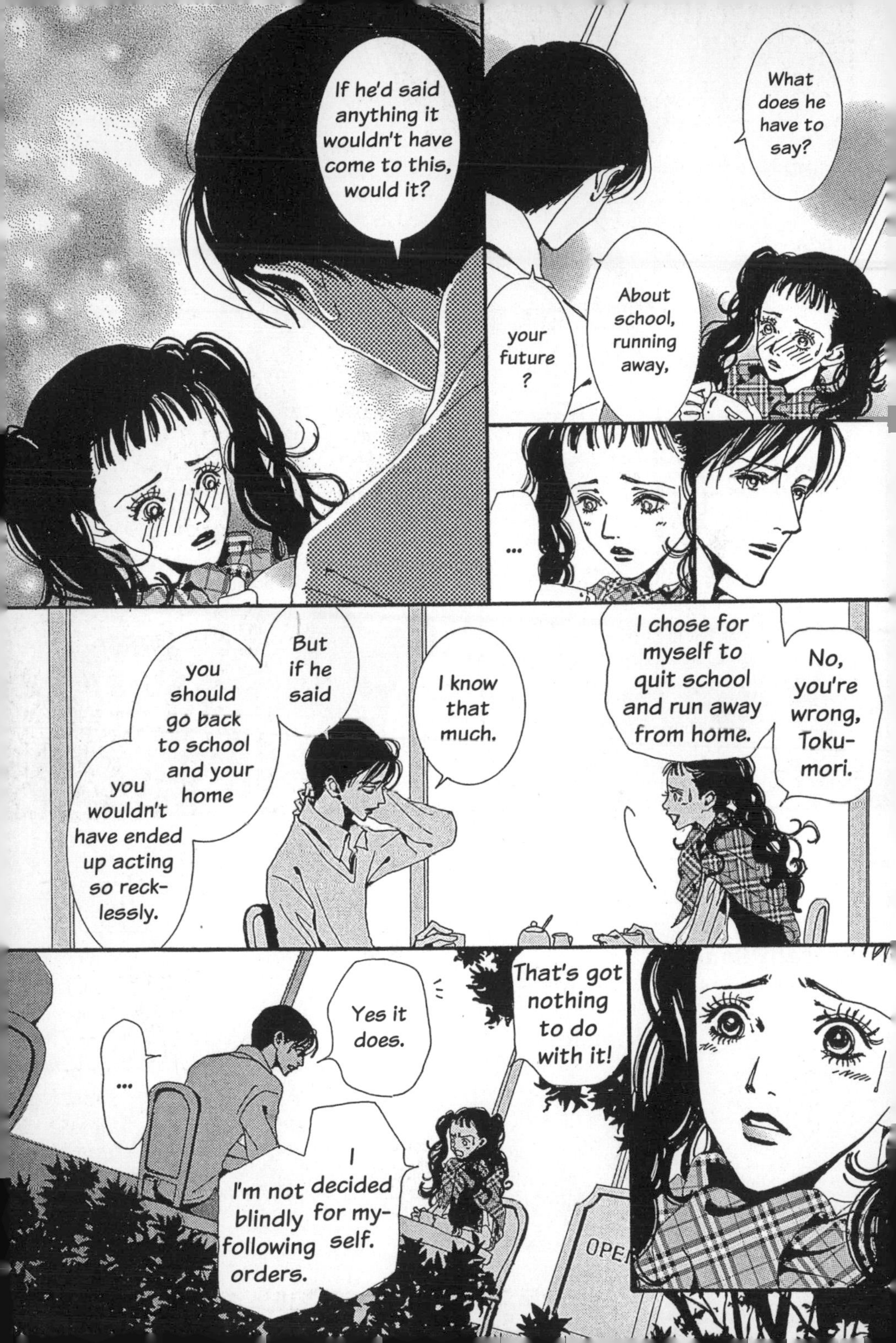
What does he have to say?
About school, running away,
your future?
...
If he'd said anything it wouldn't have come to this, would it?
No, you're wrong, Toku-mori.
I chose for myself to quit school and run away from home.
I know that much.
But if he said
you should go back to school and your home
you wouldn't have ended up acting so reck-lessly.
That's got nothing to do with it!
Yes it does.
...
I decided for my-self.
I'm not blindly following orders.

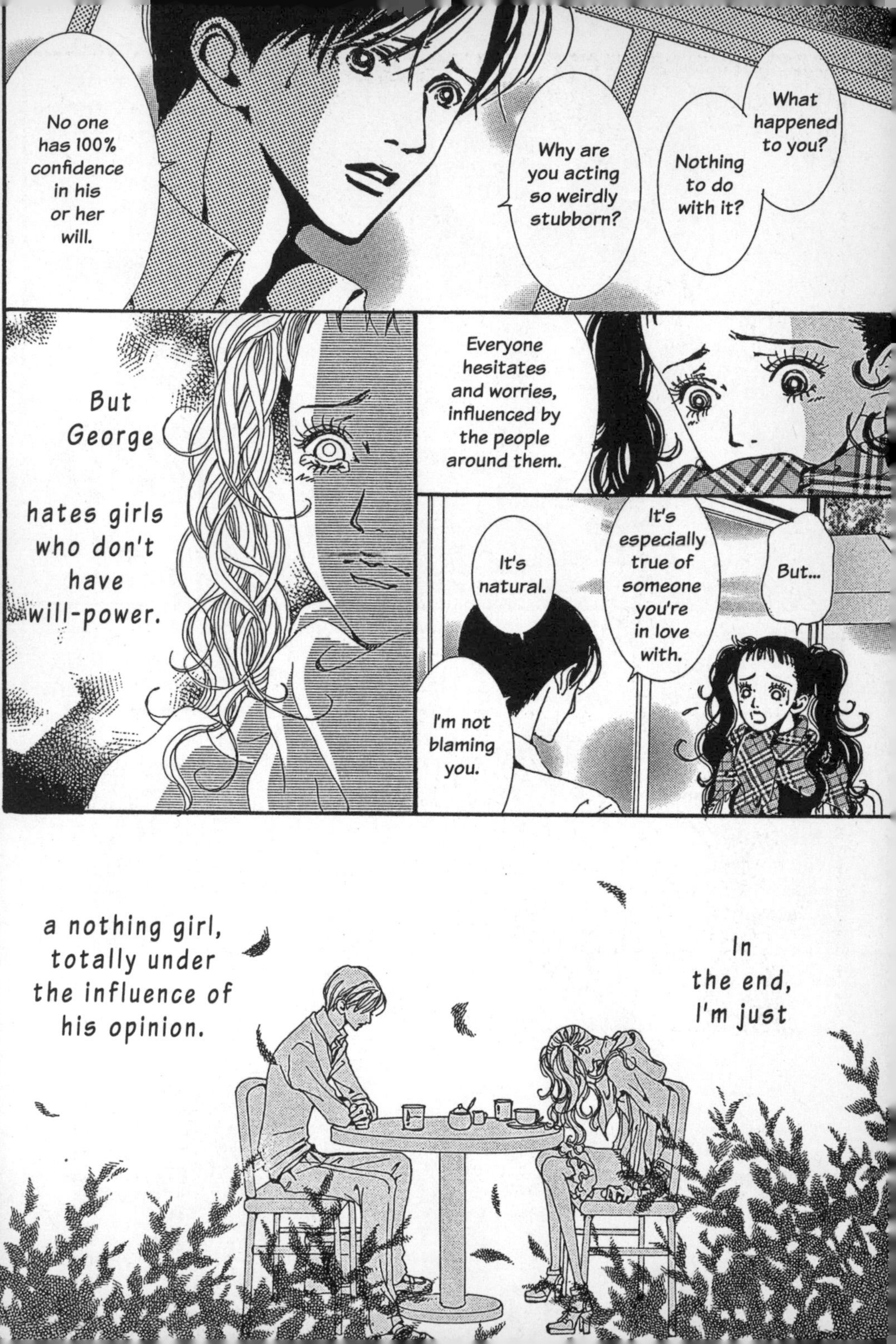
What happened to you?
Nothing to do with it?
Why are you acting so weirdly stubborn?
No one has 100% confidence in his or her will.
Everyone hesitates and worries, influenced by the people around them.
But...
It's especially true of someone you're in love with.
It's natural.
I'm not blaming you.
But George
hates girls who don't have will-power.
In the end, I'm just
a nothing girl, totally under the influence of his opinion.

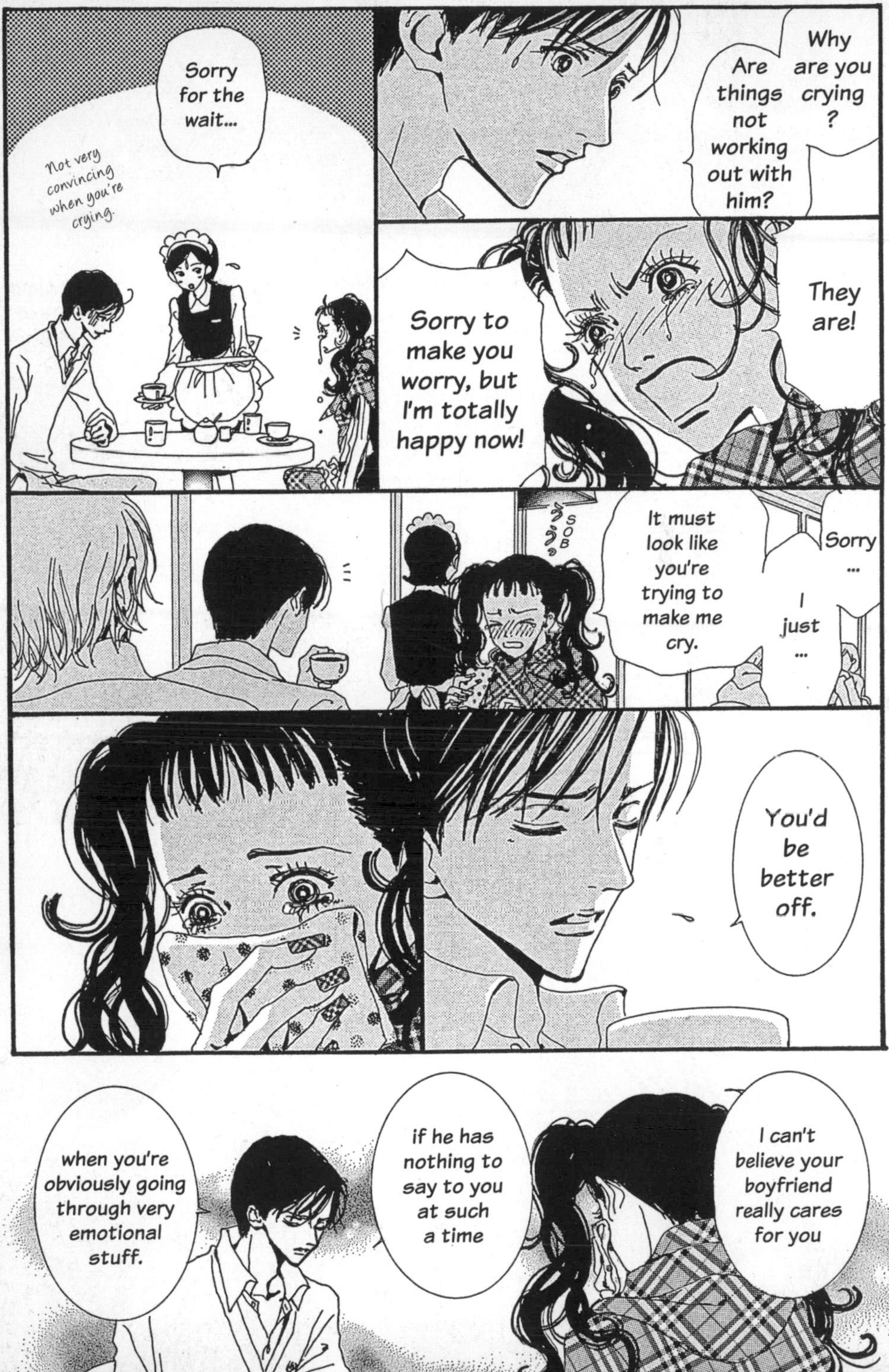
Why are you crying?
Are things not working out with him?
They are!
Sorry to make you worry, but I'm totally happy now!
Sorry for the wait...
Not very convincing when you're crying.
Sorry... I just...
It must look like you're trying to make me cry.
SOB
You'd be better off.
I can't believe your boyfriend really cares for you
if he has nothing to say to you at such a time
when you're obviously going through very emotional stuff.

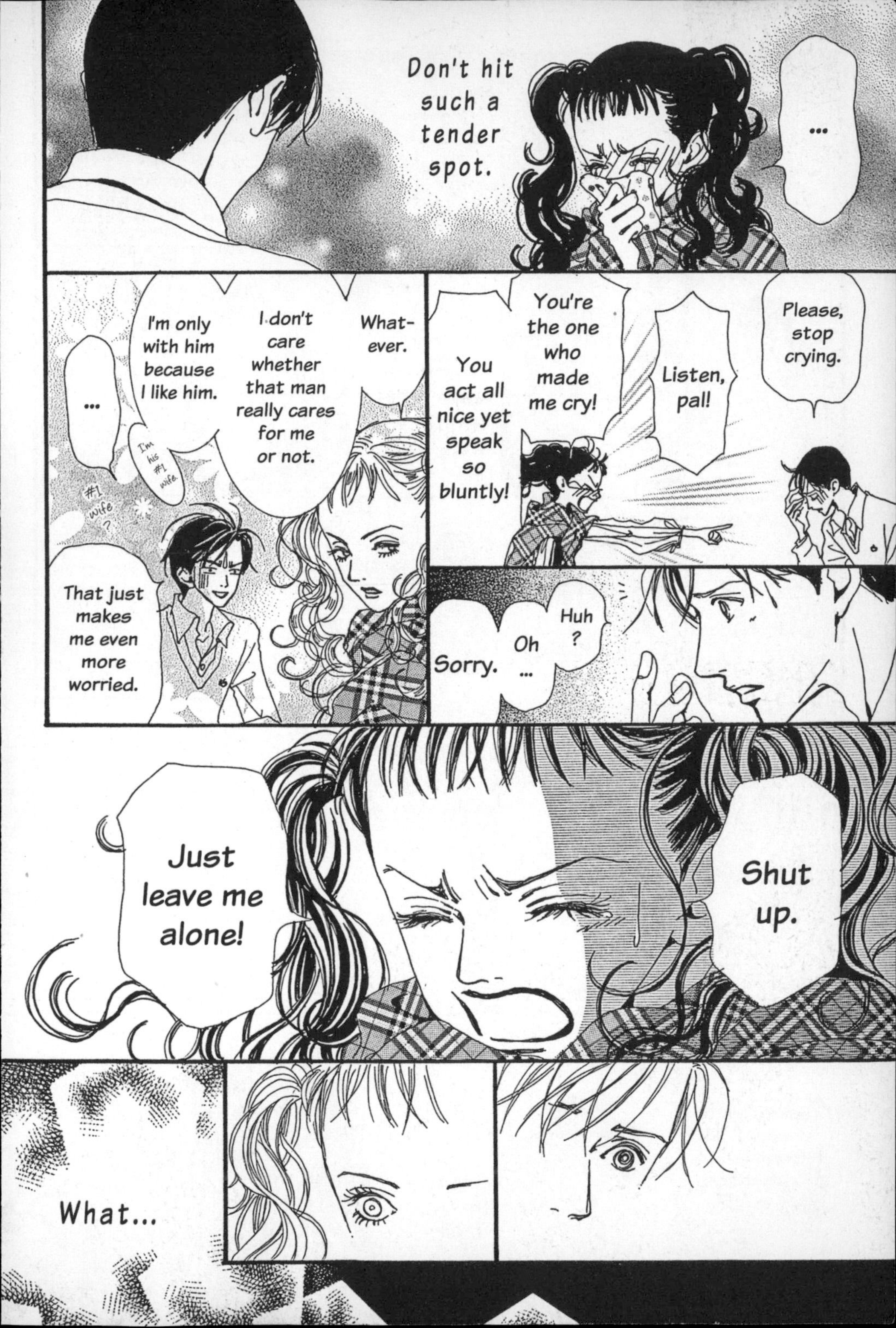
...
Don't hit such a tender spot.
Please, stop crying.
Listen, pal!
You're the one who made me cry!
You act all nice yet speak so bluntly!
Huh?
Oh...
Sorry.
What-ever.
I don't care whether that man really cares for me or not.
I'm only with him because I like him.
I'm his #1 wife.
...
#1 wife?
That just makes me even more worried.
Shut up.
Just leave me alone!
What...

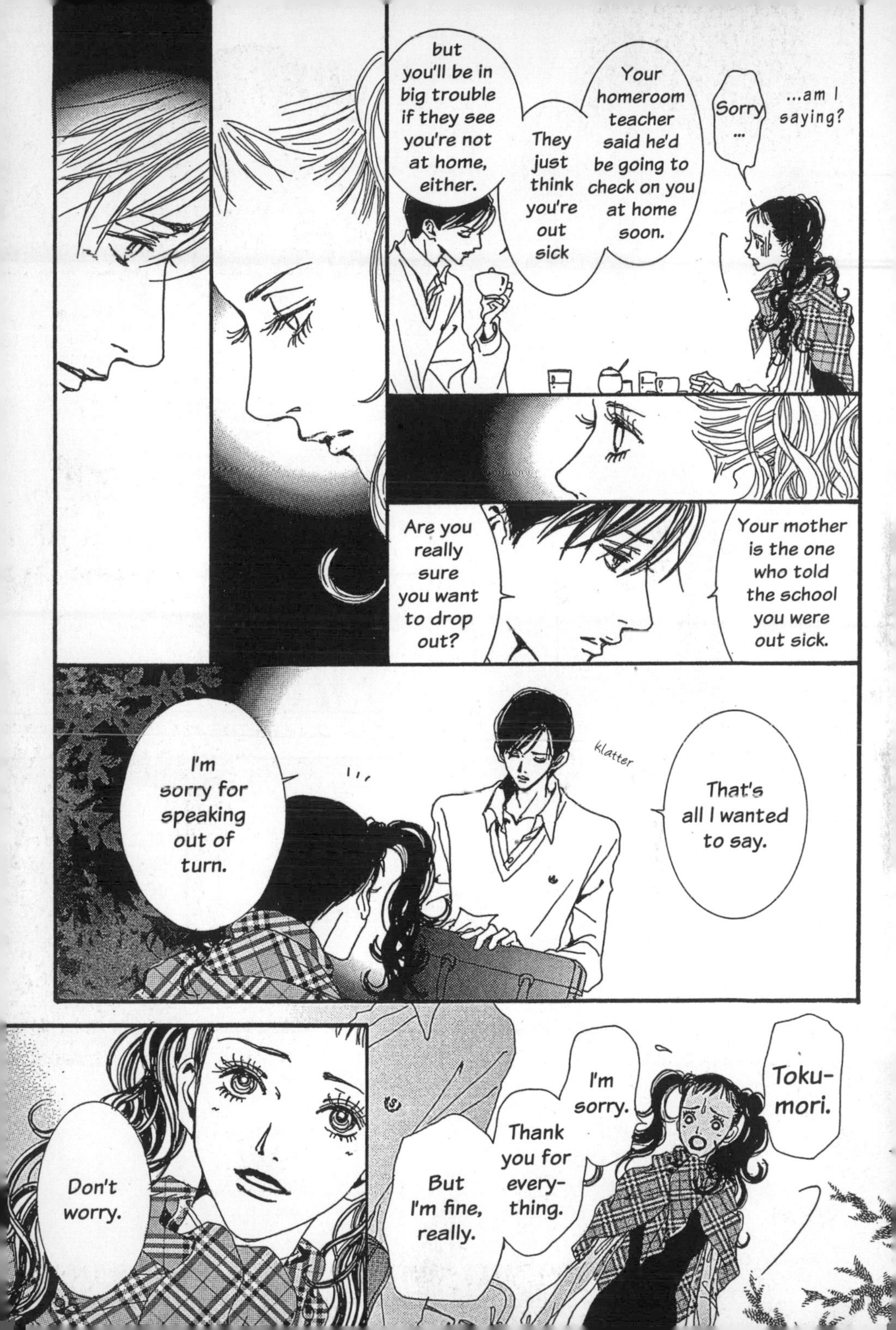
...am I saying?
Sorry...
Your homeroom teacher said he'd be going to check on you at home soon.
They just think you're out sick
but you'll be in big trouble if they see you're not at home, either.
Your mother is the one who told the school you were out sick.
Are you really sure you want to drop out?
That's all I wanted to say.
klatter
I'm sorry for speaking out of turn.
Toku-mori.
I'm sorry.
Thank you for every-thing.
But I'm fine, really.
Don't worry.

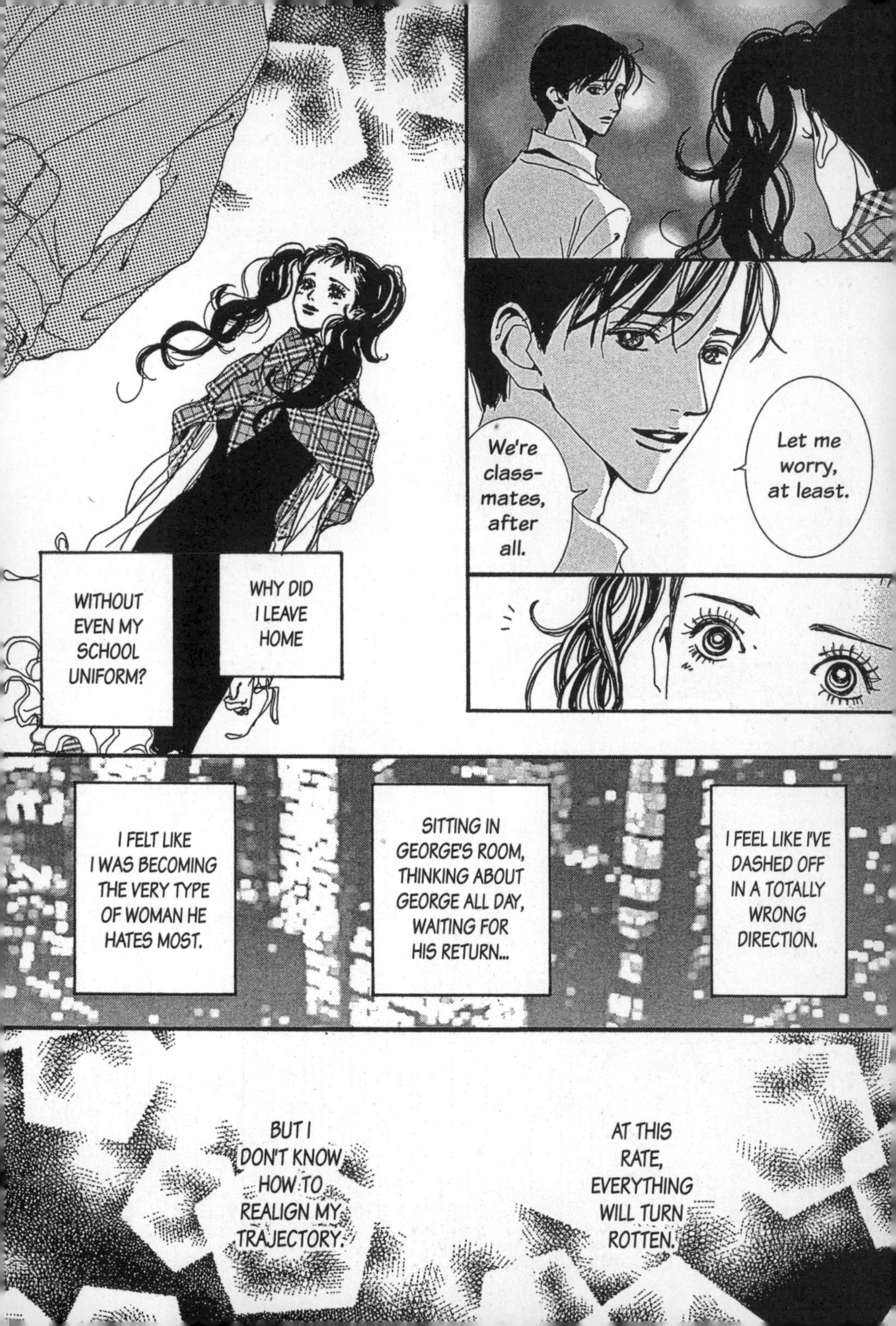
Let me worry, at least.
We're class-mates, after all.
WHY DID I LEAVE HOME
WITHOUT EVEN MY SCHOOL UNIFORM?
I FEEL LIKE I'VE DASHED OFF IN A TOTALLY WRONG DIRECTION.
SITTING IN GEORGE'S ROOM, THINKING ABOUT GEORGE ALL DAY, WAITING FOR HIS RETURN...
I FELT LIKE I WAS BECOMING THE VERY TYPE OF WOMAN HE HATES MOST.
AT THIS RATE, EVERYTHING WILL TURN ROTTEN.
BUT I DON'T KNOW HOW TO REALIGN MY TRAJECTORY.

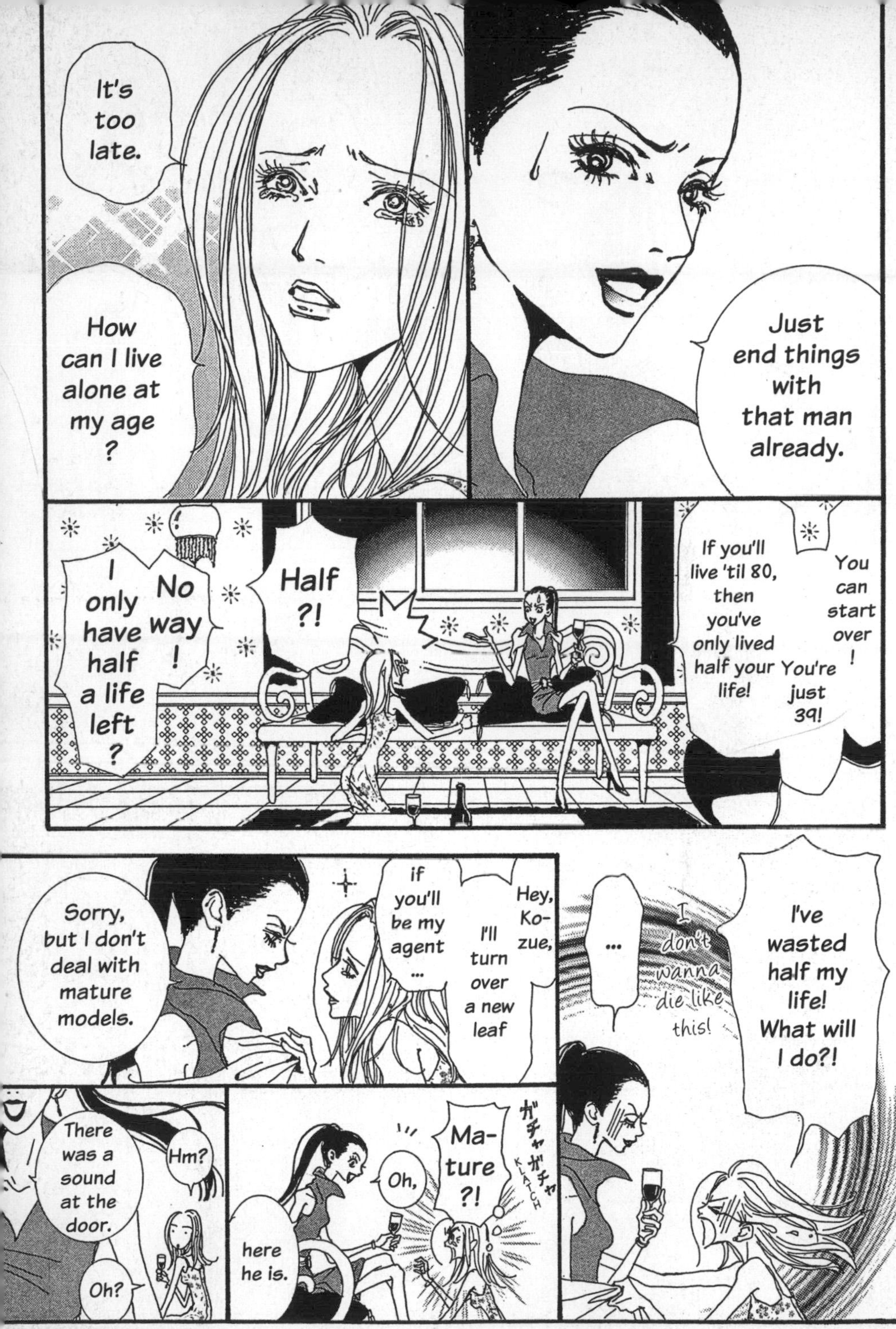
Just end things with that man already.
It's too late.
How can I live alone at my age?
You can start over!
If you'll live 'til 80, then you've only lived half your life!
You're just 39!
Half?!
No way!
I only have half a life left?
I've wasted half my life! What will I do?!
I don't wanna die like this!
...
Hey, Kozue,
if you'll be my agent...
I'll turn over a new leaf
Sorry, but I don't deal with mature models.
ガチャガチャ
KLATCH
Ma-ture?!
Oh,
here he is.
Hm?
There was a sound at the door.
Oh?

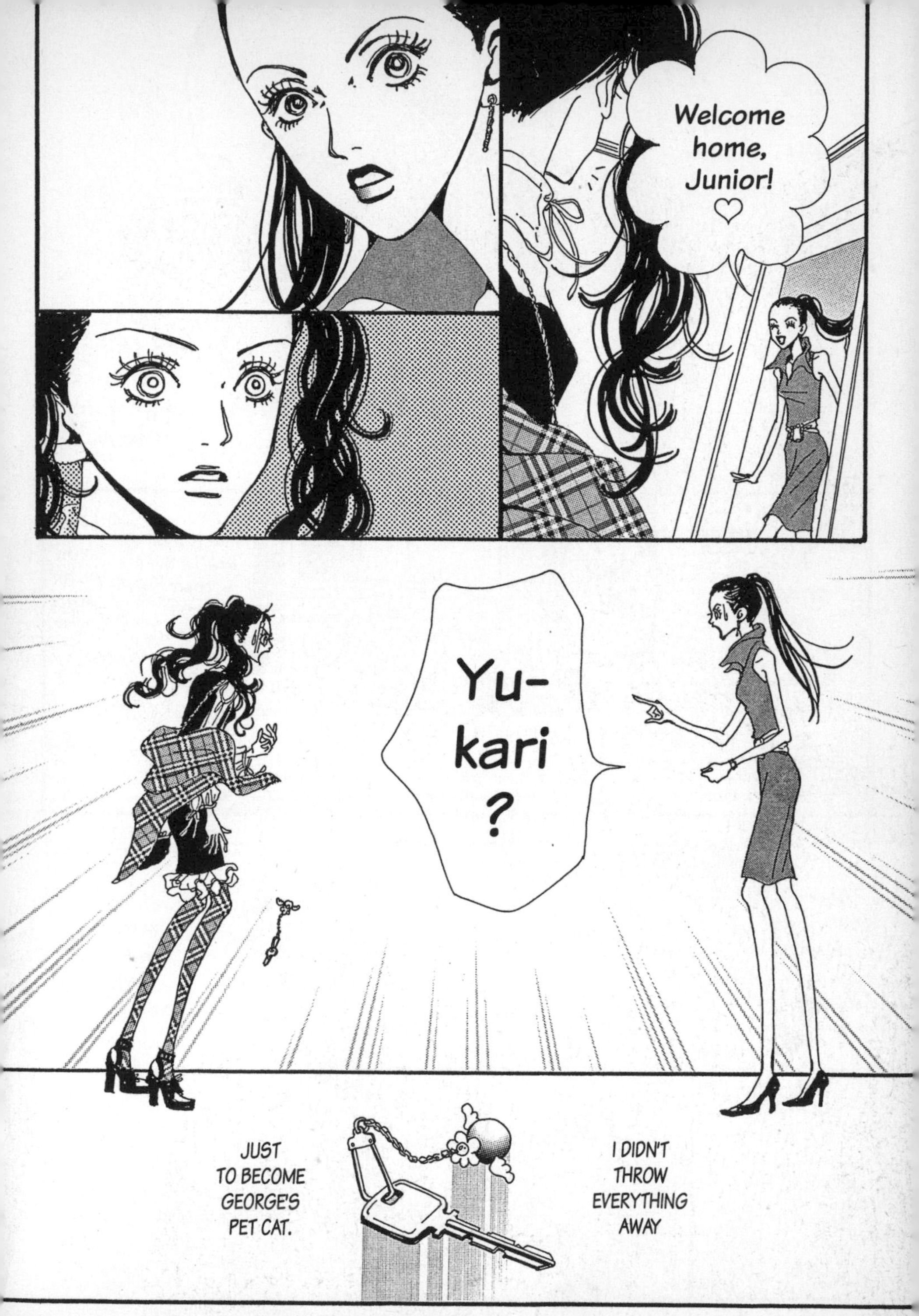
Welcome home, Junior! ♡
Yu-kari?
I DIDN'T THROW EVERYTHING AWAY
JUST TO BECOME GEORGE'S PET CAT.

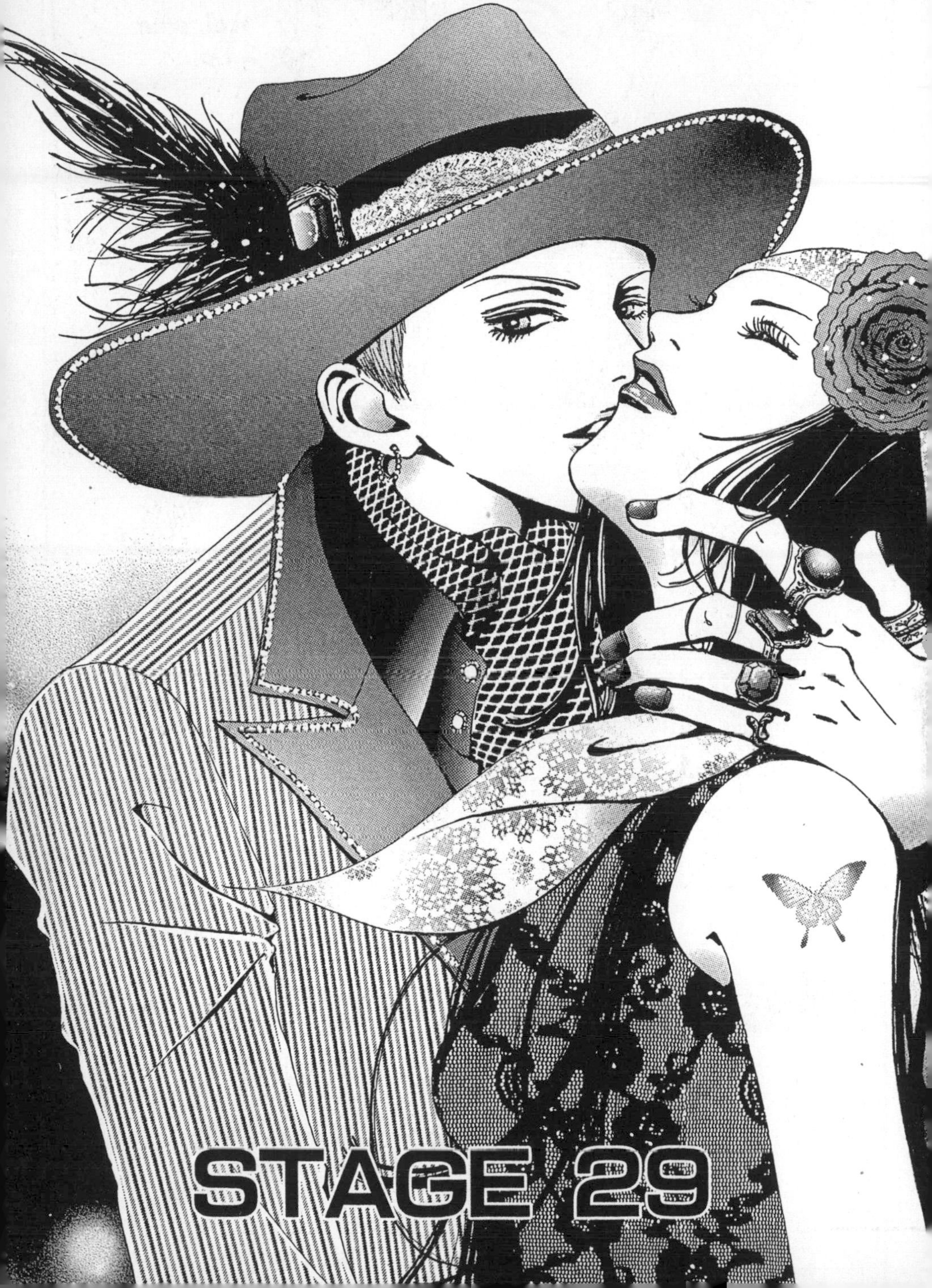
STAGE 29

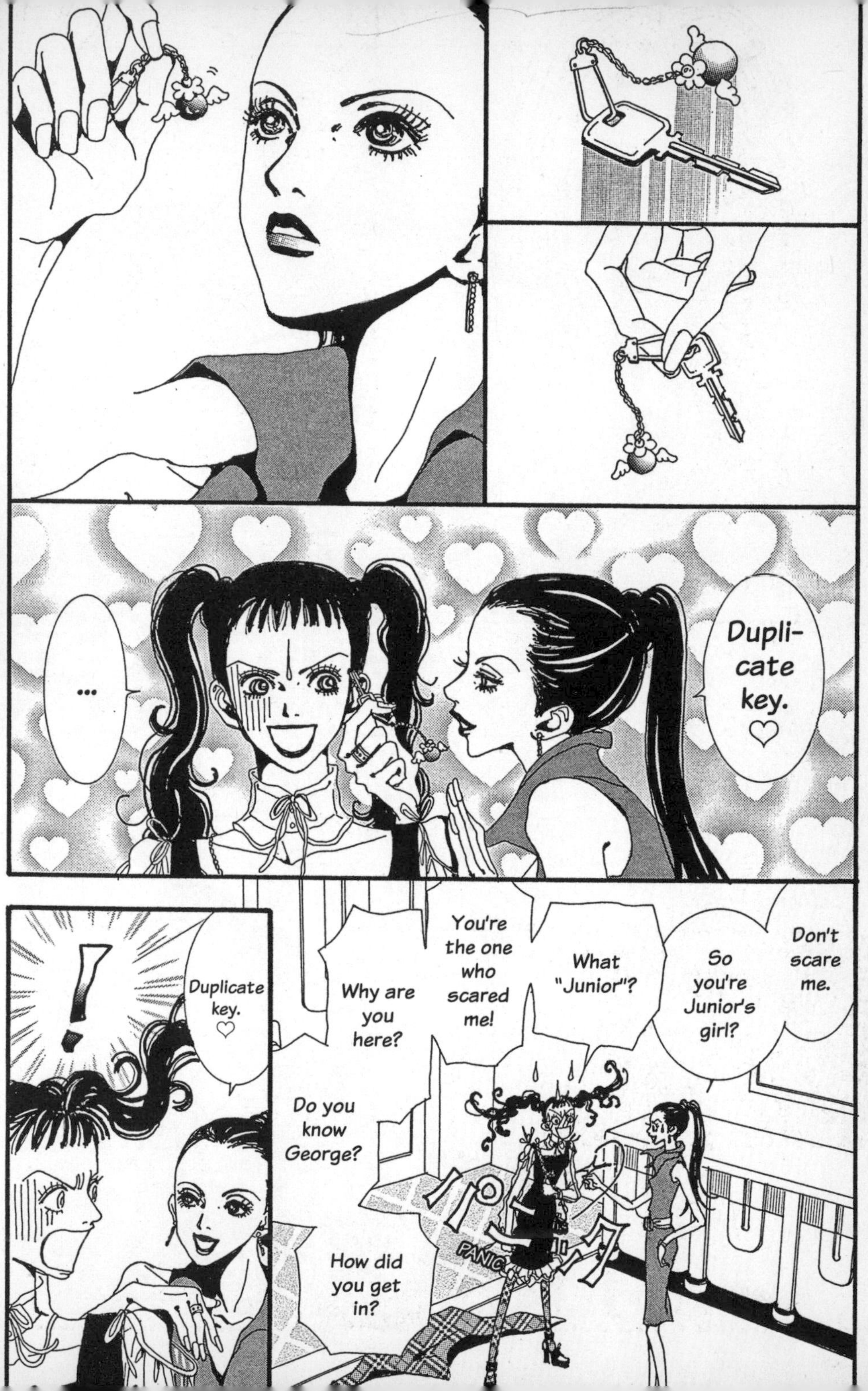
Dupli-cate key. ♡
...
Don't scare me.
So you're Junior's girl?
What "Junior"?
You're the one who scared me!
Why are you here?
Do you know George?
How did you get in?
PANIC
Duplicate key. ♡
!

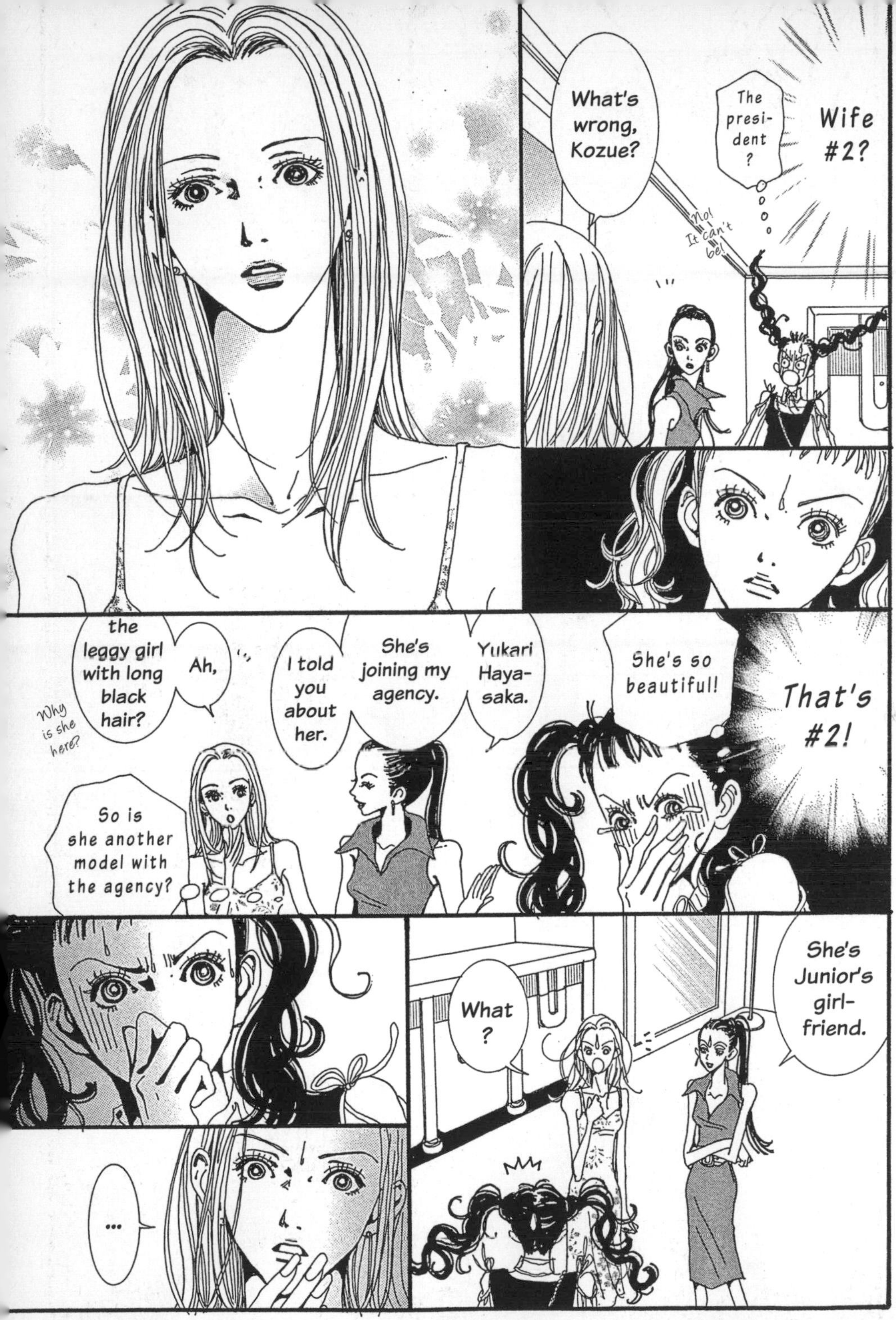
Wife #2?
The president?
What's wrong, Kozue?
No! It can't be!
That's #2!
She's so beautiful!
Yukari Hayasaka.
She's joining my agency.
I told you about her.
Ah,
the leggy girl with long black hair?
Why is she here?
So is she another model with the agency?
She's Junior's girl-friend.
What?
...

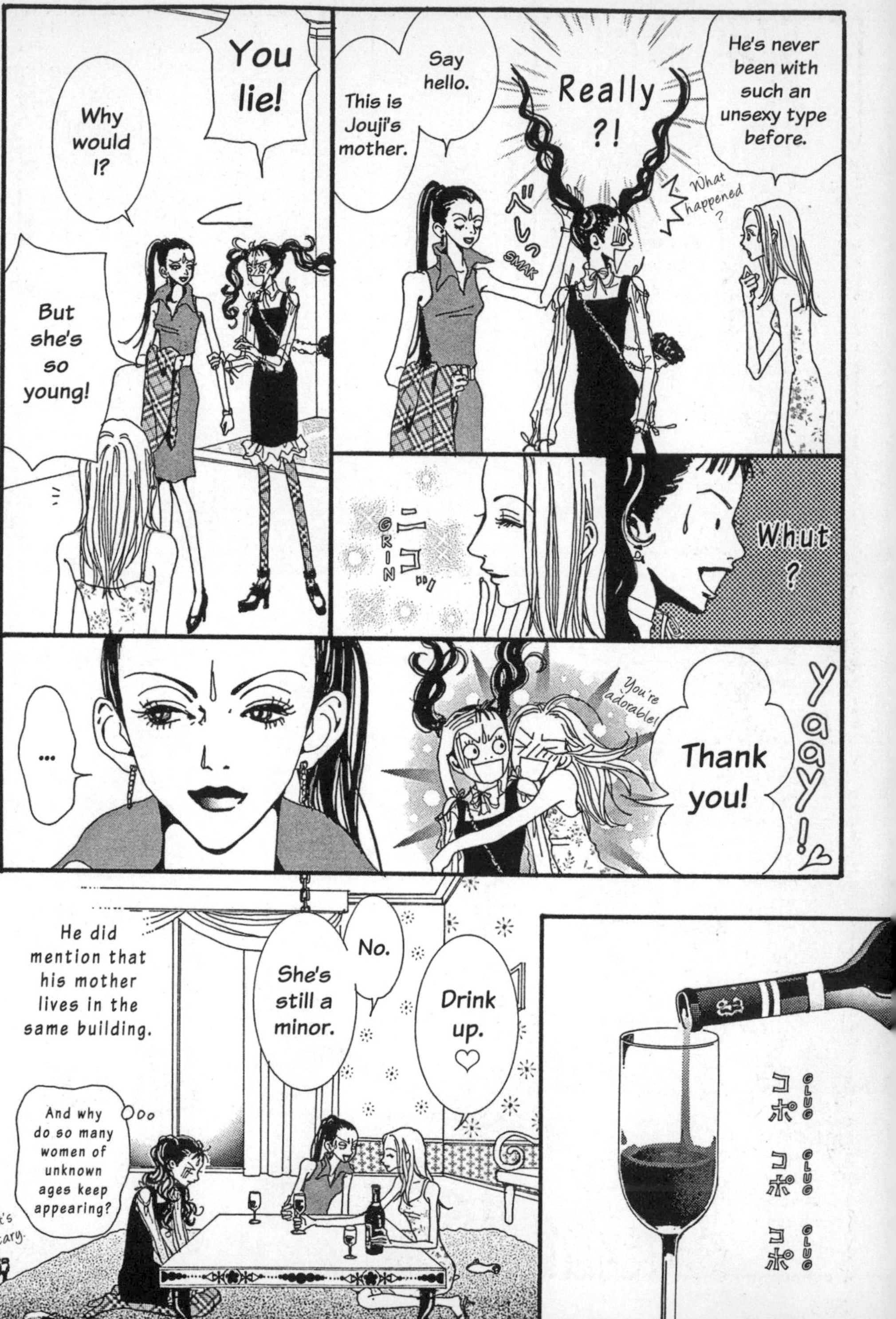
He's never been with such an unsexy type before.
What happened?
Really?!
Say hello.
This is Jouji's mother.
ベし
SMAK
You lie!
Why would I?
But she's so young!
Whut?
ニコッ
GRIN
Yaaay!♥
Thank you!
You're adorable!
...
コポ
GLUG
コポ
GLUG
コポ
GLUG
Drink up. ♡
No.
She's still a minor.
He did mention that his mother lives in the same building.
And why do so many women of unknown ages keep appearing?
It's scary.

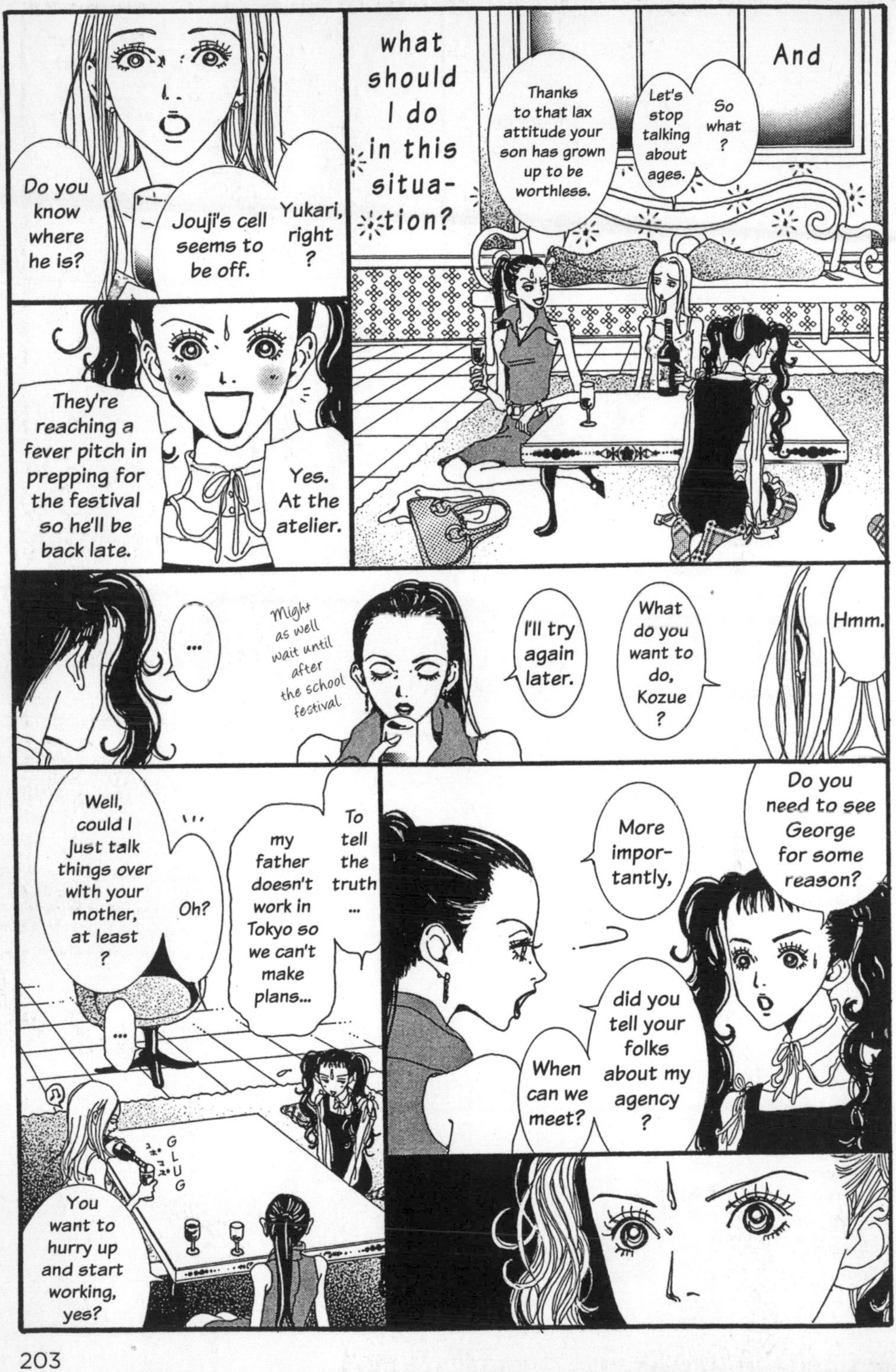
And
So what?
Let's stop talking about ages.
Thanks to that lax attitude your son has grown up to be worthless.
what should I do in this situation?
Yukari, right?
Jouji's cell seems to be off.
Do you know where he is?
Yes. At the atelier.
They're reaching a fever pitch in prepping for the festival so he'll be back late.
Hmm.
What do you want to do, Kozue?
I'll try again later.
Might as well wait until after the school festival
...
Do you need to see George for some reason?
More importantly,
did you tell your folks about my agency?
When can we meet?
To tell the truth ...
my father doesn't work in Tokyo so we can't make plans...
Oh?
...
Well, could I just talk things over with your mother, at least?
...
GLUG
You want to hurry up and start working, yes?

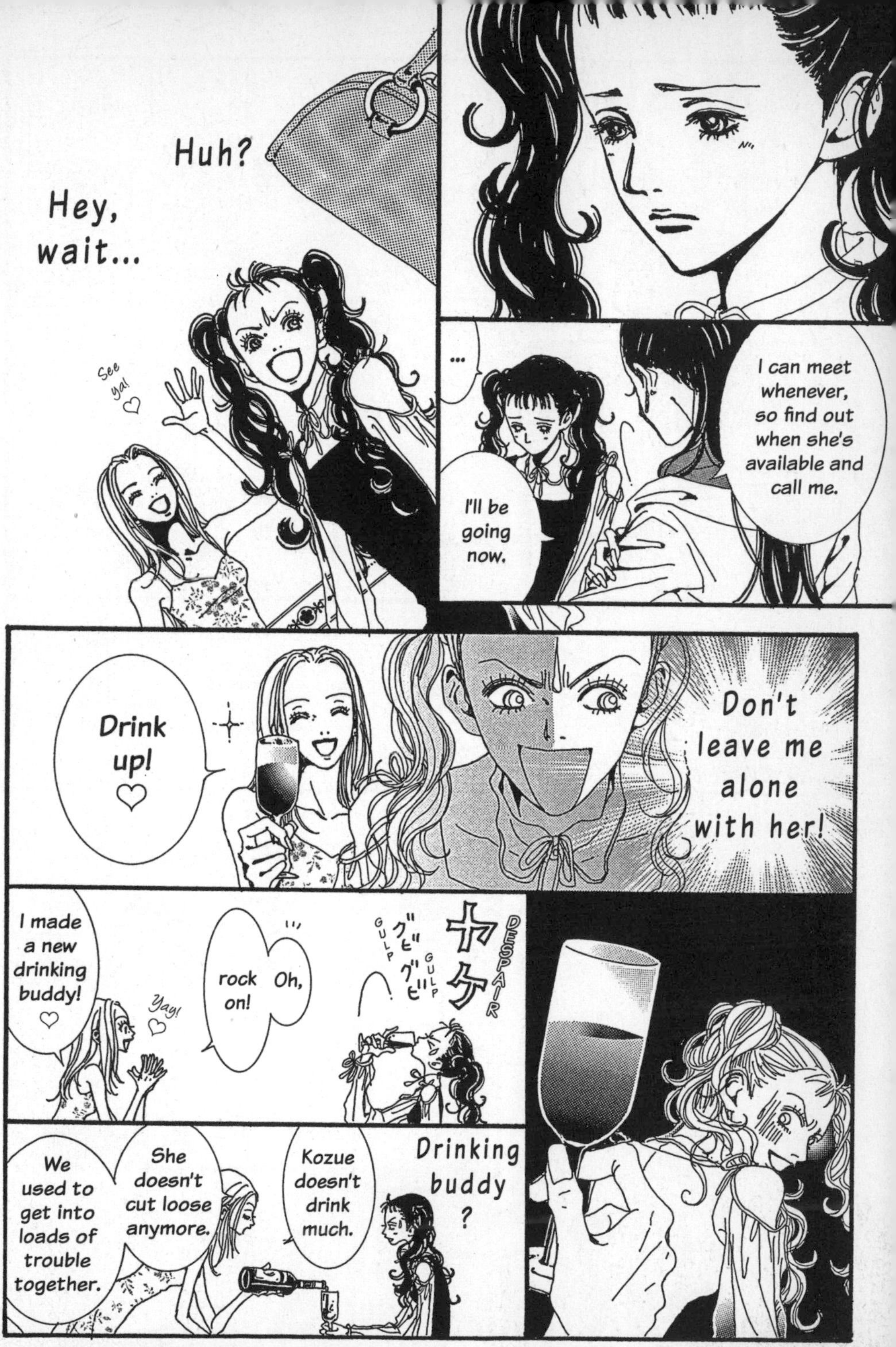
I can meet whenever, so find out when she's available and call me.
...
I'll be going now.
Huh?
Hey, wait...
See ya! ♡
Don't leave me alone with her!
Drink up! ♡
ヤケ DESPAIR
グビ GULP
グビ GULP
Oh, rock on!
I made a new drinking buddy! ♡
Yay! ♡
Drinking buddy?
Kozue doesn't drink much.
She doesn't cut loose anymore.
We used to get into loads of trouble together.

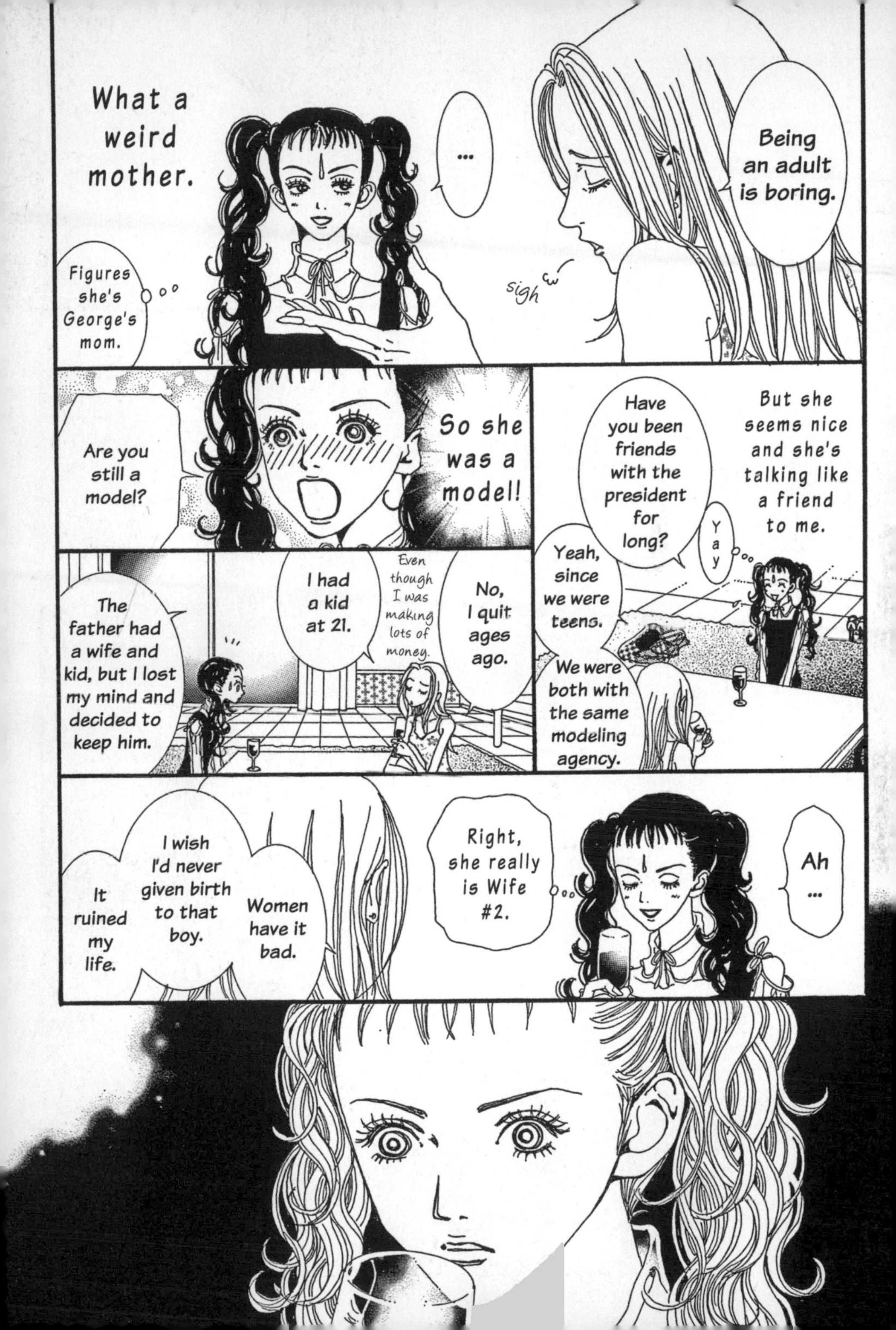
Being an adult is boring.
sigh
...
What a weird mother.
Figures she's George's mom.
But she seems nice and she's talking like a friend to me.
Have you been friends with the president for long?
Yay
Yeah, since we were teens.
We were both with the same modeling agency.
So she was a model!
Are you still a model?
No, I quit ages ago.
Even though I was making lots of money.
I had a kid at 21.
The father had a wife and kid, but I lost my mind and decided to keep him.
Ah ...
Right, she really is Wife #2.
Women have it bad.
I wish I'd never given birth to that boy.
It ruined my life.

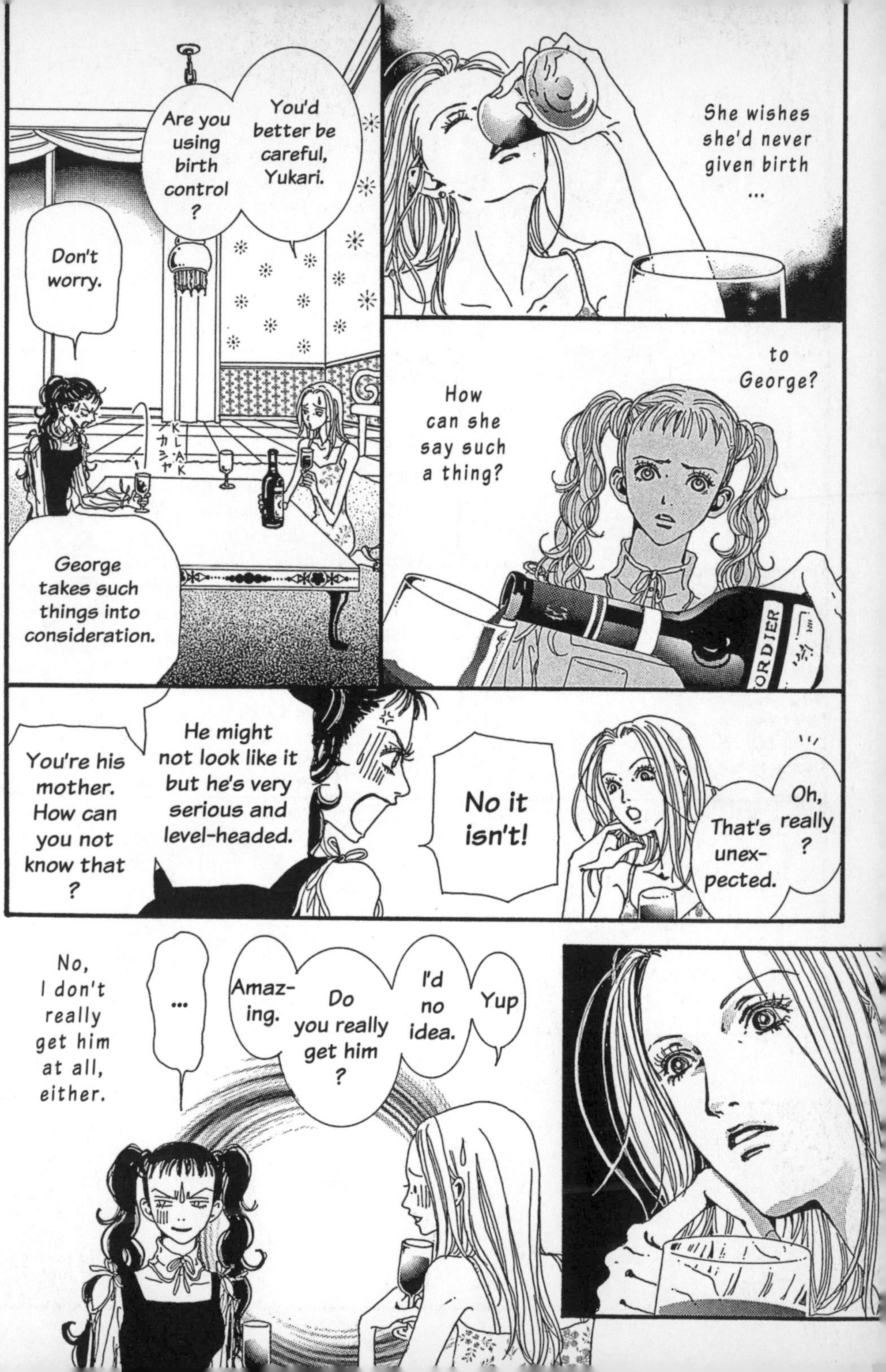
She wishes she'd never given birth ...
How can she say such a thing?
to George?
You'd better be careful, Yukari.
Are you using birth control?
Don't worry.
カシャ
KLAK
George takes such things into consideration.
Oh, really?
That's unexpected.
No it isn't!
He might not look like it but he's very serious and level-headed.
You're his mother. How can you not know that?
Yup
I'd no idea.
Do you really get him?
Amazing.
...
No, I don't really get him at all, either.

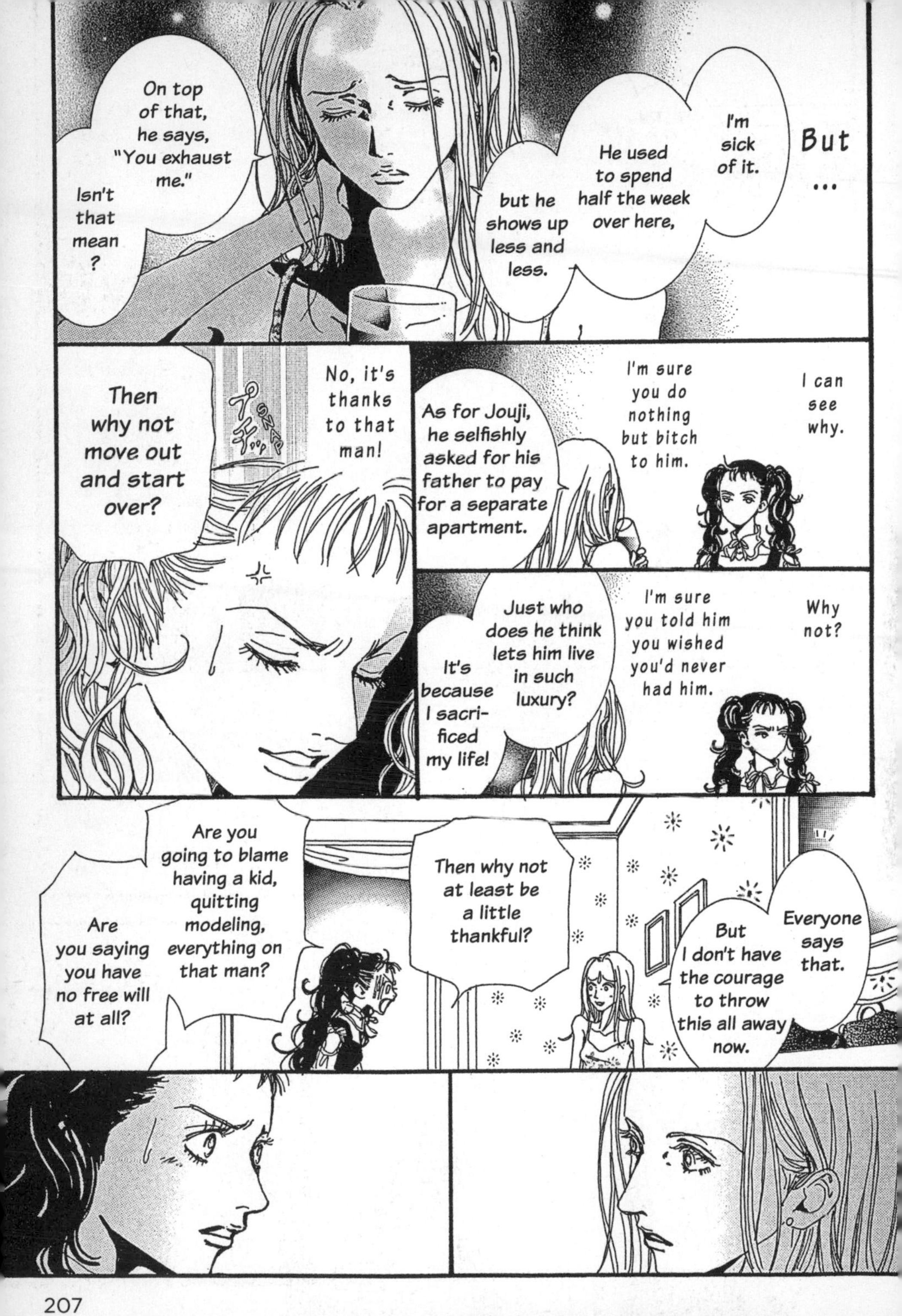
But ...
I'm sick of it.
He used to spend half the week over here,
but he shows up less and less.
On top of that, he says, "You exhaust me."
Isn't that mean ?
I can see why.
I'm sure you do nothing but bitch to him.
As for Jouji, he selfishly asked for his father to pay for a separate apartment.
Why not?
I'm sure you told him you wished you'd never had him.
Just who does he think lets him live in such luxury?
It's because I sacrificed my life!
No, it's thanks to that man!
SNAP
Then why not move out and start over?
Everyone says that.
But I don't have the courage to throw this all away now.
Then why not at least be a little thankful?
Are you going to blame having a kid, quitting modeling, everything on that man?
Are you saying you have no free will at all?

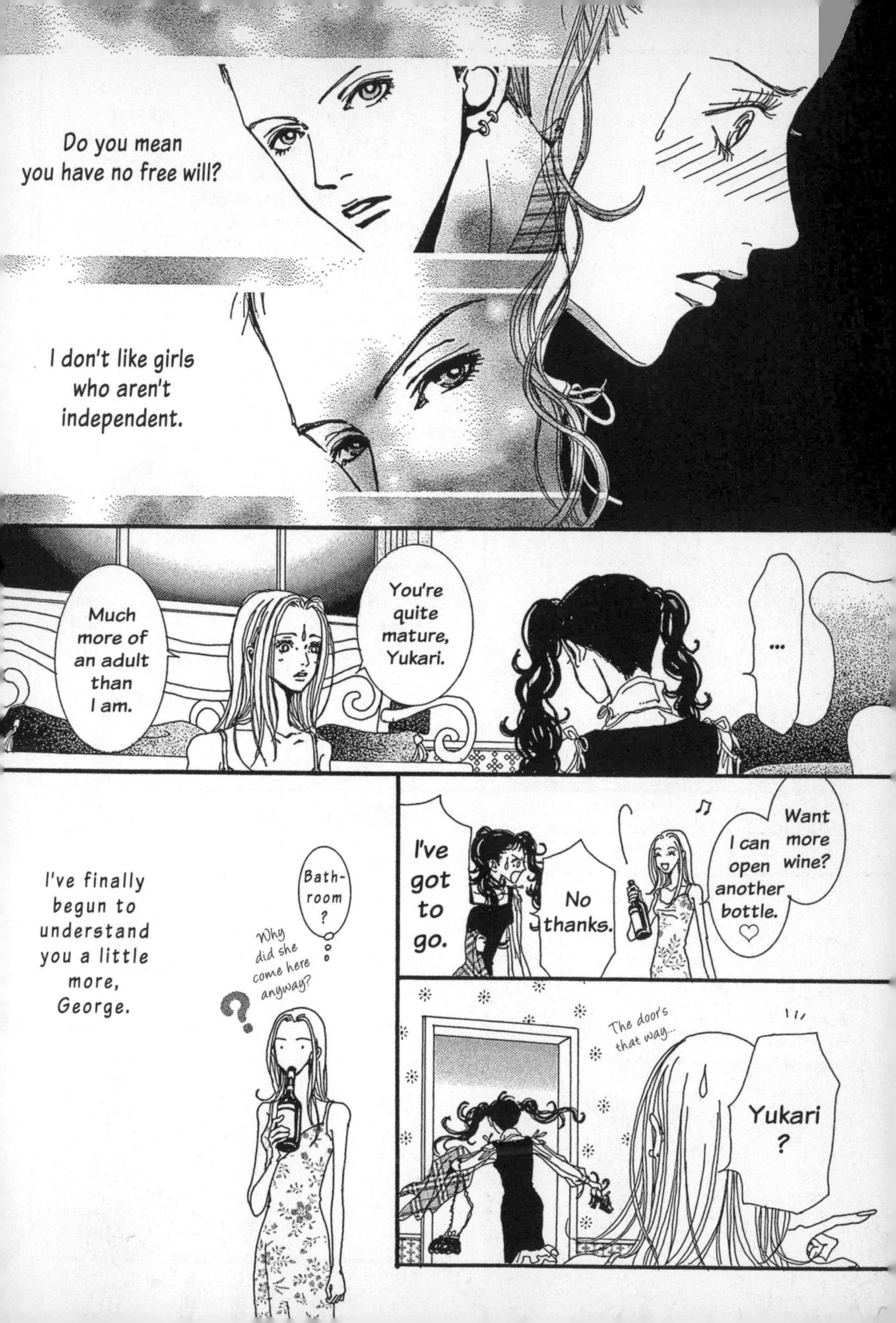

Do you mean you have no free will?
I don't like girls who aren't independent.
...
You're quite mature, Yukari.
Much more of an adult than I am.
Want more wine?
I can open another bottle. ♡
♫
No thanks.
I've got to go.
Yukari?
The doors that way...
Bathroom?
Why did she come here anyway?
?
I've finally begun to understand you a little more, George.

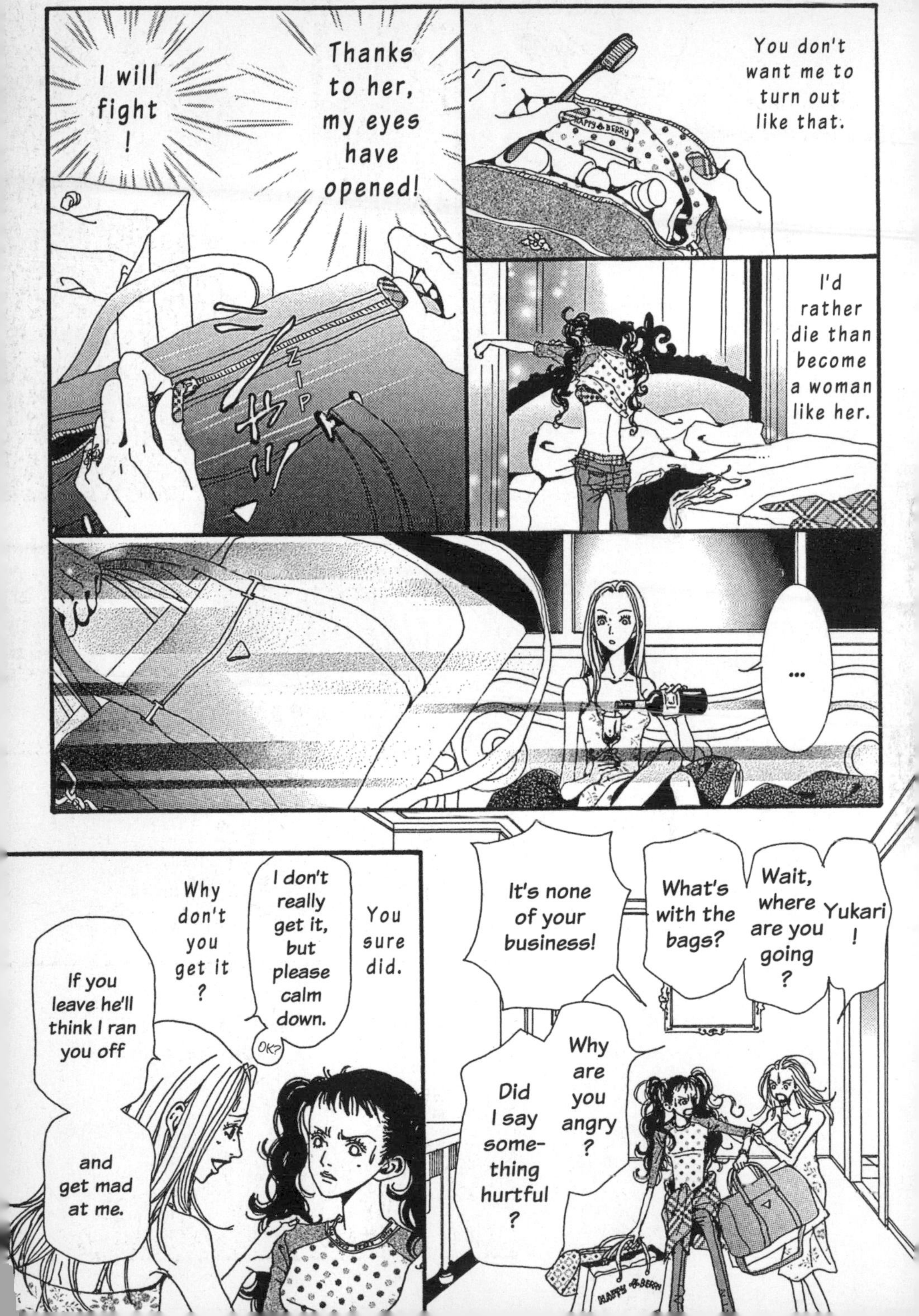
You don't want me to turn out like that.
I'd rather die than become a woman like her.
Thanks to her, my eyes have opened!
I will fight!
ZIP
...
Yukari!
Wait, where are you going?
What's with the bags?
It's none of your business!
Why are you angry?
Did I say something hurtful?
You sure did.
I don't really get it, but please calm down.
OK?
Why don't you get it?
If you leave he'll think I ran you off
and get mad at me.

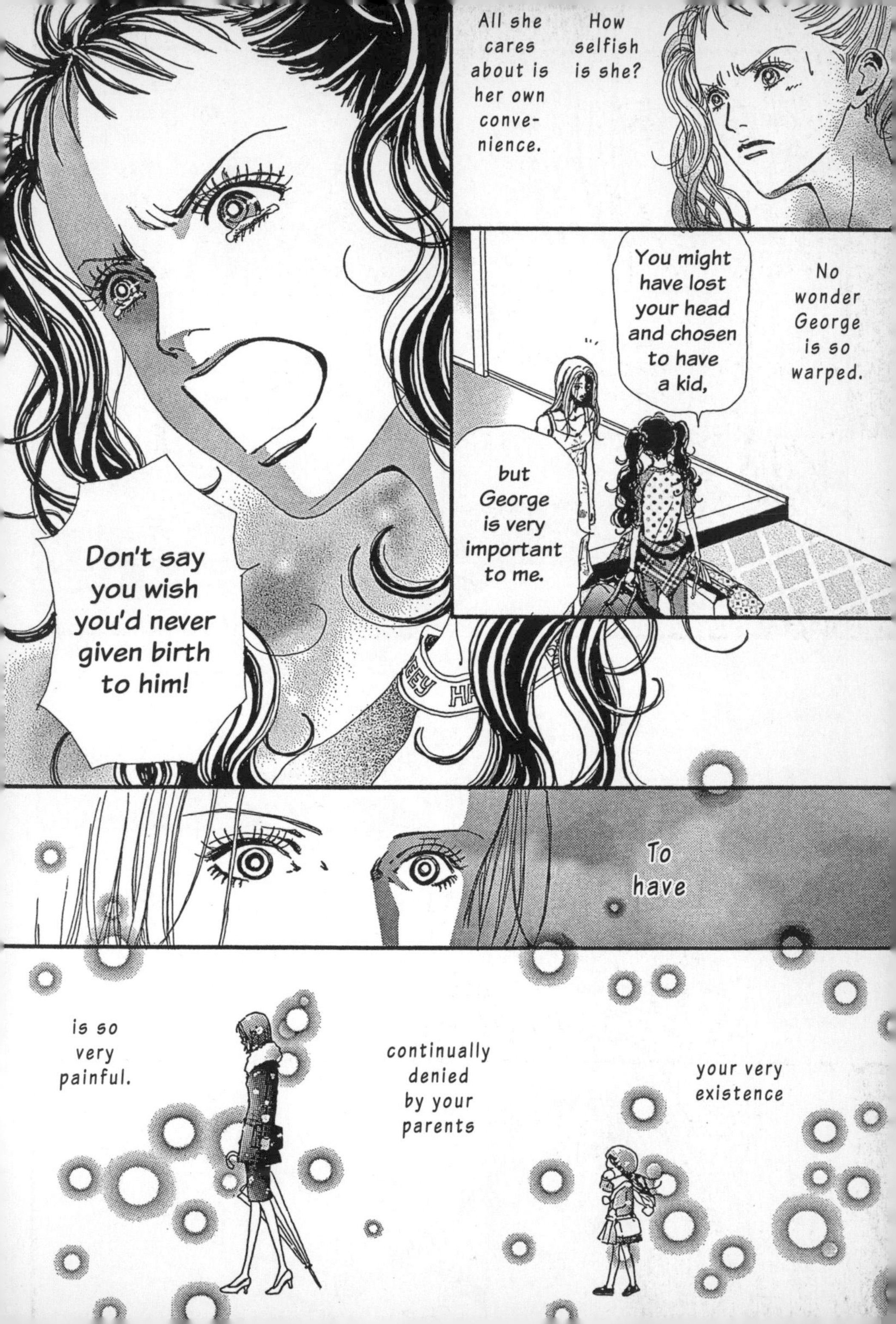
How selfish is she?
All she cares about is her own convenience.
No wonder George is so warped.
You might have lost your head and chosen to have a kid,
...
but George is very important to me.
Don't say you wish you'd never given birth to him!
To have
your very existence
continually denied by your parents
is so very painful.

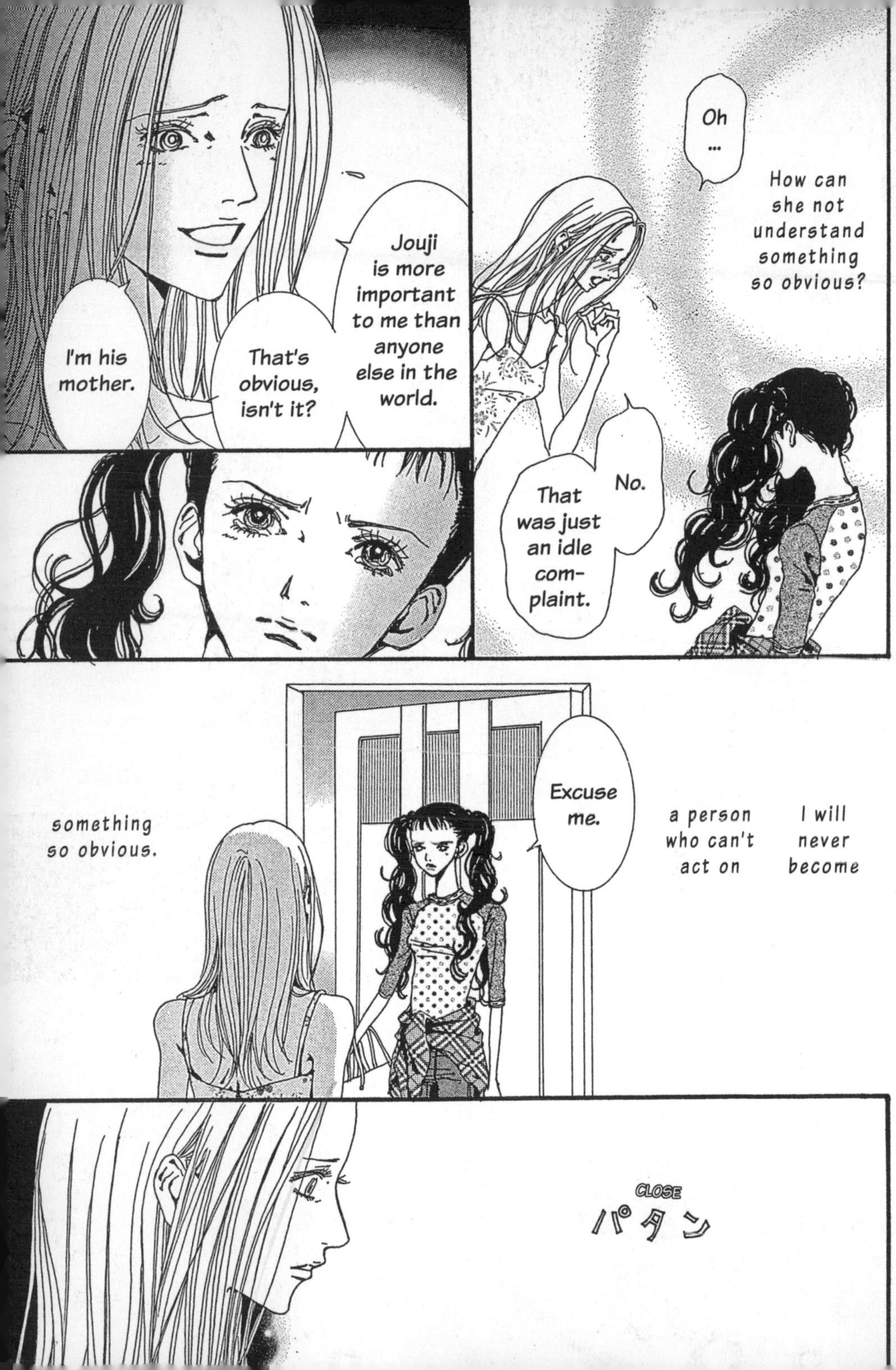
Oh ...
How can she not understand something so obvious?
No.
That was just an idle complaint.
Jouji is more important to me than anyone else in the world.
That's obvious, isn't it?
I'm his mother.
I will never become
a person who can't act on
Excuse me.
something so obvious.
CLOSE
パタン

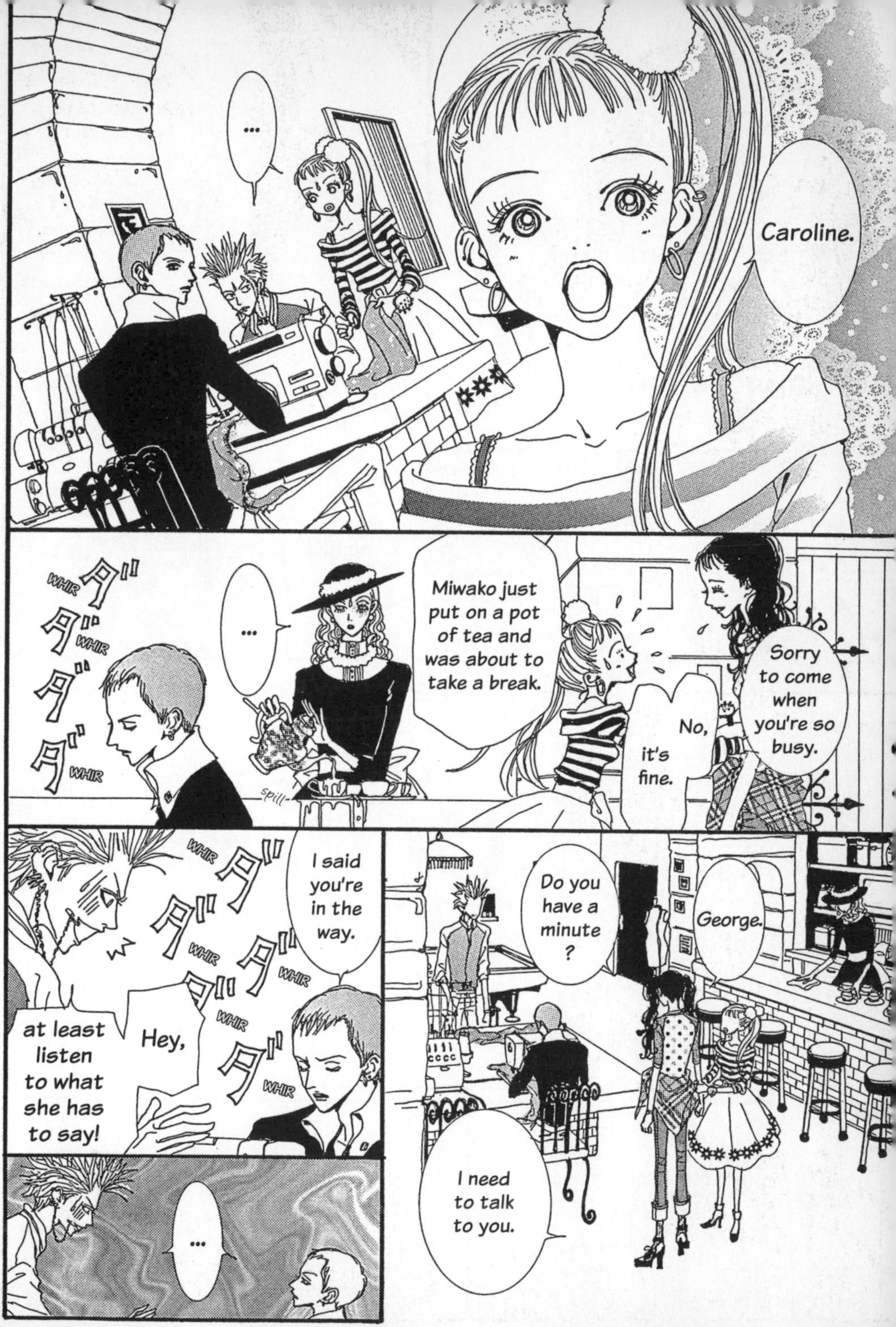
Caroline.
...
Sorry to come when you're so busy.
No, it's fine.
Miwako just put on a pot of tea and was about to take a break.
...
WHIR
WHIR
WHIR
spill
George.
Do you have a minute?
I need to talk to you.
I said you're in the way.
WHIR
WHIR
WHIR
WHIR
Hey, at least listen to what she has to say!
...

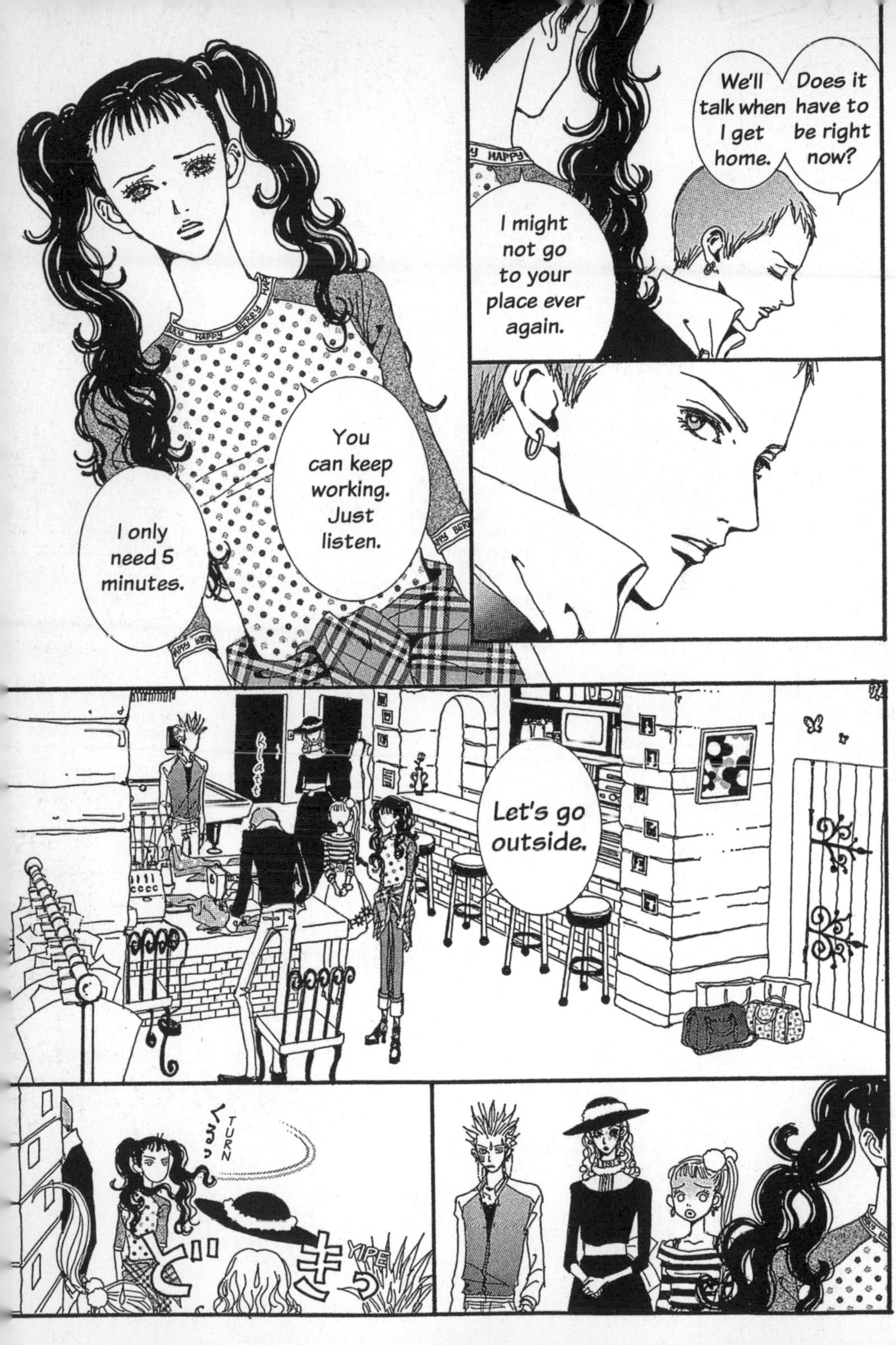

Does it have to be right now?
We'll talk when I get home.
I might not go to your place ever again.
You can keep working. Just listen.
I only need 5 minutes.
Klatt
Let's go outside.
TURN
YIPE

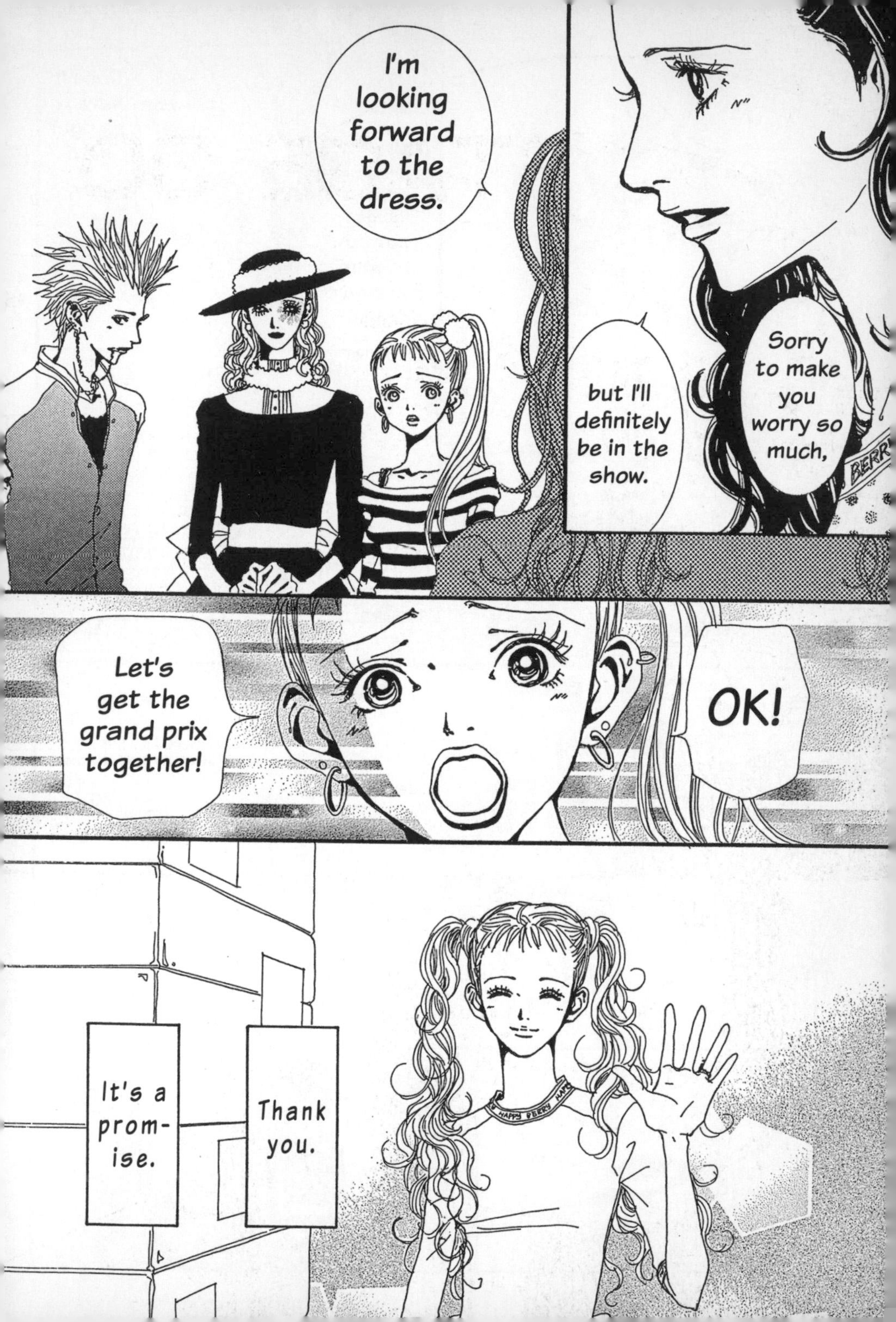
Sorry to make you worry so much,
but I'll definitely be in the show.
I'm looking forward to the dress.
OK!
Let's get the grand prix together!
Thank you.
It's a prom-ise.

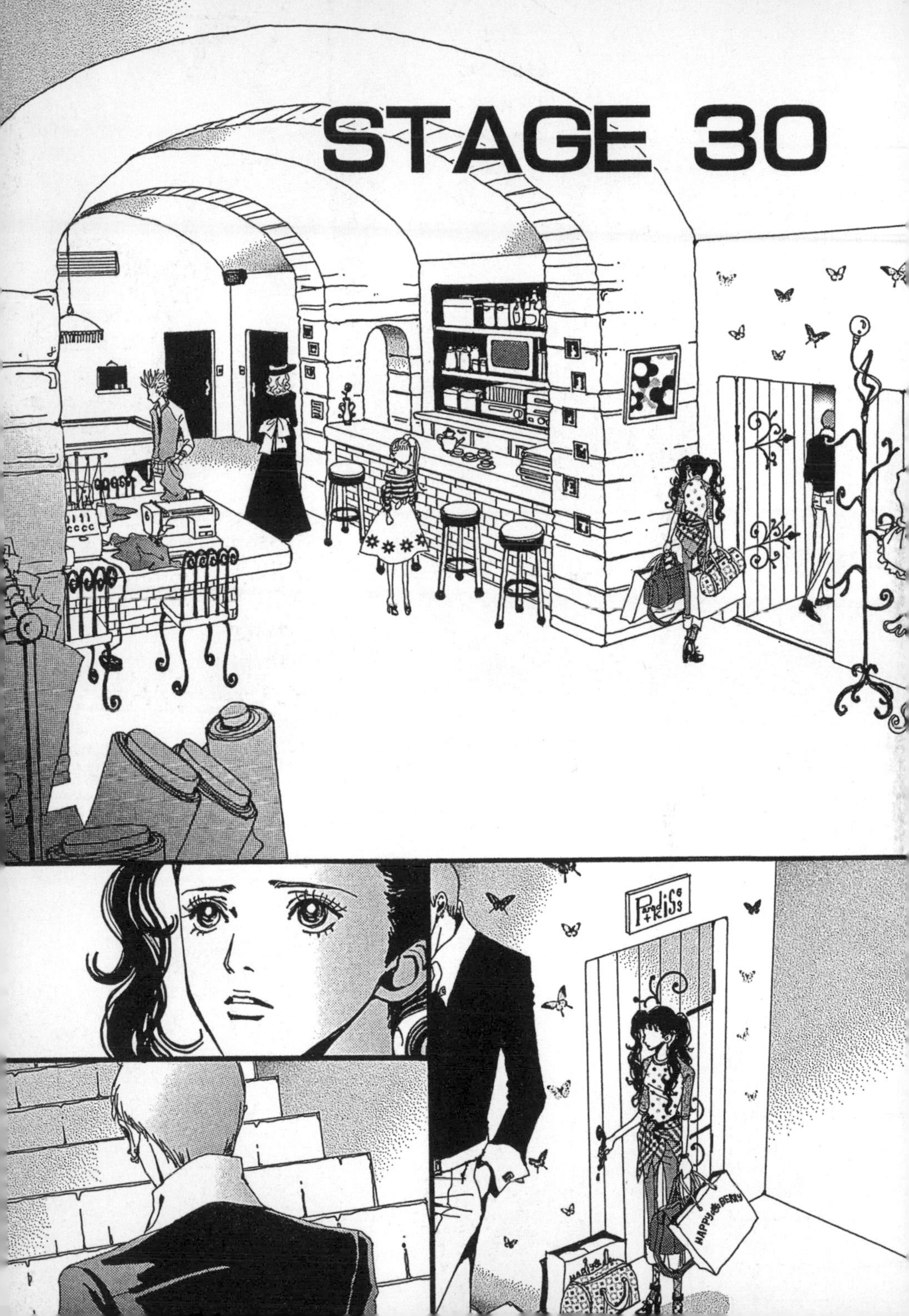
STAGE 30
HAPPY BERRY

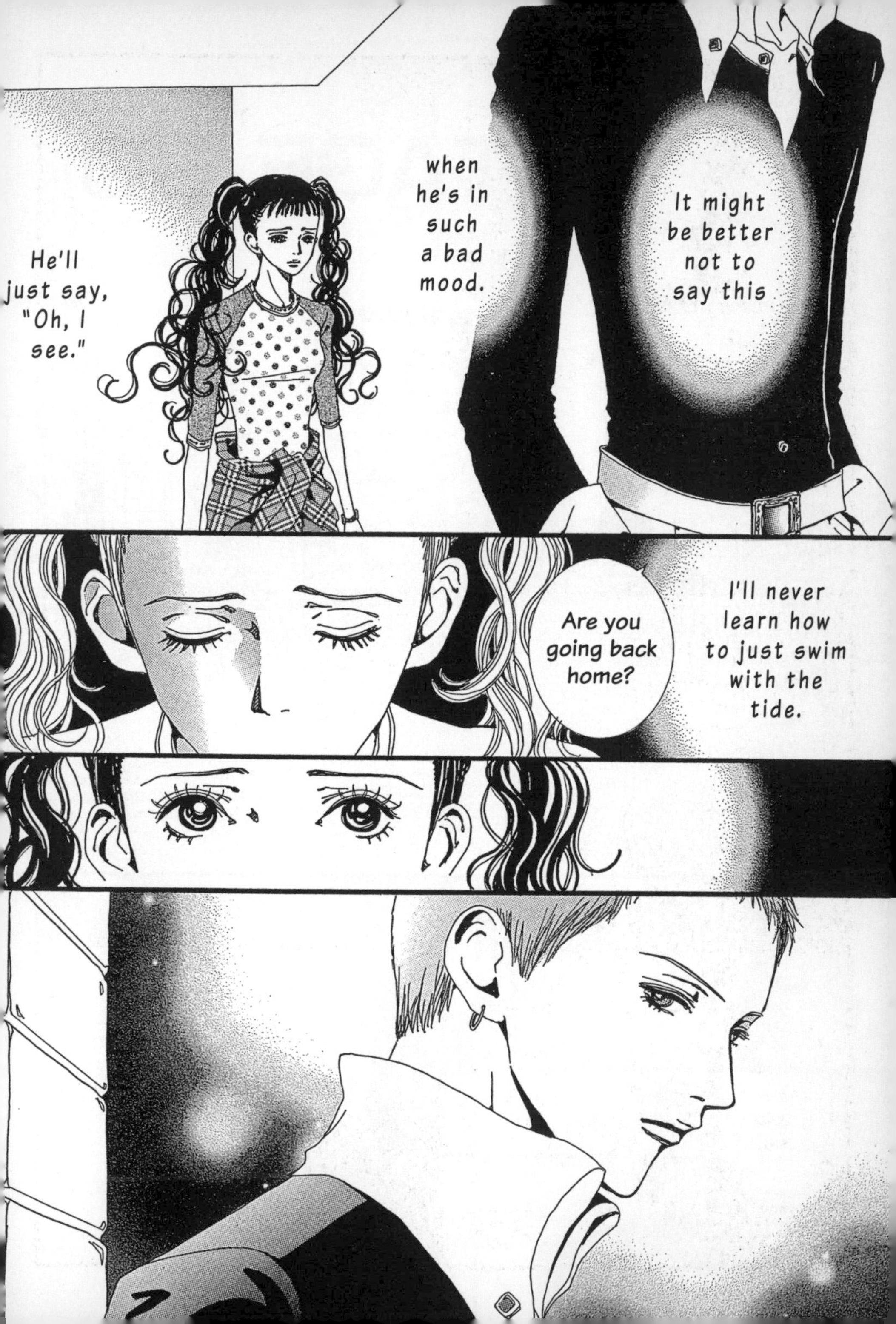
It might be better not to say this
when he's in such a bad mood.
He'll just say, "Oh, I see."
I'll never learn how to just swim with the tide.
Are you going back home?

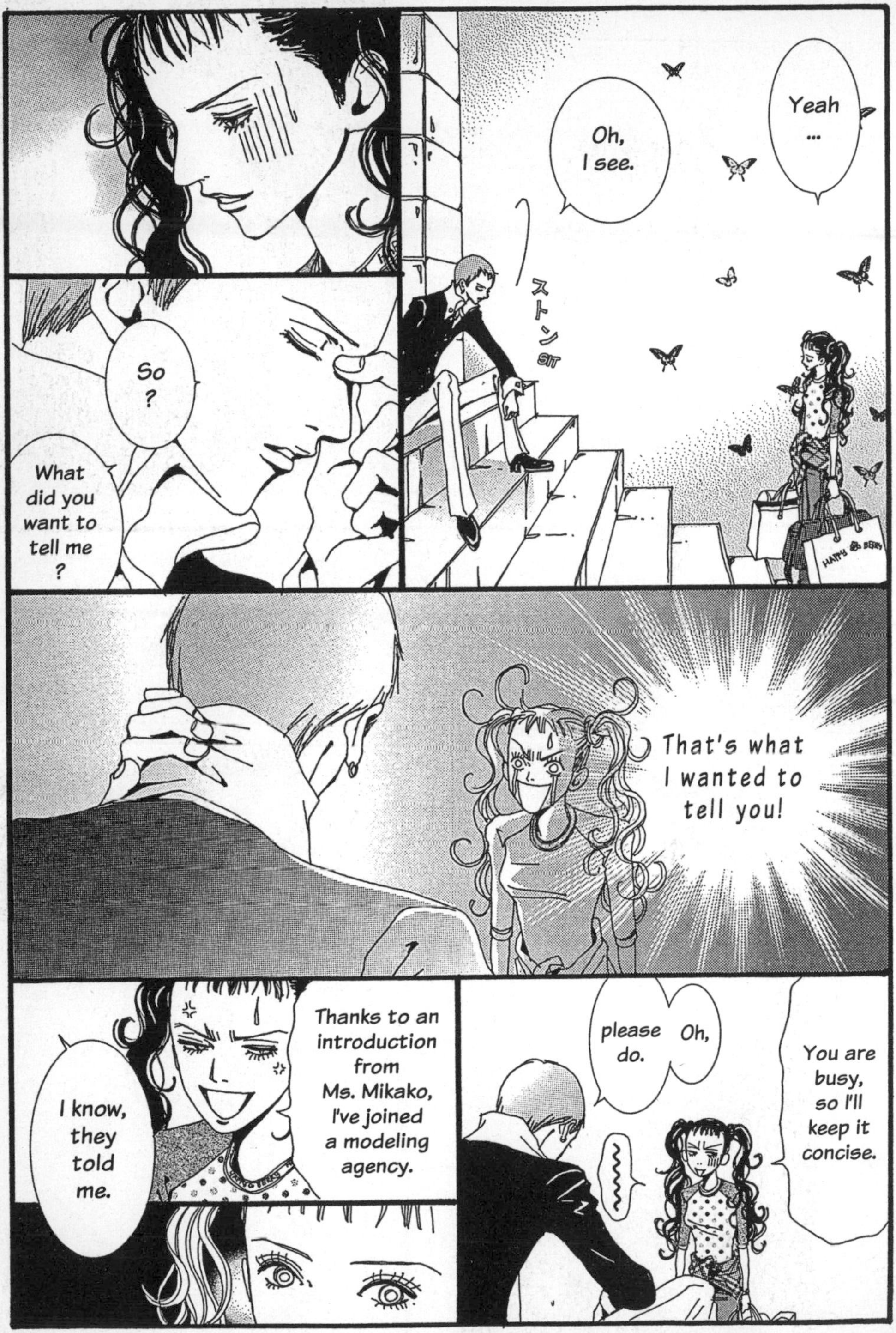
Yeah ...
Oh, I see.
ストン
SIT
So ?
What did you want to tell me ?
That's what I wanted to tell you!
You are busy, so I'll keep it concise.
Oh,
please do.
Thanks to an introduction from Ms. Mikako, I've joined a modeling agency.
I know, they told me.

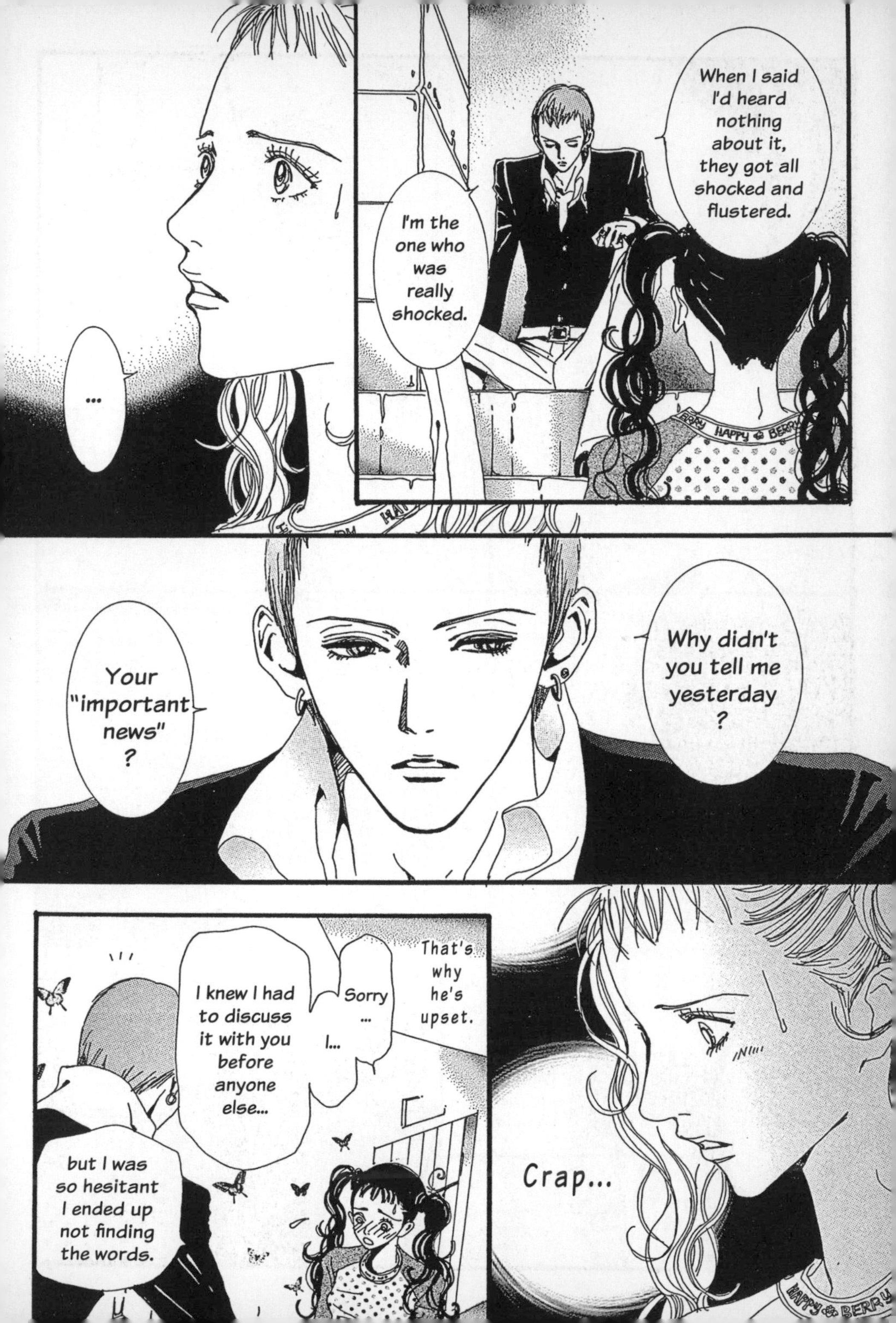
When I said I'd heard nothing about it, they got all shocked and flustered.
I'm the one who was really shocked.
BERRY HAPPY BERRY
...
Why didn't you tell me yesterday ?
Your "important news" ?
Crap...
That's why he's upset.
Sorry ... I...
I knew I had to discuss it with you before anyone else...
but I was so hesitant I ended up not finding the words.

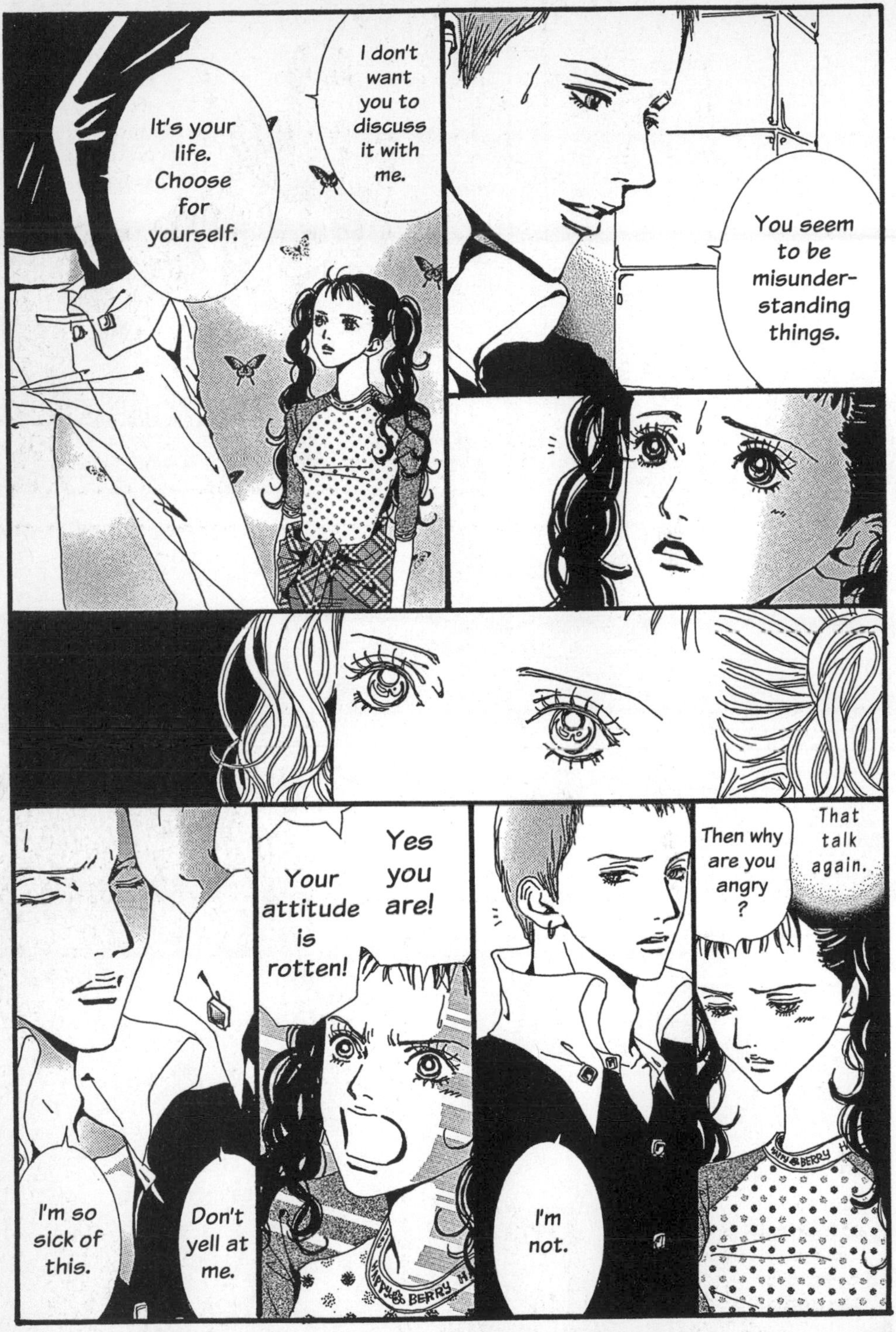

You seem to be misunderstanding things.
I don't want you to discuss it with me.
It's your life. Choose for yourself.
That talk again.
Then why are you angry?
I'm not.
Yes you are!
Your attitude is rotten!
Don't yell at me.
I'm so sick of this.

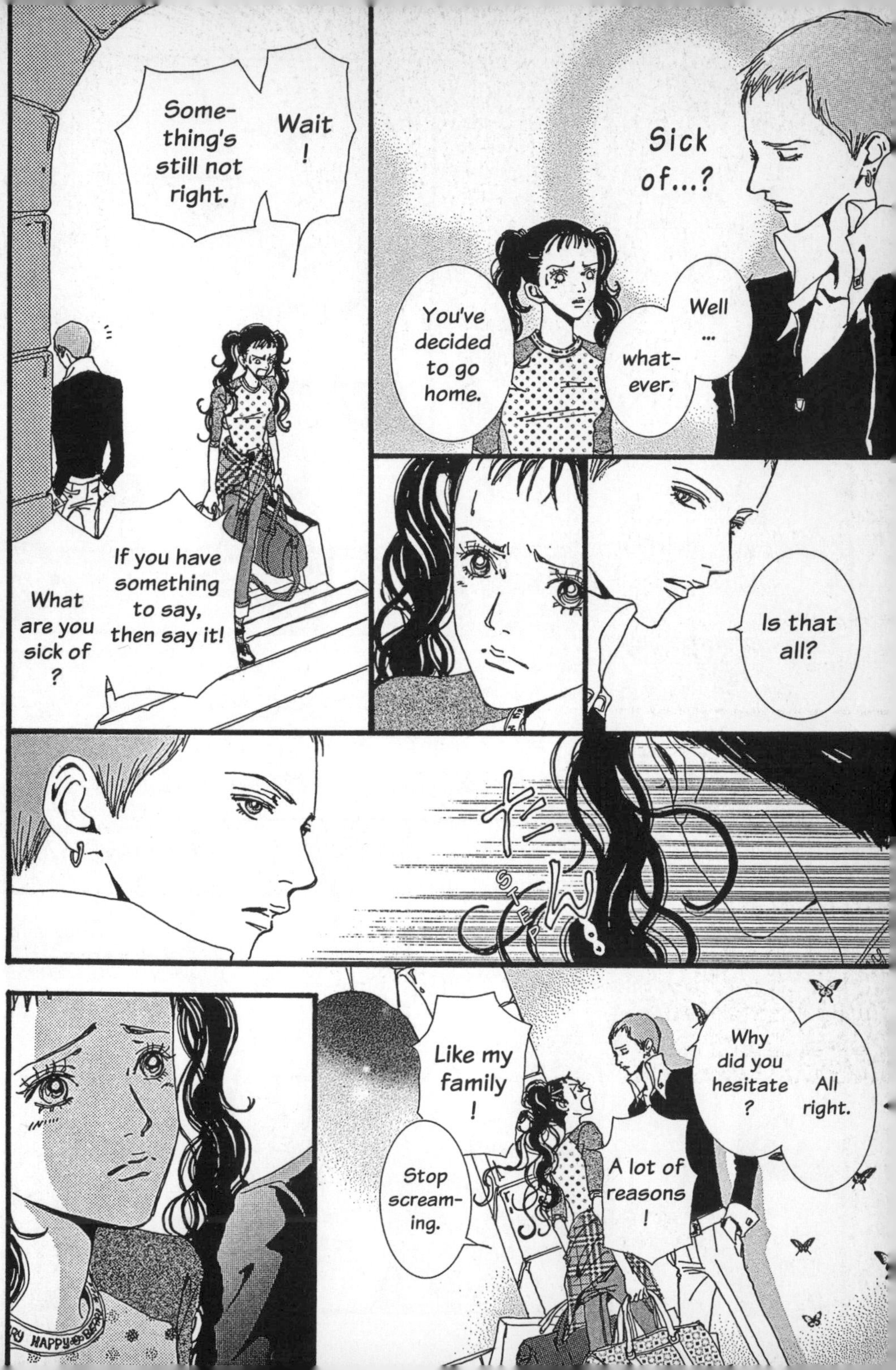

Sick of...?
Well ... whatever.
You've decided to go home.
Is that all?
Wait!
Something's still not right.
If you have something to say, then say it!
What are you sick of?
STEP
All right.
Why did you hesitate?
A lot of reasons!
Like my family!
Stop screaming.

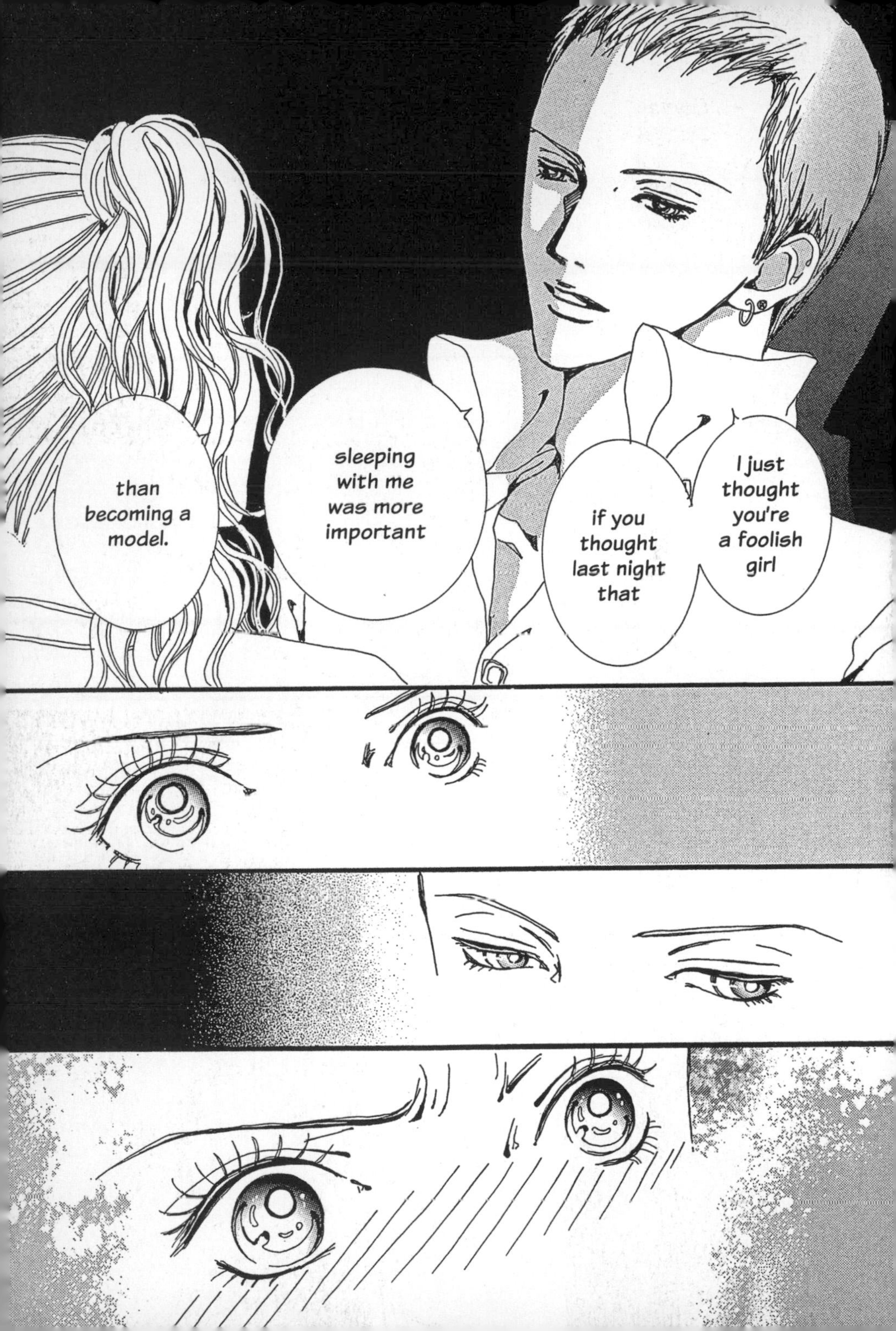
I just thought you're a foolish girl
if you thought last night that
sleeping with me was more important
than becoming a model.

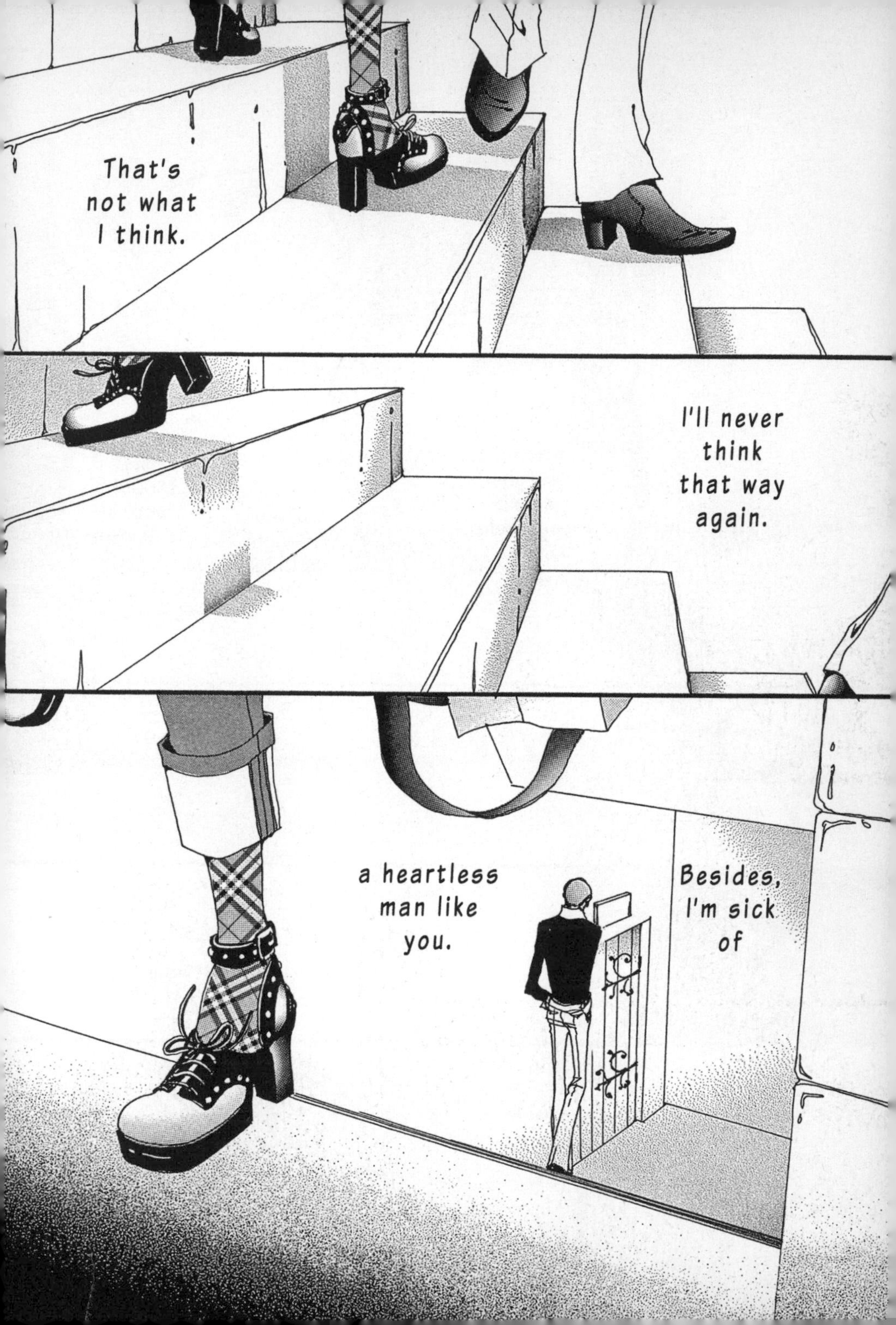
That's not what I think.
I'll never think that way again.
Besides, I'm sick of
a heartless man like you.

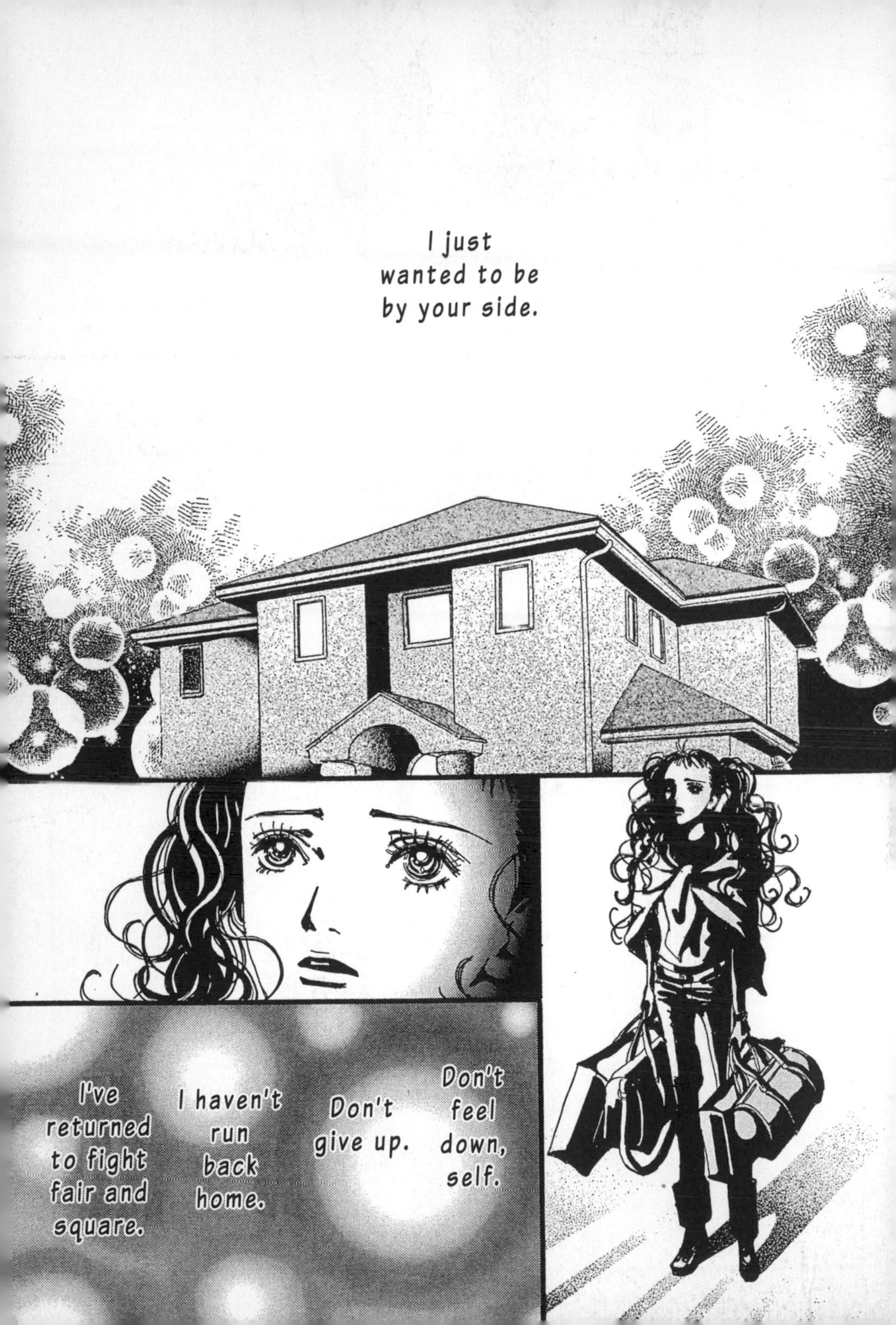
I just wanted to be by your side.
Don't feel down, self.
Don't give up.
I haven't run back home.
I've returned to fight fair and square.

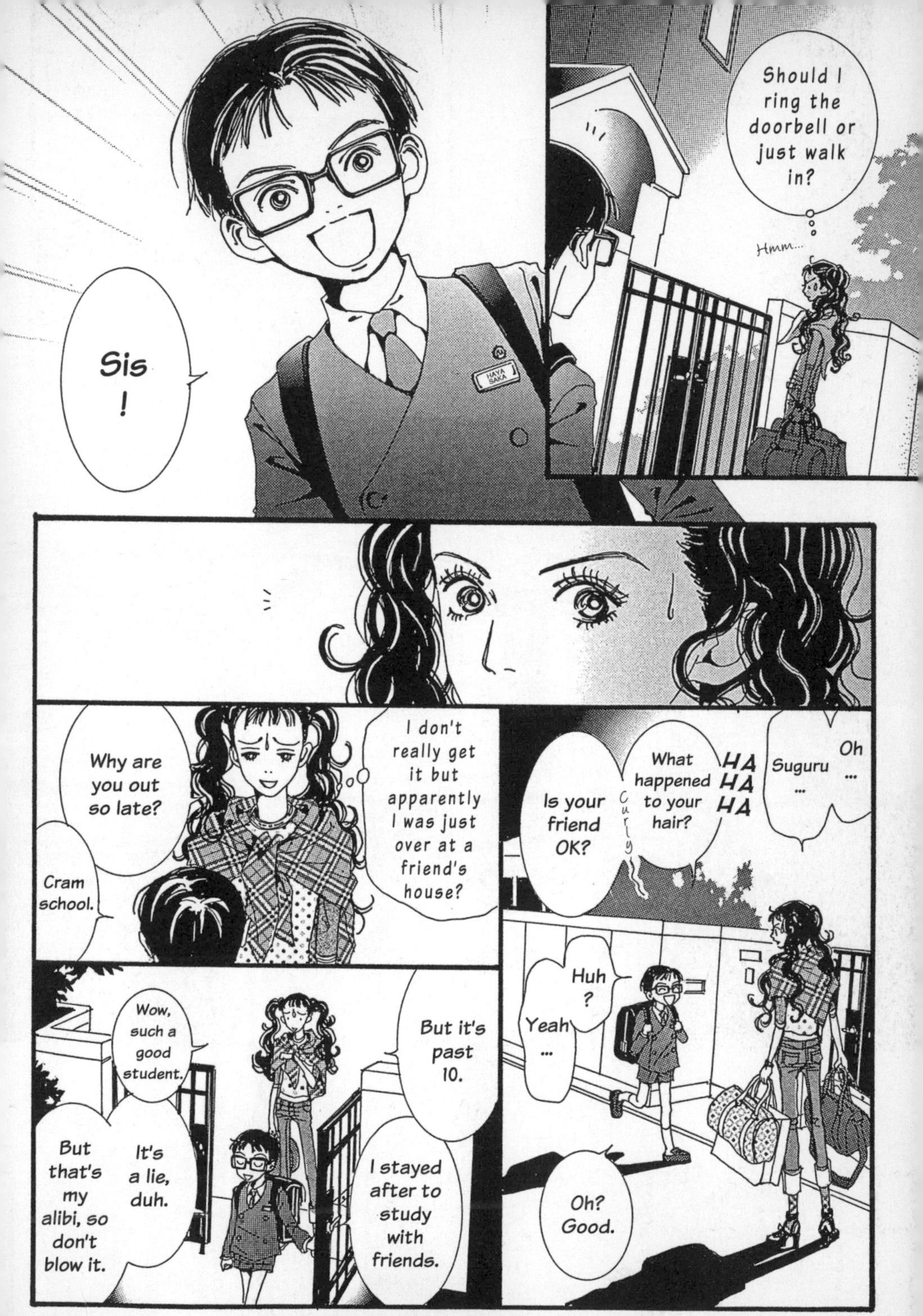
Should I ring the doorbell or just walk in?
Hmm...
Sis!
Oh ...
Suguru ...
HA HA HA
What happened to your hair?
Curly
Is your friend OK?
Huh?
Yeah ...
Oh? Good.
I don't really get it but apparently I was just over at a friend's house?
Why are you out so late?
Cram school.
But it's past 10.
Wow, such a good student.
I stayed after to study with friends.
It's a lie, duh.
But that's my alibi, so don't blow it.

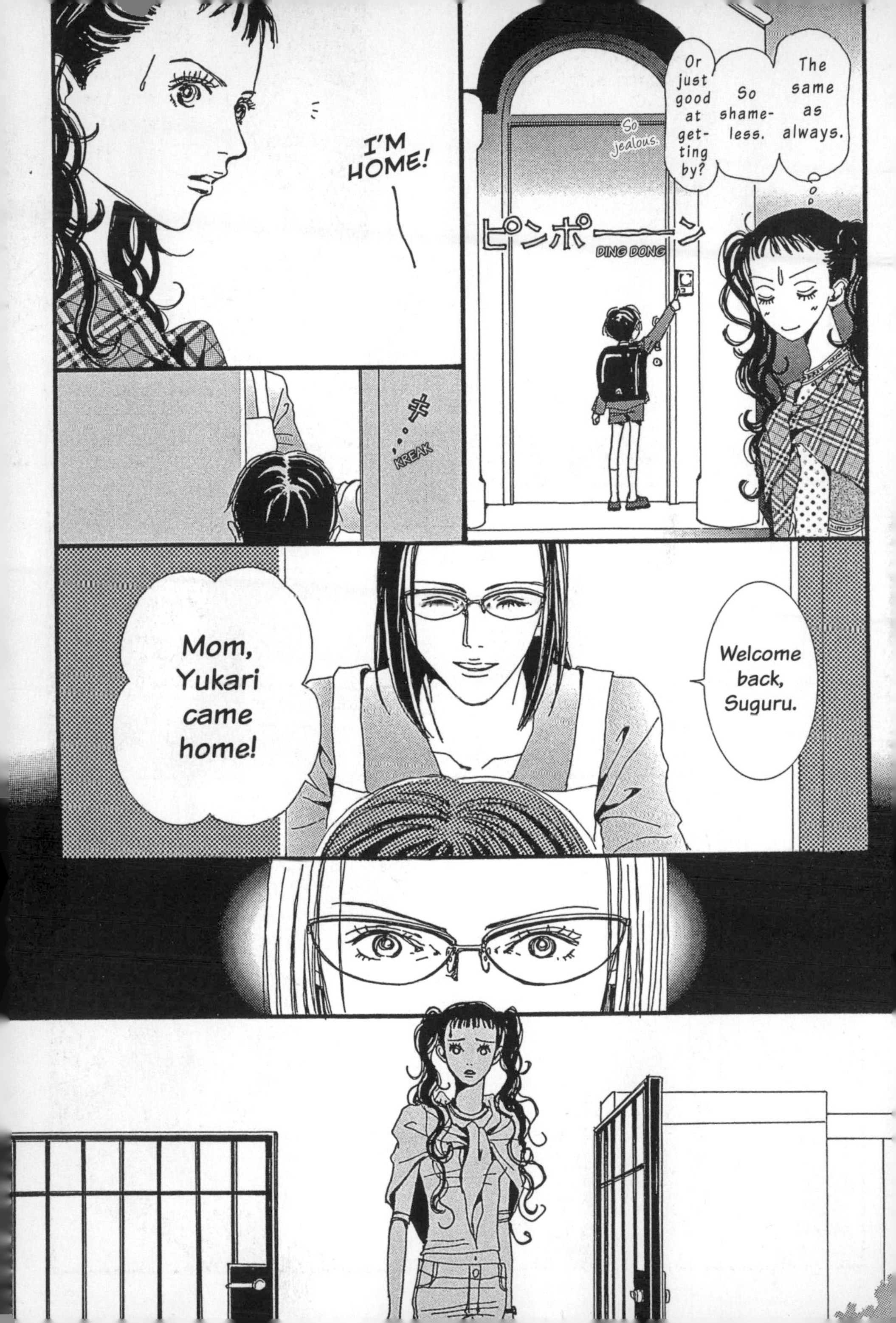
The same as always.
So shame-less.
Or just good at get-ting by?
So jealous.
ピンポーーン
DING DONG
I'M HOME!
ギ
KREAK
Welcome back, Suguru.
Mom, Yukari came home!

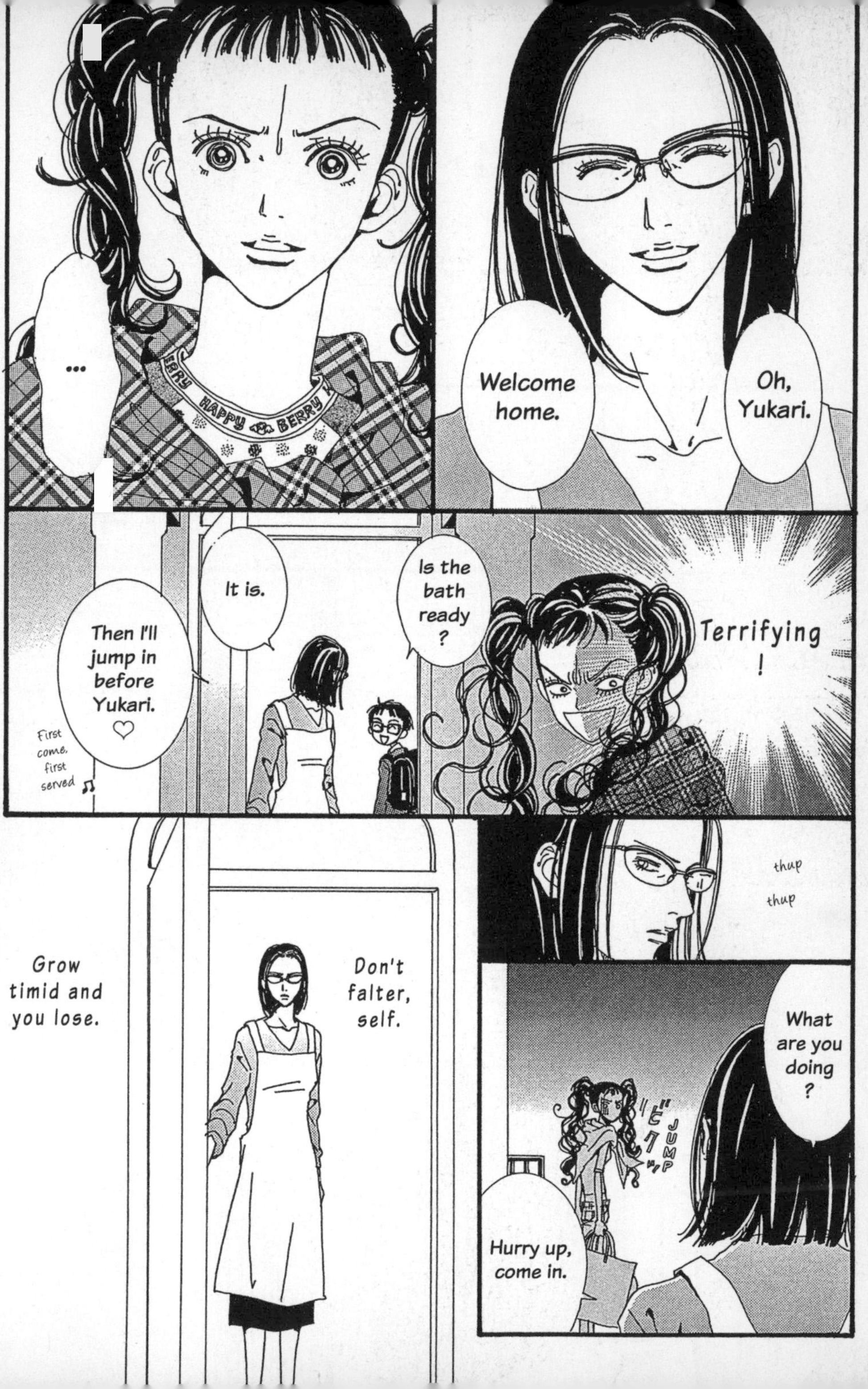
Oh, Yukari.
Welcome home.
...
HAPPY BERRY
Terrifying!
Is the bath ready?
It is.
Then I'll jump in before Yukari. ♡
First come, first served ♫
thup
thup
What are you doing?
JUMP
Hurry up, come in.
Don't falter, self.
Grow timid and you lose.

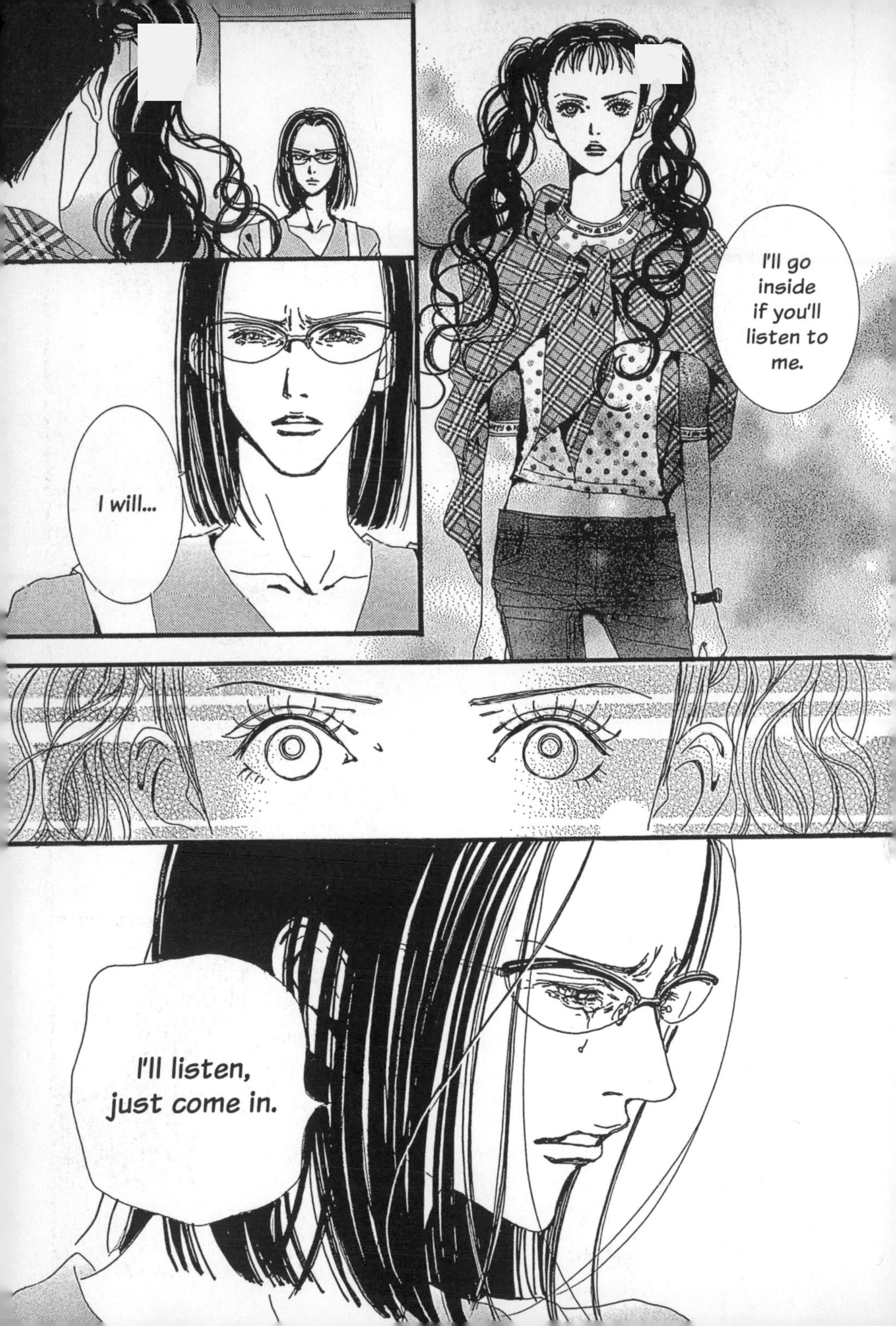
I'll go inside if you'll listen to me.
I will...
I'll listen, just come in.

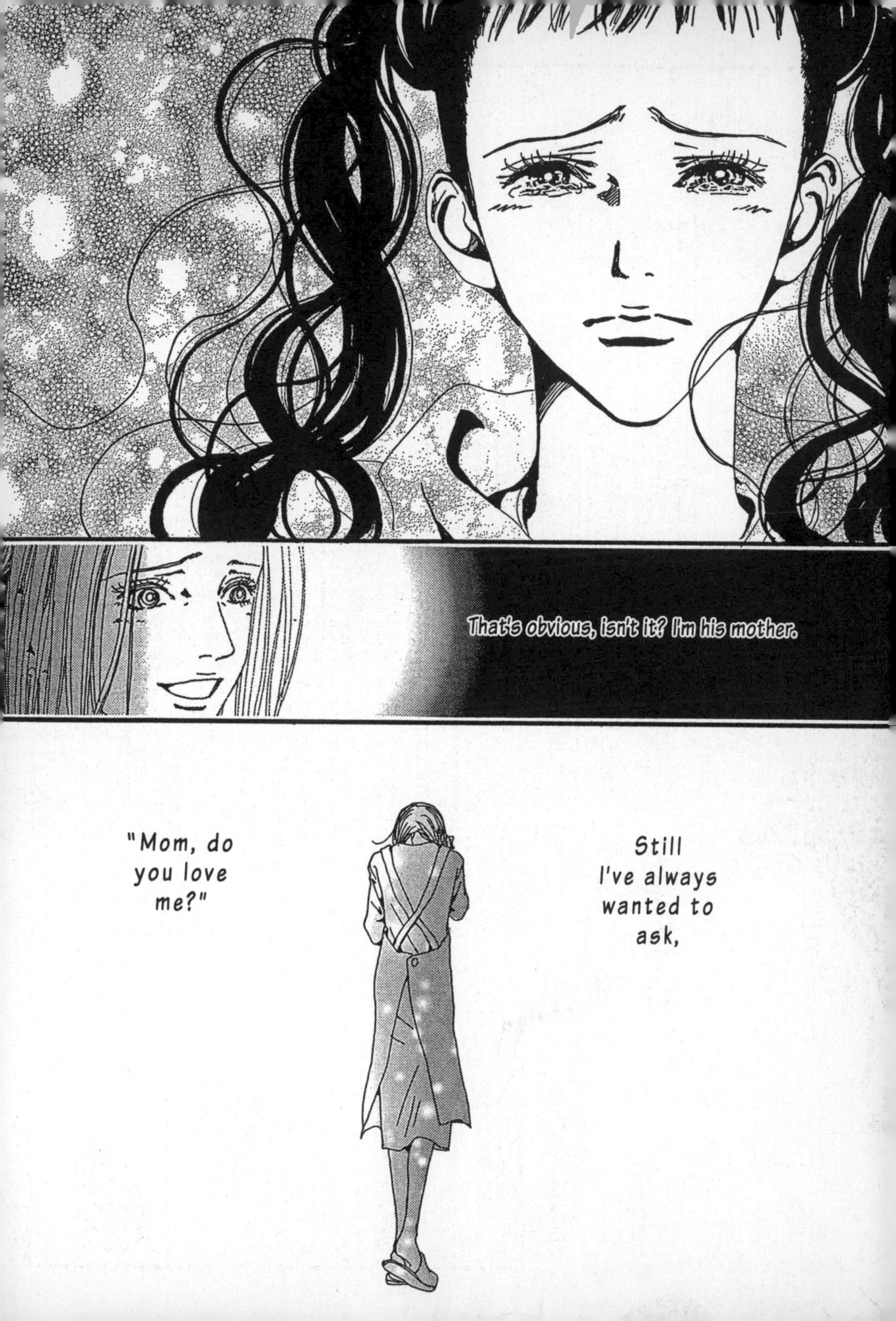
That's obvious, isn't it? I'm his mother.
Still I've always wanted to ask,
"Mom, do you love me?"

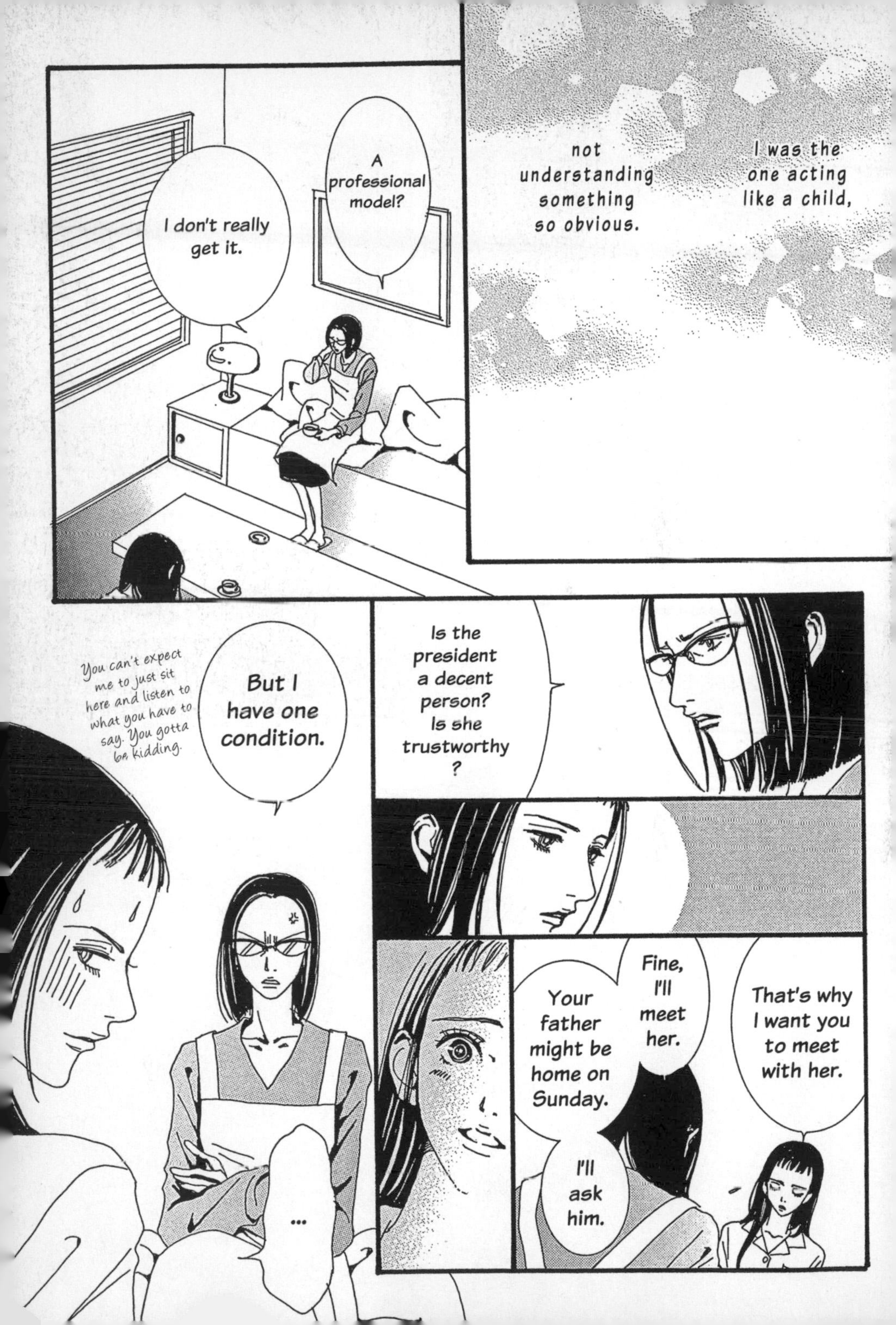

I was the one acting like a child,
not understanding something so obvious.
A professional model?
I don't really get it.
Is the president a decent person? Is she trustworthy?
That's why I want you to meet with her.
Fine, I'll meet her.
Your father might be home on Sunday.
I'll ask him.
But I have one condition.
You can't expect me to just sit here and listen to what you have to say. You gotta be kidding.
...

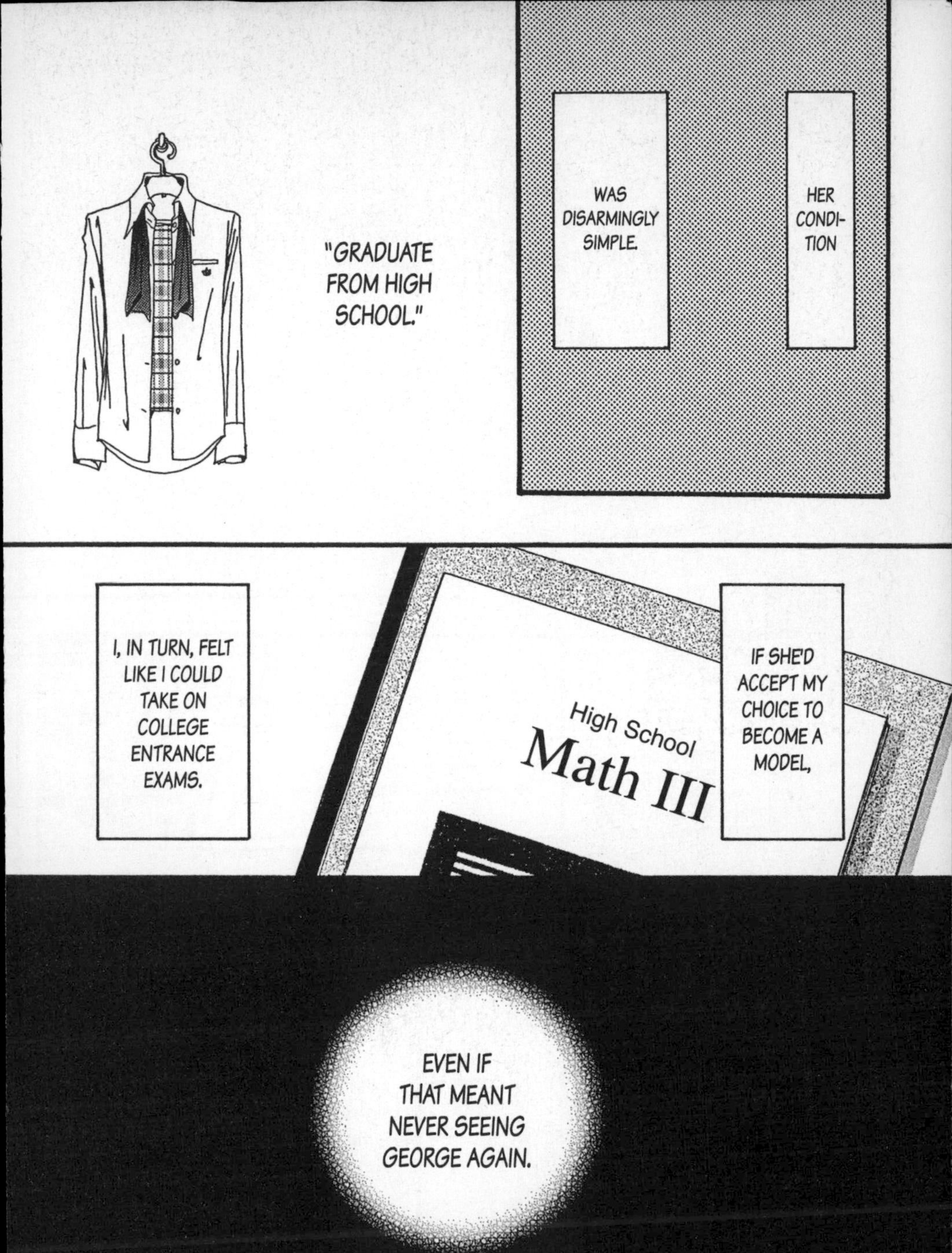

HER CONDITION
WAS DISARMINGLY SIMPLE.
"GRADUATE FROM HIGH SCHOOL."
IF SHE'D ACCEPT MY CHOICE TO BECOME A MODEL,
High School Math III
I, IN TURN, FELT LIKE I COULD TAKE ON COLLEGE ENTRANCE EXAMS.
EVEN IF THAT MEANT NEVER SEEING GEORGE AGAIN.

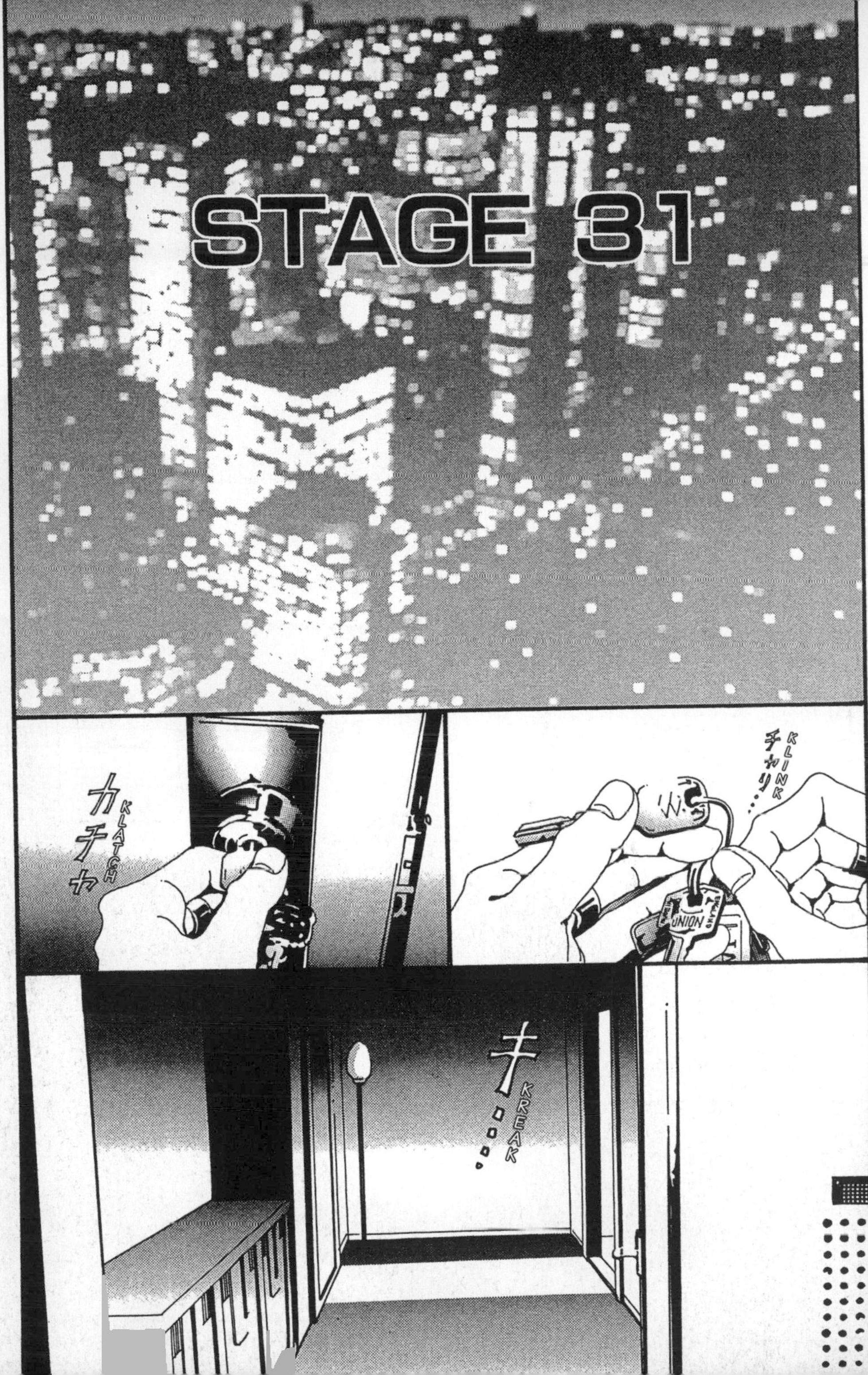
STAGE 31
チャリ…
KLINK
UNION
カチャ
KLATCH
キ…
KREAK

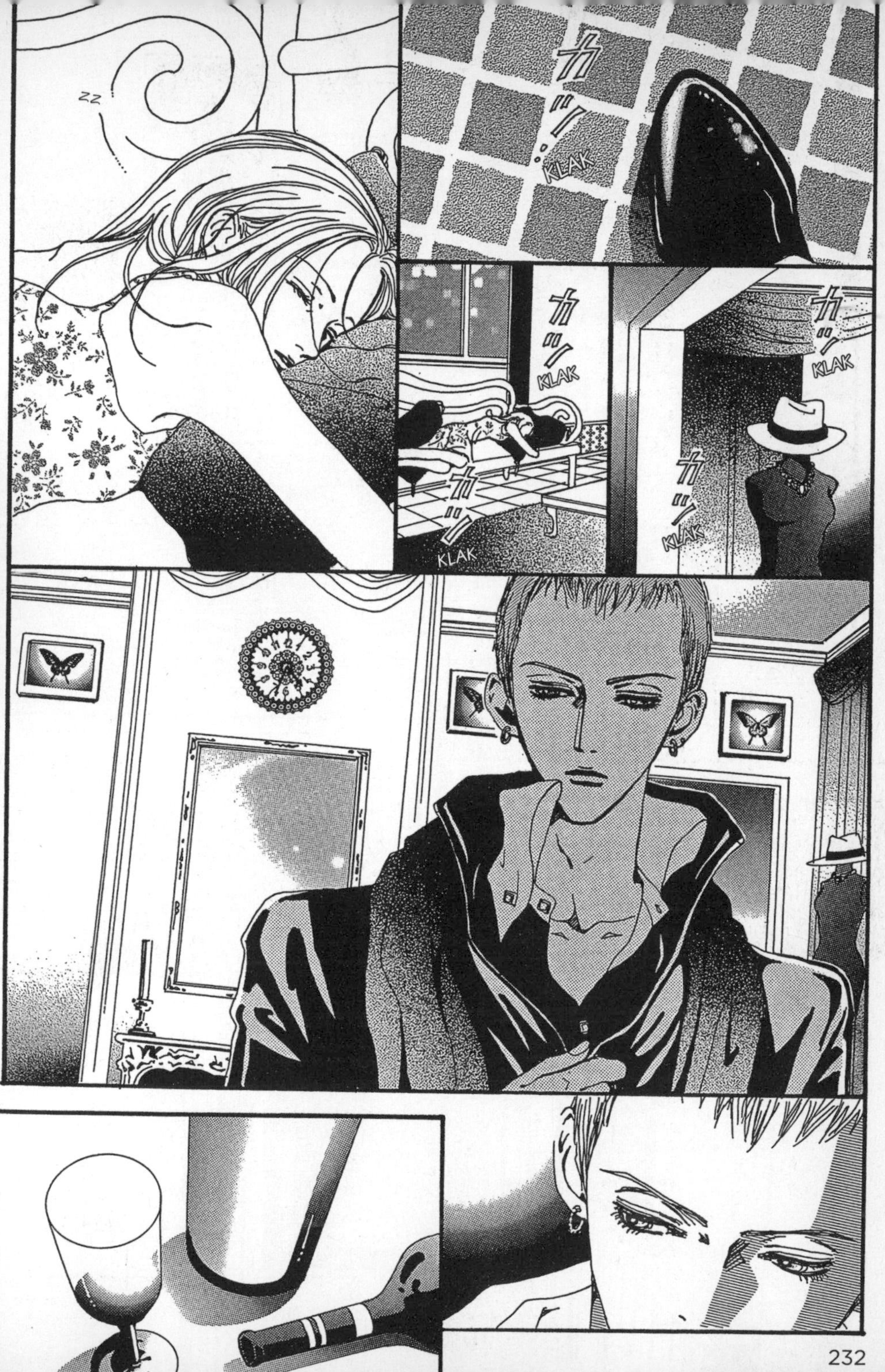

カッ…
KLAK
カッ
KLAK
カッ
KLAK
カッ
KLAK
カッ
KLAK
zz

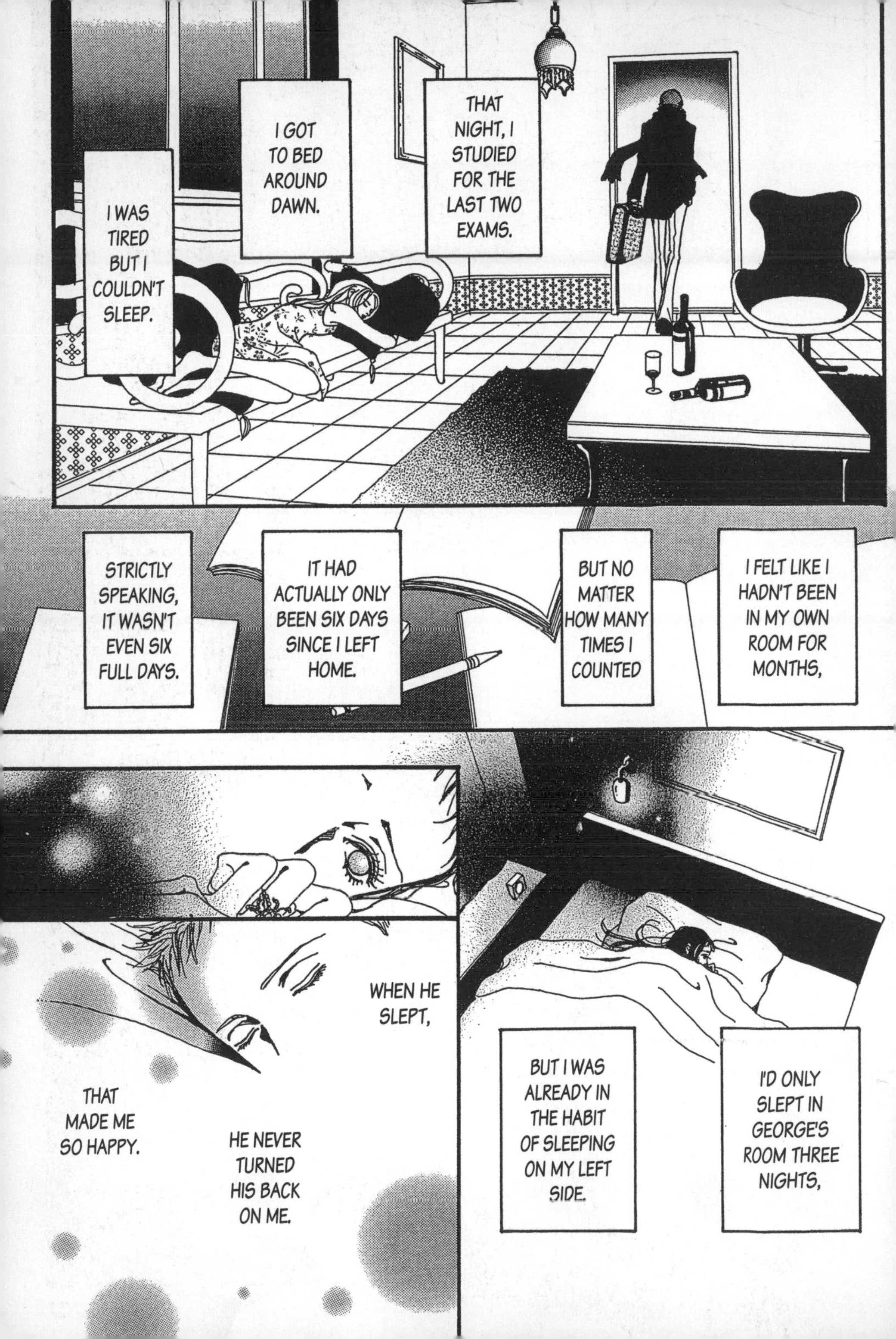
THAT NIGHT, I STUDIED FOR THE LAST TWO EXAMS.
I GOT TO BED AROUND DAWN.
I WAS TIRED BUT I COULDN'T SLEEP.
I FELT LIKE I HADN'T BEEN IN MY OWN ROOM FOR MONTHS,
BUT NO MATTER HOW MANY TIMES I COUNTED
IT HAD ACTUALLY ONLY BEEN SIX DAYS SINCE I LEFT HOME.
STRICTLY SPEAKING, IT WASN'T EVEN SIX FULL DAYS.
I'D ONLY SLEPT IN GEORGE'S ROOM THREE NIGHTS,
BUT I WAS ALREADY IN THE HABIT OF SLEEPING ON MY LEFT SIDE.
WHEN HE SLEPT,
HE NEVER TURNED HIS BACK ON ME.
THAT MADE ME SO HAPPY.

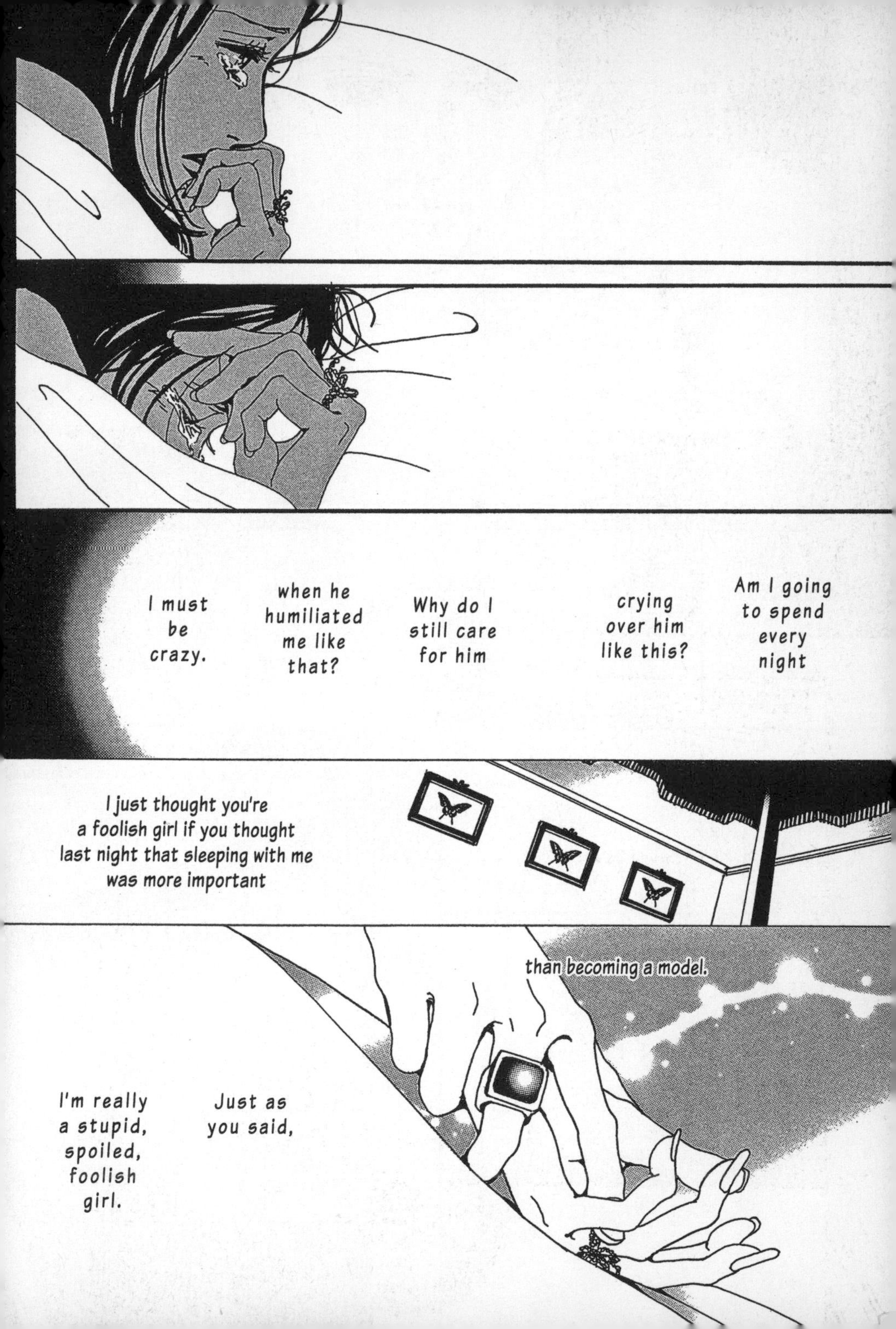
Am I going to spend every night
crying over him like this?
Why do I still care for him
when he humiliated me like that?
I must be crazy.
I just thought you're a foolish girl if you thought last night that sleeping with me was more important
than becoming a model.
Just as you said,
I'm really a stupid, spoiled, foolish girl.

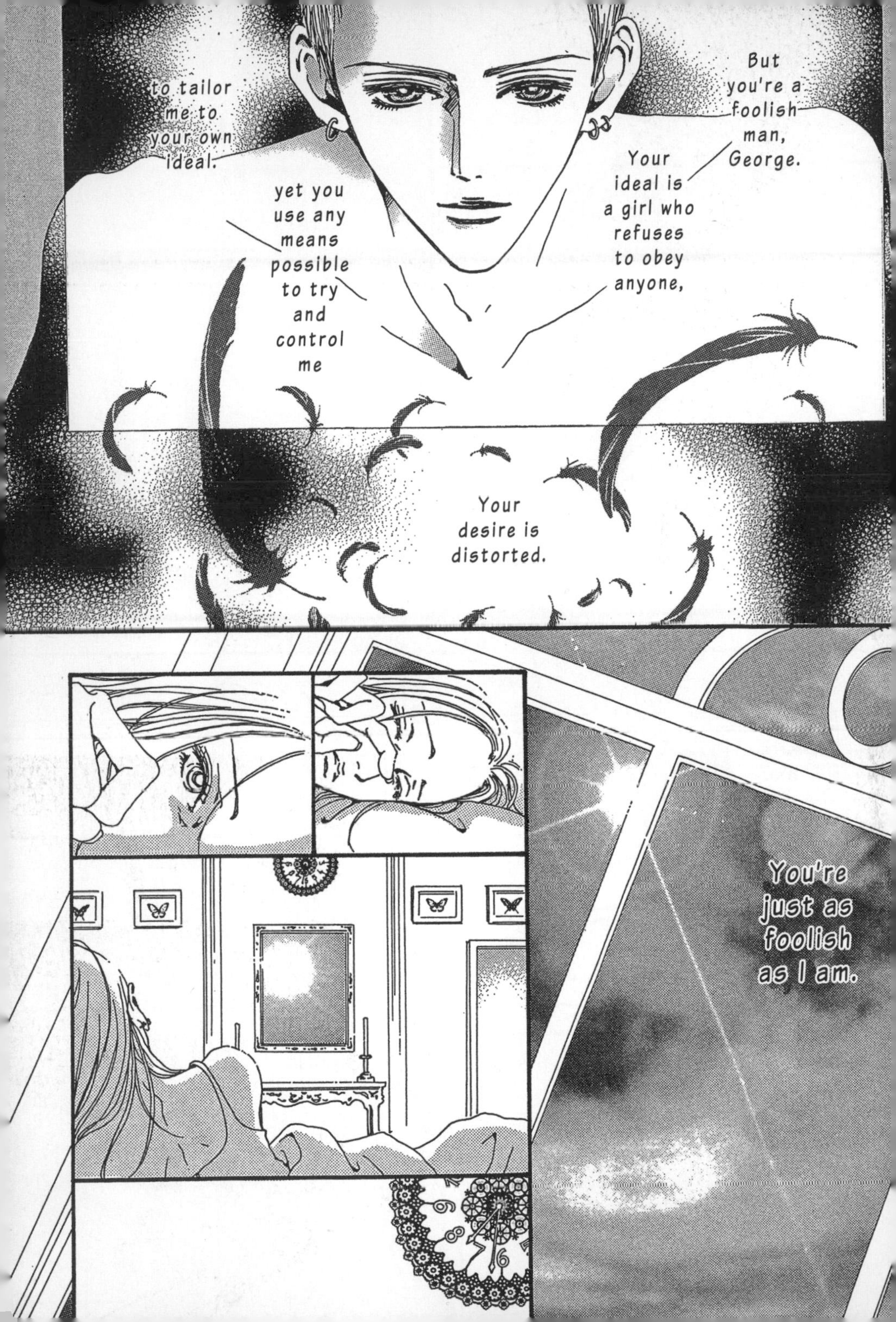
But you're a foolish man, George.
Your ideal is a girl who refuses to obey anyone,
yet you use any means possible to try and control me
to tailor me to your own ideal.
Your desire is distorted.
You're just as foolish as I am.

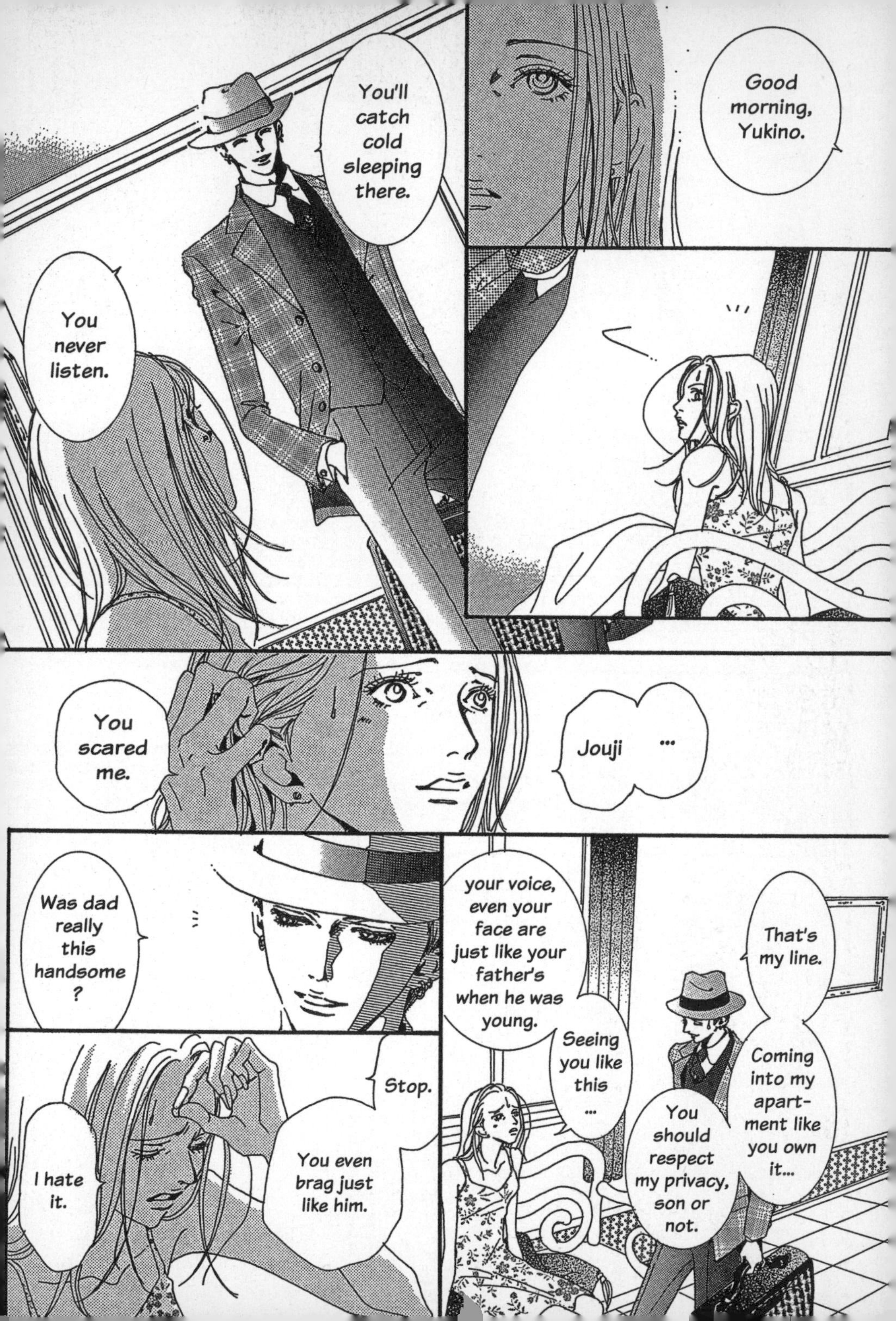
Good morning, Yukino.
...
You'll catch cold sleeping there.
You never listen.
Jouji ...
You scared me.
That's my line.
Coming into my apart-ment like you own it...
You should respect my privacy, son or not.
Seeing you like this ...
your voice, even your face are just like your father's when he was young.
Was dad really this handsome ?
Stop.
You even brag just like him.
I hate it.

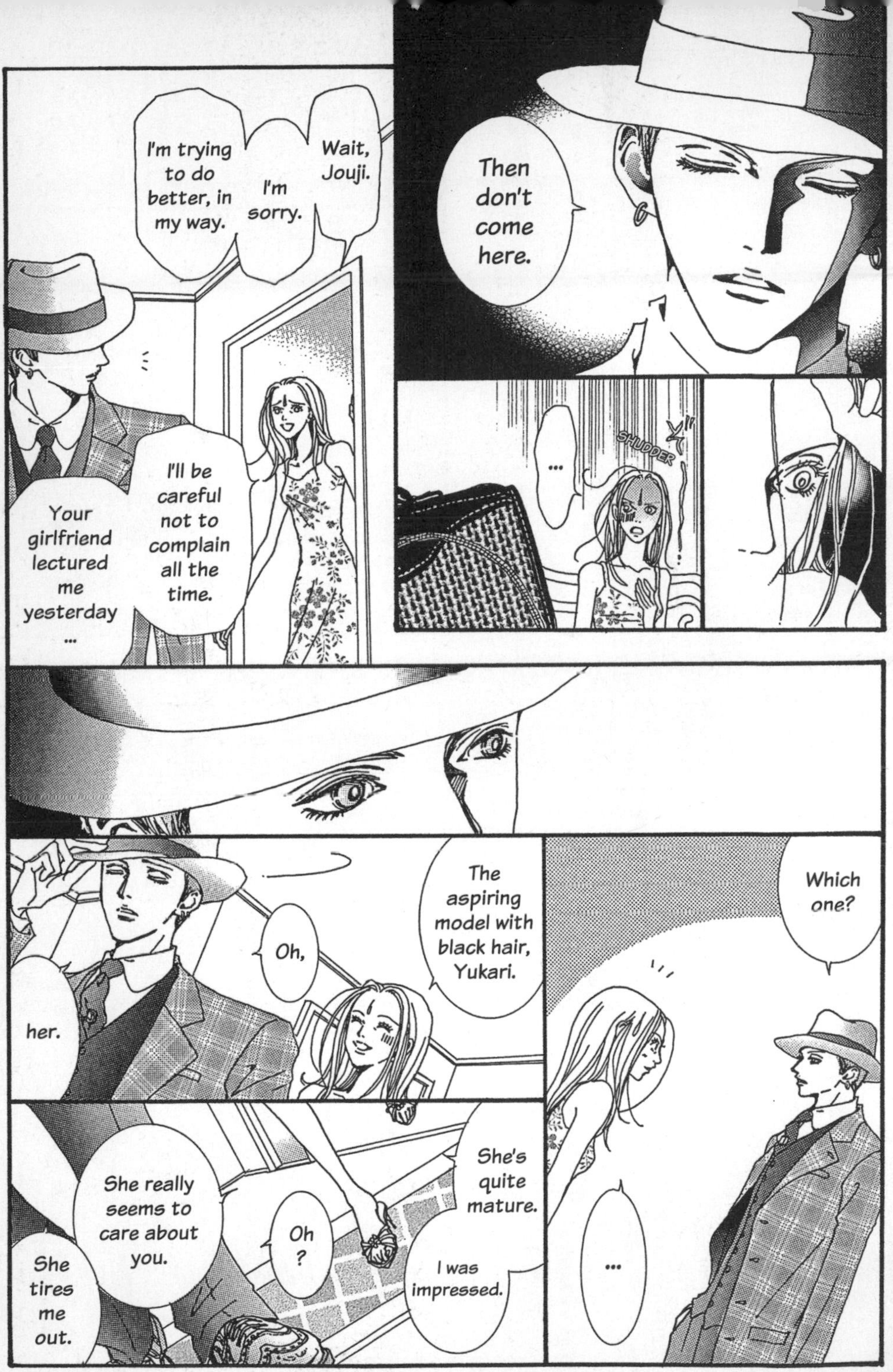
Then don't come here.
...
SHUDDER
Wait, Jouji.
I'm sorry.
I'm trying to do better, in my way.
I'll be careful not to complain all the time.
Your girlfriend lectured me yesterday ...
Which one?
...
The aspiring model with black hair, Yukari.
Oh,
her.
She's quite mature.
I was impressed.
Oh ?
She really seems to care about you.
She tires me out.

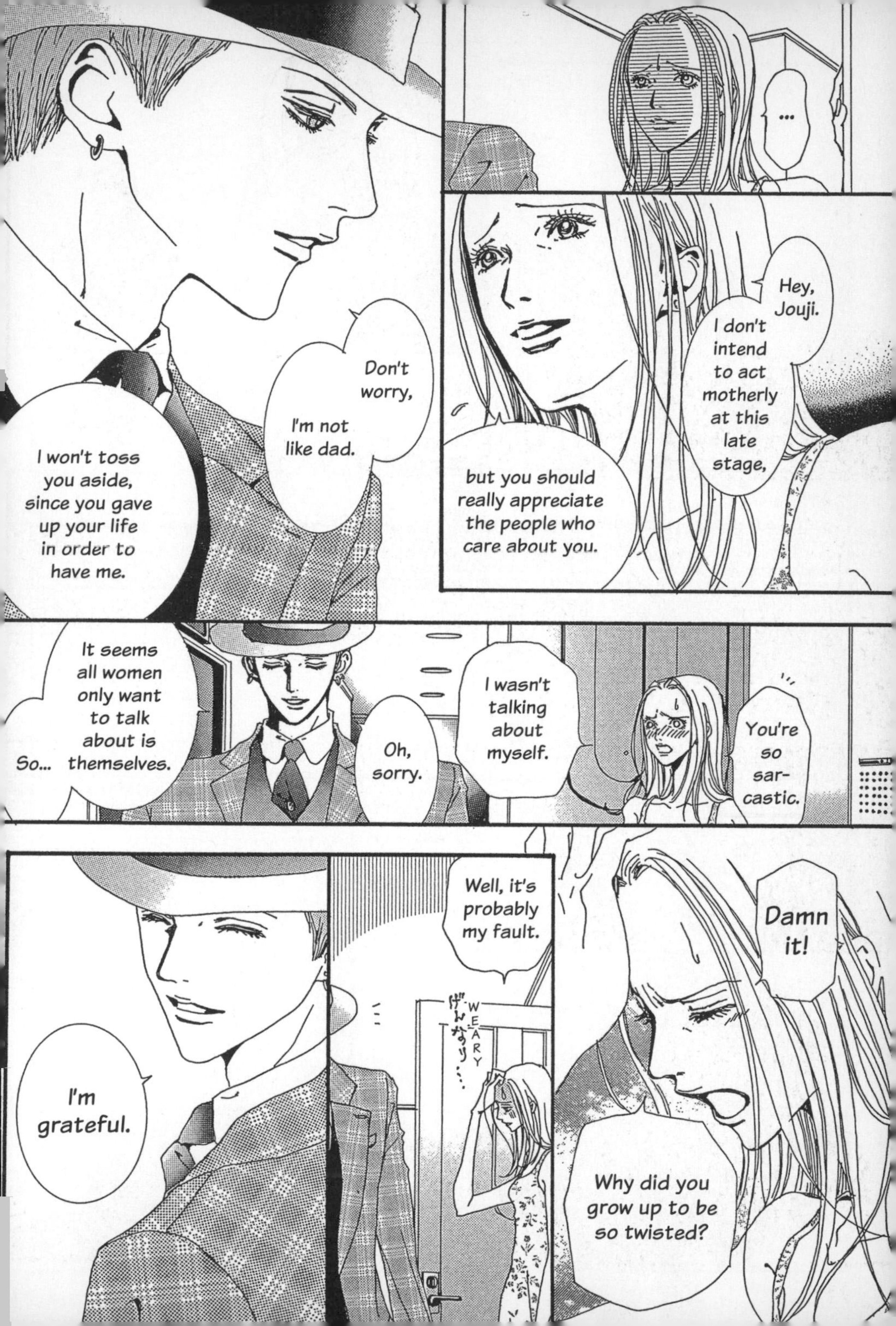
...
Hey, Jouji. I don't intend to act motherly at this late stage,
but you should really appreciate the people who care about you.
Don't worry,
I'm not like dad.
I won't toss you aside, since you gave up your life in order to have me.
You're so sar-castic.
I wasn't talking about myself.
Oh, sorry.
It seems all women only want to talk about is themselves.
So...
Damn it!
Why did you grow up to be so twisted?
Well, it's probably my fault.
WEARY
I'm grateful.

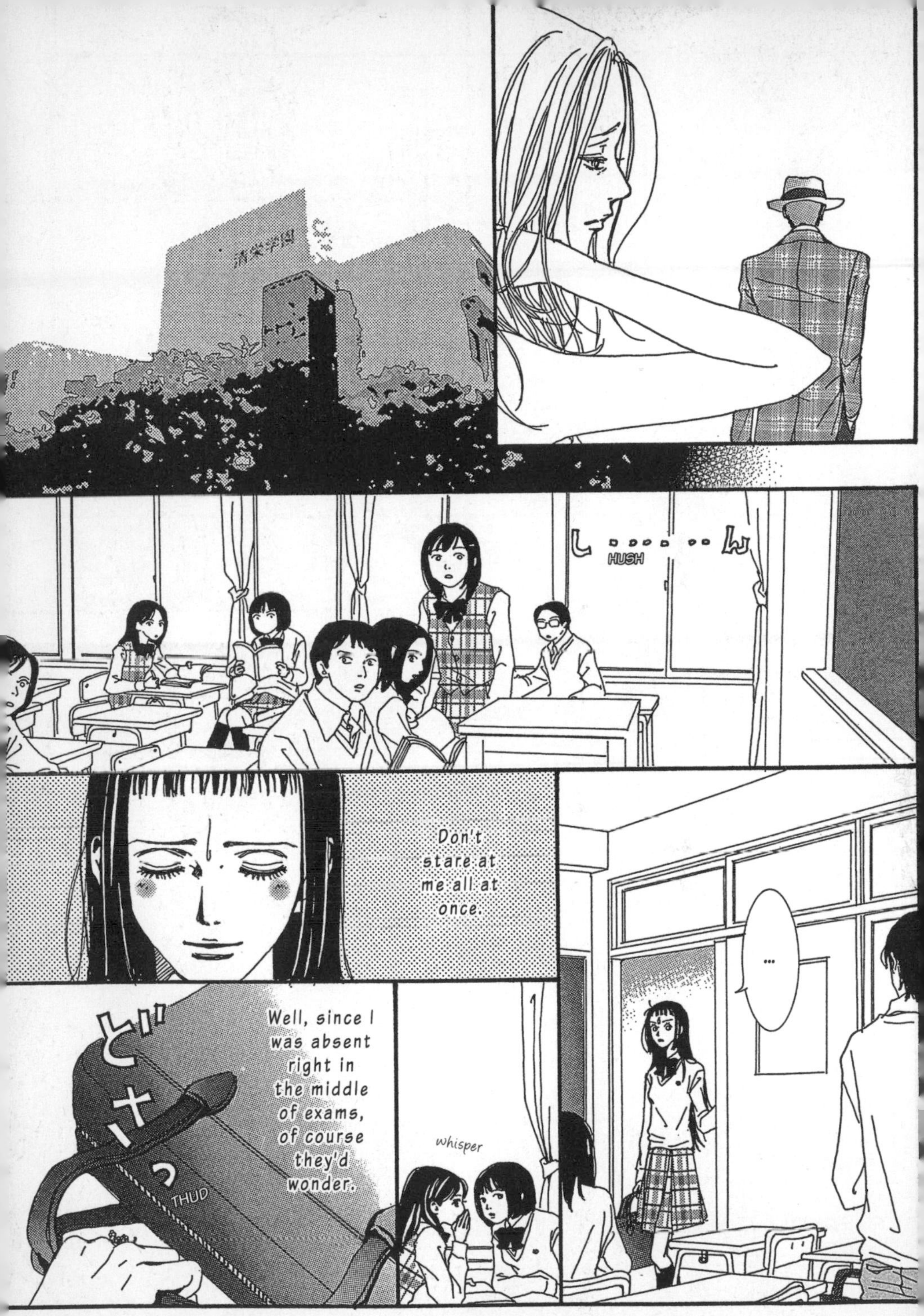

し……ん
HUSH
…
Don't stare at me all at once.
whisper
Well, since I was absent right in the middle of exams, of course they'd wonder.
とさっ
THUD

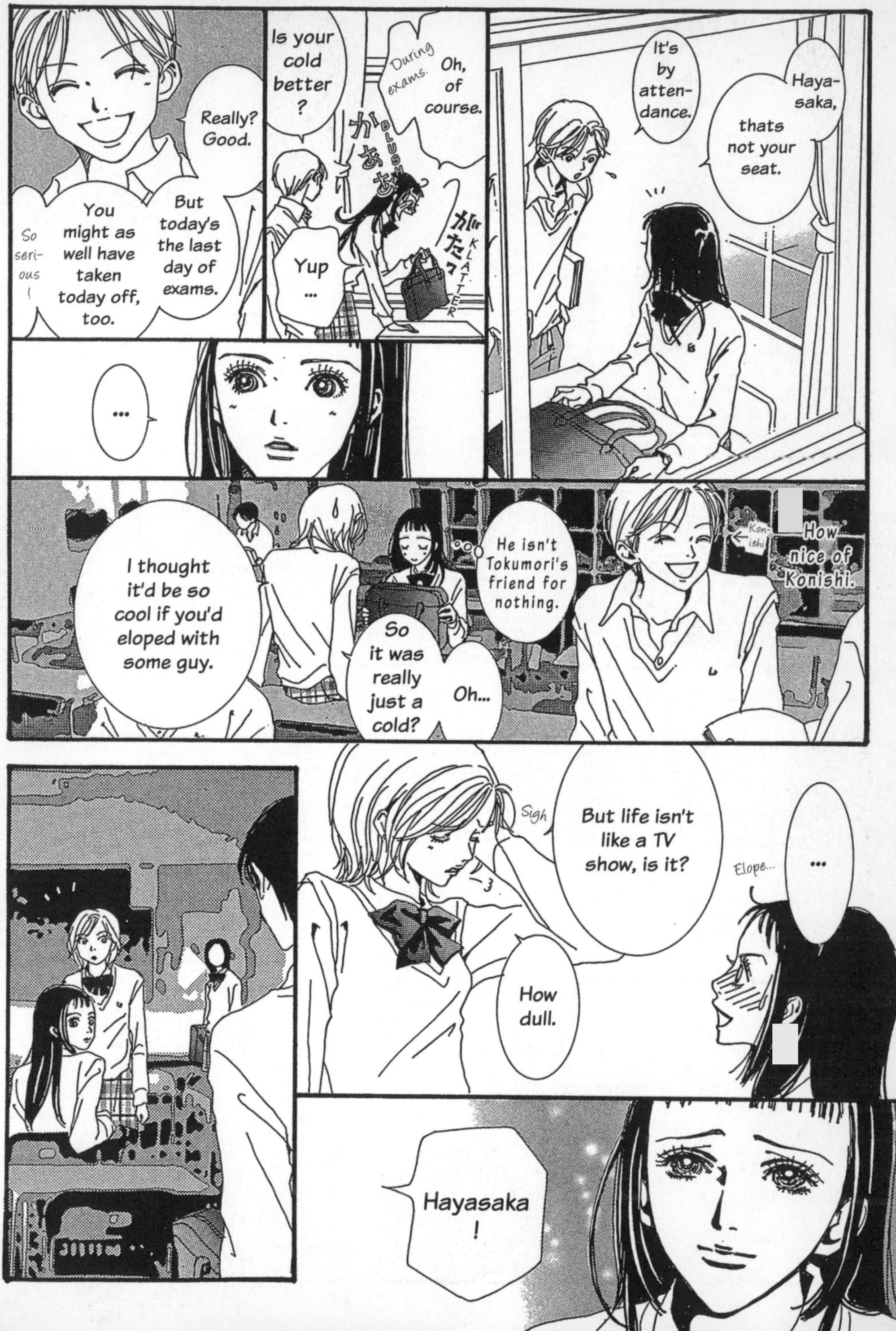
Haya-saka, thats not your seat.
It's by attendance.
Is your cold better?
During exams.
Oh, of course.
BLUSH
Yup ...
KLATTER
Really? Good.
But today's the last day of exams.
You might as well have taken today off, too.
So serious!
...
How nice of Konishi.
Konishi
He isn't Tokumori's friend for nothing.
Oh...
So it was really just a cold?
I thought it'd be so cool if you'd eloped with some guy.
...
Elope...
But life isn't like a TV show, is it?
Sigh
How dull.
Hayasaka!

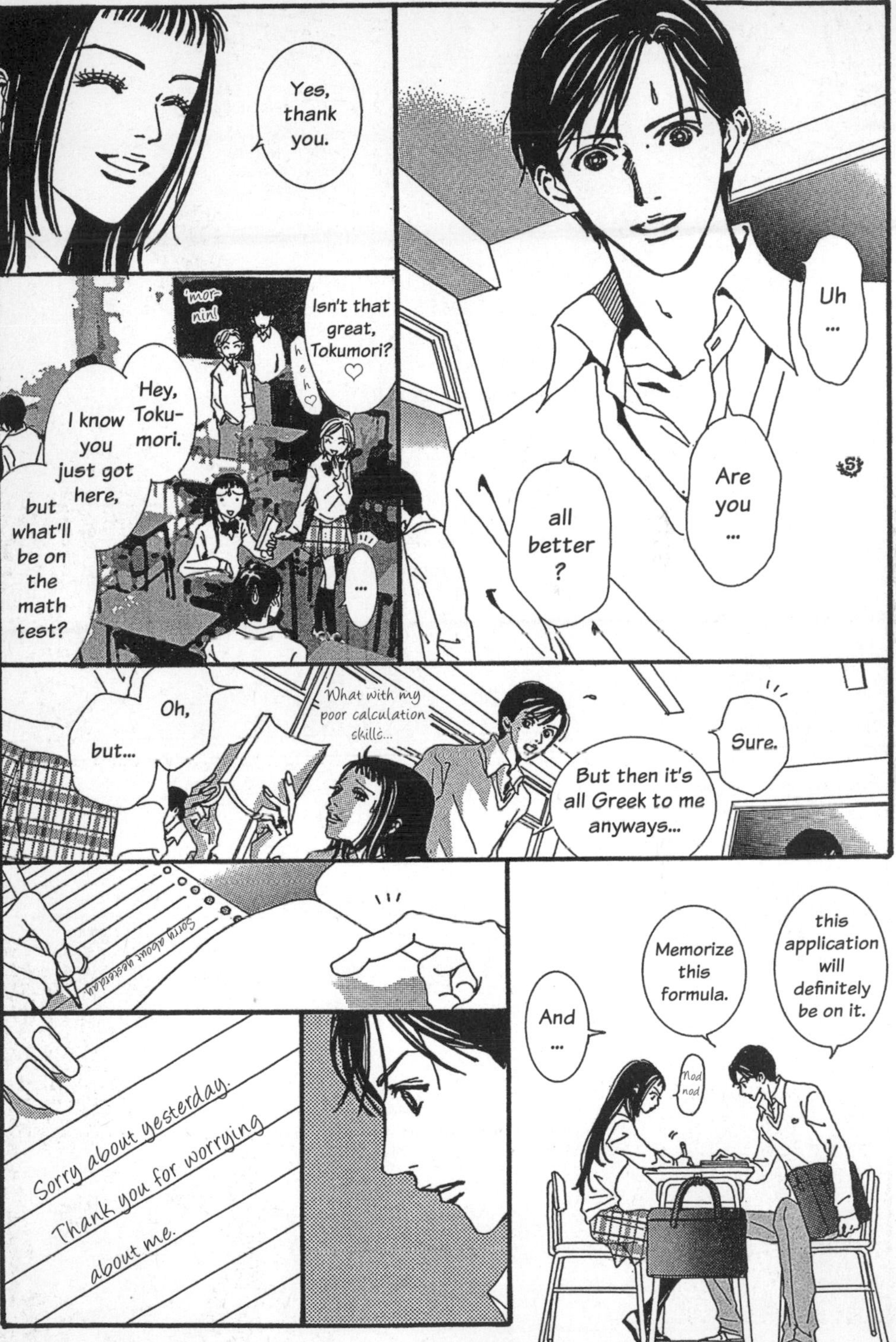

Uh ...
Are you ...
all better ?
Yes, thank you.
'mor-nin!
Isn't that great, Tokumori? ♡
heh♡
Hey, Tokumori.
I know you just got here,
but what'll be on the math test?
...
Sure.
But then it's all Greek to me anyways...
What with my poor calculation skills...
Oh,
but...
this application will definitely be on it.
Memorize this formula.
Nod nod
And ...
Sorry about yesterday
Sorry about yesterday.
Thank you for worrying about me.

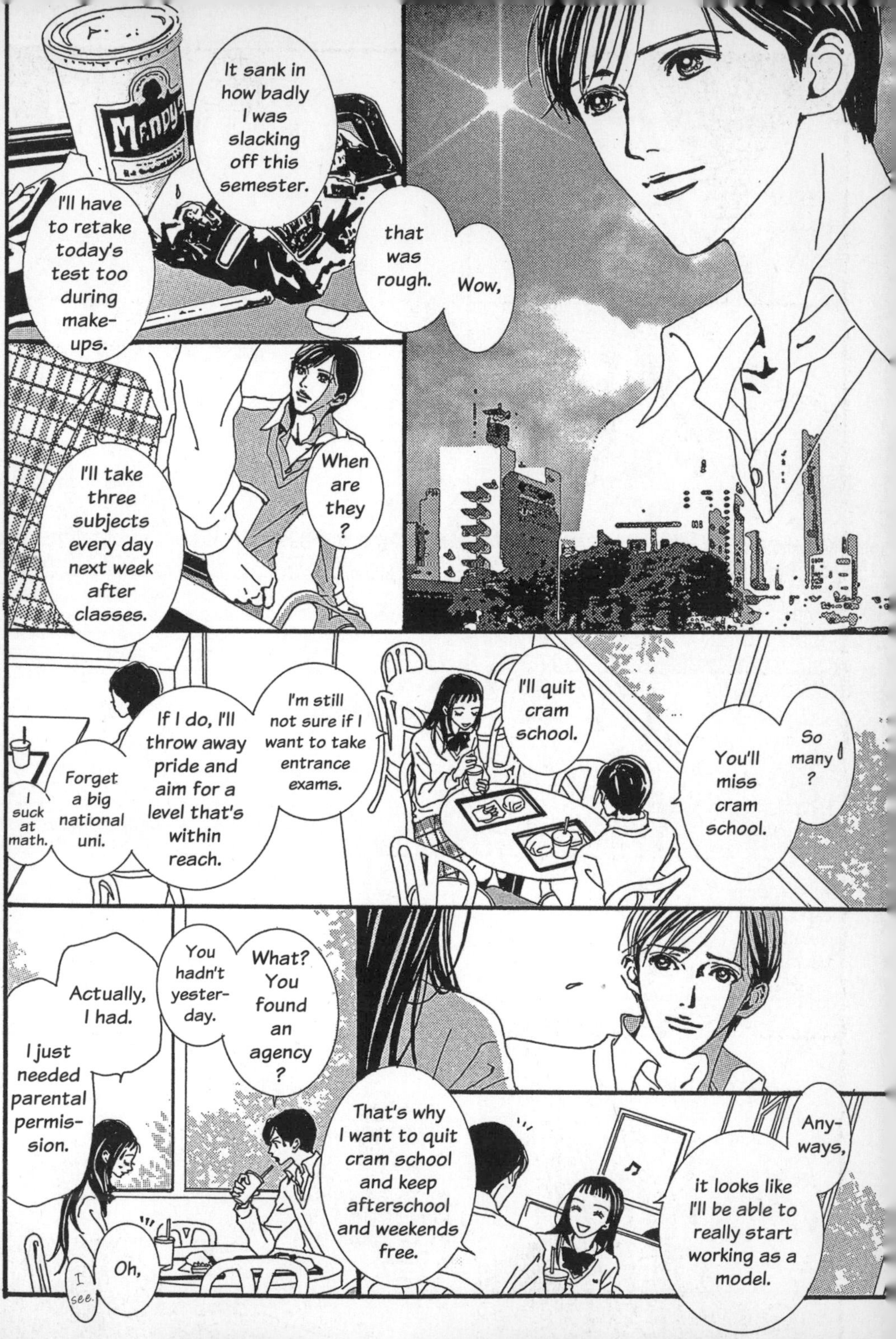
Wow,
that was rough.
It sank in how badly I was slacking off this semester.
I'll have to retake today's test too during make-ups.
When are they?
I'll take three subjects every day next week after classes.
So many?
You'll miss cram school.
I'll quit cram school.
I'm still not sure if I want to take entrance exams.
If I do, I'll throw away pride and aim for a level that's within reach.
Forget a big national uni.
I suck at math.
Any-ways,
it looks like I'll be able to really start working as a model.
That's why I want to quit cram school and keep afterschool and weekends free.
What? You found an agency?
You hadn't yester-day.
Actually, I had.
I just needed parental permis-sion.
Oh,
I see.

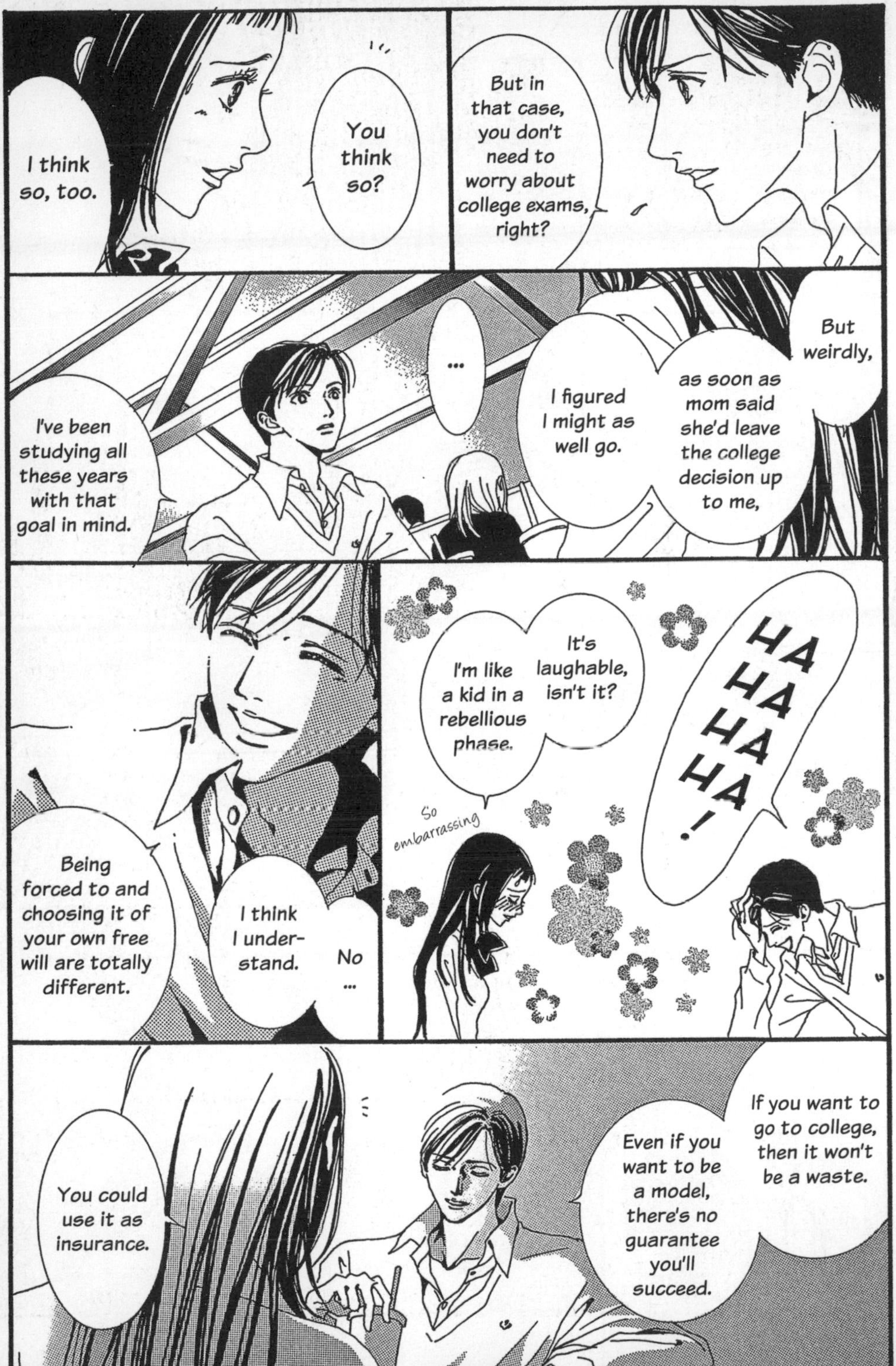

But in that case, you don't need to worry about college exams, right?
You think so?
I think so, too.
But weirdly,
as soon as mom said she'd leave the college decision up to me,
I figured I might as well go.
...
I've been studying all these years with that goal in mind.
HAHAHAHA!
It's laughable, isn't it?
I'm like a kid in a rebellious phase.
So embarrassing
No ...
I think I understand.
Being forced to and choosing it of your own free will are totally different.
If you want to go to college, then it won't be a waste.
Even if you want to be a model, there's no guarantee you'll succeed.
You could use it as insurance.

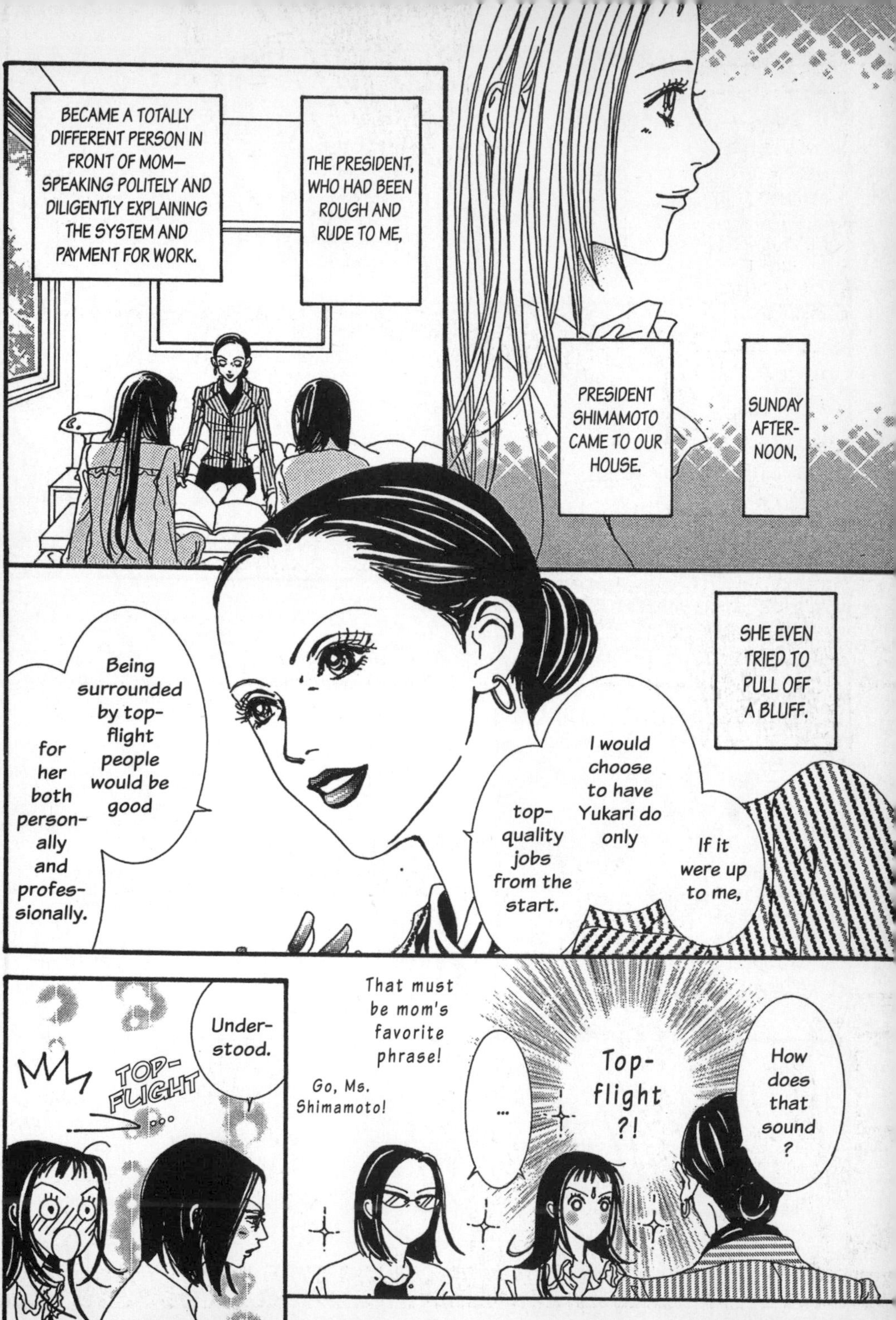
SUNDAY AFTERNOON,
PRESIDENT SHIMAMOTO CAME TO OUR HOUSE.
THE PRESIDENT, WHO HAD BEEN ROUGH AND RUDE TO ME,
BECAME A TOTALLY DIFFERENT PERSON IN FRONT OF MOM— SPEAKING POLITELY AND DILIGENTLY EXPLAINING THE SYSTEM AND PAYMENT FOR WORK.
SHE EVEN TRIED TO PULL OFF A BLUFF.
If it were up to me,
I would choose to have Yukari do only
top-quality jobs from the start.
Being surrounded by top-flight people would be good
for her both personally and professionally.
How does that sound?
Top-flight?!
...
That must be mom's favorite phrase!
Go, Ms. Shimamoto!
Understood.
TOP-FLIGHT...

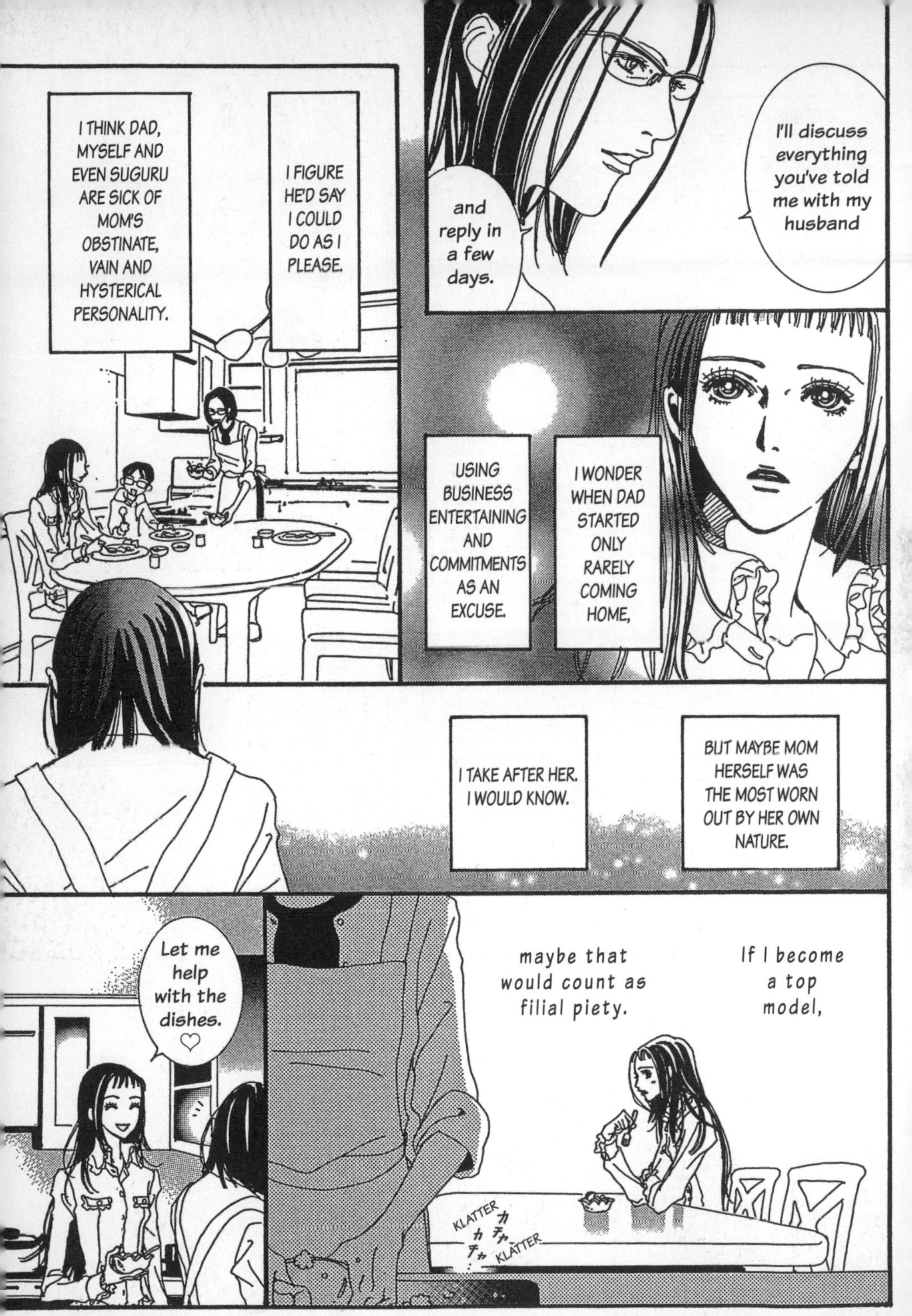
I'll discuss everything you've told me with my husband
and reply in a few days.
I WONDER WHEN DAD STARTED ONLY RARELY COMING HOME,
USING BUSINESS ENTERTAINING AND COMMITMENTS AS AN EXCUSE.
I FIGURE HE'D SAY I COULD DO AS I PLEASE.
I THINK DAD, MYSELF AND EVEN SUGURU ARE SICK OF MOM'S OBSTINATE, VAIN AND HYSTERICAL PERSONALITY.
BUT MAYBE MOM HERSELF WAS THE MOST WORN OUT BY HER OWN NATURE.
I TAKE AFTER HER. I WOULD KNOW.
If I become a top model,
maybe that would count as filial piety.
KLATTER カチャ
カチャ KLATTER
Let me help with the dishes. ♡

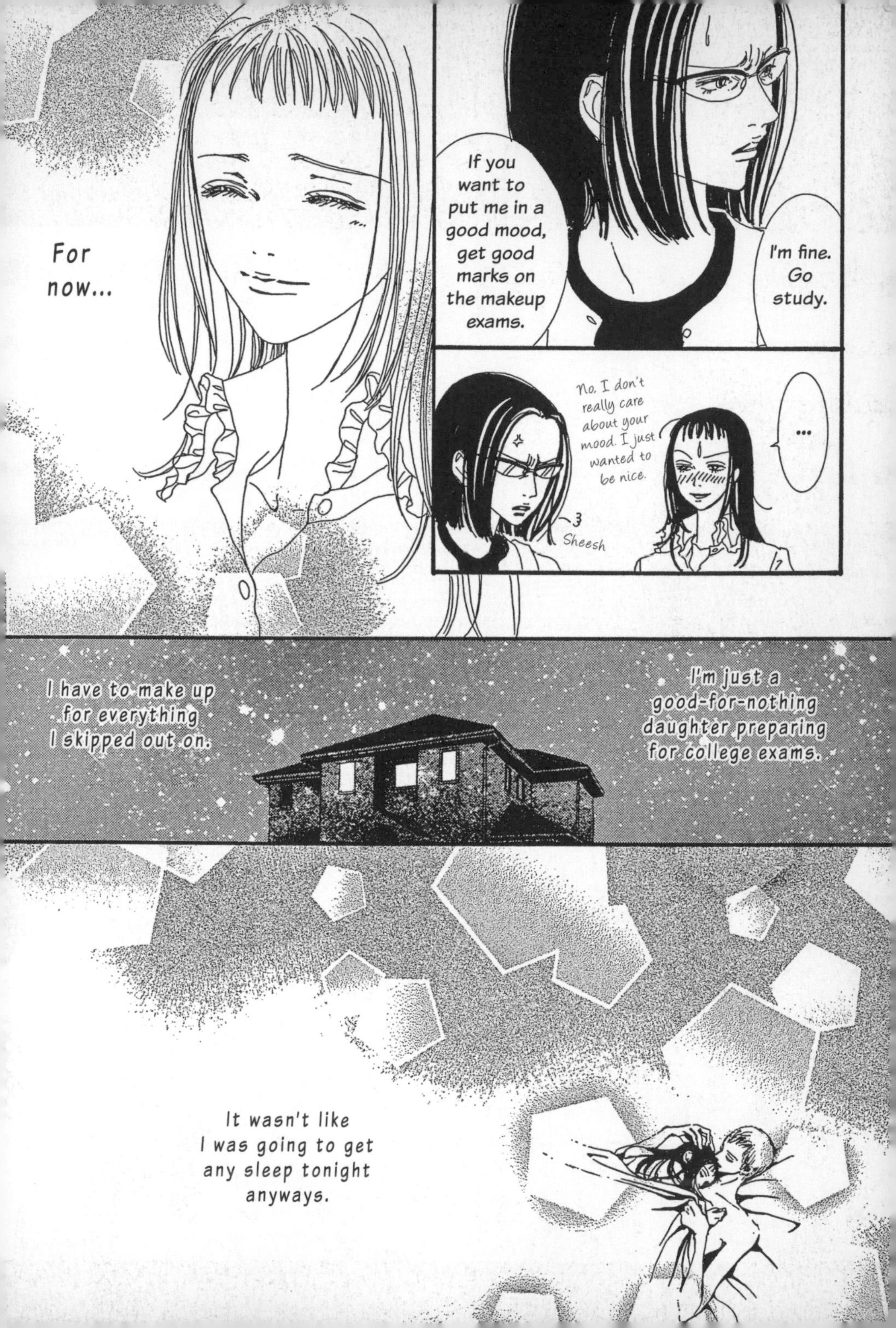
I'm fine. Go study.
If you want to put me in a good mood, get good marks on the makeup exams.
...
No, I don't really care about your mood. I just wanted to be nice.
Sheesh
For now...
I'm just a good-for-nothing daughter preparing for college exams.
I have to make up for everything I skipped out on.
It wasn't like I was going to get any sleep tonight anyways.

STAGE 32

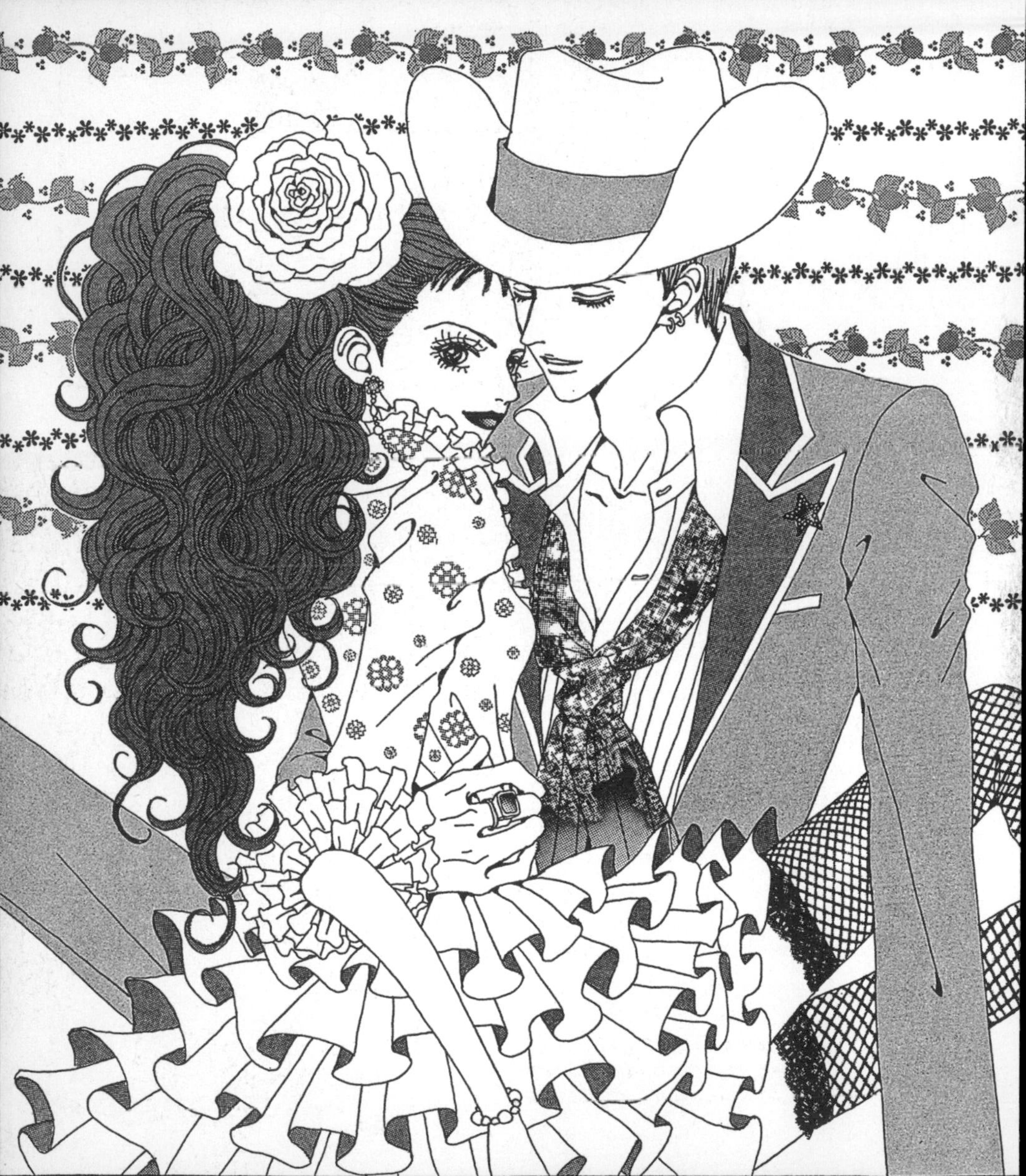

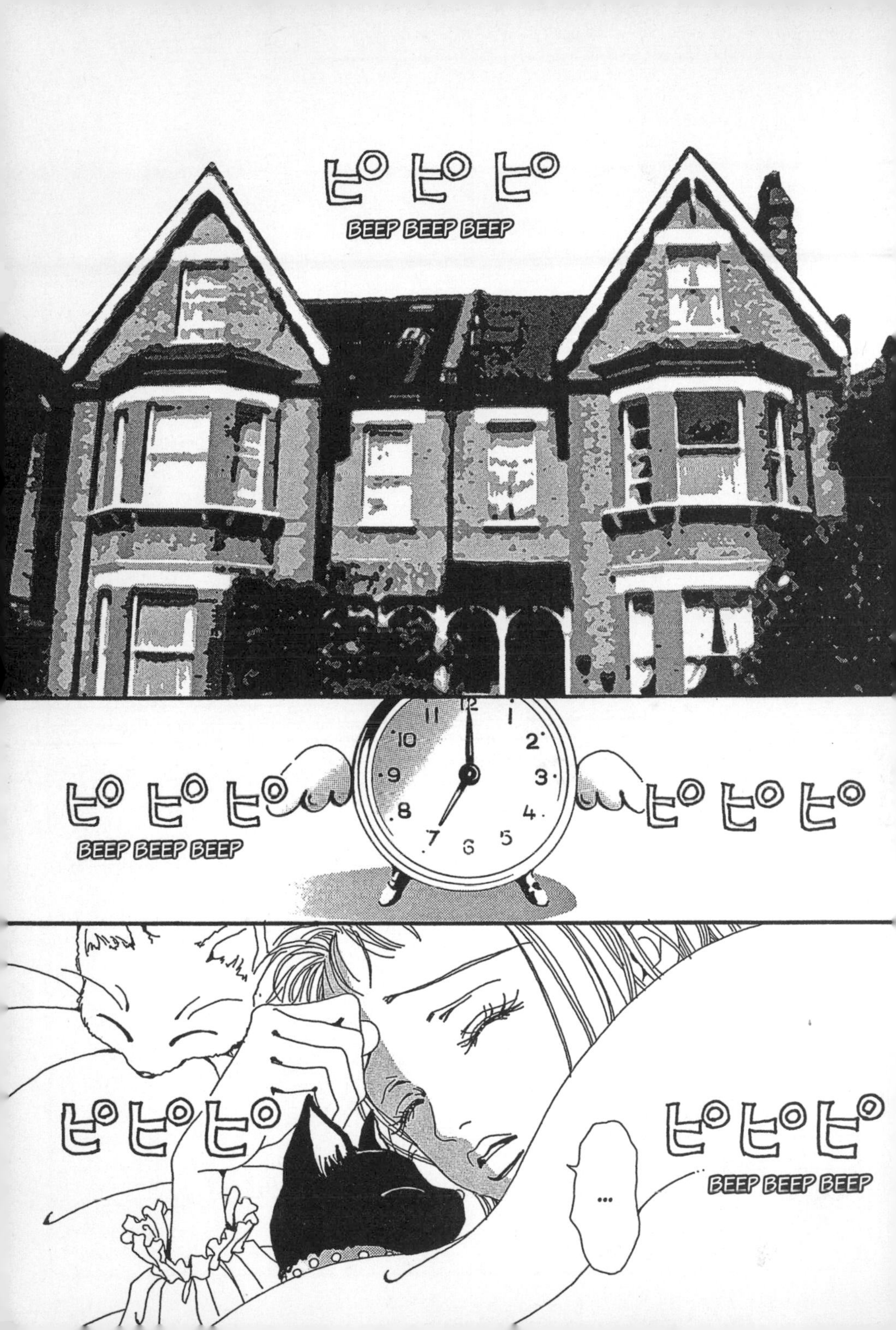

ピ ピ ピ
BEEP BEEP BEEP
ピ ピ ピ
ピ ピ ピ
BEEP BEEP BEEP
ピピピ
BEEP BEEP BEEP
...
ピピピ

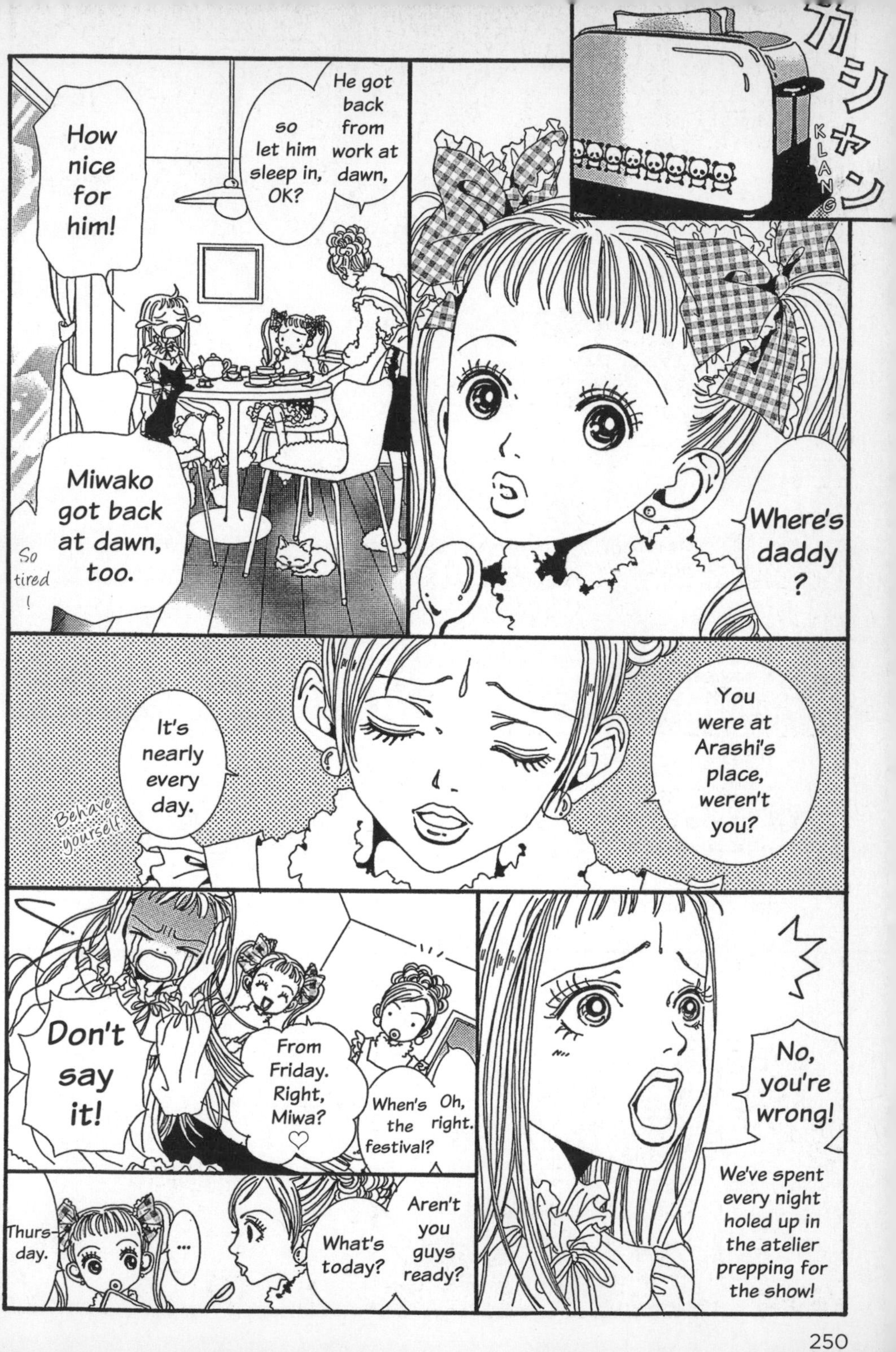
カシャーン
KLANG
Where's daddy?
He got back from work at dawn,
so let him sleep in, OK?
How nice for him!
Miwako got back at dawn, too.
So tired!
You were at Arashi's place, weren't you?
It's nearly every day.
Behave yourself.
No, you're wrong!
We've spent every night holed up in the atelier prepping for the show!
Oh, right.
When's the festival?
From Friday. Right, Miwa? ♡
Don't say it!
Aren't you guys ready?
What's today?
...
Thurs-day.

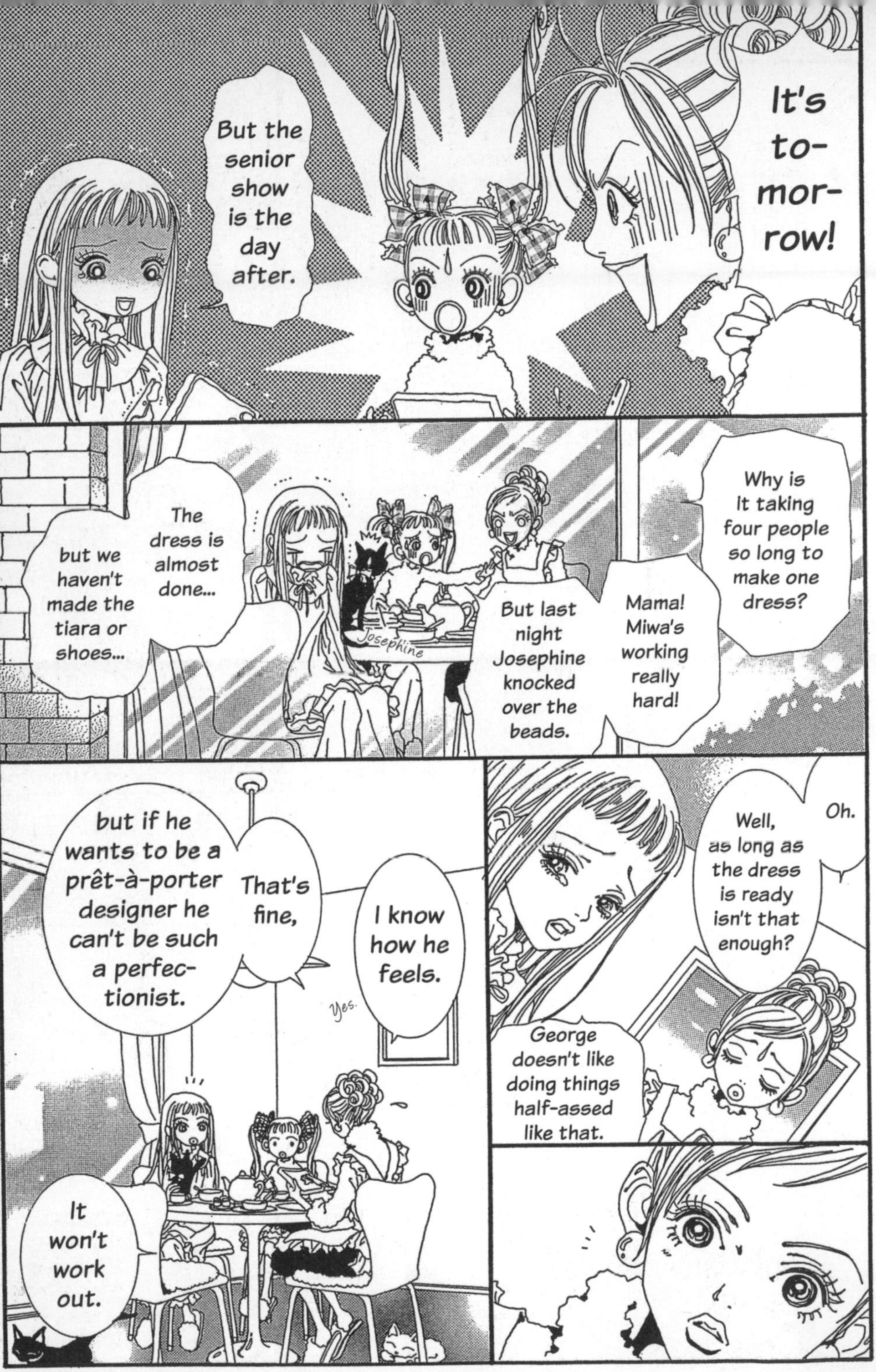
It's to-mor-row!
But the senior show is the day after.
Why is it taking four people so long to make one dress?
Mama! Miwa's working really hard!
But last night Josephine knocked over the beads.
The dress is almost done...
but we haven't made the tiara or shoes...
Josephine
Oh.
Well, as long as the dress is ready isn't that enough?
George doesn't like doing things half-assed like that.
I know how he feels.
That's fine,
but if he wants to be a prêt-à-porter designer he can't be such a perfectionist.
Yes.
It won't work out.

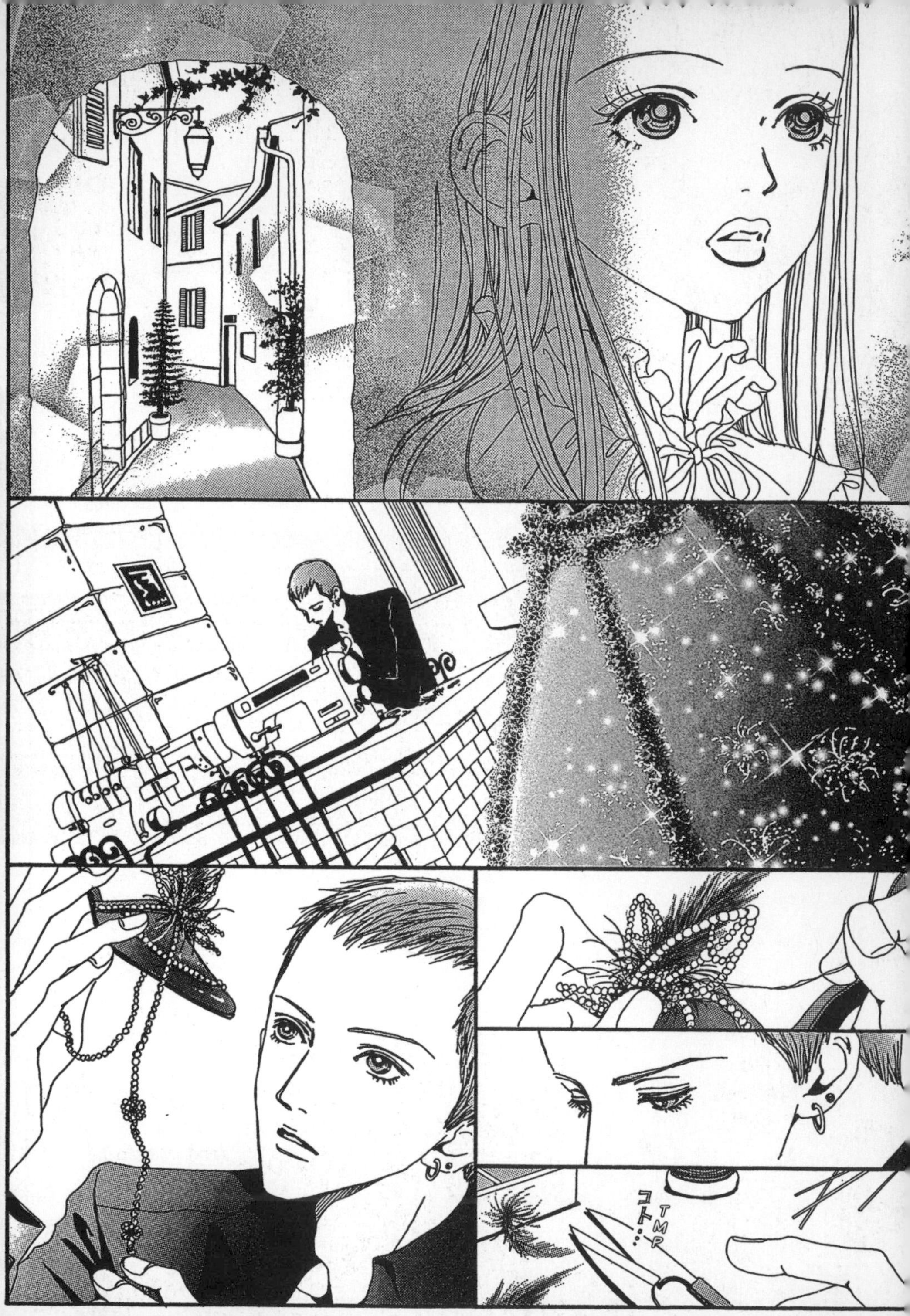
TMP
コト…

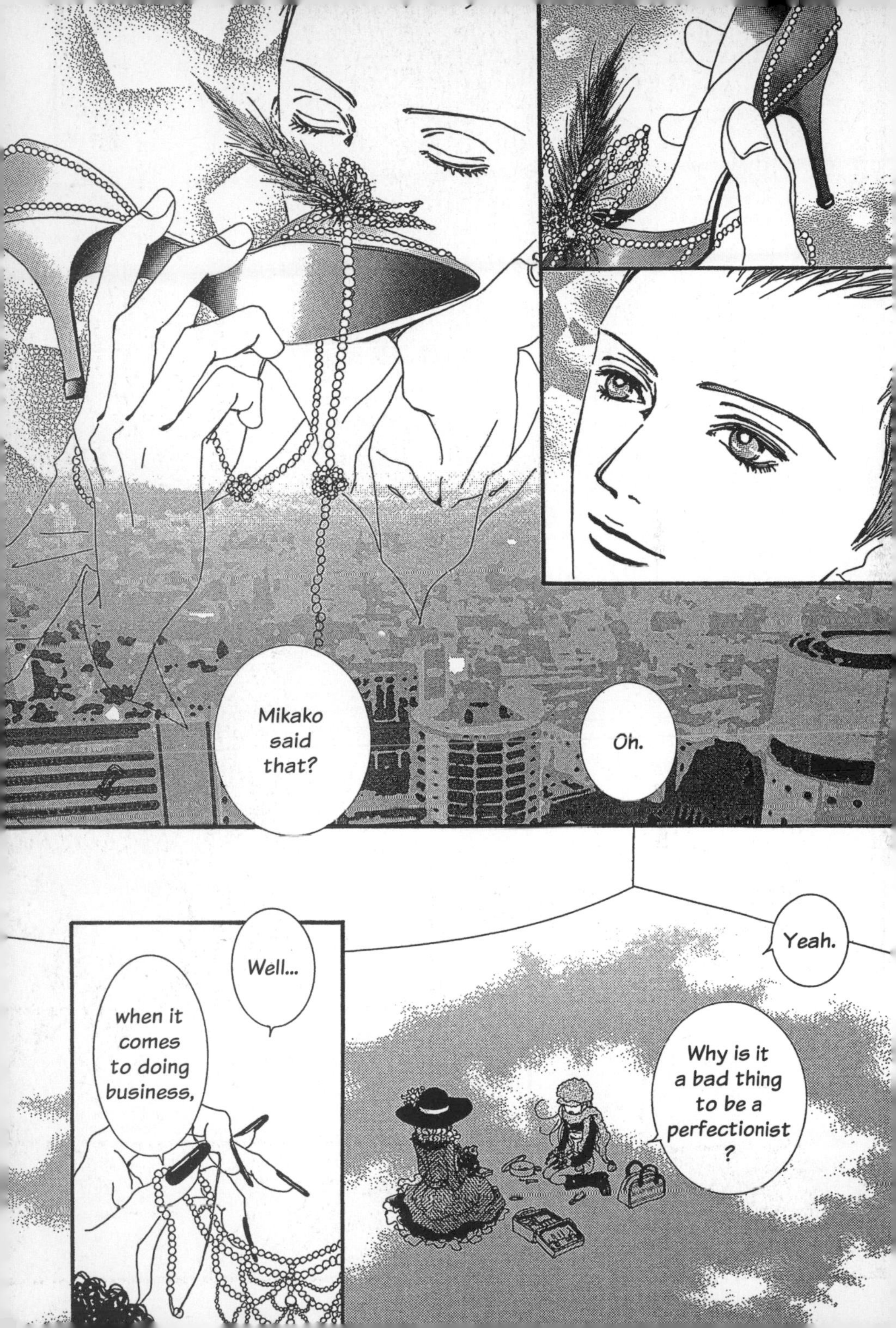
Oh.
Mikako said that?
Yeah.
Why is it a bad thing to be a perfectionist?
Well...
when it comes to doing business,

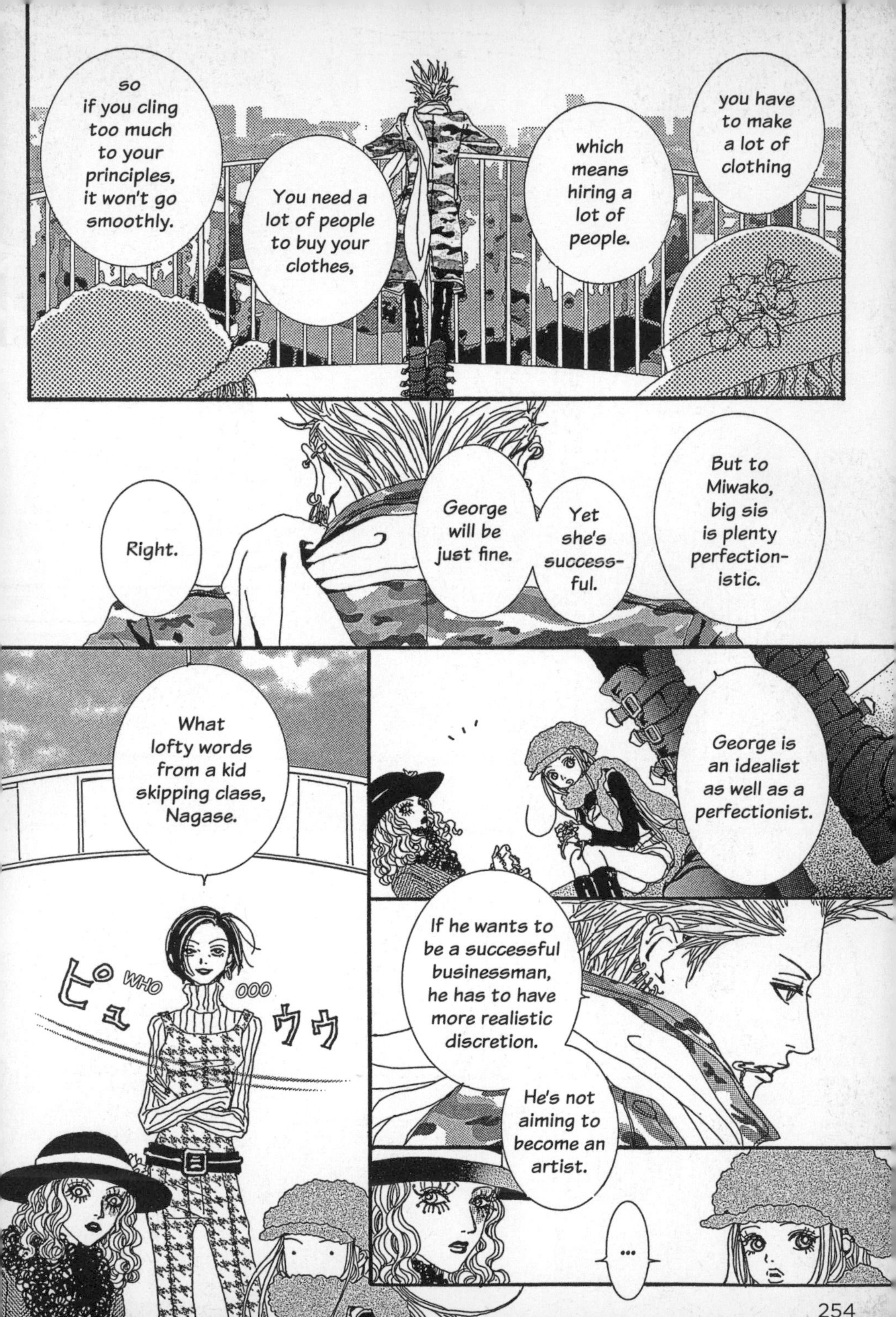
you have to make a lot of clothing
which means hiring a lot of people.
You need a lot of people to buy your clothes,
so if you cling too much to your principles, it won't go smoothly.
But to Miwako, big sis is plenty perfectionistic.
Yet she's successful.
George will be just fine.
Right.
George is an idealist as well as a perfectionist.
If he wants to be a successful businessman, he has to have more realistic discretion.
He's not aiming to become an artist.
...
What lofty words from a kid skipping class, Nagase.
ピュウウ
WHO OOO

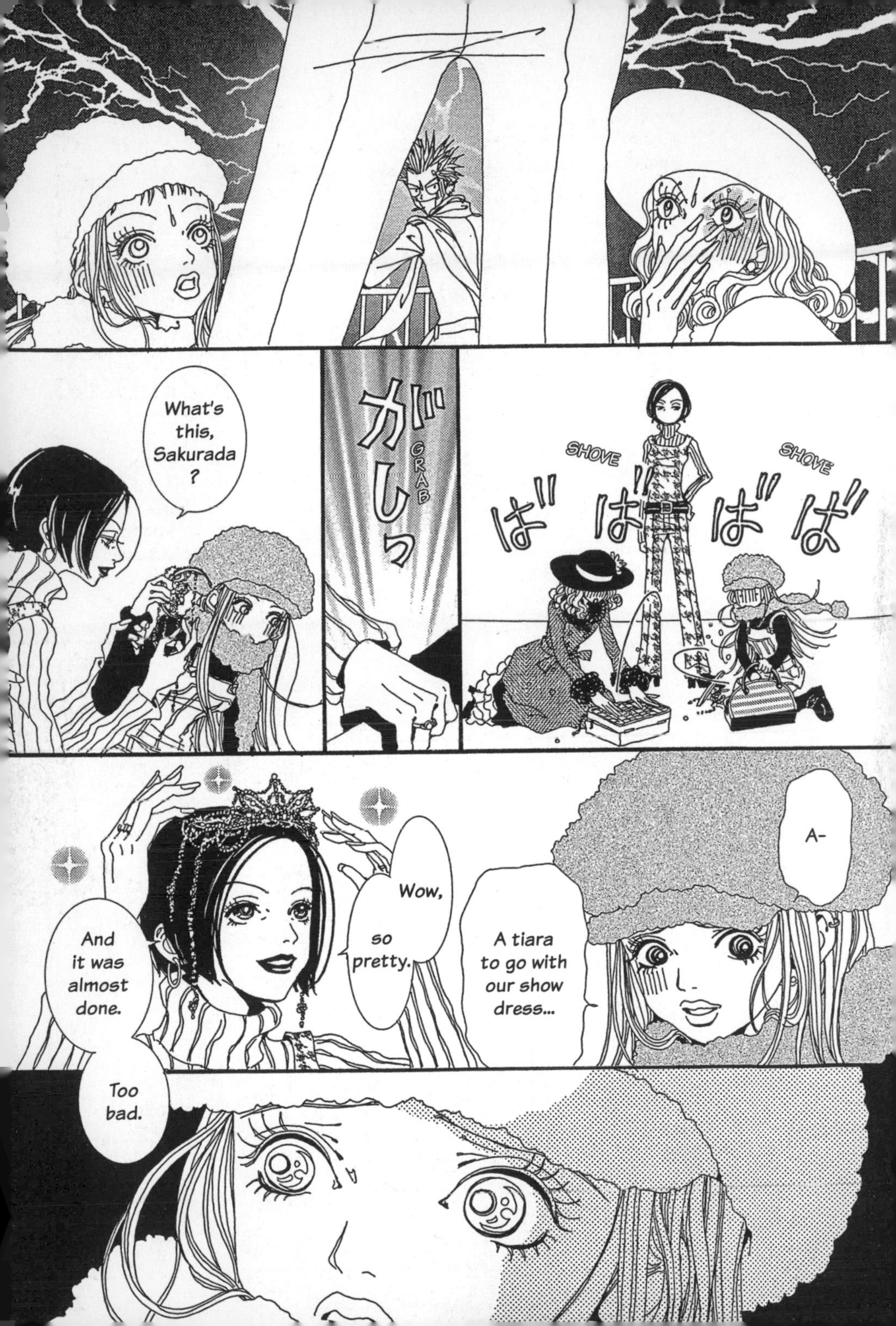
SHOVE
SHOVE
ばばばば
がしっ
GRAB
What's this, Sakurada?
A-
A tiara to go with our show dress...
Wow, so pretty.
And it was almost done.
Too bad.

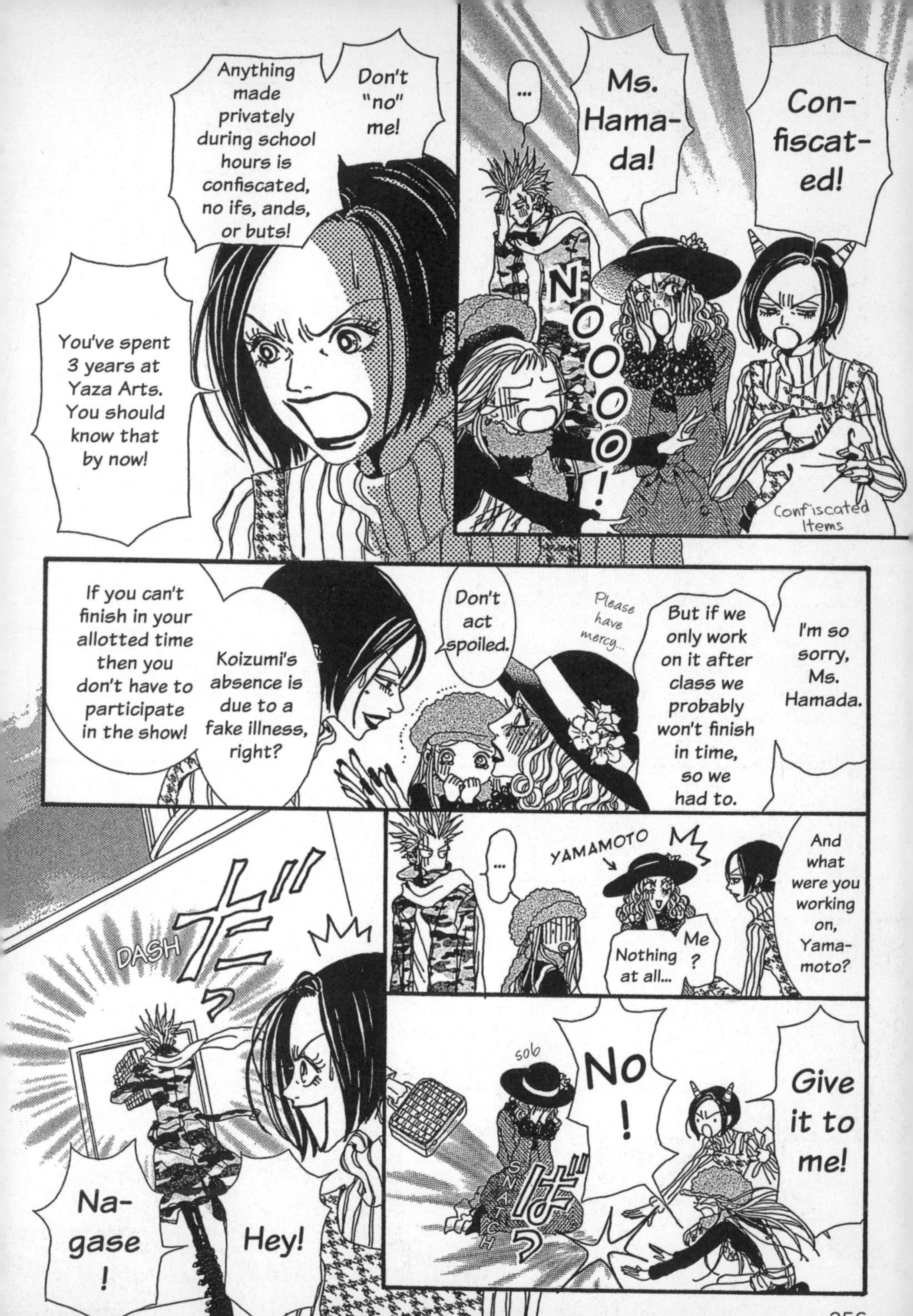
Con-fiscat-ed!
Ms. Hama-da!
...
NOOOOO!
Confiscated Items
Don't "no" me!
Anything made privately during school hours is confiscated, no ifs, ands, or buts!
You've spent 3 years at Yaza Arts. You should know that by now!
I'm so sorry, Ms. Hamada.
But if we only work on it after class we probably won't finish in time, so we had to.
Please have mercy...
Don't act spoiled.
Koizumi's absence is due to a fake illness, right?
If you can't finish in your allotted time then you don't have to participate in the show!
And what were you working on, Yamamoto?
Me?
Nothing at all...
YAMAMOTO
...
Give it to me!
No!
SNATCH
sob
DASH
Hey!
Na-gase!

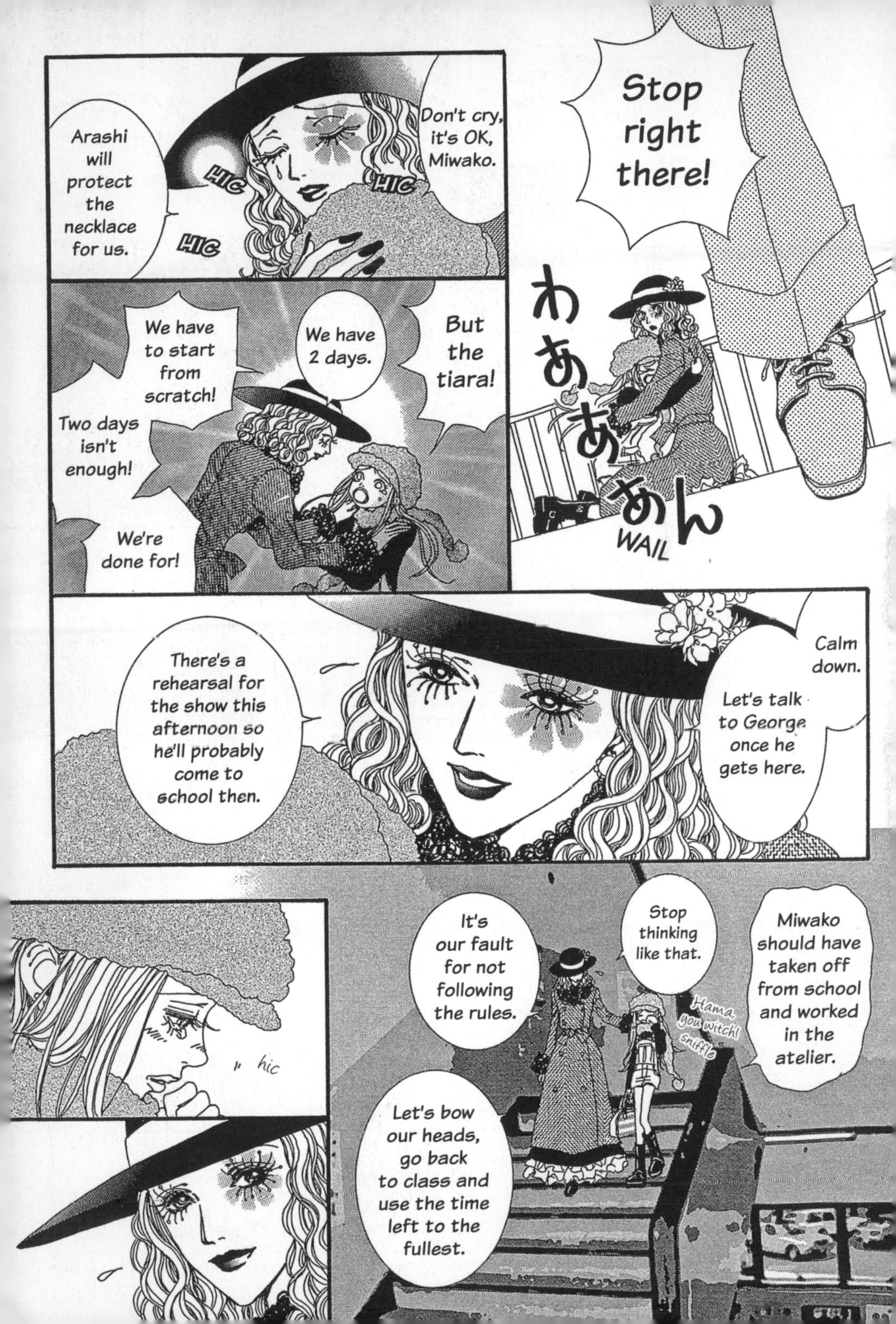

Stop right there!
わあああん
WAIL
Don't cry, it's OK, Miwako.
HIC
HIC
Arashi will protect the necklace for us.
HIC
But the tiara!
We have 2 days.
We have to start from scratch!
Two days isn't enough!
We're done for!
Calm down.
Let's talk to George once he gets here.
There's a rehearsal for the show this afternoon so he'll probably come to school then.
Miwako should have taken off from school and worked in the atelier.
Stop thinking like that.
Hama, you witch! sniffle
It's our fault for not following the rules.
Let's bow our heads, go back to class and use the time left to the fullest.
hic

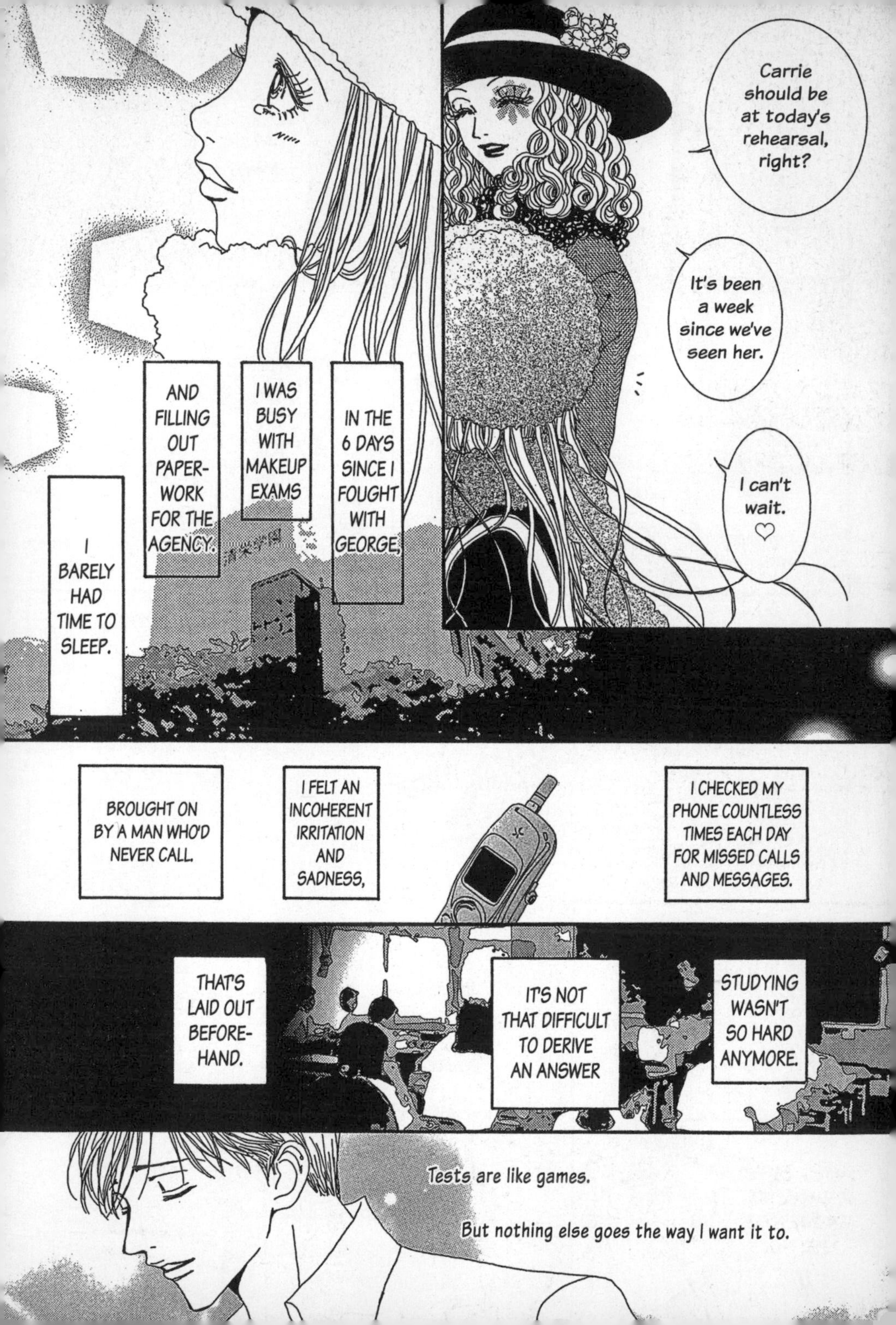
Carrie should be at today's rehearsal, right?
It's been a week since we've seen her.
I can't wait. ♡
IN THE 6 DAYS SINCE I FOUGHT WITH GEORGE,
I WAS BUSY WITH MAKEUP EXAMS
AND FILLING OUT PAPER-WORK FOR THE AGENCY.
I BARELY HAD TIME TO SLEEP.
I CHECKED MY PHONE COUNTLESS TIMES EACH DAY FOR MISSED CALLS AND MESSAGES.
I FELT AN INCOHERENT IRRITATION AND SADNESS,
BROUGHT ON BY A MAN WHO'D NEVER CALL.
STUDYING WASN'T SO HARD ANYMORE.
IT'S NOT THAT DIFFICULT TO DERIVE AN ANSWER
THAT'S LAID OUT BEFORE-HAND.
Tests are like games.
But nothing else goes the way I want it to.

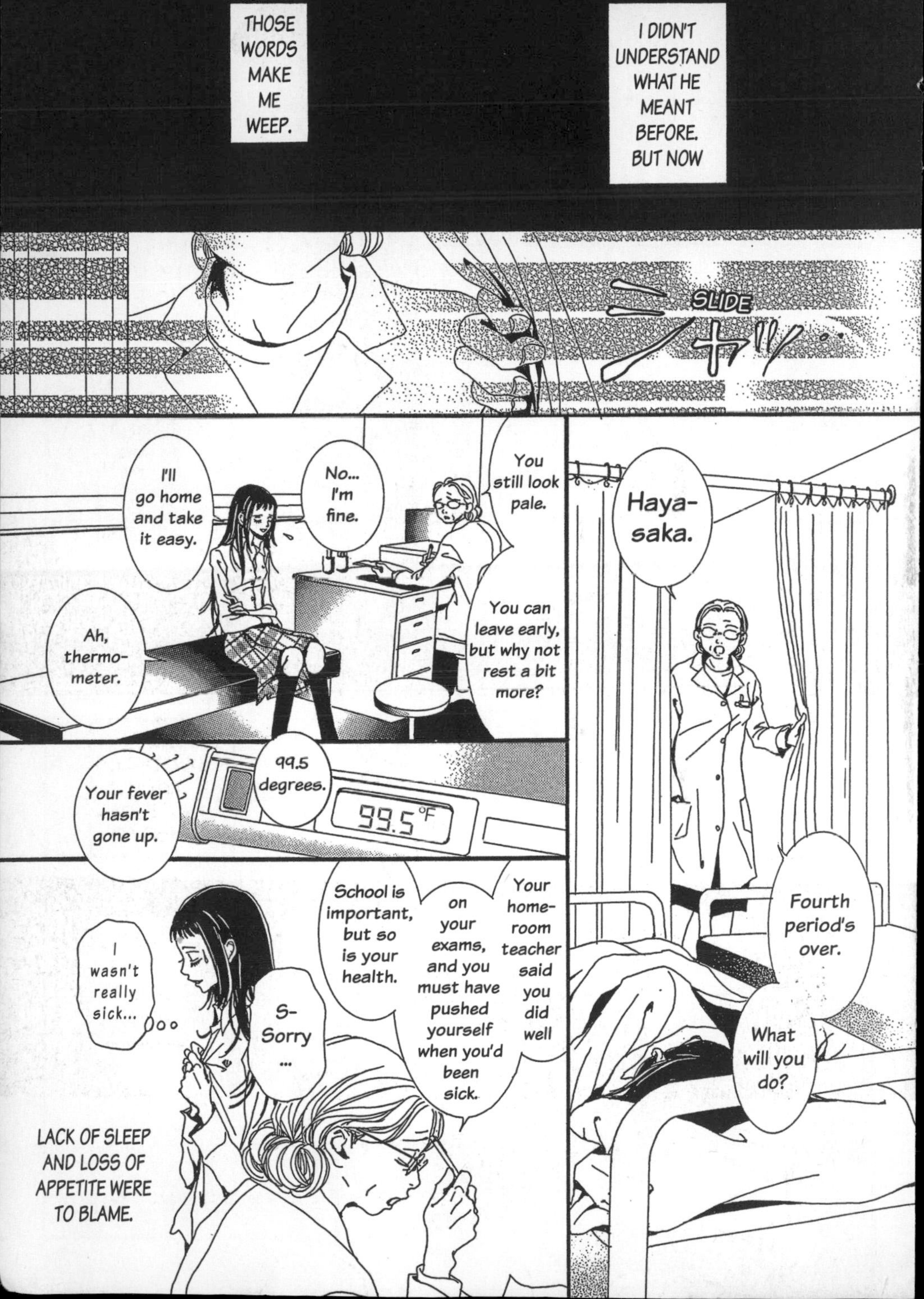

I DIDN'T UNDERSTAND WHAT HE MEANT BEFORE. BUT NOW
THOSE WORDS MAKE ME WEEP.
SLIDE
Haya-saka.
Fourth period's over.
What will you do?
You still look pale.
No... I'm fine.
I'll go home and take it easy.
You can leave early, but why not rest a bit more?
Ah, thermometer.
99.5 degrees.
99.5 °F
Your fever hasn't gone up.
Your home-room teacher said you did well
on your exams, and you must have pushed yourself when you'd been sick.
School is important, but so is your health.
S-Sorry ...
I wasn't really sick...
LACK OF SLEEP AND LOSS OF APPETITE WERE TO BLAME.

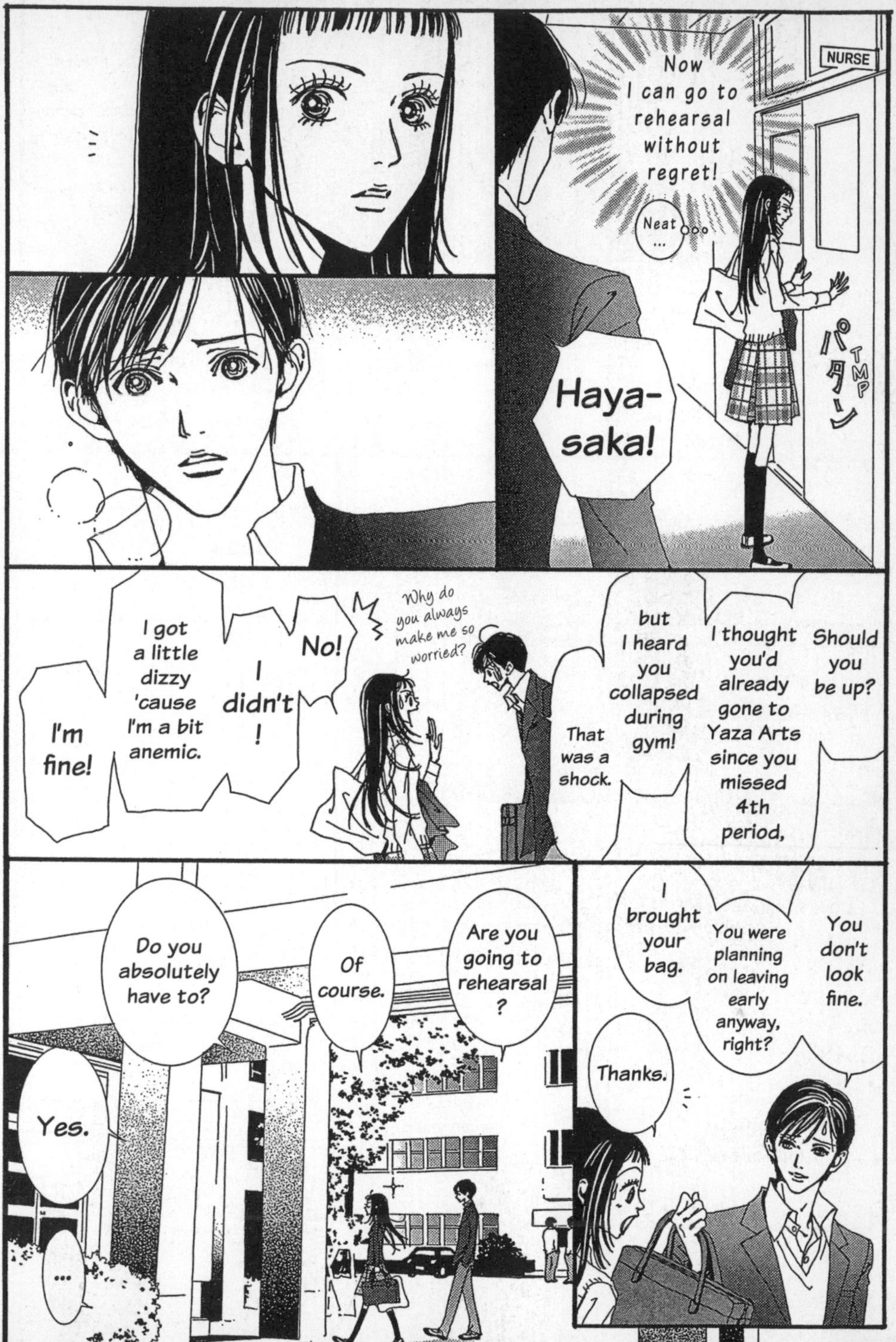
NURSE
Now I can go to rehearsal without regret!
Neat ...
パタン
TMP
Haya-saka!
Should you be up?
I thought you'd already gone to Yaza Arts since you missed 4th period,
but I heard you collapsed during gym!
That was a shock.
Why do you always make me so worried?
No!
I didn't!
I got a little dizzy 'cause I'm a bit anemic.
I'm fine!
You don't look fine.
You were planning on leaving early anyway, right?
I brought your bag.
Thanks.
Are you going to rehearsal?
Of course.
Do you absolutely have to?
Yes.
...

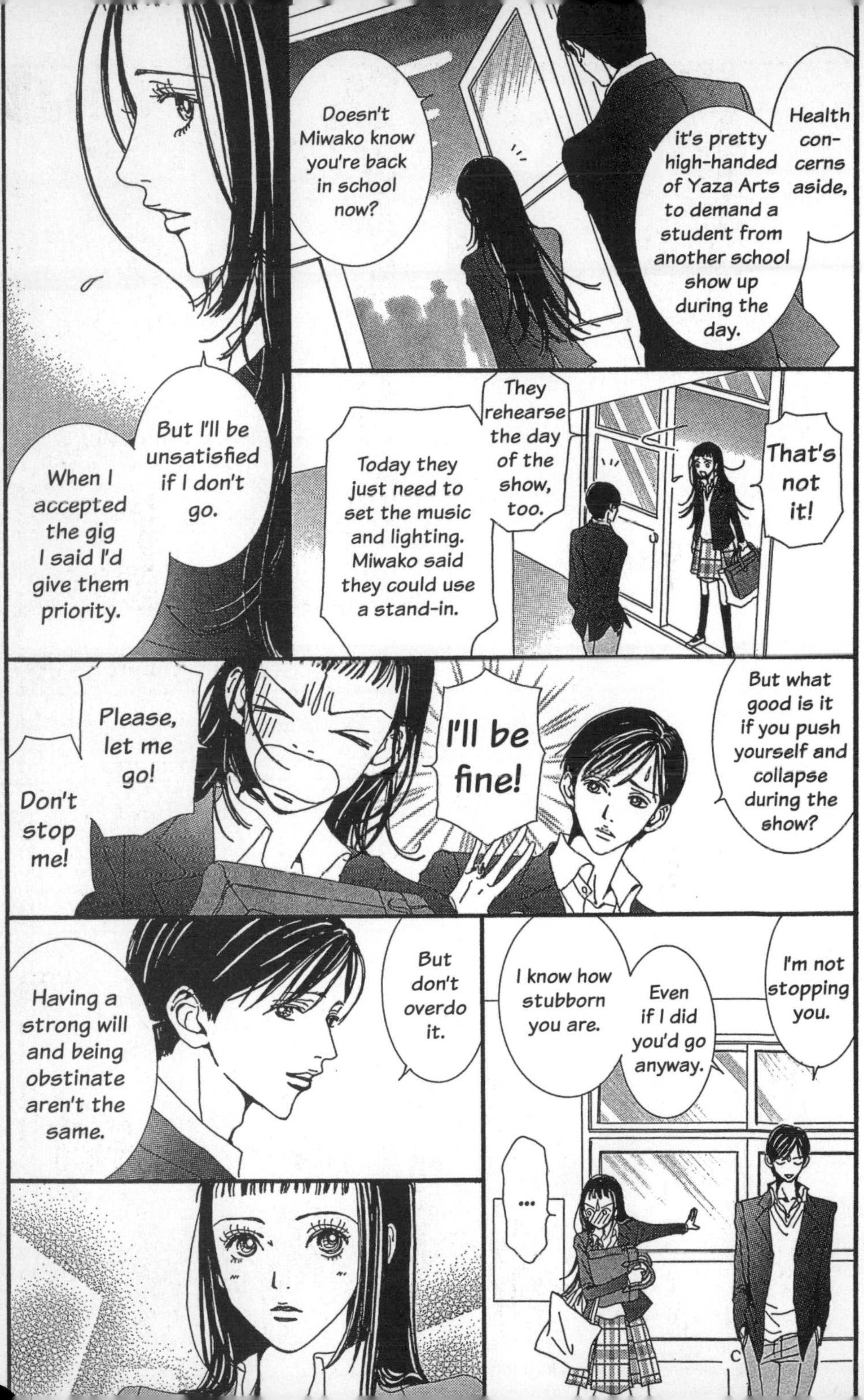
Health concerns aside,
it's pretty high-handed of Yaza Arts to demand a student from another school show up during the day.
Doesn't Miwako know you're back in school now?
That's not it!
They rehearse the day of the show, too.
Today they just need to set the music and lighting. Miwako said they could use a stand-in.
But I'll be unsatisfied if I don't go.
When I accepted the gig I said I'd give them priority.
But what good is it if you push yourself and collapse during the show?
I'll be fine!
Please, let me go!
Don't stop me!
I'm not stopping you.
Even if I did you'd go anyway.
I know how stubborn you are.
...
But don't overdo it.
Having a strong will and being obstinate aren't the same.

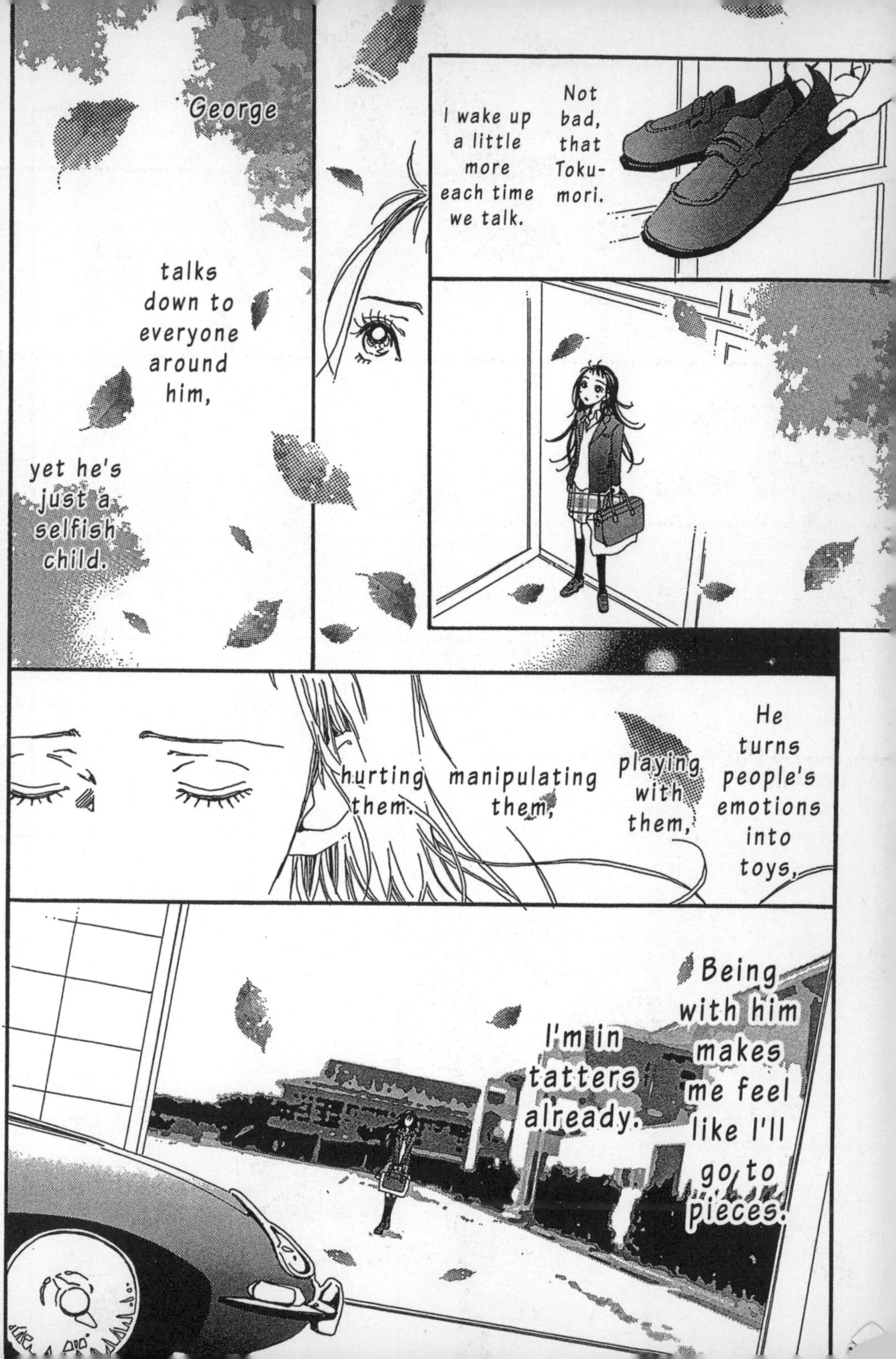
Not bad, that Toku-mori.
I wake up a little more each time we talk.
George
talks down to everyone around him,
yet he's just a selfish child.
He turns people's emotions into toys,
playing with them,
manipulating them,
hurting them.
Being with him makes me feel like I'll go to pieces.
I'm in tatters already.

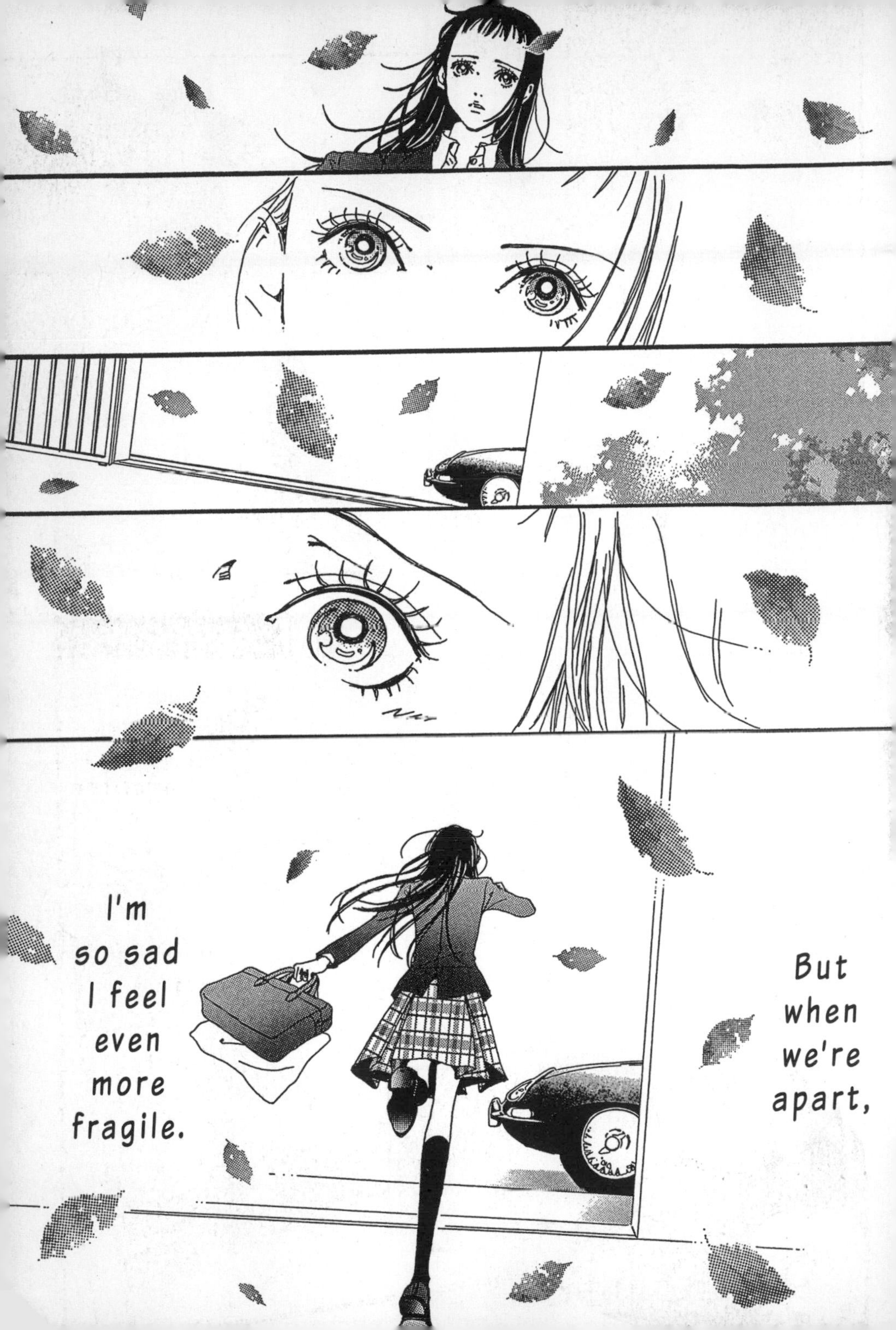
But when we're apart,
I'm so sad I feel even more fragile.

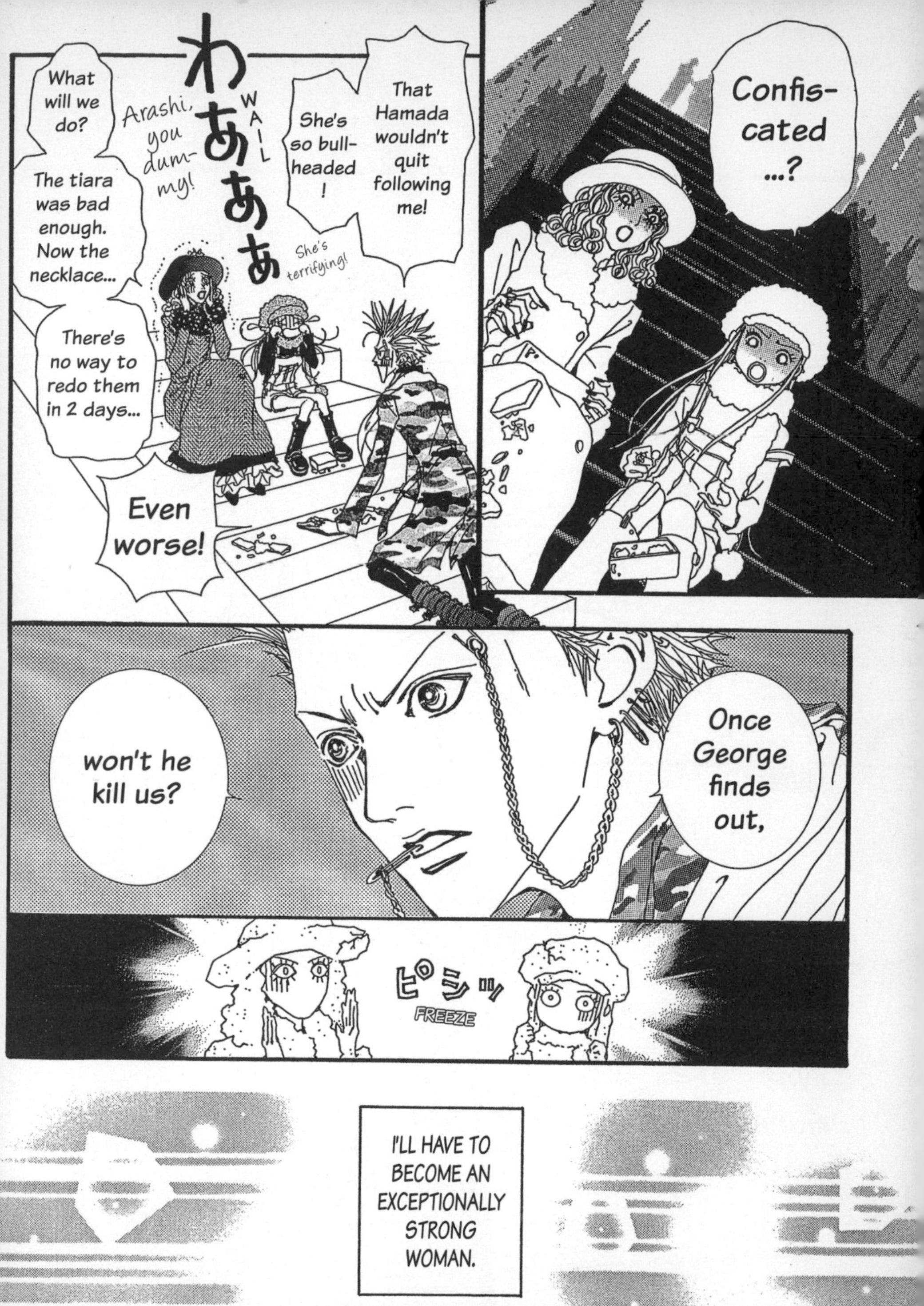

Confis-cated ...?
That Hamada wouldn't quit following me!
She's so bull-headed!
She's terrifying!
わあああ
WAIL
Arashi, you dum-my!
What will we do?
The tiara was bad enough. Now the necklace...
There's no way to redo them in 2 days...
Even worse!
Once George finds out,
won't he kill us?
ピシッ
FREEZE
I'LL HAVE TO BECOME AN EXCEPTIONALLY STRONG WOMAN.

*To be
continued in*
**Part
3**

Paradise Kiss, Part 2

by Ai Yazawa

Production: Grace Lu   Nicole Dochych
       Hiroko Mizuno   Daniela Yamada
       Jeremy Kahn   Chewei Fan

© 2001, 2002 by Yazawa Manga Seisakusho
All rights reserved.
First published in Japan in 2001, 2002 by SHODENSHA PUBLISHING CO., LTD., Tokyo
English translation rights arranged with SHODENSHA PUBLISHING CO., LTD.,
through Tuttle-Mori Agency, Inc., Tokyo

Translation copyright © 2012 Vertical, Inc.
Published by Vertical, Inc., New York

This is a work of fiction.

ISBN: 978-1-935654-72-8

Manufactured in the United States of America

First Vertical Edition

Vertical, Inc.
451 Park Avenue South 7th Floor
New York, NY 10016
www.vertical-inc.com

WRONG WAY

Japanese books, including manga like this one,
are meant to be read from right to left.
So the front cover is actually the back cover, and vice versa.
To read this book, please flip it over
and start in the top right-hand corner.
Read the panels, and the bubbles in the panels,
from right to left,
then drop down to the next row and repeat.
It may make you dizzy at first, but forcing your brain to do things
backwards makes you smarter in the long run.
We swear.